Beginning
Java

Ivor Horton

Wrox Press Ltd.®

Beginning Java

Published by Wrox Press Ltd. 30 Lincoln Road, Olton, Birmingham, B27 6PA , UK.
Printed in Canada
1 2 3 4 5 TRI 99 98 97

ISBN 1-861000-27-8

Trademark Acknowledgements

Wrox has endeavored to provide trademark information about all the companies and products mentioned in this book by the appropriate use of capitals. However, Wrox cannot guarantee the accuracy of this information.

Java and all Java-based trademarks and logos are trademarks or registered trademarks of Sun Microsystems, Inc. in the U.S. and other countries.

Credits

Author
Ivor Horton

Contributing Authors
Ron Phillips—JDBC
William Bilow Jr—RMI
Kerry Hammil—Java Tools

Additional Material
Mark Edwards—JDBC
Shy Cohen—Networking

Editors
Timothy Briggs
Simon Gilks
Chris Ullman
Anthea Elston

Technical Reviewers
Rick Anderson
Bill Bilow
Ramesh Chandak
Shy Cohen
Mark Edwards
Jim Frost

Technical Reviewers
Kerry Hammil
John Harris
Rex Jaeschke
Ken Litwak
Darren Millin
Tom Mitchell
Will Powell
Mark Robinson
Rick Stones
Julian Templeman
Dorai Thodla
Larry Rodrigues
Nick West

Cover/Design/Layout
Andrew Guillaume
Graham Butler

Index
Simon Gilks
Caroline Parks
Nancy Humphreys
Richard Evans

For the picture of Borobudur, thanks to Steve Gill of Contact Net Services, Perth, Australia
(Email steve@contact.net.au)

A Note from the Author

In all my *Beginning...* books, my objective is to minimize what, in my judgment, are the three main hurdles the aspiring programmer must face: getting to grips with the jargon that pervades every programming language and environment, understanding the *use* of the language elements (as opposed to what they are), and appreciating how the language is applied in a practical context.

Jargon is an invaluable and virtually indispensable means of communication for the competent amateur as well as the expert professional, so it can't be avoided. My approach is to ensure that the beginner understands what the jargon means and gets comfortable with using it in context. In that way, they can use the documentation that comes along with most programming products more effectively, and can also feel competent to read and learn from the literature that surrounds most programming languages.

Comprehending the syntax and effects of the language elements are obviously essential to learning a language, but I believe illustrating *how* the language features work and *how* they are used are equally important. Rather than just use code fragments, I always try to provide the reader with practical working examples that show the relationship of each language feature to specific problems. These can then be a basis for experimentation, to see at firsthand the effects of changing the code in various ways.

The practical context needs to go beyond the mechanics of applying individual language elements. To help the beginner gain the competence and confidence to develop their own applications, I aim to provide them with an insight into how things work in combination and on a larger scale than a simple example with a few lines of code. That's why I like to have at least one working example that builds over several chapters. In that way it's possible to show something of the approach to managing code as well as how language features can be applied together.

Finally, I know the prospect of working through a book of doorstop proportions can be quite daunting. For that reason it's important for the beginner to realize three things that are true for most programming languages. First, there *is* a lot to it, but this means there will be a greater sense of satisfaction when you've succeeded. Second, it's great fun, so you really will enjoy it. Third, it's a lot easier than you think, so you positively *will* make it.

Ivor Horton

Beginning

Java

Chapter 2: Programs, Data, Variables and Calculation   **29**

Chapter 3: Loops and Logic   **65**

Chapter 13: Drawing in a Window   585

Chapter 14: Extending the GUI   657

Beginning
Java

Welcome

Welcome to *Beginning Java*, a comprehensive and easy-to-use tutorial guide to learning the Java language and the Java platform API, and developing programs using the JDK 1.1.

In this book, as well as teaching you Java, we aim to give you an introduction to the wide variety of topics that will be relevant to you as a Java programmer. We've structured the book so that you learn Java programming in a carefully designed and logical set of steps, and at each stage you will be building on what you have learnt at the previous stage.

Who is this Book For?

The word *Beginning* in the title refers more to the style of the book's teaching, than to your skill level. Each aspect of Java is explained and illustrated in sufficient detail to suit a newcomer to the Java language, but it is also intended to prove adequate for a relative newcomer to programming. If you have very little programming experience, or you have programming expertise in other areas but want to learn Java, then this book is for you.

We assume, as a minimum, that you know something about programming, in that you understand at least the fundamental concepts of how programs work. However, you don't need to have significant prior programming experience to use the book successfully, though if you have, you'll get along faster. The pace of the book is fairly rapid, without stinting on any of the necessary explanations of how Java works.

Java programming is a huge, and rapidly expanding, area, so in this book we aim to provide you with a comprehensive understanding of the language, plus enough understanding of Java application contexts to give you a solid 'beginning' in each of these core areas. With an understanding of the topics in this book, you can start to write fully featured and effective Java programs.

Introduction

What's Covered in this Book

The book aims to teach you Java programming following a logical format:

▶ First, it covers some of the main terms and concepts that underpin programming in Java. Without these we're getting nowhere fast.

▶ Second, it provides you a clear explanation of the features of the Java language—the basic data types, the control structures which manipulate data, the object-oriented features of the language, the way runtime errors are handled and how threads are used. This doesn't just explain what the language elements do, but also how you can apply them in practice.

▶ Third, it gives you an extensive introduction to the key packages in the Java class library—the `io`, `util`, `awt`, `awt.event`, `applet`, `net`, `sql` and `rmi` packages are covered. All of these are illustrated with fully working examples.

▶ Fourth, it guides you through creating a larger application, Sketcher, applying the Java language capabilities and the Java class library in a realistic context, and with detailed information about some important considerations you need to have in mind when applying what you have learned.

▶ Fifth, it shows how you can use the tools that come with the JDK 1.1.

As we progress through these topics, we aim to introduce the theory, and then illustrate it with an appropriate example and a clear explanation. You can learn quickly on a first read, and look back over things to brush up on all the essential elements again if you need to.

The small examples in each chapter are designed mainly to illustrate a class and its methods, or some new piece of theory in action. They focus specifically on showing you how the particular language feature or method works. However, in the chapters covering the AWT, alongside the simple examples, a large sample project is developed—a sketching application with menus, toolbars, a status panel, the ability to draw a number of elements, handle text, print and save sketches. This will give you a much better understanding of how you apply Java in practical projects of your own, something that's hard to appreciate from any number of more trivial examples.

To help you get the most from the chapters, we would really like you to try out the examples as you read. Type them in yourself, even if you have downloaded the source code. It really does make a difference. The examples also provide a good base for experimentation and will hopefully inspire you to create programs of your own. It's important to try things out—you will learn as much (if not more) from your mistakes as you will from the things that work first time.

What You Need to Use this Book

You'll need at least version 1.1.1 of the JDK available from JavaSoft. Other hardware and software requirements for most of the chapters is fairly minimal, basically a copy of a text editor and a command line window from which to run the Java tools. The detailed requirements for the book are covered in Appendix A.

Conventions

To help you get the most from the text and keep track of what's happening, we've used a number of conventions throughout the book.

For instance,

For Your Information (FYI) boxes contains extra tit-bits and asides which add to the discussion.

When discussing code, we have two conventions:

Background, which is used to hold asides on programming code.

while,

> *These boxes hold important, not-to-be-forgotten information which is directly relevant to the surrounding text.*

When we introduce them, we **highlight** important words. We show keyboard strokes like this: *Ctrl-A.*

The command line and terminal output is shown as:

```
C:\> java ShowStyle
When the command line is shown, it's in the above style, whereas
terminal output is in this style.
```

while text for windowed applications, such as on buttons, is shown as OK and Cancel.

We present code in four different ways. Firstly, variables, Java keywords, methods and classes are referenced in the text using a **code style**.

Definitions of Java methods and structures are shown in definition boxes. For example:

```
if(life==good)
{
   DoSomething;          // Italics show that words should be replaced
   DoSomethingElse;      // with something more meaningful
}
```

```
Lastly in our code examples, the code foreground style shows new,
important,
   pertinent code;
while code background shows code that's less important in the present
context,
   or has been seen before.
```

One point we should make about how code is shown in the book is that sometimes string literals (denoted by inverted commas) go over two lines. When you type this in, the string literal should be on one line, without any returns, otherwise the compiler will complain. We use the ♭ symbol to show that the string continues.

We'll presage example code with a Try It Out, which is used to split the code up where that's helpful, to highlight the component parts and to show the progression of the application. When it's important, we also follow the code with a How It Works to explain any salient points of the code in relation to previous theory. We find these two conventions help break up the more formidable code listings into more palatable morsels.

Tell Us What You Think

We've worked hard to make this book as useful to you as possible, so we'd like to get a feel for what it is you want and need to know, and what you think about how we've presented things to you.

Return the reply card in the back of the book, and you'll register this copy of Beginning Java with Wrox Press, and be put on our mailing list for information on the latest Wrox products.

We appreciate feedback on our efforts and take both criticism and praise on board in our future editorial efforts. If you've anything to say, let us know on:

Feedback@wrox.com
or at
http://www.wrox.com

Introducing Java

This chapter will give you an appreciation of what the Java language and some of its core libraries are all about. Understanding the details that we'll introduce in this chapter is not important at this stage; you'll see all of them again in greater depth in later chapters of the book. It is important that you understand the general ideas we'll be covering throughout the book, as well as the contexts in which you can use Java programs and the different types of program applicable in these contexts.

In this chapter you will learn:

▶ The basic characteristics of the Java language

▶ How Java programs work on your computer

▶ Why Java programs are portable between different computers

▶ The basic ideas behind object-oriented programming

▶ How a simple Java program looks and how you can run it using the Java Development Kit

▶ How to use HTML to include a Java program in a web page

What is Java All About?

Java is an innovative programming language that enables you to write programs that you can embed in Internet web pages, as well as programs that you can run normally on any computer that supports Java. You can even write programs that will work both as applets and applications.

Being able to embed executable code in a web page introduces a vast range of exciting possibilities. Instead of being a passive presentation of text and graphics, a web page can be interactive in any way that you want. You can include animations, games, interactive transaction processing—the possibilities are unlimited. Of course, embedding program code in a Web page creates special security requirements.

You need to be confident that, if you receive such code from a variety of sources and you execute it, it will not do anything that might interfere with the operation of your computer, or damage the data you have on your system. Java implicitly incorporates measures to minimize the possibility of such occurrences.

Aside from its ability to create programs that can be embedded in a web page, perhaps the most important characteristic of Java is that it was designed from the outset to be machine independent. Java programs will run unchanged on any computer that supports Java. Of course, there is still the slight possibility of the odd glitch, because you are ultimately dependent on the implementation of Java on any particular machine, but Java programs are intrinsically more portable than programs written in other languages.

Possibly the next most important characteristic of Java is that it is **object-oriented**. The object-oriented approach to programming is also an implicit feature of all Java programs, so we will be looking at what this implies later in this chapter. Not only is Java object oriented, but it manages to avoid many of the difficulties and complications that are inherent in some other object-oriented languages, so you will find it very straightforward and easy to learn.

Learning Java

Java is not difficult, but there is a great deal to it. In this book, the sequence in which you learn how the language works, and how you apply it, has been carefully structured so that you can gain expertise and confidence with programming in Java through a relatively easy and painless process. Consequently, you won't be writing Java to be embedded in web pages right away. While it may be an appealing idea, this would be like learning to swim by jumping in the pool at the deep end. Generally, there is good evidence that, by starting in the shallow end of the pool and learning how to float before you try to swim, the chance of you drowning is minimized, and there is a high expectation that you will end up a competent swimmer.

Java Programs

As we have already noted, there are two kinds of programs you can write in Java. Programs that are to be embedded in a Web page are called Java **applets**, and ordinary standalone programs are called Java **applications**. You can further subdivide Java applications into **console applications,** which only support character output to your computer screen, and **windowed Java applications** that can create and manage multiple windows, and use the typical graphical user interface (GUI) mechanisms of windows-based programs.

While you are learning the Java language basics, we will be using console applications as examples illustrating how things work, because we can then focus on the specifics of the language without worrying about any of the complexity involved in creating and managing windows. Once you are comfortable with applying the language, we'll proceed to windowed application and applet examples.

Learning Java—the Road Ahead

Before starting out, it is always helpful to have an idea of where you are heading and what route you should take, so let's take a look at a brief road map of where you will be going with Java. There are six broad stages you will be progressing through in learning Java using this book:

1   The first stage is this chapter. It sets out some fundamental ideas about the structure of Java programs and how they work. This includes such things as what object-oriented programming is all about, and how an executable program is created from a Java source file. Getting these concepts straight at the outset will make learning to write Java programs that much easier for you.

2   Next you will learn how statements are put together, what facilities you have for storing basic data in a program, how you perform calculations and how you make decisions based on the results of them. These are the nuts and bolts you need for the next stages.

3   In the third stage you will learn about classes—how you define them and how you can use them. By the time you are through this stage you will have learnt the basics of how the Java language works so you will be ready to progress further into how you can use it. The remaining stages involve applying what you have learnt and using the standard support capabilities that are implemented in Java. These enable you to write applications with a graphical user interface, and applets that are embedded in a web page.

4   In the fourth stage, you will learn how you can segment your application into several pieces that can execute concurrently. This is important for when you want to include several applets in a Web page, but you don't want one applet to have to wait for another to finish executing, before it can start. You may want a fancy animation to continue running while you play a game for example, with both programs sitting in the same web page.

5   In the fifth stage you will learn in detail how you implement an application with a graphical user interface using windows, and how you handle interactions with the user in this context. When you finish this stage you will be equipped to write your own fully fledged applications in Java.

6   In the last stage you will apply most of what you have learned in the previous stages to write practical Java applications and applets. Here, too, we'll be looking at other features that Java provides; for instance, the ability to communicate via networks, talk to databases and to call Java objects remotely. When you get to here you should be a knowledgeable Java programmer. The rest is down to experience.

Throughout this book we will be using complete examples to explore how Java works. You should create and run all of the examples, even the simplest, and don't be afraid to experiment with them. If you are not quite clear on anything, try changing an example around to see what happens, or better still, write an example of your own. If you are uncertain how some aspect of Java that you have already covered works, don't look it up right away—try it out. Making mistakes is a great way to learn.

The Java Environment

You can run Java programs on a wide variety of computers using a range of operating systems. Your Java program will run just as well on a PC running Windows 95 as it will on a Sun Solaris workstation. This is possible because a Java program does not execute directly on your computer. It runs on a standardized hypothetical computer called the **Java virtual machine** which is emulated inside your computer by a program.

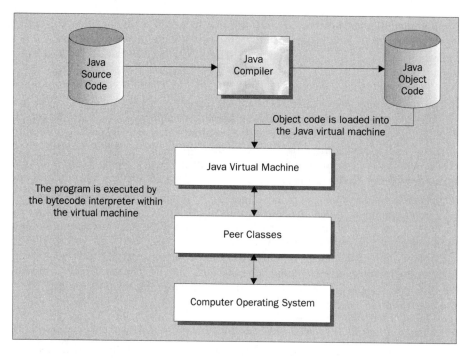

The Java source code that you write is converted by a Java compiler to a binary program consisting of **bytecodes**. Bytecodes are machine instructions for the Java virtual machine. When you execute a Java program, a program called the **Java interpreter** inspects and deciphers the bytecodes for it, checks it out to ensure that it has not been tampered with and is safe to execute, and then executes the actions that they specify within the Java virtual machine. A Java interpreter can run stand-alone, or it can be part of a web browser such as Netscape or Explorer where it can be invoked automatically to run applets in a web page.

Because your Java program consists of bytecodes rather than native machine instructions, it is completely insulated from the particular hardware on which it is run. Any computer that has the Java environment implemented will work as well as any other, and because the Java interpreter sits between your program and the physical machine, it can prevent unauthorized actions in the program from being executed.

There is usually a penalty for all this flexibility and protection, and that is in the speed of execution. An interpreted Java program will typically run at only one tenth of the speed of an equivalent program using native machine instructions. In programs that are not computation intensive—which is usually the case with the sort of program you would want to include in a web page, for example, you really won't notice this. If you happen to have a Java environment which supports **just-in-time (JIT) compilation** of your programs, you will not suffer the penalty in any event. JIT compilers convert and cache your Java programs to native machine instructions as they are loaded. Your programs will take a little longer to load of course, but once loaded they execute at maximum speed.

Java Program Development

There are a number of excellent Java program development environments available, including products from Sun, Microsoft, Borland and Symantec. These all provide very friendly environments for creating and editing your source code, and compiling and debugging your programs. While it isn't the easiest to use, the lowest cost development package for Java programs is undoubtedly the Java Development Kit (JDK) from Sun, because it is free. You can download this for a variety of different hardware platforms and operating systems from the Sun Java web site at **http://www.javasoft.com**

Running a Java Application

Java source code is always stored in files with the extension **.java**. Once you have created the source code for a program and saved it in a **.java** file, you need to process the source using a Java compiler. Using the compiler that comes with the JDK, you would do this with the following command:

```
javac MyProgram.java
```

Here, **javac** is the name of the Java compiler, and **MyProgram.java** is the name of the program source file. Note that the **javac** is case-sensitive. Assuming your program contains no errors, the compiler generates a bytecode program that is the equivalent of your source code. This is stored in a file with the same name as the source file, but with the extension **.class**. Java executable modules are always stored in a file with the extension **.class**.

If you are using some other product to develop your Java programs, you will probably be using a more user-friendly, graphical interface for compiling your programs that won't involve entering commands such as that shown above. The file name extensions for your source file and the object file that results from it will be just the same however.

To execute the bytecode program in the **.class** file with the Java interpreter in the JDK, you enter the command:

```
java MyProgram
```

The bytecode instructions are analyzed and executed by the Java interpreter. The Java virtual machine is identical in all computer environments supporting Java, so you can be sure your program is completely portable. As we already said, your program will run just as well on a Unix Java implementation as it will on that for Windows 95, MacOS or any other operating system that supports Java.

Note that the Java compiler in the JDK will compile both applications and applets. However, an applet is not executed in the same way as an application. You must embed an applet in a web page before it can be run. You can then execute it either within a Java-enabled web browser, or by using the **appletviewer** provided in the JDK.

If you have compiled an applet and you have included it in a web page stored as **MyApplet.html** in the current directory on your computer, you can execute it by entering the command:

```
appletviewer MyApplet.html
```

So how do you put an applet in a web page?

The Hypertext Markup Language

The HyperText Mark-up Language, or **HTML** as it is commonly known, is used to describe a web page. If you want a good, compact, reference guide to HTML, I recommend the book *Instant HTML* by Steve Wright, published by Wrox Press (ISBN 1-861000-76-6). You can also get the latest from **http://www.w3.org**. Here we will just gather just enough on HTML so that you can run a Java applet.

When you define a web page as an HTML document, it is stored in a file with the extension **.html**. An HTML document consists of a number of elements, and each element is identified by **tags**. The document will begin with **<HTML>** and end with **</HTML>**. These delimiters, **<HTML>** and **</HTML>**, are tags, and each element in an HTML document will be enclosed between a similar pair of tags between angle brackets. All element tags are case insensitive, so you can use upper or lower case, or even a mixture of the two, but by convention they are capitalized so they stand out from text and URLs. Here is an example of an HTML document consisting of a title and some other text:

```
<HTML>
<HEAD>
<TITLE>This is the title of the document</TITLE>
</HEAD>
<BODY>
You can put whatever text you like here. The body of a document can
contain all kinds of other HTML elements, including <B>Java applets</B>.
Note how each element always begins with a start tag identifying the
element, and ends with an end tag that is the same as the start tag but
with a slash added. The pair of tags around Java applets will display the
text as bold.
</BODY>
</HTML>
```

There are two elements that can appear directly within the **<HTML>** element, a **<HEAD>** element and a **<BODY>** element, as in the example above. The **<HEAD>** element provides information about the document, and is not strictly part of it. The text enclosed by the **<TITLE>** element tags that appears here within the **<HEAD>** element, will be displayed as the window title when the page is being viewed.

Other element tags can appear within the **<BODY>** element, and they include tags for headings, lists, tables, links to other pages and Java applets. There are some elements that do not require an end tag because they are considered to be empty. An example of this kind of element tag is **<HR>** which specifies a horizontal rule; a line across the full width of the page. You can use the **<HR>** tag to divide up a page and separate one type of element from another. You will find a comprehensive list of available HTML tags in the book I mentioned earlier.

For many element tag pairs, you can specify an **element attribute** in the starting tag which defines additional or qualifying data about the element. This is how a Java applet is identified in an **<APPLET>** tag.

Try It Out—Adding an Applet to an HTML Document

1 Here is an example of how you include a Java applet in an HTML document:

```
<HTML>
<HEAD>
<TITLE> A Simple Program </TITLE>
</HEAD>
<BODY>
<HR>
<APPLET   code = "MyFirstApplet.class"   width = 300   height = 200 >
</APPLET>
<HR>
</BODY>
</HTML>
```

2 Here is the Java source code for a simple applet:

```
import java.applet.Applet;
import java.awt.Graphics;

public class MyFirstApplet extends Applet
{
  public void paint(Graphics g)
  {
    g.drawString("To climb a ladder, start at the bottom rung", 20, 90);
  }
}
```

*Note that Java is case sensitive. You can't enter **public** with a capital **P**—if you do the program won't compile. This applet will just display a message.*

The mechanics are irrelevant here—it's just to illustrate how an applet goes into an HTML page.

3 If you compile this code and save the previous HTML page specification in the file **MyFirstApplet.html** in the same directory as the Java applet code, you can run the applet using **appletviewer** from the JDK with the command:

```
appletviewer MyFirstApplet.html
```

This will display a window something like that shown here:

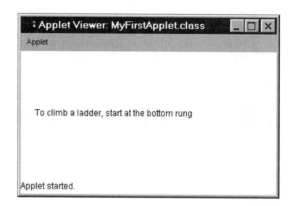

How It Works

Looking at the HTML file, the two shaded lines between tags for horizontal lines specify that the applet to be executed is **MyFirstApplet.class**. The file containing the bytecodes for the applet is specified as an attribute in the **<APPLET>** tag. The other two attributes define the width and height of the region on the screen that will be used by the applet when it executes. These are mandatory.

In this particular case, the window is produced under Windows 95. Under other operating systems it is likely to look a little different since Java 'takes on' the style of the platform it is running on. Since the height and width of the window for the applet is specified in pixels, the physical dimensions of the window will depend on the resolution and size of your monitor.

Object-Oriented Programming in Java

As we said at the beginning of this chapter, Java is an object-oriented language. When you use a programming language that is not object-oriented, you must express the solution to every problem essentially in terms of numbers and characters—the basic kinds of data that you can manipulate in the language. In an object-oriented language like Java, things are different. Of course, you still have numbers and characters to work with—these are referred to as the **basic data types**—but you can define other kinds of entities that represent some aspect of your particular problem. You solve your problem in terms of the entities or objects that occur in, or define, the problem in real life. This not only affects how a program is structured, but also the terms in which the solution to your problem is expressed. If your problem concerns baseball players, your Java program is likely to have **BaseballPlayer** objects in it. If you are producing a program dealing with fruit production in California, it may well have objects that are **Oranges** in it. Apart from seeming to be inherently sensible, object-oriented programs are usually easier to understand.

In Java almost everything is an object. If you haven't delved into object-oriented programming before, or maybe because you have, you may feel this is a bit daunting. But fear not. Objects in Java are particularly easy. So easy in fact that we are going to start out by understanding some of the ideas behind Java objects right now. In that way you will be on the right track from the outset.

This doesn't mean we are going to jump in with all the precise nitty-gritty of Java that you need to describe and use objects. We are just going to get the concepts straight at this point. We will do this by taking a stroll through the basics using the odd bit of Java code where it helps the ideas along. All the code we use here will be fully explained in later chapters. Concentrate on getting the notion of objects clear first. Then we can ease into the specific practical details as we go along.

So What Are Objects?

Anything can be thought of as an object. Objects are all around you. You can consider **Tree** to be a particular class of objects, and then the tree in my yard which I call **myOak**, the tree in your yard which I call **thatDarnedTree**, and a **generalSherman**, the well-known redwood, could be instances of **Tree**. In other words, they are objects of the class **Tree**. Note how we drop into the jargon here—<u>class</u> is a term which describes a specification for a collection of objects with common properties. A class is a specification—expressed as a piece of program code—which defines what goes to make up a particular sort of object. Of course, you will define this specification to fit what you want to do. There are no absolutes here. You design your classes to suit your needs. For my trivial problem, the specification of a **Tree** class might just consist of its name and its height. If you are an arboriculturalist, then your problem with trees may require a much more complex class, or more likely, set of classes, that involve a mass of arboreal characteristics.

Every object that your program uses will have a corresponding class definition somewhere for objects of that type. This is true in Java as well as in other object-oriented languages. The basic idea of a class in programming parallels that of classifying things in the real world. It is a convenient and well defined way to group things together.

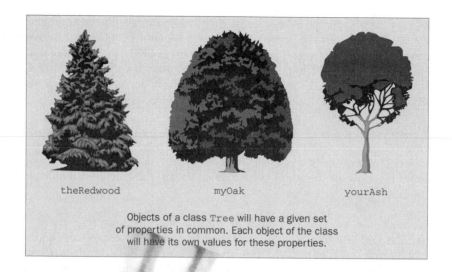

theRedwood   myOak   yourAsh

Objects of a class Tree will have a given set
of properties in common. Each object of the class
will have its own values for these properties.

An **instance** of a class is a technical term for an object of that class. **Tree** is a specification for a type of object and **yourAsh** is an object constructed to that specification, so **yourAsh** would be an instance of the class **Tree**. Once you have a class defined, then you can come up with objects, or instances of that class. This raises the question of what differentiates an object of a given class, a **Tree** class object say, from an object which is not a **Tree** class object. In other words, what sort of information defines a class?

What Defines a Class of Objects?

A class definition lists all the parameters that you need to define an object of that particular class—at least, so far as your needs go. Someone else might choose a larger or smaller set of parameters to define the same sort of object—it all depends on what they want to do with that object. You will decide what aspects of the objects you need to include to define that particular class of object, and you will choose them depending on the kinds of problems that you want to address using the objects of the class.

Let's think about a specific class of objects. For a class **Hat** for example, you might use just two parameters in the definition. You could include the name of a hat as a string of characters such as **"Fedora"** or **"Baseball cap"**, and its size as a numeric value. The parameters that define an object of a class are referred to as **instance variables** or **attributes** of a class. The instance variables can be basic types of data such as numbers, but they could also be objects. For example, the name of a **Hat** object could be of type **String**—the class **String** defines objects that are strings of characters.

Of course there are lots of other things you could include to define a **Hat** if you wanted to; **color**, for instance, which might be another string of characters such as **"Blue"**. To specify a class you just decide what set of attributes suit your needs, and those are what you use. This is called **data abstraction** in the parlance of the object-oriented aficionado, because you just abstract the attributes you want to use from the myriad possibilities for a typical object.

In Java the definition of the class **Hat** would look something like:

```
class Hat {
   // Stuff defining the class in detail goes here.
   // This could specify the name of the hat, the size,
   // maybe the color, and whatever else
   // you felt was necessary.
}
```

The name of the class follows the word **class**, and the details of the definition appear between the curly braces.

> *Because the word* **class** *has this special role in Java it is called a keyword, and it is reserved for use only in this context. There are lots of other keywords in Java that you will pick up as we go along. You just need to remember that you must not use any of them for any other purposes.*

We won't go into the detail of how the class **Hat** is defined, since we don't need it at this point. The lines appearing between the braces above are not code, they are actually **program comments**, since they begin with two successive slashes. Anything on a line that follows two successive slashes in your Java programs will be ignored, so you will use this to add explanations to your programs. Generally the more useful comments you can add to your programs, the better. We will also see, in Chapter 2, that there are other ways you can write comments in Java.

Each object of your class will have a particular set of values defined that characterize that particular object. You could have an object you could refer to as **CowboyHat** which might be defined by values such as **"Stetson"** for the name of the hat, **"White"** for the color, and the size as 7.

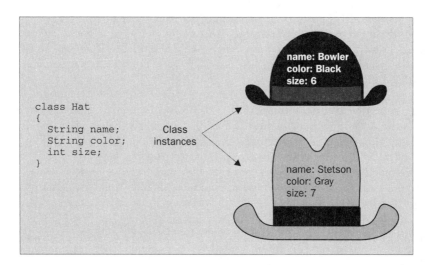

The parameters defining an object are not necessarily fixed values though. You would expect the name and size attributes for a **Hat** object to stay fixed, but you could have other attributes such as one you might call **state** for example, which could indicate whether the hat was on or off the owner's head, or even **owner**, which would record the owner's name so the value stored as the attribute **owner** would change when the hat was sold.

Operating on Objects

There is another kind of information that is included in the definition of a class, which is the fundamental difference between a class and the complex data types that you find in some other programming languages. This specifies what you can do with an object of the class—that is, it defines the operations that are possible on objects of the class. Clearly for objects to be of any use in a program, you need to decide what you can do with them. This will depend on what sort of objects you are talking about, the attributes they contain and how you intend to use the objects of the class.

To take a very simple example, if your objects were numbers, of type **Integer** for example, it would be reasonable to plan for the usual arithmetic operations; add, subtract, multiply and divide, and probably a few others you can come up with. On the other hand it would not make sense to have operations for calculating the area of an **Integer**, boiling an **Integer**, or for putting an **Integer** object on. There are lots of classes where these would make sense, but not those dealing with integers.

While we're on this topic, it is interesting to reflect that your computer cannot directly add 2 to 2.5 and get a correct result because these are inherently different types of numbers—the number 2 is an integer whereas 2.5 is a decimal value (or to use the proper jargon in Java—a **floating point value**). Java does not support the operation that can deal with this situation, and so the Java compiler will complain.

Your computer can add integers to integers since it has an built-in instruction, or method for doing this, so 2+3 is no problem. It can also add floating point values together too, as long as the hardware supports such operations, so it can calculate 3.6+2.5 with ease. With 2+2.5 things are a little more complicated. Your computer has no direct operation to handle this because 2 and 2.5 are not the same sort of thing. We know they are numbers, but your computer doesn't deal with numbers, it deals with two subclasses of numbers—integers and floating point numbers.

Before your computer can do the arithmetic, the value 2 must first be converted from an integer value to a floating point value. Then 2.0+2.5 can be calculated using the standard floating point add operation to produce the result as a floating point value. It all works just like class objects really. The only operations that are possible between objects are those that you have defined, and this goes for objects of the same class as well as those of different classes. If you want to be able to combine objects of different classes in various ways, you must define the methods that do this within the classes concerned.

Coming back to our **Hat** class, you might want to have operations that you could refer to as **putHatOn** and **takeHatOff,** which would have meanings that are fairly obvious from their names, and do make sense for **Hat** objects. However, these operations would only be effective if a **Hat** object also had another defining value that recorded whether it was on or off; then these operations on a particular **Hat** object could set this value for the object. To determine whether your **cowboyHat** was on or off, you would just need to look at this value. Conceivably you might also have an operation **changeColor** by which you could set the color of a particular **Hat** object to a new color. The effect of this operation would be to change the color specification for the **Hat** object being operated on. Of course, to do this your hat must be made of the new Sensocolortex™ fabric which enables you to change the color by remote control—or else you will have to just plunge it into a bucket of dye. The illustration shows two operations applied in succession to a **Hat** object.

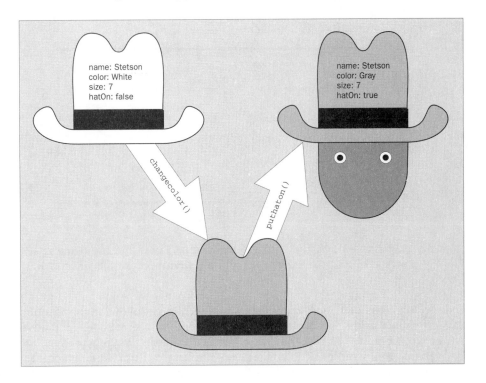

You may be wondering at this point how an operation for a class is defined. As we shall see in detail a bit later, it boils down to a self-contained block of program code called a **method** that is identified by the name you give to it. You can pass data items—which can be integers, floating point numbers, character strings or class objects—to a method, and a method can return a data item as a result. Performing an operation on an object amounts to 'executing' the method that defines the operation for the object.

> *Of course, the only operations you can perform on an instance of a particular class are those defined within the class, so the usefulness and flexibility of a class is going to depend on the thought that you give to its definition. We will be looking into these considerations a bit more in Chapter 5 when we get into the detail of how you define classes.*

Let's take a look at an example of a complete class definition. The code for the class **Hat** we have been talking about might look like the following:

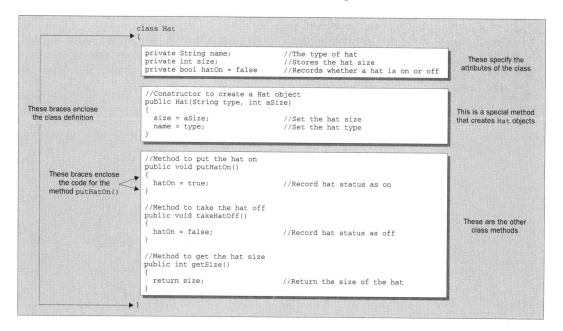

This code would be saved in a file with the name **Hat.java**—the file name is always the same as the class name, and the extension will be **.java** because the file contains source code.

The code for the class definition appears between the braces following the identification for the class, as shown in the illustration. The code for each of the methods in the class also appears between braces. The class has three instance variables, **size**, **name** and **hatOn**, and this last variable is always initialized as **false**. The keyword **private**, which has been applied to each instance variable, ensures that only code within the methods of the class can access or change the values of these directly.

> *Methods of a class can also be specified as **private**. Being able to prevent access to some members of a class from outside is an important facility. It protects the internals of the class from being changed or used incorrectly. Someone using your class in another program can only get access to the bits you want them to have access to. This means that you can change how the class works internally—the **private** methods that is—without affecting other programs that may use it.*

The color of the hat that we had in the earlier example has been omitted here just to keep the code short.

The class also has four methods, so you can do four different things with a **Hat** object. One of these is a special method called a **constructor** which creates a **Hat** object—this is the method with the name, **Hat**, that matches the class name. The items between the parentheses that follow the name of the constructor specify data that is to be passed to the method when it is executed.

> *Of course, in practice you might need to define a few other methods for the class to be useful; you might want to compare* **Hat** *objects for example, to see if one was larger than another. However, at the moment you just need to get an idea of how the code looks. The details are of no importance here, as we will be delving into all this in Chapter 5.*

Java Program Statements

As you saw in the **Hat** class example, the code for each method in the class appears between braces, and it consists of **program statements**. As you can see, each program statement is terminated by a semicolon. A statement in Java can spread over several lines if necessary, since the end of each statement is defined by the semicolon, not the end of the line. Here is a Java program statement:

```
hatOn = false;
```

If you wanted to, you could also write this as:

```
hatOn =
          false;
```

You can generally include spaces and tabs, and spread your statements over multiple lines to enhance readability, but sensible constraints apply. You can't put a space in the middle of a name for instance. If you write **hat On**, for example, the compiler will read this as two words.

Encapsulation

At this point we can introduce another bit of jargon you can use to impress or bore your friends—**encapsulation**. Encapsulation refers to hiding items of data and methods within an object by specifying them as **private** in the definition of the class. In the **Hat** class we defined earlier, the instance variables, **name, size** and **hatOn** were encapsulated. They were only accessible through the methods defined for the class. Being able to encapsulate members of a class in this way is important for the security and integrity of class objects. You may have a class with data members which can only take on particular values. By hiding the data members and forcing the use of a method to set or change the values, you can ensure that only legal values are set.

We mentioned earlier another major advantage of encapsulation—the ability to hide the implementation of a class. By only allowing limited access to the members of a class, you can have the freedom to change the internals of the class with necessitating changes to programs that use the class. As long as external characteristics of the methods that can be called from outside the class remain unchanged, the internal code can be changed in any way that you want.

A particular object, for instance a **cowboyHat**, will incorporate, or encapsulate, the **name**, the **size** of the object, and the status of the hat in the instance variable **hatOn**. Only the constructor, and the **putHatOn()**, **takeHatOff()** and **getSize()** methods can be accessed externally.

> *Whenever we are referring to a method in the text, we will add a pair of parentheses after the method name to distinguish it from other names within the code. A method always has parentheses in its definition and in its use in a program, as we shall see, so it makes sense to represent it in this way in the text.*

Classes and Data Types

Programming is concerned with specifying how data of various kinds is to be processed, massaged, manipulated or transformed. Since classes define the types of objects that a program will work with, you can consider defining a class to be the same as defining a data type. Thus **Hat** is a type of data, as is **Tree**, and any other class you care to define. Java also contains a library of standard classes which provide you with a whole range of programming tools and facilities. For the most part then, your Java program will process, massage, manipulate or transform class objects.

There are some basic types of data in Java that are not classes as we noted at the beginning. We will go into these in the next chapter, but they are essentially data types for numeric values such as 99 or 3.75, for single characters such as 'A' or '?', and for logical values that can be **true** or **false**. Java also has classes that correspond to the basic types for reasons that we will see later on. Every other entity in your Java program will be an object of a class—either a class that you define yourself, a class supplied as part of the Java environment or a class that you obtain from somewhere else, such as from a specialized support package.

Classes and Subclasses

Many sets of objects that you might define in a class can be subdivided into more specialized subsets that can also be represented by classes, and Java provides you with the ability to define one class as a version of another. Again, this reflects real life. There are always lots of ways of dividing a cake—or a forest. **Conifer** for example could be a subclass of the class **Tree**. The **Conifer** class would have all the instance variables and methods of the **Tree** class, plus some additional instance variables and/or methods that make it a **Conifer** in particular. You would refer to the **Conifer** class as a **subclass** of the class **Tree**, and the class **Tree** as a **superclass** of the class **Conifer**.

When you define a class such as **Conifer** using another class such as **Tree** as a starting point, the class **Conifer** is said to be **derived** from the class **Tree**, and the class **Conifer** **inherits** all the attributes of the class **Tree**.

Why Java is Object-Oriented

As we said at the outset, object-oriented programs are written using objects which model the problem being solved. Your pinball machine simulator may well define and use objects of type **Table**, **Ball**, **Flipper** and **Bumper**. This has tremendous advantages, not only in terms of easing the development process, but also in any future expansion of such a program. Java provides a whole range of standard classes to help you in the development of your program, and you can develop your own generic classes to provide a basis for developing programs that are of particular interest to you.

Because an object includes the methods that can operate on it as well as the data that defines it, programming using objects is much less prone to error. Your object-oriented Java programs should be more robust than the equivalent in a procedural programming language. Object-oriented programs take a little longer to design than programs that do not use objects since you must take care in the design of the classes that you will need, but the time required to write the code is sometimes substantially less than that for procedural programs. Object-oriented programs are also much easier to maintain and extend.

Java Program Structure

To summarize the necessary elements of a program structure:

▶ A Java program always consists of a number of classes.

▶ There is at least one class in every program, and there can be many.

▶ You typically put the program code for each class in a separate file, and you must give each file the same name as that of the class that is defined within it.

▶ A Java source file must also have the extension **.java**. Thus your file containing the class **Hat** will be called **Hat.java** and your file containing the class **BaseballPlayer** must have the file name **BaseballPlayer.java**.

A typical program will consist of several files as illustrated in the following diagram.

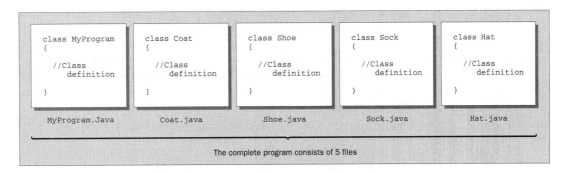

This program clearly majors on apparel with four of the five classes being clothing related. Each source file will contain a class definition and all of the files that go to make up the program will be stored in the same directory. The source files for your program will contain all the code that you wrote, but this is not everything that is ultimately included in the program. There will also be code from the **Java standard class library** that we mentioned earlier, so let's take a peek at what that can do.

Java's Class Library

A library in Java is a collection of classes—usually providing related facilities—that you can use in your programs. The Java class library provides you with a whole range of goodies, some of which are essential for your programs to work at all, and some of which just make writing your Java programs easier. The class library covers a lot of ground so we won't be going into it detail here, but we will be looking into how to apply many of the facilities it provides throughout the book.

Since the class library is a set of classes, it is stored in sets of files where each file contains a class definition. The classes are grouped together into related sets that are called **packages**, and each package is stored in a separate directory. A class in a package can access any of the other classes in the package. A class in another package may or may not be accessible. We will learn more about this in Chapter 5.

The package name is based on the path to the directory in which the classes belonging to the package are stored. Classes in the package **java.lang** for example are stored in the directory path **java\lang** (or **java/lang** under Unix). This path is relative to a directory specified by the **CLASSPATH** environment variable, so you must always ensure that **CLASSPATH** is defined appropriately for you system, otherwise the Java interpreter will not be able to find the standard system classes.

Java includes an ever growing number of standard packages—23 at the last count. Some of the packages you will meet most frequently are:

Package Name	Description
java.lang	These classes support the basic language features and includes classes for handling arrays and strings. Classes in the package are always available directly in your programs by default because this package is always automatically loaded with your program.
java.io	Classes for input and output operations.
java.util	This package contains utility classes of various kinds, including classes for managing data.
java.applet	These classes are used for implementing applets.
java.awt	Classes in this package support windowed applications in Java.
java.awt.event	The classes in this package are used in the implementation of windowed application to handle events in your program. Events are things like moving the mouse, pressing the left mouse button or clicking on a menu item.

As noted above, you can use any classes from the **java.lang** package in your programs by default. To use classes from the other packages, you will typically use an **import** statement for each package that you need. This will allow you to reference the classes by the simple class name. Without an **import** statement you would need to specify the full path to each class each time you refer to it. This would make your program code rather cumbersome, and certainly less readable.

Java Applications

Every Java application contains a class definition which contains a method called **main()**. ✓ You can call the class whatever you want, but the method which is executed first in an application is always called **main()**. When you run your Java application this method will typically cause methods belonging to other classes to be executed, but the simplest possible Java program consists of one class containing just the method **main()**.

We'll see how this works by taking a look at just such a Java program. You need to enter the program code using your favorite plain text editor, or if you have a Java development system with an editor, you can enter the code for the example using that. When you have entered the code, save the file with the same name as that used for the class and the extension **.java**. For this example the file name will be **OurFirstProgram.java**. The code for the program is:

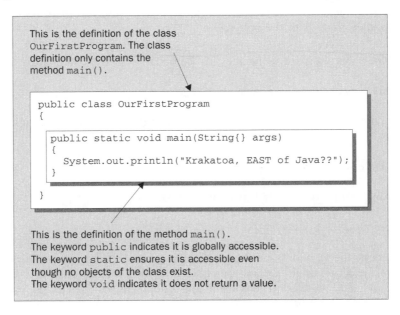

This is the definition of the class `OurFirstProgram`. The class definition only contains the method `main()`.

```
public class OurFirstProgram
{

  public static void main(String{} args)
  {
    System.out.println("Krakatoa, EAST of Java??");
  }

}
```

This is the definition of the method `main()`.
The keyword `public` indicates it is globally accessible.
The keyword `static` ensures it is accessible even though no objects of the class exist.
The keyword `void` indicates it does not return a value.

The program consists of a definition for a class we have called **OurFirstProgram**. The class definition only contains one method, the method **main()**. The first line of the definition for the method **main()** is always of the form:

```
public static void main(String[] args)
```

Our version of the method has only one executable statement:

```
System.out.println("Krakatoa, EAST of Java??");
```

So what does this statement do? Let's work through it from left to right:

> ▶ **System** is the name of a standard class that contains variables and methods for supporting simple keyboard input and character output to the display. It is contained in the package **java.lang** so it is always accessible just by using the simple class name, **System**.

> ▶ The object **out** represents the standard output stream - your display screen, and is a data member of the class **System**. This member is referenced by using the class name **System** separated from the member name **out** by a period—**System.out**.

> ▶ The bit at the rightmost end of the statement, **println("Krakatoa, EAST of Java??")**, calls the **println()** method that belongs to the object **out**, and that outputs the text string that appears between the parentheses to your display. This demonstrates one way in which you can call a class method—by using the object name followed by the method name, with a period separating them. The text between the parentheses following the name of a method is information that is passed to the method when it is executed; as we said, for **println()** it is the text we want to output to the screen.

You can compile this program using the JDK compiler with the command:

```
javac OurFirstProgram.java
```

and you can execute the program once you have compiled it successfully with the command:

```
java OurFirstProgram
```

When you run the program, it will display the text:

```
Krakatoa, EAST of Java??
```

For completeness, the keywords **public**, **static**, and **void**, that appear in the method definition are explained briefly in the annotations to the program code, but you need not be concerned if they still seem a bit obscure at this point. We will be coming back to all these in much more detail later on.

Java and Unicode

Programming to support languages that use anything other than the Latin character set has always been a major problem. There are a variety of 8-bit character sets defined for many national languages, but if you want to combine the Latin character set and Cyrillic, for example, in the same context, things can get difficult. If you want to handle Japanese as well it becomes impossible with an 8-bit character set. Unicode is a standard character set, developed to accommodate the characters necessary for all languages. It uses a 16-bit code to represent a character so each character occupies two bytes and up to 65,535 non-zero characters can be distinguished. With so many character codes available, there are enough to allocate each national character set its own set of codes, including character sets such as Kanji, which requires thousands of character codes.

Java supports Unicode internally to represent characters and strings, so the potential is there for a comprehensive international language capability. There are still a number of practical constraints on implementing international applications in Java, but we will not be going into these in this book. The normal ASCII set that you will be familiar with corresponds to the first 255 characters of the Unicode set, so apart from the fact that each character occupies two bytes, you can ignore the fact that you are handling Unicode characters.

Summary

In this chapter we have looked at the basic characteristics of Java, and how portability between different computers is achieved. We have also introduced the elements of object-oriented programming.

The essential points we have covered in this chapter are:

- Java applets are programs designed to be embedded in an HTML document. Java applications are stand-alone programs. Java applications can be console programs that only support text output to the screen, or they can be windowed applications with a graphical user interface.

- Java programs are implicitly object-oriented

- Java source code is stored in files with the extension `.java`

- Java programs are compiled to bytecodes, which are instructions for the Java Virtual Machine. The Java Virtual Machine is the same on all the computers on which it is implemented, thus ensuring the portability of Java programs

- Java object code is stored in files with the extension `.class`

- Java programs are executed by the Java interpreter which analyses the bytecodes and carries out the operations they specify

- The Java Development Kit supports the compilation and execution of Java applications and applets

Programs, Data, Variables and Calculation

In this chapter we'll look at the entities in Java that aren't objects. This will give you all the elements of the language necessary to perform numerical calculations, and this we will do with a few working examples.

By the end of this chapter you will have learned:

- How to declare and define variables of the basic integer and floating point types
- How to write an assignment statement
- How integer and floating point expressions are evaluated
- How to output data from a console program
- How mixed integer and floating point expressions are evaluated
- What casting is and when you must use it
- What **boolean** variables are
- What determines the sequence in which operators in an expression are executed
- How to include comments in your programs

Data and Variables

A **variable** is a named piece of memory that you use to store information—a piece of data of some description. Each named piece of memory that you define in your program will only be able to store data of one particular type. If you define a variable to store integers, you can't use it to store a decimal value. If you've defined a variable that you'll use to refer to a **Hat** object, you can only use it to refer to a **Hat** object. With the type of data fixed for each variable, the compiler is able to check that, when you use a variable in your program, it isn't being used in a manner or a context that is inappropriate to its type. If a method in your program is supposed to process integers, the compiler will be able to detect when you inadvertently try to use it with some other kind of data, for example a decimal value or a string.

> ✓ *Before you can use a variable, you must specify its name and type in a declaration. This will associate a name with data of a specific type stored in the computer's memory, and allow you to manipulate that data using its name within some code. Before we look at how you write a declaration for a variable, we should consider what flexibility you have in choosing a name.*

Variable Names

The name you choose for a variable, or indeed the name you choose for anything in Java is called an **identifier**. An identifier can be any length, but it must start with a letter, an underscore, or a dollar sign. The rest of an identifier can include any characters except those used as operators in Java (such as **+**, **-**, or *****), but you will be generally better off if you stick to letters, digits, and underscore characters. Java is a case-sensitive language so the names **republican** and **Republican** are not the same. You must not include blanks or tabs in the middle of a name, so **Betty May** is out, but you could have **BettyMay** or even **Betty_May**. Note that you can't have **7Up** as a name as you can't start a name with a digit. Of course, you can have **sevenUp** as an alternative.

Subject to the restrictions we've mentioned, you can name a variable almost anything you like, except for one additional restraint—you can't use keywords in Java as a name for something. We saw some keywords in the previous chapter and we'll learn a few more in this chapter. If you want to know what they all are, a complete list appears in Appendix 1. Obviously, it makes sense to choose names for your variables that give a good indication of the sort of data that they hold. If you want to record the size of a hat for example, **hatSize** isn't a bad choice for a variable name. It's a common convention in Java to start ✓ variable names with a lower-case letter, and where you have a name that combines several words to capitalize the first letter of each word, as in **hatSize**, or **moneyWellSpent**. You're in no way obliged to follow this convention but since the rest of the Java world does, it helps to do so.

Each variable can only store one particular type of data, determined by the **data type** of that variable. You specify the type of a particular variable by using a **type name** in the variable declaration, which is a statement we'll come to shortly in this chapter.

A lot of your variables will be used to reference objects, but let's leave those on one side for the moment. The only things in Java that aren't objects are variables that correspond to one of eight basic data types defined within the language. These fundamental types allow you to define variables for storing:

- ▶ Numeric values which can be either integer or floating point
- ▶ Variables which store a single Unicode character
- ▶ Logical variables that can assume the values **true** or **false**

All of the type names for the basic variable types are keywords in Java so you mustn't use them for other purposes. Let's take a closer look at each of the basic data types and get a feel for how we can use them.

Integer Data Types

There are four types of variables that you can use to store integer data. All of these are signed, that is they can store both negative and positive values. The four integer types differ in the range of values they can store, so the choice of type for a variable depends on the range of data values you are likely to need.

The four integer types in Java are:

Data Type	Description
byte	Variables of this type can have values from –128 to +127 and occupy 1 byte in memory.
short	Variables of this type can have values from –32768 to 32767 and occupy 2 bytes in memory.
int	Variables of this type can have values from –2147483648 to 2147483647 and occupy 4 bytes in memory.
long	Variables of this type can have values from –9223372036854775808 to 9223372036854775807 and occupy 8 bytes in memory.

The range of values that can be stored by each type is always the same, regardless of what kind of computer you're using. This is also true of the other basic types that we will come across in this chapter, and has the rather useful effect that your program will execute in the same way on computers that may be quite different. This is not necessarily the case with other programming languages.

Integer Values

A value in Java is referred to as a **literal**. So 1, 10.5, and "This is text" are all examples of literals. Any integer literal that you specify is of type **int** by default. Thus 1, –9999, 123456789 are all literals of type **int**. The minus sign in the negative number –9999 is called the **unary –** and, conversely, there is also an **unary +**, but that is optional for positive constants. If you want to define an integer of type **long**, you need to append an **L** to the value. The values **1L**, **-9999L**, and **123456789L** are all of type **long**. You can also use a lower case letter **1**, but don't—it's too easily confused with the digit **1**. If the integer you specify is too big to store as an **int**, **3000000000** for example, it will be stored as type **long**, regardless of whether you put an **L** at the end.

> *You're perhaps wondering how you explicitly specify literals of type **byte** or **short**. It's simple really—you can't. But as we shall see a bit later, there's a good reason— usually they just aren't necessary in Java.*

Integer literals can also be specified to base 16, in other words as hexadecimal numbers. Hexadecimal literals in Java have **0x** in front of them and follow the usual convention of using the letters **A** to **F** (or **a** to **f**) to represent digits with values 10 to 15 respectively. In case you're a little rusty on hexadecimal values, here are some examples:

`0x100`	$1 \times 16^2 + 0 \times 16^1 + 0 \times 16^0$	which is 256 in decimal
`0x1234`	$1 \times 16^3 + 2 \times 16^2 + 3 \times 16^1 + 4 \times 16^0$	which is 4660 in decimal
`0xDEAF`	$13 \times 16^3 + 14 \times 16^2 + 10 \times 16^1 + 15 \times 16^0$	which is 57007 in decimal
`0xCAB`	$12 \times 16^2 + 10 \times 16^1 + 11 \times 16^0$	which is 3243 in decimal

You will typically use hexadecimal literals when you want to define a particular sequence of binary digits—usually called a **bit pattern**. We'll see this when we come to looking into operations that combine bit patterns a little later in this chapter.

Declaring Integer Variables

We can declare a variable of type **long** with the statement:

```
long bigOne;
```

This statement is a **declaration** for the variable **bigOne**. This specifies that the variable **bigOne** will store a value of type **long**. When this statement is compiled, 8 bytes of memory will be allocated for the variable **bigOne**. It's a good idea to initialize each variable as you declare it so you always know what values your variables start out with. By default, uninitialized integer variables will be 0. To declare *and* initialize the variable **bigOne**, you just write:

```
long bigOne = 999999999L;
```

This statement is not just a declaration; it's also a **definition** for the variable **bigOne**, since it establishes a value for it. The variable will be set to the value following the equals sign. And as we just saw, all integer literals of type **long** must have an **L** appended to them to differentiate them from other integer constants. If you forget the **L**, here the statement will still compile, but the literal will be stored as type **int** and then converted to **long** before being stored in **bigOne**—so you'll be executing an extra unnecessary step.

> *You can declare a variable just about anywhere in your program; that's not to say that you shouldn't care where you declare variables. We'll be discussing the dos and don'ts of program structure in Chapter 5. You must, however, declare a variable before you use it in a calculation. The placement of the declaration has an effect on whether a particular variable is accessible at a given point in a program, and we'll look deeper into the significance of this in the next chapter. Note that if you try to use a variable that hasn't had a value assigned to it in a calculation, your program will not compile.*

You can declare and define multiple variables in a single statement. For example:

```
long bigOne = 999999999L, largeOne = 100000000L;
```

Here we've declared two variables of type **long**. A comma separates the variables. You can declare as many variables as you like in a single statement as long as each one is separated by commas. It's usually better, though, to stick to declaring one variable in each statement as it helps to make your programs easier to read. A possible exception is perhaps with variables that are closely related—an x,y coordinate pair representing a point for example, which you might reasonably declare as:

```
long xCoord=0L, yCoord=0L;        // Point coordinates
```

On the same line as the declaration of these two variables, we have a comment following the double slash explaining what they are about. Everything following the double slash is ignored by the compiler.

> *Explaining in comments what your variables are for is a good habit to get into, as it can be quite surprising how something that was as clear as crystal when you wrote it is as clear as mud a few weeks later.*

There are other ways in which you can add comments to your programs which we'll look at a little later in this chapter.

Variables of other integer types are declared in a similar manner to those of type **long**. For example, to declare a variable **myNumber** of type **int**, you write:

```
int myNumber = 12345;
```

Here we initialize **myNumber** with the value 12345. Integer constants of types other than **long** are written with just their numeric value—no **L** appended. Naturally, you must be sure that an initializing constant is within the range of the type concerned, otherwise the compiler will complain. Your compiler is intelligent enough to recognize that you can't get a quart into a pint pot, or, alternatively, a **long** constant into a variable of type **int**, **short**, or **byte**.

To complete the set we can declare a variable of type **byte** and one of type **short** with the following two statements:

```
byte luckyNumber = 7;
short smallNumber = 1234;
```

Most of the time you'll find that variables of type **int** will cover your needs for dealing with integers, with **long** ones being necessary now and again when you have some really big integer values to deal with. Variables of type **byte** and **short** do save a little memory, but unless you have very large numbers of values of these types to store, the memory you save won't be worth worrying about.

Floating Point Data Types

Values which aren't integral are stored as **floating point** numbers. A floating point number has a fixed number of digits of accuracy but with a very wide range of values. This is possible because the decimal point can 'float'. For example, the values 0.000005, 500.0, and

5000000000000.0 can be written as 5×10^{-6}, 5×10^2, and 5×10^{12} respectively—we have just one digit, 5—but we move the decimal point around.

There are two basic floating point types in Java: **float** and **double**. These give you a choice in the number-of-digits precision available to represent your data values, and thus, in the range of values that can be accommodated:

Data Type	Description
float 4	Variables of this type can have values from –3.4E38 (-3.4×10^{38}) to +3.4E38 ($+3.4 \times 10^{38}$) and occupy 4 bytes in memory. Values are represented with approximately 7 digits accuracy.
double 8	Variables of this type can have values from –1.7E308 (-1.7×10^{308}) to +1.7E308 ($+1.7 \times 10^{308}$) and occupy 8 bytes in memory. Values are represented with approximately 15 digits accuracy. The smallest non-zero value that you can have is roughly $\pm 4.9 \times 10^{-324}$.

FYI   **All floating point operations and the definition for values of type float and type double in Java conform to the IEEE 754 standard.**

As with integer calculations, floating point calculations in Java will produce the same results on any computer.

Floating Point Constants

When you're specifying floating point literals, Java handles them as type **double** by default, so 1.0 and 345.678 are both of type **double**. To specify a value of type **float**, you just append an **f** or an **F** to the value, so 1.0f and 345.678F are both constants of type **float**.

When you need to write very large or very small floating point values, you'll usually want to write them with an exponent—that is, as a decimal value multiplied by a power of 10. You can do this in Java by writing the number as a decimal value, followed by an **E** or an **e** preceding the power of 10 that you require. For example, the distance of the earth to the sun is approximately 149600000 kilometers which is more conveniently written as 1.496E8. Since the **E** (or **e**) precedes the exponent, this is equivalent to 1.496×10^8. At the opposite end of the scale, the mass of an electron is around 0.0000000000000000000000000009 grams. This is much more convenient, not to say more readable, when it's written as 9.0E–28.

Declaring Floating Point Variables

You declare floating point variables in a similar way to that we've already used for integers. We can declare and initialize a variable of type **double** with the statement:

```
double sunDistance = 1.496E8;
```

Declaring a variable of type **float** is much the same. For example:

```
float electronMass = 9E-28F;
```

You can of course declare more than one variable of a given type in a single statement:

```
float hisWeight = 185.2F, herWeight = 108.5F;
```

Now that we know how to declare and initialize variables of the basic types, we're nearly ready to write a program. We just need to look at how to calculate and store the results of a calculation.

Arithmetic Calculations

You store the result of a calculation in a variable by using an **assignment statement**. An assignment statement consists of a variable name followed by an arithmetic expression followed by a semicolon. Here's a simple example of an assignment statement:

```
fruit = apples + oranges;          // Calculate the total fruit
```

The value of the expression to the right of the = sign is calculated, and stored in the variable that appears to the left of the equals sign. In this case, the values in the variables **apples** and **oranges** are added together and the result is stored in the variable **fruit**.

You can write multiple assignments in a single statement. Suppose you have three variables **a**, **b**, and **c**, of type **int**, and you want to set all three to 777. You can do this with the statement:

```
a = b = c = 777;
```

Now let's look in more detail at how we can perform calculations with integers.

Integer Calculations

The basic operators you can use on integers are **+**, **-**, ***** and **/**, which have the usual meanings—add, subtract, multiply and divide. The priority or **precedence** that applies when an expression using these operators is evaluated is the same as you learned in school. Multiplication and division are executed before any addition or subtraction operations, so the expression,

```
20 - 3*3 - 9/3
```

will produce the value 8, since it is equivalent to 20 – 9 – 3.

As you will also have learned in school, you can use parentheses in arithmetic calculations to change the sequence of operations. Expressions within parentheses are always evaluated first, starting with the innermost when they are nested. Therefore the expression,

$$(20 - 3) * (3 - 9) / 3$$

is equivalent to $17*(-6)/3$ which gives us -34.

We can now try out some simple arithmetic in a console application:

Try It Out—Apples and Oranges (or Console Yourself)

1 Key in this example and save it in a file **Fruit.java**. You'll remember from the last chapter that each file will contain a class, and that the name of the file will be the same as that of the class with the extension **.java**.

```java
public class Fruit
{
  public static void main(String[] args)
  {
    // Declare and initialize three variables
    int oranges = 5;
    int apples = 10;
    int fruit = 0;

    fruit = oranges + apples;    // Calculate the total fruit

    System.out.println("A totally fruity program");
    // Display the result
    System.out.println("Total fruit is " + fruit);
  }
}
```

2 Depending on what sort of Java environment you're working in, the output may not be displayed long enough for you to see it. If this is the case, you can add a few lines of code to get the program to wait until you press *Enter* before it ends. The additional lines to do this are shown shaded in the following listing:

```java
import java.io.IOException;  // For code that delays ending the program
public class Fruit
{
  public static void main(String[] args)
  {
    // Declare and initialize three variables
    int oranges = 5;
    int apples = 10;
    int fruit = 0;

    fruit = oranges + apples;    // Calculate the total fruit

    System.out.println("A totally fruity program");
    // Display the result
```

```
    System.out.println("Total fruit is " + fruit);
    // Code to delay ending the program
    System.out.println("(press Enter to exit)");
    try
    {
      System.in.read();              // Read some input from the keyboard
    }
    catch (IOException e)            // Catch the input exception
    {
      return;                        // and just return
    }
  }
}
```

The stuff between parentheses following **main()**—the **String[] args**—provides a means of accessing what is passed to the program from the command line when you run it. We'll be going into this in detail later on so you can just ignore it for now. You must always include it though in the first line of **main()**.

All that the additional code in the body of the **main()** method does is to wait until you press *Enter* before ending the program. If necessary, you can include this in all of our console programs to make sure they don't disappear before you can read the output. It won't make any difference to how the rest of the program works. We'll defer discussing in detail what is happening in this bit of code that we've added until we get to the topic of exceptions in Chapter 7.

If you run this program with the additional code, the output will be similar to the following window:

Here are the basic elements in the original version of the program:

```
                                                              This specifies that main()
                                                              is accessible from outside
      public class Fruit                                              of the class
      {
                                                              This specifies that main()
        public static void main(String[] args)               exists without any objects
        {                                                          being defined
          //Declare and initialize three variables           This specifies that main()
          Int oranges = 5;                                    does not return a value
          int apples = 10;
          int fruit = 0;                                      Execution starts with
Executable code                                                    this statement
for main()      fruit = oranges + apples     //Calculate the total fruit
                                                              This displays the
          System.out.println("A totally fruity program");     first output line
          System.out.println("Total fruit is " + fruit);    // Display the result
        }                                                     This displays the
                                                              second output line
      }
```

Our program consists of just one class, **Fruit**, and the class has no instance variables and just one method, **main()**. Remember that an instance variable is a variable within the class definition that will typically have different values for different objects of the class, and a method is a named block of code within the class definition that defines an operation for the class.

Execution of an application always starts at the first executable statement in the method **main()**. There are no objects of our class **Fruit** defined, but the method **main()** can still be executed because we have specified it as **static**. The method **main()** is always specified as **public** and **static** and with the return type **void**. We can summarize the effects of these on the method as:

public   Specifies that the method is accessible from outside of the class.

static   Specifies that the method is to be executable, even though no class objects have been created. (Methods that are not **static** must executed for a particular object of the class as we will see.)

void   Specifies that the method does not return a value.

The first three statements in **main()** declare the variables **oranges**, **apples** and **fruit** to be of type **int** and initialize them to the values 5, 10, and 0 respectively. The next statement adds the values stored in **oranges** and **apples**, and stores the result, 15, in the variable **fruit**.

Producing Output

The next two statements use the method **println()** which displays text output. The statement looks a bit complicated but it breaks down quite simply:

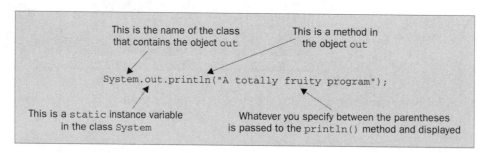

The text between double quotes, **"A totally fruity program"** is a character string. Whenever you need a string constant, you just put the sequence of characters between double quotes.

You can see from the annotations above how you execute methods that belong to an object. Here we execute the method **println()** which belongs to the object **out**, which, in turn, is an instance variable of the class **System**. Since the object **out** is **static**, it will exist even if there are no objects of type **System** in existence. This is analogous to the use of the keyword **static** for the method **main()**. If you guessed from the last example that to call the **putHatOn()** method for an object **cowboyHat** of the **Hat** class that we introduced in Chapter 1, you would write,

```
        cowboyHat.putHatOn();
```

you would be right. Don't worry if you didn't though. We'll be going into this again when we get to look at classes in detail. For the moment, any time we want to output something as text to the console, we will just write,

```
    System.out.println( whateverWeWantToDisplay );
```

with whatever data we want to display plugged in between the parentheses.

Thus the second statement in our example,

```
    System.out.println("Total fruit is " + fruit);
```

outputs the character string **Total fruit is** followed by the value of **fruit** converted to characters which is **15**. So what's the **+** doing here—it's not arithmetic we are doing, is it? No, but the plus has a special effect when used with character strings: it joins them together. But **fruit** is not a string, is it? No, but **"Total fruit is "** is, and this causes the compiler to decide that the whole thing is an expression working on character strings. It therefore converts fruit to a character string to be compatible with the string **"Total fruit is "** and tacks it on the end. The composite string is then passed to the **println()** method. "Dashed clever, these compilers."

If you wanted to output the value of **oranges** as well, you could write:

```
    System.out.println("Total fruit is " + fruit
                  + " and oranges = " + oranges);
```

Try it out if you like. You should get this output:

```
    Total fruit is 15 and oranges = 5
```

Integer Division and Remainders

When you divide one integer by another, if the result is not exact any remainder is discarded. So 3/2, for example, produces the result 1, and 11/3 produces the result 3.

Of course, there are circumstances where you may want the remainder and on these occasions you can calculate the remainder using the modulus operator, **%**. If you wanted to know how many fruit were left after dividing the total by 4, you could write:

```
    int remainder = 0;
    remainder = fruit % 4;    // Calculate the remainder after division by 4
```

You could add this to the program too if you want to see the modulus operator in action. The modulus operator has the same precedence as multiply and divide, and is therefore executed in an expression before any add or subtract operations.

The Increment and Decrement Operators

If you want to increment an integer variable you can use the operator **++**. For example, if you have an integer variable count declared as,

```
int count = 10;
```

you can then write the statement,

```
++count;      // Add 1 to count
```

which will increase the value of count to 11. If you want to decrease the value of count by 1 you can use the decrement operator, --:

```
--count;      // Subtract 1 from count
```

At first sight, this doesn't seem to have much of an advantage over writing:

```
count = count - 1;      //Subtract 1 from count
```

but the one big advantage of the increment and decrement operators is that you can use them in an expression.

Try It Out—Incrementing Oranges

Try changing the arithmetic statement calculating the sum of **apples** and **oranges** in the previous example:

```
public class Fruit
{
  public static void main(String[] args)
  {
    // Declare and initialize three variables
    int oranges = 5;
    int apples = 10;
    int fruit = 0;

    // Increment oranges and calculate the total fruit
    fruit = ++oranges + apples;

    System.out.println("A totally fruity program");
    // Display the result
    System.out.println("Value of oranges is " + oranges);
    System.out.println("Total fruit is " + fruit);
  }
}
```

Running the program you should see:

```
A totally fruity program
Value of oranges is 6
Total fruit is 16
```

How It Works

The lines that have been altered or added have been highlighted. In addition to the change to the **fruit** calculation, an extra statement has been added to output the final value of oranges. The value of **oranges** will be increased to 6 before the value of apples is added, so the value of fruit will be 16. You can try the decrement operation in the example as well.

A further property of the increment and decrement operators is that they work differently in an expression depending on whether you put the operator in front of the variable, or after it. When you put the operator in front of a variable, as in the example we have just seen, it's called the **prefix form**. The converse case, with the operator following the variable, is called the **postfix form**. If you change the statement in the example to,

```
fruit = (oranges++) + apples;
```

and run it again, you'll find that **oranges** still ends up with the value 6, but the total stored in **fruit** has reverted to 15. This is because the effect of the postfix increment operator is to change the value of **oranges** to 6 after the original value, 5, has been used in the expression to supply the value of **fruit**. The postfix decrement operator works similarly, and both operators can be applied to any type of integer variable.

The parentheses in the expression **(oranges++) + apples** are not strictly necessary. You could write it as **oranges++ + apples**, or even as **oranges+++apples** and it will still mean the same thing but it is less obvious what you mean, especially in the latter case. It's a good idea to add parentheses to clarify things when there's some possibility of confusion. ✓

Computation with Shorter Integer Types

With arithmetic expressions using variables of type **byte** or **short**, the calculation is carried out with 32-bit arithmetic, and the result will be a 32-bit number. As a consequence, if you change the types of the variables **oranges**, **apples**, and **fruit** in the original version of the program to **short** for example,

```
short oranges = 5;
short apples = 10;
short fruit = 0;
```

then the program will no longer compile. The problem is with the statement:

```
fruit = oranges + apples;
```

Since the expression **oranges + apples** produces a 32-bit result, the compiler can't store this value in **fruit**, as the variable **fruit** is only 16-bits long. You must modify the code to convert the result of the addition back to a 16-bit number. You do this by changing the statement to:

41

```
fruit = (short)(oranges + apples);
```

The statement now calculates the sum of **oranges** and **apples** and then converts or **casts** it to the type **short** before storing it in **fruit**. This is called an **explicit cast**, and the conversion process is referred to as **casting**. The cast applies to whatever is to the right of **(short)** so the parentheses around the expression **oranges + apples** are necessary. Without them the cast would only apply to the variable **oranges** which is a **short** anyway, and the code would still not compile. Similarly, if the variables here were of type **byte**, you would need to cast the result of the addition to the type **byte**.

The effect of the cast to **short** is to just take the least significant 16 bits of the result, discarding the most significant 16 bits. For the cast to type **byte** only the least significant 8 bits are kept. This means that if the magnitude of the result is such that more than 16 bits are necessary to represent it (or 8 bits in the case of a cast to **byte**), your answer will be wrong. You'll get no indication from the compiler that this has occurred so you should avoid explicit casts unless they are absolutely essential.

To recap, an integer arithmetic involving a value of type **long** will be carried using 64-bit values—numbers that are not of type long will be cast to **long**. All other integer arithmetic involving types other than **long** is carried out with 32-bit values. Thus, you only really need to consider two kinds of integer literals:

- The type **long** for operations with 64-bit values where the value has an **L** appended
- The type **int** for operations with 32-bit values for all other cases where there is no **L** at the end of the number

Errors in Integer Arithmetic

If you divide an integer value by zero an exception will be thrown. An exception is the way of signaling errors in Java that we'll discuss in detail in Chapter 7. Using the **%** operator with a variable or expression for the right-hand operand that has a zero value will also cause an exception to be thrown.

Bitwise Operations

Of course, as you probably already know, all these integer variables we have been talking about are represented internally as binary numbers. A value of type **int** consists of 32 binary digits, known to computer fans as **bits**. You can combine integer values by logically combining or operating on their bits using the **bitwise operators**. Four bitwise operators are available to work on integers:

&	Bitwise AND	|	Bitwise OR
^	Bitwise XOR	~	Bitwise complement

Each of these operators works with individual bits as follows:

▶ The ~ operator is the NOT operator, and takes a single operand (a value that an operator is applied to is called an **operand**) in which it inverts all the bits, so that each 1 bit becomes 0, which is *NOT* 1, and each 0 bit becomes 1 which is *NOT* 0.

▶ The **&** operator is the AND operator, and combines corresponding bits in its two operands such that if the first bit *AND* the second bit are 1, the result is 1— otherwise the result is 0.

▶ The **|** operator is the OR operator, and combines corresponding bits such that if either one bit *OR* the other is 1, then the result is 1. Only if both bits are 0 is the result is 0.

▶ The **^** operator, is the exclusive OR (XOR) operator, and combines corresponding bits such that if both bits are the same the result is 0, otherwise the result is 1.

You can see the effect of these operators in the following examples.

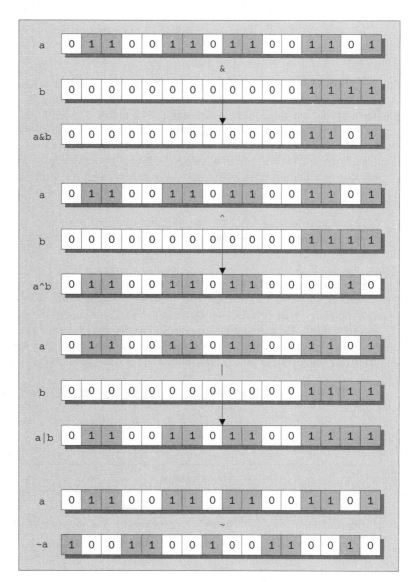

The illustration shows the binary digits that make up the operands and the results. It is not a very convenient way to write binary numbers, but neither is the normal decimal value when you're using bitwise operators. A very handy shorthand way of writing binary values is to express them as hexadecimal numbers, which are to base 16, because you can convert from binary to hexadecimal, and vice versa, very quickly. We saw how to write hexadecimal numbers in Java earlier in this chapter. Let's briefly look at how you convert between binary and hexadecimal.

Converting from binary to hexadecimal is easy. Each group of four binary digits corresponds to one hexadecimal digit. You just work out what the value of each four bits is and write the appropriate hexadecimal digit. For example, the value of **a** from the illustration is:

Binary	0110	0110	1100	1101
Decimal value	6	6	12	13
Hexadecimal	6	6	C	D

So the value of the variable **a** in hexadecimal is **0x66CD**, where the **0x** prefix indicates that it is a hexadecimal value. The variable **b** in the illustration has the hexadecimal value **0x000F**. If you think of the variable **b** as a **mask** applied to **a**, you can view the **&** operator as keeping bits unchanged where the mask is 1 and setting the rest to 0. **Mask** is a term used to refer to a particular configuration of bits designed to select out specific bits when it's combined with a variable using a bitwise operator. So if you want to select a particular bit out of an integer variable, just *AND* it with a mask with that bit set to 1 and all the others as 0.

You can also look at what the **&** operator does from another perspective—it forces a bit to 0, if the corresponding mask bit is 0. Similarly, the **|** operator forces a bit to be 1 when the mask bit is 1.

The **&** and **|** are the most frequently used of these operators, mainly for dealing with variables where the individual bits are used as **state indicators** of some kind for things that can be either true or false, or on or off. You could use a single bit as a state indicator determining whether something should be displayed—with the bit as 1, or not displayed—with the bit as 0. A single bit can be selected using the **&** operator; for example, to select the third bit in a variable **indicators**, you can write:

```
thirdBit = indicators&0x4;      // Select the 3rd bit
```

We can illustrate how this works if we assume the variable **indicators** contains the hexadecimal value **0xFF07**:

	Hexadecimal	Binary			
indicators	0xFF07	1111	1111	0000	0111
mask value	0x4	0000	0000	0000	0100
indicators&0x4	0x0004	0000	0000	0000	0100

All these values should have 32 bits and we are only showing 16 bits here, but you will see how it works from this anyway. The mask value will set all the bits in indicators to zero except for the third bit. Here, the result of the expression is non-zero because the third bit in **indicators** is 1.

On the other hand, if the variable **indicators** contained the value **0xFF09** the result would be different:

	Hexadecimal	Binary			
indicators	0xFF09	1111	1111	0000	1001
mask value	0x4	0000	0000	0000	0100
indicators&0x4	0x0000	0000	0000	0000	0000

The result of the expression is now zero because the third bit of indicators is zero.

To set a particular bit on, you can use the | operator, so to set the third bit in **indicators** on, you can write:

```
indicators = indicators|0x4;   // Set the 3rd bit on
```

We can see how this applies to the last value we had for indicators:

	Hexadecimal	Binary			
indicators	0xFF09	1111	1111	0000	1001
mask value	0x4	0000	0000	0000	0100
indicators|0x4	0FF0D	1111	1111	0000	1101

As you can see, the effect is just to switch the third bit of indicators on. All the others are unchanged. Of course, if it was already on, it would stay on.

To set a bit off you need to use the **&** operator again, with a mask that has 0 for the bit you want as 0, and 1 for all the others. To set the third bit of **indicators** off you could write:

```
indicators = indicators&~0x4;   // Set the 3rd bit off
```

With **indicators** having the value **0xFF07**, this would work as follows:

	Hexadecimal	Binary			
indicators	0xFF07	1111	1111	0000	0111
mask value	0x4	0000	0000	0000	0100
~0x4		1111	1111	1111	1011
indicators&!0x4	0FF0D	1111	1111	0000	1101

The ^ operator has the slightly surprising ability to interchange two values without moving either value somewhere else. If you execute three statements:

```
a = a^b;
b = a^b;
a = a^b;
```

this will interchange the values of the integers **a** and **b**. We can try this out with a couple of arbitrary values for **a** and **b**, **0xD00F** and **0xABAD** respectively—again we'll just look at 16 bits for each variable. The first statement will change **a** to a new value:

	Hexadecimal		Binary		
a	0xD00F	1101	0000	0000	1111
b	0xABAD	1010	1011	1010	1101
a from a^b	07BA2	0111	1011	1010	0010

Now the next statement which calculates a new value of **b** using the new value of **a**:

	Hexadecimal		Binary		
a	07BA2	0111	1011	1010	0010
b	0xABAD	1010	1011	1010	1101
b from a^b	0xFF0D	1101	0000	0000	1111

So **b** now has a value that looks remarkably like the value that **a** started out with. Let's look at the last step which calculates a new value for **a** using the new value of **b**:

	Hexadecimal		Binary		
a	07BA2	0111	1011	1010	0010
b	0xFF0D	1101	0000	0000	1111
b from a^b	0xABAD	1010	1011	1010	1101

Lo and behold, the value of **a** is now the original value of **b**. In the old days when all programmers had beards, when computers were driven by steam, and when memory was measured in bytes rather than megabytes, this mechanism could be quite useful since you could interchange two values in memory without having to have extra memory locations available. So if antique computers are your thing this may turn out to be a valuable technique.

*Don't forget—all of these bitwise operators can only be applied to integers. They don't work with any other type of value. As with the arithmetic expressions, the bitwise operations are carried out with 32 bits for integers of type **short** and of type **byte**, so a cast to the appropriate type is necessary for the result of the expression on the right of the assignment operator.*

Shift Operations

Another mechanism that you have for working with integer variables at the bit level is **shifting**. You can shift the bits in an integer to the right or the left. You can envisage shifting binary digits right or left as dividing or multiply by powers of two. Shift the binary value of 3, which is 0011, to the left one bit multiplies it by two. It becomes binary 0110 which is 6. Shifting it to the right by one bit divides it by 2—it becomes binary 0001 which is 1.

Java has three shift operators:

    <<   Shift left, filling with zeros from the right

    >>   Shift right, propagating the sign bit from the left

    >>>   Shift right, filling with zeros from the left

The effect of the operators is shown in the following illustration.

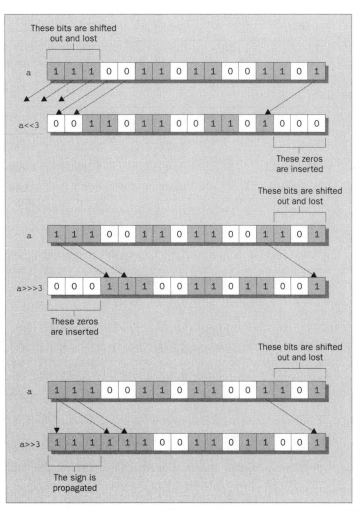

Of course, if the high order bit in the **>>** operation in the illustration was zero, there would be three zeros at the leftmost end of the result. If you haven't come across shift operations before you may be wondering why you have an extra shift-right operation that propagates the leftmost bit. It's related to the notion of a shift as multiplying or dividing by a power of 2, and to how negative integers are represented on the majority of computers.

The sign of a binary number is indicated by the leftmost bit. If it is 1 the value is negative, and if it's zero the value is positive. However, there's a bit more to it than that. Negative integers are usually represented in two's complement form (to form the two's complement of a binary number, flip all the bits and add 1). We can obtain the two's complement representation of –16 as a **short** value from + 16, as follows:

	Hexadecimal	Binary			
+16	0x0010	0000	0000	0001	0000
flip the bits		1111	1111	1110	1111
Value 1 to add	0x0001	0000	0000	0000	0001
–16	0xFFF0	1111	1111	1111	0000

It doesn't look much like –16, but it is. To show that this really is –16 we can add 30 to it. We should get 14 as a result:

	Hexadecimal	Binary			
–16	0xFFF0	1111	1111	1111	0000
30 to add	0x001E	0000	0000	0001	1110
Result is 14	0x000E	0000	0000	0000	1110

So it works.

If you shift –16 right by two, you would expect the result to be –4 since each bit shift is equivalent to shifting the binary point. However if you use the operator **>>>** for this, the result will be:

```
0011 1111 1111 1100
```

which is nothing like –4. In fact it's 16,380. The leftmost bit in a binary integer is the sign bit. If you use the operator **>>** which propagates the sign (that is, fills in the new bits introduced on the left with whatever the sign bit is), the result is:

```
1111 1111 1111 1100
```

which is –4, the result you would expect.

You can check that this is indeed –4 by flipping the bits and adding 1 to get the two's complement. You should end up with 4.

Floating Point Calculations

The four basic arithmetic operators, **+**, **-**, *****, **/**, are also available for use in floating point expressions. We can try some of these out in another version of the **Fruit** program we'll call **AverageFruit**:

Try It Out—Average Fruit

Make the following changes to the **Fruit.java** file, and save this as **AverageFruit.java**. If necessary, you can add in the code we used earlier to make the program wait for the *Enter* key to be pressed before finishing.

```
public class AverageFruit
{
  public static void main(String[] args)
  {
    // Declare and initialize three variables
    double oranges = 50.0E-1;
    double apples = 1.0E1;
    double averageFruit = 0.0;

    averageFruit = (oranges + apples) / 2.0;

    System.out.println("A totally fruity program");
    System.out.println("Average fruit is " + averageFruit);
  }
}
```

This will produce the output:

```
A totally fruity program
Average fruit is 7.5
```

The program just computes the average number of fruits by dividing the total by 2.0.

 As you can see, we've used various representations for the initializing values for the variables in the program, which are now of type **double**. It's not the ideal way to write 5.0 but at least it demonstrates that you can write a negative exponent value.

Other Floating Point Operators

You can use **++** and **--** with floating point variables, and they have the same effect as with integer variables, <u>incrementing or decrementing</u> the floating point variable to which they are applied by 1.0. You can use them in prefix or postfix form, and their operation in each case is the same as with integer variables.

You can apply the <u>modulus</u> operator, **%**, to floating point values too. For the operation,

```
floatOperand1%floatOperand2
```

the result will be the floating point remainder after dividing **floatOperand2** into **floatOperand1** an integral number of times. For example, the expression **12.6%5.1** will give the result 2.4.

Error Conditions in Floating Point Arithmetic

There are two error conditions that are signaled by a special result value being generated. One occurs when a calculation produces a value which is <u>outside the range</u> that can be represented, and the other arises when the result is <u>mathematically indeterminate</u>, such as when your calculation is effectively dividing zero by zero.

To illustrate the first kind of error we could use a variable to specify the number of types of fruit. We could define the variable,

```
double fruitTypes = 2.0;
```

and then rewrite the calculation as:

```
averageFruit = (oranges + apples) / fruitTypes;
```

This in itself isn't particularly interesting, but if we happened to set **fruitTypes** to 0.0, the output from the program would be:

```
A totally fruity program
Average fruit is Infinity
```

The value **Infinity** indicates a positive but effectively infinite result, in that it is greater than the largest number that can be represented as type **double**. A negative infinite result would be output as –Infinity. You don't actually need to divide by zero to produce this effect; any calculation which generates a value outside the data type's range will have the same effect. Repeatedly dividing by a very small number such as 1.0E–300 will result in an out-of-range result, for example.

If you want to see what an indeterminate result looks like, you can replace the statement to calculate **averageFruit** with:

```
averageFruit = (oranges - 5.0)/(apples-10.0);
```

This statement doesn't make much sense but it will produce an indeterminate result. The value of **averageFruit** will be output as <u>NaN</u>. This value is referred to as **Not-a-Number**. A variable with an indeterminate value will contaminate any subsequent expression in which it is used, to produce the same result.

A value that is **Infinity** or **-Infinity** will be unchanged when you add, subtract, or multiply by finite values, but if you divide any finite value by **Infinity** or **-Infinity** the result will be zero.

Mixed Arithmetic Expressions

You can mix values of the basic types together in a single expression. The way mixed expressions are treated is governed by some simple rules that apply to each operator in such an expression. The first rule that applies is the one that is used:

> If either operand is of type **double**, the other is converted to **double** before the operation is carried out.

> If either operand is of type **float**, the other is converted to **float** before the operation is carried out.

> If either operand is of type **long** the other is converted to **long** before the operation is carried out.

If neither operand is **double**, **float** or **long**, they must be **int**, **short**, or **byte**, so they use 32-bit arithmetic as we saw earlier.

Explicit Casting

It may well be that the default treatment of mixed expressions listed above is not what you want. For example, if you have a **double** variable **result**, and you compute its value using two **int** variables **three** and **two** with the values 3 and 2, with the statement,

```
result = 1.5 + three/two;
```

the value stored will be 2.5. You may have wanted the term **three/two** to produce the value 1.5 so the overall result would be 3.0. You could do this using an explicit cast:

```
result = 1.5 + (double)three/two;
```

This causes the value stored in **three** to be converted to **double** before the divide operation takes place. Then rule 1 applies for the divide operation, and the operand **two** is also converted to double before the divide is executed. Hence the value of **result** will be 3.0.

 FYI You can cast any of the basic types to any other, but you need to take care that you don't lose information when you do so. Obviously casting from a larger integer type to a smaller has the potential for losing information, as does casting any floating point value to an integer. Casting from **double** to **float** can also produce effective infinity when the original value is greater than 10^{38}.

Casting in Assignments

When the result of an expression on the right of an assignment statement differs from the type on the left of the assignment, an automatic cast will be applied as long as there's no possibility of losing information. If you think of the basic types we've seen so far, as being in the sequence,

byte ➔ **short** ➔ **int** ➔ **long** ➔ **float** ➔ **double**

then an automatic conversion will be made as long as it is upwards through the sequence, that is, from left to right. If you want to go in the opposite direction, from **double** to **float** or **long** for example, then you must use an explicit cast.

The op= Operators

The **op=** operators are used in statements of the form,

```
lhs op= rhs;
```

where **op** can be any of the operators **+**, **-**, *****, **/**, **%**, plus some others you haven't seen yet. The above is a shorthand representation of the statement:

```
lhs = lhs op (rhs);
```

The right-hand side is in brackets because it is worked out first—then the result is combined with the left-hand side using the operation, **op**. Let's look at a few examples of this to make sure it's clear. To increment an **int** variable **count** by 5 you can write,

```
count += 5;
```

which is equivalent to:

```
count = count + 5;
```

Of course the expression to the right of the **op=** operator can be anything that is legal in the context, so the statement,

```
result /= a % b/(a + b);
```

is equivalent to:

```
result = result/(a % b/(a + b));
```

The bitwise operators can also be used in the **op=** form. Setting the third bit in the variable indicators that we saw earlier would usually be written as,

```
indicators |= 0x4;
```

although there's nothing wrong with the original statement we wrote. The one above is just a bit more concise.

The complete set of **op=** operators appears in the precedence table later in this chapter.

Mathematical Functions

Sooner or later you're likely to need mathematical functions in your programs, even if it's only obtaining an absolute value or calculating a square root. Java provides a range of methods that support such functions as part of the standard library stored in the package **java.lang**, and all these are available in your program automatically. The methods that support various additional mathematical functions are implemented in the class **Math**, so to reference a particular function you need to write **Math** and a period in front of the function name. To use **sqrt()**, for example, which calculates the square root of whatever you place between the parentheses, you would write **Math.sqrt(aNumber)**. *e.g.*

The class **Math** includes a range of methods for standard trigonometrical functions. These are:

Method	Function	Argument	Result
sin(arg)	sine of the argument	Of type **double** in radians	Of type **double**
cos(arg)	cosine of the argument	Of type **double** in radians	Of type **double**
tan(arg)	tangent of the argument	Of type **double** in radians	Of type **double**
asin(arg)	$\sin^{-1}$ (arc sine) of the argument	Of type **double**	Of type **double** in radians
acos(arg)	$\cos^{-1}$ (arc cosine) of the argument	Of type **double**	Of type **double** in radians

Table Continued on Following Page

53

Method	Function	Argument	Result
`atan(arg)`	tan⁻¹ (arc tangent) of the argument	Of type `double`	Of type `double` in radians
`atan2(arg1,arg2)`	tan⁻¹ (arc tangent) of `arg1/arg2`	Both of type `double`	Of type `double` in radians

As with all methods, the argument or arguments which you put inside the parentheses following the method name, can be any expression that produces a value of the required type. If you aren't familiar with these trigonometric operations you can safely ignore them.

You also have a range of numerical functions that are implemented in the class `Math`. These are:

Method	Function	Argument	Result
`abs(arg)`	Calculates absolute value of the argument	Can be of type `int`, `long`, `float` or `double`	The same type as the argument
`max(arg1,arg2)`	Returns the larger of the two arguments	Can be of type `int`, `long`, `float` or `double`	The same type as the argument
`min(arg1,arg2)`	Returns the smaller of the two arguments	Can be of type `int`, `long`, `float` or `double`	The same type as the argument
`ceil(arg)`	Returns the smallest integer that is greater than or equal to the argument	Of type `double`	Of type `double`
`floor(arg)`	Returns the largest integer that is less than or equal to the argument	Of type `double`	Of type `double`
`round(arg)`	Calculates the nearest integer to the argument value	Of type `float` or `double`	Of type `int` for a `float` argument, of type `long` for a `double` argument
`rint(arg)`	Calculates the nearest integer to the argument value	Of type `double`	Of type `double`
`IEEEremainder (arg1,arg2)`	Calculates the remainder when `arg1` is divided by `arg2`	Both of type `double`	Of type `double`

FYI The `IEEERemainder()` method produces the remainder from `arg1` after dividing `arg2` into `arg1` the integral number of times that is closest to the exact value of `arg1/arg2`.

Where more than one type of argument is noted in the table, there are actually several methods, one for each type of argument, but all having the same name. We'll see how this is possible in Java when we look into implementing class methods in Chapter 5.

The mathematical functions available in the class `Math` are:

Method	Function	Argument	Result
`sqrt(arg)`	Calculates the square root of the argument	Of type `double`	Of type `double`
`pow(arg1,arg2)`	Calculates the first argument raised to the power of the second argument $\text{arg1}^{\text{arg2}}$	Both of type `double`	Of type `double`
`exp(arg)`	Calculates **e** raised to the power of the argument e^{arg}	Of type `double`	Of type `double`
`log(arg)`	Calculates the natural logarithm(base **e**) of the argument	Of type `double`	Of type `double`
`random()`	Returns a pseudorandom number between 0.0 and 1.0	None	Of type `double`

The Math class also defines **double** values for **e** and π, which you can access as **Math.E** and **Math.PI** respectively.

Let's try out a sample of the contents of the class **Math** in an example to make sure we know how they are used.

Try It Out—The *Math Class*

Type in the following program, which will calculate the radius of a circle in feet and inches, given that it has an area of 100 square feet.

```java
public class MathCalc
{
  public static void main(String[] args)
  {
```

```
      // Calculate the radius of a circle
      // which has an area of 100 square feet
      double radius = 0.0;
      double circleArea = 100.0;
      int feet = 0;
      int inches = 0;
      radius = Math.sqrt(circleArea/Math.PI);
      feet = (int)Math.floor(radius);      // Get the whole feet and nothing
                                           // but the feet
      inches = (int)Math.round(12.0*(radius - feet));
      System.out.println("The radius of a circle with area " +
                      circleArea + " square feet is\n " +
                      feet + " feet " + inches + " inches");
   }
}
```

Save the program as **MathCalc.java**. When you compile and run it, you should get:

```
The radius of a circle with area 100 square feet is
 5 feet 8 inches
```

How It Works

The first calculation, after defining the variables we need, uses the **sqrt()** method to calculate the radius. Since the area of a circle, with radius r, is given by the formula πr^2, the radius must be $\sqrt{(area/\pi)}$, and we specify the argument to the **sqrt()** method as the expression **circleArea/Math.PI**, where **Math.PI** references the value of π. The result is in feet as a **double** value. To get the number of whole feet we use the **floor()** method. Note that the cast to **int** is essential, otherwise you'll get an error message from the compiler.

Lastly, we get the number of inches by subtracting the value for whole feet from the original radius, multiplying the fraction of a foot by 12 to get the equivalent inches, and then rounding the result to the nearest integer using the **round()** method.

Note how we output the result. We specify the combination (or concatenation) of strings and variables as an argument to the **println()** method. The statement is spread over three lines for convenience here. The output will be on two lines. The \n in the output specifies a newline character. Any time you want the next bit of output on a newline, just add \n to the output string.

Storing Characters

Variables of the type **char** store a single character. They each occupy 16 bits—2 bytes—in memory because all characters in Java are stored as Unicode. To declare and initialize a character variable **myCharacter** you would use the statement:

```
char myCharacter = 'X';
```

This initializes the variable with the Unicode character representation of the letter **'X'**. You must put the single quotes around a character in a statement—**'X'**. This is necessary to enable the compiler to distinguish between the character **'X'** and the variable with the name **X**.

If you're using an ASCII text editor you will only able to enter characters directly that are defined within ASCII. You can define Unicode characters by specifying the hexadecimal representation of the character codes in an **escape sequence**. An escape sequence is simply an alternative means of specifying a character, often by its code. A backslash indicates the start of an escape sequence, and you create an escape sequence for a Unicode character by preceding the four hexadecimal digits of the character by **\u**. Since the Unicode coding for the letter X is 0x0058 (the low order byte is the same as the ASCII code), you could also declare and define **myCharacter** with the statement:

```
char myCharacter = '\u0058';
```

You can enter any Unicode character in this way, although it isn't exactly user-friendly for entering a lot of characters.

FYI   **You can get more information on the full Unicode character set on the Internet by visiting http://www.unicode.org/.**

Because the backslash indicates the beginning of an escape sequence in a character string, you must use an escape sequence to specify a backslash character itself, ****. You can define a single quote with the escape sequence **\'**, and a double quote with **\"**. For example, to produce the output:

```
"I'm at breaking point", he snapped.
```

You could write:

```
System.out.println("\"I\'m at breaking point\", he snapped.");
```

There are other escape characters you can use to define control characters:

\b	Backspace
\n	New line
\r	Carriage return
\t	Tab

You can perform arithmetic on **char** variables. With **myCharacter** set to **X**, the statement,

```
myCharacter += 1;     // Increment to next character
```

will assign **myCharacter** the value **Y**. You could use the increment operator **++** to increase the code stored in **myCharacter** by just writing:

```
    ++myCharacter;          // Increment to next character
```

You can use variables of type **char** in an arithmetic expression. It doesn't necessarily make a whole lot of sense, but you could write,

```
    char aChar = 0;
    char bChar = '\u0028';
    aChar = (char)(2*bChar + 8);
```

which will leave **aChar** holding the code for **x**—which is 0x0058.

Boolean Variables

Boolean variables are variables that can only have one of two values, **true** or **false**. You can define a **boolean** variable, **state**, with the statement:

```
    boolean state = true;
```

This statement also initializes the variable **state** with the value **true**. You can also set a **boolean** variable in an assignment statement. For example, the statement,

```
    state = false;
```

sets the value of the variable **state** to **false**.

At this point we can't do much with a **boolean** variable, other than to set its value to **true** or **false**, but as you will see in the next chapter booleans become much more useful in the context of decision making in a program.

> *One point you should note is that **boolean** variables differ from the other basic data types in that they can't be cast to any other basic type, and the other basic types can't be cast to **boolean**.*

Operator Precedence

We've already recapped the idea of there being a pecking order for operators, which determines the sequence in which they are executed in a statement. We can now formalize the position by classifying all the operators present in Java. Each operator in Java has a set priority or precedence in relation to the others, as shown in the following table. Operators with a higher precedence are executed before those of a lower precedence, and where two or more operators are of equal precedence they are executed in a particular sequence called the <u>associativity</u> of the operators. Order of precedence in the table is highest at the top down to lowest at the bottom:

Operators	Associativity
(), [], .	left to right
unary +, unary −, ++, −−, ~, !, **(type)**	right to left
*, /, %	left to right
+, −	left to right
<<, >>, >>>	left to right
< ,<= , >, >=, instanceof	left to right
==, !=	left to right
&	left to right
^	left to right
|	left to right
&&	left to right
||	left to right
? :	left to right
=, +=, −=, *=, /=, %=, <<=, >>=, >>>=, &=, |=, ^=	right to left

Most of the operators that appear in the table you have not seen yet, but you will meet them all in this book eventually, and it is handy to have them all gathered together in a single precedence table that you can refer back to when necessary.

Operators that appear in the same box in the table are of equal precedence. The sequence of execution of operators with equal precedence in a statement is determined by the associativity of the group. If the associativity is left to right, they are executed in sequence starting with the leftmost and ending with the rightmost. Right to left associativity runs in the opposite direction. For example, if you write the statement,

```
a = b + c + 10;
```

the left-to-right associativity of the group to which the + operator belongs implies that this is effectively:

```
a = (b + c) + 10;
```

On the other hand = and **op=** are right-to-left associative, so if you have **int** variables **a**, **b**, **c**, and **d** each initialized to 1, the statement,

```
a += b = c += d = 10;
```

sets **a** to 12, **b** and **c** to 11 and **d** to 10. The statement is equivalent to:

```
a += (b = (c += (d = 10)));
```

Note that these statements are intended to illustrate how associativity works, and are not a recommended approach to coding.

You'll probably find that you'll learn the precedence and associativity of the operators in Java by just using them in your programs. You may need to refer back to the table from time to time, but as you gain experience you'll gain a feel for where the operators sit and eventually you will automatically know when you need parentheses and when you don't.

Program Comments

We've been adding comments in all our examples so far, so you already know that everything following // in a line is ignored by the compiler (except when the // appears in a character string between double quotes, of course). Another use for // is to comment out lines of code. If you want to remove some code from a program temporarily, you just need to add // at the beginning of each line you want to eliminate.

It's often convenient to include multiple lines of comment in a program, at the beginning of a method to explain what it does for example. An alternative to using // at the beginning of each line in a block of comments is to put /* at the beginning of the first comment line and */ at the end of the last comment line. Everything between the /* and the next */ will be ignored. By this means you can annotate your programs like this for example:

```
/****************************************
 * This is a long explanation of        *
 * some particularly important          *
 * aspect of program operation.         *
 ****************************************/
```

Of course, you can frame blocks like this in any way that you like, or even not at all, just so long as there is /* at the beginning and */ at the end.

Documentation Comments

You can also include comments in a program that are intended to produce separate documentation for the program. These are called **documentation comments**. The documentation is produced by processing a program containing documentation comments with a program called **javadoc**. The documentation generated is in the form of hypertext web pages that can be viewed using a browser. A fuller discussion of the possible documentation comments can be found in Appendix B. For now, we will just describe the topic in sufficient detail for you to recognize documentation comments when you see them.

A documentation comment begins with /** and ends with */. An example of a simple documentation comment is:

```
/**
 * This is a documentation comment.
 */
```

Any asterisks at the beginning of each line in a documentation comment are ignored, as are any spaces preceding the first *****.

A documentation comment can also include HTML tags, as well as special tags beginning with **@** that are used to document methods and classes in a standard form. The **@** is followed by a keyword that defines the purpose of the tag. You can use the following keywords:

@author	Used to define the author of the code.
@deprecated	Used in the documentation of library classes and methods to indicate that they have been superseded and generally shouldn't be used in new applications.
@exception	Used to document exceptions that the code can throw and the circumstances which can cause this to occur.
@param	Used to describe the parameters for a method.
@return	Used to document the value returned from a method.
@see	Used to specify cross references to some other part of the code such as another class or a method. It can also reference a URL.
@version	Used to describe the current version of the code.

You can use any HTML tags within a documentation comment except for the heading tags, **H1** and **H2**. The HTML tags you insert are used to structure and format the documentation appropriately when it is viewed, and **javadoc** will add HTML tags to format the comments that include the special **@** tags that we mentioned above.

Summary

In this chapter you have seen all of the basic types of variables available in Java. The discussion of **boolean** variables will be more meaningful in the context of the next chapter since their primary use is in decision making and modifying the sequence of execution of a program.

The important points you have learned in this chapter are:

- The integer types are **byte**, **short**, **int**, and **long**, occupying 1, 2, 4 and 8 bytes respectively

- Variables of type **char** occupy 2 bytes and can store a single Unicode character code

- Integer expressions are evaluated using 64-bit operations for variables of type **long**, and using 32-bit operations for all other integer types. You must therefore add a cast for all assignment operations storing a result of type **byte**, **short**, or **char**

- A cast will be automatically supplied where necessary for **op=** assignment operations

- The floating point types are **float** and **double**, occupying 4 and 8 bytes respectively

▶ Values that are outside the range of a floating point type are represented by a special value that is displayed as either Infinity or − Infinity

▶ Where the result of a floating point calculation is indeterminate, the value is displayed as NaN. Such values are referred to as **Not-a-Number**

▶ Variables of type **boolean** can only have either the value **true**, or the value **false**

▶ The order of execution of operators in an expression is determined by their precedence. Where operators are of equal precedence, the order of execution is determined by their associativity

Exercises

1 Write a console program to define and initialize a variable of type **byte** to 1, and then successively multiply it by 2 and display its value 8 times. Explain the reason for the last result.

2 Write a console program to declare and initialize a **double** variable with some value such as 1234.5678, then retrieve the integral part and store it in a variable of type **long**, and the first four digits of the fractional part and store it in an integer of type **short**. Display the value of the **double** variable by outputting the two values stored as integers.

3 The diameter of the sun is approximately 865,000 miles. The diameter of the earth is approximately 7600 miles. Use the methods in the class Math to calculate:

the volume of the earth in cubic miles
the volume of the sun in cubic miles
the ratio of the volume of the sun to the volume of the earth

and then output the three values. Treat both the earth and the sun as spheres. The volume of a sphere is given by the formula $4/3\pi r^3$ where r is the radius.

Loops and Logic

In this chapter we'll look at how you make decisions and choices in your Java programs. You'll also learn how to make your programs repeat a set of actions until a specific condition is met. We'll cover:

- How you compare data values
- How you can define logical expressions
- How you can use logical expressions to alter the sequence in which program statements are executed
- How you can select different expressions depending on the value of a logical expression
- How to choose between options in a fixed set of alternatives
- How long your variables last
- How you can repeat a block of code a given number of times
- How you can repeat a block of code as long as a given logical expression is true
- How you can break out of loops and statement blocks

All your programs of any consequence will use at least some, and often most, of the language capabilities and programming techniques we'll cover in this chapter, so make sure you have a good grasp of them.

But first, how do we make decisions in code, and so affect the way the program runs?

Making Decisions

As a fundamental element in all your programs, you need to be able to make decisions like "*if* the bank balance is fat, buy the car with the go-faster stripes, *else* renew the monthly bus ticket". In programming terms this requires the ability to make comparisons between variables, constants and the values of expressions, and then to execute one group of statements or another, depending on the result of the comparison. Let's look first at how we make comparisons.

Making Comparisons

Java provides you with six relational operators for comparing two data values. Those data values can be variables, constants, or expressions drawn from Java's primitive data types: **byte**, **short**, **int**, **long**, **char**, **float** or **double**:

Relational Operators	Description
>	Produces the value **true** if the left operand is **greater than** the right operand, and **false** otherwise.
>=	Produces the value **true** if the left operand is **greater than or equal to** the right operand, and **false** otherwise.
==	Produces the value **true** if the left operand is **equal to** the right operand, and **false** otherwise.
!=	Produces the value **true** if the left operand is **not equal to** the right operand, and **false** otherwise.
<=	Produces the value **true** if the left operand is **less than or equal to** the right operand, and **false** otherwise.
<	Produces the value **true** if the left operand is **less than** the right operand, and **false** otherwise.

As you see, each operator produces either the value **true**, or the value **false**, and so is eminently suited to the business of making decisions.

If you wish to store the result of a comparison, you should use a **boolean** variable. We saw how to declare these in the previous chapter. For example, you can define a **boolean** variable **state** and you can set its value in an assignment as follows:

```
boolean state = false;
state = x - y < a + b;
```

The value of the variable **state** will be set to **true** in the assignment if **x-y** is less than **a+b**, and to **false** otherwise.

To explain the above expression a little more, take a look back to the precedence table for operators you saw in the last chapter, where you'll see that the comparison operators are all of lower precedence than the arithmetic operators, so arithmetic will always be completed before any comparisons are made. This means that the expression,

```
x - y == a + b
```

will produce the result **true** if **x - y** is equal to **a + b**.

Note that if you create an expression using relational operators using operands of differing types, values will be promoted in the same way as we saw in the last chapter for mixed arithmetic expressions. So if **aDouble** is of type **double**, and **number** is of type **int**, in the following expression,

```
aDouble < number + 1
```

the value produced by **number + 1** will be calculated as type **int**, then this value will be promoted to type **double** before comparing it with the value of **aDouble**.

The if Statement

The **if** statement, in its simplest configuration, takes this form,

```
if(expression)
   statement;
```

where **expression** can be any expression that produces a value **true** or **false**. You can see a graphical representation of the logic of this in the following diagram:

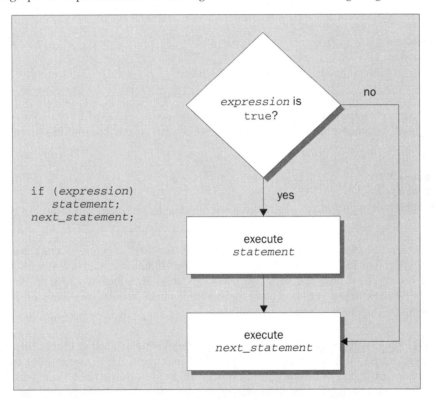

If the value of **expression** is **true**, the **statement** on the line after the **if** is executed, otherwise it is ignored. Here's a simple practical example of this:

```
if(number%2 != 0)          // Test if number is odd
   ++number;               // If so make it even
```

The **if** tests whether the value of **number** is odd by comparing the remainder, after dividing by 2, with 0. If the remainder isn't equal to 0, the value of **number** is odd, so we add 1 to make it even. If the value of **number** is even, the statement incrementing **number** will not be executed.

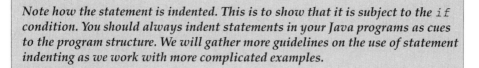

Note how the statement is indented. This is to show that it is subject to the `if` condition. You should always indent statements in your Java programs as cues to the program structure. We will gather more guidelines on the use of statement indenting as we work with more complicated examples.

Statement Blocks

In general, wherever you can have one executable statement in Java, you can replace it with a block of statements enclosed between braces instead. So a statement block between braces can also be nested in another statement block to any depth. This means that we can use a statement block within the basic **if** statement that we just saw. The **if** statement can equally well take this form, and must do so, if several statements depend on the expression being **true**:

```
if(expression)
{
  statement 1;
  statement 2;
  ...         ;
}
```

Now if the value of **expression** is **true**, all the statements enclosed in the following block will be executed. Of course, if you don't put the braces in to enclose the block, so that it looks like this,

```
if(expression)
  statement 1;
  statement 2;
  ...         ;
```

it isn't a statement block any more and therefore only the first statement, **statement 1**, will be executed when the **if** expression is **true**. Note that indenting is just a visual cue to the logic. It has no effect on how the program code executes. This looks as though the sequence of statements belongs to the **if**, but only the first one does because there are no braces. The indenting is just plain wrong here.

In this book, we'll adopt the convention of aligning the bounding braces for a block and indenting all the statements within the block from the braces so that they are easily identified as belonging to the block. There are other conventions which you can use if you prefer, the most important consideration being that you are consistent.

As a practical example of an **if** statement that includes a statement block, we could write:

```
if(number%2 != 0)            // Test if number is odd
{
  // If so make it even and output a message
  ++number;
  System.out.println("Number was forced to be even and is now " + number);
}
```

Now both statements between the braces are executed if the **if** expression is **true**, and neither of them is executed if the **if** expression is **false**.

Statement blocks are more than just a convenient way of grouping statements together—they effect the life and accessibility of variables. We'll learn more about statement blocks when we discuss variable scope later in this chapter. In the meantime, let's look a little deeper into what we can do with the **if** statement.

The else Clause

We can extend the basic **if** statement by adding an **else** clause, as we did at the beginning of the chapter when lack of money meant we had to settle for a bus pass. This provides a second choice of statement, or statement block that is executed when the **expression** in the **if** statement is **false**. You can see the syntax of this clause, and how the program's control flow works, in the following diagram:

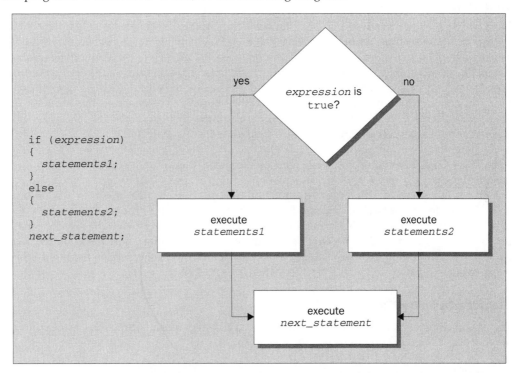

We can apply this in a console program:

Try It Out—If-Else

When you've entered the program text, save it in a file called **NumberCheck.java**. Run it a few times to see what results you get.

```
public class NumberCheck
{
```

```
    public static void main(String[] args)
    {
      int number = 0;
      number = 1 + (int)(99.*Math.random()); // Get a random integer
                                              //          between 1 & 100

      if(number%2 == 0)                       // Test if it is even
        // It is even
        System.out.println("You have got an even number, " + number);
      else
        // It is odd
        System.out.println("You have got an odd number, " + number);
    }
  }
```

How It Works

We saw the method **random()** in the standard class **Math** in the previous chapter. It returns a random value of type **double** between 0.0 and 1.0, so when we multiply the value returned by 99.0, we'll get a random value between 0.0 and 99.0. We convert this value to type **int** with the explicit cast, **(int)**, which will discard any fractional part of the number and produce a random integer between 0 and 99. Lastly, we add 1 to this, so we'll store a random integer between 1 and 100 in the variable **number**. We generate the program output in the **if** statement. If the value of **number** is even, the first **println()** call is executed, otherwise the second **println()** call in the **else** clause is executed.

Note the use of indentation here. The braces enclosing the definition of the class **NumberCheck** are aligned and the statements within the class definition are indented from the braces bounding it. This is just the method **main()** which also has braces bounding its code. The code for **main()** is indented from the position of the braces. The lines for the **if** and the **else** clause are also further indented. This makes it very easy to see the structure of the code. It's evident that **main()** is within the class definition, and the code for **main()** is clearly distinguished. You can also see immediately which statement is executed when the if expression is **true**, and which applies when it is **false**.

Nested if Statements

The statement that is executed when either the **if** or the **else** expressions are **true** can be another **if** statement. This will enable you to express such convoluted logic as "*if* my bank balance is healthy then I will buy the car *if* I have my check book with me, *else* I will buy the car *if* I can get a loan from the bank". An **if** statement that is nested inside another can also itself contain a nested **if**. You can continue nesting **if**s one inside the other like this for as long as you know what you're doing.

To illustrate the nested **if** statement, we can modify the previous example:

```
  if(number%2 == 0)                       // Test if it is even
  {
    if(number < 50)                  // Output a message if number is < 50
      System.out.println("You have got an even number < 50, " + number);
  }
  else
    System.out.println("You have got an odd number, " + number); // It is
  odd
```

Now the message for an even value is only displayed if the value of **number** is also less than 50.

The braces around the nested **if** are necessary here because of the **else** clause. This constrains the nested **if** in the sense that if it had an **else** clause, it would have to appear between the braces enclosing the nested **if**. If the braces were not there, the program would still compile and run but the logic would be different. Let's see how.

With nested **if**s, the question of which **if** statement a particular **else** clause belongs to often arises. If we remove the braces from the code above, we have this:

```
  if(number%2 == 0)                       // Test if it is even
    if(number < 50 )                 // Output a message if number is < 50
      System.out.println("You have got an even number < 50, " + number);

    else
      System.out.println("You have got an odd number, " + number); // It is
          odd
```

This has substantially changed the logic from what we had before. The **else** clause now belongs to the nested **if** that tests whether **number** is less than fifty, so the second **println()** call is only executed for **even** numbers that are greater than fifty. This is clearly not what we wanted since it makes nonsense of the output in this case, but it does illustrate the rule for connecting **else**s to **if**s:

> An **else** *always belongs to the nearest preceding **if** that isn't in a separate block, and isn't already spoken for by another **else**.*

You need to take care that the indenting of statements with nested **if**s is correct. It's easy to convince yourself that the logic is as indicated by the indentation, even when this is completely wrong.

Let's try the **if-else** combination in another program:

Try It Out—Deciphering Characters the Hard Way

Create the class **LetterCheck**, and code its **main()** method as follows:

```
public class LetterCheck
{
  public static void main(String[] args)
  {
    char symbol = 'A';
    symbol = (char)(127.0*Math.random());    // Generate a random
                                             //    character

    if(symbol >= 'A')                        // Is it A or greater?
    {
      if(symbol <= 'Z')                      // yes, so is it Z or less?
        // Then it is a capital letter
        System.out.println("You have the capital letter " + symbol);
      else                                   // It is not Z or less
        if(symbol >= 'a')                    // So is it a or greater?
          if(symbol <= 'z')                  // Yes, so is it z or less?
            // Then it is a small letter
            System.out.println("You have the small letter " + symbol);
          else                               // It is not less than z
            System.out.println("The code is greater than a but it's not a
                letter");
        else
          System.out.println("The code is less than a and it's not a
              letter");
    }
    else
      System.out.println("The code is less than A so it's not a letter");
  }
}
```

How It Works

This program figures out whether the character stored in the variable **symbol** is an upper-case letter, a lower-case letter or some other character. The program first generates a random character with a numeric code between 0 and 127 which corresponds to the characters in basic 7-bit ASCII character set. You'll find the ASCII character codes in Appendix C. The Unicode coding for the ASCII characters is numerically the same as the ASCII code values. Within these characters, the letters **'A'** to **'Z'** are represented by a contiguous group of ASCII codes with decimal values from 65–90, and the small letters are represented by another contiguous group with ASCII code values that have decimal values from 97–122. So to convert any capital letter to a small letter, you just need to add 32 to the character code.

The **if** statements are a bit convoluted so let's look at a diagram of the logic.

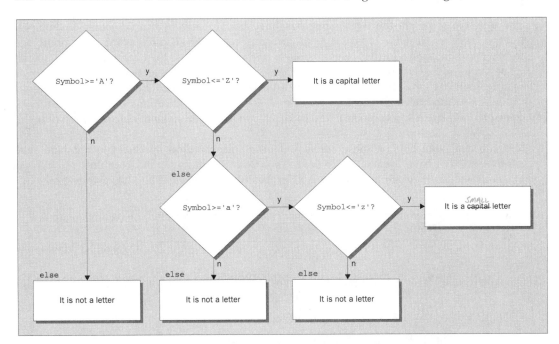

We have four **if** statements altogether. The first **if** tests whether **symbol** is **'A'** or greater. If it is, it could be a capital letter, a small letter, or possibly something else. But if it isn't, it is not a letter at all, so the **else** for this **if** statement towards the end of the program produces a message to that effect.

The nested **if** statement, which is executed if **symbol** is **'A'** or greater, tests whether it is **'Z'** or less. If it is, then **symbol** definitely contains a capital letter and the appropriate message is displayed. If it isn't then it may be a small letter, so another **if** statement is nested within the **else** clause of the first nested **if**, to test for this possibility.

The **if** statement in the **else** clause tests for **symbol** being greater than **'a'**. If it isn't, we know that **symbol** is not a letter and a message is displayed. If it is, another **if** checks whether **symbol** is **'z'** or less. If it is we have a small letter, and if not we don't have a letter at all.

You will have to run the example a few times to get all the possible messages to come up. They all will—eventually.

Having carefully crafted our convoluted and cumbersome condition checking, now's the time to reveal that there's a much easier way.

Logical Operators

The tests we've put in the **if** expressions have been relatively simple so far, except perhaps for the last one. Real life is typically more complicated. You'll often want to combine a number of conditions so that you execute a particular course, for example, if they are all **true** simultaneously. You can ride the roller coaster if you're over twelve years old, over four feet tall *and* less than six feet six. Failure on any count and it's no go. Sometimes, though, you may need to test for any one of a number of conditions being **true**, for example, you get a lower price entry ticket if you're under sixteen, or over sixty-five.

You can deal with both of these cases, and more, using **logical operators** to combine several expressions that have a value **true** or **false**. Because they operate (combine and compare) **boolean** values they are also referred to as **boolean operators**. There are five logical operators:

Symbol	Long name
&	logical AND
&&	conditional AND
|	logical OR
||	conditional OR
!	logical negation (NOT)

These are very simple, the only point of potential confusion being the fact that we have the choice of two operators each for AND and OR. We'll first consider what each of these are used for in general terms, then we'll look at how we can use them in an example.

Boolean AND Operations

You can use either AND operator, **&&** or **&**, where you have two logical expressions that must both be **true** for the result to be **true**—that is, you want to be rich *and* healthy. Either operator will produce the same result from the logical expression. We'll come back to how they are different in a moment. First, let's explore how they are used. All of the following discussion applies equally well to **&** as well as **&&**.

Let's see how logical operators can simplify the last example. You could use the **&&** operator if you were testing a variable of type **char** to determine whether it contained an upper-case letter. The value being tested must be both greater than or equal to **'A'** AND less than or equal to **'Z'**. Both conditions must be **true** for the value to be a capital letter. Taking the example from our previous program, with a value stored in a **char** variable **symbol**, we could implement the test for an upper-case letter in a single **if** by using the **&&** operator:

```
if(symbol >= 'A' && symbol <= 'Z')
    System.out.println("You have the capital letter " + symbol);
```

If you take a look at the precedence table back in Chapter 2, you'll see that the relational operators will be executed before the **&&** operator, so parentheses aren't necessary. Here, the output statement will be executed only if both of the conditions combined by the operator **&&** are **true**. However, as we've said before, it's a good idea to add parentheses if they make the code easier to read. It also helps to avoid mistakes.

The effect of a logical operator is often shown using what is called a **truth table**. This gives the operator result for all possible combinations of operands. The truth table for **&&** (it's the same for **&**) is as follows:

&&	false	true
false	false	false
true	false	true

The row headings on the left and the column headings at the top represent the two values of the logical expressions to be combined by the operator **&&**. Thus, to determine the result of combining a **true** condition with a **false** condition, select the row with **true** at the left and the column with **false** at the top, and look at the intersection of the row and column for the result, which in this case is **false**. In fact, the rule for the **&&** operator is very simple and you probably don't need the table. The result of **&&** is **true** only if both operands are **true**, otherwise the result is **false**.

We could rewrite the set of **if**s from the last example as:

Try It Out—Deciphering Characters the Easy Way

Replace the outer **if-else** loop and its contents in **LetterCheck.java** with the following:

```
if(symbol >= 'A' && symbol <= 'Z')          // Is it a capital letter?
   System.out.println("You have the capital letter " + symbol);
else
   if(symbol >= 'a' && symbol <= 'z')        // or is it a small letter?
     System.out.println("You have the small letter " + symbol);
   else                                      // It is not less than z
     System.out.println("The code is not a letter");
```

How It Works

Using the **&&** operator has condensed the example down quite a bit. We now can do the job with two **if**s, and it's certainly easier to follow what's happening.

You might want to note that when the statement in an **else** clause is another **if**, the **if** is sometimes written on the same line as the **else**, as in:

```
if(symbol >= 'A' && symbol <= 'Z')        // Is it a capital letter
   System.out.println("You have the capital letter " + symbol);
else if(symbol >= 'a' && symbol <= 'z')      // or is it a small letter?
   System.out.println("You have the small letter " + symbol);
else                                     // It is not less than z
   System.out.println("The code is not a letter");
```

I think it's clearer as before though, so I prefer not to do this.

&& versus &

So what distinguishes **&&** from **&**? The difference between them is that the conditional **&&** will not bother to evaluate the right-hand operand if the left-hand operand is **false**, since the result is already determined in this case to be **false**. This can make the code a bit faster when the left-hand operand is **false**.

For example, consider the following statements:

```
int number = 50;
if(number < 40 && (3*number - 27) > 100)
   System.out.println("number = " + number);
```

Here the expression **(3*number - 27)>100** will never be executed since the expression **number<40** is always **false**. On the other hand, if you write the statements as,

```
int number = 50;
if(number<40 & (3*number - 27) > 100)
   System.out.println("number = " + number);
```

the effect is different. The whole logical expression is always evaluated, so even though the left-hand operand of the **&** operator is false and the result is a foregone conclusion once that is known, the right-hand operand **(3*number - 27)>100** will still be evaluated. So, we can just use **&&** all the time to make our programs a bit faster and forget about **&**, right? Wrong. Most of the time you can use **&&**, but there are occasions when you'll want to be sure that the right-hand operand is evaluated.

This situation can arise when the right-hand expression involves calling a method that modifies some variables somewhere else—it will be clearer how a method can do this when we get to discuss methods in Chapter 5. If you use **&&** and the left-hand operand is **false**, such variables will not be modified; if you use **&** the method will always be called and the variables will be modified. The behavior of the program is vastly different depending on which operator you use.

Logical OR

The OR operators, **|** and **||**, apply when you have two conditions and you want a **true** result if either or both of them are **true**. The conditional OR, **||**, has a similar effect to the conditional AND, in that it omits the evaluation of the right-hand operand when the left-hand operand is true.

Let's take an example. If you get a reduced entry ticket price if you are under sixteen years of age or over sixty-five, we can test for the eligibility of the reduction using the following `if`:

```
if(age < 16 || age> 65)
   ticketPrice *= 0.9;          // Reduce ticket price by 10%
```

Clearly in this case both conditions can't be true.

We can also construct a truth table for the `||` operator which also applies for `|`:

`||`	false	true
false	false	true
true	true	true

As you can see, you only get a **false** result if both conditions are **false,** so you don't really need a table to work this out either. You might conclude that the only use for truth tables with these operators is to demonstrate that you don't need them! However, they do summarize quite concisely how the operands combine.

Logical NOT

The third logical operator, `!`, takes one operand with a value, **true** or **false**, and inverts it. So if the value of a **boolean** variable, **state**, is **true**, then the expression `!state` has the value **false**, and if it is **false** then `!state` becomes **true**. To take the example of a simple expression, if an integer variable **x** has the value 10, in the code below,

```
int x = 10;
boolean isXSmall = !(x > 5);
```

`isXSmall` is **false**, since `x > 5` is **true**.

We could also apply the `!` operator in an expression that was a favorite of Charles Dickens:

```
!(Income>Expenditure)
```

If this expression is **true**, the result is misery, at least as soon as the bank starts bouncing your checks.

Of course, you can use any of the logical operators in combination if necessary. If the theme park decides to give a discount on the price of entry to anyone who is under twelve years old and under forty-eight inches tall, or someone who is over sixty-five and over seventy-two inches tall, you could apply the discount with this test:

```
if((age < 12 && height < 48) || (age > 65 && height > 72))
   ticketPrice *= 0.8;              // 20% discount on the ticket price
```

The parentheses aren't strictly necessary here as **&&** has a higher precedence than **||**, but adding the parentheses makes it clearer how the comparisons combine and makes it a little more readable.

FYI Don't confuse the bitwise operators **&**, **|**, and **!**, with the logical operators that look the same. Which type of operator you're using in any particular instance is determined by the type of the operands that you use it with. The bitwise operators apply to integer types and produce an integer result. The logical operators apply to operands that have **boolean** values and produce a result of type **boolean**—true or false. You can use both bitwise and logical operators in an expression if it's convenient to do so.

Character Testing Using Standard Library Methods

Though testing characters using logical operators is a useful way of demonstrating how these operators work, in practice there's an easier way. The Java class library provides a range of methods to do the sort of testing for particular sets of characters such as letters or digits that we have been doing with **if** statements. They are all available within the class **Character** which is automatically available in your programs.

Let's digress to see how we would use the **Character** class in our previous example, replacing the **if** statement in our **LetterCheck** program.

Try It Out—Deciphering Characters Trivially

Replace the code body of the **LetterCheck** class with the following code:

```
if(Character.isUpperCase(symbol))
  System.out.println("You have the capital letter " + symbol);
else
  if(Character.isLowerCase(symbol))
    System.out.println("You have the small letter " + symbol);
  else
    System.out.println("The code is not a letter");
```

How It Works

The **isUpperCase()** method returns **true** if the **char** value passed to it is upper case, and **false** if it isn't. Similarly, the **isLowerCase()** method returns **true** if the **char** value passed to it is lower case.

The following table shows some of the other methods included in the class **Character** which you may find useful for testing characters. In each case the argument to be tested is of type **char**, and goes between the parentheses following the method name:

Method	Description
`isDigit()`	Returns the value **true** if the argument is a digit (0 to 9) and **false** otherwise.
`isLetter()`	Returns the value **true** if the argument is a letter, and **false** otherwise.
`isLetterOrDigit()`	Returns the value **true** if the argument is a letter or a digit, and **false** otherwise.
`isSpace()`	Returns the value **true** if the argument is white space which is any one of the characters: space(`' '`), tab (`'\t'`), newline (`'\n'`), carriage return (`'\r'`), form feed (`'\f'`) The method returns **false** otherwise.

You'll find information on other methods in the **Character** class in the **javadoc** documentation for the class that's part of the Java Development Kit. We'll be revisiting the **Character** class in Chapter 5.

The Conditional Operator

The **conditional operator** is sometimes called the ternary operator because it involves three operands. It's best understood by looking at an example. Suppose we have two variables of type **int**, **a** and **b**, and we want to assign the greater of the values stored in **a** and **b** to a third variable also of type **int**, **c**. We can do this with this statement:

```
c = a>b ? a : b;            // Set c to the greater of a and b
```

The conditional operator has a logical expression as its first argument, in this case **a>b**. If this expression is **true**, the operand which follows the **?** symbol—in this case **a**—is selected as the value resulting from the operation. If the expression **a>b** is **false,** the operand which comes after the colon—in this case **b**—is selected as the value. Thus, the result of this conditional expression is **a**, if **a** is greater than **b**, and **b** otherwise. This value is then stored in **c**. The use of the conditional operator in this assignment statement is equivalent to the **if** statement:

```
if(a > b)
   c = a;
else
   c = b;
```

Remember though that the conditional operator is an operator, and not a statement. The conditional operator can be written generally as:

```
logical_expression ? expression1 : expression2
```

If the *logical_expression* evaluates as **true**, the result is the value of *expression1*. If it evaluates to **false**, the result is the value of *expression2*.

There are lots of circumstances where the conditional operator can be used, and a common application of it is to control output, depending on the result of an expression or the value of a variable. You can vary a message by selecting one text string or another depending on the condition specified.

Try It Out—Conditional Plurals

Type in the following code which will add the 's' to the end of 'hat' when you have more than one hat:

```
public class ConditionalOp
{
  public static void main(String[] args)
  {
    int nHats = 1;      // Number of hats
    System.out.println("I have " + nHats + " hat" + (nHats == 1?
        ".":"s."));

    nHats++;            // Increment number of hats
    System.out.println("I have " + nHats + " hat" + (nHats == 1?
        ".":"s."));
  }
}
```

The output from this program will be:

```
I have 1 hat.
I have 2 hats.
```

How It Works

The result of the conditional operator is a string containing just a period when the value of **nHats** is 1, and a string containing an **s** and a period in all other cases. The effect of this is to cause the output statement to automatically adjust the output between singular and plural. You can use the same technique in other situations, such as where you need to choose between **he** or **she**, for example, as long as you're able to specify a logical expression to differentiate the situation where you should use one rather than the other.

The switch Statement

The **switch** statement enables you to select from multiple choices based on a set of fixed values for a given expression. The expression must produce a result of type **char**, **byte**, **short** or **int**, otherwise the statement will not compile. It operates rather like a physical rotary switch in that you can select one of a fixed number of choices. For example, on some makes of washing machine you choose between the various possible machine settings in this way, with positions for cotton, wool, synthetic fiber and so on, which you select by turning the knob to point to the option that you want.

A **switch** statement reflecting this logic would be:

```
switch(wash)
{
  case 1:                          // wash is 1 for Cotton
    System.out.println("Cotton selected");
    break;
  case 2:                          // wash is 2 for Linen
    System.out.println("Linen selected");
    break;
  case 3:                          // wash is 3 for Wool
    System.out.println("Wool selected");
    break;
  default:                         // Not a valid value for wash
    System.out.println("Selection error");
    break;
}
```

In the **switch** statement, the selection is determined by the value of an expression that you specify, which is enclosed between the parentheses after the keyword **switch**. In this case, it's the variable **wash** which would need to have been declared as of type **char**, **byte**, **short**, or **int**. You define the possible switch positions by one or more **case values**, also called **case labels**, that are delimited using the keyword **case**. All the case values for a switch are enclosed between the braces for the **switch** statement and they can appear in any order. In our example above we've used three case values. A particular case value is selected if the value of the **switch** expression is the same as that of the particular case value.

When a particular case is selected, the statements which follow that case value are executed. So if **wash** has the value 2, the statement that follows,

```
case 2:                          // wash is 2 for Linen
```

is executed.

When a **break** statement is executed here, it causes the next statement to be the one following the closing brace for the **switch**. If you don't put a **break** statement at the end of the case value statements, the statements for the next case in sequence will be executed. The **break** after the **default** statements in our example isn't strictly necessary, but it does protect against the situation when you might add another case value at the end of the **switch** statement block, and overlook the need for the **break** at the end of the last case.

There's a case value for each possible choice in the **switch**, and they must all be unique. The **default** case we have in the example above is, in general, optional. It's selected when the value of the expression for the **switch** doesn't correspond with any of the case values that have been defined. If you don't specify a **default** case and the value of the **switch** expression doesn't match any of the case values, execution continues at the statement following the closing brace of the **switch** statement.

We can illustrate the logic of the general **switch** statement in a flow chart.

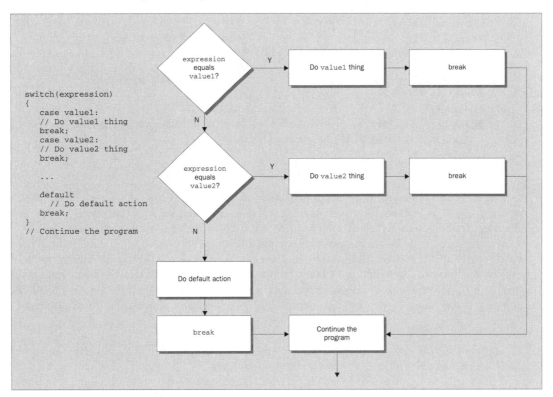

Each **case** value is compared with the value of expression. If one matches the code for that case is executed and the **break** branches to the first statement after the switch. If you don't include the break statements, the logic is quite different.

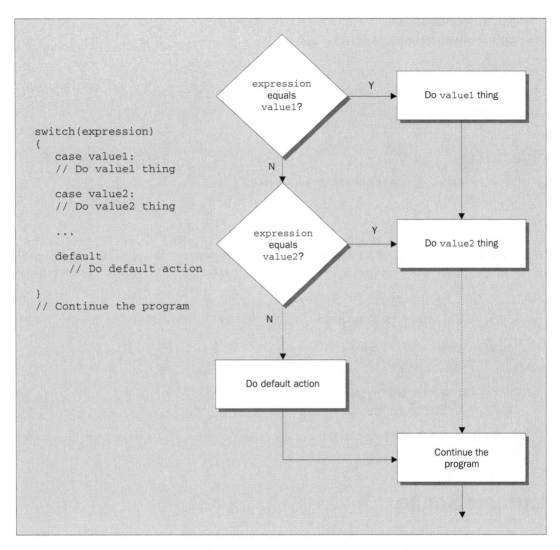

```
switch(expression)
{
    case value1:
    // Do value1 thing

    case value2:
    // Do value2 thing

    ...

    default
       // Do default action

}
// Continue the program
```

Now when a case label value is equal to the switch expression, the code for that case and all the other cases that follow are executed, including that for the default case if that also follows the case selected. This isn't usually what you want, so make sure you don't forget the break statements.

You can arrange to execute the same statements for several case labels, as in the following **switch** statement:

```
char yesNo = 'N';
// more program logic...

switch(yesNo)
{
  case 'n':
  case 'N':
    System.out.println("No selected");
    break;
  case 'y':
  case 'Y':
    System.out.println("Yes selected");
    break;
}
```

Here the variable **yesNo** receives a character from the keyboard 'somehow'. You want a different action depending on whether the user enters **'Y'** or **'N'** but you want to be able to accept either upper- or lower-case entries. This **switch** does this just by putting the case values together.

Of course, you could also implement this logic using **if** statements:

```
if(yesNo=='n' || yesNo=='N')
  System.out.println("No selected");
else
  if(yesNo=='y' || yesNo=='Y')
    System.out.println("Yes selected");
```

I prefer the **switch** statement as I think it's easier to follow, but you can decide which you prefer.

Variable Scope

Every variable that we've declared so far in program examples has been defined within the context of a method, the method **main()**. Variables that are declared within a method are called **local variables**, as they are only accessible locally, that is within the confines of the method in which they are declared. However, they aren't necessarily accessible everywhere in the code for the method in which they are declared. Look at the example in the illustration below that illustrates nested blocks inside a method.

```
{
    int a = 1;                          // Declare and define a

    // Reference to a is OK here
    // Reference to b here is an error
    {

        // Reference to a here is OK
        // Reference to b here is still an error

        int b = 2;                      // Declare and define b

        // References to a and b are OK here - b exists now

    }
    // Reference to b is an error here - it doesn't exist
    // Reference to a is still OK though

}
```

A variable doesn't exist before its declaration, so you can only refer to it after it has been declared. It continues to exist until the end of the block in which it is defined, and that includes any blocks nested within the block containing its declaration. The variable **b** only exists within the inner block. After the brace at the end of the inner block, **b** no longer exists so you can't refer to it. The variable **a** is still around though since it survives until the last brace.

So, the rule for accessibility of local variables is simple. They are only accessible from the point in the program where they are declared to the end of the block that contains the declaration. At the end of the block in which they are declared they cease to exist. We can demonstrate this with an example:

Try It Out—Scoping

First define and initialize the variable **outer**, then start an inner block. Within that block, define the variable **inner**. When the block closes you'll need to redefine **inner** to use it once more.

```
public class Scope
{
  public static void main(String[] args)
  {
    int outer = 1;                      // Exists throughout the method

    {
```

```
          // You cannot refer to a variable before its declaration
          // System.out.println("inner = " + inner); // Uncomment this for
                                                              an error

        int inner = 2;
        System.out.println("inner = " + inner);      // Now it is OK
        System.out.println("outer = " + outer);      // and outer is still
                                                              here
         // All variables defined in the enclosing outer block still exist,
         // so you cannot redefine them here
         // int outer = 5;                          // Uncomment this for an error
      }

      // Any variables declared in the inner block no longer exist
      // so you cannot refer to them
      // System.out.println("inner = " + inner);    // Uncomment this for
        an error

      // The previous inner block does not exist so you can define a new
        one
      int inner = 3;
      System.out.println("inner = " + inner);   // ... and output its value
      System.out.println("outer = " + outer);   // outer is still around
   }
}
```

As it stands, this program will produce the output:

```
inner = 2
outer = 1
inner = 3
outer = 1
```

If you uncomment any or all of the three statements as suggested, it won't compile:

```
C:\>javac Scope.java
Scope.java:11: Undefined variable: inner
   System.out.println("inner = " + inner); // Uncomment this for an error
                                   ^
1 error


C:\>javac Scope.java
Scope.java:19: Variable 'outer' is already defined in this method.
        int outer = 5;                          // Uncomment this for an error
            ^
1 error


C:\>javac Scope.java
Scope.java:23: Undefined variable: inner
   System.out.println("inner = " + inner); // Uncomment this for an error
                                   ^
1 error
```

How It Works

The method **main()** in this program has one block nested inside the block containing the code for the method. The variable **outer** is defined right at the start, so you can refer to this anywhere within the method **main()**, including inside any nested blocks. You aren't allowed to re-declare a variable, so the commented statement that re-declares **outer** within the inner block will cause a compiler error, if you remove the double slash at the beginning of the line.

The variable **inner** is defined inside the nested block with the initial value 2, and you can refer to it anywhere from its declaration to the end of the inner block. After the closing brace of the inner block, the variable **inner** no longer exists, so the first commented output statement is illegal. However, since the variable **inner** has expired, we can declare another one with the same name and with the initial value 3.

Note that all this is just to demonstrate the lifetime of local variables. It isn't good practice to redefine variables that have expired, because of the potential for confusion. Also, although we've used just variables of type **int** in the example above, scoping rules apply to variables of any type.

There are other variables called class variables which have much longer lifetimes when they are declared in a particular way. The variables PI and E in the standard library class, Math, are examples of these. They hang around as long as your program is executing. We'll see more about these in Chapter 5.

Loops

A loop allows you to execute a statement or block of statements repeatedly. The need to repeat a block of code arises in almost every program. If you did the first exercise at the end of the last chapter, you would have come up with a program along the lines of:

```java
public class TryExample2_1
{
  public static void main(String[] args)
  {
    byte value = 1;
    value *= 2;
    System.out.println("Value is now " + value);
    value *= 2;
    System.out.println("Value is now " + value);
    value *= 2;
    System.out.println("Value is now " + value);
    value *= 2;
    System.out.println("Value is now " + value);
    value *= 2;
    System.out.println("Value is now " + value);
    value *= 2;
    System.out.println("Value is now " + value);
    value *= 2;
```

```
        System.out.println("Value is now " + value);
        value *= 2;
        System.out.println("Value is now " + value);
    }
}
```

You had to enter the same pair of statements eight times. This is quite unrealistic in practice. If the program for the company payroll had to include separate statements for each employee, it would never get written. You could have used a loop and saved yourself a lot of trouble. The method **main()** to do the same as the code above could be written as:

```
public static void main(String[] args)
{
  byte value = 1;
  for(int i = 0; i < 8; i++)
  {
    value *= 2;
    System.out.println("Value is now " + value);
  }
}
```

The **for** loop statement causes the statements in the following block to be repeated eight times. The number of times it is to be repeated is determined by the stuff between parentheses following the keyword **for**—we'll see how in a moment. The point is you could repeat the same block of statements as many times as you want—a thousand or a million—it is just as easy and it doesn't require any more lines of code.

There are three kinds of loop statements you can use:

The **for** loop

```
for(control stuff)
{
  // statements
}
```

The control of the **for** loop appears in parentheses following the keyword **for**. This loop is usually controlled by a counter, although it can be used in other ways. You can count up or down using an integer or a floating point counter, and execution continues as long as the count condition you've specified is **true**. When the count condition is **false**, execution continues with the statement following the loop block.

The **while** loop

```
while(expression)
{
  // statements
}
```

This loop executes as long as a given logical expression is **true**. When the expression is **false**, execution continues with the statement following the loop block. The expression is tested at the beginning of the loop, so if it is initially **false**, the loop statement block will not be executed at all.

The **do-while** loop

```
do
{
   // statements
}while(expression);
```

This loop is similar to the **while** loop, except that the expression controlling the loop is tested at the end of the loop block. This means that the loop block is executed at least once, even if the expression is initially **false**.

We can contrast the basic logic of the three kinds of loop in a diagram.

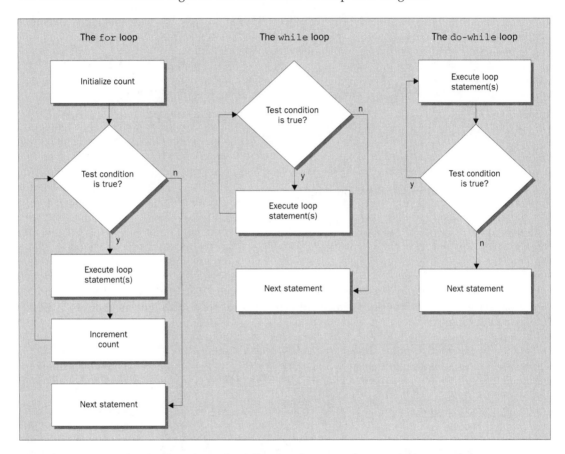

This shows quite clearly that the only difference between the **while** loop and the **do-while** loop is where the test is carried out.

Let's explore each of these in turn and see how they are used in practice.

Try It Out—The *for* Loop

Let's start with a simple example. Suppose you want to calculate the sum of the integers from 1 to a given value. You can do this using the **for** loop as in the following example:

```
public class ForLoop
{
  public static void main(String[] args)
  {
    int limit = 20;                  // Sum from 1 to this value
    int sum = 0;                     // Accumulate sum in this variable

    // Loop from 1 to the value of limit, adding 1 each cycle
    for(int i = 1; i <= limit; i++)
      sum += i;                      // Add the current value of i to sum
    System.out.println("sum = " + sum);
  }
}
```

This program will produce the output:

```
sum = 210
```

but you can try it out with different values for **limit**.

How It Works

All the work is done in the **for** loop. The loop counter is **i**, and this is declared and initialized within the **for** loop statement. The syntax of the **for** loop is shown in the following diagram:

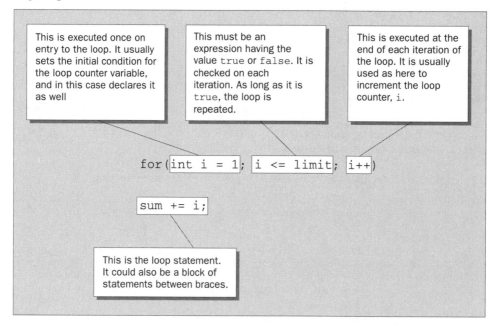

As you see, there are three elements that control the operation of a **for** loop, and they appear between the parentheses that follow the keyword **for**. In sequence their purpose is to:

▶ Set the initial conditions for the loop, particularly the loop counter

▶ Specify the condition for the loop to continue

▶ Increment the loop counter

They are always separated by semicolons.

The first control element is executed when the loop is first entered. Here we declare and initialize the loop counter **i**. Because it's declared within the loop, it will not exist outside of it. If you try to output the value of **i** after the loop with a statement such as:

```
System.out.println("Final value of i = " + i);  // Will not work outside
                                                           the loop
```

you will find that the program will not compile. If you need to initialize and or declare other variables for the loop, you can do it here by separating the declarations by commas. For example, we could write:

```
for(int i = 1, j = 0; i <= limit; i++)
   sum += i * j++;                    // Add the current value of i*j to sum
```

We initialize an additional variable **j**, and to make the loop vaguely sensible, we've modified the value to add the sum to **i*j++** which is the equivalent of **i*(i-1)** in this case. Note that **j** will be incremented after the product **i*j** has been calculated. You could declare other variables here, but note that it wouldn't make sense to declare **sum** at this point. If you can't figure out why, delete the original declaration of **sum** and put it in the **for** loop instead to see what happens. The program won't compile—right? After the loop ends the variable **sum** no longer exists, so you can't output its value.

The second control element in a **for** loop is a logical expression which is checked at the beginning of each iteration through the loop. If the expression is **true**, the loop continues, and as soon as it is **false** the loop is finished. In our program the loop ends when **i** is greater than the value of **limit**.

The third control element in a **for** loop typically increments the loop variable, as we have in our example. You can also put multiple expressions here too, so we could rewrite the above code fragment, which added **j** to the loop, as:

```
for(int i = 1, j = 0; i <= limit; i++, j++)
   sum+=i*j;                          // Add the current value of i*j to sum
```

Again, there can be several expressions here, and they don't need to relate directly to the control of the loop. We could even rewrite the original loop for summing integers so that the summation occurs in the loop control element:

```
for(int i = 1; i <= limit; sum += i, i++);
```

Now the loop statement is empty. It doesn't really improve things though and there are hazards in writing the loop this way. If you forget the semicolon the next statement will be used as the loop statement which is likely to cause chaos. Another potential problem arises if you happen to reverse the sequence of adding to **sum** and incrementing **i**, as follows:

```
for(int i = 1; i <= limit; i++, sum += i);    // Wrong!!!
```

Now you'll generate the wrong answer. This is because the expression **i++** will be executed before **sum += i**, so the wrong value of **i** is used.

You can omit any or all of the elements that control the **for** loop. It's up to you to make sure it does what you want. We could write the loop in our program as:

```
for(int i = 1; i <= limit; )
  sum += i++;                              // Add the current value of i to sum
```

We have simply transferred the incrementing of **i** from the **for** loop control to the loop statement. The **for** loop works just as before. However, this isn't a good way to write the loop, as it makes it much less obvious how the loop counter is incremented.

Counting Using Floating Point Values

You can use a floating point variable as the loop counter if you need to. This may be needed when you're calculating the value of a function for a range of fractional values. Suppose you wanted to calculate the area of a circle with values for the radius from 1–2 in steps of 0.2. You could write this as:

```
for(double radius = 1.0; radius <= 2.0; radius += 0.2)
{
  System.out.println("radius = " + radius + " area = " +
      Math.PI*radius*radius);
}
```

This will produce the output:

```
radius = 1.0 area = 3.141592653589793
radius = 1.2 area = 4.523893421169302
radius = 1.4 area = 6.157521601035994
radius = 1.5999999999999999 area = 8.04247719318987
radius = 1.7999999999999998 area = 10.178760197630927
radius = 1.999999999999998 area = 12.566370614359169
```

The area has been calculated using the formula πr^2 using the standard value **PI** which is 3.14159265358979323846. Although we intended the values of **radius** to increment from 1.0 to 2.0 in steps of 0.2, they don't. The value of radius is never exactly 2.0 or any of the other intermediate values, because 0.2 can't be represented exactly as a binary floating point value. If you doubt this, and you're prepared to deal with an infinite loop, change the loop to:

```
// BE WARNED - THIS LOOP DOES NOT END
for(double radius = 1.0; radius != 2.0; radius += 0.2)
{
  System.out.println("radius = " + radius + " area = " +
      Math.PI*radius*radius);
}
```

If the value of **radius** reaches 2.0, the condition **radius!=2.0** will be **false** and the loop will end, but unfortunately it doesn't. Its last value before 2 will be approximately 1.999... and the next value will be something like 2.1999... and so it will never be 2.0. From this we can deduce a golden rule:

> *Do not use tests that depend on an exact value for a floating point variable to control a loop.*

Try It Out—The while Loop

We can write the program for summing integers again using the **while** loop, so you can see how the loop mechanism differs from the **for** loop.

```
public class WhileLoop
{
  public static void main(String[] args)
  {
    int limit = 20;                 // Sum from 1 to this value
    int sum = 0;                    // Accumulate sum in this variable
    int i = 1;                      // Loop counter

    // Loop from 1 to the value of limit, adding 1 each cycle
    while(i <= limit)
      sum += i++;                   // Add the current value of i to sum
    System.out.println("sum = " + sum );
  }
}
```

You should again get the result:

```
sum = 210
```

How It Works

The **while** loop is controlled wholly by the logical expression that appears between the parentheses that follow the keyword **while**. The loop continues as long as this expression has the value **true**, and how it ever manages to arrive at the value **false** to end the loop is up to you. You need to be sure that something in the loop will eventually result in this expression being **false**. Otherwise you have an infinite loop.

In our example, how the loop ends is clear. We have a simple count as before, and we increment **i** in the loop statement that accumulates the sum of the integers. Sooner or later **i** exceeds the value of **limit** and the **while** loop will end. You don't always need to use the testing of a count limit as the loop condition. You can use any logical condition you want.

And last, but not least, we have the **do-while** loop.

Try It Out—The *do-while* Loop

As we said at the beginning of this topic, the **do-while** loop is much the same as the **while** loop, except for the fact that the continuation condition is checked at the end of the loop. We can write an integer summing program with this kind of loop:

```
public class DoWhileLoop
{
  public static void main(String[] args)
  {
    int limit = 20;                  // Sum from 1 to this value
    int sum = 0;                     // Accumulate sum in this variable
    int i = 1;                       // Loop counter

    // Loop from 1 to the value of limit, adding 1 each cycle
    do
      sum += i++;                    // Add the current value of i to sum
    while(i <= limit);

    System.out.println("sum = " + sum);
  }
}
```

How It Works

As in the other loops, the loop statement:

```
sum += i++;                         // Add the current value of i to
sum
```

could equally well be a statement block.

Note the semicolon after the **while** condition here. This is part of the loop statement so you must not forget to put it in. The primary reason for using this loop over the **while** loop would be if you want to be sure that the loop code always executes at least once.

Nested loops

You can nest loops of any kind one inside another to any depth. Let's look at an example where we nest **for** loops. A factorial of an integer n is the product of all the integers from 1 to n. It is written as n! Our example will calculate the factorial of every integer from 1 to a given limit:

Try It Out—Calculating Factorials

Enter the following code with the two **for** loops:

```
public class Factorial
{
  public static void main(String[] args)
  {
    long limit = 20;   // Calculate factorial of integers up to this value
    long factorial = 1;   // Calculate factorial in this variable

    // Loop from 1 to the value of limit
    for(int i = 1; i <= limit; i++)
    {
      factorial = 1;        // Initialize factorial
      for(int j = 2; j <= i; j++)
        factorial *= j;
      System.out.println(i + "!" + " is " + factorial);
    }
  }
}
```

This program will produce the output:

```
1! is 1
2! is 2
3! is 6
4! is 24
5! is 120
6! is 720
7! is 5040
8! is 40320
9! is 362880
10! is 3628800
11! is 39916800
12! is 479001600
13! is 6227020800
14! is 87178291200
15! is 1307674368000
16! is 20922789888000
17! is 355687428096000
18! is 6402373705728000
19! is 121645100408832000
20! is 2432902008176640000
```

How It Works

The outer loop, controlled by **i**, walks through all the integers from 1 to the value of **limit**. In each iteration of the outer loop, the variable **factorial** is initialized to 1 and the nested loop calculates the factorial of the current value of **i** using **j** as the control counter which runs from 2 to the current value of **i**. The resulting value of **factorial** is then displayed, before going to the next iteration of the outer loop.

95

Although we have nested a **for** loop inside another **for** loop here, as we said at the outset, you can nest any kind of loop inside any other.

 If you've been concentrating, you may well have noticed that you don't really need nested loops to display the factorial of successive integers. You can do it with a single loop that multiplies the current factorial value by the loop counter. However, this would be a very poor demonstration of a nested loop.

The continue Statement

There are situations where you may want to skip all or part of a loop iteration. Suppose we want to sum the values of the integers from 1 to some limit, except that we don't want to include integers that are multiples of three. We can do this using an **if** and a **continue** statement:

```
for(int i = 1; i <= limit; i++)
{
  if(i % 3 == 0)
    continue;                    // Skip the rest of this iteration
  sum += i;                      // Add the current value of i to sum
}
```

The **continue** statement is executed in this example when **i** is an exact multiple of 3. It causes the rest of the current loop iteration to be skipped. Program execution continues with the next iteration if there is one, and if not, with the statement following the end of the loop block. The **continue** statement can appear anywhere within a block of loop statements. You may even have more than one **continue** in a loop.

The Labeled continue Statement

Where you have nested loops, there's a special form of the **continue** statement that enables you to stop executing the inner loop—not just the current iteration of the inner loop—and continue at the beginning of the next iteration of the outer loop. This is called the **labeled continue statement**.

To use the labeled continue statement, you need to identify the loop statement for the outer loop with a **statement label**. A statement label is simply an identifier that's used to reference a statement. A statement label appears at the beginning of the statement line and is separated from the statement by a colon. Let's look at an example:

Try It Out—Labeled continue

We could add a labeled **continue** statement to omit the calculation of factorials of odd numbers greater than 10. This isn't the best way to do this, but it does demonstrate how the labeled **continue** statement works:

```
public class Factorial
{
  public static void main(String[] args)
  {
    long limit = 20;  // Calculate factorial of integers up to this value
    long factorial = 1;   // Calculate factorial in this variable

    // Loop from 1 to the value of limit
    OuterLoop:
    for(int i = 1; i <= limit; i++)
    {
      factorial = 1;                    // Initialize factorial
      for(int j = 2; j <= i; j++)
      {
        if(i > 10 && i % 2 == 1)
          continue OuterLoop;           // Transfer to the outer loop
        factorial *= j;
      }
      System.out.println("!" + i + " is " + factorial);
    }
  }
}
```

How It Works

The outer loop has the label **OuterLoop**. In the inner loop, when the condition in the **if** statement is **true**, the labeled **continue** is executed causing an immediate transfer to the beginning of the next iteration of the outer loop.

In general, you can use the labeled **continue** to exit from an inner loop to any enclosing outer loop, not just the one immediately enclosing the loop containing the labeled **continue** statement.

Using the break Statement in a Loop

We've seen how to use the **break** statement in a **switch** block. Its effect is to exit the **switch** block and continue execution with the first statement after the switch. You can also use the **break** statement to break out from a loop when you need to. To demonstrate this we'll write a program to find prime numbers. In case you've forgotten, a prime number is an integer that isn't exactly divisible by any number less than itself, other than 1 of course.

Try It Out—Calculating Primes I

1 Start with the **main()** method in the class **Primes**, and declare **nValues** and **isPrime**. Then start a **for** loop that will loop through all integers from 2 to **nValues**.

```
public class Primes
{
  public static void main(String[] args)
```

```
{
  int nValues = 50;              // The maximum value to be checked
  boolean isPrime = true;        // Is true if we find a prime

  // Check all values from 2 to nValues
  for(int i = 2; i <= nValues; i++)
  {
```

2 Then we try dividing **i** by all integers less than its value.

```
    isPrime=true;                    // Assume the current i is prime

    // Try dividing by all integers from 2 to i-1
    for(int j = 2; j < i; j++)
    {
      if(i % j == 0)        // This is true if j divides exactly
      {
        isPrime = false;    // If we got here, it was an exact division
        break;              // so exit the loop
      }
    }
```

3 The final section prints out any primes.

```
    // We can get here through the break, or through completing the loop
    if(isPrime)                  // So is it prime?
      System.out.println(i);     // Yes, so output the value
    }
  }
}
```

You should get the output:

```
2
3
5
7
11
13
17
19
23
29
31
37
41
43
47
```

How It Works

There are much more efficient ways to calculate primes, but this does demonstrate the **break** statement in action. The basic idea of the program is to go through the integers from 2 to the value of **nValues**, and check each one to see if it has an integer divisor less than the number being checked. The outer loop indexed by **i** steps through the possible values, and the inner loop, indexed by **j**, checks whether any integer less than the value being checked is an exact divisor.

The checking is done in the **if** statement in the inner loop. If **j** divides **i** exactly **i%j** will be 0, so **isPrime** will be set to **false**, and the **break** will be executed to exit the inner loop. The next statement to be executed will be the **if** statement after the closing brace of the inner loop block. You can also reach this point by a normal exit from the loop, so it is necessary to check the value of **isPrime** to see whether we do have a prime.

This example could be simplified if we used the labeled **continue** instead of the **break** statement:

Try It Out—Calculating Primes II

Try the following changes to the code in the **Primes** class.

```
public class Primes
{
  public static void main(String[] args)
  {
    int nValues = 50;                 // The maximum value to be checked

    // Check all values from 2 to nValues
    OuterLoop:
    for(int i = 2; i <= nValues; i++)
    {
      // Try dividing by all integers from 2 to i-1
      for(int j = 2; j < i; j++)
      {
        if(i%j == 0)                  // This is true if j divides exactly
          continue OuterLoop;         // so exit the loop
      }
      // We only get here if we have a prime
      System.out.println(i);          // so output the value
    }
  }
}
```

How It Works

We no longer need the **isPrime** variable to indicate whether we have a prime, as we can only reach the output statement through a normal exit from the inner loop. When this occurs it means we have a prime. If we get an exact divisor, implying the current value of **i** is not prime, the labeled **continue** transfers immediately to the next iteration of the outer loop. The output from this version of the program is the same as before.

Breaking Infinite Loops

You'll find that sometimes you'll need to use a loop where you don't know in advance how many iterations are required. This can arise when you're processing external data items that you might be reading in from a file for example, and you don't know in advance how many there are. You can often use a **while** loop in these circumstances with the loop condition determining when the loop should end, but sometimes it can be convenient to use an infinite loop instead, with a **break** statement to end the loop.

Try It Out—Calculating Primes III

Suppose we want our primes program to generate a given number of primes, rather than check up to a given integer value. We can code this as follows:

```java
public class FindPrimes
{
  public static void main(String[] args)
  {
    int nPrimes = 50;                // The maximum number of primes required

    // Check all values from 2 to nValues
    OuterLoop:
    for(int i = 2; ; i++)            // This loop runs forever
    {
      // Try dividing by all integers from 2 to i-1
      for(int j = 2; j < i; j++)
      {
        if(i % j == 0)               // This is true if j divides exactly
          continue OuterLoop;        // so exit the loop
      }
      // We only get here if we have a prime
      System.out.println(i);         // so output the value
      if(--nPrimes == 0)             // Decrement the prime count
        break;                       // It is zero so we have them all
    }
  }
}
```

How It Works

This program is very similar to the previous version. The principal differences are that **nPrimes** contains the number of primes required so the program will produce the first 50 primes instead of finding the primes between 2 and 50, and that the outer loop controlled by **i** has the loop condition omitted, so the loop will continue indefinitely.

As we find each prime, the value is displayed, after which the value of **nPrimes** is decremented in the **if** statement:

```
if(--nPrimes == 0)          // Decrement the prime count

  break;                    // It is zero so we have them all
```

The **break** statement will be executed when **nPrimes** has been decremented to zero, and this will exit the indefinite loop.

The Labeled break Statement

Java also makes a labeled **break** statement available to you. This enables you to jump immediately to the statement following the end of the enclosing statement block or to the loop that's identified in the labeled **break** statement. This mechanism is shown in the following diagram:

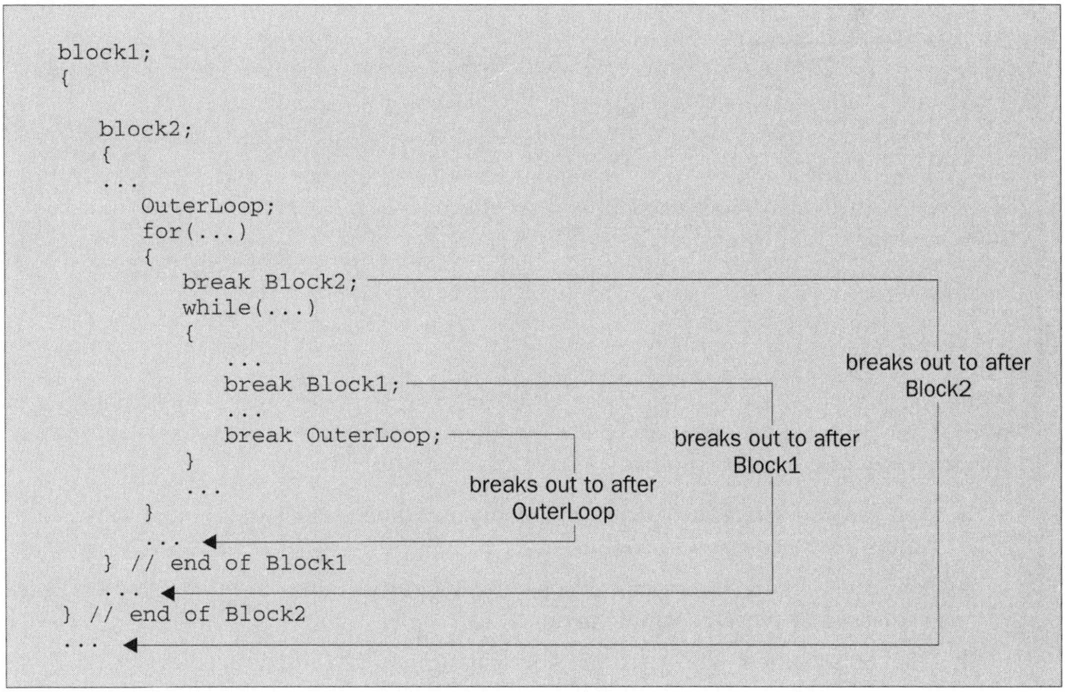

```
block1;
{

  block2;
  {
  ...
    OuterLoop;
    for(...)
    {
      break Block2; ─────────────────────────────────────┐
      while(...)                                          │
      {                                                   │
        ...                                   breaks out to after
        break Block1; ──────────────────────┐      Block2
        ...                                  │
        break OuterLoop; ──────────┐  breaks out to after
      }                            │        Block1
      ...              breaks out to after
    }                      OuterLoop
    ... ◄──────────────────────────┘
  } // end of Block1
  ... ◄──────────────────────────────────────┘
} // end of Block2
... ◄────────────────────────────────────────────────────┘
```

As the labeled **break** enables you to break out to the statement following any enclosing block or loop, you just need to add a label to the beginning of the relevant block or loop, and use that label in the **break** statement.

We could have used a labeled **break** statement in the previous example:

```
public class FindPrimes
{
  public static void main(String[] args)
```

```
      {
        int nPrimes = 50;                 // The maximum number of primes required

        // Check all values from 2 to nValues
        OuterLoop:
        for(int i = 2; ; i++)             // This loop runs forever
        {
          // Try dividing by all integers from 2 to i-1
          for(int j = 2; j < i; j++)
          {
            if(i % j == 0)                // This is true if j divides exactly
              continue OuterLoop;         // so exit the loop
          }
          // We only get here if we have a prime
          System.out.println(i);         // so output the value
          if(--nPrimes == 0)              // Decrement the prime count
            break OuterLoop;              // It is zero so we have them all
        }
        // break OuterLoop goes to here
      }
    }
```

It works in exactly the same way as before. The labeled **break** ends the loop operation beginning with the label `OuterLoop`, and so effectively branches to the point indicated by the comment.

Summary

In this chapter you have learned about all of the essential mechanisms for making decisions in Java. You have also learned all of the looping facilities that you have available when programming. The essential points we have covered are:

- You can use **relational operators** to compare values, and such comparisons result in values of either **true** or **false**

- You can combine basic comparisons and logical variables in more complex logical expressions by using **logical operators**

- The **if** statement is a basic decision-making tool in Java. It enables you to choose to execute a block of statements if a given logical expression has the value **true**. You can optionally execute another block of statements if the logical expression is **false** by using the **else** keyword

- You can use the **conditional operator** to choose between two expressions depending on the value of a logical expression

- You can use the **switch** statement to choose from a fixed number of alternatives

- The variables in a method come into existence at the point at which you declare them, and cease to exist after the end of the block that immediately encloses their declaration

▶ You have three options for repeating a block of statements: a **for** loop, a **while** loop, or a **do-while** loop

▶ The **continue** statement enables you to skip to the next iteration in the loop containing the **continue** statement

▶ The labeled **continue** statement enables you to skip to the next iteration in a loop enclosing the labeled **continue** that's identified by the label. The loop doesn't have to be the one immediately enclosing the labeled **continue**

▶ The **break** statement enables you to break out of the loop or a block of statements in which it appears

▶ The labeled **break** statement enables you to break out of the loop or a block of statements that encloses it that's identified by the label. This isn't necessarily the block that encloses it directly

Exercises

1 Write a program to display a random choice from a set of six choices for breakfast (you could use any set, for example, scrambled eggs, waffles, fruit, cereal, toast or yogurt).

2 When testing whether an integer is a prime, it is sufficient to try to divide by integers up to the square root of the number being tested. Rewrite the program example from this chapter to use this approach.

3 A lottery requires that you select six different numbers from the integers 1 – 49. Write a program to do this for you and generate five sets of entries.

4 Write a program to generate a random sequence of capital letters that does not include vowels.

Arrays and Strings

In this chapter you will start to use Java objects. You will first be introduced to arrays which enable you to deal with a number of variables of the same type through a single variable name, and then you will look at how to handle character strings. By the end of this chapter you will have learned:

- What arrays are and how you declare and initialize them
- How you access individual elements of an array
- How you can use individual elements of an array
- How to declare arrays of arrays
- How you can create arrays of arrays with different lengths
- How to create **String** objects
- How to create and use arrays of **String** objects
- What operations are available for **String** objects
- What **StringBuffer** objects are and how they relate to operations on **String** objects
- What operations are available for **StringBuffer** objects

Some of what we discuss in this chapter relates to objects, and as we haven't yet covered in detail how a class (or object definition) is defined we'll have to skate over some points. All will be revealed in Chapter 5.

Arrays

With the basic built-in Java data types we've seen in the last few chapters, each identifier corresponds to a single variable. But when you want to handle sets of values of the same type—the first 1000 primes, for example—you really don't want to have to name them individually. What you need is an **array**.

An array is a named set of variables of the same type. Each variable in the array is called an **array element**. To reference a particular element in an array you use the array name combined with an integer value called an **index**. The index for an array element is the offset of that particular element from the beginning of the array. The first element will have an index of 0, the second will have an index of 1, the third an index of 2 and so on.

You aren't obliged to create the array itself when you declare the array variable. The array variable is an object distinct from the array itself. You could define the integer array variable, **primes**, with the statement:

```
int[] primes;            // Declare an integer array variable
```

The variable **primes** is now a placeholder for an integer array that you've yet to define. No memory is allocated to hold the array itself at this point. We'll see in a moment that to create the array itself we must specify its type and how many elements it is to contain. The square brackets following the type in the previous statement indicates that the variable is for referencing an array, and not for storing a single value of type **int**.

You may come across an alternative notation for declaring an array variable:

```
int primes[];            // Declare an integer array variable
```

This is exactly equivalent to the previous statement so you can use either notation. Many programmers prefer the original notation, as **int[]** tends to indicate more clearly that the type is an **int** array.

Once you've declared an array variable, you can define an array that it will reference:

```
primes = new int[10];    // Define an array of 10 integers
```

You could also declare the array variable, and define the array of type **int** to hold 10 prime numbers with a single statement, as shown in the following illustration:

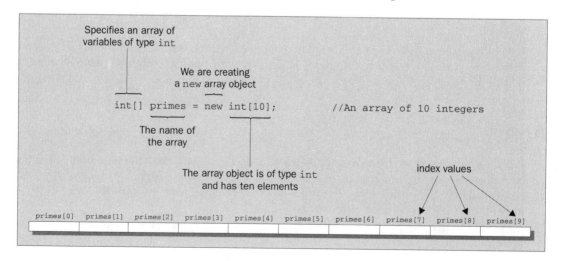

The first part of the definition specifies the type of the array. The type name, **int** in this case, is followed by an empty pair of square brackets to indicate you're declaring an array rather than a single variable of type **int**. The part following the equals sign defines the array. The keyword **new** indicates that you're allocating new memory for the array, and the **int[10]** part specifies you want capacity for ten variables of type **int** in the array.

Before we go any further, let's clarify a bit of terminology we've been using in this discussion—a declaration for an array just defines the variable name. So the statement,

```
int[] myArray;
```

is a declaration for the array name, **myArray**. No memory has been allocated to store the array itself and the number of elements hasn't been defined.

The statement,

```
int[] myArray = new int[100];
```

is a definition, since the array size is specified.

You refer to an element of the array by using the array name followed by the element's index value, enclosed between square brackets. You can specify an index value by any expression that produces a result of type **int**. The fact that our array is also of type **int** is coincidental. The index must be of type **int** for an array of **float** values for example. If you use a value of type **long** as an index, you'll get an error message from the compiler, but you'll recall from Chapter 2 that expressions involving values of type **short** and type **byte** produce a result of type **int**, so you can use those in an index expression.

As you can see in the diagram, the first element of the array is **primes[0]**; you reference the fifth element in the array as **primes[4]**, and the maximum index value is one less than the number of elements in the array. Java checks that the index values you use are valid. If you use an index value that is less than 0, or greater than the index value for the last element in the array, an **exception** will be thrown—throwing an exception is just the way errors at execution time are signaled and there are different types of exceptions for signaling various kinds of errors. The exception in this case is called an **IndexOutOfBoundsException**. We'll be looking in detail at exceptions in Chapter 7.

The array, **primes**, is referred to as a **one-dimensional array**, since each of its elements are referenced using one index running from 0 to 9. We'll see later that arrays can have two or more dimensions, the number of dimensions being the same as the number of indexes required to access an element of the array. Since each element in the **primes** array is an **int** variable requiring 4 bytes, the whole array will occupy 40 bytes. When an array is created like this, all the array elements are initialized to zero.

Reusing Array Variables

An array variable is actually an object which can reference different arrays at different points in your program. Suppose you've declared and defined the variable **primes** as before:

```
int[] primes;
primes = new int[10];        // Allocate an array of 10 integer elements
```

This produces an array of ten elements of type **int**. A bit later in your program you may want the array variable **primes** to refer to a larger array, with 50 elements say. You would simply write:

```
primes = new int[50];        // Allocate an array of 50 integer elements
```

When this statement is executed, the previous array of 10 elements is discarded, along with the data values you may have stored in it, as illustrated here.

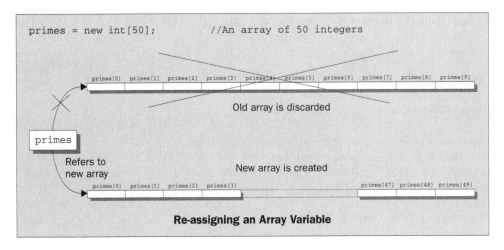

Re-assigning an Array Variable

The array variable, **primes**, now points to a new integer array with fifty elements, with index values running from 0 to 49. Although you can change the array that an array variable references, all the arrays must correspond to the declared type of the array variable. Your variable **primes**, for example, can only reference arrays of type **int**.

We've used an **int** array throughout so far, but everything applies equally well to **long** or **double** or to any of the basic data types. More than that, you can create arrays of any other type of object, including the classes that you'll be defining yourself in Chapter 5.

Initializing Arrays

You can initialize an array with your own values when you declare it, and thus determine how many elements it will have. Following the declaration of the array variable, simply add an equals sign followed by the list of element values enclosed between braces. For example, if you write,

```
int[] primes = {2, 3, 5, 7, 11, 13, 17};     // An array of 7 elements
```

the array is created with sufficient elements to store all of the initializing values that appear between the braces, seven in this case. If you specify initializing values for an array, you must include values for all the elements. If you only want to set some of the array elements to values explicitly, you should use an assignment statement for each element. For example:

```
int[] primes = new int[100];
primes[0] = 2;
primes[1] = 3;
```

The first statement declares and defines an integer array of one hundred elements, all of which will be initialized to zero. The two assignment statements then set values for the first two array elements.

You can also initialize an array with an existing array. For example, you could declare the following array variables,

```
long[] even = {2L, 4L, 6L, 8L, 10L};
long[] value = even;
```

where the array **even** is used to initialize the array **value** in its declaration. This has the effect shown here.

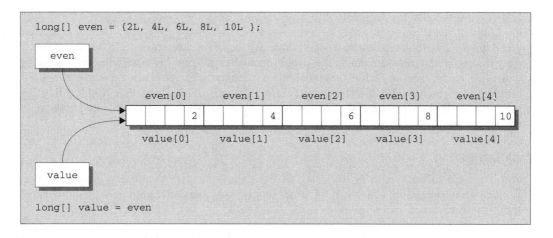

You've created two array variables, but you only have one array. Both arrays refer to the same set of elements and you can access the elements of the array through either variable name—for example, **even[2]** refers to the same variable as **value[2]**.

Using Arrays

You can use array elements in expressions in exactly the same way as you might use a single variable of the same data type. For example, if you declare an array **samples**, you can fill it with random values between 0.0 and 100.0 with the following code:

```
double[] samples = new double[50];      // An array of 50 double values
for(int i = 0; i < 50; i++)
  samples[i] = 100.0*Math.random();     // Generate random values
```

109

To show that array elements can be used in exactly the same way as ordinary variables, you could write:

```
double result = (samples[10]*samples[0] -
                               Math.sqrt(samples[49]))/samples[29];
```

This is a totally arbitrary calculation of course, but with the right numbers inserted it can calculate anything you like. More sensibly, to compute the average of the values stored in the **samples** array, you could write:

```
double average = 0.0;          // Variable to hold the average

for(int i = 0; i < 50; i++)
   average += samples[i];       // Sum all the elements

average /= 50.0;                // Divide by the total number of elements
```

Within the loop we accumulate the sum of all the elements of the array **samples** in the variable **average**. We then divide this sum by the number of elements.

Notice how we use the length of the array, 50, all over the place. It appears in the **for** loop, and in floating point form as a divisor to calculate the average. When you use arrays you'll often find that references to the length of the array are strewn all through your code. And if you later want to change the program, to handle one hundred elements for instance, you need to be able to decide whether any particular value of 50 in the code is actually the number of elements, and therefore should be changed to 100, or if it is a value that just happens to be the same and should be left alone. Java helps you avoid this problem, as we'll now see.

Array Length

You can refer to the length of the array using **length**, a data member of the **array** object. For our array **samples**, we can refer to its length as **samples.length**. We could use this to write the calculation of the average as:

```
double average = 0.0;          // Variable to hold the average
for(int i = 0; i < samples.length; i++)
   average += samples[i];       // Sum all the elements
average /= samples.length;      // Divide by the total number of elements
```

Now the code is independent of the number of array elements. If you change the number of elements in the array, the code will automatically deal with that. You'll also see in Chapter 6 that being able to obtain the length of an array in this way is very convenient in the context of coding your own class methods that process arrays.

Let's try out an array in an improved program to calculate prime numbers:

Try It Out—Even More Primes

Try out the following code derived, in part, from the code we used in Chapter 3.

```java
public class MorePrimes
{
  public static void main(String[] args)
  {
    long[] primes = new long[20];  // Array to store primes
    primes[0] = 2;                 // Seed the first prime
    primes[1] = 3;                 // and the second
    int count = 2;                 // Count of primes found - up to now
                                   // which is also the array index
    long number = 5;               // Next integer to be tested

    outer:
    for( ; count < primes.length; number += 2)
    {
      // The maximum divisor we need to try is square root of number
      long limit = (long)Math.ceil(Math.sqrt((double)number));

      // Divide by all the primes we have up to limit
      for(int i = 1; i < count && primes[i] <= limit; i++)
        if(number%primes[i] == 0)        // Is it an exact divisor?
          continue outer;                // yes, try the next number

        primes[count++] = number;        // We got one!
    }

    for(int i=0; i < primes.length; i++)
      System.out.println(primes[i]);     // Output all the primes
  }
}
```

This program computes as many prime numbers as the capacity of the array **primes** will allow.

How It Works

Any number that isn't a prime must be a product of prime factors, so we only need to divide a candidate by prime numbers that are less than, or equal to the square root of the candidate to test for whether it is prime. The math isn't really that difficult. For every factor a number has that is greater that the square root of the number, the result of division by this factor is another factor that is less than the square root. You perhaps can see this more easily with a specific example. The number 24 has a square root that is a bit less than 5. You can factorize it as 2x12, 3x8, 4x6, then we come to cases where the first factor is greater that the square root so the second is less, 6x4 etc., and so we are repeating the pairs of factors we already have.

We first declare the array primes to be of type **long**, and define it as having twenty elements. We set the first two elements of the **primes** array to 2 and 3 respectively to start the process off, as we'll use the primes we have in the array as divisors when testing a new candidate. The variable, **count**, is the total number of primes we've found, so this starts out as 2. Note that we use **count** as the **for** loop counter, so we omit the first expression between parentheses in the loop statement as **count** has already been set.

The candidate to be tested is stored in **number**, with the first value set as 5. The **for** loop statement, labeled **outer**, counts in steps of two, since we don't want to check even numbers. The **for** loop ends when count is equal to the length of the array. We test the value in **number** in the inner **for** loop by dividing **number** by all of the prime numbers we have in the **primes** array that are less than, or equal to the square root of the candidate. If we get an exact division the value in **number** is not prime, so we go immediately to the next iteration of the outer loop via the **continue** statement.

If we get no exact division, we exit normally from the inner loop and execute the statement:

```
primes[count++] = number;     // We got one!
```

Because **count** is the number of values we have stored, it also corresponds to the index for the next free element in the **primes** array. Thus we use **count** as the index to the array element in which we want to store the value of **number**, and then increment **count**.

When we've filled the **primes** array, the outer loop will end and we'll output all the values in the array. Note that, because we've used the **length** member of the **primes** object whenever we need the number of elements in the array, changing the number of elements in the definition of the array to generate a larger or smaller number of primes is simple.

Arrays of Arrays

We've only worked with one-dimensional arrays up to now, that is arrays that use a single index. Why would you ever need the complications of using more indexes to access the elements of an array?

Suppose that you have a fanatical interest in the weather, and you are intent on recording the temperature each day at ten separate geographical locations throughout 1997. Once you've sorted out the logistics of actually collecting this information, you can use an array of 10 elements corresponding to the number of locations, where each of these elements is an array of 365 elements to store the temperature values. You would declare this array with the statement:

```
float[][] temperature = new float[10][365];
```

This is called a **two-dimensional array**, since it has two dimensions: one with index values running from 0 to 9, and the other with index values from 0 to 364. The first index will relate to a geographical location, and the second index corresponds to the day of the year. That's much handier than a one-dimensional array with 3650 elements, isn't it?

The organization of the two-dimensional array is shown in the following diagram.

	temperature[0][0]	temperature[0][1]	temperature[0][2]		temperature[0][363]	temperature[0][364]
temperature[0]						
	temperature[1][0]	temperature[1][1]	temperature[1][2]		temperature[1][363]	temperature[1][364]
temperature[1]						
	temperature[9][0]	temperature[9][1]	temperature[9][2]		temperature[9][363]	temperature[9][364]
temperature[9]						

```
float[] [] temperature = new float[10] [365];
```

There are 10 arrays, each having 365 elements. In referring to an element, the first square brackets enclose the index for a particular array, and the second pair of square brackets enclose the index value for an element within that array. So to refer to the temperature for day 100 for the sixth location, you would use **temperature[5][99]**. Since each **float** variable occupies 4 bytes, the total space required to store the elements of this two-dimensional array is 10x365x4 bytes, which is a total of 14,600 bytes. The array has some additional overhead itself.

For a fixed second index value in a two-dimensional array, varying the first index direction is often referred to as accessing a **column** of the array. Similarly, fixing the first indexing and varying the second, you access a **row** of the array. The reason for this terminology is apparent from the last diagram.

You could just as well have used two statements to create the last array: one to declare the array variable, and the other to create the array:

```
float [][] temperature;              // Declare the array variable
temperature = new float[10][365];    // Create the array
```

The first statement declares the array variable temperature for two-dimensional arrays of type **float**. The second statement creates the array with ten elements, each of which is an array of 365 elements.

Let's exercise this two-dimensional array in a program to calculate the average annual temperature for each location.

Try It Out—The Weather Fanatic

In the absence of real samples, we'll generate the temperatures as random values between –10° and 35°. This assumes we're recording temperatures in degrees Centigrade. If you prefer Fahrenheit you could use 14° – 95° to cover the same range of temperatures.

```java
public class WeatherFan
{
  public static void main(String[]args)
  {
    float[][] temperature = new float[10][365]; // Temperature array

    // Generate temperatures
    for(int i = 0; i < temperature.length; i++)
      for(int j = 0; j < temperature[0].length; j++)
        temperature[i][j] = (float)(45.0*Math.random() - 10.0);

    // Calculate the average per location
    for(int i = 0; i < temperature.length; i++)
    {
      float average = 0.0f;      // Place to store the average

      for(int j = 0; j < temperature[0].length; j++)
        average += temperature[i][j];

      // Output the average temperature for the current location
      System.out.println("Average temperature at location "
              + (i+1) + " = " + average/(float)temperature[0].length);
    }
  }
}
```

How It Works

After declaring the array, **temperature**, we fill it with random values using nested **for** loops. Note how **temperature.length** used in the outer loop refers to the length of the first dimension, 10 in this case. In the inner loop we use **temperature[0].length** to refer to the length of the second dimension, 365. We could use any index value here, **temperature[9].length** would have been just as good, since the lengths of the rows of the array are all the same.

The **Math.random()** method generates a value of type **double** between 0.0 and 1.0. This value is multiplied by 45.0 in the expression for the temperature, which results in values between 0.0 and 45.0. Subtracting 10.0 from this value gives us the range we require, −10.0 to 35.0.

We then use another pair of nested **for** loops, controlled in the same way as the first, to calculate the averages of the stored temperatures. The outer loop iterates over the locations and the inner loop sums all the temperature values for a given location. Before the execution of the inner loop, the variable **average** is declared and initialized, and this is used to accumulate the sum of the temperatures for a location in the inner loop. After the inner loop has been executed, we output the average temperature for each location, identifying the locations by numbers 1 to 10, one more than the index value for each location. Note that the parentheses around **(i+1)** here are essential. To get the average we divide the variable **average** by the number of samples which is **temperature[0].length** which is the length of the array holding temperatures for the first location. Again, we could use any index value here since as we've seen they all return the same value, 365.

Arrays of Arrays of Varying Length

When you create an array of arrays, the arrays don't need to be all the same length. You could declare an array variable sample with the statement,

```
float[][] sample;              // Declare an array of arrays
```

which declares the array object sample of type **float**. You can then define the number of elements in the first dimension with the statement:

```
sample = new float[6][];       // Define 6 elements, each is an array
```

We now have six elements allocated, each of which can hold a one-dimensional array. You can define these arrays individually if you want:

```
sample[2] = new float[6];    // The 3rd array has 6 elements
sample[5] = new float[101];  // The 6th array has 101 elements
```

This defines two of the arrays. Obviously, you can't use an array until it has been defined, but you could use these two and define the others later.

If you wanted the array, **sample**, to have a triangular shape, with one element in the first row, two elements in the second row, three in the third row, and so on, you could define the arrays in a loop:

```
for(int i = 0; i < sample.length; i++)
   sample[i] = new float[i+1];      // Allocate each array
```

The effect of this is to produce an array layout that's shown here.

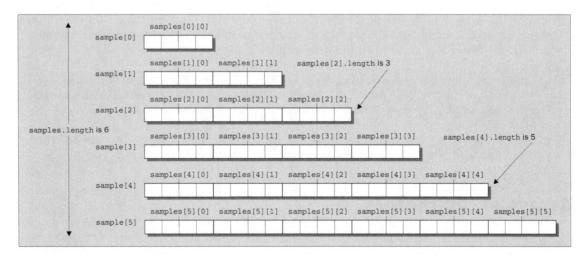

The total of 21 elements in the array will occupy 84 bytes. When you need a two-dimensional array with rows of varying length, allocating them to fit the requirement can save a considerable amount of memory compared to just using rectangular arrays where the row lengths are all the same.

To check out that the array is as shown, you could implement this in a console program, and display the **length** member for each of these arrays.

Multidimensional Arrays

You aren't limited to two-dimensional arrays either. If you're an international Java Bean grower with multiple farms across several countries, you could arrange to store the results of your bean counting in the array declared and defined in the statement:

```
long[][][] beans = new long[5][10][30];
```

The array **beans** has three dimensions. It provides for holding bean counts for each of up to thirty fields per farm, with ten farms per country in each of five countries.

You can envisage this as just a three-dimensional array, but remember that **beans** is an array of five elements, each of which holds a two-dimensional array, and each of these two-dimensional arrays can be different. For example, if you really want to go to town, you can declare the array **beans** with the statement;

```
long[][][] beans = new long[3][][];   // Three two dimensional arrays
```

Each of the three elements in the first dimension of **beans** can hold a different two-dimensional array, so you could specify the first dimension of each explicitly with the statements:

```
beans[0] = new long[4][];
beans[1] = new long[2][];
beans[2] = new long[5][];
```

These three arrays have elements which hold a one-dimensional array, and you can also specify the sizes of these independently. Note how the empty square brackets indicate there's still a dimension undefined. You could give the arrays in each of these elements random dimensions between 1 and 7 with the following code:

```
for(int i = 0; i < beans.length; i++)          // Vary over 1st dimension
  for(int j = 0; j < beans[i].length; j++)     // Vary over 2nd dimension
    beans[i][j] = new long[(int)(1.0 + 6.0*Math.random())];
```

If you can find a sensible reason for doing so, or if you're just a glutton for punishment, you can extend this to four or more dimensions.

Arrays of Characters

All our arrays have been numeric so far. Of course, you can also have arrays of characters. For example, we can declare an array variable of type **char** to hold 50 characters with the statement:

```
char[] message = new char[50];
```

We could also define an array of type **char** by the characters it holds:

```
char[]  vowels = { 'a', 'e', 'i', 'o', 'u'};
```

This defines an array of five elements, initialized with the characters appearing between the braces. This is fine for things like vowels, but what about proper messages?

Using an array of type **char**, you can write statements such as:

```
char[] sign = {'F', 'l', 'u', 'e', 'n', 't', ' ',
               'G', 'i', 'b', 'b', 'e', 'r', 'i', 's', 'h', ' ',
               's', 'p', 'o', 'k', 'e', 'n', ' ',
               'h', 'e', 'r', 'e'};
```

Well, you get the message—just, but it's not a very friendly way to deal with it. It looks like a collection of characters, which is what it is. What we really need is something which is a bit more integrated—something that looks like a message, but still gives us the ability to get at the individual characters if we want. What we need is a **String**.

Using Strings

You'll need to use character strings in most of your programs, if only to output error messages. Of course, there are many other contexts in which you'll be using strings; for example, in headings, names, addresses, product descriptions—the list is endless. In Java, strings are objects of the class **String**. The **String** class is a standard class that comes with Java, and it's specifically designed for creating and processing strings.

String Constants

You've already made extensive use of string constants for output. Just about every time the **println()** method was used in an example, we used a string constant as the argument. A **string constant** is a sequence of characters between double quotes:

```
"This is a string constant!"
```

It's literally a **String** constant—a constant object of the class **String** that the compiler creates for use in your program.

Some characters can't be entered explicitly from the keyboard for inclusion in a string constant. You can't include a double quote, for example, as this is used to indicate where a string constant begins and ends. You can't include a new line character by pressing the *Enter* key since this will move the cursor to a new line. All of these characters are provided in the same way as **char** constants—you use an escape sequence. All the escape sequences you saw when we looked at **char** constants apply to strings. You use **\"** for a double quote, **\n** for a new line character, **\t** for a tab character, and **** for a backslash. The statement,

```
System.out.println("This is \na string constant!");
```

will produce the output:

```
This is
a string constant!
```

Like values of type **char**, strings are stored internally as Unicode characters so you can also include Unicode character codes as escape sequences of the form **\unnnn** where **nnnn** are the four hexadecimal digits of the Unicode coding for a character.

You'll recall from our preliminary discussion of classes and objects in Chapter 1 that a class usually contains data and methods and this is also true of the class **String**. The sequence of characters included in the string is the class data, and the methods in the class **String** enable you to process the data in a variety of ways. We won't go into the detail of how the class is defined. We'll deal with that in Chapter 5. In this chapter we'll concentrate on how we can create and use objects of the class **String**. You know how to define a **String** constant. The next step is to learn how a **String** variable is defined.

Creating String Objects

Just to make sure there's no confusion in your mind, a **String** variable is simply an object of the class **String**. You declare a **String** variable in much the same way as you define a variable of one of the basic types. You can also initialize it in the declaration, which is generally a good idea:

```
String myString = "My inaugural string";
```

This declares the variable **myString** as type **String**, and initializes it with the value **"My inaugural string"**. You can store another string in a **String** variable, once you've declared it, by using an assignment. For example, we can change the value of our **String** variable **myString** with the statement:

```
myString = "Strings can be knotty";
```

The effect of this is illustrated here:

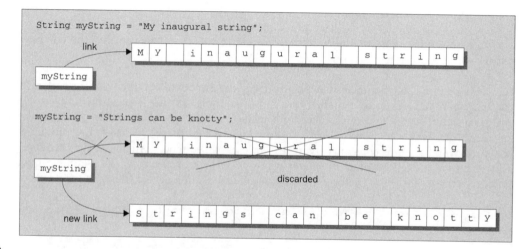

The variable **myString** is distinct from the characters that make up the string itself. As we saw with array objects, the variable **myString** acts as a sort of reference to the string it contains at any time. When we declare and initialize **myString**, it is linked to the initializing string value. When we execute the assignment statement, the original link is severed, the old string is discarded, and the variable **myString** is connected to the new string value. This means that you can't extend the string that's stored in a variable of type **String**. To change the value of a **String** variable you throw away the old string and connect it to a new one. The distinction between a **String** variable and the string it references isn't apparent most of the time, but we'll see situations later in this chapter where it's important to understand this, so keep it in mind.

Of course, if you declare a variable of type **String** without initializing it,

```
String anyString;      // Uninitialized String variable
```

then it doesn't have a value. You just have a variable of type **String** to which you can assign a value.

Arrays of Strings

Since string variables are objects, you can create arrays of strings. You declare an array of **String** objects with the same mechanism that we used to declare arrays of elements for the basic types. You just use the type **String** in the declaration. For example, to declare an array of five **String** objects, you could use the statement:

```
String[] names = new String[5];
```

We can try this out with a small example:

Try It Out—Twinkle, Twinkle, Lucky Star

Let's create a console program to generate your lucky star for the day.

```
public class LuckyStars
{
  public static void main(String[] args)
  {
    String[] stars = {
                      "Robert Redford"   , "Marilyn Monroe",
                      "Boris Karloff"    , "Lassie",
                      "Hopalong Cassidy", "Trigger"
                     };
    System.out.println("Your lucky star for today is "
            + stars[(int)( stars.length*Math.random())%6]);
  }
}
```

119

How It Works

This program creates the array **stars**, of type **String**. The array length will be set to however many initializing values appear between the braces in the declaration statement, six in this case. We select a random element from the array by creating a random index value. Multiplying the random number produced using the method **Math.random** (with a value somewhere between 0.0 and 1.0) by the length of the array, we'll get a value between 0.0 and 6.0. We don't actually want the value ever to be 6.0, since this would produce an illegal index value, so use the modulus operator, **%**, to make sure that we only get values from 0 – 5. If the value 1.0 happens to be returned from the **random()** method, this will be multiplied by the length of the **stars** array which is 6 to produce 6.0. After casting this value to type **int**, we generate the remainder after dividing by 6 using the **%** operator, so the value 6 will produce 0.

You might be tempted to use the expression,

```
(int)(( stars.length -1)*Math.random())
```

for the index value to the **stars** array, but this would be incorrect—at least, in the context of what we want to do here. Sure, it would produce values between 0 and 5, but the value 5 would be a relatively rare occurrence—certainly much less likely than the other values 0, 1, 2, 3, and 4. Why is this?

As you know, the cast to **int** produces the nearest integer less than or equal to the value being cast. This means that 0.0 will produce 0, so will 0.1, 0.3, 0.456789, or any other value that is less than 1.0. Similarly, 4.9 will produce 4, so will 4.0001 or 4.9999, or any number that is less than 5.0 and greater than or equal to 4.0—there are millions of them. The case of 5 is different. Only exactly 5.0 will produce 5. This will happen once in a blue moon, so poor old Trigger will hardly ever come up.

The code as written in the example produces the numbers 0 – 5 with equal likelihood, although there's a tiny extra bias towards 0, because 6.0 will produce 0, as well as any of the numbers less than 1.0.

Operations on Strings

There are many kinds of operations that can be performed on strings, but we can start with one you've used already, joining strings together, often called **string concatenation**.

Joining Strings

For this you use the **+** operator, just as you've been doing with the argument to the **println()** method throughout this book. The simplest use of this is to join two strings together:

```
myString = "The quick brown fox" + " jumps over the lazy dog";
```

This will join the two strings on the right of the assignment, and store the result in the **String** variable **myString**.

Let's see how some variations on the use of the **+** operator with **String** objects work:

Try It Out—String Concatenation

Enter the following code for the class **JoinStrings**:

```
public class JoinStrings
{
  public static void main(String[] args)
  {
    String firstString = "Many ";
    String secondString = "hands ";
    String thirdString = "make light work";

    String myString;             // Variable to store results

    // Join three strings and store the result
    myString = firstString + secondString + thirdString;
    System.out.println(myString);

    // Convert an integer to String and join with two other strings
    int numHands = 99;
    myString = numHands + " " + secondString + thirdString;
    System.out.println(myString);

    // Combining a string and integers
    myString = "fifty five is " + 5 + 5;
    System.out.println(myString);

    // Combining integers and a string
    myString = 5 + 5 + " is ten";
    System.out.println(myString);
  }
}
```

If you run this example, it will produce some interesting results:

```
Many hands make light work
99 hands make light work
fifty five is 55
10 is ten
```

How It Works

The first line of output is quite straightforward. It simply joins the three string values stored in the **String** variables **firstString**, **secondString** and **thirdString** into a single string, and stores this in the variable **myString**.

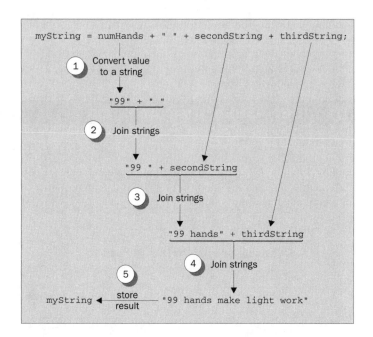

The second line of output is a use of the **+** operator we've used regularly with the `println()` method, but clearly something a little more complicated is happening, as illustrated here:

Behind the scenes, the value of the variable **numHands** is being converted to a string that represents this value as a decimal. This is prompted by the fact that it's combined with the string, **" "**. Dissimilar types can't be operated on, so one operand must be converted to the type of the other for the operation to be possible. After the conversion has been done we have an expression combining four strings using the **+** operator. If you look back at the table of operator precedences, you'll see that the associativity of the operator **+** is from left to right, so the strings are combined in pairs starting from the left, as shown in the diagram.

The left-to-right associativity of the **+** operator is important in understanding the next two lines of output. The two statements involved in creating these strings look very similar. Why does **5+5** result in **"55"** in one statement, and **"10"** in the other? The reason is illustrated below.

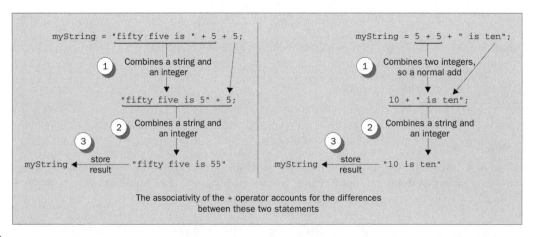

The essential difference between the two is that the first statement always has at least one operand of type **String**, so each of the integers is converted to type **String** individually. In the second statement the first operation is an arithmetic add, as both operands are integers.

The conversion of values of the basic types to type **String** is actually accomplished by using a **static** method **valueOf()** in the class **String**. A value of one of the basic types is passed to the method as an argument and it returns the **String** equivalent. There's a version of **valueOf()** for each of the basic types and the correct one for any particular type is selected automatically. All of this happens automatically when you're concatenating strings using the **+** operator.

Comparing Strings

Here's where the difference between the **String** variable and the string it references will become apparent. To compare variables of the basic types for equality you use the **==** operator. This does **not** apply to **String** objects (or any other objects). The expression,

```
string1 == string2
```

will check whether the two string variables refer to the same string. If they reference separate strings, this expression will have the value **false**, regardless of whether the strings happen to be the same. We can demonstrate this with a little example:

Try It Out—Two Strings, Identical but not the Same

1 In the following code, we test to see whether **string1** and **string3** refer to the same string.

```
public class MatchStrings
{
  public static void main(String[] args)
  {
    String string1 = "Too many ";
    String string2 = "cooks";
    String string3 = "Too many ";

    // Display the contents of the strings
    System.out.println("string3 is now: " + string3);
    System.out.println("string1 is now: " + string1);

    if(string1 == string3)      // Now test for identity
      System.out.println("string1 and string3 point to the same string");
    else
      System.out.println(
                  "string1 and string3 do not point to the same string");
```

2 Now we do the same again, but make **string1** and **string3** refer to two identical but separate strings:

```
string3 = string1 + string2;
string1 += "cooks";

// Display the contents of the strings
System.out.println("\n\nstring3 is now: " + string3);
System.out.println("string1 is now: " + string1);

if(string1 == string3)        // Now test for identity
  System.out.println("string1 and string3 point to the same string");
else
  System.out.println(
            "string1 and string3 do not point to the same string");
  }
}
```

This will produce the output:

```
string3 is now: Too many
string1 is now: Too many
string1 and string3 point to the same string

string3 is now: Too many cooks
string1 is now: Too many cooks
string1 and string3 do not point to the same string
```

How It Works

The variables **string3** and **string1** are both initialized with the string constant **"Too many "**. The compiler will only create one copy of this constant, as constants can't be modified, and makes both variables refer to this copy. There's no risk in this since, as we saw, you can't change the string that a **String** variable refers to: you can only make it refer to another string. The result of executing the first **if** statement shows that they do indeed point to the same string.

Next we change the values of **string1** and **string3**. Because these values are the result of an operation involving variables they each refer to separate strings—which happen in this case to be identical. This is clear from the second block of output where you can see the strings are the same, but the **else** clause of the **if** statement is executed indicating that the **string1** and **string3** objects do indeed refer to separate strings.

Testing for Equality

To compare two **String** variables, that is to decide whether the strings they reference are equal or not, you use the method **equals()** which is defined in the **String** class. To check for equality between two strings ignoring the case of the string characters, you use the method **equalsIgnoreCase()**. Let's put these in the context of an example to see how they work.

Try It Out—String Identity

Make the following changes to the **CompareStrings.java** file of the previous example:

```
public class CompareStrings
{
  public static void main(String[] args)
  {
    String string1 = "Too many ";
    String string2 = "cooks";
    String string3 = "Too many ";

    // Display the contents of the strings
    System.out.println("string3 is now: " + string3);
    System.out.println("string1 is now: " + string1);

    if(string1.equals(string3))      // Now test for equality
      System.out.println(
                    "string1 and string3 refer to identical strings");
    else
      System.out.println(
              "string1 and string3 do not refer to identical strings");

    string1 += string2;    // Join string2 to string1

    // Compare a String variable with a constant
    System.out.println("string1.equals(\"Too many cooks\") has the value"
                    + string1.equals("Too many cooks"));

    string1 = "Cooks";      // Set string1 to a new value
    // Compare two string variables ignoring case
    System.out.println("string1.equalsIgnoreCase(string2) has the value "
                    + string1.equalsIgnoreCase(string2));
  }
}
```

If you run this example, you should get the output:

```
string3 is now: Too many
string1 is now: Too many
string1 and string3 point to identical strings
string1.equals("Too many cooks") has the value true
string1.equalsIgnoreCase(string2) has the value true
```

How It Works

Before we look in detail at how the program works, let's take some time to look at the method calls peppering the code.

In the **if** expression, we've called the method **equals()** of the object **string1** to test the condition. This is the syntax we've been using to call the method **println()** in the object **out**. In general, to call a method belonging to an object you write the object name, then a period, then the name of the method. The parentheses following the method name enclose the information to be passed to the method, **string3** in this case. The general form for calling a method for an object is shown here.

```
                        Name of the
                          method
                       _____
   objectName  .  methodName  ( arg1, arg2, ... )

   Object owning          Expressions specifying data to be
   the method                 passed to the method
```

FYI   We'll learn more about this in Chapter 6, when we look at how to define our own classes. For the moment, just note that you don't necessarily need to pass any arguments to a method. On the other hand there can be several. It all depends on how the method was defined in the class.

The **equals()** method requires one argument, and it returns **true** if the value passed in the parentheses (**string3** in the code for this Try It Out) is identical to the string pointed to by the **String** object that owns the method, in this case **string1**. As you may have already guessed, we could just as well call the **equals()** method for the object **string3**, and pass **string1** as the argument. In this case, the expression to call the method would be,

```
string3.equals(string1)
```

and we would get exactly the same result.

Looking at the program code, after outputting the values of **string3** and **string1**, the next line shows that calling the **equals()** method for **string1** with **string3** as the argument returns **true**. After the **if**, we join **string1** and **string2** to form a new string, and store this in **string1**. We then compare the value of **string1** with a string constant in the statement:

```
System.out.println("string1.equals(\"Too many cooks\") has the value "
                            + string1.equals("Too many cooks"));
```

This looks busy because we must use **\"** to include each of the double quotes in the string constant:

```
"string1.equals(\"Too many cooks\") has the value "
```

The argument to **println()** method is the concatenation of this string constant and the string representation of the value of the expression:

```
string1.equals("Too many cooks")
```

This calls the **equals()** method belonging to **string1** and compares the value of **string1** with **"Too many cooks"**. As the output indicates, this returns **true**. In this example we used a string constant as the argument to the method **equals()**, but it could equally be any expression that results in an object of type **String**.

Checking the Start and End of a String

You can test whether a string starts with a particular character sequence by using the method **startsWith()**. If **String1** has been defined as **"Too many cooks"**, the expression **String1.startsWith("Too")** will have the value **true**. So would the expression **String1.startsWith("Too man")**. A complementary method **endsWith()** checks for what appears at the end of a string.

Sequencing Strings

You'll often need to place strings in order, for example, when you have a collection of names for instance. Testing for equality doesn't help—what you need is the method **compareTo()** in the class **String**. This method compares the **String** object from which it is called with the argument passed to it, and returns an integer which is negative if the string object is less than the argument passed, zero if the string object is equal to the argument, and positive if the string object is greater than the argument. It isn't that obvious what the terms 'less than', 'equal to', and 'greater than' mean when applied to strings, so let's go into that a bit.

Strings are compared in the **CompareTo()** method by comparing individual corresponding characters, starting with the first character in each string, until two corresponding characters are found to be different or the last character in the shorter string is reached. Individual characters are compared by comparing their numeric values—so two characters are equal if the numeric value of the Unicode characters are equal, and one is greater than the other if the Unicode character for one is greater than the other.

One string is greater than another if it has a character greater than the corresponding character in the other string, and all the previous characters were equal. So if **string1** has the value **"mad dog"**, and **string2** has the value **"mad cat"**, then the expression,

```
string1.compareTo(string2);
```

will return a positive value as a result of comparing the fifth characters in the strings, the **'d'** in **string1** with the **'c'** in **string2**.

What if the corresponding characters in both strings are equal up to the end of the shorter string, but the other string has more characters? In this case the longer string is greater than the shorter string, so **"catamaran"** is greater than **"cat"**.

127

One string is less than another string if it has a character less than the corresponding character in the other string, and all the other characters are equal. Thus the expression:

```
string2.compareTo(string1);
```

will return a negative value.

Two strings are equal if they contain the same number of characters and corresponding characters are identical. In this case the **compareTo()** method returns 0.

We can try the **compareTo()** method in a simple example:

Try It Out—Ordering Strings

1 Enter the following code with some simple strings:

```java
public class SequenceStrings
{
  public static void main(String[] args)
  {
    String string1 = "A";
    String string2 = "To";
    String string3 = "Z";

    // Compare string1 with string3
    if(string1.compareTo(string3) < 0)
      System.out.println("string1" + "(" + string1 + ")" +
                          " is less than string3" + "(" + string3 + ")");
    else
      if(string1.compareTo(string3) > 0)
        System.out.println("string1" + "(" +  string1 + ")" +
                            " is greater than string3" +
                            "(" + string3 + ")");
      else
        System.out.println("string1 is equal to string3");
```

2 Copy the last nested **if** statements and change them to compare **string2** and **string1**.

```java
    if(string2.compareTo(string1) < 0)
      System.out.println("string2" + "(" + string2 + ")" +
                          " is less than string1" + "(" + string1 + ")");
    else
      if(string2.compareTo(string1) > 0)
        System.out.println("string2" + "(" + string2 + ")" +
                            " is greater than string1"+
                            "(" + string1 + ")");
      else
        System.out.println("string2 is equal to string1");
```

128

```
    }
  }
```

The example will produce the output:

```
string1(A) is less than string3(Z)
string2(To) is greater than string1(A)
```

How It Works

You should have no trouble with this example. It declares and initializes three **String** variables: **string1**, **string2**, and **string3**. We then have an **if** and a nested **if** to compare **string1** with **string3**. We compare **string2** with **string1** in the same way.

As with the **equals()** method, the argument to the method **compareTo()** can be any expression that results in a **String** object.

Accessing String Characters

When you're processing strings, sooner or later you'll need to access individual characters in a **String** object. To refer to a particular character in a string you use an index of type **int** that is the offset of the character position from the beginning of the string. This is exactly the same principle as we used for referencing an array element. The first character in a string is at position 0, the second is at position 1, the third is at position 2, and so on. However, although the principle is the same, the practice isn't. You can't use square brackets to access characters in a string—you must use a method.

Extracting String Characters

You can extract a character from a **String** object by using the method **charAt()** which accepts an argument which is the offset of the character position from the beginning of the string—in other words an index. If you attempt to use an index that is less than 0 or greater than the index for the last position in the string, you'll cause an error. In fact, it will result in an **exception** being thrown. We'll discuss exactly what exceptions are, and how you should deal with them in Chapter 7. For the moment, just note that the specific exception thrown in this case is called **StringIndexOutOfBoundsException**.

To avoid errors, you obviously need to be able to determine the length of a **String** object. To get this you use the method **length()**. Note that this is different from the way you obtained the length of an array. Here you're calling a method, **length()** in the class **String**, whereas with an array you were accessing a data member, **length**. We can explore the use of the **charAt()** and **length()** methods in the **String** class with an example.

Try It Out—Getting at Characters in a String

In the following code the soliloquy is analyzed character by character to determine the vowels, spaces and letters used.

```
public class StringCharacters
{
  public static void main(String[] args)
  {
    // Text string to be analyzed
    String text = "To be or not to be, that is the question;"
                + "Whether 'tis nobler in the mind to suffer"
                + " the slings and arrows of outrageous fortune,"
                + " or to take arms against a sea of troubles,"
                + " and by opposing end them?";

    int spaces  = 0,     // Count of spaces
        vowels  = 0,     // Count of vowels
        letters = 0;     // Count of letters

    // Analyze all the characters in the string
    for(int i = 0; i < text.length(); i++)
    {
      // Check for vowels
      char ch = Character.toLowerCase(text.charAt(i));
      if(ch == 'a' || ch == 'e' || ch == 'i' || ch == 'o' || ch == 'u')
        ++vowels;

      //Check for letters
      if(Character.isLetter(ch))
        ++letters;

      // Check for spaces
      if(Character.isWhitespace(ch))
        ++spaces;
    }

    System.out.println("The text contained vowels:     "
        + vowels + "\n"
        + "                          consonants: " + (letters-vowels) + "\n"
        + "                          spaces:     " + spaces);
  }
}
```

Running the example, you'll see:

```
The text contained vowels:     59
                    consonants: 93
                    spaces:     37
```

How It Works

The **String** variable, **text**, is initialized with the quotation you see. All the counting of letter characteristics is done in the **for** loop, which is controlled by the index **i**. The loop continues as long as **i** is less than the length of the string, which is returned by the method **text.length()**.

Starting with the first character, which has the index value 0, each character is retrieved from the string by calling its **charAt()** method. The loop index **i** is used as the index to the character position string. The method returns the character at index position **i,** as a value of type **char**, and we convert this to lower case, where necessary, by calling the **static** method **toLowerCase()** in the class **Character**. We've already met this method once, in Chapter 3. The character to be converted is passed as an argument and the method returns either the original character, or if it is upper case, the lower-case equivalent. This enables us to deal with the string in just one case.

There's an alternative to using the **toLowerCase()** method in the class **Character**. The class **String** also contains a method **toLowerCase()** that will convert a whole string and return the converted string. You could convert the string text to lower case with the statement:

```
text = text.toLowerCase();     // Convert string to lower case
```

This statement replaces the original string with the lower-case equivalent. If you wanted to retain the original, of course, you could store the lower-case string in another variable of type **String**. For converting strings to upper case, the class **String** also has a method **toUpperCase**() which is used in the same way.

The **if** expression checks for any of the vowels by ORing the comparisons for the five vowels together. If the expression is **true** we increment the **vowels** count. To check for a letter of any kind we use the **isLetter()** method in the class **Character**, and accumulate the total letter count in the variable **letters**. This will enable us to calculate the number of consonants by subtracting the number of vowels from the total number of letters. Lastly, the loop code checks for a space by using the **isWhitespace()** method in the class **Character**. This method returns true if the character passed as an argument is a Unicode whitespace character. As well as spaces, whitespace in Unicode also includes horizontal and vertical tab characters, new line, carriage return, and form feed characters. After the **for** loop ends, we just output the results.

Using startsWith() with an Offset

The method **startsWith()** that we mentioned earlier also comes in a version that accepts an additional argument that is an offset from the beginning of the string being checked. The check for the matching character sequence then begins at that offset position. If you've defined a string as:

```
String string1 = "The Ides of March";
```

then the expression **String1.startsWith("Ides", 4)** will have the value **true**.

Searching Strings for Characters

There are two methods available to you in the class **String**, that will search a string, **indexOf()** and **lastIndexOf()**. Both of these come in four different flavors to provide a range of search possibilities. The basic choice is whether you want to search for a single character, or for a substring; so let's look first at the options for searching a string for a given character.

To search a string, **text**, for a single character, **'a'** for example, you could write:

```
int index = 0;              // Position of character in the string
index = text.indexOf('a'); // Find 1st index position containing 'a'
```

The method **indexOf()** will search the contents of the string, **text**, forwards from the beginning, and return the index position of the first occurrence of **'a'**. If **'a'** isn't found, the method will return the value –1.

> *This is characteristic of both the search methods in the class* String. *They always return either the index position of what is sought, or –1 if the search objective isn't found. Clearly it's important that you check the index value returned for –1 before you use it to index a string, otherwise you'll get an error when you don't find what you're looking for.*

If you wanted to find the last occurrence of **'a'** in the **String** variable, **text**, you just use the method **lastIndexOf()**:

```
index = text.lastIndexOf('a');  // Find last index position containing
'a'
```

The method searches the string backwards, starting with the last character in the string. The variable **index** will therefore contain the index position of the last occurrence of **'a'**, or –1 if it isn't found.

We can find the first and last occurrences of a character, but what about the ones in the middle? Well, there's a variation of both the above methods that has a second argument to specify a 'from position'—from which to start the search. To search forwards from a given position, **startIndex**, you would write:

```
index = text.indexOf('a', startIndex);
```

This version of the method **indexOf()** searches the string for the character specified by the first argument, starting with the position specified by the second argument. You could use this to find the first **'b'** that comes after the first **'a'** in a string with the statements:

```
int aIndex = -1;                         // Position of 1st 'a'
int bIndex = -1;                         // Position of 1st 'b' after 'a'
aIndex = text.indexOf('a');              // Find 1st 'a'
if(aIndex >= 0 && aIndex < text.length()-1)
  bIndex = text.indexOf('b', ++aIndex); // Find 1st 'b' after 1st 'a'
```

Once we've the index value from the initial search for **'a'**, we need to check that **'a'** was really found by verifying that **aIndex** isn't negative, and we also need to ensure that it isn't the last character in the string by confirming that **aIndex** is less than the index value for the last string character.

We can then search for `'b'` from the position following `'a'`. As you can see, the second argument of this version of the method `indexOf()` is separated from the first argument by a comma. Since the second argument is the index position from which the search is to start, and `aIndex` is the position at which `'a'` was found, we should increment `aIndex` to the position following `'a'` before using it in the search for `'b'` to avoid checking for `'b'` in the position we already know contains `'a'`.

Searching for Substrings

The methods `indexOf()` and `lastIndexOf()` also come in versions that accept a string as the first argument, and will search for this string rather than a single character. In all other respects they work in the same way as the character searching methods we've just seen. The complete set of `indexOf()` methods is:

Method	Description
`indexOf(int ch)`	Returns the index position of the first occurrence of the character **ch** in the **String** for which the method is called. If the character, **ch** doesn't occur, –1 is returned.
`indexOf(int ch, int index)`	Same as the method above, but with the search starting at position **index**. If the value of index is outside the legal limits for the **String** object, –1 is returned.
`indexOf(String str)`	Returns the index position of the first occurrence of the substring, **str**, in the **String** object for which the method is called. If the character, **ch** doesn't occur, –1 is returned.
`indexOf(String str, int index)`	Same as the method above, but with the search starting at position **index**. If the value of index is outside the legal limits for the **String** object, –1 is returned.

The four flavors of the `lastIndexOf()` method have the same parameters as the four versions of the `indexOf()` method. The difference is that the last occurrence of the character or substring that is sought is returned.

We can show them at work in an example:

Try It Out—Exciting Concordance Entries

We'll use the `indexOf()` method to search the quotation we used in the last example for `"and"` and the `lastIndexOf()` method for `"the"`.

```
public class FindCharacters
{
  public static void main(String[] args)
  {
    // Text string to be analyzed
```

```
String text = "To be or not to be, that is the question;"
            + " Whether 'tis nobler in the mind to suffer"
            + " the slings and arrows of outrageous fortune,"
            + " or to take arms against a sea of troubles,"
            + " and by opposing end them?";

    int andCount = 0;                  // Count of number of and's
    int theCount = 0;                  // Count of number of the's

    int index = -1;                    // Current index position

    String andStr = "and";             // Search substring
    String theStr = "the";             // Search substring

    // Search forwards for "and"
    index = text.indexOf(andStr);      // Find 1st "and"
    while(index >= 0)
    {
      ++andCount;
      index += andStr.length();        // Step to position after last and
      index = text.indexOf(andStr, index);
    }

    // Search backwards for "the"
    index = text.lastIndexOf(theStr);    // Find last "the"
    while(index >= 0)
    {
      ++theCount;
      index -= theStr.length();        // Step to position before last the
      index = text.lastIndexOf(theStr, - -index);
    }

    System.out.println("The text contains " + andCount + " and's\n"
                     + "The text contains " + theCount + " the's");
  }
}
```

The program will produce the output:

```
The text contains 2 and's
The text contains 5 the's
```

FYI If you were expecting the `"the"` count to be 3, note that there's one instance in `"whether"` and another in `"them"`. If you want to find three, you need to search for `" the "`.

How It Works

We define the **String** variable, **text**, as before, and set up two counters, **andCount** and **theCount**, for the two words. The variable **index** will keep track of the current position in the string. We then have **String** variables **andStr** and **theStr** holding the substrings we will be searching for.

To find the instances of **"and"**, we first find the index position of the first occurrence of **"and"** in the string **text**. If this index is negative, **text** doesn't contain **"and"**, and the **while** loop will not execute as the condition is false on the first iteration. Assuming there is at least one **"and"**, the **while** loop block is executed and **andCount** is incremented for the instance of **"and"** we've just found. The method **indexOf()** returns the index position of the first character of the substring, so we have to move the index forward to the character following the last character of the substring we've just found. This is done by adding the length of the substring, as shown here:

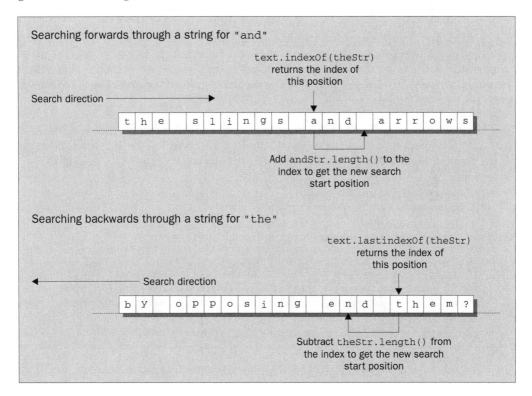

We can then search for the next occurrence of the substring by passing the new value of **index** to the method **indexOf()**. The loop continues as long as the index value returned isn't –1.

To count the occurrences of the substring **"the"** the program searches the string, **text**, backwards, by using the method **lastIndexOf()** instead of **indexOf()**. This works in much the same way, the only significant difference being in the decrementing of the value of **index**, instead of incrementing it. This is because the next occurrence of the substring has to be at least that many characters back from the first character of the substring we've just found. If the string, **"the"**, happened to occur at the beginning of the string we're searching, the **lastIndexOf()** method would be called with a negative value for **index**. This wouldn't cause any problem—it would just result in –1 being returned in any event.

Extracting Substrings

The **String** class includes a method, **substring()**, that will extract a substring from a string. There are two versions of this method. The first version will extract a substring consisting of all the characters from a given index position to the end of the string. This works as illustrated in the following code fragment:

```
String place = "Palm Springs";
String lastWord = place.substring(5);
```

After executing these statements, **lastWord** will contain the string **"Springs"**. The substring is copied from the original to form a new string. This is useful when a string has basically two constituent substrings, but a more common requirement is to extract several substrings from a string where each substring is separated from the next by a special character such as a comma, a slash, or even just a space. The second version of **substring()** will help with this.

You can extract a substring from a string by specifying the index positions of the first character in the substring, and one beyond the last character of the substring, as arguments to the method **substring()**. With the variable **place** being defined as before, the statement,

```
String segment = place.substring(7, 11);
```

will result in the variable **segment** being set to the string **"ring"**.

> The **subString()** method isn't like the **indexOf()** method when it comes to illegal index values. With either version of the method **substring()** if you specify an index that's outside the bounds of the string, you'll get an error. As with the **charAt()** method, **substring()** will throw a **StringIndexOutOfBoundsException** exception.

We can see how **substring()** works with a more substantial example:

Try It Out—Word for Word

We can use the **indexOf()** method in combination with the **substring()** method to extract a sequence of substrings that are separated by spaces from a single string:

```
public class ExtractSubstring
{
```

```java
public static void main(String[] args)
{
  String text = "To be or not to be";      // String to be segmented
  int count = 0;                            // Number of substrings
  char separator = ' ';                     // Substring separator

  // Determine the number of sub-strings
  int index = 0;
  do
  {
    ++count;                                // Increment count of substrings
    ++index;                                // Move past last position
    index = text.indexOf(separator, index);
  }while(index != -1);

  // Extract the sub-string into an array
  String[] subStr = new String[count];      // Allocate for substrings
  index = 0;                                 // Substring start index
  int endIndex = 0;                          // Substring end index
  for(int i = 0; i < count; i++)
  {
    endIndex = text.indexOf(separator,index); // Find next separator

    if(endIndex == -1)                       // If it is not found
      subStr[i] = text.substring(index);     // extract to the end
    else                                     // otherwise
      subStr[i] = text.substring(index, endIndex);  // to end index

    index = endIndex + 1;                    // Set start for next cycle
  }

  // Display the sub-strings
  for(int i = 0; i < subStr.length; i++)
    System.out.println(subStr[i]);
}
}
```

When you run this example, you should get the output:

```
To
be
or
not
to
be
```

How It Works

After setting up the string **text** to be segmented into substrings, a **count** variable to hold the number of substrings, and the separator character, **separator**, the program has three distinct phases.

The first phase counts the number of substrings by using the **indexOf()** method to find separators. The number of separators is always one less than the number of substrings. For instance, with two substrings there will be one separator, and with three substrings there will be two separators. By using the **do-while** loop, we ensure that the value of **count** will be one more than the number of separators.

The second phase extracts the substrings in sequence from the beginning of the string, and stores them in an array of **String** variables that has **count** elements. Following each substring from the first to the penultimate is a separator, so we use the version of the **substring()** method that accepts two index arguments for these. The last substring is signaled by a failure to find the separator character when **index** will be –1. In this case, we use the **substring()** method with a single argument to extract the substring through to the end of the string, **text**.

The third phase simply outputs the contents of the array by displaying each element in turn, using a **for** loop.

Modifying String Objects

There are a couple of methods that can modify a **String** object and return a new **String** object. They don't change the original string of course. To replace one specific character with another throughout a string, you can use the **replace()** method. For example, to replace each space in our string, **text**, with a slash, you could write:

```
String newText = text.replace(' ', '/');      // Modify the string text
```

The first argument of the **replace()** method specifies the character to be replaced, and the second argument specifies the character that is to be substituted in its place. We have stored the result in a new variable **newText** here, but naturally you could save it back in the original **String** variable, **text**, if you wanted.

To remove whitespace (spaces, tabs, newlines) from the beginning and end of a string (but not the interior) you can use the **trim()** method. You could apply this to a string as follows,

```
String sample = "   This is a string   ";
String result = sample.trim();
```

after which the **String** variable **result** will contain the string **"This is a string"**. This can be useful when you're segmenting a string into substrings and the substrings may contain leading or trailing blanks. For example, this might arise if you were analyzing an input string that contained values separated by one or more spaces.

Creating Character Arrays from String Objects

You can create an array of variables of type **char** from a **String** variable by using the **toCharArray()** method in the class **String**. Because this method returns an array of type **char**, you only need to declare the array variable of type **char**—you don't need to allocate the array. For example:

```
String text = "To be or not to be";
char[] textArray;                     // Declare the array variable
textArray = text.toCharArray();       // Create the array from the string
```

The **toCharArray()** method will return an array containing the characters of the **String** variable **text**, one per element, so **textArray[0]** will contain **'T'**, **textArray[1]** will contain **'o'**, **textArray[2]** will contain **' '**, and so on.

You can also extract a substring as an array of characters using the method **getChars()**, but in this case you do need to create an array that's large enough to hold the characters. The method **getChars()** has four parameters. In sequence, these are:

- Index position of the first character to be extracted (type **int**)
- Index position following the last character to be extracted (type **int**)
- The name of the array to hold the characters extracted (type **char[]**)
- The index of the array element to hold the first character (type **int**)

You could copy a substring from text into an array with the statements:

```
String text = "To be or not to be";
char[] textArray = new char[3];
text.getChars(9, 12, textArray, 0);
```

This will copy characters from **text** at index positions 9 – 11 inclusive, so **textArray[0]** will be **'n'**, **textArray[1]** will be **'o'**, and **textArray[2]** will be **'t'**.

You can also extract characters into a **byte** array using the **getBytes()** method in the class **String**. This converts the original string characters into the character encoding used by the underlying operating system—which is usually ASCII. For example:

```
String text = "To be or not to be";          // Define a string
byte[] textArray = text.getBytes();           // Get equivalent byte array
```

The **byte** array **textArray** will contain the same characters as in the **String** object, but stored as 8-bit characters.

Creating String Objects from Character Arrays

The **String** class also has a static method, **copyValueOf()**, to create a **String** object from an array of type **char[]**. You'll recall that a static method of a class can be used even if no objects of the class exist. Suppose you have an array defined as:

```
char[] textArray = {'T', 'o', ' ', 'b', 'e', ' ', 'o', 'r', ' ',
                    'n', 'o', 't', ' ', 't', 'o', ' ', 'b', 'e' };
```

You can then create a **String** object with the statement:

```
String text = String.copyValueOf(textArray);
```

This will result in the object, **text**, referencing the string **"To be or not to be"**.

Another version of the **copyValueOf()** method can create a string from a subset of the array elements. It requires two additional arguments to specify the index of the first character in the array to be extracted and the count of the number of characters to be extracted. With the array defined as previously, the statement,

```
String text = String.copyValueOf(textArray, 9, 3);
```

extracts 3 characters starting with **textArray[9]**, so **text** will contain the string **"not"** after this operation.

StringBuffer Objects

String objects can't be changed, but we've been creating strings that are combinations and modifications of existing **String** objects, so how is this done? Java has another standard class for defining strings, **StringBuffer**, and a **StringBuffer** object can be altered directly. Strings that can be changed are often referred to as **mutable strings** whereas a **String** object is an **immutable string**. Java uses objects of the class **StringBuffer** internally to perform many of the operations on **String** objects. You can use a **StringBuffer** object whenever you need a string that you can change directly.

So when do you use **StringBuffer** objects rather than **String** objects? **StringBuffer** objects come into their own when you're transforming strings—adding, deleting, or replacing substrings in a string. Operations will be faster and easier using **StringBuffer** objects. If you have static strings, which perhaps you occasionally need to concatenate, then **String** objects will be the best choice. Of course, if you want to you can mix the use of both in the same program.

Creating StringBuffer Objects

You can create a **StringBuffer** object that contains a given string with the statement:

```
StringBuffer aString = new StringBuffer("A stitch in time");
```

This declares a **StringBuffer** object, **aString**, and initializes it with the string **"A stitch in time"**. You must use the syntax when initializing a **StringBuffer** object of the keyword **new**, the **StringBuffer** class name and the initializing value between parentheses. You can't just use the string as the initializing value as we did with **String** objects. This is because there's rather more to a **StringBuffer** object than just the string that it contains initially, and of course a string constant is a **String** object by definition.

You can create the **StringBuffer** variable in much the same way as you created a **String** variable:

```
StringBuffer myString;
```

This variable doesn't point to anything until you initialize it with a defined `StringBuffer` object. For example, you could write:

```
myString = new StringBuffer("Many a mickle makes a muckle");
```

which will initialize it with the string specified. You can also initialize a `StringBuffer` variable with an existing `StringBuffer` object:

```
myString = aString;
```

Both `myString` and `aString` will now point to a single `StringBuffer` object.

The Capacity of a StringBuffer Object

The `String` objects that we've been using each contain a fixed string, and memory is allocated to accommodate however many Unicode characters are in the string. A `StringBuffer` object is a little different. It contains a block of memory called a **buffer** which may or may not contain a string, and if it does, the string need not occupy all of the buffer. Once you've created a `StringBuffer` object, you can find the length of the string it contains, by using the `length()` method for the object:

```
int theLength = aString.length();
```

If the object, `aString`, was defined as in the previous declaration, the variable `theLength` will have the value 16—the number of characters in the string. However, the capacity of the object is larger, as illustrated in the diagram.

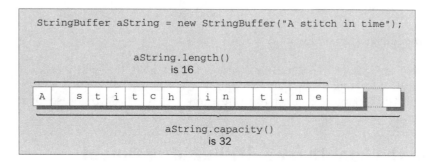

Both the capacity and the length are in units of Unicode characters, so twice as many bytes will be occupied in memory.

You can create a `StringBuffer` object with a given capacity by specifying the capacity when you declare it:

```
StringBuffer newString = new StringBuffer(50);
```

This will create an object, `newString`, with the capacity to store 50 characters. If you omitted the capacity value in this declaration, the object would have a default capacity of sixteen characters.

A **String** object is always a fixed string, so capacity is irrelevant—it's always just enough to hold the characters in the string. A **StringBuffer** object is a container in which you can store any string and therefore has a capacity—a potential for storing strings up to a given size. The capacity is unimportant in the sense that it's just a measure of how much memory is available to store Unicode characters at this instant. You can get by without worrying about the capacity of a **StringBuffer** object though. The capacity required to cope with what your program is doing will always be provided automatically. It just gets increased as necessary.

On the other hand the capacity of a **StringBuffer** object is important in the sense that it affects the amount of overhead involved in storing and modifying a string in a **StringBuffer** object. If the capacity is small, and you store a string that is long, or you add to an existing string significantly, extra memory will need to be allocated, which will take time.

To find out what the capacity of a **StringBuffer** object is, you use the **capacity()** method for the object:

```
int theCapacity = aString.capacity();
```

This method will return the number of Unicode characters the object can currently hold. For **aString** defined as shown, this will be 32. When you create a **StringBuffer** object containing a string, its capacity will be 16 characters greater than the minimum necessary to hold the string.

The **ensureCapacity()** method enables you to change the default capacity of a **StringBuffer** object. You specify the minimum capacity you need as the argument to the method, for example:

```
aString.ensureCapacity(40);
```

If the current capacity of the **aString** object is less than 40, this will increase the capacity of **aString** by allocating a new larger buffer, but not necessarily with a capacity of 40. The capacity will be the larger of either the value you specify—40 in this case, or twice the current capacity plus 2, which is 66, given that **aString** is defined as before.

Changing the Length for a StringBuffer Object

You can change the length of the string contained in a **StringBuffer** object with the method **setLength()**. Note that the length is a property of the string the object holds, as opposed to the capacity, which is a property of the string buffer. When you increase the length for a **StringBuffer** object, the extra characters will contain **'\u0000'**. If you decrease the length, the string will be truncated. If **aString** contains **"A stitch in time"**, the statement,

```
aString.setLength(8);
```

will result in **aString** containing the string **"A stitch"**, and the value returned by the **length()** method will be 8. The characters that were cut from the end of the string by this operation are lost.

To increase the length to what it was before, you could write:

```
aString.setLength(16);
```

Now **aString** will contain

```
"A stitch\u0000\u0000\u0000\u0000\u0000\u0000\u0000\u0000"
```

The **setLength()** method doesn't affect the capacity of the object unless you set the length to be greater than the capacity. In this case the capacity will be increased to accommodate the new string length to a value that's twice the original capacity plus two. If the capacity of **aString** is 66, executing the statement,

```
aString.setLength(100);
```

will set the capacity of the object, **aString**, to 134.

You must not specify a negative length. If you do a **StringIndexOutOfBoundsException** exception will be thrown.

Adding to a StringBuffer Object

The **append()** method enables you to add a string to the end of the existing string stored in a **StringBuffer** object. This method comes in quite a few flavors, but perhaps the simplest adds a **String** constant to a **StringBuffer** object.

If we've defined a **StringBuffer** object with the statement,

```
StringBuffer aString = new StringBuffer("A stitch in time");
```

we can add to it with the statement,

```
aString.append(" saves nine");
```

after which **aString** will contain **"A stitch in time saves nine"**. The length of the string contained in the **StringBuffer** object will be increased by the length of the string that you add, and if necessary the capacity will increase automatically, so you don't need to worry about running out of space.

The **append()** method returns the extended **StringBuffer** object, so you could also assign it to another **StringBuffer** object. Instead of the previous statement, you could have written:

```
StringBuffer bString = aString.append(" saves nine");
```

Now both **aString** and **bString** point to the same **StringBuffer** object.

If you take a look at the operator precedence table back in Chapter 2, you'll see that the . operator (sometimes called the **member selection operator**) that we use to execute a particular method for an object has left-to-right associativity. You could therefore write:

```
StringBuffer proverb = new StringBuffer();      // Capacity is 16
proverb.append("Many").append(" hands").append(" make").
                                       append(" light").append("
work.");
```

The second statement is executed from left to right, so that the string contained in the object **proverb** is progressively extended until it contains the complete string. The expression **proverb.append("Many")** will result in **proverb** containing the string **"Many"**. The next **append(" hands")** will be applied to this version of **proverb**, so proverb will then contain **"Many hands"**. The other **append()** method calls are applied successively until finally the object **proverb** contains the string **"Many hands make light work"**.

Appending a Substring

Another version of the **append()** method will add part of a **String** object to a **StringBuffer** object. This version of **append()** requires you to specify two additional arguments, the index position of the first character to be appended, and the total number of characters to be appended. This operation is shown in the diagram.

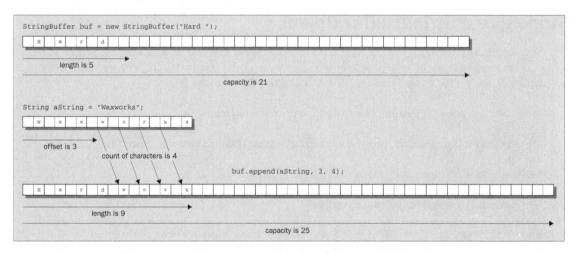

This operation appends a substring of **aString** consisting of four characters starting at index position 3 to the **StringBuffer** object, **buf**. The capacity of **buf** is automatically increased by the length of the appended substring, if necessary.

Appending Basic Types

You've a set of versions of the **append()** method that will enable you to **append()** any of the basic types to a **StringBuffer** object. These will accept an argument of any of the types: **boolean**, **char**, **byte**, **short**, **int**, **long**, **float** or **double**. In each case, the value is converted to a string equivalent of the value which is appended to the object, so a **boolean** variable will be appended as either **"true"** or **"false"**, and for numeric types the string will be a decimal representation of the value. For example:

```
StringBuffer buf = new StringBuffer("The number is ");
long number = 999;
buf.append(number);
```

will result in **buf** containing the string **"The number is 999"**.

There's nothing to prevent you from appending constants to a **StringBuffer** object. For example, if you now execute the statement,

```
buf.append(12.34);
```

the object, **buf**, will contain **"The number is 99912.34"**.

There's also a version of the **append()** method which accepts an array of type **char** as an argument. The contents of the array are appended to the **StringBuffer** object as a string. A further variation on this enables you to append a subset of the elements from an array of type **char** by using two additional arguments, one to specify the index of the first element to be appended, and another to specify the total number of elements to be appended. An example of how you might use this is:

```
char[] text = { 'i', 's', ' ', 'e', 'x', 'a', 'c', 't', 'l', 'y'};
buf.append(text, 2, 8);
```

This will append the string **" exactly"** to **buf**, so after executing this statement **buf** will contain **"The number is 99912.34 exactly"**.

You may be somewhat bemused by the plethora of **append()** method options, so let's drag together all the possibilities. You can append any of the following types to a **StringBuffer** object:

boolean	char	String	Object	int	long	float
double	byte	short				

You can also append an array of type **char[]**, and a subset of the elements of an array of type **char[]**. In each case the **String** equivalent of argument is appended to the string in the **StringBuffer** object.

We haven't discussed type **Object**—it's here for the sake of completeness. You'll learn about this type of object in Chapter 6.

Creating a String Object from a StringBuffer Object

You can produce a **String** object from a **StringBuffer** object by using the **toString()** method of the **StringBuffer** class. This method creates a new **String** object and initializes it with the string contained in the **StringBuffer** object. For example, to produce a **String** object containing the proverb that we created in the previous section, you could write:

```
String saying = proverb.toString();
```

The object, **saying**, will contain **"Many hands make light work"**.

The **toString()** method is used extensively by the compiler together with the **append()** method to implement the concatenation of **String** objects. When you write a statement such as,

```
String saying = "Many" + " hands" + " make" + " light" + " work";
```

the compiler will implement this as:

```
String saying = new StringBuffer().append("Many").append(" hands").
                                  append(" make").append(" light").
                                  append(" work").toString();
```

The expression to the right of the **=** sign is executed from left to right, so the segments of the string are appended to the **StringBuffer** object that is created until finally the **toString()** method is invoked to convert it to a **String** object. **String** objects can't be modified, so any alteration or extension of a **String** object will involve the use of a **StringBuffer** object which can be changed.

Inserting Strings

To insert a string into a **StringBuffer** object, you use the **insert()** method of the object. The first argument specifies the index of the position in the object where the first character is to be inserted. For example, if **buf** contains the string **"Many hands make light work"**, the statement,

```
buf.insert(4, " old");
```

will insert the string **" old"** starting at index position 4, so **buf** will contain the string **"Many old hands make light work"** after executing this statement.

There are versions of the **insert()** method that will accept a second argument of any of the same range of types that apply to the **append()** method, so you can use any of the following with the **insert()** method:

boolean	char	String	Object	int	long	float
double	byte	short				

You can also insert an array of type **char[]**, but there's no provision for inserting a subset of an array of type **char[]**. In each case the string equivalent of the second argument is inserted starting at the index position specified by the first argument.

Extracting Characters from a StringBuffer Object

The `StringBuffer` includes the `charAt()` and `getChars()` methods, both of which work in the same way as the methods of the same name in the class `String` which we've already seen. The `charAt()` method extracts the character at a given index position, and the `getChars()` method extracts a range of characters and stores them in an array of type `char` starting at a specified index position. You should note that there's no equivalent to the `getBytes()` method for `StringBuffer` objects.

Other StringBuffer Operations

You can change a single character in a `StringBuffer` object by using the `setCharAt()` method. The first argument indicates the index position of the character to be changed, and the second argument specifies the replacement character. For example, the statement,

```
buf.setCharAt(3, 'Z');
```

will set the fourth character in the string to `'Z'`.

You can completely reverse the sequence of characters in a `StringBuffer` object with the `reverse()` method. For example, if you define the object with the declaration,

```
StringBuffer palindrome = new StringBuffer("never odd or even");
```

you can then transform it with the statement,

```
palindrome.reverse();
```

which will result in `palindrome` containing the useful phrase `"neve ro ddo reven"`.

Summary

You should now be thoroughly familiar with how to create and use arrays. Most people have little trouble dealing with one-dimensional arrays, but arrays of arrays are a bit trickier so try to practice using these.

You've also acquired a good knowledge of what you can do with `String` and `StringBuffer` objects. Most operations with these objects are very straightforward and easy to understand. Being able to decide which methods you should apply to the solution of specific problems is a skill that will come with a bit of practice.

The essential points that we've discussed in this chapter are:

▶ You use an array to hold multiple values of the same type, identified through a single variable name

▶ You reference an individual element of an array by using an index value of type **int**. The index value for an array element is the offset of that element from the first element in the array

▶ An array element can be used in the same way as a single variable of the same type

▶ You can obtain the number of elements in an array by using the **length** member of the array object

▶ An array element can also contain an array, so you can define arrays of arrays, or arrays of arrays of arrays…

▶ A **String** object stores a fixed character string that can't be changed. However, you can assign a given **String** variable to a different **String** object

▶ You can obtain the number of characters stored in a **String** object by using the **length()** method for the object

▶ The **String** class provides methods for joining, searching, and modifying strings— the modifications being achieved by creating a new **String** object

▶ A **StringBuffer** object can store a string of characters that can be modified

▶ You can get the number of characters stored in a **StringBuffer** object by calling its **length()** method, and you can find out what the current maximum number of characters it can store by using its **capacity()** method

▶ You can change both the length and the capacity for a **StringBuffer** object

▶ The **StringBuffer** class contains a variety of methods for modifying **StringBuffer** objects

▶ You can create a String object from a **StringBuffer** object by using the **toString()** method of the **StringBuffer** object

Exercises

1 Create an array of **String** variables and initialize the array with the names of the months from January through December. Create an array containing 12 random decimal values between 0.0 and 100.0. Display the names of each month along with the corresponding decimal value. Calculate and display the average of the 12 decimal values.

2 Write a program to create a rectangular array containing a multiplication table from 1x1 up to 12x12. Output the table as 13 columns with the numeric values right aligned in columns. (The first line of output will be the column headings, the first column with no heading, then the numbers 1 – 12 for the remaining columns. The first item in each of the succeeding lines is the row heading which ranges from 1 – 12.)

3 Write a program that sets up a **String** variable containing a paragraph of text of your choice. Extract the words from the text and sort them into alphabetical order. Display the sorted list of words. You could use a simple sorting method called the **bubble sort**. The process for sorting an array into ascending order is as follows:

▶ Starting with the first element in the array compare successive elements (0 and 1, 1 and 2, 2 and 3, and so on).

▶ If the first element of any pair is greater than the second, interchange the two elements.

▶ Repeat the process for the whole array until no interchanges are necessary. The array elements will now be in ascending order.

4 Set up an array of ten **String** variables each containing an arbitrary string of the form day/month/year, for example 29/10/97. Analyze each element in the array and output the date represented in the form Wednesday 29th October 1997.

Defining Classes

In this chapter we will explore the heart of the Java language—classes. Classes specify the objects you use in object-oriented programming. These form the basic building blocks of any Java program, as we saw in Chapter 1. Every program in Java involves classes, since the code for a program can only appear within a class definition.

We will now explore the details of how a class definition is put together, how to create your own classes and how to use classes to solve your own computing problems. And in the next chapter we'll extend this to look at how object-oriented programming helps us work with related classes.

By the end of this chapter you will have learned:

- What a class is, and how you define one
- How to implement class constructors
- How to define class methods
- What method overloading is
- What a recursive method is and how it works
- How to create objects of a class
- What packages are and how you can create and use them
- What access attributes are and how you should use them in your class definitions
- When you should add the **finalize()** method to a class
- What native methods are

What is a Class?

As you saw in Chapter 1, a class is a prescription for a particular kind of object. We can use the class definition to create objects of that class type, that is, to create objects that incorporate all the components specified as belonging to that class.

> *In case that's too abstract, look back to the last chapter, where we used the **String** class. This is JavaSoft's ultimate definition for a string object, with every conceivable requirement built in, to make **String** objects indispensable and string handling within a program easy.*

In essence a class definition is very simple. There are just two kinds of element that you can include in a class definition:

> **variables**—The elements that differentiate one object of the class from another.
> **methods**—The operations you can perform for the class—these determine what you can do to, or with, objects of the class. Methods operate on the variables of the class.

The variables in a class definition can be of any of the basic types, or they can be objects of any class, including the one that you are defining.

The methods in a class definition are named, self-contained blocks of code, that typically operate on the variables that appear in the class definition. Note though, that this doesn't necessarily have to be the case, as you might have guessed from the **main()** methods we have written in all our examples up to now.

Variables in a Class Definition

An object of a class is also referred to as an **instance** of that class. When you create an object, the object will contain all the variables that were included in the class definition. However, the variables in a class definition are not all the same. There are two kinds. One kind of class variable is associated with each object uniquely—each instance of the class will have its own copy of each of these variables, with its own value assigned. These differentiate one object from another—they give an object its individuality. The other kind of class variable is associated with the class, and is shared by all objects of the class. There is only one copy of each of these kinds of variables no matter how many class objects are created.

Because this is extremely important to understand, let's summarize the two kinds of variables that you can include in your classes:

Instance variables	Each object of the class will have its own copy of each of the instance variables that appear in the class definition. Each object will have its own values for each instance variable. The name 'instance variable' originates from the fact that an object is an 'instance' of a class. An instance variable is declared within the class definition in the usual way, with a type name and a variable name.

Class variables

A given class will only have one copy of each of its class variables, and these will be shared between all the objects of the class. The class variables exist even if no objects of the class have been created. They belong to the class, but they are included as part of every object of the class. If the value of a class variable is changed, the new value is available in all the objects of the class. This is quite different from instance variables where changing a value for one object does not affect the values in other objects. A class variable must be declared using the keyword **static** preceding the type name.

For an illustration of the difference between the two, look at the following diagram.

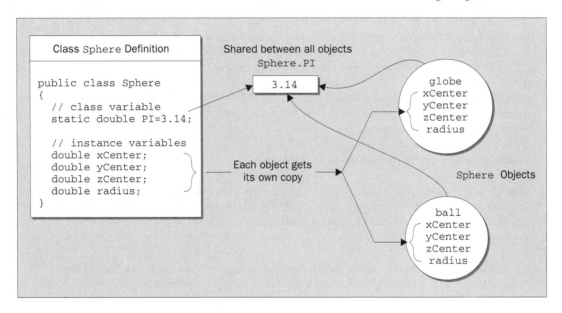

This shows a schematic of a class **Sphere** with one class variable **PI**, and four instance variables, **radius**, **xCenter**, **yCenter** and **zCenter**. Each of the objects, **globe** and **ball** will have their own variables, **radius**, **xCenter**, **yCenter** and **yCenter**, but both will share a single copy of the class variable **PI**.

Why would you need two kinds of variables in a class definition? The instance variables are clearly necessary since they are the parameters that distinguish a particular object. The radius and the coordinates of the position of the center of the sphere are fundamental to determining how big a particular **Sphere** object is, and where it is in space. However, although the variable **PI** is a fundamental parameter for a sphere—to calculate the volume for example—it would be wasteful to store a value for **PI** in every object, since it is always the same. Incidentally, it is also available from the standard class **Math**. So one use for class variables is to hold constant values such as π that are common to all objects of the class.

Another use for class variables is to track data values that are common to all objects of a class, and that need to be available even when no objects have been defined. For example, if you wanted to keep a count of how many objects of a class have been created in your program, you would define the variable storing the count as a class variable. It would be essential to use a class variable, because you would still want to be able to use your **count** variable even when no objects had been declared.

Methods in a Class Definition

The methods that you define for a class provide the actions that can be carried out using the variables specified in the class definition.

Analogous to the variables in a class definition, there are two varieties of methods, **instance methods** and **class methods**. You can execute class methods even when no objects of a class exist, whereas instance methods can only be executed in relation to a particular object, so if no objects exist, there are no instance methods to be executed. Again, like class variables, class methods are declared using the keyword **static**.

Since class methods can be executed when there are no objects in existence, they cannot refer to instance variables. This is quite sensible if you think about it—trying to operate with variables that might not exist is bound to cause trouble. In fact the Java compiler won't let you try. If you reference an instance variable in the code for a class method, it won't compile—you'll just get an error message.

The class **Sphere** might well have an instance method **volume()** to calculate the volume of a particular object. It might also have a class method **objectCount()** to return the current count of how many objects have been created. If no objects exist, you could still call this method and get the count, 0.

> *Note that, although instance methods are specific to objects of a class, there is only ever one copy of an instance method in memory, as it would be extremely expensive to replicate all the instance methods for each object. This raises the question as to how this is consistent with instance methods being specific to an object, but we will defer exploring this until a little later in this chapter.*

Perhaps the most common use for class methods is when a class is just used to contain a bunch of methods, rather than as a specification for objects. All executable code in Java has to be within a class, but there are lots of general utility functions that you need that don't necessarily have an object association—calculating a square root, for instance, or generating a random number. For example, the mathematical functions that are implemented as class methods in the standard class **Math**, don't relate to class objects at all—they operate on values of the basic types. You don't need objects of type **Math**, you just want to use the methods from time to time, and you can do this as we saw in Chapter 2. The class **Math** also contains some class variables containing useful mathematical constants such as e and π.

So, if you wanted to calculate the square root of π you could access the class method **sqrt()** and the class variable **PI** as follows:

```
double rootPi = Math.sqrt(Math.PI);
```

Defining Classes

To define a class you use the keyword **class** followed by the name of the class, followed by a pair of braces enclosing the details of the definition.

Try It Out—The *Sphere* **Class**

The definition of the class **Sphere** could be:

```
class Sphere
{
  static final double PI = 3.14;  // Class variable that has a fixed value
  static int count = 0;           // Class variable to count objects

  // Instance variables
  double radius;                  // Radius of a sphere

  double xCenter;                 // 3D coordinates
  double yCenter;                 // of the center
  double zCenter;                 // of a sphere

  // Instance method to calculate volume
  double volume()
  {
    return 4.0/3.0*PI*radius*radius*radius;
  }

  // Plus the rest of the class definition...
}
```

You name a class using an identifier of the same sort you've been using for variables. By convention though, class names in Java begin with a capital letter. If you adopt this approach, you will be consistent with most of the code you will come across.

How It Works—Defining Data Members of the Class

The keyword **static** in the first line of the definition specifies the variable **PI** as a class variable. The variable **PI** is also initialized with the value 3.14. The keyword **final** tells the compiler that you do not want the value of this variable to be changed—you want its final value to be 3.14—so the compiler will check that this variable is not modified anywhere in your program. Obviously this is a very poor value for π. You would normally use **Math.PI** which is defined to twenty decimal places—close enough for most purposes

> *Whenever you want to fix the value stored in a variable, that is, make it a constant, you just need to declare the variable with the keyword **final** and specify its initial value. By convention, constants have names in capital letters.*

The next variable, **count**, is also declared with the keyword **static**. All objects of the **Sphere** class will share one copy of **count**, and one of **PI**. We have initialized the variable count to 0, but since it is not declared with the keyword **final**, we can change its value. It wouldn't make much sense if we couldn't alter its value.

The next four variables in the class definition are instance variables as they don't have the keyword **static** applied to them. Each object of the class will have its own separate instance of each of these variables storing the radius and the coordinates of the center of the sphere. Although we haven't put initial values for these variables here, we could do so if we wanted.

Next we have an instance method, **volume()**. This method is an instance method because the keyword **static** does not appear in the definition of the method. There has to be something missing from the definition of the **Sphere** class—there is no way to set the value of **radius** and the other instance variables when a particular **Sphere** object is created. There is nothing to update the value of **count** either.

Adding these things to the class definition involves using methods, so we now need to look at how a method is put together.

Defining Methods

We have been producing versions of the method **main()** since Chapter 1, so you already have an idea of how a method is constructed. Nonetheless, we will go through from the beginning to make sure everything is clear.

The basic structure of a method is shown below.

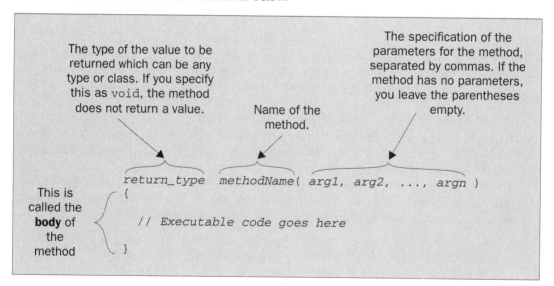

When you specify the return type for a method, you are defining the type for the value that will be returned by the method when you execute it. The method must always return a value of this type. To define a method that does not return a value, you specify the return type as **void**. Something called an **access attribute** can optionally precede the return type in a method definition, but we will defer looking into this until later in this chapter.

The parameters to a method appear between parentheses following the method name. These specify what information is to be passed to the method when you execute it. They are optional, and a method that does not require any such information just has an empty pair of parentheses.

Returning from a Method

To return a value from a method when its execution is complete you use a **return** statement, for example:

```
return return_value;    // Return a value from a method
```

After executing the **return** statement, the program continues from the point where the method was called. The value, **return_value**, returned by the method can be any expression that produces a value of the type specified for the return value in the declaration of the method. Methods that return a value—that is methods declared with a return type other than **void**—must always finish by executing a **return** statement. Note, though, that you can put several **return** statements within a method if the logic requires this.

If a method does not return a value, you can just use the keyword **return** by itself to end execution of the method:

```
return;    // Return from a method
```

Note that, for methods that do not return a value, falling through the closing brace enclosing the body of the method is equivalent to executing a **return** statement.

The Parameter List

The **parameter list**, which appears between the parentheses following the method name, specifies the type of each value that can be passed as an argument to a method, and the variable name that is to be used in the body of the method to refer to the value passed. The difference between a **parameter** and an **argument** is sometimes confusing because people often use them interchangeably.

- ▶ A parameter has a name and appears in the parameter list in the definition of a method.

- ▶ An argument is a value passed to a method when it is executed, and the value of the argument is referenced by the parameter name during execution of the method.

This is illustrated in the diagram below.

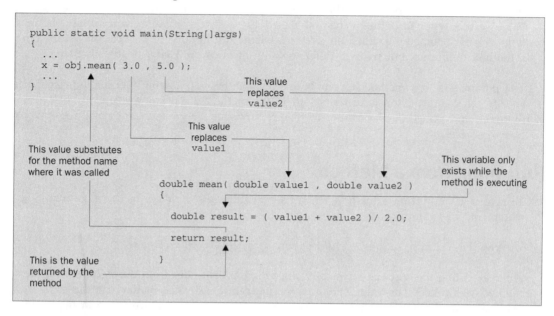

Here we have the definition of a method **mean()**. Naturally this can only appear within the definition of a class, but the rest of the class definition has been omitted so as not to clutter up the diagram. You can see that the method accepts two arguments, **value1**, and **value2**, both of which are of type **double**. Since this method has not been defined as **static**, you can only call it for an object of the class containing the method. We call **mean()** in our example for the object **obj**.

When you call the method from another method (from **main()** in this case, but it could be from some other method), the values of the arguments passed are the initial values assigned to the corresponding parameters. You can use any expression you like for an argument when you call a method, as long as the value it produces is of the same type as the corresponding parameter in the definition of the method. With our method **mean()**, both parameters are of type **double**, so both argument values must always be of type **double**.

> *The method **mean()** declares the variable **result**, which only exists within the body of the method. The variable is created each time you execute the method and it is destroyed when execution of the method ends. All the variables that you declare within the body of a method are local to the method, and are only around while the method is being executed.*

How Argument Values are Passed

You need to be clear about how your argument values are passed to a method, otherwise you may run into problems. In Java, all argument values that belong to one of the basic types are transferred to a method using what is called the **pass-by-value** mechanism, which is illustrated next.

```
public static void main(String[]args)
{
    int i = 10;                                         i
    ...                                             ┌──────┐
    int x = obj.change(i);                          │  10  │
    ...                                             └──────┘
}
                                                    copy of i
                                                 ┌──────────┐
                                                 │    10    │
                                                 └──────────┘
                                                      │ j refers to the
                                    acts on           │ copy
                                             int change( int j)
                                             {
            This statement
            modifies the copy,                   ++j;
            not the original
                                                 return j;

                                             }
```

All this means is that for each argument value that you pass to a method, a copy is made, and it is the copy that is passed and referenced through the parameter name, not the original value. This means that if you use a variable of any of the basic types as an argument, the method cannot modify the value of this variable in the calling program. In the example shown, the method **change()** will modify the copy of **i** that is created automatically, so the value of **j** that is returned will be 11 and this will be stored in **x**. However, the original value of **i** will remain at 10.

FYI | While the pass-by-value mechanism applies to all basic types of arguments, the effect for objects is different from that for variables of the basic types. You can change an object, as we shall see a little later in this chapter, because a reference to the object is passed to the method, not the object itself.

Defining Class Methods

You define a class method by adding the keyword **static** to its definition. For example, the class **Sphere** could have a class method to return the value stored in the static variable, **count**:

```
static int getCount()
{
    return count;   // Return current object count
}
```

This method needs to be a class method because we want to be able to get at the count of the number of objects even when it is zero.

> Note that you cannot refer to any of the instance variables in the class within a
> *static* method. This is because your *static* method may be executed when no
> objects of the class have been created, and therefore no instance variables exist.

Accessing Class Data Members in a Method

An instance method can access any of the data members of the class, just by using the
appropriate name. Take another look at the example of the class **Sphere**:

```
class Sphere
{
  static final double PI = 3.14;  // Class variable that has a fixed value
  static int count = 0;           // Class variable to count objects

  // Instance variables
  double radius;                  // Radius of a sphere

  double xCenter;                 // 3D coordinates
  double yCenter;                 // of the center
  double zCenter;                 // of a sphere

  // Instance method to calculate volume
  double volume()
  {
    return 4.0/3.0*PI*radius*radius*radius;
  }

  // Plus the rest of the class definition...
}
```

The method **volume()** uses the class variable **PI** and the instance variable **radius** in the
calculation. Each object of the class will have its own separate set of instance variables, so
how is the instance variable for a particular object selected?

The Variable this

Every instance method has a variable with the name **this**, which refers to the current
object for which the method is being called. This is used implicitly by the compiler when
your method refers to an instance variable of the class. For example, when the method
volume() refers to the instance variable **radius**, the compiler will insert the **this** object
reference, so that the reference will be equivalent to **this.radius**. When you execute a
statement such as:

```
double ballVolume = ball.volume();
```

where **ball** is an object of the class **Sphere**, the variable **this** in the method **volume()**
will refer to the object **ball**, so the instance variable **radius** for this particular object will
be used in the calculation.

 We mentioned earlier that only one copy of each instance method for a class exists in memory, even though there may be many different objects. You can see that the variable **this** allows the same instance method to work for different class objects. Each time an instance method is called, the **this** variable is set to reference the particular class object to which it is being applied. The code in the method will then relate to the specific data members of the object referred to by **this**.

When you write the code for a method, we've seen that there are four different potential sources of data available to you:

▶ Arguments passed to the method which you refer to by using the parameter names.

▶ Class data members, both instance variables and class variables which you refer to by their variable names.

▶ Local variables declared in the body of the method.

▶ Values that are returned by other methods that are called.

You can use a name for a local variable in a method, or possibly a parameter, that is the same as the name of a class data member. In this case you must use the keyword **this** when you refer to the data member in the method. For example, let us suppose we wanted to add a method to change the radius of a **Sphere** object to a new radius value which is passed as an argument. We could code this as:

```
void changeRadius(double radius)
{
  // Change the instance variable to the argument value
  this.radius = radius;
}
```

In the body of the **changeRadius()** method, **this.radius** refers to the instance variable, and **radius** by itself refers to the parameter. There is no confusion in the duplication of names here. It is clear that we are receiving a radius value as a parameter and storing it in the **radius** variable for the class object.

Constructors

When you create an object of a class, a special kind of method called a **constructor** is always invoked. If you don't define a constructor for a class, the compiler will supply a default constructor which does nothing. The primary purpose of a constructor is to provide you with the means of initializing the instance variables for the object being created.

A constructor has two special characteristics which differentiate it from other class methods:

▶ A constructor never returns a value and you must not specify a return type—not even of type **void**

▶ A constructor always has the same name as the class

We could add a constructor to our class `Sphere`:

Try modifying your `Sphere` class with the shaded code:

```
class Sphere
{
  static final double PI = 3.14; // Class variable that has a fixed value
  static int count = 0;          // Class variable to count objects

  // Instance variables
  double radius;                 // Radius of a sphere

  double xCenter;                // 3D coordinates
  double yCenter;                // of the center
  double zCenter;                // of a sphere

  // Class constructor
  Sphere(double theRadius, double x, double y, double z)
  {
    radius = theRadius;          // Set the radius

    // Set the coordinates of the center
    xCenter = x;
    yCenter = y;
    zCenter = z;
    ++count;                     // Update object count
  }

  // Instance method to calculate volume
  double volume()
  {
    return 4.0/3.0*PI*radius*radius*radius;
  }
}
```

How It Works

As you can see, the constructor has the same name as the class and has no return type specified. A constructor can have any number of parameters, including none. In this case we have four parameters, and each of the instance variables is initialized with the value of the appropriate parameter. Here is a situation where we might have used the name **radius** for the parameter, in which case we would need to use the keyword **this** to refer to the instance variable of the same name. The last action of our constructor is to increment the class variable, **count**, by 1, so that **count** accumulates the total number of objects created.

Creating Objects of a Class

When you declare a variable of type **Sphere** with the statement:

```
Sphere ball;        // Declare a variable
```

no constructor is called and no object is created. All you have created at this point is the variable **ball** which can reference an object of type **Sphere**, if and when you create one.

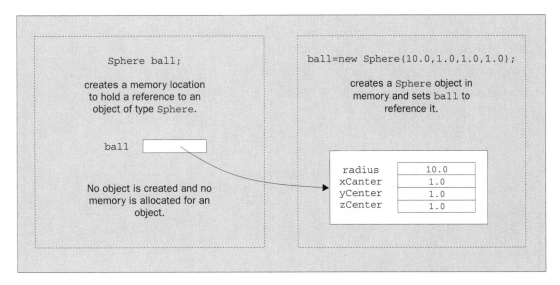

You will recall from our discussion of **String** objects and arrays that the variable and the object it references are distinct entities. To create an object of a class you must use the keyword **new** followed by a call to a constructor. To initialize **ball** with an object, you could write:

```
ball = new Sphere(10.0, 1.0, 1.0, 1.0);   // Create a sphere
```

Now we have a **Sphere** object with a radius of 10.0 located at the coordinates (1.0, 1,0, 1.0). The object is created in memory and will occupy sufficient memory to accommodate all the data necessary to define the object. The variable **ball** will record where in memory the object is—it acts as a reference to the object.

Of course, you can do the whole thing in one step, with the statement:

```
Sphere ball = new Sphere(10.0, 1.0, 1.0, 1.0);   // Create a sphere
```

which creates the variable **ball** and the **Sphere** object to which it refers.

You can create another variable that refers to the same object as **ball**:

```
Sphere myBall = ball;
```

Now the variable **myBall** refers to the same object as **ball**. We have only one object still, but we have two different variables that reference it. You could of course, have as many variables as you like referring to the same object.

The separation of the variable and the object has an important effect on how objects are passed to a method, so we need to look at that.

Passing Objects to a Method

When you pass an object as an argument to a method, the mechanism that applies is called **pass-by-reference**, because a copy of the reference contained in the variable is transferred to the method, not the object itself. The effect of this is shown in the following diagram.

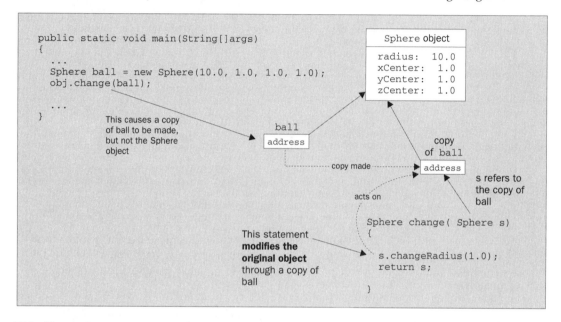

This illustration presumes we have defined a method in the class **Sphere** that will alter the radius value for an object, and that we have a method **change()** in some other class that calls the method **changeRadius()**. When the variable **ball** is used as an argument to the method **change()**, the pass-by-reference mechanism causes a copy of **ball**, **s**, to be made. The variable **ball** just stores a reference to the **Sphere** object, and the copy contains that same reference and therefore refers to the same object. No copying of the actual object occurs.

Since the copy of **ball** refers to the same object as the original, when the **changeRadius()** method is called the original object will be changed. You need to keep this in mind when writing methods that have objects as parameters because this is not always what you want.

In the example shown, the method **change()** returns the modified object. In practice you would probably want this to be a distinct object, in which case you would need to create a new object from **s**. You will see how you can write a constructor to do this a little later in this chapter.

> *Remember that this only applies to objects. If you pass a variable of type **int** or **double** to a method for example, a copy of the value is passed. You can modify the value passed as much as you want in the method, but it won't affect the original value.*

The Lifetime of an Object

The lifetime of an object is determined by the variable that references it. If we have the declaration:

```
Sphere ball = new Sphere(10.0, 1.0, 1.0, 1.0);    // Create a sphere
```

the **Sphere** object that the variable **ball** refers to will die when the variable **ball** goes out of scope. This will be at the end of the block containing this declaration. Where an instance variable refers to an object, the object survives as long as the instance variable owning the object survives.

 FYI A slight complication can arise with objects though. As you have seen, several variables can reference a single object. In this case the object survives as long as there is still a variable in existence which references the object.

You can reset a variable to point to nothing by setting its value to **null**. If you write the statement:

```
ball = null;
```

the variable ball no longer points to an object, and assuming there is no other object referencing it, the **Sphere** object it originally pointed to is destroyed.

The process of disposing of objects is called **garbage collection**. Garbage collection is automatic in Java, but this doesn't necessarily mean that objects disappear from memory straight away. It can be some time after the object becomes inaccessible to your program. This won't affect your program directly in any way. It just means you can't rely on memory occupied by an object that is done with being available immediately. For the most part it doesn't matter; the only circumstances where it might would be if your objects were very large, millions of bytes say, or you were creating and getting rid of very large numbers of objects.

Defining and Using a Class

To put what we know about classes to use, we can use our **Sphere** class in an example.

Try It Out—Using the Sphere Class

1 You will be creating two files. The first is the file **CreateSpheres.java** which will contain the class definition with the method **main()**, where execution of the program starts. The second is the file **Sphere.java** which will contain the definition of the class **Sphere**.

Both files will need to be in the same directory or folder—I suggest you name the directory **CreateSpheres**. Then copy the last version of **Sphere.java** to the directory.

2 Enter the following code for the file `CreateSpheres.java`:

```
public class CreateSpheres
{
  public static void main(String[] args)
  {
    System.out.println("Number of objects = " + Sphere.getCount());
    Sphere ball = new Sphere(4.0, 0.0, 0.0, 0.0);    // Create a sphere
    System.out.println("Number of objects = " + ball.getCount());
    Sphere globe = new Sphere(12., 1.0, 1.0, 1.0);  // Create a sphere
    System.out.println("Number of objects = " + Sphere.getCount());

    // Output the volume of each sphere
    System.out.println("ball volume = " + ball.volume());
    System.out.println("globe volume = " + globe.volume());
  }
}
```

Compile the source files and then run `CreateSpheres`, and you should get the output:

```
Number of objects = 0
Number of objects = 1
Number of objects = 2
ball volume = 267.94666666666666
globe volume = 7234.559999999999
```

How It Works

The `Sphere` class definition includes a constructor and the method `volume()` to calculate the volume of a particular sphere. It also contains the `static` method, `getCount()`, we saw earlier, which returns the current value of the class variable `count`. We need to define this method as `static` since we want to able to call it regardless of how many objects have been created, including the situation when there are none.

The method `main()` in the `CreateSpheres` class puts the class `Sphere` through its paces. When the program is compiled, the compiler will look for a file `Sphere.java` to provide the definition of the class `Sphere`. As long as this file is in the current directory the compiler will be able to find it.

The first thing the program does is to call the `static` method `getCount()`. Because no objects exist, you must use the class name to call it at this point. We then create the object `ball`, which is a `Sphere` object with a radius of 4.0 and its center at the origin point, (0.0, 0.0, 0.0). The method `getCount()` is called again, this time using the object name to demonstrate that you can call a `static` method of an object. Another `Sphere` object, `globe`, is created with a radius of 12.0. The `getCount()` method is called again, this time using the class name. Static methods are usually called using the class name because in most situations where you would use such a method, you cannot be sure that any objects exist. After all, the reason for calling this particular method would be to find out how many objects exist.

The program then outputs the volume of both objects by calling the `volume()` method for each object in the argument to the `println()` method calls.

Method Overloading

Java allows you to define several methods in a class with the same name, as long as each method has a set of parameters that is unique. This is called **method overloading**.

The name of a method together with the type and sequence of the parameters form the **signature** of the method, and the signature of each method in a class must be distinct to allow the compiler to determine exactly which method you are calling at any particular point.

Note that the return type has no effect on the signature of a method. You cannot differentiate between two methods just by the return type. This is because the return type is not apparent when you call a method. For example, if you write a statement such as:

```
Math.round(value);
```

there is no way of knowing what the return type of the method **round()** is supposed to be. Therefore if there were several versions of the method **round()**, and the return type was the only distinguishing aspect of the method signature, the compiler would be unable to determine which version of **round()** you wanted to use.

There are many circumstances where it is convenient to use method overloading. You have already seen that the standard class **Math** contains two versions of the method **round()**, one that accepts an argument of type **float**, and the other that accepts an argument of type **double**. You can see now that method overloading makes this possible. It would be rather tedious to have to use a different name for each version of **round()** when they both do essentially the same thing. One context in which you will regularly need to use overloading is when you write constructors for your classes.

Multiple Constructors

In most situations, you will need to generate objects of a class from different sets of initial defining data. If we just consider our class **Sphere**, we could conceive of a need to define a **Sphere** object in a variety of ways. You might well want a constructor that accepted just the (x, y, z) coordinates of a point, and have a **Sphere** object created with a default radius of 1.0. Another possibility is that you may want to create a default **Sphere** with a radius of 1.0 positioned at the origin, so no arguments would be specified at all. This requires two constructors in addition to the one we have already written.

Try It Out—Multiple Constructors for the *Sphere* Class

1 The code for the extra constructors would be:

```
class Sphere
{
  // First Constructor and variable declarations
```

```
      // Construct a unit sphere at a point
      Sphere(double x, double y, double z)
      {
        xCenter = x;
        yCenter = y;
        zCenter = z;
        radius = 1.0;
      }

      // Construct a unit sphere at the origin
      Sphere()
      {
        xCenter = 0.0;
        yCenter = 0.0;
        zCenter = 0.0;
        radius = 1.0;
      }

    // The rest of the class as before...
}
```

2 If you add the following statements to the **CreateSpheres** class, you can test out the new constructors:

```
Sphere eightBall = new Sphere(10.0, 10.0, 0.0);
Sphere oddBall = new Sphere();
```

3 Note that if you wanted a constructor which defined a **Sphere** object at a point by specifying the diameter, you have a problem. You might try to write it as:

```
      // Illegal constructor!!!
      // This WON'T WORK because it has the same signature as the original!!!
      Sphere(double diameter, double x, double y, double z)
      {
        xCenter = x;
        yCenter = y;
        zCenter = z;
        radius = diameter/2.0;
      }
```

Try compiling this and you'll get a compile-time error.

4 You could get around the problem in this case by using type **float** for the first parameter:

```
      // This will work because it has a different signature from the others
      Sphere(float diameter, double x, double y, double z)
      {
        xCenter = x;
        yCenter = y;
```

```
        zCenter = z;
        radius = (double)diameter/2.0;
    }
```

How It Works

When you create a **Sphere** object, the compiler will select the constructor to use based on the types of the arguments you have specified. So the first of the new constructors is used in the first statement, as its signature is different from the original constructor. The second statement clearly selects the last constructor as no arguments are specified.

It is the number and types of the parameters which affects the signature of a method, not the parameter names. The third constructor has four arguments of type **double**, so its signature is identical to the first constructor we wrote for the class. This is not permitted and you'll get a compile-time error. When the number of parameters is the same in two overloaded methods, at least one pair of corresponding parameters must be of different types.

In the fourth constructor, since the instance variable **radius** is of type **double**, the value of **diameter** is converted to type **double**. In this case you could leave out the explicit cast, and the conversion would be inserted by the compiler anyway. So the last statement could be written as:

```
    radius = diameter/2.0;
```

Duplicating Objects

When we were looking at how objects were passed to a method, we came up with a requirement for duplicating an object. The need to produce an identical copy of an object occurs surprisingly often.

 Java provides a **clone()** method, but the details of using it must wait for the next chapter.

Suppose you declare a **Sphere** object with the following statement:

```
    Sphere eightBall = new Sphere(10.0, 10.0, 0.0);
```

Later in your program you want to create a new object **newBall**, which is identical to the object **eightBall**. If you write:

```
    Sphere newBall = eightBall;
```

this will compile OK but it won't do what you want. You will remember from our discussion of **String** objects that the variable **newBall** will reference the same object as **eightBall**. You will not have a distinct object. The variable **newBall** of type **Sphere** is created but no constructor is called, so no new object is created.

Of course, you could create **newBall** by specifying the same arguments to the constructor as you used to create **eightBall.** However, in general it may be that **eightBall** has been modified in some way during execution of the program, so you don't know that its instance variables have the same values—for example, the position might have changed. This presumes we have some other class methods which alter the instance variables. You could fix this by writing a constructor that will accept an existing **Sphere** object as an argument:

```
// Create a sphere from an existing object
Sphere(Sphere oldSphere)
{
  radius = oldSphere.radius;
  xCenter = oldSphere.xCenter;
  yCenter = oldSphere.yCenter;
  zCenter = oldSphere.yCenter;
}
```

This works by copying the values of the instance variables of the **Sphere** object, passed as an argument, to the corresponding instance variables of the new object.

Now you can create **newBall** as a distinct object by writing:

```
Sphere newBall = new Sphere(eightBall);  // Create a copy of eightBall
```

Let's recap what we have learned about methods and constructors with another example.

Using Objects

Let's create an example to do some simple 2D geometry which will give us an opportunity to use more than one class. We will define two classes, a class of point objects and a class of line objects, and then use these to find the point at which the lines intersect. We will call the example **TryGeometry**, so this will be the name of the directory or folder in which you should save the program files.

Try It Out—The Point Class

We first define a basic class for point objects:

```
class Point
{
  // Coordinates of the point
  double x;
  double y;

  // Create a point from coordinates
  Point(double xVal, double yVal)
```

```
  {
    x = xVal;
    y = yVal;
  }

  // Create a point from another Point object
  Point(Point oldPoint)
  {
    x = oldPoint.x;     // Copy x coordinate
    y = oldPoint.y;     // Copy y coordinate
  }

  // Move a point
  void move(double xDelta, double yDelta)
  {
    // Parameter values are increments to the current coordinates
    x += xDelta;
    y += yDelta;
  }

  // Calculate the distance to another point
  double distance(Point aPoint)
  {
    return Math.sqrt(
        (x - aPoint.x)*(x - aPoint.x) + (y - aPoint.y)*(y - aPoint.y) );
  }

  // Output the point position
  void show()
  {
    System.out.println("Point is at position " + x + "," + y);
  }
}
```

You should save this as `Point.java` in the directory `TryGeometry`.

How It Works

This is a simple class that has just two instance variables, **x** and **y**, which are the coordinates of the **Point** object. At the moment we have two constructors, one which will create a point from a coordinate pair passed as arguments, and the other which will create a new **Point** object from an existing one.

There are three methods included in the class. The method **move()** moves a **Point** to another position by adding an increment to each of the coordinates. The method **distance()** calculates the distance from the current **Point** object to the **Point** object passed as an argument. This uses the Pythagorean theorem to compute the distance as shown next.

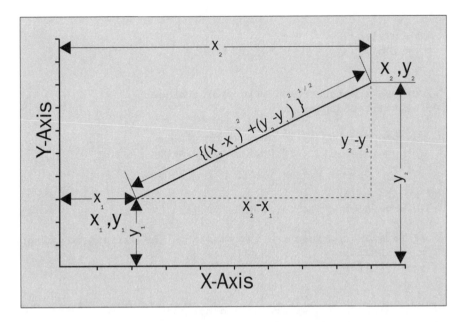

Finally we have a method **show()** that returns a string representation of the coordinates of the current point.

Try It Out—The *Line Class*

We can use **Point** objects in the definition of the class **Line**:

```java
class Line
{
  Point start;    // Start point of line
  Point end;      // End point of line

  // Create a line from two points
  Line(Point start, Point end)
  {
    this.start = start;
    this.end = end;
  }

  // Create a line from two coordinate pairs
  Line(double xStart, double yStart, double xEnd, double yEnd)
  {
    start = new Point(xStart, yStart);    // Create the start point
    end = new Point(xEnd, yEnd);          // Create the end point
  }

  // Calculate the length of a line
  double length()
```

```
     {
        return start.distance(end);   // Use the method from the Point class
     }
   }
```

You should save this as **Line.java** in the directory **TryGeometry**.

How It Works

You shouldn't have any difficulty with this class definition as it is very straightforward. The class **Line** stores two **Point** objects as instance variables. There are two constructors for **Line** objects, one accepting two **Point** objects as arguments, the other accepting the (x, y) coordinates of the start and end points. You can see how we use the variable **this** to differentiate the class instance variables **start** and **end** from the parameter names in the constructor.

Note how the constructor that accepts **Point** objects works:

```
   // Create a line from two points
   Line(Point start, Point end)
   {
     this.start = start;              // Dependent on external object!!!
     this.end = end;                  // Dependent on external object!!!
   }
```

The important thing you should notice here is that the way the constructor is implemented could cause problems that might be hard to track down. It's the same problem of an object variable being separate from the object to which it refers. In this version no new points are created. The **start** and **end** members of the object refer to the **Point** objects passed as parameters. If these were changed outside the class, by using the **move()** method for example, this would 'silently' modify the **Line** object. You might consciously decide that this is what you want, so the **Line** object continues to be dependent on its associated **Point** objects, for instance in a drawing package. But, in general, you should avoid implicit dependencies between objects.

It would be much better written as:

```
   // Create a line from two points
   Line(Point start, Point end)
   {
     this.start = new Point(start);
     this.end = new Point(end);
   }
```

With this version of the constructor, two new **Point** objects are created which will be identical to, but independent of, the objects passed to the constructor. We will try the **Line** class out with the original constructor to see the effect, and then change it to the better version. First we need to be able to get the point at the intersection of two lines.

We've now defined two classes. In these class definitions, we've included the basic data the object of that class will eventually use. We've also defined some methods which we think will be useful. And we've added constructors for a variety of input parameters. Note how the **Point** class is used in **Line** class, because two **Point** objects naturally define the extent of a line. To further demonstrate how classes can interact, and how to use this to solve computing problems, let's devise a method to calculate the intersection of two **Line** objects.

Creating a Point from Two Lines

We could add this method as a constructor in the **Point** class. The diagram below illustrates how the mathematics works out.

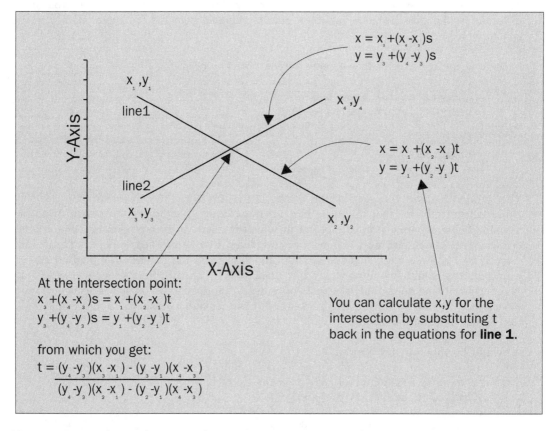

You can ignore the mathematics if you want to, as it is not the most important aspect of the example. If you are willing to take the code in the new constructor on trust, then skip to the Try It Out section next.

FYI

On the other hand you shouldn't find it hard if you can still remember what you did in high school. One way to get the intersection of two lines is to use equations like those shown. These are called parametric equations because they use a parameter value (s or t) as the variable for determining points on each line. The parameters s and t vary between 0 and 1 to give points on the lines between the defined start and end points. When a parameter s or t is 0 the equations give the coordinates of the start point of each line, and when the parameter value is 1 you get the end point of the line.

Where the lines intersect, the equations for the lines must produce the same (x, y) values, so, at this point, the right hand sides of the equations for x for the two lines must be equal, and the same goes for the equations for y. This will give you two equations in s and t, and with a bit of algebraic juggling you can eliminate s to get the equation shown for t. You can then replace t in the equations defining line 1 to get x and y for the intersection point.

Try It Out—Calculating the Intersection of Two Lines

We can use these results to write the additional constructor we need for the **Point** class. Add the following code to the definition in **Point.java**:

```java
// Create a point as the intersection of two lines
Point(Line line1, Line line2)
{
  double num =
    (line2.end.y - line2.start.y)*(line2.start.x - line1.start.x) -
    (line2.end.x - line2.start.x)*(line2.start.y - line1.start.y);

  double denom =
    (line2.end.y - line2.start.y)*(line1.end.x - line1.start.x) -
    (line2.end.x - line2.start.x)*(line1.end.y - line1.start.y);

  x = line1.start.x + (line1.end.x - line1.start.x)*num/denom;
  y = line1.start.y + (line1.end.y - line1.start.y)*num/denom;
}
```

How It Works

The constructor accepts two **Line** objects as arguments. In the code, the local variables **num** and **denom** are the numerator and denominator in the expression for **t** in the diagram. We then use these values to calculate the **x** and **y** coordinates for the intersection.

175

FYI If the lines are parallel, the denominator in the equation for t will be zero, something you should really check for in the code. For the moment, we will ignore it and end up with cordinates that are `Infinity` if it occurs.

Note how we get at the values of the coordinates for the **Point** objects defining the lines. For example, for the object **line1**, **line1.start** refers to the **Point** object and the beginning of the line. Therefore **line1.start.x** refers to its x coordinate, and **line1.start.y** accesses its y coordinates.

Now we have a **Point** class which we can use to calculate the intersection point of two objects of our **Line** class. We need a program to test the code out.

Try It Out—The `TryGeometry` Class

We can demonstrate the two classes we have defined, with the following code in the method **main()**:

```
public class TryGeometry
{
  public static void main(String[] args)
  {
    Point start = new Point(0.0, 1.0);
    Point end = new Point(5.0, 6.0);
    Line line1 = new Line(start, end);          // Create a line

    Line line2 = new Line(0.0, 3.0, 3.0, 0.0); // Create another line
    new Point(line1, line2).show();             // Show the intersection

    // Now move the end start and show the new intersection
    end.move(1.0, -5.0);
    new Point(line1, line2).show();             // No change...
  }
}
```

The program will produce the output:

```
Point is at position 1.0,2.0
Point is at position 2.0,1.0
```

How It Works

We first create two **Point** objects, which we will use in the creation of the object **line1**. We then use the other constructor in the class **Line** to create **line2** from two pairs of coordinates.

The next statement creates a new **Point** object at the intersection of the two lines, **line1** and **line2**, and calls its **show()** method to output its coordinates. As you see, we are not obliged to save an object when we create it. Here we just use it to call its **show()** method.

176

We use the **move()** method in the class **Point** to modify the coordinates of the object, **end**, that we used to create **line1**. We then get the intersection of the two lines again. This will demonstrate that **line1** is dependent on the object **end.**

Now change the constructor in the **Line** class to create new points to define the line, as we saw earlier, and run the example again. The output will be:

```
Point is at position 1.0,2.0
Point is at position 1.0,2.0
```

Changing the **end** object doesn't affect the line now. We get exactly the same intersection point after we move the point **end**. This is because we took care to create new **Point** objects to store in the instance variables for a **Line** object.

> *This is very important. When you use instance variables that refer to objects in a class definition, you must always be conscious of the possibility of creating objects that are dependent on external objects. You will usually want to take care to create independent copies of any objects used to initialize instance variables of a class.*

Recursion

The methods you have seen so far have been called from within other methods, but a method can also call itself—something referred to as **recursion**. Clearly you must include some logic in a recursive method so that it will eventually stop calling itself. We can see how this might be done with a simple example.

We can write a method that will calculate integer powers of a variable, in other words, evaluate x^n, or $x*x...*x$ where x is multiplied by itself n times.

Try It Out—Calculating Powers

Here is the complete program including the recursive method, **power()**:

```
public class PowerCalc
{
  public static void main(String[] args)
  {
    double x = 5.0;
    System.out.println(x + " to the power 4 is " + power(x,4));
    System.out.println("7.5 to the power 5 is " + power(7.5,5));
    System.out.println("7.5 to the power 0 is " + power(7.5,0));
    System.out.println("10 to the power -2 is " + power(10,-2));
  }
```

```java
  // Raise x to the power n
  static double power(double x, int n)
  {
    if(n > 1)
      return x*power(x, n-1);   // Recursive call
    else if(n < 0)
      return 1.0/power(x, -n);  // Negative power of x
    else
      return n == 0 ? 1.0 : x;  // When n is 1 return x, otherwise 1.0
  }
}
```

This program will produce the output:

```
5.0 to the power 4 is 625.0
7.5 to the power 5 is 23730.46875
7.5 to the power 0 is 1.0
10 to the power -2 is 0.01
```

How It Works

The method **power()** has two parameters, the value **x** and the power **n**, which for positive values of **n** is the number of **x** values to be multiplied together. The method performs four different actions depending on the value of **n**:

n>1	A recursive call to **power()** is made with **n** reduced by 1, and the value returned is multiplied by **x**.
n<0	x^{-n} is equivalent to $1/x^n$ so this is the expression for the return value. This involves a recursive call to **power()** with the sign of **n** reversed.
n=0	x^0 is defined as 1, so this is the value returned.
n=1	x^1 is **x**, so **x** is returned.

Just to make sure the process is clear we can work through the sequence of events as they occur in the calculation of 5^4.

Level	Description	Relevant Code

1	The first call of the **power()** method passes 5.0 and 4 as arguments. Since the second argument, **n**, is greater than 1, the **power()** method is called again in the **return** statement, with the second argument reduced by 1.	`Power(5.0, 4)`
		`{`
		`  if(n > 1)`
		`    return 5.0*power(5.0, 4-1);`
		`  . . .`
		`}`

Level	Description	Relevant Code

2	The second call of the **power()** method passes 5.0 and 3 as arguments. Since the second argument, n, is still greater than 1, the **power()** method is called again in the **return** statement with the second argument reduced by 1.	```Power(5.0, 3)```
		
		```{```
		
		``` if(n > 1)```
		
		``` return 5.0*power(5.0, 3-1);```
		
		``` ...```
		
		```}```

3	The third call of the **power()** method passes 5.0 and 2 as arguments. Since the second argument, **n**, is still greater than 1, the **power()** method is called again, with the second argument again reduced by 1.	```Power(5.0, 2)```
		
		```{```
		
		``` if(n > 1)```
		
		``` return 5.0*power(5.0, 2-1);```
		
		``` ...```
		
		```}```

4	The fourth call of the **power()** method passes 5.0 and 1 as arguments. Since the second argument, **n**, is not greater than 1, the value of the first argument, 5.0, is returned to level **3**.	```Power(5.0, 1)```
		
		```{```
		
		``` if(n > 1)```
		
		``` ...```
		
		``` else```
		
		``` return 5.0;```
		
		```}```

3	Back at level **3**, the value returned, 5.0, is multiplied by the first argument, 5.0, and returned to level **2**.	```Power(5.0, 2)```
		
		```{```
		
		``` if(n>1)```
		
		``` ...```
		
		``` else```
		
		``` return 5.0*5.0;```
		
		```}```

2	Back at level **2**, the value returned, 25.0, is multiplied by the first argument, 5.0, and returned to level **1**.	```Power(5.0, 3)```
		
		```{```
		
		``` if(n > 1)```
		
		``` ...```
		
		``` else```
		
		``` return 5.0*25.0;```
		
		```}```

Table Continued on Following Page

Level	Description	Relevant Code

1	Back at level **1**, the value returned, 125.0, is multiplied by the first argument, 5.0, and 625.0 is returned as the result of calling the method in the first instance.	`Power(5.0, 4)`
		
		`{`
		
		`  if(n > 1)`
		
		`  . . .`
		
		`  else`
		
		`    return 5.0*125.0;`
		
		`}`

This shows that the method **power()** is called four times in all. The calls cascade down through four levels until the value of n allows a value to be returned. The return values ripple up through the levels until we are eventually back at the top, and 625.0 is returned to the original calling point.

As a rule, you should only use recursion where there are evident advantages in the approach, as there is quite of lot of overhead in recursive method calls. This particular example could be more easily programmed as a loop and it would execute much more efficiently. One example of where recursion can be applied very effectively is in the handling of data structures such as trees. Unfortunately these aren't good illustrations of how recursion works, because of their complexity.

Understanding Packages

Packages are fundamental to Java programs so make sure you understand this section. Packages are implicit in the organization of the standard classes as well as your own programs, and they influence the names you can use for classes and the variables and methods they contain.

Essentially a **package** is a named collection of classes. The purpose of grouping classes in a package is to make it easy to add the classes in a package into your program code. One aspect of this is that the names used for classes in one package cannot interfere with the names of classes in another package, or your program, because the class names in a package can be qualified by the package name.

Every class in Java is contained in a package, including all those we have defined in our examples. You haven't see any references to package names so far because we have been implicitly using the default package, which doesn't have a name, to hold our classes.

All of the standard classes in Java are contained within packages. The package that contains all the standard classes we have used so far is called **java.lang**. You haven't seen any explicit reference to this in your code either, because this package is automatically available to your programs since some of its classes are used in every program. There are other packages containing standard classes which you will need to include explicitly, as you will see.

Packaging up Your Classes

Putting one of your classes in a package is very simple. You just add a package statement as the first statement in the file containing the class definition. A package statement consists of the keyword **package**, followed by the package name, and is terminated by a semi-colon. If you want the classes in a package to be accessible outside the package, you must declare the class using the keywords **public class** in your class definition. Classes definitions that aren't preceded by the keyword **public** are only accessible to classes within the same package.

For example, to include the class **Sphere** in a package called **Geometry**, the contents of the file **Sphere.java** would need to be:

```
package Geometry;

public class Sphere
{
   // Details of the class definition
}
```

You can put comments preceding the package statement, but other than that it must be the first statement in the file. Each class that you want to include in the package **Geometry** must contain the same package statement at the beginning, and you should save all the files for the classes in the package in a directory with the same name as the package, that is **Geometry**.

Packages and the Directory Structure

Packages are actually a little more complicated than they appear at first sight, because a package is intimately related to the directory structure in which it is stored. You already know that the definition of a class **ClassName** must be stored in a file with the name **ClassName.java**, and that all the files for classes within a package **PackageName** must be included in a directory with the name **PackageName**.

A package need not have a single name. You can specify a package name as a sequence of names separated by periods. For example, you might have developed several collections of classes dealing with geometry, one dealing with 2D shapes and another with 3D shapes perhaps. In this case you might include the class **Sphere** in a package with the statement:

```
package Geometry.Shapes3D;
```

and the class for circles in a package using the statement:

```
package Geometry.Shapes2D;
```

In this situation, the packages are expected to be in the directories **Shapes3D** and **Shapes2D**, and both of these must be sub-directories of **Geometry**. In general, you can have as many names as you like separated by periods to identify a package, but the name must reflect the directory structure where the package is stored.

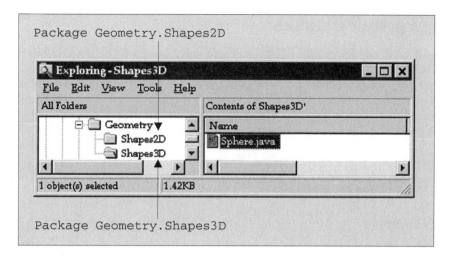

Package Geometry.Shapes2D

Package Geometry.Shapes3D

The directory and sub-directories containing your package must be stored in one of the directories that appear in the **CLASSPATH** environment variable if you want Java to be able to access the classes to compile or incorporate them into one of your programs. Note that it is up to you to make sure the classes in your package are in the right directory. Java will not prevent you from saving a file in a directory that is quite different from that appearing in the package statement.

The **CLASSPATH** environment variable must, at least, contain the path to the standard classes supplied with Java. For example, you would typically set it under Windows 95 by adding the command:

```
set CLASSPATH=.;C:\Java\lib\classes.zip
```

to your **autoexec.bat** file.

Under Unix, the equivalent to this might be:

```
CLASSPATH=.:/usr/local/java/lib/classes.zip
```

If you want to store your own packages in a different path, you need to add your path to the **CLASSPATH** environment variable. For example, if you are storing your packages in the path **C:\MyPackages** so that the package **PackageName** is located in **C:\MyPackages\PackageName**, you would need to change the **CLASSPATH** environment variable definition under Windows 95 to:

```
set CLASSPATH=.;C:\MyPackages;C:\java\lib\classes.zip
```

If you're using Unix you would define it with the command:

```
CLASSPATH=.:/home/ivorh/MyPackages:/usr/local/java/lib/classes.zip
```

If you're using the Sun Java Development Kit, you can override the **CLASSPATH** environment variable by specifying the **-classpath** option when you execute the Java compiler. If you don't set the class path in this way, or if you forget to set the **CLASSPATH** environment variable, or you set it incorrectly, Java will not be able to find the classes in any new packages.

Adding Classes from a Package to your Program

Assuming they have been defined with the **public** keyword, you can add all or any of the classes in a package to the code in your program by using an **import statement**. To add all the classes in the package **Geometry.Shapes3D** to a program, you just need to add an import statement after the package statement in the file:

```
import Geometry.Shapes3D.*;    // Include all classes from this package
```

The keyword **import** is followed by the specification of what you want to import. The wildcard, *****, following the period after the package name selects all the classes in the package, rather like selecting all the files in a directory.

If you want to add a particular class rather than an entire package, you specify its name explicitly in the **import** statement:

```
import Geometry.Shapes3D.Sphere;  // Include the class Sphere
```

So the import statement gives you the choice of selecting either all classes in a package, or just one. If you want to select just a few classes from a package you can add an import statement for each.

> Note that the *** can only be used to select all the classes in a package. You can't use *Geometry. ** to select all the packages in the directory *Geometry*.

Packages and Names in your Programs

A package creates a self-contained environment for naming your classes. This is the primary reason for having packages in Java. You can specify the names for classes in one package without worrying about whether the same names have been used elsewhere. Java makes this possible by treating the package name as part of the class name—actually as a prefix. This means that the class **Sphere** in the package **Geometry.Shapes3D** has the full name **Geometry.Shapes3D.Sphere**. If you don't use an import statement to incorporate the class in your program, you can still make use of the class by calling it with its full class name. If you needed to do this with the class **Sphere**, you might declare a variable with the statement:

```
Geometry.Shapes3D.Sphere ball =
                new Geometry.Shapes3D.Sphere(10.0, 1.0, 1.0, 1.0);
```

which is rather verbose, and certainly doesn't help the readability of the program.

In most circumstances, you will import a class so you don't need to use the fully qualified name. The name **Sphere** will suffice when you have an **import** statement adding the class to your program code. However, one situation can arise where you will need to use a qualified name. If you are using two classes with the same name that obviously reside in separate packages, you can only import one of them. To use the other you will need to use the qualified name. This is a good reason to avoid using a name for one of your classes that corresponds with the name of one of the standard Java classes: if you don't you will need to use the qualified name when you refer to the standard class in your program.

Standard Packages

All of the standard classes that are provided with Java are stored in standard packages. There is a growing list of standard packages but the ones you may hear about quite frequently are:

`java.lang`	Contains classes that are fundamental to Java (e.g. the **Math** class) and all of these are available in your programs automatically. You do not need an **import** statement to include them.
`java.io`	Contains classes supporting input/output operations
`java.awt`	Contains classes that support Java's graphical user interface (GUI). It enables you to create window-based applications, as well as the menus and dialogs that go along with them.
`java.awt.event`	Contains classes that support event handling.
`java.awt.image`	Contains classes to support image processing.
`java.awt.peer`	Defines the interfaces that transform the Java GUI class method calls to their native implementations on a particular platform. You will not normally be concerned with the contents of this package, and we will not discuss it further in this book.
`java.applet`	This contains classes that enable you to write applets—programs that are embedded in a Web page.
`java.util`	This contains classes that support a range of standard operations for managing collections of data, accessing date and time information, and analyzing strings.
`java.util.zip`	Contains classes to support the creating of `.jar` (Java ARchive) files.
`java.net`	This contains classes to support networking operations.
`java.rmi`	Contains classes to support remote method invocation—calling methods of a Java program in a separate virtual machine.
`java.security`	Contains classes to enhance the security in Java program, supporting such things as cryptography and digital signatures.
`java.sql`	Contains classes that support database access using standard SQL.
`java.beans`	Contains classes supporting the development of software components in Java that can be plugged together through a standard interface.

Standard Classes Encapsulating the Basic Data Types

As well as the classes **String** and **StringBuffer** which you saw in the previous chapter, the package **java.lang** includes classes that allow you to define objects that encapsulate each of the basic data types in Java. These classes are:

Boolean	Character	Byte
Short	Integer	Long
Float	Double	

Each of these classes encapsulates the corresponding basic type, and includes methods for manipulating and interrogating objects of the class, and for converting between **String** objects and values of the encapsulated basic type. Another use for these classes is when you want to pass a value of a basic type by reference rather than by value.

As you have seen, passing a variable by value makes it impossible to modify the value in the calling program. By using an object of type **Long** for example as a parameter to a method instead of a variable of type **long**, you will be able to alter the value of the object that is passed to the method since an object is passed by reference, not by value.

The classes encapsulating the numeric basic types each contain the **static final** constants **MAX_VALUE** and **MIN_VALUE** that define the maximum and minimum values that can be represented. They also have **toString()** methods that enable the automatic conversion of class objects to type **String**, when you concatenate them with other **String** objects. Conversely there are methods to convert from a **String** to a basic type. For example, the **parseInt()** member of the class **Integer** accepts a **String** representation of an integer as an argument, and returns the equivalent value as type **int**.

The classes **Float** and **Double** contain the methods **isInfinite()** and **isNaN()** which accept an argument of type **float** or **double**. These provide the means for you to test whether a variable of a basic floating point type contains an infinite value (as a result of division by zero), or a value that is not a number (**NaN**—the result of 0/0).

Controlling Access to Class Members

We have not yet discussed how accessible class members are outside a class. You know that from inside a class method you can refer to any of the variables and any other methods defined in the class. The degree to which variables and methods within a class are accessible from other classes depends on whether the classes are in the same package, and on what **access attributes** you have specified for the members of a class.

Using Access Attributes

Within a given package, any class has direct access to any other class name—for declaring variables, for example—but the variables and methods that are members of that other class are not necessarily accessible. The accessibility of these are controlled by **access attributes**. You have four possibilities when specifying an access attribute, including what we have used in our examples so far—that is, not to specify anything at all—and each possibility has a different effect overall. The options you have for specifying the accessibility of a variable or a method in a class are:

Attribute	Permitted access
No access attribute	From any class in the same package.
`public`	From any class anywhere.
`private`	No access from outside the class at all.
`protected`	From any class in the same package and from any sub-class anywhere.

The table shows you how the access attributes you set for a class determine the parts of the Java environment from which you can access a class member. Inside a class, an instance method can access any member of the class, and a **static** method can access any **static** member of the class. We will discuss sub-classes in the next chapter, so don't worry about these for the moment. We will be coming back to how and when you use the **protected** attribute then. Note that **public**, **private**, and **protected** are all keywords.

This may sound more complicated than it actually is. Look at the next diagram, which shows the access allowed between classes within the same package.

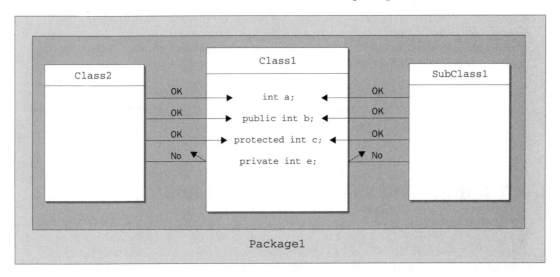

Within a package, only the **private** members of the class **Class1** can't be directly accessed by a method in another class, **Class2**. If the other class is a sub-class of the class in question, as is the case with **SubClass1**, it is only the **private** members of **Class1** that can't be referenced.

The next diagram shows the situation where the classes seeking access are in different packages.

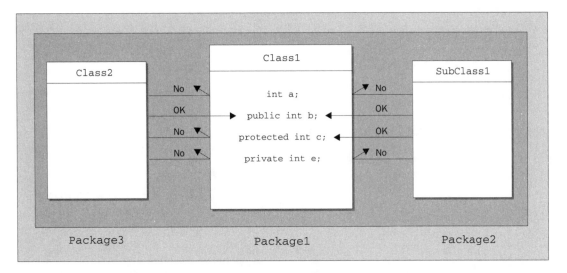

Here access is more restricted. The only members of **Class1** that can be accessed from an ordinary class, **Class2**, in another package are those specified as **public**. Bear in mind that the class, **Class1**, must also have been defined with the attribute **public**. From a sub-class of **Class1** in another package, the members of **Class1** without an access attribute cannot be reached, and neither can the **private** members—these can never be accessed externally under any circumstances.

Specifying Access Attributes

As you probably gathered from the diagrams we just looked at, to specify an access attribute for a class member, you just add the keyword to the beginning of the declaration. Here is the **Point** class you saw earlier, but now with access attributes defined for its members:

Try It Out—Accessing the Point Class

Make the following changes to your **Point** class. If you save it in a new directory, do make sure **Line.java** is copied there as well.

```java
public class Point
{
    // Coordinates of the point
    private double x;
    private double y;

    // Create a point from its coordinates
    public Point(double xVal, double yVal)
    {
        x = xVal;
        y = yVal;
    }
```

```
  // Create a Point from an existing Point object
public Point(Point aPoint)
  {
    x = aPoint.x;
    y = aPoint.y;
  }

  // Create a point as the intersection of two lines
public Point(Line line1, Line line2)
  {
    double num =
          (line2.end.y - line2.start.y)*(line2.start.x - line1.start.x) -
          (line2.end.x - line2.start.x)*(line2.start.y - line1.start.y);

    double denom =
          (line2.end.y - line2.start.y)*(line1.end.x - line1.start.x) -
          (line2.end.x - line2.start.x)*(line1.end.y - line1.start.y);

    x = line1.start.x + (line1.end.x - line1.start.x)*num/denom;
    y = line1.start.y + (line1.end.y-line1.start.y)*num/denom;
  }

  // Move a point
public void move(double xDelta, double yDelta)
  {
    // Parameter values are increments to the current coordinates
    x += xDelta;
    y += yDelta;
  }

  // Calculate the distance to another point
public double distance(Point aPoint)
  {
    return Math.sqrt(
          (x - aPoint.x)*(x - aPoint.x) + (y - aPoint.y)*(y - aPoint.y) );
  }

  // Display the point position
public void show()
  {
    System.out.println("Point is at position " + x + "," + y);
  }
}
```

How It Works

Now the instance variables **x** and **y** cannot be accessed or modified from outside the class. The only way these can be set or modified is through methods within the class, either with constructors, or the **move()** method. If it was necessary to make the values of **x** and **y** available, a simple function would do the trick. For example:

```
public double getX()
{ return x; }
```

Couldn't be simpler really, could it?

Choosing Access Attributes

As you can see from the table of access attributes, all the classes we have defined so far have had members that are freely accessible within the same package. This applies both to the methods and the variables that were defined in the classes. This is not good object-oriented programming practice. As we said in Chapter 1, one of the ideas behind objects is to keep the data members encapsulated so they cannot be modified by all and sundry, even from other classes within the same package. On the other hand, the methods in your classes generally need to be accessible. They provide the outside interface to the class and define the set of operations that are possible with objects of the class. Therefore in the majority of situations with simple classes (i.e. no sub-classes), you should be explicitly specifying your class members as either **public** or **private**, rather than omitting the access attributes.

Broadly, unless you have good reasons for declaring them otherwise, the variables in a class should be **private** and the methods that will be called from outside the class should be **public**. Even where access to the values of the variables from outside a class is necessary, you don't need to make them **public** or leave them without an access attribute. As we've just seen, you can provide access quite easily by adding a simple **public** method to return the value of a data member.

Of course, there are always exceptions:

▶ If you have data members that have been specified as **final** so that their values are fixed, and they are likely to be useful outside the class, you might as well declare them to be **public**.

▶ You may well have methods in a class that are only intended to be used internally by other methods in the class. In this case you should specify these as **private**.

▶ In a class like the standard class, **Math**, which is just a convenient container for utility functions and standard data values, you will want to make everything **public**.

All of this applies to simple classes. We will see in the next chapter, when we will be looking at sub-classes, that there are some further aspects of class structure that you must take into account.

Using a Package and Access Attributes

Let's put together an example that uses a package that we will create. We can put the **Point** and **Line** classes that we defined earlier in a package we could call **Geometry**. We can then write a program that will import these classes and test them.

Try It Out—Packaging up the Line and Point Classes

1 Remember that you need to ensure the path to the directory **Geometry** appears in the **CLASSPATH** environment variable setting before you try compiling either of these two classes. Then the compiler knows where to search for **Geometry.Point** and **Geometry.Java**.

2 To include the class **Point** in the package, the code will be:

```java
package Geometry;

public class Point
{
  // Coordinates of the point
  private double x;
  private double y;

  // Create a point from its coordinates
  public Point(double xVal, double yVal)
  {
    x = xVal;
    y = yVal;
  }

  // Create a Point from an existing Point object
  public Point(Point aPoint)
  {
    x = aPoint.x;
    y = aPoint.y;
  }

  // Create a point as the intersection of two lines
  public Point(Line line1, Line line2)
  {
    double num =
      (line2.getEnd().y - line2.getStart().y)*
        (line2.getStart().x - line1.getStart().x) -
      (line2.getEnd().x - line2.getStart().x)*
        (line2.getStart().y - line1.getStart().y);

    double denom =
      (line2.getEnd().y - line2.getStart().y)*
        (line1.getEnd().x - line1.getStart().x) -
      (line2.getEnd().x - line2.getStart().x)*
        (line1.getEnd().y - line1.getStart().y);

    x = line1.getStart().x +
        (line1.getEnd().x - line1.getStart().x)*num/denom;
    y = line1.getStart().y +
        (line1.getEnd().y - line1.getStart().y)*num/denom;
  }
```

```
  // Move a point
  public void move(double xDelta, double yDelta)
  {
    // Parameter values are increments to the current coordinates
    x += xDelta;
    y += yDelta;
  }

  // Calculate the distance to another point
  public double distance(Point aPoint)
  {
    return Math.sqrt(
        (x - aPoint.x)*(x - aPoint.x) + (y - aPoint.y)*(y - aPoint.y) );
  }

  // Display the point position
  public void show()
  {
    System.out.println("Point is at position " + x + "," + y);
  }
}
```

3 The **Line** class needs to be amended in a similar way:

```
package Geometry;

public class Line
{
  private Point start;    // Start point of line
  private Point end;      // End point of line

  // Create a line from two points
  public Line(Point start, Point end)
  {
    this.start = new Point(start);
    this.end = new Point(end);
  }

  // Create a line from two coordinate pairs
  public Line(double xStart, double yStart, double xEnd, double yEnd)
  {
    start = new Point(xStart, yStart);   // Create the start point
    end = new Point(xEnd, yEnd);         // Create the end point
  }

  // Calculate the length of a line
  public double length()
  {
    return start.distance(end);  // Use the method from the Point class
  }
```

```
    public Point getEnd(){ return end; }        // Return the end point
    public Point getStart(){ return start; }    // Return the start point
}
```

How It Works

Looking first at the `Point` class, there are a few more changes that we have made to the class definition. All these are necessary if the class is to be available through an `import` statement. The package statement at the beginning defines the package it belongs to. Naturally, you still have to save it in the correct directory, `Geometry`. Without the attribute `public`, the class `Point` would not be available to classes outside the package `Geometry`.

Since we will declare the instance variables in the class `Line` as `private`, they will not be accessible directly. We will need to add the methods `getStart()` and `getEnd()` to the `Line` class to make the `Point` object values available. These methods are used in the `Point` constructor that creates a `Point` from two `Line` objects.

The `Line` class hasn't been updated since our first example, so we first have to sort out the access attributes. The two instance variables are now declared as `private`, so they can no longer be accessed from outside the class. All of the methods have been declared as `public` to ensure that they can be accessed from anywhere. We have also declared the class as `public` and added the `package` statement to specify that it is in the package `Geometry`.

We can now write the program that is going to import the package we have just created.

Try It Out—Testing the Geometry Package

We can just create a succession of points, create a line joining each pair of successive points in the sequence, and then calculate the total line length.

```
import Geometry.*;      // Import the Point and Line classes

public class TryPackage
{
  public static void main(String[] args)
  {
    double[][] coords = { {1.0, 0.0}, {6.0, 0.0}, {6.0, 10.0},
                          {10.0,10.0}, {10.0, -14.0}, {8.0, -14.0}};

    // Create an array of points and fill it with Point objects
    Point[] points = new Point[coords.length];
    for(int i = 0; i < coords.length; i++)
      points[i] = new Point(coords[i][0],coords[i][1]);

    // Create an array of lines and fill it using Point pairs
    Line[] lines = new Line[points.length - 1];
    double totalLength = 0.0;                 // Store total line length here
    for(int i = 0; i < points.length - 1; i++)
    {
      lines[i] = new Line(points[i], points[i+1]); // Create a Line
```

```
        totalLength += lines[i].length();              // Add its length
    }

    // Output the total length
    System.out.println("Total line length = " + totalLength);
  }
}
```

You should save this as **TryPackage.java** in the directory **TryPackage**. When you compile and run it you should see:

```
Total line length = 45.0
```

How It Works

This example is a handy review of how you can define arrays, and also shows that you can declare an array of objects in the same way as you declare an array of one of the basic types. The dimensions of the array of arrays, **coords**, are determined by the initial values that are specified between the braces. The first dimension is determined by the number of values within the outer braces. Each of the elements in the array is itself an array of length 2, with each pair of element values being enclosed within their own braces. Since there are six sets of these, we have an array of 6 elements, each of which is itself an array of two elements. Each of these elements correspond to the (x, y) coordinates of a point.

> *You can see from this that, if necessary, you can create an array of arrays with each row having a different number of elements. The length of each row is determined by the number of initializing values that appear, so they could all be different in the most general case.*

We declare an array of **Point** objects with the same length as the number of (x, y) pairs in the **coords** array. This array is filled with **Point** objects in the **for** loop, which we created using the pairs of coordinate values from the **coords** array.

Since each pair of **Point** objects will define a **Line** object, we need one less element in the array **lines** than we have in the **points** array. We create the elements of the lines array in the second **for** loop using successive **Point** objects, and accumulate the total length of all the line segments by adding the length of each **Line** object to **totalLength** as it is created. Finally, we output the value of **totalLength**, which in this case is 45.

Note that the import statement adds the classes from the package **Geometry** to our program. These classes can be added to any application using the same import statement.

Inner Classes

All the classes we have defined so far have been separate from each other—each stored away in its own file. Not all classes have to be defined like this. You can put the definition of one class inside the definition of another class. The inside class is called an **inner class**, and the outside class is called a **top-level class**. The inner class can itself be a top-level class to another class, if need be (we'll see an example of this in Chapter 13).

The idea is to keep relevant classes near to the top-level class, particularly when their function is to support the top-level class. Inner classes make life easier for the programmer by allowing access to the members of the enclosing class.

We can see how this works with an example. We will create a class **MagicHat** that will define an object containing a variable number of rabbits. We will put the definition for the class **Rabbit** inside the definition of the class **MagicHat**. The basic structure of **MagicHat.java** will be:

```
public class MagicHat
{
  // Definition of the MagicHat class...

  // Inner class to define a rabbit
  class Rabbit
  {
    // Definition of the Rabbit class...
  }
}
```

Try It Out—Rabbits Out of Hats

1 Let's add the detail of the **MagicHat** class definition:

```
public class MagicHat
{
  private String hatName;      // Name of the hat
  private Rabbit rabbits[];     // Rabbits in the hat

  // Constructor for a hat
  public MagicHat(String hatName)
  {
    this.hatName = hatName;     // Store the hat name
    rabbits = new Rabbit[1 + (int)(4.*Math.random())]; // Random rabbits

    for(int i = 0; i < rabbits.length; i++)
      rabbits[i] = new Rabbit();                    // Create the rabbits
  }

  // String representation of a hat
  public String toString()
  {
    // Hat name first...
    String hatString = "\n" + hatName + " contains:\n";

    for(int i = 0; i < rabbits.length; i++)
      hatString += "\t" + rabbits[i] + " ";  // Add the rabbits strings
    return hatString;
  }
```

```
  // Inner class to define a rabbit
  class Rabbit
  {
    // Definition of the Rabbit class...
  }
}
```

2 We can now add the definition of the **Rabbit** class. When we create a **Rabbit** object, we want it to have a unique name so we can distinguish one rabbit from another. We can generate unique names from a set of fixed names with an integer appended that is different each time the base name is repeated. Here's what we need to add for the **Rabbit** class definition:

```
public class MagicHat
{
  static private String rabbitNames[] = {"Floppsy", "Gnasher", "Thumper"};
  static private int rabbitNamesCount[] = {0,0,0};

  // Definition of the MagicHat class - as before...

  // Inner class to define a rabbit
  class Rabbit
  {
    private String name;                      // Name of the rabbit

    // Constructor for a rabbit
    public Rabbit()
    {
      int index = (int)(3.*Math.random())%3;  // Get random name index
      name = rabbitNames[index] + (++rabbitNamesCount[index]);
    }

    // String representation of a rabbit
    public String toString()
    {
      return name;
    }
  }
}
```

3 We can use the following application class to try out our inner class:

```
public class TryInnerClass
{
  static public void main(String[] args)
  {
    // Create three magic hats and output them
    System.out.println(new MagicHat("Gray Topper"));
    System.out.println(new MagicHat("Black Topper"));
    System.out.println(new MagicHat("Baseball Cap"));
  }
}
```

When I ran the program, I got the output:

```
Gray Topper contains:
        Floppsy1        Thumper1        Gnasher1        Thumper2

Black Topper contains:
        Thumper3

Baseball Cap contains:
        Floppsy2        Thumper4        Floppsy3
```

You are likely to get something different.

How It Works

A **MagicHat** object has two private data members, a **String** variable, **hatName**, to store the name of the hat, and an array of **Rabbit** objects. Each object will contain a random number of rabbits. The constructor for a **MagicHat** object stores the name of the hat and generates a **Rabbit** array with at least one, and up to five, elements. This array is then filled with rabbits. The class also has a method **toString()** method which returns a **String** object containing the name of the hat and the names of all the rabbits in the hat. This assumes the **Rabbit** class also has a **toString()** method defined. We will be able to use the **toString()** implicitly in an output statement when we come to use the **MagicHat** class.

The base names we use to generate rabbit names are defined in the **static** array **rabbitNames[]**. The count for each base name which we will append to the base name to produce a unique name is stored in the **static** array **rabbitNamesCount[]**. Both of these are defined in the **MagicHat** class. Why not in the **Rabbit** class—after all, that's where we use them? There are two reasons. Firstly, the example demonstrates quite nicely that an inner class can refer to any of the class members of the top-level class, even when they are **private**. Secondly, and rather more importantly, an inner class cannot have **static** members, so we have no choice in the matter.

The **Rabbit** class has a single data member, **name**, to store a name. This is initialized in the constructor. A random base name is selected from the **rabbitNames[]** array using an index value between 0 and 3. We then append the current count for the name incremented by 1, so successive uses of any base name **Gnasher** for example, will produce names **Gnasher1**, **Gnasher2** and so on. The **toString()** method for the class just returns the name for the **Rabbit** object.

The method **main()** in **TryInnerClass** just creates three **MagicHat** objects and outputs the string representation of each of them. Putting the object as an argument to the **println()** method will call the **toString()** method for the object automatically, and the **String** object that is returned will be output to the screen.

Using an Inner Class outside the Top-Level Class

You can create objects of an inner class outside the top-level class containing the inner class, but only in the context of an object of the top-level class. Thus the inner class objects are always associated with a top-level class object.

Try It Out—Rabbits Breaking Free

We can see how this works by modifying the method **main()** in **TryInnerClass** to create another **MagicHat** object, and then create a **Rabbit** object for it:

```
static public void main(String[] args)
{
  // Create three magic hats and output them
  System.out.println(new MagicHat("Gray Topper"));
  System.out.println(new MagicHat("Black Topper"));
  System.out.println(new MagicHat("Baseball Cap"));

  MagicHat oldHat = new MagicHat("Old hat");         // New hat object
  MagicHat.Rabbit rabbit = oldHat.new Rabbit();      // Create rabbit object
  System.out.println(oldHat);                        // Show the hat
  System.out.println("\nNew rabbit is: " + rabbit);  // Display the rabbit
}
```

I got the output:

```
Gray Topper contains:
        Thumper1

Black Topper contains:
        Gnasher1          Gnasher2          Floppsy1          Gnasher3

Baseball Cap contains:
        Thumper2          Thumper3          Thumper4

Old hat contains:
        Floppsy2          Gnasher4

New rabbit is: Floppsy3
```

How It Works

The new code first creates a **MagicHat** object, **oldHat**. This will have its own rabbits. We then use this object to create an object of the class **MagicHat.Rabbit**. This is how an inner class name is referenced—with the top-level class name as a qualifier. You can only call the constructor for the inner class by qualifying it with a **MagicHat** object name. This is because an inner class can refer to members of the top-level class—including instance members. Therefore, an instance of the top-level class must exist for this to be possible. Note how the top-level object is used in the constructor call. The object name qualifier goes before the keyword **new** which precedes the constructor call for the inner class. This creates an object, **rabbit**, in the context of the object, **oldHat**. This doesn't mean **oldHat** has **rabbit** as a member. It just means that if top-level members are used in the inner class, they will be the members for **oldHat**. You can see from the example that the name of the new rabbit is not part of the **oldHat** object.

We will come back to inner classes in Chapter 12 when we'll be learning about writing windows-based programs in Java. They are used quite extensively to make some operations in this context easier to implement.

197

The finalize() Method

You have the option of including a method **finalize()** in a class definition. This method is called automatically by Java before an object is finally destroyed and the space it occupies in memory is released. Please note that this may be some time after the object is inaccessible in your program. When an object goes out of scope, it is dead so far as your program is concerned, but the Java virtual machine may not get around to disposing of the remains until later. When it does, it calls the **finalize()** method for the object. The form of the **finalize()** method is:

```
protected void finalize()
{
   // Your clean-up code...
}
```

This method is useful if your class objects use resources that require some special action when they are destroyed. Typically these are resources that are not within the Java environment that are not guaranteed to be released by the object itself. This means such things as graphics resources—fonts or other drawing related resources that are supplied by the host operating system, or external files on the hard disk. Leaving these around after an object is destroyed wastes system resources, and in some circumstances—with graphics resources under Windows 95 for instance—if you waste enough of them, your program, and possibly other programs on the system, may stop working. For most classes this is not necessary, but if an object opened a disk file for example, but did not guarantee its closure, you would want to make sure that the file was closed when the object was destroyed. You could implement the **finalize()** method to take care of this.

Note that when variables go out of scope, although you can no longer use the objects they pointed to, they may not be destroyed immediately. You cannot rely on an object being destroyed when it is no longer available to your program code. The Java virtual machine will only get rid of unwanted objects and free the memory they occupy if it runs out of memory, or if there is no activity within your program—for example when waiting for input. As a result objects may not get destroyed until execution of your program ends. You also have no guarantee as to when a **finalize()** method will be called. All you are assured of is that it will be called before the memory that the object occupied is freed. Nothing time-sensitive should be left to the **finalize()** method.

One consequence of this is that there are circumstances where this can cause problems, that is, when you don't allow for the possibility of your objects hanging around. For example, suppose you create an object in a method that opens a file, and rely on the `finalize()` method to close it. If you then call this method in a loop, you may end up with a large number of files open at one time, since the object that is created in each call of the method will not necessarily be destroyed immediately on return from the method. This introduces the possibility of your program attempting to have more files open simultaneously than the host operating system allows. In this situation, you need to make sure a file is closed when you are done with it, by including an object method to close it explicitly, for example `close()`.

Native Methods

It is possible to include a method in a class that is implemented in some other programming language, such as C or C++, external to the Java Virtual Machine. To specify such a method within a class definition you use the keyword **native** in the declaration of the method. For example:

```
public native long getData();      // Declare a method that is not in Java
```

Of course the method will have no body in Java since it is defined elsewhere, where all the work is done, so the declaration ends with a semi-colon.

The major drawback to using native methods in Java is that your program will no longer be portable. Security requirements for applets embedded in Web pages require that the code must all be written in Java, so using native methods in an applet is simply not possible. Since the primary reasons for using Java are the portability of the code and the ability to produce applets, the need for you to add native methods to your Java programs will be minimal. We will therefore not delve any deeper into this topic.

Summary

In this chapter you have learned all the essentials of defining your own classes. You can now create your own class types to fit the context of the problems you are dealing with. We will build on this in the next chapter to enable you to add more flexibility to the operations on your class objects by showing you how to realize polymorphism.

The important points you have covered in this chapter are:

- A class definition specifies the variables and methods that are members of the class

- Each class must be saved in a file with the same name as the class, and with the extension **.java**

- Class variables are declared using the keyword **static**, and one instance of each class variable is shared amongst all objects of a class

- Each object of a class will have its own instance variables—these are variables declared without using the keyword **static**

- Methods that are specified as **static** can be called even if no class objects exist, but a **static** method cannot refer to instance variables

- Methods that are not specified as **static** can access any of the variables in the class directly

- Recursive methods are methods that call themselves

- Access to members of a class is determined by the access attributes that are specified for each of them. These can be **public**, **private**, **protected**, or nothing at all

- Classes can be grouped into a package. If a class in a package is to be accessible from outside the package the class must be declared using the keyword **public**

- To designate that a class is a member of a package you use a **package** statement at the beginning of the file containing the class definition

- To add classes from a package to a file you use an **import** statement immediately following any package statement in the file

- A native method is a method implemented in a language other than Java. Java programs containing native methods cannot be applets and are no longer portable

Exercises

1 Define a class for rectangle objects defined by two points, the top-left and bottom-right corners of the rectangle. Include a constructor to copy a rectangle, a method to return a rectangle object that encloses the current object and the rectangle passed as an argument, and a method to display the defining points of a rectangle. Test the class by creating four rectangles and combining these cumulatively to end up with a rectangle enclosing them all. Output the defining points of all the rectangles you create.

2 Define a class, **yfiLength**, to represent a length measured in yards, feet, and inches, each stored as integers. Include methods to add and subtract objects, to multiply and divide an object by an integer value, to calculate an area resulting from the product of two objects, and to compare objects. Include a constructor that accepts three arguments, yards, feet, and inches, a constructor that accepts one integer argument in inches, a constructor that accepts one **double** argument in yards, and a constructor that accepts no arguments, which creates an object with the length set to zero. Check the class by creating some objects and testing the class operations.

3 Define a class, **tpoWeight**, to represent a weight in tons, pounds, and ounces, and include a similar range of methods and constructors as the previous example. Demonstrate this class by creating and combining some class objects.

4 Put both the previous classes in a package called **Measures**. Import this package into a program that will calculate and display the total weight of 200 carpets of size 12 feet by 7 feet 6 inches and that weigh 40 ounces per square yard, plus 60 carpets that are 11 feet 6 inches by 15 feet and that weigh 50 ounces per square yard.

Extending Classes and Inheritance

A very important part of object-oriented programming is that which allows you to create a new class based on a class that has already been defined. The class you use as the base for your new class can be either a class you yourself have defined, a standard class in Java, or a class defined by someone else—perhaps from a package supporting a specialized application area.

This chapter focuses on how you can reuse existing classes by creating new classes based on them, and explores the ramifications of using this facility, and the additional capabilities it provides. We will also delve into an important related topic, interfaces, and how you can use them.

In this chapter you will learn:

- How to reuse classes by defining a new class based on an existing class
- What class inheritance is
- What polymorphism is and how to define your classes to take advantage of it
- What an abstract method is
- What an abstract class is
- What an interface is and how you can define your own interfaces
- How to use interfaces in your classes
- How interfaces can help you implement polymorphic classes

Using Existing Classes

Let's start by understanding the jargon. Defining a new class based on an existing class is called **derivation**. The new class, or **derived class**, is referred to as a **direct sub-class** of the class from which it is derived. The original class is called a **base class** because it forms the base for the definition of the derived class. The original class is also referred to as a **super-class** of the derived class. Just to confuse things, a super-class can itself be a sub-class of another class, which will then be an indirect super-class of the lowest derived class. This is illustrated in the following diagram:

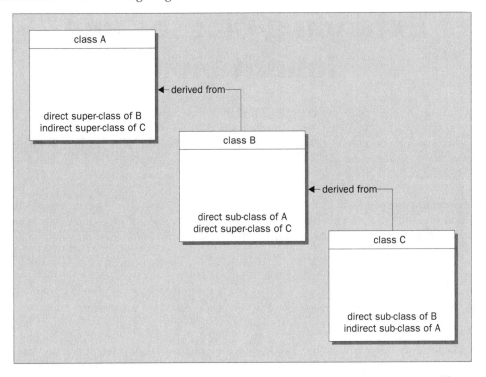

This shows just three classes in a hierarchy, but there can be as many as you like.

Let's consider a more concrete example. We could define a class **Dog** that could represent a dog of any kind. This might contain a data member identifying the name of a particular dog such as "Lassie" or "Pooch" and another data member identifying the breed, such as "Border Collie" or "Pyrenean Mountain Dog". From the **Dog** class, we could derive a **Spaniel** class that represented a dog which was a spaniel. The breed would be "Spaniel" for all instances of the class **Spaniel**, although in general the name for each spaniel would be different. The **Spaniel** class might have some data members that characterize other spaniel specifics.

A **Spaniel** object is clearly a specialized instance of a **Dog** object. This reflects real life. A spaniel is obviously a dog, but it has some unique characteristics of its own which distinguish it from dogs that are not spaniels.

When you derive a new class from a base class, the process is additive. Any members you add to the new class are in addition to those already defined in the base class. Your new class will contain both. For our **Spaniel** class derived from **Dog**, the data members to hold the name and the breed that are defined for the class **Dog** would automatically be in the class **Spaniel**. The inclusion of members of the base class in a derived class so that they are accessible in that derived class is called **class inheritance**.

> *However, bear in mind that not all members of the base class are necessarily accessible in the derived class. That depends on the member's access attributes, which we looked at in the last chapter.*

Let's be clear from the start what inheritance means. An inherited member of a derived class is a full member of that class. When you define a method in your derived class, you can refer to the inherited members of the class, if they're accessible, in just the same way as any member that you've declared in the derived class. We need to take a closer look at how inheritance works, and how the access attribute of a base class member affects its visibility in a derived class.

Class Inheritance

We need to consider two aspects of defining and using a derived class:

- Which members of the base class are inherited in the derived class
- What you get when you create an object of the derived class

Inheriting Data Members

The next diagram shows which access attributes permit a class member to be inherited in a sub-class. It shows what happens when the sub-class is defined in the same package as the base class, and when the sub-class is defined in a package different from that containing the base class.

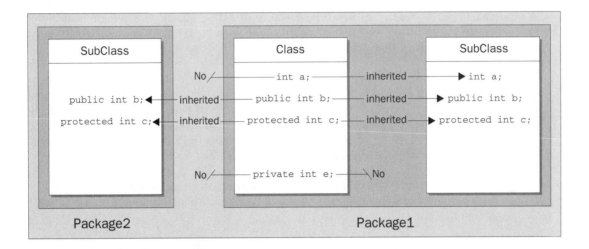

Note that to derive a class from outside the package containing the base class, the base class must be declared as `public`. If a class is not declared as `public` it cannot be reached directly from outside the package.

As you can see, a sub-class that you define in the same package as its base inherits everything except for **private** data members of the base. If you define a sub-class outside the package containing the base class, the **private** data members are not inherited, and neither are any data members in the base class that you have declared with the default access attribute. Members defined as **private** in the base class are never inherited under any circumstances.

The inheritance rules apply to class variables as well as instance variables—you recall that class variables are variables that you have declared as **static**. So for example, a variable that you declare as **private** and **static** in the base class is not inherited in a derived class, whereas a variable that you declare as **protected** and **static** will be inherited.

Inherited Methods

Ordinary methods in a base class, that is, methods that are not constructors, are inherited in a derived class in the same way as the data members of the base class. Those methods that you declare as **private** in a base class are not inherited, and those that you declare without an access attribute are only inherited if you define the derived class in the same package as the base class. The rest are all inherited.

Constructors are different. Constructors in the base class are never inherited, regardless of their attributes.

Objects of a Derived Class

We said at the beginning of the chapter that a derived class extends a base class. This is not just jargon—it really does do this. Inheritance is about what members of the base class are *accessible* in a derived class, not what members of the base class *exist* in a derived class object. An object of a sub-class will contain *all* the members of the original base class, plus any new members defined in the derived class:

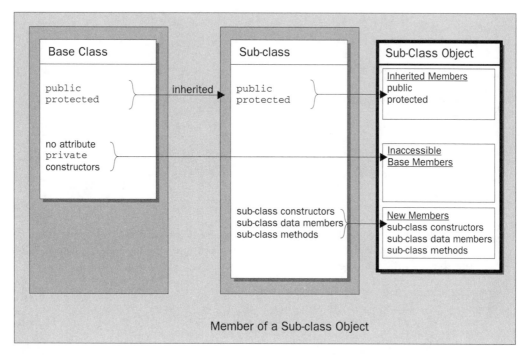

The base members are all there—you just can't access some of them in the methods that you define for the derived class. The fact that you can't access some of the base class members does not mean that they are just excess baggage—they are essential members of your derived class objects, necessary for the base class to continue functioning. The base class methods which are inherited in a derived class can access all the base class members, including those that are not inherited.

Though the base class constructors are not inherited in your derived class, you can still call them to initialize the base class members when necessary. More than that, if you don't call a base class constructor from your derived class constructor, the compiler will try to arrange to do it for you.

To understand this a bit better, let's take a look at how it works in practice.

Try It Out—Deriving a Class

1 Let's take a simple example. Suppose we have defined a class to represent an animal:

```java
public class Animal
{
  private String type;

  public Animal(String aType)
  {
    type = new String(aType);
  }

  public void show()
  {
    System.out.println("This is a " + type);
  }
}
```

2 We now want to create another class based on the class **Animal** to define dogs. We can do this immediately, without affecting the definition of the class **Animal**. We could write the definition of the class **Dog** as:

```java
public class Dog extends Animal
{
  private String name;      // Name of a Dog!
  private String breed;     // Dog breed

  public Dog(String aName)
  {
    super("Dog");           // Call the base constructor
    name = aName;           // Supplied name
    breed = "Unknown";      // Default breed value
  }

  public Dog(String aName, String aBreed)
  {
    super("Dog");           // Call the base constructor
    name = aName;           // Supplied name
    breed = aBreed;         // Supplied breed
  }
}
```

3 We can try out our class **Dog** with the following code:

```java
public class TestDerived
{
  public static void main(String[] args)
```

```
   {
     Dog aDog = new Dog("Fido", "Chihuahua"); // Create a dog
     Dog starDog = new Dog("Lassie");          // Create a Hollywood dog
     aDog.show();                              // Let's hear about it
     starDog.show();                           // and the star
   }
 }
```

The example produces the rather boring output:

```
This is a Dog
This is a Dog
```

How It Works

You use the keyword **extends** in the definition of a sub-class to identify the name of the super-class. The class **Dog** will only inherit the method **show()** from the class **Animal**, since the **private** data member and the constructor cannot be inherited. We have added two new instance variables in the derived class—**name**, to hold the name of the particular dog, and **breed**, to store the kind of dog.

Derived Class Constructors

The sub-class has two constructors, one that just accepts an argument for the name of a dog, and the other that accepts both a name and the breed of the **Dog** object. For a derived class object, we need to make sure that the **private** base class member, **type**, is properly initialized. The statement in the derived class constructor that does this is:

```
super("Dog");        // Call the base constructor
```

This calls the constructor that we defined in the class **Animal**. This will initialize the **private** member, **type**, to **"Dog"**. The super-class constructor is always called in this way in the sub-class, using the name **super** rather than the constructor name **Animal**. This is necessary because the constructor is not inherited, so you cannot call it directly from within the sub-class. The keyword **super** has other uses in a derived class, as we will see later in this chapter.

Calling the Base Class Constructor

You should always call an appropriate base class constructor from the constructors in your derived class, and it should always be the first statement in the body of the derived class constructor.

If the first statement in a derived class constructor is not a call to a base class constructor, the compiler will insert a call to the default constructor for the base class:

```
super();    // Call the default base constructor
```

Unfortunately, this can result in a compiler error, even though the offending statement has been inserted automatically. So how does this come about?

When you define your own constructor in a class, as is the case for our class, **Animal**, no default constructor is created by the compiler. It assumes you are taking care of all the details of object construction, including any requirement for a default constructor. If you have not defined your own default constructor in a base class—that is, a constructor that has no parameters—when the compiler inserts a call to the default constructor, you will get a message that the constructor is not there.

In the test code, we create two **Dog** objects, and then call the **show()** method for each. You could try commenting out the call to **super()** in the constructors to the derived class to see the effect of the compiler's efforts to call the default base class constructor.

We have called the inherited method **show()** successfully, but this only knows about the base class data members. At least we know that the **private** member, **type**, is being set up properly. What we really need though, is a version of **show()** for the derived class.

Try It Out—Overriding a Base Class Method

We can add the definition of a new version of **show()** to the definition of the derived class, **Dog**:

```
// Show a dog's details
public void show()
{
  System.out.println("It's " + name + " the " + breed);
}
```

With this change to the example, the output will now be:

```
It's Fido the Chihuahua
It's Lassie the Unknown
```

How It Works

This method **overrides** the base class method because it has the same signature. You will recall from the last chapter that the signature of a method is determined by its name and the parameter list. So, now when you call the method **show()** for a **Dog** object, this method will be called—not the base class method.

> Note that you are obliged to declare this method as `public`. When you override a base class method, you cannot change the access attributes of the new version of the method to be more stringent than that of the base class method that it overrides.

Of course, ideally we would like to output the member, **type**, of the base class, but we can't reference this in the derived class, because it is not inherited. However, we can still call the base class version of **show()**.

We can rewrite the derived class version of **show()** to call the base method:

```
// Show a dog's details
public void show()
{
  super.show();    // Call the base method
  System.out.println("It's " + name + " the " + breed);
}
```

Running the example again will produce the output:

```
This is a Dog
It's Fido the Chihuahua
This is a Dog
It's Lassie the Unknown
```

How It Works

The keyword **super** is used to identify the base class version of **show()** that is hidden by the derived class version. You use the same notation to refer to super-class data members that are hidden by derived class data members with the same name.

Choosing Base Class Access Attributes

You now know the options that are available to you in defining the access attributes for classes you expect to use to define sub-classes. You know what effect the attributes have on class inheritance, but how do you decide which you should use?

There are no hard and fast rules—what you choose will depend on what you want to do with your classes in the future, but there are some guidelines you should bear in mind. They follow from basic object-oriented principles:

▶ The methods that make up the external interface to a class should be declared as **public**. As long as there are no overriding methods defined in a derived class, **public** base class methods will be inherited and fully available as part of the external interface to the derived class. You should not normally make data members **public** unless they are constants intended for general use

▶ If you expect other people will use your classes as base classes, your classes will be more secure if you keep data members **private**, and provide **public** methods for accessing and manipulating them. In this way you control how a derived class object can affect the base class data members

▶ Making base class members **protected** allows them to be accessed from other classes in the same package, but prevents direct access from a class in another package. Base class members that are **protected** are inherited in a sub-class. You can use this option when you have a package of classes within which you want uninhibited access to the data members of any class, because they operate in a closely coupled way, for instance, but, in other packages, you want free access to be limited to sub-classes

⯈ Omitting an access attribute for a class member makes it directly available to other classes in the same package, while preventing it from being inherited in a sub-class that is not in the same package—so it is effectively **private** when viewed from another package. A minor disadvantage with the default access attribute is that it can be set by omission—something you can quite easily do unintentionally

Polymorphism

Class inheritance is not just about reusing classes that you have already defined as a basis for defining a new class. It also adds enormous flexibility to the way in which you can program your applications, with a mechanism called **polymorphism**.

What is polymorphism? The word *polymorphism* means the ability to assume several different forms or shapes. In programming terms it means the ability of a single variable to call different methods, depending on what the variable contains.

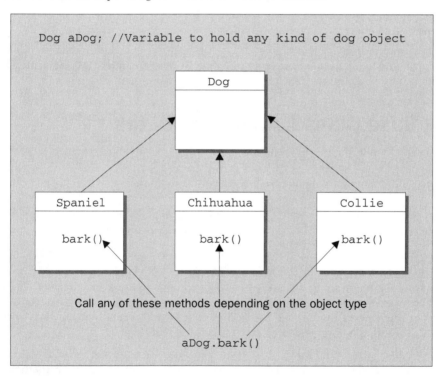

Polymorphism involves two things:

⯈ Firstly, it involves using a variable of a single type, typically a variable of a base class type, to store objects of any of a number of derived classes. An example of this might be might be using a variable of type **Dog** to store objects of type **Spaniel**, type **Chihuahua** or type **Collie**, where these are all classes derived from **Dog**

▶ Secondly, it involves the automatic use of the object stored in the base class variable to select a method from one of the derived classes, dependent on the object's class. The kind of object stored is not known until the program executes, so the choice of which class's method to execute is made dynamically, when the program is running. The variable of type **Dog** can do different things, depending on what kind of object (breed of dog) it contains

As we will see, this introduces a whole new level of capability in programming using objects.

Polymorphism is a direct consequence of being able to create a sub-class, and is one of the most powerful tools in object-oriented programming. More than that, polymorphism is fundamental to the idea of object-oriented programming. Normally, the method which is to be executed for a particular object is fixed by the compiler, so that it is always the same whenever you execute your program. This is often referred to as **static**, or **early**, **binding**.

When you have defined several sub-classes of a common base class, each containing a definition of a method with the same signature as a given base class method, polymorphism enables you to defer the decision about which of these methods is to be called for a class variable until runtime, when it will depend on the kind of object to which the variable is referring. This is sometimes referred to as **dynamic**, or **late**, **binding**, because the method to be executed is selected dynamically when you run your program. This means that a single variable can be used to call different methods depending on what type of object it references.

Using Polymorphism

A crucial feature of polymorphism is the ability to assign an object of a sub-class to a variable that you have declared as being of the base class type. If you declare the variable:

```
Animal theAnimal;     // Declare an animal variable
```

You can quite happily make this refer to an object of any of the sub-classes of the class **Animal**. For example, you could use it to reference an object of type **Dog**:

```
theAnimal = new Dog("Rover");
```

As you might expect, you could also initialize the variable **theAnimal** when you declare it:

```
Animal theAnimal = new Dog("Rover");
```

This **object casting** applies quite generally. You can make a variable of a base class point to an object of any class that you have derived, directly or indirectly, from the base. We can see what magic can be wrought with this by extending our previous example. We can add a new method to the class **Dog** which will output the sound a **Dog** makes, and we can add a couple of new sub-classes which will relate to some other kinds of animals.

Try It Out—Enhancing the Dog *Class*

1 First of all we will enhance the class **Dog**:

```
public class Dog extends Animal
{
   // Rest of the class as before...

   // A barking method
   public void sound()
   {
     System.out.println("Woof    Woof");
   }
}
```

2 We can also derive a class **Cat** from the class **Animal**:

```
public class Cat extends Animal
{
   private String name;      // Name of a cat
   private String breed;     // cat breed

   public Cat(String aName)
   {
     super("Cat");           // Call the base constructor
     name = aName;           // Supplied name
     breed = "Unknown";      // Default breed value
   }

   public Cat(String aName, String aBreed)
   {
     super("Cat");           // Call the base constructor
     name = aName;           // Supplied name
     breed = aBreed;         // Supplied breed
   }

   // Show a cat's details
   public void show()
   {
     super.show();           // Call the base method
     System.out.println("It's " + name + " the " + breed);
   }

   // A miaowing method
   public void sound()
   {
     System.out.println("Miiaooww");
   }
}
```

3 Just to make it a crowd, we can derive another class—of ducks:

```
public class Duck extends Animal
{
  private String name;      // Ducky name
  private String breed;     // Duck breed

  public Duck(String aName)
  {
    super("Duck");          // Call the base constructor
    name = aName;           // Supplied name
    breed = "Unknown";      // Default breed value
  }

  public Duck(String aName, String aBreed)
  {
    super("Duck");          // Call the base constructor
    name = aName;           // Supplied name
    breed = aBreed;         // Supplied breed
  }

  // Show a duck's details
  public void show()
  {
    super.show();           // Call the base method
    System.out.println("It's " + name + " the " + breed);
  }

  // A quacking method
  public void sound()
  {
    System.out.println("Quack quackquack");
  }
}
```

4 You can fill out the whole farmyard if you need the practice, but three kinds of animal will do to show you how polymorphism works. We need to make one change to the class **Animal**. To select a method **sound()** dynamically, it needs to be a member of the base class. We can add a content-free version of **sound()** to the class **Animal**:

```
class Animal
{
  // Rest of the class as before...

  // Dummy method to be implemented in the derived classes
  public void sound(){}
}
```

5 To give the classes a workout, we can create an array of type **Animal** and populate its elements with different sub-class objects. We can then select an object randomly from the array so that there is no possibility that the type of the object selected is known ahead of time:

```java
public class TryPolymorphism
{
  public static void main(String[] args)
  {
    // Create an array of three different animals
    Animal[] theAnimals = { new Dog("Rover", "Poodle"),
                            new Cat("Max", "Abyssinian"),
                            new Duck("Daffy","Aylesbury")};

    Animal petChoice;                          // Choice of pet

    // Make five random choices of pet
    for(int i = 0; i < 5; i++)
    {
      // Create a random index from 0 to theAnimals.length-1
      int index = (int)(theAnimals.length*Math.random() - 0.001);

      petChoice = theAnimals[index];        // Pick from the array

      System.out.println("\nYour choice:");
      petChoice.show();                      // Display the details
      petChoice.sound();                     // Get the pet's reaction
    }
  }
}
```

I get the output:

```
Your choice:
This is a Dog
It is a Poodle called Rover
Woof    Woof

Your choice:
This is a Dog
It is a Poodle called Rover
Woof    Woof

Your choice:
This is a Duck
It is a Aylesbury called Daffy
Quack quackquack

Your choice:
This is a Duck
It is a Aylesbury called Daffy
Quack quackquack
```

```
Your choice:
This is a Cat
It is a Abyssinian called Max
Miiaooww
```

The chances are that you will get a different set, and a different set again when you rerun the example. The example clearly shows that the methods are being selected at runtime, depending on which object happens to get stored in the variable **petChoice**.

How It Works

The array **theAnimals** contains a **Dog** object, a **Cat** object and a **Duck** object. We select objects randomly from this array in the **for** loop, and store the selection in **petChoice**. We can then call the **show()** and **sound()** methods using the object stored.

Note that the definition of the method **sound()** in the **Animal** class has no statements in the body, so it will do nothing if it is executed. We will see a little later in this chapter how we can avoid including the empty definition for the method.

Polymorphism is a fundamental part of object-oriented programming. We will be making extensive use of polymorphism in many of the examples we'll be developing later in the book, and you will find that you will often need to use it in your own applications and applets. This is not all there is to polymorphism in Java, however, and we will come back to it again later in this chapter.

Multiple Levels of Inheritance

As we indicated at the beginning of the chapter, there is nothing to prevent a derived class being used as a base class. For example, we could derive a class **Spaniel** from the class **Dog** without any problem:

Try It Out—A Spaniel Class

1 Start the **Spaniel** class off with this minimal code:

```
class Spaniel extends Dog
{
  public Spaniel(String aName)
  {
    super(aName, "Spaniel");
  }
}
```

2 To try this out, you can add a **Spaniel** object to the array **theAnimals** in the previous example, by changing the statement to:

```
Animal[] theAnimals = { new Dog("Rover", "Poodle"),
                        new Cat("Max", "Abyssinian"),
                        new Duck("Daffy","Aylesbury"),
                        new Spaniel("Fido")};
```

Try running the example again.

3 Finally add a **show()** method to the definition of the class **Spaniel**, and recompile and run the **TryPolymorphism** again:

```
class Spaniel extends Dog
{
  public Spaniel(String aName)
  {
    super(aName, "Spaniel");
  }

  public void show()
  {
    System.out.println("Spaniel show method called");
    super.show();                // Call the base (Dog) method, show()
  }
}
```

How It Works

The class **Spaniel** will inherit members from the class **Dog**, including the members of **Dog** that are inherited from the class **Animal**. The class **Dog** is a direct super-class, and the class **Animal** is an indirect super-class of the class **Spaniel**. The only additional member of **Spaniel** is the constructor. This just calls the **Dog** class constructor passing the value of **aName** and the **String** object **"Spaniel"** to it.

If you run the **TryPolymorphism** class after the second stage, you should get a choice of the **Spaniel** object from time to time. Thus the class **Spaniel** is also participating in the polymorphic selection of the methods **show()** and **sound()**, which in this case are inherited from the parent class, **Dog**.

In the final section, you define the method **show()** in the class **Spaniel**. This version of the method will be called if the object referenced by **petChoice** is of type **Spaniel**. When the **Spaniel** object is chosen, you will see that the **show()** method you have added is called, and this calls the same method in the class **Dog**, which in turn calls its base class **show()** method from the class **Animal**.

> *Note that you can continue to derive classes from derived classes to any depth you require.*

The Universal Super-Class

I must now reveal something I have been keeping from you. *All* the classes that you define are sub-classes by default—whether you like it or not. All your classes have a standard class, **Object**, as a base, so **Object** is a super-class of every class. You never need to specify the class **Object** as a base in the definition of your classes—it happens automatically.

There are some interesting consequences of having **Object** as a universal super-class. For one thing, a variable of type **Object** can hold an object of any class. This is useful when you want to write a method that needs to handle objects of unknown type. You can use a variable of type **Object** as a parameter to a method to receive an object, and then include code in the method that figures out what kind of object it actually is (we will see something of the tools that will enable you to do this a little later in this chapter).

Of course, your classes will inherit members from the class **Object**. These all happen to be methods, of which seven are **public**, and two are **protected**. The seven **public** methods are:

Method	Purpose
toString()	This method returns a **String** object that describes the current object. This will be the name of the class, followed by '**@**' and the hexadecimal representation for the object. This method is called automatically when you concatenate objects with **String** variables using **+**. You can over ride this method in your classes to return your own **String** object for your class.
getClass()	This method returns an object of type **Class** that identifies the class of the current object. We will see a little more about this later in this chapter.
equals()	This method compares the current object with the object referred to by an **Object** variable passed as an argument. It returns **true** only if both objects are one and the same (not just equal—they must be same object).
hashCode()	This method calculates a hash code value for an object and returns it as type **int**. Hash code values are used in classes defined in the package **java.util** for storing objects in hash tables. We will learn more about this in Chapter 9.
notify()	This is used to wake up a thread associated with the current object. We will discuss this in Chapter 10 when we look into how threads work.
notifyAll()	This is used to wake up all threads associated with the current object. We will discuss this in Chapter 10 when we look into what threads are, and how they work.
wait()	This method causes a thread to wait for a change in the current object. There are three overloaded versions of this method. We will discuss this method in Chapter 10.

The two **protected** methods your classes inherit from **Object** are:

Method	Purpose
clone()	This will create an object that is a copy of the current object regardless of type. This can be of any type as an **Object** variable can refer to an object of any class. Note that this does not always do precisely what you want, as we will see later in this section.
finalize()	This is the method that is called when an object is destroyed. As you have seen in the last chapter, you can override this to add your own clean-up code. You must, however, make a call to **super.finalize()** at the end of your implementation, so any finalization in any super-classes occurs unaffected

Implementing the toString() Method

You can see what the **toString()** method, inherited from the class **Object**, will output for an object of one of your classes by adding a couple of statements to the end of **main()** in the previous example:

```
Spaniel aSpaniel = new Spaniel("Mitzi");
System.out.println("\n" + aSpaniel);
```

Since the argument to the method, **println()**, must be a **String** object, the compiler calls the **toString()** method for the object **aSpaniel**, which at the moment is the **toString()** method inherited from the class **Object**. This will produce the output:

```
Spaniel@d40bf0
```

If you don't like this, it is very easy to implement your own **toString()** method for a class, but you need to keep in mind how you are going to use it. As an example, you could add the following implementation to the **Spaniel** class we defined earlier:

```
public String toString()
{
  return "This is a Spaniel " + super.toString();
}
```

Note that you must specify the method as **public**, since the method is **public** in the class **Object**. If you forget to put the access attribute, the compiler will flag it as an error. This method just calls the **toString()** method in the base class, **Dog**, by using the **super** keyword, and concatenates its return value with the string **"This is a Spaniel "**.

We can code the **toString()** method in the class **Dog** as:

```
public String toString()
{
  return "Dog called " + name;
}
```

This just returns the string **"Dog called "** with the value of **name** added to the end of it. You can now rerun the example once more, and the two extra statements will produce the output:

```
This is a Spaniel Dog called Mitzi
```

The compiler now calls the **toString()** method for the object **aSpaniel** that we defined in the class. This then calls the **toString()** method defined in the base class, **Dog**. The method defined in the class **Object** is no longer involved in the process since it has been overridden by the versions we have supplied.

Determining the Type of an Object

The **getClass()** method that all your classes inherit from **Object** will return an object of type **Class** that identifies the class of an object. If you have a variable, **pet**, of type **Animal** that might refer to an object of type **Dog**, **Cat**, **Duck**, or even **Spaniel**, then to figure out what sort of thing it really is, you could write the following statements:

```
Class objectType = pet.getClass();              // Get the class type
System.out.println(objectType.getName());       // Output the class name
```

The method **getName()** is a member of the class **Class** which returns the fully qualified name of the class as a **String** object, so the second statement will output the name of the class for the **pet** object. If **pet** referred to a **Duck** object, this would output:

```
Duck
```

This is the fully qualified name in this case, as the class is in the default package which has no name. For a class defined in a named package, the class name would be prefixed with the package name. If you just wanted to output the class identity, you need not keep the **Class** object. You can just combine both statements into one:

```
System.out.println(pet.getClass().getName());   // Output the class name
```

Members of the Class Class

When your program is executing, instances of the class **Class** exist representing each of the classes and interfaces in your program. The primary use of the class **Class** is in representing the class of an object, and this we can obtain by calling the **getClass()** method for the object, as we have just discussed. However, you also get a number of other useful methods with an object of class **Class**:

Method	Purpose
`forName()`	You pass the name of a class as a **String** object to this method, and it returns a **Class** object for the class with the name you have supplied. If no class of the type you specify exists, a **ClassNotFoundException** exception will be thrown.
`newInstance()`	This method will call the default constructor for the class represented by the current **Class** object, and will return the object created as type **Object**. Unless you want to store the result in a variable of type **Object**, you must cast the object to the appropriate type. When things don't work as they should, this method can throw two exceptions—**InstantiationException** or **IllegalAccessException**. If you use this method and don't provide for handling the exceptions, your program will not compile. We'll learn how to deal with this in the next chapter.

`getSuperclass()`	This method returns a **Class** object for the super-class of the class for the current **Class** object. For example, for the **Class** object **objectType** for the variable **pet** we just defined, this would return a **Class** object for the class **Animal**. You could output the name of the super-class with the statement:
	
	``java
	System.out.println(pet.getClass()
	                  .getSuperclass().getName());
	``
	
	Where your class is not a derived class, the method will return a **Class** object for the class **Object.**

`isInterface()`	This method returns **true** if the current object represents an interface. We will discuss interfaces a little later in this chapter.
`getInterface()`	This method will return an array of **Class** objects that represent the interfaces implemented by the class.
`toString()`	This method returns a **String** object representing the current **Class** object. For example, for the **Class** object, **objectType**, corresponding to the **pet** variable we created, this would output: `class Duck`

Copying Objects

As you saw in the summary at the beginning of this section, the **protected** method, **clone()**, that is inherited from the class **Object**, will create a new object that is a copy of the current object. It does this by creating a new object of the same type as the current object, and setting each of the variables in the new object to the same value as the corresponding variables in the current object.

However, when the variables in the original object refer to class objects, those objects are not automatically duplicated when the clone is created. This can result in confusion, as it is not typically what you want to happen, since both the old and the new class objects can now be modifying a single shared object, and not recognizing that this is occurring. In order to get round this, you either need to construct a copy, as we saw in the last chapter, or explicitly clone the objects referred to from within the class.

We can see this more clearly if we take a simple specific instance, just to illustrate the point.

Try It Out—Cloning Dogs

1 Let's suppose we define a class **FlexiDog** that has a method that allows the name to be changed:

```java
public class FlexiDog extends Animal implements Cloneable
{
  private String name;                      // Name of a Dog!
  private String breed;                     // Dog breed

  // Constructor
  public FlexiDog(String aName, String aBreed)
  {
    super("FlexiDog");
    name = aName;                           // Supplied name
    breed = aBreed;                         // Supplied breed
   }

  // Change the dog's name
  public void setName(String aName)
  {
    name = aName;                           // Change to the new name
  }

  // Get the dog's name
  public String getName()
  {
    return name;
  }

  // Show a dog's details
  public void show()
  {
    super.show();                           // Call the base method
    System.out.println("It's " + name + " the " + breed);
  }
 }
```

By implementing the `Cloneable` interface we are indicating we are happy to clone objects of this class. Make sure that you copy the `Animal` class to the same directory as `FlexiDog`.

We now define a class `PetDog` that contains a `FlexiDog` object as a member, and that is also cloneable.

*In practice, this class wouldn't just wrap up the **FlexiDog** functionality, but would contain such useful information as favorite food, and the pet dog's abode. But we keep it simple to show off how to clone class objects within a class.*

```java
public class PetDog implements Cloneable
{
  FlexiDog thePet;                                    // The pet dog

  // Constructor
  public PetDog(String name, String breed)
  {
    thePet = new FlexiDog(name, breed);              // Initialize thePet
  }

  // Change the name of the pet
  public void setName(String name)
  {
    thePet.setName(name);
  }

  // Get the name of the pet dog
  public String getName()
  {
    return thePet.getName();
  }

  // Override inherited clone() to make it public
  public Object clone() throws CloneNotSupportedException
  {
    return super.clone();
  }
}
```

To make it possible to clone a `PetDog` object, we override the inherited `clone()` method with a `public` version that just calls the inherited version. Note that the inherited method 'throws' the `CloneNotSupportedException` so we must declare the method as shown—otherwise it won't compile. We will be looking into what exceptions are in the next chapter.

3 We can now create a `PetDog` object with the statement:

```java
PetDog myPet = new PetDog("Fang", "Chihuahua");
```

4 Of course, after seeing my pet, you want one just like it, so we can clone him:

```
PetDog yourPet = (PetDog)myPet.clone();
```

Now we have individual **PetDog** objects, that regrettably contain references to the same **FlexiDog** object. The **clone()** method will create the new **PetDog** object, **yourPet**, and copy the reference to the **FlexiDog** object from the **thePet** data member in **myPet** to the member with the same name in **yourPet**.

5 If you decide that you prefer the name **"Gnasher"** for **yourPet**, we can change the name of your pet with the statement:

```
yourPet.setName("Gnasher");
```

Unfortunately my pet will also have the name **"Gnasher"** because under the covers we both share a common **FlexiDog**.

6 If you want to demonstrate this, you can put all the classes together in an example, with the following class:

```
// Test cloning
public class ClonePets
{
  public static void main(String[] args)
  {
    try
    {
      PetDog myPet = new PetDog("Fang", "Chihuahua");
      System.out.println("myPet: " + myPet.getName());
      PetDog yourPet = (PetDog)myPet.clone();
      yourPet.setName("Gnasher");
      System.out.println("myPet: " + myPet.getName());
    }
    catch(CloneNotSupportedException e)
    {
      System.out.println(e);
    }
  }
}
```

> *Don't worry about the try and catch blocks—these are necessary to deal with the exception that we mentioned earlier. You will learn all about exceptions in Chapter 7.*

If you run it the example will output the name for **myPet** before and after the name for **yourPet** has been changed.

```
myPet: Fang
myPet: Gnasher
```

Unless you really want to share objects between the variables in two separate objects, it is necessary to clone the object. To do this you can add a constructor to your class to create a new class object from an existing object that also copies any objects referred to by members of the original object. You saw how to do this in the previous chapter. Alternatively, you can implement your own public version of `clone()` to override the inherited version that explicitly clones the various objects. Let's see how we could avoid **yourPet** interfering with **myPet**:

Try it Out—Cloning Dogs II

1 First we need to make sure that the object referenced by the variable **thePet**, of type **FlexiDog**, in a **PetDog** object, is cloned within the **PetDog** class's `clone()` method:

```
public Object clone() throws CloneNotSupportedException
{
  PetDog pd;

  pd = (PetDog)super.clone();
  pd.thePet = (FlexiDog)thePet.clone();
  return pd;
}
```

2 Now we need to add the **FlexiDog.clone()** method we've just called:

```
public Object clone() throws CloneNotSupportedException
{
  return super.clone();
}
```

Now when you run the example, you'll get the output:

```
myPet: Fang
myPet: Fang
```

How It Works

We have added a `clone()` method to the **FlexiDog** class which is identical to the one we originally used in **PetDog**. The 'improved' `clone()` method in the **PetDog** class just calls the **FlexiDog.clone()** method to get a copy of the object referenced by **thePet** in the original object—so now we have two **FlexiDog** objects, the original and one we can use as the new pet. The **PetDog.clone()** method casts the reference returned by **FlexiDog.clone()** from type **Object** to type **FlexiDog**. This reference is then stored in **thePet** variable in the new **PetDog** class object.

If you use the inherited `clone()` method in your class, you must do what we did in the example—declare that your class implements the **Cloneable** interface, and implement a public version that at least calls the base class version. You must also prepare to catch any **CloneNotSupportedException**s that may be thrown. We will look into interfaces in more detail later in this chapter.

Casting Objects

You can cast an object to another class type, but only if the object type and the class type you are casting to are in the same hierarchy of derived classes. For example, earlier in this chapter we defined the classes **Animal**, **Dog**, **Spaniel**, **Cat** and **Duck**, and these classes are related in the hierarchy shown below:

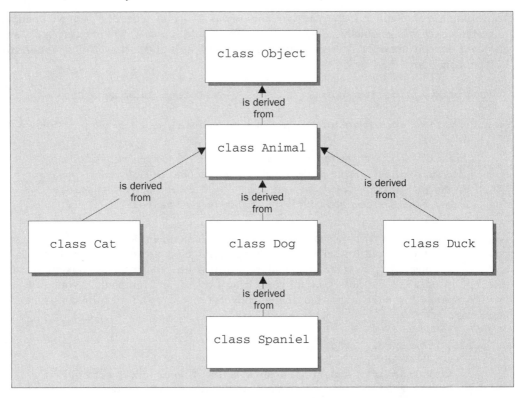

You can cast an object of a class upwards through its direct and indirect super-classes. For example, you could cast an object of type **Spaniel** directly to type **Dog**, type **Animal** or type **Object**. You could write:

```
Spaniel aPet = new Spaniel("Fang");
Animal theAnimal = (Animal)aPet;    // Cast the Spaniel to Animal
```

When you are assigning an object to a variable of a super-class, you do not have to include the cast. You could write the assignment as:

```
Animal theAnimal = aPet;            // Cast the Spaniel to Animal
```

and it would work just as well.

When you cast an object to a super-class, Java retains full knowledge of the actual class to which the object belongs. If this were not the case, polymorphism would not be possible. Since information about the original type of an object is retained, you can cast down a hierarchy as well, but you must always explicitly write the cast, and the object must be a legitimate instance of the class you are casting to—that is, the class you are casting to must be the original class of the object, or must be a super-class of the object.

For example, you could cast the variable **theAnimal** above to type **Dog** or type **Spaniel**, since the object was originally a **Spaniel**, but you could not cast it to **Cat** or **Duck**, since an object of type **Spaniel** does not have **Cat** or **Duck** as a super-class. To cast **theAnimal** to type **Dog**, you would write:

```
Dog aDog = (Dog)theAnimal;          // Cast from Animal to Dog
```

Now the variable **aDog** refers to an object of type **Spaniel**, that also happens to be a **Dog**.

> Note that you can only use the variable **aDog** to call the polymorphic methods from the class **Spaniel** that override methods that exist in **Dog**. You can't call methods that are not defined in the class **Dog**. If you want to call a method that is in the class **Spaniel** and not in the class **Dog**, you must first cast **aDog** to type **Spaniel**.

Although you cannot cast between unrelated objects, from **Spaniel** to **Duck** for instance, you can always achieve a conversion by writing a suitable constructor where it makes sense to do so. You just write a constructor in the class to which you want to convert, and make it accept an object of the class you are converting from as an argument. If you really thought **Spaniel** to **Duck** was a reasonable conversion, you could add the constructor to the **Duck** class:

```
public Duck(Spaniel aSpaniel)
{
  // Back legs off, and staple on a beak of your choice...
  super("Duck");             // Call the base constructor
  name = aSpaniel.getName();
  breed = "Barking Coot";  // Set the duck breed for a converted Spaniel
}
```

This assumes you have added a method, **getName()**, in the class **Dog** which will be inherited in the class **Spaniel**, and which returns the value of **name** for an object. This constructor accepts a **Spaniel** and turns out a **Duck**.

When to Cast Objects

You will need to cast objects in both directions through a class hierarchy. For example, whenever you execute methods polymorphically, you will be storing objects in a variable of a super-class type, and calling methods in a sub-class of the super-class. This generally will involve casting the sub-class objects up through the hierarchy to the super-class. Another reason you might want to cast up through a hierarchy is to pass an object of several possible subclasses to a method. You could pass a **Dog**, **Duck** or **Cat** to a method as type

Animal, for instance. Casting upwards through a class hierarchy is automatic when you store an object of a sub-class in a variable of a super-class type—you don't need to write an explicit cast.

The reason you might want to cast down through a class hierarchy is to execute a method unique to a particular class. If the **Duck** class has a method **layEgg()** for example, you can't call this using a variable of type **Animal**, even though it references a **Duck** object. Casting downwards through a class hierarchy always requires an explicit cast.

Try It Out—Laying an Egg

1 We'll amend the **Duck** class and use it along with the **Animal** class in an example. Add **layEgg()** to the **Duck** class as:

```
public Duck extends Animal
{
  public void layEgg()
  {
    System.out.println("Egg laid");
  }

  // Rest of the class as before...
}
```

2 If you now try to use this with the code:

```
public class LayEggs
{
  public static void main(String[] args)
  {
    Duck aDuck = new Duck("Donald", "Eider");
    Animal aPet = aDuck;                    // Cast the Duck to Animal
    aPet.layEgg();                          // This won't compile!
  }
}
```

you will get a compiler message to the effect that **layEgg()** is not found in the class **Animal**.

3 Since you know this object is really a **Duck**, you can make it work by writing the call to **layEgg()** in the code above as:

```
    ((Duck)aPet).layEgg();                 // This works fine
```

The object pointed to by **aPet** is first cast to type **Duck**, then the result of the cast is used to call the method **layEgg()**. Of course, if the object were not of type **Duck**, the cast would cause an exception to be thrown.

> *In general, you should avoid casting objects explicitly as much as possible, since it increases the potential for an invalid cast and therefore can make your programs unreliable. Most of the time you should find that if you design your classes carefully, you can avoid the need for casting.*

Using instanceof

There are circumstances when you may not know what sort of object you are dealing with. This can arise if an object is passed to a method as a variable of type **Object** for example, and you then need to cast it to a sub-class. If you try to make an illegal cast, an exception will be thrown and your program will end. One way to obviate this situation is to test that the object is of the type you expect before you make the cast using the operator **instanceof**. For example, suppose you have a variable, **pet**, of type **Animal**, and you want to cast it to type **Duck**. You could code this as:

```
Duck aDuck;                          // Define a duck

if(pet instanceof Duck)
   aDuck = (Duck)pet;                // It is a duck so the cast is OK
```

If **pet** does not refer to a **Duck** object, an attempt to cast the object referenced by **pet** to **Duck** would cause an exception to be thrown. This code fragment will only execute the cast if **pet** does refer to a **Duck** object.

Designing Classes

A basic problem in object-oriented programming is deciding how the classes in your program should interrelate. You can create a hierarchy of classes by deriving classes from a super-class that you have defined, adding methods and data members to specialize the sub-classes. You can also define a set of classes which are not hierarchical, but which have data members that are themselves class objects. And of course, you can have class hierarchies which contain data members that are class objects. Quite often you will have a choice between defining your classes as a hierarchy, or defining classes which have members that are class objects. Which is the best approach to take?

Like all questions of this kind, there are no clear-cut answers. If object-oriented programming was a process that we could specify by a fixed set of rules, we could get the computer to do it. There are some guidelines though, and some contexts in which the answer may be more obvious.

The need to use polymorphism is a primary reason for using sub-classes. This is the essence of object-oriented programming. Having a range of related objects that can be treated equivalently can greatly simplify your programs. You have seen how having various kinds of animals specified by classes derived from a common base class **Animal** allows us to treat the operations on different types of animal as though they are the same, and how we can get different results depending on what kind of animal is being dealt with—all automatically.

Derivation versus Class Membership

Many situations involve you in making judgments about the design of your classes, and the way to go may well boil down to a question of personal preference. Let's try to see how the options look in practice by considering a simple example. Suppose we want to define a class **PolyLine** to represent lines consisting of one or more connected segments, as illustrated in the diagram.

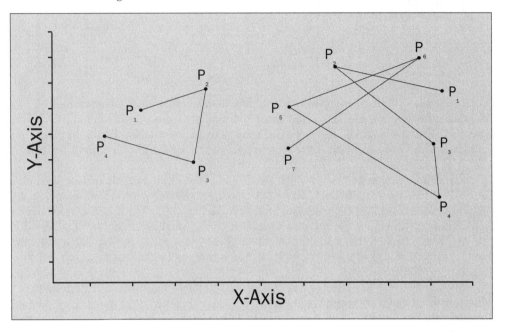

This shows two polylines, one defined by four points, the other defined by seven points.

Clearly it will be helpful if we represent points as objects of a class **Point**. Points are well-defined objects that will occur in the context of all kinds of geometric entities. We have seen a class for points earlier that we put in the package **Geometry**. Rather than repeat the whole thing, we will define the bare bones we need in this context:

```
public class Point
{
   // Coordinates of the point
   protected double x;
   protected double y;

   // Create a point from its coordinates
   public Point(double xVal, double yVal)
   {
      x = xVal;
      y = yVal;
   }
```

```
    // Create a point from another point
    public Point(Point point)
    {
      x = point.x;
      y = point.y;
    }

    // Convert a point to a string
    public String toString()
    {
      return x + "," + y;
    }
  }
```

Both data members will be inherited in any sub-class because they are specified as **protected** and they are also insulated from interference from outside the class's package. The **toString()** method will allow **Point** objects to be concatenated to a **String** objects for automatic conversion—in an argument passed to the **println()** method, for example.

The next question you might ask is, "Should I derive the class **PolyLine** from the class **Point**?". This has a fairly obvious answer. A polyline is clearly not a kind of point, so it is not logical to derive the class **PolyLine** from the **Point** class. This is an elementary demonstration of what is often referred to as the **'is a'** test. If you can say that one kind of object 'is a' specialized form of another kind of object, you may well have a good case for a derived class (but not always—there may be other reasons not to!). If not, you don't.

The complement to the 'is a' test is the **'has a'** test. If one object 'has a' component that is an object of another class, you have a case for a class member. A **House** object 'has a' door, so a **Door** variable (or class if you preferred) is likely to be a member of the class **House**. Our **PolyLine** class will contain several points, which looks promising, but we should look a little more closely at how we might store them, as we do have some options.

Designing the PolyLine Class

With the knowledge we have of Java, an array of **Point** objects looks like a good candidate to be a member of the class. It has some disadvantages though. A common requirement with polylines is to be able to add a segment or two to an existing object. With an array storing the points, we will need to create a new array each time we add a segment, then copy all the points from the old array to the new one. This could be time consuming if we have a **PolyLine** object with a lot of segments.

We have another option. We could create a **linked list** of points. A linked list of objects is an arrangement where each object in the list has a reference to the next object. As long as you have a variable containing the first **Point** object, you can access all the points in the list, as shown in the diagram:

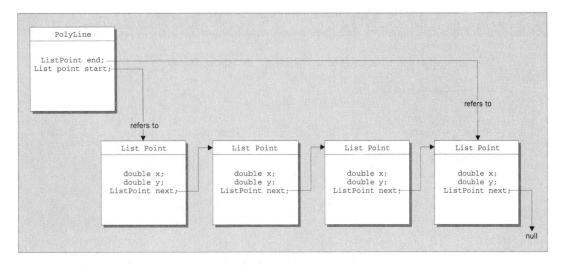

This illustrates the basic structure of a linked list of points. The points are stored as **ListPoint** objects.

You have three approaches you could take to define the **ListPoint** class, and there are arguments in favor of all three.

▶ You could define the **ListPoint** class with the members shown in the diagram, with the x and y coordinates stored explicitly. The main argument against this would be that we have already encapsulated the properties of a point in the **Point** class, so why not use that

▶ You could regard a **ListPoint** object as something that contains a **Point** object, plus a member that refers to the next **ListPoint** object in the list. This is not an unreasonable approach, it is easy to implement and not inconsistent with an intuitive idea of a **ListPoint**

▶ You could view a **ListPoint** object as a specialized kind of **Point**

The best option looks like the second approach to defining the **ListPoint** class. We will implement the **ListPoint** class with a data member of type **Point**, which defines a basic point with its coordinates. A **ListPoint** object will have an extra data member, **next**, which will be a **ListPoint** variable. For each object in the list, bar the last, **next** will contain a reference to the next object in the list. For the last object in the list, the variable **next** will be **null**.

We can define the **ListPoint** class using the class **Point** with the code:

```java
public class ListPoint
{
  ListPoint next;                    // Refers to next point in the list
  Point point;                       // The point for this list point

  // Constructor to create an object from coordinates
  public ListPoint(double x, double y)
  {
    point = new Point(x, y);         // Call Point constructor
    next = null;                     // Set next as end point
  }

  // Constructor to create an object from a Point object
  public ListPoint(Point point)
  {
    this.point = new Point(point);   // Call Point constructor
    next = null;                     // Set next as end point
  }

  // Set the pointer to the next ListPoint
  public void setNext(ListPoint next)
  {
    this.next = next;                // Store the next ListPoint
  }

  // Get the next point in the list
  public ListPoint getNext()
  {
    return next;                     // Return the next ListPoint
  }

  // Return class name & coordinates
  public String toString()
  {
    return "ListPoint " + point;
  }
}
```

How It Works

We have two ways to create **ListPoint** objects, using a pair of coordinates and using an existing **Point** object. In each case, the constructor uses the appropriate **Point** class constructor to initialize the data member, **point**. The data member, **next**, should contain a reference to the next **ListPoint** in the list, and since that is not defined here, we set next to **null**.

The `setNext()` method will enable the next data member to be set for the existing last point in the list, when a new last point is added. A reference to the new `ListPoint` object will be passed as an argument to the method. The `getNext()` method enables the next point in the list to be determined, so this method is the means by which we can iterate through the entire list.

By implementing the `toString()` method for the class, we enable the automatic creation of a `String` representation for a `ListPoint` object when required. Concatenating the object, `point`, to the string will automatically invoke the `toString()` method for `point`.

FYI If you were to put this class in a package along with the PolyLine class, you would probably want to omit the public specification for the ListPoint class, to prevent unnecessary access from outside the package, while providing public access to the PolyLine class.

Try It Out—The *PolyLine* Class

1 We can define the `PolyLine` class as:

```
public class PolyLine
{
  private ListPoint start;        // First ListPoint in the list
  private ListPoint end;          // Last ListPoint in the list

  // Construct a polyline from an array of points
  public PolyLine(Point[] points)
  {
    // Create a one point list
    start = new ListPoint(points[0]);   // 1st point is the start
    end = start;                        // as well as the end

    // Now add the other points
    for(int i = 1; i < points.length; i++)
      addPoint(points[i]);
  }

  // Add a Point object to the list
  public void addPoint(Point point)
  {
    ListPoint newEnd = new ListPoint(point);  // Create a new ListPoint
    end.setNext(newEnd);       // Set next variable for old end as new end
    end = newEnd;              // Store new point as end
  }

  // Output the polyline
  public void show()
  {
    System.out.println("Polyline points are:");
```

```
      ListPoint nextPoint = start;          // Set the 1st point as start
      while(nextPoint != null)
      {
        System.out.println(nextPoint);       // Output the current point
        nextPoint = nextPoint.getNext();     // Make the next point current
      }
    }
  }
```

2 You might want to be able to add a point to the list by specifying a coordinate pair.
You could overload the **addPoint()** method to do this:

```
// Add a point to the list
public void addPoint(double x, double y)
{
  ListPoint newEnd = new ListPoint(x, y);   // Create a new ListPoint
  end.setNext(newEnd);     // Set next variable for old end as new end
  end = newEnd;            // Store new point as end
}
```

3 You might also want to create a **PolyLine** object from an array of coordinates. The
constructor to do this would be:

```
// Construct a polyline from an array of coordinate
public PolyLine(double[][] coords)
{
  // Create a one point list
  start = new ListPoint(coords[0][0], coords[0][1]);// 1st pt is start
  end = start;                                       // as well as end

  // Now add the other points
  for(int i = 1; i < coords.length ; i++)
    addPoint(coords[i][0], coords[i][1]);
}
```

How It Works

The **PolyLine** class has the data members **start** and **end** that we saw in the diagram.
These will reference the first and last points of the list. The constructor accepts an array of
Point objects and starts the process of assembling the object by creating a list containing
one **ListPoint** object produced from the first element in the array. It then uses the
addPoint() method to add all the remaining points in the array to the list.

Adding a point to the list is deceptively simple. All the **addPoint()** method does is create
a **ListPoint** object from the **Point** object passed as an argument, sets the **next** member of
the old end point in the list to refer to the new point, and finally stores the new end point
in the member **end**.

The method **show()** will output the **PolyLine** object as a list of point coordinates. The
compiler will arrange to use the **toString()** method that we defined for **ListPoint** objects
to generate the argument to the **println()** method. Note how the **next** member of the

`ListPoint` objects controls the loop that runs through the list. When the last `ListPoint` object is reached, the **next** member will be returned as **null**, and the **while** loop will end.

Try It Out—Using `PolyLine` Objects

We can create a simple example to illustrate how to use the `PolyLine` class:

```java
public class TryPolyLine
{
  public static void main(String[] args)
  {
    // Create an array of coordinate pairs
    double[][] coords = { {1., 1.}, {1., 2.}, { 2., 3.},
                          {-3., 5.}, {-5., 1.}, {0., 0.} };

    // Create a polyline from the coordinates and display it
    PolyLine polygon = new PolyLine(coords);
    polygon.show();

    // Add a point and display the polyline again
    polygon.addPoint(10., 10.);
    polygon.show();

    // Create Point objects from the coordinate array
    Point[] points = new Point[coords.length];
    for(int i = 0; i < points.length; i++)
      points[i] = new Point(coords[i][0],coords[i][1]);

    // Use the points to create a new polyline and display it
    PolyLine newPoly = new PolyLine(points);
    newPoly.show();
  }
}
```

Remember that all three classes, **Point**, **ListPoint**, and **PolyLine** need to be together in the same directory as this class. If you have keyed everything in correctly, the program will output three **PolyLine** objects. The first and the third will be the same, with the coordinates from the **coords** array. The second will have the extra point, (**10**, **10**), at the end.

Generalizing the Linked List

The implementation of the polyline example works well enough, but the code is specific to the problem—we couldn't use the linked list we have implemented to store anything else. But linked lists are not just for storing points. You could use a linked list to store all kinds of objects, dogs, shapes, fruit or whatever you like. You might even want to have a linked list containing a mixture of things—an inventory of the items in a house for example. Can we implement a linked list so that we could use it as a general purpose storage facility? You bet we can.

Let's put together a general purpose linked list, and then use it to store polylines as before. Put this in a new directory as we will implement it as a whole new example.

Try It Out—Defining a List Item

The key to implementing a general purpose linked list is the **Object** class that we discussed earlier in this chapter. Because the **Object** class is a super-class of every class, a variable of type **Object** can be used to store any kind of object. We could re-implement the **ListPoint** class in the form of a **ListItem** class:

```java
public class ListItem
{
  ListItem next;              // Refers to next item in the list
  Object item;                // The item for this ListItem

  // Constructor
  public ListItem(Object item)
  {
    this.item = item;         // Store the item
    next = null;              // Set next as end point
  }

  // Set the pointer to the next ListItem
  public void setNext(ListItem next)
  {
    this.next = next;         // Store reference to the next item
  }

  // Get the next item in the list
  public ListItem getNext()
  {
    return next;
  }

  // Get the object for this item
  public Object getObject()
  {
    return item;
  }

  // Return class name & object
  public String toString()
  {
    return "ListItem " + item;
  }
}
```

How It Works

It's quite similar to the **ListPoint** class. We only need one constructor that accepts an object of type **Object** as an argument. The **toString()** method assumes that the object referenced by item implements a **toString()** method. We won't use the **toString()** method when we come to use the general linked list we are implementing, but it is a good idea to implement the **toString()** method for your classes anyway. If you do, class objects can always be output using the **println()** method which is very handy for debugging.

We have an new method, **getObject()**, to obtain the object stored as part of the list item. We will use this in the class that represents the linked list to provide a means to iterate through the objects in the list.

We can now use objects of this class in a definition of a class that will represent a linked list.

Try It Out—Defining a Linked List

This will be similar to the **PolyLine** class, but simpler and more general:

```
public class LinkedList
{
  private ListItem start;              // First ListIem in the list
  private ListItem end;                // Last ListIem in the list
  private ListItem current;            // The current item for iterating

  // Constructor to create a list containing one object
  public LinkedList(Object item)
  {
    start = new ListItem(item);        // item is the start
    end = start;                       // as well as the end
  }

  // Construct a linked list from an array of objects
  public LinkedList(Object[] items)
  {
    // Create a one item list
    start = new ListItem(items[0]);    // 1st item is the start
    end = start;                       // as well as the end

    // Now add the other items
    for(int i = 1; i < items.length; i++)
      addItem(items[i]);
  }

  // Add an item object to the list
  public void addItem(Object item)
  {
    ListItem newEnd = new ListItem(item); // Create a new ListItem
    end.setNext(newEnd);               // Set next variable for old end as new end
    end = newEnd;                      // Store new item as end
  }
```

```
    // Get the first object in the list
    public Object getFirst()
    {
      current = start;
      return start.getObject();
    }

    // Get the next object in the list
    public Object getNext()
    {
      current = current.getNext();      // Get the reference to the next item
      return current == null ? null : current.getObject();
    }
  }
```

How It Works

This is essentially the same organization as the **PolyLine** class but will create a linked list containing any object types. The class has data members to track the first and last items in the list, plus the member, **current**, which will be used to iterate through the list. We have two class constructors, one to create a list with a single object that can be added to via the **addItem()** method, and another to create a list from an array of objects. This latter list can also be added to of course.

The **addItem()** method works as the **addPoint()** method did in the **PolyLine** class. It creates a new **ListItem** object, and updates the next member of the previous last item to refer to the new one.

The **getFirst()** and **getNext()** methods are intended to be used in combination to access all the objects stored in the list. The **getFirst()** method returns the object stored in the first **ListItem** object in the list, and sets the **current** data member to refer to the first **ListItem** object. After calling the **getFirst()** method, successive calls to the **getNext()** method will return subsequent objects stored in the list. The method updates **current** to refer to the next **ListItem** object, each time it is called. When the end of the list is reached, **getNext()** returns **null**.

We can now define the **PolyLine** class so that it uses a **LinkedList** object.

Try It Out—Using the General Linked List

All we need to do is to put a **LinkedList** variable as a class member that we initialize in the class constructors, and implement all the other methods we had in the previous version of the class to used the **LinkedList** object:

```
public class PolyLine
{
  LinkedList polyline;        // The linked list of points
```

```java
    // Construct a polyline from an array of coordinate pairs
    public PolyLine(double[][] coords)
    {
      Point[] points = new Point[coords.length];  // Array to hold points

      // Create points from the coordinates
      for(int i = 0; i < coords.length ; i++)
        points[i] = new Point(coords[i][0], coords[i][1]);

      // Create the polyline from the array of points
      polyline = new LinkedList(points);
    }

    // Construct a polyline from an array of points
    public PolyLine(Point[] points)
    {
      polyline = new LinkedList(points);          // Create the polyline
    }

    // Add a Point object to the list
    public void addPoint(Point point)
    {
      polyline.addItem(point);                          // Add the point to the list
    }

    // Add a point from a coordinate pair to the list
    public void addPoint(double x, double y)
    {
      polyline.addItem(new Point(x, y));        // Add the point to the list
    }

    // Output the polyline
    public void show()
    {
      System.out.println("Polyline points are:");

      // Set the 1st point as start
      Point nextPoint = (Point)polyline.getFirst();

      // Output the points
      while(nextPoint != null)
      {
        System.out.println(nextPoint);            // Output the current point
        nextPoint = (Point)polyline.getNext(); // Get the next point
      }
    }
}
```

You can test this using the same code as the previous example—with the **TryPolyLine.java** file. Just copy this file and **Point.java** to the directory for this example.

How It Works

The **PolyLine** class implements all the methods that we had in the class before, so the **main()** method in the **TryPolyLine** class works just the same. Under the covers, the methods in the **PolyLine** class work a little differently. The work of creating the linked list is now in the constructor for the **LinkedList** class. All the **PolyLine** class constructors do is assemble a point array if necessary, and call the **LinkedList** constructor. Similarly, the **addPoint()** method just creates a **Point** object from the coordinate pair it receives, and passes it to the **addItem()** method for the **LinkedList** object, **polyline**.

Note that the cast from **Point** to **Object**, when the **addItem()** method is called, is automatic. A cast from any class type to type **Object** is always automatic because the class is up the class hierarchy—remember that all classes have **Object** as a base. In the **show()** method, we must insert an explicit cast to store the object returned by the **getFirst()** or the **getNext()** method. This cast is down the hierarchy so you must specify the cast explicitly.

You could use a variable of type **Object** to store the objects returned from **getFirst()** and **getNext()**, but this would not be a good idea. You would not need to insert the explicit cast, but you would lose a valuable check on the integrity of the program. You put objects of type **Point** into the list, so you would expect objects of type **Point** to be returned. An error in the program somewhere could result in an object of some other type being inserted. If the object is not of type **Point**—due to the said program error, for example—the cast to type **Point** will fail and you will get an error message. A variable of type **Object** can store anything, so if you use this and something other than a **Point** object is returned, it would not register at all in this case.

Abstract Classes

In the class **Animal**, we had to introduce a version of the method **sound()** that did nothing, just because we wanted to call the **sound()** method in the sub-class objects dynamically. The method **sound()** has no meaning in the context of the generic class **Animal**, so implementing it does not make much sense. This situation often arises in object-oriented programming. You will find yourself creating a super-class from which you will derive a number of sub-classes, just to take advantage of polymorphism.

To cater for this, Java has **abstract classes**. An abstract class is a class in which one or more methods are declared but not defined. The bodies of these methods are omitted, because, as in the case of the method **sound()** in our class **Animal**, implementing the methods does not make sense. Since they have no definition, they are called abstract. The declaration for an abstract method ends with a semi-colon, and you specify the method with the keyword **abstract** to identify it as such. To define an abstract class you use the keyword **abstract** in front of the class name.

We could have defined the class **Animal** as an abstract class by amending it as follows:

```
public abstract class Animal
{
  private String type;
```

```
    public Animal(String aType)
    {
      type = new String(aType);
    }

    public void show()
    {
      System.out.println("This is a "+type);
    }

    public abstract void sound();    // Abstract method
  }
```

The previous program will work just as well with these changes. It doesn't matter whether you prefix the class name with **public abstract** or **abstract public**, they are equivalent, but you should be consistent in your usage. The sequence **public abstract** is typically preferred. The same goes for the declaration of an abstract method, but both **public** and **abstract** must precede the return type specification, which is **void** in this case.

An **abstract** method cannot be **private** since a **private** method cannot be inherited, and therefore cannot be redefined in a sub-class.

You cannot instantiate an object of an abstract class, but you can declare a variable for it. With our new abstract version of the class **Animal**, we can still write:

```
  Animal thePet;    // Declare an Animal variable
```

just as we did in the **TryPolymorphism** class. We can then use this variable to store objects of the sub-classes, **Dog**, **Spaniel**, **Duck** and **Cat**.

When you derive a class from an abstract base class, you don't have to define all the abstract methods in the sub-class. In this case the sub-class will also be abstract and you won't be able to declare any objects of the sub-class either. If a class is abstract, you must use the **abstract** keyword when you define it, even if it only inherits an abstract method from its super-class. Sooner or later you must have a sub-class that contains no abstract methods. You can then create objects of this class.

Using the final Modifier

We have already used the keyword **final** to fix the value of a static data member of a class. You can also apply this keyword to the definition of a method, and to the definition of a class.

It may be that you want to prevent a sub-class from overriding a method in your class. When this is the case, simply declare that method as **final**. Any attempt to override a **final** method in a sub-class will result in the compiler flagging the new method as an error. For example, you could declare the method **addPoint()** as **final** within the class, **PolyLine**, by writing its definition in the class as:

```
public final void addPoint(Point point)
{
  ListPoint newEnd = new ListPoint(point);  // Create a new ListPoint
  end.setNext(newEnd);    // Set next variable for old end as new end
  end = newEnd;           // Store new point as end
}
```

Any class derived from **PolyLine** would not be able to redefine this method. Obviously an **abstract** method cannot be declared as **final**, since an **abstract** method must be defined in a sub-class.

If you declare a class as **final**, you prevent any sub-classes from being derived from it. To declare the class **PolyLine** as **final**, you would define it as:

```
public final class PolyLine
{
  // Definition as before...
}
```

If you now attempt to define a class based on **PolyLine** you will get an error message from the compiler. An abstract class cannot be declared as **final** since this would prevent the abstract methods in the class from ever being defined.

Interfaces

In the classes that we derived from the class **Animal**, we had a common set of methods, consisting of the methods **show()** and **sound()**, that were implemented individually in each of the sub-classes. The method names and arguments were the same in each class, and both the methods could be called polymorphically. The main point to defining the class **Animal** first, and then deriving the classes **Dog**, and **Cat**, and so on from it, was to be able to use the methods **show()** and **sound()** in this way. When all you want is a set of methods to be implemented in a number of classes so that you can call them polymorphically, you can dispense with the base class, and achieve the same end result more simply by using a Java facility called an **interface**. This is just one aspect of what you can do using an interface, so we should start by examining what an interface is, and then look at what we can do with it.

An **interface** is essentially a collection of constants and abstract methods that you can **implement** in a class—that is, write the code for the body of each of the methods. If a class implements an interface, the constants are available directly in the class, and the methods are included in the class and are typically defined in the class definition. An interface can contain just constants, just abstract methods, or both.

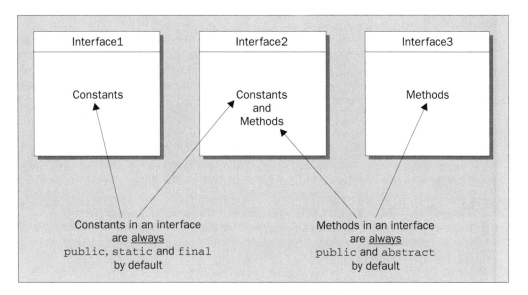

The methods in an interface are always **public** and **abstract**, so you do not need to specify them as such—indeed, it is considered to be bad programming practice to specify any attributes for them at all. The constants in an interface are always **public**, **static** and **final**, so you do not need to specify the attributes for these either.

The syntax for defining an interface is very much like that of a class.

Try It Out—Defining Interfaces

1 Here is an interface containing only constants:

```
public interface ConversionFactors
{
  double INCH_TO_MM = 25.4;
  double OUNCE_TO_GRAM = 28.349523125;
  double POUND_TO_GRAM = 453.5924;
  double HP_TO_WATT = 745.7;
  double WATT_TO_HP = 1.0/HP_TO_WATT;
}
```

2 You might also want to define an interface containing methods for conversion:

```
public interface Conversions
{
  double inchToMM(double inches);
  double ounceToGram(double ounces);
  double poundToGram(double pounds);
  double HPToWatt(double hp);
  double wattToHP(double watts);
}
```

How It Works

An interface is defined just like a class, but using the keyword **interface** rather than the keyword **class**. The name that you give to an interface must be different from the name of any other interface or class in the same package. The members of the interface, constants and methods, appear between braces. All the variables **INCH_TO_MM**, **OUNCE_TO_GRAM**, **POUND_TO_GRAM, HP_TO_WATT** and **WATT_TO_HP**, are **public**, so they are accessible outside the interface. Incidentally, they are also available outside the package containing the interface in this case, since the interface is declared as **public**. They're also **static** and **final** so they cannot be altered. You have no choice about this. Constants defined in an interface always have these attributes. The names given to these use capital letters to indicate that they are **static final** and cannot be altered—this is a common convention in Java.

> *The only explicit access attribute you can use with an interface definition is* public. *This makes the interface accessible outside the package containing it. If you omit the keyword* public, *your interface is only accessible from within its containing package.*

Since the constants in an interface are all **final**, you must initialize them. If you don't, the compiler will complain. You can define the value of one constant in terms of a preceding constant, as in the definition of **WATT_TO_HP**. If you try to use a constant that is defined later in the interface—for example if the definition for **WATT_TO_HP** appeared first—your code will not compile.

As you see, the **Conversions** interface only defines the signature for each method. It is up to the class that implements the interface to supply the code for each method.

Extending Interfaces

You can define one interface based on another by using the keyword **extends** to identify the base interface name. This is essentially the same form we use to derive one class from another. For example, the interface **Conversions** perhaps would be more useful if it contained the constants that the interface **ConversionFactors** contains.

Try It Out—Inheriting Interfaces

We could do this by defining the interface **Conversions** as:

```
public interface Conversions extends ConversionFactors
{
  double inchToMM(double inches);
  double ounceToGram(double ounces);
  double poundToGram(double pounds);
  double HPToWatt(double hp);
  double wattToHP(double watts);
}
```

How It Works

Now the interface **Conversions** also contains the members of the interface **ConversionFactors**, and any class implementing the **Conversions** interface will have the constants from **ConversionFactors** available to implement the methods. The interface **ConversionFactors** is referred to as a **super-interface** of the interface **Conversions**.

An interface can use the contents of several other interfaces. To define an interface that includes the members of several other interfaces, you just specify the names of the interfaces separated by commas following the keyword **extends**. For example,

```
public interface MyInterface extends HisInterface, HerInterface
{
  // Interface members - constants and abstract methods...
}
```

Now **MyInterface** will incorporate all the methods and constants that are members of **HisInterface** and **HerInterface**. Some care is necessary if you do this. If both super-interfaces have a method with the same signature, that is, with identical name and parameters, they must also have the same return type, otherwise the compiler will report an error. This is because it would be impossible for a class to implement both, as they have the same signature.

Implementing an Interface

To implement an interface in a class, you just add the keyword, **implements**, followed by the interface name after the class name in the class definition. Then you need to implement each of the methods declared in the interface definition. Let's look at what sort of effort is involved in implementing interfaces in a class.

For example, we can implement the interface **ConversionFactors** in a class **MyClass**.

Try It Out—Implementing an Interface

1 Simply define the class as:

```
public class MyClass implements ConversionFactors
{
  // Definition of the class...

  double poundsWeight;     // A weight in pounds

  public double getMetricWeight()
  {
    return poundsWeight*POUND_TO_GRAM;
  }
}
```

2   When the interface contains methods, the class has a bit more work to do. It needs to implement the methods that are in the interface. For example, we can implement the **Conversions** interface in the class, **MyClass** as follows:

```
public class MyClass implements Conversions
{
   // Definition of the class...

   // Implementation of the methods in the interface
   public double inchToMM(double inches)
   {
     return inches*INCH_TO_MM;
   }

   public double ounceToGram(double ounces)
   {
     return ounces*OUNCE_TO_GRAM;
   }

   public double poundToGram(double pounds)
   {
     return pounds*POUND_TO_GRAM;
   }

   public double HPToWatt(double hp)
   {
       return hp*HP_TO_WATT;
   }

   public double wattToHP(double watts)
   {
     return watts*WATT_TO_HP;
   }
}
```

3   We could omit the implementation of one or more of the methods from the interface in the class **MyClass**, but in this case we would need to declare the class as **abstract**:

```
public abstract class MyClass implements Conversions
{
   // Definition of the class...

   // Implementation of the methods in the interface
   public double inchToMM(double inches)
   {
     return inches*INCH_TO_MM;
   }

   public double ounceToGram(double ounces)
   {
```

```
        return ounces*OUNCE_TO_GRAM;
    }

    // other method definitions not included here...
}
```

How It Works

The first section shows an ordinary class implementing interfaces, but it could equally well be a derived class or an **abstract** class. All the constants defined in the interface, **ConversionFactors** are available in **MyClass** as though they were data members of the class. You can reference them freely in any of the methods in the class. Because they are **public**, they will also be accessible members of objects of type **MyClass**.

As you see, each of the abstract methods that are members of the **Conversion** interface are defined in the second version of **MyClass**, and the constants from the super-interface, **ConversionFactors**, are available for use in our class. Every method declared in the interface should have a definition within the class if you are going to create objects of the class.

> Since the methods in an interface are, by definition, `public`, you must use the `public` keyword when you define them in your class, otherwise your code will not compile. To recap, the implementation of an interface method must not have an access specifier that is more restrictive than that implicit in the abstract method declaration, and you can't get less restrictive than `public`.

Where several classes are implementing the same interface, they will typically have different ways of implementing the methods. That obviously doesn't apply to the sort of methods we have in the **Conversions** interface. However, you might have an interface declaring a method **show()** that is supposed to display an entity. If the interface was implemented in classes defining geometric shapes, the implementation of a **show()** method for a **Circle** object would be quite different from that for a **Curve** object.

Of course, you don't have to implement every method in the interface. With the third, abstract version of **MyClass**, you cannot create objects of the class **MyClass**, and you must define a sub-class of **MyClass** that implements the remaining methods in the interface. The declaration of the class as **abstract** is mandatory when you don't implement all of the methods that are declared in an interface. The compiler will complain if you forget to do this.

Now we know how to use interfaces in code, we can tie up something we met earlier in this chapter, when we were looking at the standard class **Object**. We mentioned that, to use the inherited method **clone()**, you need to implement the interface **Cloneable**. In fact this interface is empty, so all you need to do to implement it in a class is to specify that the class in question implements it in the class declaration. This means that you just need to write something like:

```
public MyClass implements Cloneable
{
  // Detail of the class...
}
```

Using Interfaces

What you have seen up to now has primarily illustrated the mechanics of creating an interface and incorporating it into a class. The really interesting question is—what should you use interfaces for?

We have already illustrated one use for interfaces. An interface is a very handy means of packaging up constants. You can use an interface containing constants in any number of different classes that have access to the interface. All you need to do is make sure the class implements the interface, and all the constants it contains will be available, since the constants are **static** and so will be shared among all objects of a class.

We also hinted at a more important use at the beginning of this discussion. Interfaces enable you to make use of polymorphism without necessarily defining sub-classes. This is an extremely useful and powerful facility. Let's have a look at how this works.

Interfaces and Polymorphism

When we first introduced the idea of a class, we referred to the **public** methods in a class as 'the interface to the class'. Where several classes share a common set of methods with given signatures, but with possibly different implementations, you can separate the set of methods common to the classes into an **interface**, and this interface can then be implemented by each of the classes.

Earlier in this chapter we implemented several classes with a common set of methods by defining them as sub-classes of a base class from which the sub-classes inherited the common methods. This enabled us to take advantage of the flexibility provided by dynamic binding. We can achieve exactly the same effect by defining an interface and implementing this interface in each class. Our example using the class **Animal** called the methods in the sub-classes dynamically. We can see how polymorphism works with an interface by implementing the same example with the classes **Dog**, **Spaniel**, **Cat**, and **Duck**, but using an interface to specify the common methods, rather than the base class **Animal**.

> *In case you think that the use of interfaces renders class inheritance less than useful, note that a base class is still useful for implementing functionality common to all its sub-classes. An interface, however, allows the method signatures for code implementation to be specified, so that polymorphism will work. If you're unconvinced, take a look at the Java class hierarchy in the Java documentation.*

Try It Out—An Animal Interface

1 We first need to define an interface that includes the methods we want to select dynamically:

```
public interface PetOutput
{
  void sound();
  void show();
}
```

The interface, **PetOutput**, just includes the two methods that were previously in the base class **Animal**.

2 Now all we need to do is make sure each of the classes implement this interface. We won't reproduce all of the detail of each class here, as the code is much the same as before with essentially the same modifications to each of the direct sub-classes of **Animal**. Here is the definition for the class **Dog**:

```
public class Dog implements PetOutput
{
  private String name;       // Name of a dog
  private String breed;      // Dog breed

  public Dog(String aName)
  {
    name = aName;            // Supplied name
    breed = "Unknown";       // Default breed value
  }

  // Make a Duck a Dog
  public Dog(Duck aDuck)
  {
    name = aDuck.getName();
    breed = aDuck.getBreed();
  }

  public Dog(String aName, String aBreed)
  {
    name = aName;            // Supplied name
    breed = aBreed;          // Supplied breed
  }

  // Show a dog's details
  public void show()
  {
    System.out.println("It's " + name + " the " + breed);
  }
```

```
  // A barking method
  public void sound()
  {
    System.out.println("Woof    Woof");
  }

  public String getName()
  {
    return name;
  }
}
```

The **Cat** and **Duck** classes need to be modified in a similar way.

3 The definition of the class, **Spaniel**, will remain:

```
class Spaniel extends Dog
{
  public Spaniel(String aName)
  {
    super(aName, "Spaniel");
  }
}
```

4 Here is the code that tries out the classes:

```
public class TestInterface
{
  public static void main(String[] args)
  {
    PetOutput[] thePets = { new Dog("Rover", "Poodle"),
                            new Cat("Max", "Abyssinian"),
                            new Duck("Daffy","Aylesbury"),
                            new Spaniel("Fido")};

    PetOutput petChoice;

    for(int i = 0; i < 5; i++)
    {
      int index = (int)(thePets.length*Math.random() - 0.001);
      petChoice = thePets[index];
      System.out.println("\nYou have chosen:");
      petChoice.show();
      petChoice.sound();
    }
  }
}
```

How It Works

The **Dog**, **Duck** and **Cat** classes are no longer sub-classes of **Animal**. They just implement the **PetOutput** interface. We have omitted the variable, **type**, that was originally inherited from the class **Animal**. You can add it in here if you want as an instance variable of the class, and then set it in the constructors. The calls to the super-class constructors that we had in the class constructors are now not applicable, so they have been removed. The interface methods **show()** and **sound()** are defined in the class, but of course, the call to the **show()** method in the super-class no longer applies.

The **Spaniel** class is a sub-class of **Dog**, and will be implemented in the same way here as it was earlier in the chapter. Of course, the **Spaniel** class will inherit the interface methods from the super-class and they will be quite satisfactory. Even if you need to redefine the methods in this class, you won't need to explicitly specify the interface as being implemented by the class.

The relationship between the classes and the interface is shown in the next illustration.

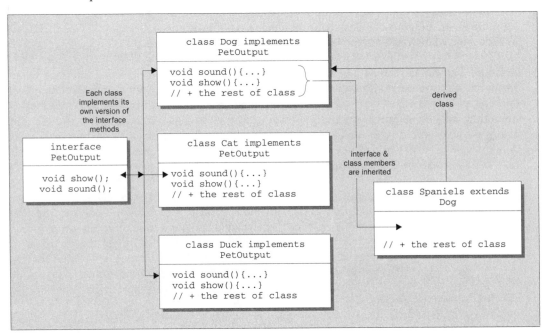

With the classes defined, all we need is the code for **main()** to test them. For polymorphism to work, we need one variable that is capable of referring to any of the four different kinds of object, **Dog**, **Spaniel**, **Duck** or **Cat**. We no longer have the base class **Animal**, so we can't use a variable of that type. However, because we are using an interface to specify the methods that are common to the classes, we can use a variable of the interface type, **PetOutput**, to store any of the class objects.

Other than that the test code works in the same way as before. A random selection from the array, **thePets**, which is now of type **PetOutput**, is stored in the variable **petChoice**, which is also of type **PetOutput**. The variable **petChoice** is then used to call the appropriate version of the methods **show()** and **sound()**. These will be selected from the class corresponding to the object referenced by the variable **petChoice**. The loop makes five random selections from the array, **thePets**.

If you declare a variable to be an interface type, such as we have for the variable **PetOutput** in our example, you can use it to reference an object of any class that is declared to implement the interface. This excludes abstract classes of course, since you cannot define an object of an abstract class, but it does include sub-classes that inherit the interface methods from a direct or indirect super-class. We can therefore use **petOutput** to refer to objects of the class **Spaniel** in our example, which inherits the interface methods from the class **Dog**.

Using Multiple Interfaces

A derived class can only have a single base class in Java. However, you are not restricted in the number of interfaces a class can implement. This introduces a further level of flexibility in how you write your programs and make use of polymorphism.

A simple use for implementing multiple interfaces in a class is to use one interface to hold application constants, and another to declare methods that you want to use polymorphically. You can put all the constant values that you need in a program into a single interface definition, and then implement the interface in any class that needs access to the constants. This only involves adding **implements** and the interface name to the first line of the class definition. You can also implement any other interfaces in these classes that declare methods that are to be executed polymorphically as and when necessary.

At a more complex level—which we will just touch on—you can have classes that implement multiple interfaces that declare methods. You can see this in action in the Java class library, if you look at the **javadoc**'d information on **java.awt.Component**, which implements three interfaces for the differing functionality it needs. To call the methods declared in a particular interface polymorphically, you will need to use a variable that is of that interface type. You cannot use this variable to call methods in any other interface that a class implements. You will always need a variable of a type corresponding to the interface that declares the method.

Summary

You should now understand polymorphism, and how to apply it. You will find that this technique can be utilized to considerable advantage in the majority of your Java programs. It will appear in many of the examples in the remaining chapters.

The important points we have covered in this chapter are:

▶ An **abstract method** is a method that has no body defined for it, and is declared using the keyword **abstract**

▶ An **abstract class** is a class that contains one or more abstract methods. It must be defined with the attribute **abstract**

▶ You can define one class based on another. This is called class derivation or inheritance. The base class is called a **super-class** and the derived class is called a **sub-class**. A super-class can also be a sub-class of another super-class

▶ A sub-class inherits certain members of its super-class. An inherited member of a class can be referenced and used as though it were declared as a normal member of the class

▶ A sub-class does not inherit the super-class constructors

▶ The **private** members of a super-class are not inherited in a sub-class. If the sub-class is not in the same package as the super-class, then members of the super-class that do not have an access attribute are not inherited

▶ The first statement in the body of a constructor for a sub-class should call a constructor for the super-class. If it does not, the compiler will insert a call for the default constructor for the super-class

▶ A sub-class can re-implement, and overload, the methods inherited from its super-class. If two or more sub-classes with a common base class re-implement a common set of methods, these methods can be selected for execution at run-time

▶ A variable of a super-class can point to an object of any of its sub-classes. Such a variable can then be used to execute the sub-class methods inherited from the super-class

▶ A sub-class of an abstract class must also be declared as **abstract** if it does not provide definitions for all of the abstract methods inherited from its super-class

▶ An interface can only contain constants and abstract methods

▶ A class can implement one or more interfaces by declaring them in the class definition, and including the code to implement each of the interface methods

▶ A class that does not define all the methods for an interface it implements, must be declared as **abstract**

▶ If several classes implement a common interface, methods declared as members of the interface can be executed polymorphically

Exercises

1 Define an abstract base class **Shape**, that includes protected data members for the (x, y) position of a shape, a public method to move a shape, and a public abstract method **show()** to output a shape. Derive sub-classes for lines, circles and rectangles. Also define the class **PolyLine** that you saw in this chapter with **Shape** as its base class. You can represent a line as two points, a circle as a center and a radius, and a rectangle as two points on diagonally opposite corners. Implement the **toString()** method for each class. Test the classes by selecting ten random objects of the derived classes then invoking the **show()** method for each. Use the **toString()** methods in the derived classes.

2 Define a class, **ShapeList**, that can store an arbitrary collection of any objects of sub-classes of the **Shape** class.

3 Implement the classes for shapes using an interface for the common methods, rather than inheritance from the super-class, while still keeping **Shape** as a base class.

4 Extend the classes **LinkedList** and **ListItem** that we defined in this chapter so that they support traversing the list backwards as well as forwards.

5 Add methods to the class **LinkedList** to insert and delete elements at the current position.

6 Implement a method in the **LinkedList** class to insert an object following an object passed as an argument. (Assume the objects stored in the list implement an **equals()** method that compares the **this** object with an object passed as an argument, and returns **true** if they are equal).

Exceptions

Java uses exceptions as a way of signaling problems when you execute a program. Since they arise in your Java programs when things go wrong, and if something can go wrong in your code, sooner or later it will, they are a very basic consideration when you are designing and writing your program code.

The reason we've been sidestepping the question of exceptions for the past six chapters is that you first need to understand classes and inheritance before you can understand what an exception is, and appreciate what happens when an exception occurs. Only when you have a good grasp of these topics can we delve into how to use and deal with exceptions in a program.

In this chapter you will learn:

- What an exception is
- How you handle exceptions in your programs
- The standard exceptions in Java
- How to guarantee that a particular block of code in a method will always be executed
- How to define and use your own types of exceptions
- How to throw exceptions in your programs

The Idea Behind Exceptions

An exception usually signals an error, and is so-called because errors in your Java programs are bound to be the exception rather than the rule—by definition! An exception doesn't always indicate an error though. An exception can also signal some exceptional event in your program that deserves special attention.

If, in the midst of the code that deals with the normal operation of the program, you try to deal with the myriad, and often highly unusual, error conditions that might arise, your program structure will soon become very complicated and difficult to understand. One major benefit of having an error signaled by an exception is that it separates the code that deals with errors from the code that is executed when things are moving along smoothly. Another positive aspect of exceptions is that they provide a way of enforcing a response to particular errors—with certain kinds of exceptions, you must include code in your program to deal with them, otherwise your code will not compile.

An **exception** in Java is an object that's created when an abnormal situation arises in your program. This exception object has data members that store information about the nature of the problem. The exception is said to be **thrown**, that is, the object identifying the exceptional circumstance is tossed, as an argument, to a specific piece of program code that has been written specifically to deal with that kind of problem. The code receiving the exception object as a parameter is said to **catch** it.

The situations that cause exceptions are quite diverse, but they fall into four broad categories:

Code or Data Errors	For example, you attempt an invalid cast of an object, you try to use an array index that's outside the limits for the array, or an arithmetic expression that has a zero divisor.
Standard Method Exceptions	For example, if you use the **substring()** method in the **String** class, it can throw a **StringIndexOutOfBoundsException** exception.
Throwing your own Exceptions	We'll see later in this chapter how you can throw a few of your own when you need to.
Java Errors	These can be due to errors in executing the Java Virtual Machine which executes your compiled program, but are usually due to an error in your program.

Before we look at how you make provision in your programs for dealing with exceptions, we should understand what kinds of exceptions can arise.

Types of Exceptions

An exception is always an object of some subclass of the standard class **Throwable**. This is true for exceptions that you define and throw yourself, as well as the standard exceptions that arise due to errors in your code. It's also true for exceptions that are thrown by methods in one or other of the standard packages.

All the standard exceptions are covered by two direct subclasses of the class **Throwable**— the class **Error** and the class **Exception**. Both these classes themselves have subclasses which identify specific exception conditions.

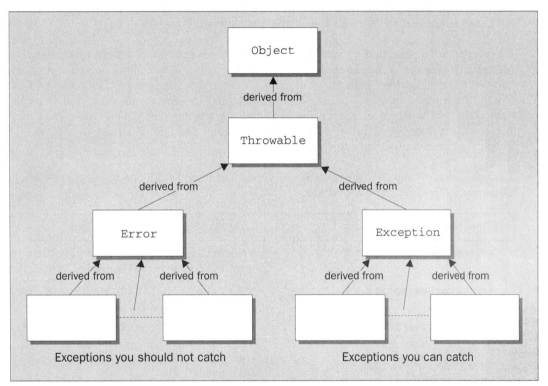

Error Exceptions

The exceptions that are defined by the class **Error** and its subclasses are characterized by the fact that they all represent error conditions from which you aren't expected to recover, and therefore you aren't expected to catch them.

You aren't prohibited from trying to deal with these exceptions, but in general there's little point in you attempting to catch any of them. Since the exceptions that correspond to objects of classes derived from **Error** are all the result of fairly catastrophic events or conditions, you can do little or nothing to recover from them during the execution of the program. Typical of the kinds of problems we're talking about here is the Java Virtual Machine running out of memory, or a class definition that can't be found during the loading of your program. In these sorts of situations, all you can usually do is just read the error message generated by the exception, and then try to figure out what might be wrong with your code to cause the exception to be thrown.

RuntimeException Exceptions

You can and should catch the exceptions that are represented by objects of classes derived from the class **Exception**. An important subset of these exceptions has the parent class **RuntimeException**, itself a subclass of the class **Exception**.

The exceptions represented by subclassing **RuntimeException** are differentiated from other exception subclasses of **Exception**, in that the compiler will not check whether your code handles these exceptions. Compare this with all other subclasses of the class **Exception** where, if a method in your program has the potential to generate an exception of some such class, you must either handle the exception, or register that your method may throw such an exception. If you don't, your program will not compile. We'll see in a moment how to specify that a method can throw an exception.

The subclasses of **RuntimeException** are defined in the standard packages **java.lang**, and **java.util**. Those in **java.lang** are:

Class Name	Exception Condition Represented
ArithmeticException	An invalid arithmetic condition has arisen such as an attempt to divide by zero.
ArrayStoreException	You've attempted to store an object in an array that isn't permitted for the array type.
ClassCastException	You've tried to cast an object to an invalid type—the object isn't of the class specified, nor is it a subclass or a superclass of the class specified.
IllegalArgumentException	You've passed an argument to a method which doesn't correspond with the parameter type.
IllegalMonitorStateException	A thread has tried to wait on the monitor for an object that the thread doesn't own. (We'll look into threads in Chapter 10).
IndexOutOfBoundsException	You've attempted to use an index that is outside the bounds of the object it is applied to. This may be an array, a **String** object, or a **Vector** object. The class **Vector** is defined in the standard package, **java.util**.

Class Name	Exception Condition Represented
NegativeArraySizeException	You tried to define an array with a negative dimension.
NullPointerException	You used an object variable containing **null**, when it should refer to an object for proper operation—for example, calling a method or accessing a data member.
SecurityException	Your program has performed an illegal operation that is a security violation. This might be trying to read a file on the local machine from an applet.

There are only two exception classes defined in **java.util**. Both of these relate to errors in using classes that we haven't discussed yet, but we'll include them here for reference purposes. These exception classes are:

Class Name	Exception Condition Represented
EmptyStackException	The class **Stack** is defined in **java.util** and we'll discuss it in Chapter 9. This exception indicates an illegal operation on an empty **Stack** object—for example, popping an element from it.
NoSuchElementException	The **Enumeration** interface is defined in **java.util** and we'll look into it in Chapter 9. This exception is thrown if you try to use the **nextElement()** method with a **Vector** object for example, when there's no next element.

Other Subclasses of Exception

For all the other classes derived from the class **Exception**, the compiler will check that you've either handled the exception in a method where the exception may be thrown, or you've indicated that the method can throw such an exception. We'll look more at what this means in the next two sections.

Exceptions of this type include:

▶ **Input/Output Errors:** The package **java.io** defines a class **IOException** that's derived from the class **Exception**. This covers the exceptions that can be thrown during input/output operations. There are four subclasses of **IOException** defined in **java.lang** which classify the problems that can occur more precisely. We'll look at these in detail in Chapter 8.

▶ **Network Operation Errors:** The package **java.net** also defines five subclasses of **IOException** which identify error conditions that can arise during network operations.

263

Specifying the Exceptions a Method Can Throw

Suppose you have a method which can throw an exception which is neither a subclass of **RuntimeException** nor **Error**, an **IOException** for example because your method involves some file input and output operations. If the exception isn't caught in the method, you must at least declare that the exception can be thrown. But how do you do that?

You do it simply by adding a **throws** clause in the definition of the method. For example, suppose we write a method that uses methods for input/output stored in the package **java.io**. You'll see in the next chapter that some of these can throw exceptions represented by objects of classes **EOFException** and **FileNotFoundException**. Neither of these are subclasses of **RuntimeException** or **Error**, and so the possibility of an exception needs to be declared. Since the method can't handle any exceptions it might throw, for the simple reason that we don't know how to do it yet, it must be defined as:

```
double myMethod() throws EOFException, FileNotFoundException
{
  // Detail of the method code...
}
```

To declare that your method can throw exceptions, you just put the **throws** keyword after the parameter list for the method, and then add the list of classes for the exceptions that might be thrown, separated by commas. This has a knock-on effect—if another method calls this method, it too must take account of the exceptions this method can throw. The calling method definition must either deal with the exceptions, or declare that it can throw these exceptions as well. It's a simple choice. You either pass the buck, or decide that the buck stops here. The reasons for this will become obvious when we look at the way a Java program behaves when it encounters an exception.

Handling Exceptions

If you want to deal with the exceptions where they occur, there are three kinds of code block that you can include in a method to handle them. These are the **try**, **catch** and **finally** blocks:

▶ A **try** block encloses code that may give rise to one or more exceptions

▶ A **catch** block encloses code that is intended to handle those exceptions

▶ The code in a **finally** block is always executed before the method ends, regardless of whether any exceptions are thrown in the **try** block

The try Block

When you want to catch an exception, the code in the method which might cause the exception to arise must be enclosed in a **try** block. You have no option about this. Code that can cause exceptions need not be in a **try** block, but in this case you can't catch the exceptions within the method in which the code appears.

A **try** block is simply the keyword **try**, followed by braces enclosing the code that can throw the exception.

```
try
{
  // Code that can throw one or more exceptions
}
```

The catch Block

You enclose the code to handle an exception in a **catch** block. The **catch** block must immediately follow the **try** block which contains the code that may throw that particular exception. A **catch** block consists of the keyword, **catch**, followed by a parameter between parentheses that identifies the type of exception that the block is to deal with. This is followed by the code to handle the exception enclosed between braces:

```
catch(ArithmeticException e)
{
  // Code to handle the exception
}
```

This **catch** block only handles **ArithmeticException** exceptions. In general, the parameter for a **catch** block must be of type **Throwable** or one of the subclasses of the class **Throwable**. If the class that you specify as the parameter type has subclasses, the **catch** block will be expected to process exceptions of that class, plus all subclasses of the class. If you specified the parameter to a **catch** block as type **RuntimeException** for example, the code in the **catch** block would be invoked for exceptions defined by the class **RuntimeException**, or any of its subclasses.

We can see how this works with a simple example. It doesn't matter what the code does—the important thing is that it throws an exception we can catch.

Try It Out—Using a *try* and a *catch* Block

The following code is really just an exhaustive log of the program's execution:

```
public class TestTryCatch
{
  public static void main(String[] args)
```

```
  {
    int i = 1;
    int j = 0;

    try
    {
      System.out.println("First try block entered");
      System.out.println(i/j);          // Divide by 0 - exception thrown
      System.out.println("Ending first try block");
    }
    // Catch the exception
    catch(ArithmeticException e)
    {
      System.out.println("Arithmetic exception caught");
    }

    System.out.println("After first try block");
    return;
  }
}
```

If you run the example, you should get the output:

```
First try block entered
Arithmetic exception caught
After first try block
```

How It Works

The variable **j** is initialized to 0, so that the divide operation in the **try** block will throw an **ArithmeticException** exception. We must use the variable **j** here because the Java compiler will not allow you to explicitly divide by zero—that is, the expression **i/0** will not compile. The first line in the **try** block will enable us to track when the **try** block is entered, and the second line will throw an exception. The third line can only be executed if the exception isn't thrown—which can't occur in this example.

This shows that when the exception is thrown, control transfers immediately to the first statement in the **catch** block. After the **catch** block has been executed, execution then continues with the statement following the **catch** block. The statements in the **try** block following the point where the exception occurred aren't executed. You could try running the example again after changing the value of **j** to 1 so that no exception is thrown. The output in this case will be:

```
First try block entered
1
Ending first try block
After first try block
```

From this you can see that the entire **try** block is executed, then execution continues with the statement after the **catch** block. Because no arithmetic exception was thrown, the code in the **catch** block isn't executed.

FYI You need to take care when adding try blocks to existing code. A try block is no different to any other block between braces when it comes to variable scope. Variables declared in a try block are only available until the closing brace for the block. It's easy to enclose the declaration of a variable in a try block, and in doing so inadvertently limit the scope of the variable and cause compiler errors.

Multiple catch Blocks

If a **try** block can throw several different kinds of exception, you can put several **catch** blocks after the **try** block to handle them. In this case, the order of the **catch** blocks can be important. When an exception is thrown, it will be caught by the first **catch** block that processes this class of exception, or a superclass of the exception.

For example, if you have a **catch** block for exceptions of type **ArithmeticException**, as well as a **catch** block for exceptions of type **Exception** as a catch-all, in the following sequence, exceptions of type **ArithmeticException** will never reach the second **catch** block as they will always be caught by the first.

```
try
{
  // try block code
}
catch(Exception e)
{
  // Generic handling of exceptions
}
catch(ArithmeticException e)
{
  // Specialized handling for these exceptions
}
```

This means that if you have **catch** blocks for several exception types in the same class hierarchy, you must put the **catch** blocks in order starting with the lowest subclass, and then progressing to the highest superclass last. Naturally, if you're only interested in generic exceptions, all the error handling code can be localized in one **catch** block for exceptions of the superclass type. So the **catch** block above that has an argument of type **Exception** will receive all exceptions of type **Exception** and exceptions of types corresponding to any subclass of **Exception**.

The finally Block

The **finally** block provides a means by which you can do any necessary cleaning up at the end of executing a **try** block. Sometimes you need to be sure that some code is run before a method exits, no matter what exceptions are thrown in the previous **try** block. A **finally** block is always executed, regardless of what happens during the execution of the method. So if a file needs to be closed, or a critical resource must be released, you can guarantee that it will be done if you put the code to do it in a **finally** block.

The **finally** block has a very simple structure:

```
finally
{
  // Clean-up code to be executed last
}
```

A **finally** block is associated with a particular **try** block, and you must locate it immediately following any **catch** blocks for the **try** block. If there are no **catch** blocks then you position the **finally** block immediately after the **try** block. If you don't do this, your program will not compile.

FYI The primary purpose for the try block is to identify code that may result in an exception being thrown. However, you can use it to contain code that doesn't throw exceptions just to obtain the convenience of using a finally block. This can be useful when the code in the try block has several possible exit points through break or return statements for example, but you always want to have a specific set of statements executed after the try block has been executed. You can just put these in a finally block.

Structuring a Method

We've looked at the blocks you can include in the body of a method, but it may not always be obvious how they are combined. The first thing to get straight is that the **try** block, any corresponding **catch** blocks, and the **finally** block all bunch together:

```
try
{
  // Code that may throw exceptions...
}
catch(ExceptionType1 e)
{
  // Code to handle exceptions of type ExceptionType1 or subclass
}
catch(ExceptionType2 e)
{
  // Code to handle exceptions of type ExceptionType2 or subclass
}

// More catch blocks if necessary...

finally
{
  // Code to be executed after try block code
}
```

The **finally** block and the **catch** blocks are optional. Of course, if you have neither then you don't really need a **try** block. You must not include other code between a **try** block and its **catch** blocks, or between the **catch** blocks and the **finally** block. You can have other code that doesn't throw exceptions after the **finally** block, and you can have multiple **try** blocks in a method. In this case, your method might be structured as shown in the following diagram.

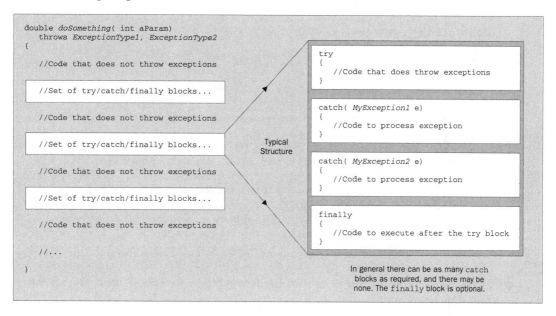

The more usual, and much more readable structure for a method is to have a single **try** block followed by all the **catch** blocks for the exceptions that need to be processed in the method, plus a **finally** block. However, Java gives you all the flexibility you're likely to need by allowing you to have as many **try** blocks as you want.

The **throws** clause that follows the parameter list for the method identifies exceptions that can be thrown in this method, but which aren't caught by any of the **catch** blocks within the method. We saw this earlier in this chapter. Exceptions that aren't caught can be thrown by code anywhere in the body of the method, that is, they need not be enclosed by **try** blocks.

Execution Sequence

We saw how the sequence of execution proceeded with the simple case of a **try** block and a single **catch** block. We also need to understand the sequence in which code is executed when we have the **try-catch-finally** combinations of blocks when different exceptions are thrown. This is easiest to comprehend by considering an example. We can use the following code to create a range of exceptions and conditions.

Try It Out—Execution Sequence of a *try* Block

1 Start by importing the **java.io.IOException** class. Then, in the **TryBlockTest** class, start the **main()** function off with the following **try** block:

```
import java.io.IOException;

public class TryBlockTest
{
  public static void main(String[] args)
  {
    int[] x = {10, 5, 0};        // Array of three integers

    // This block only throws an exception if method divide() does
    try
    {
      System.out.println("First try block in main()entered");
      System.out.println("result = " + divide(x,0));  // No error
      x[1] = 0;                   // Will cause a divide by zero
      System.out.println("result = " + divide(x,0));  // Arithmetic error
      x[1] = 1;                   // Reset to prevent divide by zero
      System.out.println("result = " + divide(x,1));  // Index error
    }
```

2 Then we write the **catch** blocks for the two types of exceptions that we can expect from the above code:

```
    catch(ArithmeticException e)
    {
    System.out.println("Arithmetic exception caught in main()");
    }
    catch(ArrayIndexOutOfBoundsException e)
    {
    System.out.println("Index-out-of-bounds exception caught in main()");
    }

    System.out.println("Outside first try block in main()");
    System.out.println("\nPress Enter to exit");
```

3 Because **read()** can throw an I/O exception it must itself be called in a **try** block and have an associated **catch** block, unless the enclosing method is declared as throwing the exception.

```
    try
    {
      System.out.println("In second try block in main()");
      System.in.read();
      return;
    }
```

```
  catch(IOException e)
  {
    System.out.println("I/O exception caught in main()");
  }
  finally
  {
    System.out.println("finally block for second try block in main()");
  }

  System.out.println("Code after second try block in main()");
}
```

4 Lastly, we come to the **divide()** method which throws these arithmetic and index-out-of-bounds exceptions

```
public static int divide(int[] array, int index)
{
  try
  {
    System.out.println("\nFirst try block in divide() entered");
    array[index + 2] = array[index]/array[index + 1];
    System.out.println("Code at end of first try block in divide()");
    return array[index + 2];
  }
  catch(ArithmeticException e)
  {
    System.out.println("Arithmetic exception caught in divide()");
  }
  catch(ArrayIndexOutOfBoundsException e)
  {
    System.out.println("Index-out-of-bounds exception caught in
           divide()");
  }
  finally
  {
    System.out.println("finally block in divide()");
  }
  System.out.println("Executing code after try block in divide()");
  return array[index + 2];
}
}
```

If you run the example it will produce the output:

```
First try block in main()entered

First try block in divide() entered
Code at end of first try block in divide()
finally block in divide()
result = 2
```

```
First try block in divide() entered
Arithmetic exception caught in divide()
finally block in divide()
Executing code after try block in divide()
result = 2

First try block in divide() entered
Index-out-of-bounds exception caught in divide
finally block in divide()
Executing code after try block in divide()
Index-out-of-bounds exception caught in main()
Outside first try block in main()

Press Enter to exit
In second try block in main()

finally block for second try block in main()
```

How It Works

All the **try**, **catch**, and **finally** blocks in the example have output statements so we can trace the sequence of execution.

The method **divide()** can throw an arithmetic exception in the **try** block if the element **array[index + 1]** of the array passed to it is 0, and can throw an **ArrayIndexOutOfBounds** exception in the **try** block if the index value passed to it is negative, or results in **index + 2** being beyond the array limits. Both these exceptions are caught in the body of the method so they will not be apparent in the calling method **main()**.

Note however that **divide()** can also throw an index-out-of-bounds exception in the last statement,

```
return array[index+2];
```

which is outside the **try** block. Because it's outside the **try** block, it will not be caught. However, we aren't obliged to declare that the method throws this exception because the **ArrayIndexOutOfBoundsException** class is a subclass of **RuntimeException**.

The method **main()** has two **try** blocks. The first **try** block encloses three calls to the method **divide()**. The first call will execute without error; the second call will cause an arithmetic exception in the method; and the third call will cause an index-out-of-bounds exception. There are two **catch** blocks for the first **try** block in **main()** to deal with these two potential exceptions.

The **read()** method in the second **try** block in **main()** can cause an input/output exception to be thrown. Since this is one of the exceptions that the compiler will check for, we must either put the statement that calls the **read()** method in a **try** block, and have a **catch** block to deal with the exception, or declare that **main()** throws the **IOException** exception. If we don't do one or the other, the program will not compile.

Using the **read()** method in this way has the effect of pausing the program until the *Enter* key is pressed. We'll be looking in detail at **read()**, and other input/output methods, in the next chapter. The class **IOException** is in the package **java.io**, so we need the **import** statement for this class because we refer to it in the **catch** block. Remember that only classes defined in **java.lang** are included in your program automatically.

Normal Execution of a Method

The first line of output from the example, **TryBlockTest**, indicates we've begun execution of the **try** block in **main()**. The next block of four lines of output from the example are the result of a straightforward execution of the method **divide()**. No exceptions occur in **divide()**, so no **catch** blocks are executed.

The code at the end of the method **divide()**, following the **catch** blocks, isn't executed because the **return** statement in the **try** block ends the execution of the method. However, the **finally** block in **divide()** is executed before the return to the calling method occurs. If you comment out the **return** statement at the end of the **divide()** method's **try** block and run the example again, you'll see that the code that follows the **finally** block will be executed.

The sequence of execution when no exceptions occur is shown in the diagram.

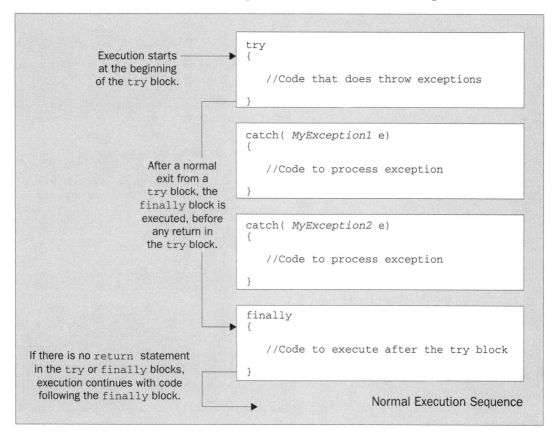

Execution starts at the beginning of the try block.

```
try
{
    //Code that does throw exceptions

}
```

```
catch( MyException1 e)
{
    //Code to process exception

}
```

After a normal exit from a try block, the finally block is executed, before any return in the try block.

```
catch( MyException2 e)
{
    //Code to process exception

}
```

```
finally
{
    //Code to execute after the try block

}
```

If there is no return statement in the try or finally blocks, execution continues with code following the finally block.

Normal Execution Sequence

The above diagram illustrates the normal sequence of execution in an arbitrary **try-catch-finally** set of blocks. If there's a **return** statement in the **try** block, this will be executed immediately after the **finally** block completes execution, so this prevents the execution of any code following the **finally** block. A **return** statement in a **finally** block will cause an immediate return to the calling point, so the code following the **finally** block wouldn't be executed in this case.

Execution when an Exception is Thrown

The next block of five lines in the output correspond to an **ArithmeticException** being thrown and caught in the method **divide()** as a result of the value of the third element in the array **x** being zero. When the exception occurs, execution of the code in the **try** block is stopped, and you can see that the code that follows the **catch** block for the exception in the method **divide()** is then executed. The **finally** block executes next, followed by the code after the **finally** block. The value in the last element of the array isn't changed from its previous value because the exception occurs during the computation of the new value, before the result is stored.

The general sequence of execution in an arbitrary **try-catch-finally** set of blocks when an exception occurs is shown here.

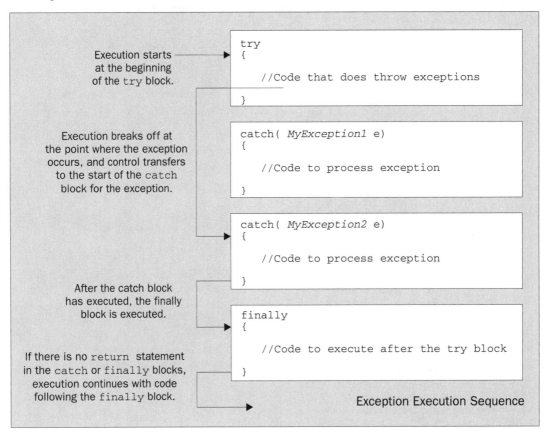

Execution of the **try** block stops at the point where the exception occurs, and the code in the **catch** block for the exception is executed immediately. If you have a **return** statement in the **catch** block, this isn't executed until the **finally** block has been executed.

Execution when an Exception is not Caught

The next block of six lines in the output are a consequence of the third call to the method **divide()**. This causes an **ArrayIndexOutOfBoundsException** to be thrown in the **try** block, which is then caught. However, the code at the end of the method which is executed after the **finally** block, throws another exception of this type. This can't be caught in the method **divide()** because the statement causing it isn't in a **try** block. Since this exception isn't caught in the method **divide()**, the method terminates immediately and the same exception is thrown in **main()** at the point where the method was called and causes the code in the relevant **catch** block in **main()** to be executed in consequence.

An exception that isn't caught in a method is always propagated upwards (or back) to the calling method. It will continue to propagate up through each level of calling method until either it is caught, or the uppermost-level method is reached. If it isn't caught at the top-level, it causes the program to terminate and a suitable message is displayed. This situation is illustrated here.

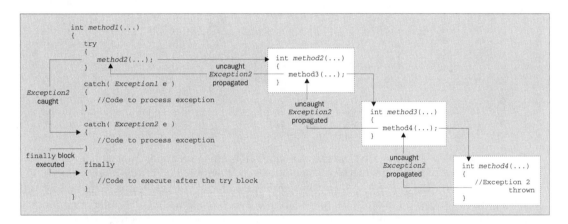

This shows **method1()** calling **method2()** which calls **method3()**, which calls **method4()** in which an exception of type **Exception2** is thrown. This exception isn't caught in **method4()** so execution of **method4()** ceases and the exception is thrown in **method3()**. It isn't caught, and continues to be rethrown until it reaches **method1()** where there's a **catch** block to handle it.

In our Try It Out, execution continues in **main()** with the output statements outside the first **try** block. The **read()** method pauses the program until you press the *Enter* key. No exception is thrown, and execution ends after the code in the **finally** block is executed. The **finally** block is tied to the **try** block that immediately precedes it, and is executed even though there's a **return** statement in the **try** block.

Nested try Blocks

We won't be going into it in detail, but you should note that you can have nested **try** blocks, as illustrated in this diagram.

```
try
{
    try
    {
        //1st inner try block code...
    }
    catch( Exception1 e )
    {
        //...
    }

    //Outer try block code...

    try
    {
        //2nd inner try block code...
    }
    catch( Exception1 e )
    {
        //try block code...
    }

}
catch( Exception2 e )
{
    //Outer catch block code...
}
```

Exceptions of type Exception2 thrown anywhere in here that are not caught, will be caught by the catch block for the outer try block.

The **catch** blocks for the outer **try** block can catch any exceptions that are thrown, but not caught, by any code within the block, including code within inner **try-catch** blocks. In the example shown, the **catch** block for the outer **try** block will catch any exception of type **Exception2**, and such exceptions could originate anywhere within the outer **try** block. The illustration shows just two levels of nesting, but if you know what you're doing, you can specify more.

Dealing with Exceptions

Well, you now understand how to put **try** blocks together with **catch** blocks and **finally** blocks in your methods, but you may be thinking at this point that it seems an awful lot of trouble to go to, just to display a message when an exception is thrown. Well, you may be right, but whether you can do very much more depends on the nature and context of the problem. In many situations a message may be the best you can do, although you can produce messages that are a bit more informative than those we've used so far in our examples.

To decide how to deal with any particular exception you need to consider two aspects of the exception:

> The information that the exception object can provide about the nature of the problem

> Where you should plan to deal with the exception in your program

Let's first look at how you can rethrow an exception to make a calling method aware that it has occurred. Then we'll look at the members of the base class for exceptions, **Throwable**, because these will be inherited by all exception classes and are therefore contained in every exception object that is thrown.

Rethrowing Exceptions

Even though you may need to recognize that an exception has occurred in a method by implementing a **catch** clause for it, this doesn't mean that that is necessarily the end of the matter. In many situations, the calling program may need to know about it, perhaps because it will affect the continued operation of the program, or maybe because the calling program is able to do something to compensate for the problem.

If you need to pass an exception on to the calling program, you can rethrow it from within the **catch** block using a **throw** statement. For example:

```
try
{
  // Code that originates an arithmetic exception
}
catch(ArithmeticException e)
{
  // Deal with the exception here
  throw e;                // Rethrow the exception to the calling program
}
```

The throw statement is just the keyword **throw** followed by the exception object to be thrown. When we get to look at how we can define our own exceptions later in this chapter, we'll be using exactly the same mechanism to throw them.

The Class Throwable

The class **Throwable** is the class from which all Java exception classes are derived, so every exception object will contain the methods defined in this class. The class **Throwable** has two constructors, a default constructor and a constructor that accepts an argument of type **String**. The **String** object that is passed to the constructor is used to provide a description of the nature of the problem causing the exception. Both constructors are **public**.

Objects of type **Throwable** contain two items of information about an exception:

▶ A message, that we have just referred to as being initialized by a constructor

▶ A record of the **execution stack** at the time the object was created

The record of the execution stack that is stored in the exception object will consist of the line number in the source code where the exception originated followed by a trace of the method calls that immediately preceded the point at which the exception occurred. This is made up of the fully qualified name for each of the methods that have been called, plus the line number in the source file where each method call occurred. The method calls are in sequence with the most recent method call appearing first. This will help you to understand how this point in the program was reached.

The **Throwable** class has four **public** methods which enable you to access the message and the stack trace:

Throwable Method	Description
getMessage()	This returns the contents of the message, describing the current exception. This will typically be the fully qualified name of the exception class (it will be a subclass of **Throwable**), and a brief description of the exception.
printStackTrace()	This will output the message and the stack trace to the standard error output stream—which is the screen in the case of a console program.
printStackTrace(PrintStream s)	This is the same as the previous method except that you specify the output stream as an argument.
to String()	This returns the message for the current exception object so the statement, **System.out.println(e);** will output the message if e is in the exception object.

There's another method, **fillInStackTrace()**, which will update the stack trace to the point at which this method is called. For example, if you put a call to this method in the **catch** block:

```
e.fillInStackTrace();
```

The line number recorded in the stack record for the method in which the exception occurred will be the line where **fillInStackTrace()** is called. The main use of this is when you want to rethrow an exception so it will be caught by the calling method, and you want to record the point at which it is rethrown. For example:

```
      e.fillInStackTrace();              // Record the throw point
      throw e;                           // Rethrow the exception
```

In practice, it's often more useful to throw an exception of your own. We'll see how you can define your own exceptions in the next section, but first, let's exercise some of the methods defined in the **Throwable** class, and see what we get.

Try It Out—Dishing the Dirt on Exceptions

The easiest way we can try out some of the methods we've just discussed is to make some judicious additions to the **catch** blocks in the **divide()** method we have in the **TryBlockTest** class example:

```
public static int divide(int[] array, int index)
{
  try
  {
    System.out.println("\nFirst try block in divide() entered");
    array[index + 2] = array[index]/array[index + 1];
    System.out.println("Code at end of first try block in divide()");
    return array[index + 2];
  }
  catch(ArithmeticException e)
  {
    System.out.println("Arithmetic exception caught in divide()\n" +
                          "\nMessage in exception object:\n\t" + e);
    System.out.println("\nStack trace output:\n");
    e.printStackTrace();
    System.out.println("\nEnd of stack trace output\n");
  }
  catch(ArrayIndexOutOfBoundsException e)
  {
    System.out.println("Index-out-of-bounds exception caught in
            divide()\n" + "\nMessage in exception object:\n\t" + e);
    System.out.println("\nStack trace output:\n");
    e.printStackTrace();
    System.out.println("\nEnd of stack trace output\n");
  }
  finally
  {
    System.out.println("finally clause in divide()");
  }
  System.out.println("Executing code after try block in divide()");
  return array[index + 2];
}
```

If you recompile the program and run it again, it will produce all the output as before, but with some extra information when exceptions are thrown in the **divide()** method. We'll show just the new output here. The additional output generated for the **ArithmeticException** will be:

```
Message in exception object:
        java.lang.ArithmeticException: / by zero

Stack trace output:

java.lang.ArithmeticException: / by zero
        at TryBlockTest.divide(TryBlockTest.java:54)
        at TryBlockTest.main(TryBlockTest.java:15)

End of stack trace output
```

The additional output generated for the **ArrayIndexOutOfBoundsException** will be:

```
Message in exception object:
        java.lang.ArrayIndexOutOfBoundsException:

Stack trace output:

java.lang.ArrayIndexOutOfBoundsException:
        at TryBlockTest.divide(TryBlockTest.java:54)
        at TryBlockTest.main(TryBlockTest.java:17)

End of stack trace output
```

How It Works

The extra lines of code in each of the **catch** blocks in the **divide()** method output the message associated with the exception object, **e**, by appending the object to the **String** argument in the call to **println()**. This invokes the **toString()** method for **e**. We have a couple of extra **println()** calls around the call to **printStackTrace()** to make it easier to find the stack trace in the output.

The first stack trace, for the arithmetic exception, indicates that the error originated at line 54 in the source file, **TryBlockText.java**, and the last method call was at line 15 in the same source file. The second stack trace provides similar information about the index-out-of-bounds exception. As you can see, with the stack trace output, it's very easy to see where the error occurred, and how this point in the program was reached.

Standard Exceptions

The majority of predefined exception classes in Java don't add further information about the conditions that created the exception. This is because additional information can only be gleaned with a prior knowledge of what sort of computation is being carried out when the exception occurs, and the only person who is privy to that is you, since you're writing the program.

This should spark the glimmer of an idea. If you need more information about the circumstances surrounding an exception, you're going to have to obtain it, and, equally important, communicate it to the appropriate point in your program. This leads to the notion of defining your own exceptions.

Defining your own Exceptions

There are two basic reasons for defining your own exception classes:

▶ You want to add information when a standard exception occurs, and you can do this by rethrowing an object of your own exception class

▶ You may have error conditions that can arise in your code that warrant the distinction of a special exception class

However, you do need to bear in mind that there's a lot of overhead in throwing exceptions, so it isn't a valid substitute for 'normal' recovery code that you would expect to be executed frequently. If you have recovery code that's going to be executed often, then it doesn't belong in a **catch** block, rather in something like an **if-then-else** loop.

Let's see how we can create our own exceptions.

Defining an Exception Class

Your exception classes must be subclasses of **Throwable**, and although you can derive them from other standard exceptions, your best policy is to derive them from the base class. This will allow the compiler to keep track of where such exceptions are thrown in your program, and check that they are either caught or declared as thrown in a method. If you use **RuntimeException** or one of its subclasses, the compiler checking for **catch** blocks of your exception class will be suppressed.

Let's go through an example of how you define an exception class:

```
public class DreadfulProblemException extends Throwable
{
  // Constructors
  public DreadfulProblemException(){ }        // Default constructor

  public DreadfulProblemException(String s)
  {
    super(s);                                // Call the base class constructor
  }
}
```

This is the minimum you need to supply. By convention, your exception should include a default constructor and a constructor that accepts a **String** object as an argument. The message stored in the superclass, **Throwable**, will automatically be initialized with the name of your class, whichever constructor for your class objects is used. The **String** passed to the constructor will be appended to the name of the class to form the message stored in the exception object.

Of course, you can add other constructors. In general, you'll want to do so, particularly when you're rethrowing your own exception after a standard exception has been thrown. In addition, you'll typically want to add instance variables to the class that store additional information about the problem, plus methods that will enable the code in a **catch** block to get at the data. Since your exception class is derived from **Throwable**, the stack trace information will be automatically available for your exceptions.

281

Throwing your Own Exception

As we saw earlier, we throw an exception with a statement that consists of the keyword **throw** followed by an exception object. This means you can throw your own exception with the statements:

```
DreadfulProblemException e = new DreadfulProblemException();
throw e;
```

The method will cease execution at this point—unless the code snippet above is in a **try** or a **catch** block with an associated **finally** clause, the contents of which will be executed before the method ends. The exception will be thrown in the calling program at the point where this method was called. The message in the exception object will just consist of the qualified name of our exception class. If you wanted to add a specific message to the exception, you could define it as:

```
DreadfulProblemException e = new DreadfulProblemException("Uh-Oh,
    ↳ trouble.");
```

We're using a different constructor here. In this case the message stored in the superclass will be a string which consists of the class name with the string passed to the constructor appended to it. The **getMessage()** method, inherited from **Throwable**, will therefore return a **String** object containing the string:

```
"DreadfulProblemException: Uh-Oh, trouble."
```

You can also create an exception object and throw it in a single statement. For example:

```
throw new DreadfulProblemException("Terrible difficulties");
```

In all the examples, the stack trace record inherited from the superclass, **Throwable**, will be set up automatically.

An Exception Handling Strategy

You need to think through what you want to achieve with the exception handling code in your program. There are no hard and fast rules. In some situations you may be able to correct a problem and enable your program to continue as though nothing happened. In other situations an error message and a fast exit will be the best approach—a fast exit being achieved by just calling the **exit()** method in the **System** class. Here we'll take a look at some of the things you need to weigh up when deciding how to handle exceptions.

Consider the last example where we handled arithmetic exceptions and index-out-of-bounds exceptions in the method, **divide()**. While this was a reasonable demonstration of the way the various blocks worked, it wasn't a satisfactory way of dealing with the exceptions in the program for two reasons. First, it doesn't make a whole lot of sense to catch the arithmetic exceptions in the **divide()** method without passing them on to the calling method—after all, it was the calling method that set the data up, and only the calling program has the potential to recover the situation. Second, by handling the exceptions completely in the

divide() method, we allow the calling program to continue execution, without any knowledge of the problem that arose. In a real situation this would undoubtedly create chaos as further calculations would proceed with erroneous data.

We could have simply ignored the exceptions in the **divide()** method. This might not be a bad approach in this particular situation, but the first problem the calling program would have is determining the source of the exception. After all, such exceptions might also arise in the calling program itself. A second consideration could arise if the **divide()** method was more complicated. There could be several places where such exceptions might be thrown, and the calling method would have a hard time distinguishing them.

An Example of an Exception Class

Another possibility is to catch the exceptions in the method where they originate, then pass them on to the calling program. You can pass them on by throwing new exceptions that provide more **granularity** in identifying the problem by having more than one exception type, or by providing additional data within the new exception type. For example, you could define more than one exception class of your own that represented an **ArithmeticException**, where each reflected the specifics of a particular situation. This situation is illustrated here.

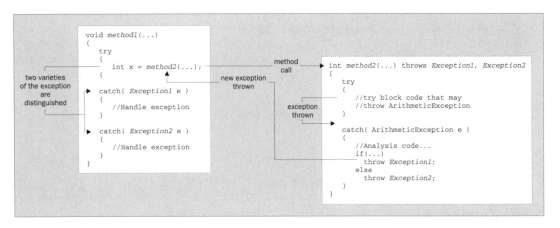

This shows how two different circumstances causing an **ArithmeticException** in **method2()**, are differentiated in the calling method, **method1()**. The method, **method2()**, can throw either an exception of type **Exception1**, or of type **Exception2**, depending on the analysis that is made in the **catch** block for the **ArithmeticException** type. The calling method has a separate **catch** block for each of the exceptions that may be thrown.

You could also define a new exception class that had instance variables that could be used to identify the problem more precisely. Let's suppose that in the last example, we wanted to provide more information to the calling program about the error that caused each exception in the **divide()** method. The primary exception can be either an **ArithmeticException** or an **ArrayIndexOutOfBoundsException**, but since we're dealing with a specific context for these errors we could give the calling program more information by throwing our own exceptions.

Let's take the **ArithmeticException** case as a model and define our own exception class that we can use in the program to help identify the reason for the error more precisely.

Try It Out—Define Your Own Exception Class

We can define the class which will correspond to an **ArithmeticException** in the method **divide()** as:

```
public class ZeroDivideException extends Throwable
{
  private int index = -1;        // Index of array element causing error

  // Default Constructor
  public ZeroDivideException(){ }

  // Standard constructor
  public ZeroDivideException(String s)
  {
    super(s);                               // Call the base constructor
  }

  public ZeroDivideException(int index)
  {
    super("/ by zero");                     // Call the base constructor
    this.index = index;                     // Set the index value
  }

  // Get the array index value for the error
  public int getIndex()
  {
    return index;                           // Return the index value
  }
}
```

How It Works

As we've derived the class from the class **Throwable**, the compiler will check that the exceptions thrown are either caught, or identified as thrown in a method. Our class will inherit all the members of the class **Throwable** so we'll get the stack trace record and the message for the exception maintained for free, and it will also inherit the **toString()** method which is satisfactory in this context, but you could override it if you wanted to.

We've added a data member, **index**, to store the index value of the zero divisor in the array passed to **divide()**. This will give the calling program a chance to fix this value if appropriate in the **catch** block for the exception. In this case the catch block would also need to include code that would enable the divide method to be called again with the corrected array.

Let's now put it to work.

Try It Out—Using the Exception Class

1 We need to use the class in two contexts—in the method **divide()** when we catch a standard **ArithmeticException**, and in the calling method, **main()**, where we need to catch the new exception. Let's modify **divide()** first:

```
public static int divide(int[] array, int index)
                                          throws ZeroDivideException
{
  try
  {
    System.out.println("First try block in divide() entered");
    array[index + 2] = array[index]/array[index + 1];
    System.out.println("Code at end of first try block in divide()");
    return array[index + 2];
  }
  catch(ArithmeticException e)
  {
    System.out.println("Arithmetic exception caught in divide()");
    throw new ZeroDivideException(index + 1);   // Throw new exception
  }
  catch(ArrayIndexOutOfBoundsException e)
  {
    System.out.println("Index-out-of-bounds index exception caught in
                        divide()");
  }
  System.out.println("Executing code after try block in divide()");
  return array[index + 2];
}
```

The first change is to add the **throws** clause to the method definition. Without this we'll get an error message from the compiler. The second change adds a statement to the **catch** block for **ArithmeticException** exceptions which throws a new exception.

2 This new exception needs to be caught in the calling method **main()**:

```
public static void main(String[] args)
{
  int[] x = {10, 5, 0};                        // Array of three integers

  // This block only throws an exception if method divide() does
  try
  {
    System.out.println("First try block in main()entered");
    System.out.println("result = " + divide(x,0));  // No error
    x[1] = 0;                      // Will cause a divide by zero
```

```
       System.out.println("result = " + divide(x,0));  // Arithmetic error
       x[1] = 1;                       // Reset to prevent divide by zero
       System.out.println("result = " + divide(x,1));  // Index error
    }
    catch(ZeroDivideException e)
    {
      int index = e.getIndex();      // Get the index for the error
      if(index > 0)                  // Verify it is valid
      {                              // Now fix up the array...
        x[index] = 1;                //  ...set the divisor to 1...
        x[index + 1] = x[index - 1]; //  ...and set the result
        System.out.println("Zero divisor corrected to " + x[index]);
      }
    }
    catch(ArithmeticException e)
    {
      System.out.println("Arithmetic exception caught in main()");
    }
    catch(ArrayIndexOutOfBoundsException e)
    {
      System.out.println
              ("Index-out-of-bounds exception caught in main()");
    }
    System.out.println("Outside first try block in main()");
  }
```

How It Works

All we need to add is the **catch** block for the new exception. We need to make sure that the index value for the divisor stored in the exception object is positive so that we don't cause another exception to be thrown when we fix up the array. We arbitrarily set the array element that contained the zero divisor to 1, and so it makes sense to set the array element holding the result to be the same as the dividend. We can then let the method **main()** stagger on.

A point to bear in mind is that the last two statements in the `try` block will not have been executed. After the `catch` block has been executed, the method continues with the code following the `try`-catch block set. In practice you would need to consider whether you should do anything about this.One possiblity is to put the whole of the `try`-catch block code in `main()` in a loop that would normally only run one iteration, but where this could be altered to run additional iterations by setting a flag in the `catch` block.

This is a rather artificial example, so what sort of circumstances could justify this kind of fixing up of the data in a program? If the data originated through some kind of instrumentation measuring physical parameters such as temperatures or pressures, it might be that the data could contain spurious zero values from time to time. Rather than abandon the whole calculation you might well want to fix these up as they occurred, and press on to process the rest of the data.

Summary

In this chapter you have learned what exceptions are and how you can deal with them in your programs. You should make sure that you consider exception handling as an integral part of developing your Java programs. The robustness of your program code depends on how effectively you deal with exceptions that can be thrown in it.

The important concepts we have explored in this chapter are:

▶ Exceptions identify errors that arise in your program.

▶ Exceptions are objects of subclasses of the class **Throwable**.

▶ Java includes a set of standard exceptions that may be thrown automatically as a result of errors in your code, or may be thrown by methods in the standard classes in Java.

▶ If a method throws exceptions that aren't caught, and aren't represented by subclasses of the class **Error**, or by subclasses of the class **RuntimeException**, then you must identify the exception classes in a **throws** clause in the method definition.

▶ If you want to handle an exception in a method, you must place the code that may generate the exception in a **try** block. A method may have several **try** blocks.

▶ Exception handling code is placed in a **catch** block that immediately follows the **try** block that contains the code that can throw the exception. A **try** block can have multiple **catch** blocks that deal with different types of exception.

▶ A **finally** block is used to contain code that must be executed after the execution of a **try** block, regardless of how the **try** block execution ends. A **finally** block will always be executed before execution of the method ends.

▶ You can throw an exception by using a **throw** statement. You can throw an exception anywhere in a method. You can also rethrow an existing exception in a **catch** block to pass it to the calling method.

▶ You can define your own exception classes by deriving them from the class **Throwable**.

Exercises

1 Write a program that will generate exceptions of type **NullPointerException**, **NegativeArraySizeException** and **IndexOutOfBoundsException**, and record the catching of each exception by displaying the message store in the exception object, and the stack trace record.

2 Add an exception class to the last example that will differentiate between the index-out-of-bounds error possibilities, rethrow an appropriate object of this exception class in **divide()**, and handle the exception in **main()**.

3 Write a program that calls a method which throws an exception of type **ArithmeticException** at a random iteration in a **for** loop. Catch the exception in the method, and pass the iteration count when the exception occurred to the calling method by using an object of an exception class you define.

4 Add a **finally** block to the method in the previous example to output the iteration count when the method exits.

Stream Input/Output

The package **java.io** is vast—it defines a large number of classes. There are also classes in the package **java.util.zip** that are strongly related to some of the classes in **java.io**. As a result, this is a heavyweight chapter. In spite of this, we still won't be able to cover all of these classes in minute detail, but we will go into enough of them so that you should be able to get to grips with the others without too much difficulty.

> **FYI** If you just want a fast track to get into window-based applications, and you are happy to get by with just file operations for objects, you can probably get by just reading the last section of this chapter that deals with writing objects to a file.

The classes in the package **java.io** provide support for transferring character and other binary data, and objects from your program to an external destination such as a file. **java.io** classes also enable you to retrieve data and objects from an external file. We have already made extensive use of the method **println()** which comes from this package, and we have also seen the method **read()**. We will now take a close look at some of the most important classes in **java.io** that support input and output, and how you can use them for storing and retrieving your Java program data.

By the end of this chapter, you will have learned:

 What a stream is and what classes Java provides to support stream operations

How to write to a stream

How you can write a file to a ZIP archive

How to read from a stream

How you can read a file from a ZIP archive

How to access a file randomly

How you can perform read and write operations on a file

How to handle inputting values of the basic Java types from the keyboard

▶ How to output numeric data to a stream in a fixed width field

▶ How to write objects to a file and read them back

Understanding Streams

Java file input and output involves using **streams**. You can write data to a stream and read data from a stream. A **stream** is an abstract representation of an input or output device that is a source or destination for data in your program. You can visualize a stream as a sequence of bytes that flows into or out of your program.

When you write data to a stream, the stream is called an **output stream**. The physical reality of the output stream—where the data goes—can be any device to which a sequence of bytes can be transferred. It will typically be either a file on your hard disk, or possibly your printer.

Note that your display screen can also be an output stream, but only at the expense of limiting it to a fraction of its true capability. When you write to your display screen as a stream, you can only display characters. You can't use its more general abilities to display graphical output. This requires more specialized support that we'll be investigating from Chapter 11 onwards.

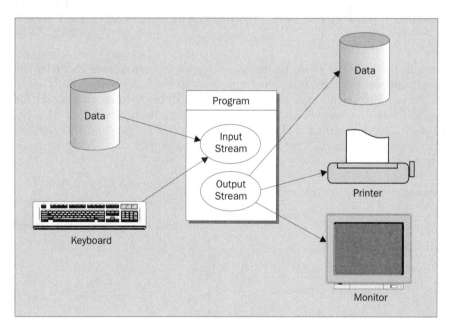

You read data from an **input stream**. In principle this can be any serial source of data but is typically a disk file, or the keyboard.

*Note that file input and output for the machine on which your program is executing is only available to Java applications under normal circumstances—not to Java applets. This is because having a Java applet embedded in a Web page with the potential to trash your hard disk, would not be acceptable to most people. As a consequence, you can expect an **IOException** to be thrown by any operation on disk files on the local machine that you include in a Java applet. However, an applet can access files on its host machine—the machine where it originated.*

The primary reason behind using the concept of a stream as the basis for input and output operations in Java is to make your program code for these operations independent of the physical device involved. This has a couple of advantages. Firstly, you don't have to worry about the detailed mechanics of each device, as this is all taken care of behind the scenes. Secondly, your program will work with a variety of disparate input/output devices without necessitating any changes to the source code.

Character Streams and Byte Streams

The `java.io` package supports two kinds of streams called **byte streams** and **character streams**. You can use byte streams when you want to store and retrieve basic types of data such as integers and floating values, as well as character strings. As you know, Java stores its characters internally as Unicode characters. When you write Unicode characters to a byte stream, each 16-bit character is written as two bytes, the high byte being written first.

Character streams are intended for use when you want to store and retrieve text—that is, strings or arrays of Unicode characters, and in particular when you want to read a text file that was not written by a Java program. When you write character strings to a character stream, the Unicode characters are automatically converted to the local representation of the characters used by the local machine, and these are then written to the file. When you read from a character stream, the data in the file is automatically converted from the local machine representation to Unicode characters. With character streams, your program reads and writes Unicode characters, but the file will contain characters in the equivalent character encoding used by the local computer.

The Classes for Input and Output

There are quite a number of classes involved in stream input and output, but as you will see, they form a very logical structure. Once you see how they are related, you shouldn't have much trouble applying them in practice. We will work through the class hierarchy from the top down, so you will be able to see how the classes hang together, and how you can easily combine them in various ways to suit different situations.

The package `java.io` contains six classes that provide the foundation for Java's support for stream I/O:

Class	Description
`File`	An object of this class represent either a file that you will access for input or output, or a directory.
`OutputStream`	The base class for byte stream output operations.
`InputStream`	The base class for byte stream input operations.
`Writer`	The base class for character stream input operations.
`Reader`	The base class for character stream input operations.
`RandomAccessFile`	This class provides support for random access to a file.

As usual, all these classes are sub-classes of the class `Object`. The classes `InputStream`, `OutputStream`, `Reader` and `Writer` are all **abstract** classes. As you are well aware by now, you cannot create instances of an abstract class—these classes only serve as a base from which to derive classes with more concrete input or output capabilities. However, don't be misled. All four of these classes declare methods that define a basic set of operations for streams that they represent, so the fundamental characteristics of how a stream is accessed is set by these classes. Although these methods are implemented in derived classes, their pattern of use is set by the arguments they accept, and the types of their return values.

We will be taking a look at each of these classes first to get an overview of how operations with streams work, and then looking in more detail at the classes that are derived from them and trying some of them out in practical examples.

> Before we get into that, though, a note of caution. Before running any of the examples in this chapter, be sure to back up the files that they operate on, and the directory that contains the files. Ideally, you should set up a separate directory for storing the files that you are using when you are testing programs.
>
> The old adage 'if anything can go wrong, it will' applies particularly in this context, as does the complementary principle 'if anything can't go wrong it will'. Remember also that the probability of something going wrong increases in proportion to the inconvenience it is likely to cause you.

The file streams that you will define using classes derived from `InputStream`, `OutputStream`, `Reader` and `Writer` are inherently serial in nature. You cannot process them randomly. For storing and retrieving data in a random access file you must use the `RandomAccessFile` class. We will also be seeing how random input and output works in practice in this chapter. Note that there is no fundamental difference between a file created as a serial byte stream and a file created using a `RandomAccessFile` object. The class object that you use to access a file only affects the ways in which you can deal with the data in the file.

A good place to start is with the `File` class, since you will use objects of this class to identify the physical file that you are going to work with whenever you define a stream object.

Defining a File

As well as enabling you to create objects that represent files or directories, the **File** class also provides several methods for you to test the objects you create. You can tell the difference between a file and a directory for example. You can also modify a **File** object in a number of ways.

When creating **File** objects, you have a choice of three constructors. The simplest accepts a **String** object as an argument, which specifies the path for a file or a directory. For example, if you are using Windows 95, you could write the statement:

```
File myDir = new File("F:\\jdk1.1\\src\\java\\io");
```

This identifies the path on my system for the directory containing the I/O package. Note that we need to use the escape character for the path separator character, \. You could equally well use the Unix separator which is a forward slash:

```
File myDir = new File("F:/jdk1.1/src/java/io");
```

This will work just as well with Windows 95, and it's a bit less cluttered. However, there is a downside. The object will store the path as you have specified it and convert it as necessary. So if you use a forward slash as the separator under Windows 95, when you invoke the **toString**() method for the object you will get back what you specified, and not the normal Windows 95 representation of a path using a backslash as a separator.

> *The last example still refers to the directory on my Windows 95 system. Of course, if you are using a Unix system, the Java directory is more likely to be at "~/java...".*

To specify a file, you just need to make sure that the string that you pass as an argument to the constructor does refer to a file. For example, the statement:

```
File myFile = new File("\\java\\src\\java\\io\\File.java");
```

sets the object **myFile** to correspond to the source file for the definition of the class **File** on the local drive.

You can also create a **File** object that represents a file by specifying the path for the directory, and the file name, separately. You just use a version of the **File** constructor that accepts two arguments. The first argument to the constructor is a **File** object that represents the directory, and the second argument is a **String** object referencing the file name. For example, to identify the source file for the definition of the class **File**, we could write:

```
File myDir = new File("F:\\java\\src\\java\\io"); // Object for directory
File myFile = new File(myDir, "File.java");       // Object for the file
```

The first statement creates a file object that is the directory for the package **io**, and the second statement creates a file object that corresponds to the file, **File.java**, in that directory.

The third constructor also accepts two arguments, but the first argument is a **String** object identifying the directory, rather than a **File** object. The second argument is still a **String** object referring to the file name. We could use this constructor to achieve the same result as the previous two statements:

```
File myFile = new File("F:\\java\\src\\java\\io", "File.java");
```

There's not a lot to choose between these last two constructors. Having a **File** object defining a directory can be useful if you intend processing more than one file in it. You can find out what files the directory contains for example.

Testing and Checking File Objects

The **File** class provides a whole bunch of methods that you can apply to **File** objects, so we will look at them grouped by the sort of thing that they do. For testing and checking **File** objects, you have the following methods available:

Method	Description
exists()	Returns **true** if the file or directory referred to by the **File** object exists, and **false** otherwise.
isDirectory()	Returns **true** if the **File** object refers to a directory, and **false** otherwise.
isFile()	Returns **true** if the **File** object refers to a file, and **false** otherwise.
isAbsolute()	Returns **true** if the file object refers to an absolute path name, and **false** otherwise. Under Windows 95, an absolute path name begins with either a drive letter followed by a colon, or by a backslash. Under Unix an absolute path is specified from the root directory down.
canRead()	Returns **true** if you are permitted to read the file referred to by the **File** object, and **false** otherwise. This method can throw a **SecurityException** if read access to the file is not permitted.
canWrite()	Returns **true** if you are permitted to write the file referred to by the **File** object, and **false** otherwise. This method may also throw a **SecurityException** if you are not allowed to write to the file.
equals()	You use this method for comparing two **File** objects for equality. If the **File** object passed as an argument to the method has the same path as the currentobject, the method returns **true**. Otherwise it returns **false**.

> *Note that all operations that involve accessing the files on the local machine can throw a **SecurityException** if access is not authorized—in an applet for instance. This is the case with the **canRead()** and **canWrite()** methods here. For a **SecurityException** to be thrown a security manager must exist on the local machine.*

The uses for these are generally obvious. To make sure it's clear how they go together, we can try some of these out with a simple example:

Try It Out—Testing for a File

Try the following source code. Don't forget the **import** statement for the **java.io** package. The example won't compile without it.

```java
import java.io.*;                      // For input & output classes

public class TryFile
{
  public static void main(String[] args)
  {
    // Create an object that is a directory
    File myDir = new File("\\jdk1.1.1\\src\\java\\io");
    System.out.println(myDir +
              (myDir.isDirectory()?" is":" is not") + " a directory.");

    // Create an object that is a file
    File myFile = new File(myDir, "File.java");
    System.out.println(myFile +
                      (myFile.exists()?" does":" does not") + " exist");
    System.out.println("You can" +
                      (myFile.canRead()?" ":"not ") + "read " + myFile);
    System.out.println("You can" +
                      (myFile.canWrite()?" ":"not ") + "write " + myFile);
    return;
  }
}
```

On my machine, the example produces the output:

```
\jdk1.1.1\src\java\io is a directory.
\jdk1.1.1\src\java\io\File.java does exist
You can read \jdk1.1.1\src\java\io\File.java
You can write \jdk1.1.1\src\java\io\File.java
```

How It Works

This program first creates an object corresponding to the directory containing the **java.io** package. You need to check the path to this directory on your own system, and insert that as the argument to the constructor if it is different.

The output statement uses the conditional operator, **?**, in conjunction with the **isDirectory()** method to display a message. If **isDirectory()** returns **true**, then **" is"** is selected. Otherwise, **" is not"** is selected. We then create another **File** object corresponding to the file **File.java** and display another message using the same sort of mechanism. Finally we use the **canRead()** and **canWrite()** methods to determine whether read or write access to the file is prevented.

With the code as written, if a **SecurityException** is thrown, it will not be caught. To provide for this you would need to put the statements involving the calls to **canRead()** and **canWrite()** in a **try** block, followed by a **catch** block for the exception. You could also try out the **/** separator with this example, and see if it makes a difference.

Accessing File Objects

You can get information about a **File** object by using the following methods:

Method	Description
getName()	Returns a **String** object containing the name of the file, but not the path name. For a **File** object representing a directory, just the directory name is returned.
getPath()	Returns a **String** object containing the path for the **File** object—including the file or directory name.
getAbsolutePath()	Returns the absolute path for the directory or file referenced by the current **File** object.
getParent()	Returns a **String** object containing the parent directory of the file or directory represented by the current **File** object.
list()	If the current **File** object represents a directory, a **String** array is returned containing the members of the directory. If the current file object is a file, **null** is returned.
length()	Returns a value of type **long** that is the length in bytes of the file represented by the current **File** object. If the current object represents a directory, zero is returned.
lastModified()	Returns a value of type **long** that represents the time that the directory or file represented by the current **File** object was last modified. Zero is returned if the file does not exist.
toString()	This returns a **String** representation of the current **File** object and is called automatically when a **File** object is concatenated with a **String** object. We have already used this method implicitly in the output statements in the previous example.
hashCode()	Returns a hash code value for the current **File** object. We will see more about what hash codes are used for in Chapter 9.

With a few changes and additions to the last example we can test some of these methods.

Try It Out—Getting More Information

1 Making the following modifications to **TryFile.java**:

```java
import java.io.*;

public class TryFile
{
  public static void main(String[] args)
  {
    // Create an object that is a directory
    File myDir = new File("\\jdk1.1.1\\src\\java\\io");
    System.out.println(myDir.getAbsolutePath() +
                (myDir.isDirectory()?" is ":"is not ") + "a directory");
    System.out.println("The parent of " + myDir.getName() +
                                    " is " + myDir.getParent());

    // Create an object that is a directory
    File myFile = new File(myDir, "File.java");
    System.out.println(myFile +
                    (myFile.exists()?" does":" does not") + " exist");
    System.out.println("You can" +
              (myFile.canRead()?" ":"not ") + "read " + myFile.getName());
    System.out.println("You can" +
              (myFile.canWrite()?" ":"not ") + "write "+myFile.getName());

    // Get the length of the file
    System.out.println("The length of " +
                          myFile.getName() + " is " + myFile.length());
    return;
  }
}
```

2 If you want to try listing the contents of a directory, you could add a few lines of code just before the **return** statement:

```java
    ...
    // Get the contents of the directory
    String[] contents = myDir.list();

    // List the contents
    if(contents!=null)
    {
      System.out.println("\nThe " + contents.length +
                " files in the directory " + myDir.getName() + " are:");
      for(int i = 0; i < contents.length; i++)
        System.out.println(contents[i]);
    }
```

```
      else
        System.out.println("\nThe directory " +
                                        myDir.getName() + " is empty");
      return;
    }
  }
```

You should not have any difficulty seeing how this works. We have modified most of the output statement to produce a little extra information about the directory and file we have specified in the **File** object. The first part of the example will now produce the output:

```
\jdk1.1.1\src\java\io is a directory
The parent of io is \jdk1.1.1\src\java
\jdk1.1.1\src\java\io\File.java does exist
You can read File.java
You can write File.java
The length of File.java is 25240
```

with the second part listing the 71 (or so) files in the **io** package.

How It Works

You can see that the **getName()** method just returns the file or the directory name, depending on what the **File** object represents. The length of **File.java** may be different on your system if you have a different release of Java from mine.

The **list()** method returns a **String** array, and each element of the array contains the name of a member of the directory, which could be a sub-directory or a file. We store the reference to array returned in our array variable, **contents**. After outputting a heading, we check that the array is not **null**, just to be on the safe side. We then list the contents of the directory in the **for** loop. If the array does happen to be **null**, we just output a message.

Filtering a File List

The **list()** method is overloaded with a version that accepts an argument that is used to filter a file list. This enables you to get a list of just those files with a given extension, or with names that start with a particular sequence of characters. The argument you pass must be a variable of type **FilenameFilter**. **FilenameFilter** is an interface that contains just the abstract method **accept()**. It is therefore defined as:

```
public interface FilenameFilter
{
  public abstract boolean accept(File directory, String filename);
}
```

The filtering of the list is achieved by the **list()** method calling the method **accept()** for every name in the raw list. If the method returns **true**, the name stays in the list, and if it returns **false** the name is not included. Obviously, the interface is just a vehicle to make the mechanism work, so you need to define your own class that implements the interface **FilenameFilter**, and then pass an object of your class to the **list()** method. We can see how this works by extending the previous example a bit further.

Try It Out—Using the `FilenameFilter` Interface

1 We can define a class to specify a file filter as:

```java
import java.io.*;                                    // For FilenameFilter

public class FileListFilter implements FilenameFilter
{
  private String name;                     // File name filter
  private String extension;                // File extension filter

  // Constructor
  public FileListFilter(String name, String extension)
  {
    this.name = name;
    this.extension = extension;
  }

  public boolean accept(File directory, String filename)
  {
    boolean fileOK = true;

    // If there is a name filter specified, check the file name
    if(name != null)
      fileOK &= filename.startsWith(name);

    // If there is an extension filter, check the file extension
    if(extension != null)
      fileOK &= filename.endsWith('.' + extension);
    return fileOK;
  }
}
```

This uses the methods `startsWith()` and `endsWith()` defined in the `String` class that we discussed in Chapter 4.

2 Now we can use this in the previous example by changing the code in `main()` that lists the contents of the directory to:

```java
    . . .
    // Define a filter for java source files beginning with F
    FilenameFilter select = new FileListFilter("F", "java");

    // Get the contents of the directory
    String[] contents = myDir.list(select);

    // List the contents
    if(contents!=null)
    {
      System.out.println("\nThe " + contents.length +
                " files in the directory " + myDir.getName() + " are:");
```

301

```
        for(int i = 0; i < contents.length; i++)
          System.out.println(contents[i]);
      }
      else
        System.out.println("\nThe directory " +
                                        myDir.getName() + " is empty");
```

When you run the code, you should get:

```
\jdk1.1.1\src\java\io is a directory
The parent of io is \jdk1.1.1\src\java
\jdk1.1.1\src\java\io\File.java does exist
You can read File.java
You can write File.java
The length of File.java is 25240

There are 12 matching files in the directory io
FileInputStream.java
FileOutputStream.java
FilterOutputStream.java
FilterInputStream.java
File.java
FilenameFilter.java
FileDescriptor.java
FileNotFoundException.java
FilterReader.java
FileWriter.java
FilterWriter.java
FileReader.java
```

How It Works

Our **FileListFilter** class has two instance variables, **name** and **extension**, which store the file name prefix and the extension which selects files to be included in a list, respectively. These variables are set by the constructor, and the value of either can be omitted when the constructor is called by specifying the appropriate argument as **null**. If you wanted a really fancy filter, you could have just one argument to the constructor so you could specify the filter as ***.java**, or **A*.java**, or even **A*.j***. You would just need a bit more code in the constructor or possibly the **accept()** method to analyze the argument. Our implementation of the **accept()** method here only returns **true** if the file name passed to it by the **list()** method has initial characters that are identical to **name**, and the file extension is the same as that stored in **extension**.

In the modified **TryFile** class, we construct an object of our filter class using the string **"F"** as the file name prefix, and the string **"java"** as the extension. This version of the example will now only list files with names beginning with **F**, and with the extension **.java**.

Modifying File Objects

There are four methods that you can use to change a **File** object in various ways, all of which return a value of type **boolean**:

Method	Description
delete()	You need to exercise caution with this method as it will delete the file represented by the current **File** object and return **true** as long as the file is deleted successfully. It won't delete directories—only files.
renameTo(File path)	The file represented by the current object will be renamed to the path represented by the **File** object, passed as an argument to the method. Note that this does *not* change the current **File** object in your program—it alters the physical file. Thus the file that the **File** object represents will no longer exist after executing this method (because the file will have a new name and possibly be located in a different directory). If the file's directory in the new path is different from the original, the file will be moved. The method will fail if the directory in the new path for the file does not exist. If the operation is successful, the value **true** will be returned, otherwise the method returns **false**.
mkdir()	Creates a directory with the path specified by the current **File** object. The method will fail if the directory in the path containing the directory to be created does not exist. The method returns **true** if it is successful, and **false** otherwise.
mkdirs()	Creates the directory represented by the current **File** object, including any parent directories that are required. It returns **true** if the new directory is created successfully, and **false** otherwise.

You should not use the **delete()** method lightly. It is all too easy in a program to delete the wrong file. However, the ability to delete a file comes in very useful in programs that use temporary files that are not required when execution is finished. Perhaps fortunately for the more error-prone programmer, Java provides no method that will delete a directory at the present time.

We will be trying out some of these methods in examples later in this chapter. Now we understand how to define physical files in a Java program, we can move on to stream operations. We will look at what we can do with byte streams first; then we will cover character streams. Since we can't read a file until we have written one, let's look at byte output streams next.

Byte Output Streams

The **OutputStream** class is an **abstract** class designed to act as a base class for all the other classes that represent a byte output stream. Classes derived from the class **OutputStream** will inherit the following five methods, all of which have a return type of **void**:

Method	Description
`write(int b)`	This is an **abstract** method that is intended to write the low order byte of the argument **b** to the output stream.
`write(byte[] b)`	This method writes the array of bytes, **b**, to the output stream.
`write(byte[] b, int offset, int length)`	This method writes **length** bytes from the array **b** to the output stream, starting with the element **b[offset]**.
`flush()`	This method forces any buffered output data to be written to the output stream. If this data is being transferred to another nested stream (we will see how this works a little later in this chapter), the nested stream will also be flushed.
`close()`	This method closes the output stream and any nested output streams.

All of these methods will throw an **IOException** if an error occurs.

Although the first version of the method **write()** is the only method that is **abstract**, the classes derived from **OutputStream** will typically implement their own versions of all of these methods, as the ones here need some improvement. The **flush()** and **close()** methods as defined in the class **OutputStream** don't actually do anything for example, and the **write()** methods that are implemented in the class simply use the version that writes one byte at a time.

FYI
As you will see, we will often create a stream object using an existing stream object, incorporating functionality from the first stream object into the second. This object can then be used to create another stream object, and so on. This is the nesting process referred to in the context of the **flush()** and **close()** methods.

A serious limitation of **OutputStream** and all the classes derived from it in the current implementation of the **java.io** package, is that there is no way to append data to an existing file. The only way you can extend an existing stream file using an **OutputStream** object is to open the file as an input stream, copy all the contents to a new output stream, then add the additional data. We will see a bit later on in this chapter that you can use a **RandomAccessFile** object to get both read and write access to a file, so this is the preferred approach when you want to update a file.

Sub-classes of OutputStream

There are five direct sub-classes of the **abstract** class **OutputStream**.

One of these, **ObjectOutputStream**, is used for writing objects to a file, and since this is a rather different process from writing ordinary data to a file, we will deal with this class separately, later in this chapter.

The other four sub-classes of **OutputStream** are shown in the next diagram. You can use three of these to create objects that represent byte output streams of different kinds. The fourth direct sub-class is a base class for further classes that you can use to extend the capabilities of the first three classes.

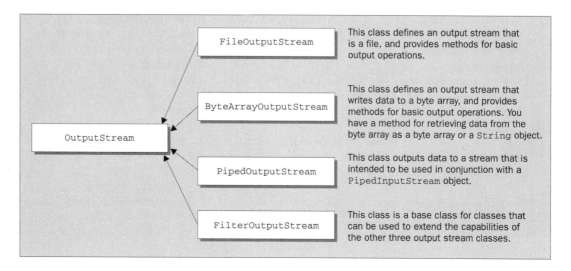

| FileOutputStream | This class defines an output stream that is a file, and provides methods for basic output operations. |

| ByteArrayOutputStream | This class defines an output stream that writes data to a byte array, and provides methods for basic output operations. You have a method for retrieving data from the byte array as a byte array or a String object. |

| PipedOutputStream | This class outputs data to a stream that is intended to be used in conjunction with a PipedInputStream object. |

| FilterOutputStream | This class is a base class for classes that can be used to extend the capabilities of the other three output stream classes. |

The basic output operations supported by these classes are the **byte** output functions supported by the **write()** methods inherited from the **OutputStream** class. They include no provision for writing other types of data to a file. To handle other types of data, you need to use one of the output filter classes that are derived from the class **FilterOutputStream**, so we will need to look at these in some detail, but first we should examine what we get with the basic output streams.

The FileOutputStream Class

You use a **FileOutputStream** object when you want to write to a physical file. To create a stream object of type **FileOutputStream**, you can pass either a **File** object to a constructor, or a **String** object that defines the path and file name. You will usually find it more convenient to use a **File** object, since you can then check the properties of the file before you try to use it. You could create an output stream with the following statements:

```
FileOutputStream file1 = new FileOutputStream("myFile.txt");
```

Alternatively, you could achieve the same result with:

```
File aFile = new File("myFile.txt");
if (!aFile.exists())
{
  FileOutputStream file1 = new FileOutputStream(aFile);
  System.out.println("myFile.txt created");
}
else
  System.out.println("myFile.txt already exists.");
```

This creates the same **FileOutputStream** object as before, but in this case we've used the methods provided by the class **File** to check whether or not the file exists before using it. Since you know that you will overwrite any data that is there, you may not want to use if it does exist.

As well as the methods inherited from the base class, a **FileOutputStream** object has a method, **getFD()** which returns an object of type **FileDescriptor** that represents the physical file. Once you have finished writing a file, the **FileDescriptor** object could be used to create byte input stream object so you could read the same file back, since the **FileInputStream** class has a constructor that accepts a **FileDescriptor** object, as we will see when we look into byte input streams. The **FileOutputStream** class also has a constructor that accepts a **FileDescriptor** object as an argument.

You cannot create a **FileDescriptor** object yourself. You can only obtain a **FileDescriptor** object by calling the **getFD()** method for a byte stream object that represents a file.

The **FileDescriptor** class also defines three public static data members **in**, **out** and **err**, which are of type **FileDescriptor**, and which correspond to the standard system input, the standard system output, and the standard error stream respectively. You can use these in the creation of byte and character stream objects.

> *Don't confuse the data members of the **FileDescriptor** class with the data members of the same name defined by the **System** class in the **java.lang** package. The **in**, **out** and **err** data members of the **System** class are of type **PrintStream**, so they have the **print()** and **println()** methods. The **FileDescriptor** data members do not.*

We will also see later in this chapter that you can use a **FileDescriptor** object to create character stream objects.

The ByteArrayOutputStream Class

You would typically use the **ByteArrayOutputStream** class when you want to transform data in some way, perhaps by using a filter output stream. Since data is written to a **byte** array that is a member of the stream object, operations are very fast and you can retrieve the contents of the **byte** array whenever you want by using methods provided by the class. Data is stored in a **ByteArrayOutputStream** object as shown below.

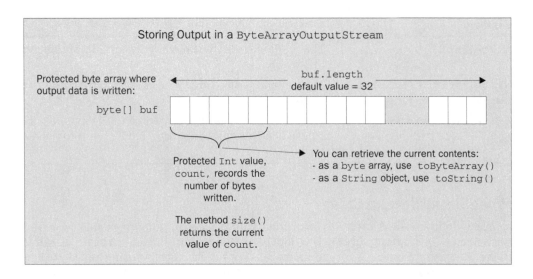

Storing Output in a `ByteArrayOutputStream`

Protected byte array where output data is written:

`byte[] buf`

`buf.length`
default value = 32

Protected `Int` value, `count`, records the number of bytes written.

You can retrieve the current contents:
- as a byte array, use `toByteArray()`
- as a `String` object, use `toString()`

The method `size()` returns the current value of `count`.

The **ByteArrayOutputStream** class has two constructors. One takes no arguments and will create an object containing a byte array of a default size of 32 bytes. The other accepts a value of type **int** as an argument which specifies the initial size of the byte array. The byte array is automatically increased in size as required, but the advantage of being able to specify in an initial size is that this avoids the overhead of frequently increasing the size when you write a lot of data to the stream. A small starting size will result in more frequent extensions to the buffer.

The **ByteArrayOutputStream** class implements the following methods:

Method	Description
`size()`	Returns the number of valid bytes in the buffer as an **int** value which is obtained from the instance variable **count**.
`reset()`	Resets the value of **count** to zero. Any bytes previously written to the buffer are lost. You use this to reset the stream object when you want to use it again. The return type is **void**.
`toByteArray()`	Returns the contents of the stream as a **byte** array of length **count**.
`toString()`	Returns the contents of the stream as a **String** object of length count. The high-order byte in each Unicode character in the string returned will be zero.
`toString(String enc)`	Returns an object of type **String** that is produced by converting the contents of the stream according to the character encoding specified by **enc**. The character encoding, **enc**, will typically correspond to the character encoding used to convert between Unicode and the host machine character codes. It can be obtained by using the **getEncoding()** method for an **OutputStreamWriter** object, as we will see later.

Table Continued on Following Page

Method	Description
`write(int b)`	This method writes the low-order byte of the argument, **b**, to the stream.
`write(byte b[], int offset, length)`	This method writes **length** bytes from the array **b** to the **int** stream, starting with **b[offset]**.
`writeTo(OutputStream out)`	This methods writes the entire contents of the stream (**count** bytes) to the output stream specified by the argument to the method.

The PipedOutputStream Class

A piped output stream is used in conjunction with a piped input stream that receives the data written to the output stream. Two independent program threads (which we will be looking at in the Chapter 10) can communicate with each other by using piped streams. A piped output stream in one thread can be connected to a piped input stream in another thread. The data written to the piped output stream can be read by the piped input stream.

There are two constructors you can use to create a **PipedOutputStream** object. The default constructor creates a stream that is not connected to a piped input stream. Before you can use it you must either call the **connect()** method of the **PipedOutputStream** object, specifying a **PipedInputStream** object as an argument, or get the **PipedInputStream** object to connect itself to the **PipedOutputStream** object. So, you must either create the **PipedInputStream** object to be connected to the output stream, or call an existing **PipedInputStream** object's **connect()** method to link it to your output stream.

More simply, the second constructor for the **PipedOutputStream** class accepts a **PipedInputStream** object as an argument, to which the output stream object will be connected.

The FilterOutputStream Classes

There are a total of nine classes that are derived from the **FilterOutputStream** class. Five of these are shown in the diagram below:

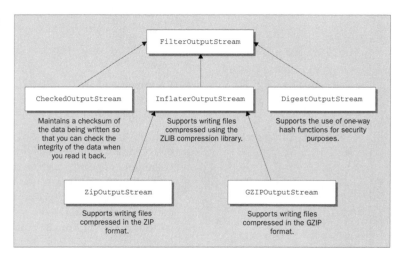

The **DigestOutputStream** class is defined in the **java.security** package. The four other sub-classes of **FilterOutputStream** shown here are defined in the **java.util.zip** package.

The **DigestOutputStream** involves the computation of one-way hash values for security purposes. Some methods involved in this are not included with Java, but must be supplied by a service provider. Further discussion of the use of this class is outside the scope of this book.

The **CheckedOutputStream** class maintains a checksum for the data that is written to the file. Creating a checksum when you write the file provides the possibility of using the checksum when you read the same data back to verify that the data is the same as was written. The **CheckedInputStream** class, which we will see later derives from the **FilterInputStream** class, complements this class for the purpose of checking that the data read is the same as was written.

The remaining three classes shown in the diagram enable you to write compressed files. We won't be going through the detail of all these, but we will try out writing a ZIP file a little later in this chapter.

Let's turn now to the two sub-classes of **FilterOutputStream** that you will use most often. They are shown in the following diagram.

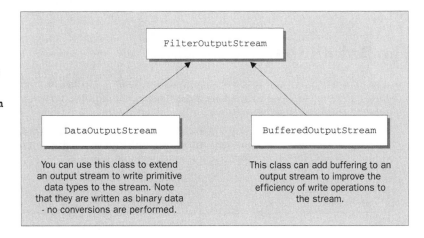

Both of these filter output stream classes are designed to augment an existing output stream class. They are intended to add function to the classes **FileOutputStream**, **PipedOutputStream** or **ByteArrayOutputStream**. Therefore, objects of the filter output stream classes cannot be created directly based on a **File** object.

To construct an object of either of these filter output classes, you must first create an object of type **FileOutputStream**, **PipedOutputStream** or **ByteArrayOutputStream**, and then use this object in the constructor for the filter output stream class of your choice.

The PrintStream Class

PrintStream is another sub-class of **FilterOutputStream**.

We have made extensive use of the **println()** method from this class in our examples up to now to output formatted information to the screen. The **out** object in the expression **System.out.println()** is of type **PrintStream**. In previous Java implementations, this was the only class available for outputting data of any of the basic types as a string. For example, an **int** value of **12345** becomes the characters **"12345"**, as generated by the **toString()** method from the class **Integer**. However, **PrintStream** has been made obsolete by the **PrintWriter** class introduced in Java 1.1 which implements output to a character stream.

PrintWriter is a significant improvement over the **PrintStream** class because it takes care of conversions between Unicode, and the character encoding on the local computer, whatever that happens to be. The old **PrintStream** class did not always work correctly. You can still use **System.out.println()** for text output to the screen without any problems though. We will be looking at the **PrintWriter** class later in this chapter.

Note that the **PrintWriter** class has no particular connection with printing—in spite of its name. Of course, you could direct a **PrintWriter** stream to a file and then arrange for the file to be redirected to your printer. However, the way you are most likely to be writing to your system printer uses a totally different mechanism that we will be looking at in Chapter 15.

The DataOutputStream Class

The **DataOutputStream** class provides methods that enable you to write any of the basic types of data, or a **String**, to a byte stream. If you are writing data to a file that is not strictly character data, then this is the class to use. All data is written as a sequence of bytes corresponding to the original binary data in memory. No conversions are done on any of the data types. The class provides you with methods for writing data of each of the basic types:

Method	Description
writeByte(int value)	Writes the low-order byte of the **int** argument to the stream.
writeBoolean(boolean value)	Writes a **boolean** value to the stream as a byte with the value 1 for **true**, and the value 0 for **false**.
writeChar(int value)	Writes the low-order two bytes of the argument to the stream.
writeShort(int value)	Writes the low-order two bytes of the argument to the stream.
writeInt(int value)	Writes the four bytes of the **int** argument to the stream.
writeLong(long value)	Writes the eight bytes of the **long** argument to the stream.

Method	Description
`writeFloat(float value)`	Writes the four bytes of the **float** argument to the stream.
`writeDouble(double value)`	Writes the eight bytes of the **double** argument to the stream.

None of these methods returns a value but any of them can throw an **IOException** *if an error occurs. As you will remember from our discussion on exceptions, this means that when you use them you must catch such errors, or at least declare that your method might throw such errors.*

Creating a DataOutputStream Object

The constructor for the **DataOutputStream** class requires an argument of type **OutputStream** that must represent a real destination for the data. You have three possibilities for this object:

Constructor Argument	Description
`PipedOutputStream`	This object will represent a connection to a **PipedInputStream** for another thread. This will connect two threads in your application and allow data to be transferred from one to the other. All data that you write to the **DataOutputStream** will be available to the connected **PipedInputStream**.
`ByteArrayOutputStream`	This object will represent an array in memory. All data that you write to the **DataOutputStream** will be written to the array in the **ByteArrayOutputStream** object.
`FileOutputStream`	This object will represent a physical file on your hard disk. Data that you write to the **DataOutputStream** will be written to the physical file.

Since the third option is by far the most useful let's look specifically at that. We have three distinct stages we need to go through to create a **DataOutputStream** object that will enable us to write a file:

▶ Create a suitable **File** object for example:

```
File aFile = new File("data.txt");
```

▶ Create a **FileOutputStream** object using the **File** object. For example:

```
FileOutputStream fStream = new FileOutputStream(aFile);
```

▶ Create the **DataOutputStream** object using the **FileOutputStream** object. For example:

```
DataOutputStream myStream = new DataOutputStream(fStream);
```

We don't have to complete these step entirely separately though. Let's see how this works out in a practical example.

Try It Out—Using the *DataOutputStream* **Class**

To write a **String** to a stream you have the method **writeChars()** available which accepts an argument of type **String**. We can try this out here. This example will create a directory, **MyData**, on your **C:** drive, and then create a file, **data.txt**, in that directory. You will need to change this if it conflicts with existing directories on your machine. Here's the code:

```java
import java.io.*;

public class TestDataStream
{
  public static void main(String[] args)
  {
    String myStr = new String("Garbage in, garbage out");
    String dirName = "c:\\MyData";            // Directory name

    try
    {
      File dir = new File(dirName);           // File object for directory

      if(!dir.exists())                       // If directory does not exist
        dir.mkdir();                          // ...create it
      else
        if(!dir.isDirectory())
          {
            System.err.println(dirName + " is not a directory");
            return;
          }

      File aFile = new File(dir, "data.txt"); // Now create the file

      // Create the byte output stream
      DataOutputStream myStream = new DataOutputStream(
                                    new FileOutputStream(aFile));
      myStream.writeChars(myStr);             // Write the string to the file
    }
    catch(IOException e)
    {
      System.out.println("IO exception thrown: " + e);
    }
  }
}
```

After you have compiled and run the program, the file, **data.txt** will contain the following:

```
G a r b a g e   i n ,   g a r b a g e   o u t
```

The spaces between the characters are because we are writing Unicode characters to the file, so two bytes are written for each character.

How It Works

We have two **String** objects defined, **myStr** that we will write to the file, and **dirName** which is the name of the directory we will create. In the **try** block we first create a **File** object to represent the directory. If this directory does not exist, the **exists()** method will return **false**, and the **mkdir()** method for **dir** will be called to create it. If the **exists()** method returns **true**, we must make sure that the **File** object represents a directory, and not a file.

Having established the directory one way or another, we create a file object **aFile** to represent the file **data.text** in the directory. We use this object as an argument to the **FileOutputStream** constructor, and we pass the object produced to the **DataOutputStream** constructor to create the object, **myStream**. Alternatively, we could combine the creation of the file object and the creation of the **DataOutputStream** object into a single composite statement:

```
DataOutputStream myStream = new DataOutputStream(
                    new FileOutputStream(new File(dir, "data.txt")));
```

Once we have the stream object, we write the string stored in **myStr** to the file **data.txt**. Of course, if you were writing several strings of varying lengths to a file you would need to include some way of knowing where the end of the string is when you come to read it back. After all, once the data is in the file, whatever it was you wrote to the file, it's just bytes. One way would be to write the length of each string to the file before you write the string. Then you can read the length and use that to read the correct number of characters for the string.

In addition to the output methods we have just seen, you also have a method **flush()** in the **DataOutputStream** class which forces any buffered output data to be written to the stream, and a method **size()** which will return the total number of bytes written to the stream as a value of type **int**. You could try this out by adding the statement:

```
System.out.println(myStream.size() + " bytes written to the file");
```

immediately following the statement that writes **myStr** to the file. You should see that 46 bytes are written to the file since the string, **myStr**, contains 23 characters.

Buffered Output Streams

You can add a buffer to an output stream to make the output operations more efficient, by using the **BufferedOutputStream** class. As you write data to a buffered stream the data is accumulated in a buffer in memory, and the data is only written to the ultimate output stream when the buffer is full. Output operations to a file are very slow compared to the time it takes to write data to a buffer in memory. Since using a buffer will reduce the number of actual output operations to the file, this will make the output faster overall. You can always cause the current contents of a buffered output stream to be written by calling the **flush()** method. Closing the stream by calling the **close()** method will also cause any residual data in the buffer to be written to the stream.

To create a buffered output stream, you pass the output stream object for the stream you want buffered, to the constructor for **BufferedOutputStream**. The default buffer size is dependent on the particular implementation of Java that you are using. For the Java 1.1 implementation under Windows 95 it is 512 bytes. You can specify the size of the buffer yourself by passing the number of bytes in the buffer as a second argument to the constructor of type **int**.

Buffer Stream Operations

The process of writing a disk file using a buffered stream is quite straightforward. Suppose we want to create an output stream that we want to use to write basic data types of data to the file. It will need to be an object of type **DataOutputStream**, as that has the methods we need to write the data. The whole process of creating the output stream that connects to the physical file is very similar to that we saw in the last example.

You first create an object of the class **File** using the name and path for the file to which you want to write. You can then use the **File** object as an argument to a constructor for a **FileOutputStream** class, to create the object that represents the physical file. Since we want the stream to be buffered, we pass this object to the **BufferedOutputStream** constructor. We finally pass the **BufferedOutputStream** object to the **DataOutputStream** object to get the stream object we will use to write the data.

We can't do it the other way round. If we create a **DataOutputStream** object first, and pass that to the **BufferedOutputStream** constructor, the object that we end up with would not contain the methods we need to write the basic data types.

We could create a buffered output stream that we will use to store primes as follows:

```
String dirName = "c:\\JunkData";        // Directory for the file
String fileName = "Primes.bin";         // The file name

File myPrimeDir = new File(dirName);     // Define directory object

if(!myPrimeDir.exists())                 // If directory does not exist
  myPrimeDir.mkdir();                    // ...create it
else
  if(!myPrimeDir.isDirectory())
  {
    System.err.println(dirName + " is not a directory");
    return;
  }
```

```
File myPrimes = new File(myPrimeDir, fileName);  // The file object

// Create a buffered data output stream for the file
DataOutputStream myFile = new DataOutputStream(
            new BufferedOutputStream(newFileOutputStream(myPrimes)));
```

We define a **File** object specifying the new file, **Primes.bin**, in the directory we have created. We then use this to create **DataOutputStream** object which we pass to the **BufferedOutputStream** constructor. We will use the **BufferedOutputStream** object to write the file. If the file already exists, we will access that (and overwrite it!), and if it doesn't it will be created automatically. Let's put this into a working example.

Try It Out—Buffered Output to a Disk File

We could add this code to the example in Chapter 4 for creating primes to see how this works. We write the primes to a file instead of writing them to the display:

```
import java.io.*;

public class TryPrimesOutput
{
  public static void main(String[] args)
  {
    long[] primes = new long[200]; // Array to store primes
    primes[0] = 2;                 // Seed the first prime
    primes[1] = 3;                 // and the second
    int count = 2;                 // count of primes found - up to now

    long number = 5;               // Next integer to be tested

    outer:
    for( ; count < primes.length; number += 2L)
    {
      // The maximum divisor we need to try is square root of number
      long limit = (long)Math.ceil(Math.sqrt((double)number));

      // Divide by all the primes we have up to limit
      for(int i = 1; i < count && primes[i] <= limit; i++)
        if(number%primes[i] == 0)           // Is it an exact divisor?
          continue outer;                   // yes, try the next number

      primes[count++] = number;    // We got one!
    }

    // Write the primes to a file
    try
    {
      String dirName = "c:\\JunkData";        // Directory for the file
      String fileName = "Primes.bin";         // The file name
```

```
           File myPrimeDir = new File(dirName);   // Define directory object

           if(!myPrimeDir.exists())                // If directory does not exist
             myPrimeDir.mkdir();                    // ...create it
           else
             if(!myPrimeDir.isDirectory())          // Verify it is a directory
             { // It is not!
               System.err.println(dirName+" is not a directory");
               return;
             }

           // Create the file object
           File myPrimes = new File(myPrimeDir, fileName);

           // Create a buffered data output stream for the file
           DataOutputStream myFile = new DataOutputStream(
                   new BufferedOutputStream(new FileOutputStream(myPrimes)));

           // Write primes to the file
           for(int i = 0; i < primes.length; i++)
             myFile.writeLong(primes[i]);

           myFile.flush();                          // Make sure all are written
           myFile.close();                          // Close the file
           System.out.println("File size = " + myFile.size());
         }
       catch(IOException e)                         // Catch any output errors
       {
         System.out.println("IOException " + e + " occurred");
       }
     }
   }
```

How It Works

The size of the array, **primes[]**, has been increased so that we create a more appreciable number of primes to be written to the file. The example uses the statements you have already seen to create the buffered stream object. All we do then is to write the primes to the stream using the **writeLong()** method. When all the primes have been written, we call **flush()** to make sure everything is sent to the stream, and then output the number of bytes written to the file that we obtain with the **size()** method. Lastly, we close the file. As you see, we include a **catch** block to catch any exceptions that occur in the write operations on the file. If we didn't do this, we would need to declare that the method **main()** may throw an **IOException**.

The object, **myFile**, will therefore be a buffered file stream with the data output stream methods available. The file will only be written each time the buffer is filled, or when the stream is flushed. In between times the write operations will just place data in the buffer—and all automatically. Easy, isn't it?

Of course, viewing this file is a waste of time—it's binary data. We will see how we can read it back a little later in this chapter.

Writing a Compressed File

To show how you can write a compressed file we will look at writing ZIP files, since that is such a common compression method. We are not going to explore every nook and cranny of the classes involved in writing ZIP files, just enough to enable you to put it into practice at a basic level, and you can take it from there. To be able to write ZIP files, we need to understand what makes the **ZipOutputStream** class tick.

There is one constructor for **ZipOutputStream** objects, and this accepts an argument of type **OutputStream**, which will typically be a **FileOutputStream** object. For example, we could define the directory to contain the ZIP file and the ZIP file name with the statements:

```
String dirName = "c:\\JunkData";      // Directory for the ZIP file
String zipName = "Primes.zip";        // The ZIP file name
```

Then, after the usual checks that everything is legitimate, we can construct the **ZipOuputStream** object with the statements:

```
File myPrimeZip = new File(myPrimeDir, zipName);  // The file object
ZipOutputStream myZipFile = new ZipOutputStream(
                               new FileOutputStream(myPrimeZip));
```

This just creates the file object as we have seen before, and uses that to create a **FileOutputStream** object which we pass to the **ZipOutputStream** constructor. This creates our object **myZipFile**, which corresponds to the physical file **Primes.zip** in the directory **C:\JunkData**.

Of course, we won't be writing data directly to this file, although it is possible to do so. A ZIP file contains one or more compressed files, and each file in the ZIP is identified by a **ZIP entry**. A ZIP entry is represented by an object of the class **ZipEntry**, which has one constructor that accepts a **String** object which will be the name of the entry. This is usually a file name. We could define a **ZipEntry** object with the statements:

```
String fileName = "Primes.bin";      // The name of the file to be
compressed
ZipEntry myZipEntry = new ZipEntry(fileName);   // The ZIP entry
```

The **ZipEntry** object also contains information about how the file should be compressed. You set this by passing a value of type **int** to the **setMethod()** method for the **ZipEntry** object. The argument can be either **ZipEntry.STORED** which will leave the entry uncompressed, or **ZipEntry.DEFLATED** which specifies that the entry should be compressed. We want the latter, so we would write:

```
myZipEntry.setMethod(ZipEntry.DEFLATED);    // Compress the file
```

Now that we have a ZIP entry defined, we must pass the information to the `ZipOutputStream` object with the statement:

```
myZipFile.putNextEntry(myZipEntry);    // Start the ZIP entry
```

This defines the next zip entry for the `ZipOutputStream` object. We can now write the ZIP entry—the file we want to add to the ZIP, and when we are done we call the `closeEntry()` for the `ZipOutputStream` object:

```
myZipFile.closeEntry();
```

This closes the entry—not the file—so we can then start a new ZIP entry corresponding to the next file we want to add to the ZIP.

So how do we write the data for the entry to the ZIP? We will usually want to write a file represented by a `DataOutputStream` object because that has the methods to write different types of data values to the file, integers, floating point values, and so on. We can arrange for this to be the case by passing our `ZipOutputStream` object to the `DataOutputStream` constructor, then when we call methods for the `DataOutputStream` object, the data will end up written to the ZIP. We construct the `DataOutputStream` object with the statement:

```
DataOutputStream myFile = new DataOutputStream(myZipFile);
```

This creates the `DataOutputStream` object from the `ZipOutputStream` object, but we can actually do a bit better than that. We can buffer the output as well by using a `BufferedOutputStream` object along the way:

```
DataOutputStream myFile = new DataOutputStream(
                            new BufferedOutputStream(myZipFile));
```

Once you have finished writing an entry in a ZIP, you can find out how many bytes were written to the ZIP by calling the `getCompressedSize()` method for the `ZipEntry` object. You can also get the size of the uncompressed file by calling the `size()` method for the `DataOutputStream` object.

The last example is a good candidate for illustrating how you can write data to a compressed ZIP file for real, particularly since all the code fragments in this section fit so well, so let's apply what we know about the `ZipOutputStream` class to write the primes directly to a compressed file.

Try It Out—Writing Primes to a ZIP File

This is going to be very easy. It's just a question of plugging the code fragments we have just been looking at into the previous example. This will write a ZIP file to the same directory as the previous example, **Prime Data**. Here's the code:

```java
import java.io.*;
import java.util.zip.*;

public class TryCompressedPrimesOutput
{
  public static void main(String[] args)
  {
    long[] primes = new long[200];   // Array to store primes
    primes[0] = 2;                    // Seed the first prime
    primes[1] = 3;                    // and the second
    int count = 2;                    // count of primes found - up to now

    long number = 5;                  // Next integer to be tested

    outer:
    for( ; count < primes.length; number += 2L)
    {
      // The maximum divisor we need to try is square root of number
      long limit = (long)Math.ceil(Math.sqrt((double)number));

      // Divide by all the primes we have up to limit
      for(int i = 1; i < count && primes[i] <= limit; i++)
        if(number%primes[i] == 0)              // Is it an exact divisor?
          continue outer;                      // yes, try the next number

      primes[count++] = number;     // We got one!
    }

    // Write the primes to a file
    try
    {
      String dirName = "c:\\JunkData";        // Directory for the ZIP file
      String zipName = "NewPrimes.zip";       // The ZIP archive name
      String fileName = "NewPrimes.bin";      // Name of the compressed file
      File myPrimeDir = new File(dirName);    // Define directory object

      if(!myPrimeDir.exists())                // If directory does not exist
        myPrimeDir.mkdir();                   // ...create it
      else
        if(!myPrimeDir.isDirectory())
        {
          System.err.println(dirName + " is not a directory");
          return;
        }

      File myPrimeZip = new File(myPrimeDir, zipName); // The file object
      ZipOutputStream myZipFile = new ZipOutputStream(
                                  new FileOutputStream(myPrimeZip));
      ZipEntry myZipEntry = new ZipEntry(fileName);
```

```
        myZipEntry.setMethod(ZipEntry.DEFLATED);    // Compress the file
        myZipFile.putNextEntry(myZipEntry);
        DataOutputStream myFile = new DataOutputStream(
                            new BufferedOutputStream(myZipFile));

    // Write primes to the file
    for(int i = 0; i < primes.length; i++)
      myFile.writeLong(primes[i]);

    myFile.flush();                        // Make sure all is written
    myZipFile.finish();                    // End the ZIP entry
    myFile.close();                        // Close the file
    System.out.println("File size = " + myFile.size());
    System.out.println("Compressed file size = " +
                                    myZipEntry.getCompressedSize());
    }
  catch(IOException e)                     // Catch any output errors
  {
    System.out.println("IOException " + e + " occurred");
  }
 }
}
```

If you compile and run this it will produce the output:

```
File size = 1600
Compressed file size = 424
```

which indicates the primes file is compressed by almost four to one.

How It Works

This uses exactly the code we saw in the text. We have an extra **String** object to define the name of the ZIP file which is used in the **File** object constructor, and the original file name is passed to the **ZipEntry** constructor to identify the file within the ZIP. Once we have created the **DataOutputStream** object, writing the data proceeds exactly as before.

When we have finished writing the data we call **flush()** for the **DataOutputStream** object to ensure any residual data is written to the file. At this point we also call **closeEntry()** for the **myZipFile** object to indicate it is the end of the current entry. Finally we call **close()** for the **DataOutputStream** object which will cause **close()** to be called for the **BufferedOutputStream** object, which in turn will cause the **close()** method for the **ZipOutputStream** object to be called.

After we have closed the file, we retrieve the size of the uncompressed file and the size of the ZIP.

Character Output Streams

Character output streams are for writing character data. Unicode characters will be automatically converted to the character coding used by the local computer on which your code is executing when the data is transferred to the stream. This contrasts with the byte output streams that we have been discussing up to now, where no conversion of characters is done. You use the character streams when you want to write text to a file, or when you want to write the string representation of your data values—**"3.1415926"** for a **double** value, for instance. You can also use a character output stream to obtain the local machine representation for a character string in your program.

All character output stream classes are derived from the **abstract** class, **Writer**. The subclasses of **Writer** are shown in the diagram.

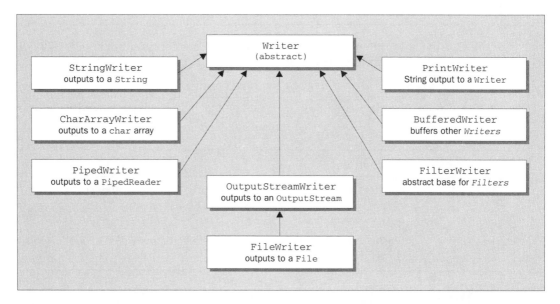

The **FilterWriter** class is an abstract class intended to be used as a base class for defining character filter streams. Writing filter stream class is outside the scope of this book, so we won't be discussing the **FilterWriter** class further.

The **PipedWriter** class defines a character stream that is connected to a **PipedReader** stream, so that two threads in a program can pass data between them. The **PipedReader** class is a character input stream class derived from the class **Reader**. We will look at character input streams later in this chapter.

The **BufferedWriter** class is used to buffer output for character streams that write a physical file. This makes the write operations much more efficient by reducing the number of writes to the physical file in just the way we saw for byte output streams. We will see how to used the **BufferedWriter** class when we look at how to write files using character stream classes.

The abstract base class for the character output streams, **Writer**, defines the following methods that will be inherited by its sub-classes:

Method	Description
write(int c)	Writes the character **c** to the stream. The return type is **void**.
write(char[] cArray)	Writes the array, **cArray**, to the stream.
write(char[] cArray, offset, int length)	Write **length** characters from the array, **cArray**, to the stream, **int** starting at the element with the index **offset**. The return type is **void**.
write(String str)	Writes the string **str** to the stream. The return type is **void**.
write(String str, int offset, int length)	Writes **length** characters from the string **str** to the stream, starting at position **offset**. The return type is **void**.

All of these methods can throw an **IOException** if an error occurs. In many cases the base class methods will be overridden in the derived classes to provide more efficient implementations.

The **Writer** class also declares two abstract methods that will be implemented in its sub-classes:

Abstract Method	Description
flush()	Flushes the stream. If the output is transferred to another stream, that stream will also be flushed, as will all nested streams. The return type is **void**.
close()	Flushes and closes the stream. All nested streams will also be flushed and closed. The return type is **void**.

Writing Characters to an Array or a String Buffer

The **StringWriter** and **CharArrayWriter** classes transfer the data written to the stream to a **StringBuffer** and an array of type **char[]** respectively, which are internal to the class object—after converting the data from Unicode to local character codes of course. Both classes have a default constructor that creates the object with the internal **StringBuffer** object or **char[]** array set to a default size. **CharArrayWriter** also has a constructor that accepts an argument of type **int** that defines the size of the internal buffer. For example, you could create a **CharArrayWriter** object with a buffer to hold 100 characters with the statement:

```
CharArrayWriter charArrayOut = new CharArrayWriter(100);
```

The **StringWriter** class defines the following methods:

Method	Description
`write(int c)`	Writes the character **c** to the buffer in the stream object. The return type is **void**.
`write(char[] cArray, int offset, int length)`	Write **length** characters from the array, **cArray**, to the buffer in the stream object, starting at the element with the index **offset**. The return type is **void**.
`write(String str)`	Writes the string **str** to the buffer in the stream object. The return type is **void**.
`write(String str, int offset, int length)`	Writes **length** characters from the string **str** to the buffer in the stream object, starting at position **offset**. The return type is **void**.
`getBuffer()`	Return the buffer in the stream object as type **StringBuffer**.
`toString()`	Returns the current contents of the buffer in the stream object as type **String**.

Several of these override methods inherited from the **Writer** class. The **CharArrayWriter** class also defines six of the methods shown above, and they work in the same way, but it doesn't re-implement **write(String str)**. The extra methods for this class are:

Method	Description
`writeTo(Writer out)`	Writes the contents of the buffer in the stream object to the stream, **out**.
`toCharArray()`	Returns a copy of the data in the buffer as type **char[]**.
`reset()`	Resets the current buffer in the stream object so that you can use it again. This saves you having to create a new stream object with a new buffer.
`size()`	Returns the current size of the buffer as type **int**.

You can use either of the classes as a means of obtaining the local machine equivalent of a Unicode string or array in your program, since both classes include methods to retrieve the contents of the internal buffer.

Connecting a Character Stream to a Byte Stream

The **OutputStreamWriter** class enables you to write character output to an object representing a byte output stream, with automatic conversion of the data being written from Unicode characters to the local machine representation of the characters. The **OutputStreamWriter** object will convert the characters written to the stream before they are transferred to the byte stream. The **OutputStreamWriter** class constructor accepts an argument of type **OutputStream**, so the destination for the converted data can be any kind of byte output stream. Once you have written the byte output stream, you can read it back as a byte input stream, and thus obtain the data in the local machine representation.

The methods defined by the `OutputStreamWriter` class for writing the data override or implement the base class methods. For writing to a byte output stream that represents a physical file, you would normally buffer the output using the `BufferedWriter` class. For example, if you wanted to write character data to the screen with automatic conversion to the local character representation, you could define a character output stream object as:

```
Writer out = new BufferedWriter(new OutputStreamWriter(System.out));
```

Using a Character Stream to Write a File

The `FileWriter` class has a constructor that accepts an object of type `File` as an argument, so you can use a `FileWriter` object to write a file. In fact you can use one of four constructors for `FileWriter` objects:

Constructor	Description
`FileWriter(File aFile)`	Create an object from the object **aFile** that represents a physical file.
`FileWriter(FileDescriptor fileDesc)`	Creates an object from a **FileDescriptor** object. A **FileDescriptor** object represents a standard system file.
`FileWriter(String fileName)`	Creates an object from the string **fileName** that is the name of a physical file.
`FileWriter(String filepath, boolean append)`	Creates an object from the string **fileName** that is the name of a physical file. If the value of **append** is **true**, data will be appended to the file if it exists—if it doesn't, a new file will be created.

As we saw earlier, the `FileDescriptor` class has public static data members of type `FileDescriptor`—**in**, **out** and **err**—that represent the standard input stream, the standard output stream, and the standard error stream respectively. You can also use a `FileDescriptor` object that was obtained from a byte stream object to create a `FileWriter` object. You would obtain this by calling the `getFD()` method for the stream object in question. There is no `getFD()` method for the `FileWriter` class.

Curiously, in the current implementation of the `java.io` package, the only `FileWriter` class constructor that will create a character output stream that you can append data to, is the last in the list above. Thus if you want to append data to a file, you have to create the stream object directly from a `String` object containing the file path.

Let's see how that works with a simple example.

Try It Out—Appending Data to a File

We will just write some proverbs to a file that we will access with the FileWriter constructor that allows us to append data. Here's the code:

```
// Appending data to a file
import java.io.*;

class WriteCharacters
{
  public static void main(String[] args)
  {
    try
    {
      String dirName = "c:\\JunkData\\"; // Directory for the output file
      String fileName = "Proverbs.txt";   // Name of the output file

      BufferedWriter out = new BufferedWriter(
                           new FileWriter(dirName + fileName, true));

      String[] sayings = { "Indecision maximixes flexibility.",
                           "Only the mediocre are always at their best.",
                           "A little knowledge is a dangerous thing.",
                           "Many a mickle makes a muckle.",
                           "Who begins too much achieves little.",
                           "Who knows most says least.",
                           "A wise man sits on the hole in his carpet."};

      // Write the proverbs to the file preceded by the string length
      for(int i = 0; i < sayings.length; i++)
      {
        out.write(sayings[i].length() + sayings[i]);
      }
      out.close();
    }
    catch(IOException e)
    {
      System.out.println("Error writing the file " + e);
    }
  }
}
```

How It Works

In the **try** block, we create a **BufferedWriter** object from a **FileWriter** object that will append data to the output file. We then create a **String** array, **sayings[]**, that contains seven proverbs. All of these are written to the stream in the **for** loop. Bearing in mind that when we want to read these back, we will have no idea where one proverb ends and the next one begins, we write the length of each proverb to the stream preceding the string for the proverb. This is done by concatenating the proverb with the value returned from the **length()** method for the string. Of course, the length will be converted to a string before it is written to the stream, so the program that reads this back will need to figure out where the length value begins and ends. After writing the proverbs, we close the stream. The **catch** block will catch any exceptions that are thrown as a result of errors writing the file.

The program doesn't produce any output, other than the file. However, you can use any program that views text files to check that it does get written as you expect. How can we tell that the append operation works? The first time you run the program, the file doesn't exist, so it will be created. You can then look at the contents. If you run the program again, the same proverbs will be appended to the file, so there will be a second set. Alternatively, you could modify the **sayings[]** array to contain different proverbs the second time around. Each time the program runs, the data will be added at the end of the existing file.

You could try changing the second argument to the **FileWriter** constructor to **false**. You will then see that each time you run the program, any existing data in the file is overwritten. This is also the case with any of the other **FileWriter** constructors. We will write a program to read this file back later in this chapter, so leave the file with some useful contents on your disk.

PrintWriter Character Streams

You can output binary numerical data such as type **int** or type **double** converted to character form by using the **PrintWriter** class. However, the output format for each data type is fixed, and you have no way to control the width of the output field or the number of digits presented. In each case it is determined by the **toString()** method applicable to the data type. If you need to alter the format of the output dynamically, you must derive your own classes to do it. We will look at an elementary approach to doing this later in this chapter.

You can create a **PrintWriter** object from a byte output stream object, or from a character stream object of type **OutputStreamWriter**. You have a choice of four constructors that you can use:

Constructors	Description
PrintWriter(OutputStream stream)	Creates a **PrintWriter** object from the **stream** object passed as an argument. This will construct an **OutputStreamWriter** internally, from the byte stream object passed as an argument.
PrintWriter(OutputStream stream, boolean flush)	Creates a **PrintWriter** object from the **stream** object passed as an argument. If the argument **flush** is **true**, the stream will be flushed automatically whenever the **println()** method is called for the stream.
PrintWriter(Writer writer)	Creates a **PrintWriter** object from the **writer** object passed as an argument. This should be an **OutputStreamWriter** object.
PrintWriter(OutputStream stream, boolean flush)	Creates a **PrintWriter** object from the **writer** object passed as an argument. If the argument **flush** is **true**, the stream will be flushed each time the **println()** method is called for the stream.

Ultimately, the **PrintWriter** object is always based on a byte stream object, since you need to have a byte output stream in order to create an **OutputStreamWriter** object. Calling either of the constructors that accept one argument is equivalent to calling the corresponding constructors with two arguments with the second argument as **false**.

The **PrintWriter** class adds a range of methods to an existing output stream that can convert data of any the basic types to a character representation of the value. The conversion in each case is fixed and is the result of calling the **toString()** method in the class from **java.lang** corresponding to the basic type, **Integer** for **int** values, **Double** for **double** values, and so on. For class objects the **toString()** method for the class is called. There are two methods that do this, the method **print()** and the method **println()**. Both of these are overloaded to accept any of the following argument types:

```
char        char[]     String     Object     boolean     int       long
float       double
```

The difference between the **print()** and **println()** methods is that the **println()** method writes an end of line character to the stream after outputting the characters for the value of its argument, whereas the **print()** method does not. There is a further version of the **println()** method which has no argument which just writes an end of line character to the stream.

The methods in the **PrintWriter** class do not throw exceptions. If an output error occurs, an internal flag is set in the object to record the event. You can check whether there have been any output errors by calling the method **checkError()**. This returns **true** if one or more errors occurred, and **false** otherwise.

We can modify the example in Chapter 4 for calculating primes to use a character output stream.

Try It Out—Displaying Primes on a Character Output Stream

Make the following changes to the source code

```java
import java.io.*;

public class PrimeCharacters
{
  public static void main(String[] args)
  {
    long[] primes = new long[20]; // Array to store primes
    primes[0] = 2;                 // Seed the first prime
    primes[1] = 3;                 // and the second
    int count = 2;                 // Count of primes found - up to now
                                   // which is also the array index
    long number = 5;               // Next integer to be tested
```

```
outer:
for( ; count < primes.length; number += 2)
{
  // The maximum divisor we need to try is square root of number
  long limit = (long)Math.ceil(Math.sqrt((double)number));

    // Divide by all the primes we have up to limit
    for(int i = 1; i < count && primes[i] <= limit; i++)
      if(number%primes[i] == 0)        // Is it an exact divisor?
        continue outer;                // yes, try the next number

    primes[count++] = number;          // We got one!
}
```

```
    // Output the primes array using a buffered stream
    PrintWriter out = new PrintWriter(
                      new BufferedWriter(
                      new FileWriter(FileDescriptor.out)));

    for(int i=0; i < primes.length; i++)
      // New line after every fifth prime
      out.print((i%5==0 ? "\n" : "  ") + primes[i]);
    out.close();                              // Close the stream
  }
}
```

This produces the output:

```
 2   3   5   7   11
13  17  19  23  29
31  37  41  43  47
53  59  61  67  71
```

How It Works

The calculation for the primes is exactly as in Chapter 4, so we won't go over that again. To output the **primes[]** array, we create the object out, which is of type **PrintWriter**. This is created from a **BufferedWriter** object so that we get buffering for the output—without this, a physical write would occur for every call to **print()**. With the buffer, a physical write will occur when the buffer is full, or when the stream is flushed, by calling the **flush()** or the **close()** method for the stream. The **BufferedWriter** object is constructed from a **FileWriter** object which is constructed from the **FileDescriptor** object **out**—this refers to the standard output device which is the screen.

Writing the array to **out** takes place in the **for** loop. We call the **print()** method for the **PrintWriter** object, **out**, for each iteration. The expression used as the argument to the **print()** method outputs two spaces before each prime value, except for every fifth value, when a newline is output instead of the two spaces.

Calling **close()** for the **PrintWriter** object will cause the **close()** method to be called for each of the nested character streams. As we saw earlier, the **close()** method flushes the stream before closing it, so any data still in the buffer for the **BufferedWriter** object will be written to the **FileWriter** stream.

The output is a little ragged. It would be nice to have it aligned in columns, so let's see how we could do that.

Formatting Printed Output

To do your own output formatting is a considerable amount of work, particularly for floating point values. It takes quite a bit of code to sort out the decimal places and exponent values and it is a little beyond the scope of this book. However, it is quite easy to line your numeric output up in columns. You can do this by defining your own sub-class of **PrintWriter**.

Try It Out—Formatting Prime Output

We will define the class so that it contains a data member containing the width of the field for a data member. The basic class definition will be:

```
import java.io.*;

public class FormatWriter extends PrintWriter
{
  private int width = 10;        // Field width required for output

  // Basic onstructor for a default field width
  public FormatWriter(Writer out)
  {
    super(out);                  // Call PrintStream constructor
  }

  // Constructor with a specified field width
  public FormatWriter(Writer out, int width)
  {
    super(out);                  // Call PrintStream constructor
    this.width = width;          // Store the field width
  }

  // Constructor with autoflush option
  public FormatWriter(Writer out, boolean autoflush)
  {
    super(out, autoflush);       // Call PrintStream constructor
  }

  // Constructor with a specified field width and autoflush option
  public FormatWriter(Writer out, boolean autoflush, int width)
  {
    super(out, autoflush);       // Call PrintStream constructor
```

```
      this.width = width;          // Store the field width
   }
}
```

How It Works

This class is intended to output data in a fixed field width. The only data member in our class **FormatWriter**, is the variable, **width**, of type **int**, which holds the output field width. Since we derive our class from **PrintWriter**, we have all the facilities of the **PrintWriter** class available. Our constructors are essentially the same as the base class constructors, with the addition of the **width** parameter to specify the number of characters required for the field width. In each of our constructors, after calling the appropriate base class constructor, we just set the **width** member. However, we have only implemented to constructors that accept a **Writer** object—you could add constructors to accept an **OutputStream** object if you need them.

At the moment, if you call **print()** or **println()** for a **FormatWriter** object, it will call the base class method, so the behavior will be exactly the same as a **PrintWriter** object. To change this we will add our own **print()** and **println()** methods that override the base class methods. First though, we will add a helper method that we can use in the implementation of our print functions.

Try It Out—Overriding *print()* and *println()*

We know that we want to output **width** characters for each value that we output. We will assume that the data value is to be right justified in the field, so all we need to do is figure out how many characters there are in each data value, subtract that from the total field width, then output that many blanks before we write the data value to the stream.

1 Since we need a character representation for each data value to do this, we will implement a method, **output()**, that will accept a **String** object as an argument, and output this object right justified in the field:

```
// Helper method for output
private void output(String str)
{
  int blanks = width - str.length();      // Number of blanks needed

  // If the length is less than the width, add blanks to the start
  if(blanks > 0)
    for (int i = 0; i < blanks; i++)
      super.print(' ');                    // Output a space
  super.print(str);                        // Use base method for output
}
```

2 We can now implement the **print()** method for **long** values in our class very easily using the **output()** method:

```
// Output type long formatted in a given width
public void print(long value)
{
  output(Long.toString(value));          // Pad to width and output
}
```

3 The `print()` method for double values will be almost identical:

```
// Output type double formatted in a given width
public void print(double value)
{
  output(Double.toString(value));        // Pad to width and output
}
```

You should be able to implement all the other versions of `print()` if you need them.

4 The `println()` method is also very simple. Here's the implementation for a `long` value:

```
// Output type long formatted in a given width plus a newline
public void println(long value)
{
  this.print(value);                     // Call current method
  super.println();                       // Call base method
}
```

5 The `println()` method for **double** values is almost identical:

```
// Output type double formatted in a given width plus a newline
public void println(double value)
{
  this.print(value);                     // Call current method
  super.println();                       // Call base method
}
```

The `println()` methods for the other data types will be much the same.

6 If you want a bit more flexibility with objects of this class, you can add a `setWidth()` member to change the field width, and perhaps a `getWidth()` member so you can find out what it is currently. The `setWidth()` method will just be:

```
public void setWidth(int width)
{
  this.width = width;
}
```

How It Works

We will only use this method inside the class, so we make it **private**. The variable blanks will contain the number of spaces that we need to output, before we output the string, **str**. The spaces are output by calling the **print()** method for the base class, **PrintWriter**, that accepts a single character as an argument. The **for** loop will output the number of spaces required. The method then outputs the string using the base class method that accepts a **String** object. If the string, **str**, has more characters than the field width, then we will just output the string. This will mess up the nice neat columns, but that's better that truncating the output.

The **print(long value)** method just calls the **toString()** method for the class **Long** to convert the value to a character string. The string is then passed to the **output()** method for output within the field width.

In the **println()** methods, we call the **print()** method for our class to output the value in the field, and then call the base class **println()** method to end the line. It is important to do this, rather than write an newline character to the stream if you want to mirror the behavior of the **PrintWriter** class. Writing a newline does not necessarily flush the stream, whereas calling the base class version of **println()** does.

With the **setWidth()** method, you can then set an individual field width for each value that you output, if necessary. You could also implement **print()** methods that accepted a width value as a second argument.

We can use the **FormatWriter** class to help us output the primes from the previous example in five tidy columns.

Try It Out—Outputting Data in Fixed Fields

We only need to modify the code at the end of the previous example so that it uses our **FormatWriter** class:

```
import java.io.*;

public class NeatPrimesOutput
{
  public static void main(String[] args)
  {
    ...
      // Divide by all the primes we have up to limit
      for(int i = 1; i < count && primes[i] <= limit; i++)
        if(number%primes[i] == 0)              // Is it an exact divisor?
          continue outer;                       // yes, try the next number

      primes[count++] = number;     // We got one!
    }
```

```
        // Output the primes array using a formatted buffered stream
        FormatWriter out = new FormatWriter(
                        new BufferedWriter(
                        new FileWriter(FileDescriptor.out)), 12);

        for(int i=0; i < primes.length; i++)
        {
          if(i%5==0)                    // New line before every fifth prime
            out.println();

          out.print(primes[i]);               // Output a prime
        }
        out.close();                         // Close the stream
      }
    }
```

Of course, this file containing class definition needs to be in the same directory as the definition for the **FormatWriter** class. This example should produce the output:

```
    2           3           5           7           11
    13          17          19          23          29
    31          37          41          43          47
    53          59          61          67          71
```

How It Works

As we want to output the data to the standard output stream, we create a **FileWriter** object from the **out** member of the **FileDescriptor** class. The **FileWriter** object is passed to a **BufferedWriter** constructor to obtain a buffered stream, and this stream is passed as the first argument to a constructor for a **FormatWriter** object. The second argument to the constructor is the field width, 12. If we omit the second argument, we will get an object with the default field width of 10.

After the stream object has been created, we output the primes in the **for** loop. Before each line of five prime values, we call the **println()** method that our **FormatWriter** class inherits from **PrintWriter**. This just outputs a newline character to the stream and flushes the buffer. After all the prime values have been written, we call **close()** to flush and close the stream.

Now that you have a reasonable idea of how to write to a stream, it's time to look at how you can read the data back.

Byte Input Streams

Byte input streams are defined using sub-classes of the abstract class, **InputStream**. Java supports **markable** streams. A markable stream is a stream where any position in the stream can be marked by calling a suitable method, so that you can return later to precisely the marked position in the stream simply by calling another suitable function. This is achieved by keeping track of how many bytes have been read from the stream. This feature makes it very easy to repeatedly process any given block of data in a file. Without the ability to mark the stream, you would have to keep track yourself of how many bytes there were from the beginning of the file to the particular block you wanted to reprocess. You would then need to return to the beginning of the file and skip that many bytes to return to the start of the block, each time you wanted to read the block again.

The classes derived from the **InputStream** class will all inherit the following methods:

Method	Description
`read()`	There are three overloaded versions of this method. The version with no arguments is abstract, and should read a single byte of data from the stream and return it as type **int**. If the operation fails, -1 is returned. All three versions will throw an **IOException** if an error occurs.
`read(byte[] buffer)`	This version reads sufficient bytes to fill the array **buffer**, or until the end of the stream is reached. The method returns the count of the number of bytes read as type **int**. If no bytes are read, -1 is returned.
`read(byte buffer, offset, int length)`	This version reads bytes into the array buffer starting at element **int buffer[offset]**. The method will read up to **length** bytes into the array, or until the end of the stream is reached, and will return the number of bytes read as type **int**. If no bytes are read, -1 will be returned.
`skip(long n)`	This method will read and discard **n** bytes from the stream, or until the end of the stream is reached, and return the number of bytes skipped as type **long**. You would use this to skip over parts of a file that you know you don't want to process.
`mark(int readlimit)`	This method marks the current position in the input stream so that you can return to it using the **reset()** method. If you read more that **readlimit** bytes from the stream after the mark has been set, the mark will be invalidated.
`reset()`	This method positions the stream at the point defined by a previous call of the **mark()** method. If the mark operation is not supported for the stream, an **IOException** will be thrown.
`markSupported()`	This method returns **true** if the **mark** operation is supported for the stream, and **false** otherwise.
`available()`	This method returns an **int** value that is the number of bytes that can be read from the current stream without blocking. If you try to read more bytes than the number returned by this method, the read operation will not return until all the data required becomes available. For example, stream input from the keyboard can be blocked until you press the *Enter* key. The method throws an **IOException** if an error occurs.
`close()`	This method closes the input stream. It throws an **IOException** if an error occurs.

Although the basic **read()** method is the only **abstract** method in the class, sub-classes will typically implement their own versions of most of these methods. Note that there is no **open()** method complementing the **close()** method. Once an input stream object has been created successfully, you can read from it immediately.

Sub-classes of InputStream

There are six classes derived directly from the abstract class, **InputStream**.

> One of these, the **ObjectInputStream** class, is specific to reading from a stream that contains class objects, including objects of classes that you define. Reading and writing objects is a rather different process from reading and writing ordinary data, so we will defer discussion of this until later in this chapter when we will look at how you can write objects of your own classes to a stream, and read them back.

We will concentrate here on the other five sub-classes of **InputStream**. You can use four of these for various kinds of stream input operations. The fifth is a base class for further classes that have can process the data from an input stream in various ways. The direct sub-classes of the class **InputStream**, excluding the **ObjectInputStream** class, are shown below.

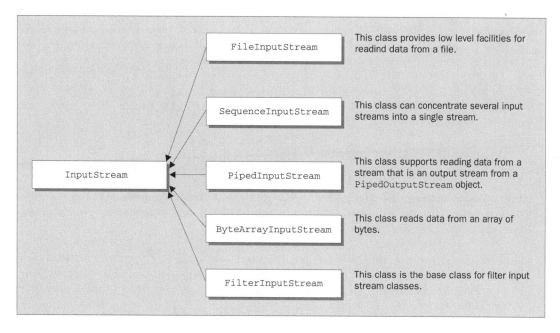

You can see that three of these sub-classes of **InputStream** enable you to define three different kinds of input stream, each with a different data source. The three options you have for a data source are: a file, a **byte** array and a piped output stream from another program process. The two other sub-classes enable you to add capabilities to an input stream. The class `SequenceInputStream` will allow you to concatenate several input streams into a single stream, and the `FilterInputStream` class is designed to be a base for deriving a number of filter stream classes.

The derived classes in the diagram, other than `FilterInputStream`, only provide the rather basic ability to read a single byte or an array of bytes from a file. This is not very convenient when you want to read data of type `double`, or a value of one of the other primitive types from a file. In this case you can use the sub-classes of `FilterInputStream` to create objects that provide more flexibility in the way data input is handled.

The classes `PipedInputStream` and `ByteArrayInputStream` are designed to complement the equivalent classes for output.

The FileInputStream Object

You can create a `FileInputStream` object corresponding to a particular disk file by passing a `File` object to the constructor for the class:

```
File myPrimes = new File("c:\\JunkData\\Primes.bin");
FileInputStream myStream = new FileInputStream(myPrimes);
```

This defines the stream `myStream`, which refers to the file that we created in the previous example using an `OutputStream` object. The `FileInputStream` constructor will throw a `FileNotFoundException` if the file is not found, so you are not obliged to test for a valid directory and file explicitly. When you create a `FileInputStream` object, you should either put the code in a try block, with a catch block to catch the exception, or define that the method containing the code throws the `FileNotFoundException`.

There is also another constructor for `FileInputStream` objects which will accept a `String` containing the file path. For example, we could create the input stream object `myStream` with the statement:

```
FileInputStream myStream =
                    new FileInputStream("c:\\JunkData\\Primes.bin");
```

This `FileInputStream` constructor will also throw a `FileNotFoundException` if the file does not exist, so you will need either a `catch` block for this exception in your method, or to declare that your method can throw this exception.

Once you have created the stream object, the file is available to be read immediately. However, all you have available are the `read()` methods that will read a single byte or a byte array from the stream. To get more capability than this you need to use a filter input stream class, as we will see a little later.

FYI   In addition to the methods defined in the base class, the `FileInputStream` also has the method, `getFD()` which returns a `FileDescriptor` object corresponding to the file that the `FileInputStream` object represents. The `FileInputStream` class has a constructor that accepts a `FileDescriptor` object, as do the `FileOutputStream`, `FileReader` and `FileWriter` classes.

Sequence Input Streams

You can combine several streams into a single stream by using the **SequenceInputStream** class. The streams are combined by effectively concatenating them head to tail in the sequence in which you specify them when you construct your **SequenceInputStream** object.

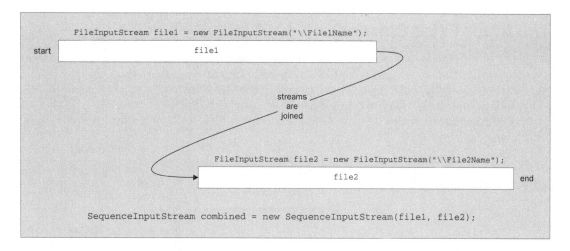

The **SequenceInputStream** class has two constructors—one which combines two stream objects into a single stream, and another which combines several. You can see the effect of combining two byte input streams, **file1** and **file2**, into a single stream, **combined**, in the diagram above. The code to create and combine the streams is shown in the diagram.

The constructor that combines several streams accepts a single argument, of type **Enumeration**. Of course, each object in the **Enumeration** must be a byte input stream. We will see how an **Enumeration** object is created in Chapter 9, but you don't really need an enumeration to concatenate multiple streams. In fact you can easily combine multiple byte input streams using the first constructor just by nesting sequence input streams. Given that we have the **SequenceInputStream** object **combined**, shown in the diagram, we could construct a stream that concatenates a further two streams to this with the statements:

```
FileInputStream file3 = new FileInputStream("\\File3Name");
FileInputStream file4 = new FileInputStream("\\File4Name");
```

```
SequenceInputStream allFour = new SequenceInputStream(combined,
                              new SequenceInputStream(file3, file4));
```

After constructing the two **FileInputStream** objects, these are combined to create a **SequenceInputStream** object which in turn is passed as the second argument to the constructor for **SequenceInputStream**. This creates the stream, **allFour**, which will be the result of concatenating all four files.

When you read from a sequence input stream, the transition from one concatenated stream to the next is automatic. When the end of one stream is reached, its **close()** method will be called, and data will then be read from the next stream, but you have no means of detecting when this occurs. So far as you are concerned you are dealing with a single seamless stream. Only when you read past the end of the last stream will an end-of-file condition be registered for the **SequenceInputStream** object. If you call the **close()** method for a **SequenceInputStream** object, all the streams making up the object will be closed.

The Input Filter Classes

There are no less than nine sub-classes of the **FilterInputStream** classes, so we will need to go through them in stages. Four of them complement the byte output stream classes we have seen, and the other five, which are not in the **java.io** package, are related to handling compressed files and to security. The direct sub-classes of the class **FilterInputStream** that are concerned with normal byte input streams are in the **java.io** package, and are shown below.

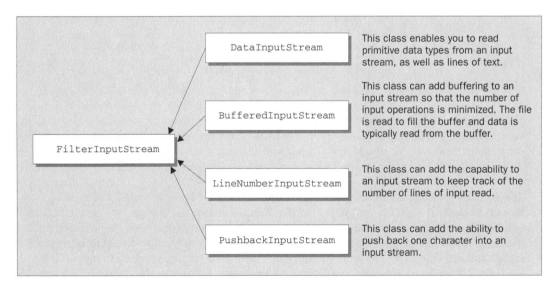

The **DataInputStream** class only supports reading data from a file in binary form. This kind of file will normally have been created by the **DataOutputStream** class methods. Within the input stream classes, you have no methods that will convert numerical data from a character stream, such as the keyboard for instance, to the integer or floating point data values. If you need to be able to read formatted numerical data from an input stream, you must implement it yourself. However, as we will see a little later in this chapter, you do get quite a bit of help from another class in the **java.io** package—**StreamTokenizer**, so it's not as difficult as it sounds.

The other five sub-classes of the **FilterInputStream** class that we mentioned at the outset, are shown in the diagram below:

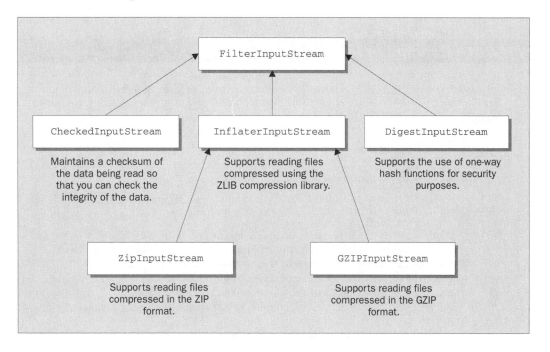

The **DigestInputStream** class is in the package **java.security**. This is quite an advanced topic so we will not be discussing this further in this book. The other four sub-classes of the **FilterInputStream** class are in the package **java.util.zip**. The **CheckInputStream** class computes a checksum for the bytes that are read from the file, and is used with files that were written using a **CheckedOutputStream** class object.

The other three classes complement the output stream classes that support compression. We will look at how we can read a ZIP and retrieve the data from the compressed file a little later in this chapter.

Reading from an Input Stream

To read from an input stream, particularly if the stream is a disk file, you will normally use one of the filter input streams. Without a filter stream, all you can read from a stream is bytes, whereas, in practice, the minimum you will want is to be able to read values of any of the basic types. Let's look first at how we can read the basic types of data values from a disk file.

Reading from a Disk File

Reading from a disk file using a filter input stream is analogous to the mechanism we saw for output streams. You need to create a **DataInputStream** object from a **FileInputStream** object that identifies the file you want to read. To see how this works in practice, we could create a program to read the file of prime numbers that we created earlier in this chapter. We will read the primes from the file using a byte input stream, and write them to the screen using a character stream.

Try It Out—Reading in the *primes.bin* File

1 Let's start by filling in the code to create the input stream object for the file:

```java
import java.io.*;

public class ReadPrimes
{
  public static void main(String[] args)
  {
    try
    {
      // Create a File object and an input stream object for the file
      String directory = "c:\\JunkData\\";      // Directory path
      String fileName = "Primes.bin";           // File name
      File myPrimes = new File(directory, fileName);
      DataInputStream primesIn = new DataInputStream(
                              new FileInputStream(myPrimes));

      // Code to read the primes from the stream goes here...
    }
    catch(FileNotFoundException e)              // Stream creation exception
    {
      System.err.println(e);
      return;
    }
  }
}
```

2 We can now add the code to read the primes from the stream and to output them to the screen. We will use a **FormatWriter** object to manage the output to the screen, so be sure to copy the **FormatWriter.java** file to the directory in which the current class file is stored. The code to read the primes from the file and display them is as follows:

```java
DataInputStream primesIn = new DataInputStream(
                            new FileInputStream(myPrimes));
```

```
      // Create a default formatted character output stream
      FormatWriter out = new FormatWriter(
                        new BufferedWriter(
                        new FileWriter(FileDescriptor.out)));

      long[] primes = new long[6];         // Array for one line of primes
      boolean EOF = false;                 // End of file flag

      while(!EOF)
      {
        int index = 0;   // Index for storing primes
        try
        {
          // Fill the array with primes from the file
          for(index = 0; index < primes.length; index++)
            primes[index] = primesIn.readLong();
        }
        catch(EOFException e)
        {
          EOF = true;                      // This will end the while loop
        }

        // Output the number of primes in the array
        for(int j = 0; j < index; j++)
          out.print(primes[j]);
        out.println();                     // Write end of line
      }
      out.close();                         // Flush and close the output stream
      primesIn.close();                    // Close the input stream
    }
    catch(FileNotFoundException e)         // Stream creation exception
    {
      System.err.println(e);
      return;
    }
    catch(IOException e)                   // File read exception
    {
      System.out.println("Error reading input file" + e );
      return;
    }
  }
}
```

The example should produce the output that begins:

2	3	5	7	11	13
17	19	23	29	31	37
41	43	47	53	59	61
67	71	73	79	83	89
97	101	103	107	109	113

127	131	137	139	149	151
157	163	167	173	179	181
191	193	197	199	211	223
227	229	233	239	241	251
257	263	269	271	277	281

Just the first few are shown here. There are 200 primes in the complete output.

How It Works

At the start of the **ReadPrimes** class, a **File** object is created from the **directory** and **fileName** strings, and this object is passed to the **FileInputStream** constructor to create a byte input stream for the file. The directory and file should be the same as that used to write primes to the file in the example earlier in this chapter. The **FileInputStream** constructor will throw a **FileNotFoundException** if the file is not found. Since we catch this exception in the **catch** block following the **try** block, we don't need to test explicitly that the directory and file name are valid.

You can check out how the **FileNotFoundException** is caught by deliberately putting an invalid file path in the call to the **File** constructor. This is not difficult because even a leading space in the file name will cause the file not to be found.

The **FileInputStream** object is passed to the **DataInputStream** constructor to create the byte stream object that we will use to read the file. This object will provide us with the methods that we need to read primitive data types from the file. The **DataInputStream** object only has the basic **read()** methods for a single byte or a byte array, that are declared in the base class, **InputStream**.

The file is read in the **while** loop, controlled by the flag, **EOF**, which we set to **false** initially. Because we read the file six values at a time, and then output them to the screen, we have included a mechanism to automatically signal when we reach the end of the file. We use the fact that the read operation will throw an **EOFException** when the end of file is reached.

We read a block of primes to fill the primes array from the file in the **try** block inside the **while** loop. As long as no **EOFException** is thrown, the code immediately following the **catch** block is executed. This writes the block of primes to the **out** stream in the **for** loop, and the **while** loop continues. The **for** loop to write the primes is controlled by the value of **index** in order to deal with the situation that can arise when the end of file is reached. If the number of values in the file is not a multiple of the size of the **primes[]** array, the array will not be full for the last line of output. The number of elements will be the value stored in the variable **index**. Note that we must declare the variable, **index**, outside the **try** block in the **while** loop, otherwise it won't exist when we output the primes.

When the **EOFException** is thrown, the **catch** block following the inner try block is executed. This will set the **EOF** flag to **true**. Thus the **while** loop will end after the current iteration, once the last line of primes has been written to **out**. If an error occurs on reading the file, an **IOException** will be thrown so we need a **catch** block for this too, at the end of the main **try** block.

Reading a ZIP Archive

You can use an object of the **ZipInputStream** class to read a ZIP archive containing compressed files. The argument to the class constructor must be an **InputStream** object that represents a physical ZIP archive. We can define an object corresponding to the ZIP we wrote containing the **primes.bin** file with the statements:

```
String dirName = "c:\\JunkData";              // Directory for the ZIP file
String zipName = "NewPrimes.zip";             // The ZIP archive name
File myPrimeZip = new File(dirName, zipName);  // The file object
ZipInputStream myZipFile = new ZipInputStream(
                                   new FileInputStream(myPrimeZip));
```

The **ZipInputStream** class defines the following methods, in addition to the constructor:

Method	Description
getNextEntry()	Returns a **ZipEntry** object for the next ZIP entry in the archive, and positions the stream at the beginning of the entry.
closeEntry()	Closes the current ZIP entry and positions the stream for reading the next entry.
read(byte[] array, int offset, int length)	Reads **length** bytes from the ZIP entry into array, starting at index position **offset** in the array. This method can throw an **IOException** if an I/O error occurs, or a **ZipException** if a ZIP file error occurs.
skip(long byteCount)	Skips over the next **byteCount** bytes in the ZIP entry. This can also throw an **IOException** or a **ZIPEXception**.
close()	Closes the ZIP input stream. This method can throw an **IOException**.

The process for reading from a ZIP entry is to call **getNextEntry()** for the **ZipInputStream** object before starting read operations. You can use the **ZipEntry** object returned to get the name of the file in the ZIP entry by calling the **getName()** method. When you are finished reading the ZIP entry, you call **closeEntry()**. Then you can call **getNextEntry()** for the next ZIP entry if there are addition entries. When you are done with the stream, you call its **close()** method to close the stream.

Of course, the basic **read()** method here is not what we want to use to read our **NewPrimes.bin** file from the archive. We want to read the prime values of type **long**, so we will need to wrap another stream around the **ZipInputStream**:

```
DataInputStream primesIn = new DataInputStream(
                           new BufferedInputStream(myZipFile));
```

Let's see how this works in practice. We can extract the ZIP file and write the contents to the screen.

Try It Out—A Prime Unzipping Example

We will use the fragments of code we have just seen to read all the primes from the archive, **NewPrimes.zip**, and write them to the standard output stream using our **FormatWriter** class. Make sure you copy **FormatWriter.java** to the directory you are using for this example.

Here's the code to read the file:

```java
import java.io.*;
import java.util.zip.*;

class ReadZippedPrimes
{
  public static void main(String[] args)
  {
    try
    {
      // Create a default formatted character output stream
      FormatWriter out = new FormatWriter(
                  new BufferedWriter(
                  new FileWriter(FileDescriptor.out)));

      String dirName = "c:\\JunkData";      // Directory for the ZIP file
      String zipName = "NewPrimes.zip";     // The ZIP archive name

      File myPrimeZip = new File(dirName, zipName);  // The file object
      ZipInputStream myZipFile = new ZipInputStream(
                                new FileInputStream(myPrimeZip));
      ZipEntry myZipEntry = myZipFile.getNextEntry();

      out.println("Compressed File is " + myZipEntry.getName());
      DataInputStream primesIn = new DataInputStream(
                            new BufferedInputStream(myZipFile));

      long[] primes = new long[6];        // Array for one line of primes
      boolean EOF = false;                // End of file flag

      while(!EOF)
      {
        int index = 0;  // Index for storing primes
        try
        {
          // Fill the array with primes from the file
          for(index = 0; index < primes.length; index++)
            primes[index] = primesIn.readLong();
```

```
        }
        catch(EOFException e)
        {
          EOF = true;                       // This will end the while loop
        }
        // Output the number of primes in the array
        for(int j = 0; j < index; j++)
          out.print(primes[j]);
        out.println();                       // Write end of line
      }

      out.close();                    // Flush and close the output stream
      primesIn.close();               // Close the input stream
    }
    catch(FileNotFoundException e)    // Stream creation exception
    {
      System.err.println(e);
      return;
    }
    catch(IOException e)              // File read exception
    {
      System.out.println("Error reading input file" + e );
      return;
    }
  }
}
```

This will output the name of the file in the archive, plus the primes:

```
Compressed File is NewPrimes.bin
     2         3         5         7        11        13
    17        19        23        29        31        37
    41        43        47        53        59        61
    67        71        73        79        83        89
    97       101       103       107       109       113
```

plus the other 170 values...

How It Works

We create the **ZipInputStream** object from a **FileInputStream** object, exactly as we saw earlier. We get the **ZipEntry** object by calling the **getNextEntry()** method for the **ZipInputStream** object, and use its **getName()** method to output the name of the file. We then create the **primesIn** stream object and read the values in much the same way as we used to read the uncompressed, **Primes.bin** file in the earlier example.

FYI
There is another class, `ZipFile`, supporting the reading of ZIP files, that is defined in the package `java.util.zip`. This is intended to ease the processing of ZIP archives that contain multiple compressed files. A `ZipFile` object can return an enumeration of all the entries in a zip so that you can then process all of them quite easily in a loop.

Character Input Streams

The character input stream classes read data from a stream as Unicode characters. Where the external source is a file, automatic character code conversion is provided by the stream object so you would use a character input stream to read a file written by a character output stream. The character input stream classes all have the abstract class **Reader** as a base. There are nine classes derived from the **Reader** class, as shown in the diagram.

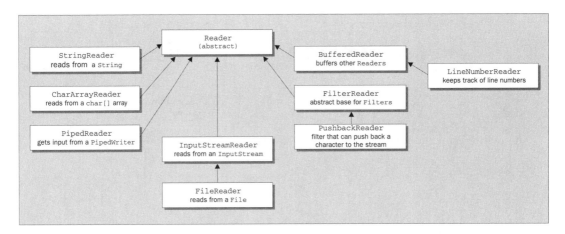

Most of the character input stream classes complement the corresponding class for a character output stream. A **PipedReader** class object is intended to be used in conjunction with a **PipedWriter** object to link two threads. The **StringReader** and **CharArrayReader** classes read from a **String** or a **char[]** array that you pass to the constructor. You use the **BufferedReader** class to buffer operation for another **Reader** object, usually a **FileReader** or a **StreamReader** which is passed to the **BufferedReader** class constructor.

To read a physical file, you can create a stream object using either the **FileReader** class or the **InputStreamReader** class. You can create a **FileReader** object from a **File** object, a **FileDescriptor** object, or a string defining the file name. You create an **InputStreamReader** object from an **InputStream** object. The **FileReader** class provides automatic conversion from the character coding used by the local computer to Unicode as the data is read.

The **PushbackReader** constructor accepts a **Reader** object as an argument—typically a **FileReader** or an **InputStreamReader** object. The **PushbackReader** stream allows you to read characters from the stream, then you can push the characters back on the stream to allow them to be read again. This gives you a read-ahead mechanism. With this mechanism you can check what is in the stream, and based on that you can select a method to process the stream after resetting the stream back to its original condition.

The methods that all the character input stream classes inherit from the **Reader** class are:

Method	Description
`read()`	Reads a character from the stream and returns it as type **int**. If the end of the stream is reached, -1 is returned.
`read(char[] array)`	Reads characters from the stream to fill **array**. The method returns the number of bytes read as type **int**, or -1 if the end of the stream is reached.
`read(char[] array, int offset, int length)`	Reads **length** characters from the stream into **array**, starting at index position **offset**. The method returns the number of bytes read as type **int**, or -1 if the end of the stream is reached.
`markSupported()`	Returns **true** if the stream is markable, and **false** otherwise.
`mark(int readAheadLimit)`	Marks the current position in the stream the argument specifies the maximum number of characters that can be read from the stream without losing track of the current mark position.
`reset()`	Resets the stream to the previous mark position. If the stream was not marked the stream may be reset to the beginning for some streams.
`ready()`	Returns **true** if the stream is ready to be read, and **false** otherwise.
`skip(long charCount)`	Skips over **charCount** characters in the stream. The method returns the numbers of characters skipped which will be less than **charCount** if the end of the stream is reached prematurely, or an input error stops the process.
`close()`	Closes the stream.

All these methods, with the exception of **markSupported()**, can throw an **IOException** if an error occurs. All the read methods will block, that is, not return to the calling point, until some characters can be read from the stream, the end of the stream is reached or an error occurs.

Reading a File as a Character Stream

We could read the file of proverbs that we wrote as an exercise for the character output streams. Remember that we wrote the string length to the file preceding the text for each proverb. However, this data is not numeric. We had to write string equivalent of the length to the file, so we have to do some work to figure out where the string length characters end, and where the proverb begins. We can do this by using a **PushBackReader** object.

We can create a **File** object for the file first:

```
String dirName = "c:\\JunkData\\";        // Directory for the output file
String fileName = "Proverbs.txt";          // Name of the output file
File input = new File(dirName, fileName);  // The file object
```

This creates a **File** object from a **String** objects for the directory and the file name. We won't need to verify that the file exists as the **FileReader** constructor will throw a **FileNotFoundException** if it doesn't.

We will buffer the **FileReader** stream by passing it to a **BufferedReader** stream constructor. We can then create the **PushBackReader** object from the **BufferedReader** object with the statement:

```
PushbackReader in = new PushbackReader(
                    new BufferedReader(
                    new FileReader(input)));
```

Each proverb in the file we want to read is always preceded by its length. We can use the special capabilities of the **PushbackReader** stream to help us deal with this. As well as the methods defined in the **Reader** base class, the **PushbackReader** class defines three methods that write characters back to the stream:

unread() Methods	Description
unread(int c)	Writes the character **c** back to the stream.
unread(char[] array)	Writes the entire contents of **array** back to the stream.
unread(char[] array, offset, int length)	Writes **length** elements of **array** back to the stream starting at **int** index position **offset**.

All of these will throw an **IOException** if an error occurs, so you should put them in a **try** block when you use them. We will be able to read the characters that correspond to the length of a proverb from the stream. When we find a character that is not a digit, we know that we have come to the end of the characters for the string length, so we can write it back to the stream. We can assemble the characters that make up the length of the proverb into a string, **number**, as follows:

```
String number = "";                    // String length as characters

// Get the characters for the length
while(Character.isDigit((char)(c = in.read())))
  number += (char)c;

// Test for end of file here - c will be -1

in.unread(c);                          // Push back the last character
```

The **read()** method for the **PushbackReader** object, **in**, returns a character from the stream as type **int**, which we store in the variable **c**. This will have the value -1 if the end of file is detected. After casting **c** to type **char**, we pass it as an argument to the **isDigit()** method in the **Character** class. This returns **true** if the character is a digit so the **while** loop will continue as long as this is the case. On each iteration of the **while** loop, we add the digit character read from the stream to the end of the string, **number**. When the **while** loop ends we will have all the digits for the length of the next proverb in the **String** object, **number**.

When the **while** loop ends, we must test for an end of file condition—indicated by **c** having the value -1. This will occur immediately after the last proverb has been read. We will fill in this detail later. If it is not the end of file, the last character read must be the first character of the proverb, so we write **c** back to the file by calling the **unread()** method for the stream object, **in**.

We now have enough information to read the next proverb:

```
char[] proverb = new char[Integer.parseInt(number)];
in.read(proverb);                                    // Read a proverb
```

This creates an array of type **char[]** that has precisely the number of elements required for the complete proverb. We convert the **String** object, **number**, to an **int** value by passing it to the **parseInt()** method from the **Integer** class. The methods in these classes paralleling the basic data types come in very handy from time to time, don't they?

Let's put all this together in a working example.

Try It Out—Using a *PushbackReader* on a Character Stream

The example will read the file, and output all the proverbs to the screen. Here's the complete program:

```
// Using the push back reader
import java.io.*;

class ReadCharacters
{
  public static void main(String[] args)
  {
    try
    {
      String dirName = "c:\\JunkData\\"; // Directory for the output file
      String fileName = "Proverbs.txt";  // Name of the output file

      File input = new File(dirName, fileName);  // The file object

      PushbackReader in = new PushbackReader(
                                    new BufferedReader(
                                    new FileReader(input)));
```

```
            boolean EOF = false;                  // End of file flag
            int c;                                // Character store
            while(!EOF)
            {
              try
              {
                String number ="";                // String length as characters

                // Get the characters for the length
                while(Character.isDigit((char)(c = in.read())))
                  number += (char)c;

                if(c==-1)                          // Check for end of file
                {
                  EOF = true;                      // Set flag
                  continue;                        // End iteration
                }
                else                               // It is not end of file so
                  in.unread(c);                    // push back the last character

                char[] proverb = new char[Integer.parseInt(number)];
                in.read(proverb);                  // Read a proverb
                System.out.println(proverb);
              }
              catch(EOFException e)
              {
                EOF = true;                        // This will end the while loop
              }
            }
          }
          catch(FileNotFoundException e)           // Stream creation exception
          {
            System.err.println(e);
            return;
          }
          catch(IOException e)                     // File read exception
          {
            System.out.println("Error reading input file" + e );
            return;
          }
        }
      }
```

The output will depend on what is in the file which will depend on how many times you ran the program that wrote it. I get the output:

```
Indecision maximixes flexibility.
Only the mediocre are always at their best.
A little knowledge is a dangerous thing.
Many a mickle makes a muckle.
```

```
Who begins too much achieves little.
Who knows most says least.
A wise man sits on the hole in his carpet.
Indecision maximixes flexibility.
Only the mediocre are always at their best.
A little knowledge is a dangerous thing.
Many a mickle makes a muckle.
Who begins too much achieves little.
Who knows most says least.
A wise man sits on the hole in his carpet.
```

How It Works

The overall read operation takes place in the while loop controlled by the **boolean** variable **EOF** which is initially **false**. Each iteration of this loop reads one proverb from the file. The variable, **EOF**, will be set to **true** if an end of file condition is recognized, and this will end the loop. The **try** block inside the **while** loop uses the code we saw earlier to read the length of the proverb, and then read the proverb itself into the array, **proverb**, of the correct size. This is written to **System.out**. Note that the **String** variable **number**, will be re-initialized on each iteration of the while loop controlled by **EOF**. Similarly, for each proverb that we read, we create a new object of type **char[]** with the appropriate number of elements.

Formatted Stream Input

As we said earlier, you can get a lot of help with formatted input from the **StreamTokenizer** class in the **java.io** package. The term **token** refers to the character representation of an item such as a number or a string, and the class has the name **StreamTokenizer** because it can read data from a stream and make the data available as a series of tokens, or data items. A token is normally either a number, which can include a minus sign, digits, and a decimal point, or it is a string which is enclosed between quotes or between double quotes. Any sequence of letters, digits, decimal points and minus signs that begins with a letter is also treated as a string token. Any other character that is not whitespace, is not enclosed within quotes or double quotes and is not part of a comment is read as **null**. The **StreamTokenizer** class will ignore Java style comments and whitespace, which by default includes newline.

You construct a **StreamTokenizer** object from a character input stream object. For example, you could construct a **StreamTokenizer** object corresponding to the standard input stream with the statement:

```
StreamTokenizer myStream = new StreamTokenizer(
                            new FileReader(FileDescriptor.out));
```

You can cause a data item to be read from the stream used to construct a **StreamTokenizer** object by calling the **nextToken()** method for the object:

```
int dataType = myStream.nextToken();
```

The data item read from the stream is stored in one of two instance variables of the **StreamTokenizer** object. If the data item is a number, it is stored in a **public** data member, **nval**, which is of type **double**. It the data item is a string, it is stored in a **public** data member, **sval**, which is of type **String**. The analysis which segments the stream into tokens is fairly simple, and the way in which an arbitrary stream is broken into tokens is illustrated below.

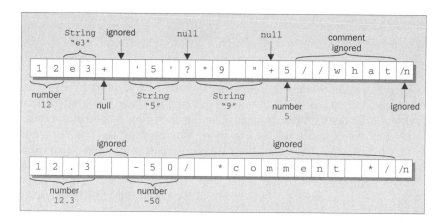

The **int** value returned by the **nextToken()** method indicates what kind of data item was read. It can be one of the following standard values which are defined in the class:

Token Value	Description
TT_NUMBER	The token is a number that has been stored in the member **nval**.
TT_WORD	The token is a string that has been stored in **sval**.
TT_EOF	The end of file has been read from the stream.
TT_EOL	An end of line character has been read. This is only set if the **eolIsSignificant()** method has been called with the argument value **true**, otherwise end of line characters are ignored.

Let's see how we can use this class to read data items from the keyboard.

Try It Out—Creating a Formatted Input Class

1 One way of reading formatted input is to derive our own class from **StreamTokenizer**. We can define a class that adds methods to return particular types of data items from the standard input stream. We can call it **FormattedInput**. Here is the basic class definition:

```
import java.io.*;

public class FormattedInput extends StreamTokenizer
```

```
{
  // Constructor
  public FormattedInput()
  {
    // Call the base class constructor for standard input
    super(new FileReader(FileDescriptor.in));
  }

  // Plus methods to read various data types...

}
```

2 All we have at the moment is the constructor. This calls the `StreamTokenizer` constructor with a `Reader` object as the argument defining the standard input stream, which is the keyboard, as the stream to be tokenized. All we need to add is the methods to read the data values that we want. We can start with a method to read values of type `int`:

```
// Method to read an int value
public int intRead()
{
  try
  {
    for(int i = 0; i < 5; i++)
    {
      if(nextToken()==TT_NUMBER)
        return (int)nval;       // Value is numeric, so return as int
      else
      {
        System.out.println("Incorrect input: " + sval +
                           " Re-enter an integer");
        continue;               // Retry the read operation
      }
    }
    System.out.println("Five failures reading an int value" +
                                  " - program terminated");
    System.exit(1);             // End the program
    return 0;
  }
  catch(IOException e)          // Error reading in nextToken()
  {
    System.out.println(e);      // Output the error
    System.exit(1);             // End the program
    return 0;
  }
}
```

3 We can test this class by adding some code to our previous example that calculates primes, `TryPrimesOutput`, to read the number of primes required from the keyboard:

```
import java.io.*;
public class TryPrimesOutput
{
  public static void main(String[] args)
  {
    FormattedInput keyboard = new FormattedInput(); // Keyboard stream

    System.out.print("Enter the number of primes required: ");
    int numPrimes = keyboard.intRead();        // Number of primes wanted
    long[] primes = new long[numPrimes];       // Array to store primes

    // Rest of the code as before...
  }
}
```

How It Works

The code for the class method is in a **try** block because the **nextToken()** method can throw an **IOException** if a read error occurs. We call **nextToken()** in the **if** statement to cause the next token to be read. If the value returned is **TT_NUMBER**, we assume it is a valid integer.

If the token read is not a number, we display a message and go to the next iteration of the **for** loop to read another token. The loop will repeat up to five times when the correct value is not present. After five failures, another message is displayed and the program is terminated by calling the static **exit()** method in the class **System**. The argument is a status code of type **int**. A non-zero value is used to indicate an error condition caused the termination.

From this model you should be able to add other methods to the class to deal with other data types.

In the test program, **TryPrimesOutput**, aside from the prompt for input, there are only two changes necessary to **main()**. The value for the number of primes required is read into the variable **numPrimes**, and we use this value to specify the number of elements in the array that stores the primes.

The input conversions supported by the **StreamTokenizer** class are fairly primitive. If you want to be able to enter floating point values with exponents, or to input numbers with a leading plus sign, you have to write your own class to do the analysis of the character string from the keyboard. At the moment, the **intRead()** method will read floating point values and just convert them to int. You could prevent this by putting an additional check in the **if** that verifies the data type:

```
if(nextToken()==TT_NUMBER && nval==(double)((long)nval))
  return (int)nval;   // Value is numeric, so return as int
else
{
  System.out.println("Incorrect input: " + sval + " Re-enter an integer");
```

```
        continue;              // Retry the read operation
  }
```

If **nval** is not an integer, casting it to **int** will truncate the fractional part, so when it is cast back to **double**, its value will be different from the original.

You don't have to worry about this when implementing a **doubleRead()** method. As long as a number was entered you can return it after casting it to **double**.

Random Access Files

If you want to access a file randomly, you must use the **RandomAccessFile** class. Even if you just want to read and update the same file, unless a character stream is sufficient for your needs, you still have to use a **RandomAccessFile** object.

There are two available constructors that you can use to create a random access file stream object, and both require two arguments. For one constructor the first argument is a **File** object that identifies the file path, and the second is a **String** object that specifies the access mode. With the other constructor, the first argument is a **String** object specifying the file path, and the second argument is a **String** defining the access mode, as before. Since you always create a **RandomAccessFile** object from a **File** object or a **String**, you cannot buffer a random access file.

The access mode can be **"r"** which indicates that you just want to read the file, or it can be **"rw"** which indicates that you want to be able to read and write the file. If you specify the mode as anything else, the constructor will throw an **IllegalArgumentException**.

To create a **RandomAccessFile** object, you could write:

```
    File myPrimes = new File("c:\\JunkData\\Primes.bin");
    RandomAccessFile myFile = new RandomAccessFile(myPrimes, "rw");
```

This will create the random access stream object, **myFile**, corresponding to the physical file **Primes.bin**, and will open it for both reading and writing. If the file does not exist with **"rw"** specified as the mode, it will be created since it is assumed you intend to write it before you try to read it. If you specify the mode as **"r"**, the file must already exist. If it doesn't, an **IOException** will be thrown by the constructor.

You can get a **FileDescriptor** object corresponding to the file that a **RandomAccessFile** object represents by calling the method **getFD()** for the stream object. You could use the **FileDescriptor** object to create another stream object for this file. You cannot create a **RandomAccessFile** object from a **FileDescriptor** object.

Input and Output Operations

The **RandomAccessFile** class supports all the read operations that are available with **DataInputStream**, and all the write operations that are defined in **DataOutputStream**. It implements the same interfaces as these two classes, so you can read and write data values that are **String** objects, or any of the basic types. You can replace the **DataInputStream** object in the earlier example which displayed the contents of the file **Primes.bin**, with a **RandomAccessFile** object, and the program will work just the same.

Apart from being able to read and write the same file, the added value you get with the **RandomAccessFile** class is the ability to change the current position in the file, so let's look at the methods we have for doing that.

Changing the File Position

The current position from the beginning of the file is the **offset** for the byte where the next read or write operation will begin. You have three methods that relate to the business of altering the current position in a file:

Method	Description
seek(long pos)	Moves the current position in the file to the offset from the beginning of the file, specified by the argument **pos**, which is of type **long**.
getFilePointer()	Returns a value of type **long** that is the current position in the file—the offset from the beginning of the file.
length()	Returns a value of type **long** that is the length of the file in bytes.

You use the method **seek()** to move the current file position to the point where you want the next read or write to start. The argument could be a value that you previously obtained using the **getFilePointer()** method, or it could be a value that you calculated based on the length of the file, and the amount of data that you write per record.

Let's see random access file streams in action in a final version of our program to compute prime numbers.

Using Random Access Files

Once we have filled the **primes** array with values, we can write the primes to a file. We can then access them when we want to check for a new prime. Once the file has been created, we can simply retrieve primes from the file if the number of primes requested is less than the total number that we have stored. To do this, we will need to change the program logic quite a bit. It will also be better if we implement the program as more than one method, so we will recreate the program from scratch.

We will put the code to test whether a number is prime in a separate method, to avoid making the method **main()** too long. This will accept the number to be tested as an argument of type **long**, and return **true** if the number is prime. We can also break out the code to output the number of primes requested in a separate method. This will be a self-contained piece of code with no return value that will use our **FormatWriter** class to display the primes in neat columns. We will also use the **FormattedInput** class that we derived from **StreamTokenizer** to handle keyboard input, so make sure you copy the files containing the definitions for these two classes to the directory for this example.

Try It Out—The Skeleton `PrimesFile` Class

The structure of the basic program class will be very simple. It will have the variables that are to be accessed by all the methods in the class as static data members, and it will have three static methods—the method **main()** where execution starts, the method to test if a number is prime and a method to output the number of primes requested:

```java
// Using a random access file to store primes
import java.io.*;

public class PrimesFile
{
  static RandomAccessFile myFile = null;// File stream
  static boolean file = false;         // True if file contains primes
  static long[] primes = new long[10];  // Array to store primes
  static int current = 0;              // Free element in primes array

  // The main computation
  public static void main(String[] args)
  {
    try
    {
      // Read the number of primes required from the keyboard...
      // Access or create the random access file...
      // Compute any primes needed that are not in the file...
      // Output the primes
    }
    catch(IOException e)
    {
      // deal with error reading the file
    }
  }

  // Test whether a number is prime
  static boolean primeTest(long number)
  {
    // Code to test for primeness...
  }

  // Method to display primes
  static void outputPrimes(long numPrimes) throws IOException
  {
    // Code to output primes...
    // We will not catch IOExceptions from file read here
  }
}
```

How It Works

We need the **import** statement for **java.io** to access the stream classes that we need. We have declared four static class variables that will be available to any method in the class.

All three methods, **main()**, **primeTest()** and **outputPrimes()**, will need access to the **RandomAccessFile** object, **myFile**. The other three class variables will be needed in **main()** as well as in the method **primeTest()**.

Just to experience both possibilities, we will add code to catch any **IOException**s that are thrown in the **primeTest()** method, but in the **outputPrimes()** method we will not catch them so they will be need to be caught in **main()**.

Try It Out—Testing for a Prime

We want the method **primeTest()** to use the primes stored in the file in the test. However, the file may be empty—this will be so the first time the program is run for instance, or if the file was deleted prior to executing the program. In this case we want the method to recognize that and just use the primes that are stored in memory in the array **primes[]**. The code to do this will be:

```
static boolean primeTest(long number)
{
  // The maximum divisor we need to try is the square root of number
  long limit = (long)Math.ceil(Math.sqrt((double)number));
  try
  {
    if(file)                      // Check whether we have primes on file...
    { // ... we do
      long prime = 0L;                       // Stores prime from file
      myFile.seek(0L);                       // Go to file start
      long primeCount = myFile.length()/8;   // Number of primes on file

      // Check the number using the primes from file
      for(int i = 0; i < primeCount; i++)
      {
        prime = myFile.readLong(); // Read a prime
        if(prime > limit)
          return true;             // No exact division - prime found
        if(number%prime == 0)
          return false;            // Exact division - not a prime
      }
    }
  }
  catch(IOException e)                        // Handle read error
  { // Exception thrown - output message
    System.out.println("Exception primeTest():\n" + e);
    System.exit(1);                           // End the program
  }

  // Otherwise check using primes in memory
  for(int i = 0; i < current; i++)
```

```
    {
      if(primes[i] > limit)
        return true;                 // No exact division - prime found
      if(number%primes[i] == 0)
        return false;                // Exact division - not a prime
    }
    return true;
  }
```

How It Works

The method uses the **file** flag to determine whether there are any primes in the file. If there are, we seek from the beginning of the file, with offset zero, and then read one prime at a time from the file. If we read a prime that is greater than **limit**, we have tested **number** against all the primes less than **limit**, so **number** must be prime and we return **true**. If we find an exact divisor, **number** is not prime so we return **false**. The code reading the file is in a **try** block so we can catch any exceptions that are thrown during input operations.

If the file is empty, we do the same test using primes from the **primes** array that we declared as a class variable. The class variable, **current**, is the index of the next free element in **primes**, so the loop variable must be less than this value.

Try It Out—Outputting Primes

Outputting primes is very simple so the method is quite short, particularly since we don't catch **IOExceptions**. You need to copy the **FormatWriter** class that we created earlier to the same directory as the example.

```
static void outputPrimes(int numPrimes) throws IOException
{
  // Create a buffered formatted output stream
  FormatWriter out = new FormatWriter(
                  new BufferedWriter(
                  new FileWriter(FileDescriptor.out)), true, 12);

  myFile.seek(0);                         // Go to file start
  for(int i = 0; i < numPrimes; i++)      // Output the primes
  {
    long prime = myFile.readLong();       // Read a prime from the file

    if(i%5 == 0)
      out.println();                      // After every 5th, a newline

    out.print(prime);                     // Output the prime
  }
  out.close();                            // Close the stream
}
```

How It Works

To pass **IOExceptions** on up to the calling class, we just add the **throws** clause to the definition of the method. Output uses our **FormatWriter** class, so you will need a copy of the source file for this class in the directory for the current program. We will output primes five to a line with a field width of 12 characters. To display the primes, we seek to the beginning of the file and read **numPrimes** primes from the file, one at a time. For every fifth prime we call **println()** for the stream object to start a new line. The primes should appear right justified in five neat columns on your display. We call the **close()** method for the object, **out**, which will flush the stream to display any primes still in the buffer, and then close it.

Try It Out—The `main()` Method

All we need now is the code for **main()** to tie it all together:

```
public static void main(String[] args)
{
  try
  {
    // Define the file to store primes
    File myPrimes = new File("c:\\JunkData\\Primes.bin");
    myFile = new RandomAccessFile(myPrimes, "rw");

    // Read the number of primes required
    FormattedInput in = new FormattedInput(); // Keyboard stream

    // Prompt for keyboard input
    System.out.print("Enter the number of primes required: ");
    int numPrimes = in.intRead();             // Number of primes required

    long count = myFile.length()/8L;  // Number of primes in the file
    long number = 0L;                 // Next number to be tested

    // Check for file contents
    if(count == 0L)
    {      // Nothing in the file
      file = false;
      primes[0] = 2;                  // Seed the first prime...
      primes[1] = 3;                  // ...and the second
      current = 2;                    // Index of next element
      count = 2L;                     // count of primes found - up to now
      number = 5L;                    // Next integer to be tested
    }
    else
    {      // Get the next number to test - the last prime + 2
      file = true;
      myFile.seek(myFile.length() - 8);
      number = myFile.readLong() + 2;
    }
```

```
            // Find additional primes required for the total primes requested
            for( ; count < numPrimes; number += 2L)
            {
              if(primeTest(number))                   // Test for a prime
              {
                primes[current++] = number;           // We got one!
                ++count;                              // Increment prime count

                if(current == primes.length)          // Check for array full
                {// Array is full so write them away
                  myFile.seek(myFile.length());       // Go to the end of the file
                  for(int i = 0; i < primes.length; i++)
                    myFile.writeLong(primes[i]);      // Write the primes
                  current = 0;                        // Set free array element index
                  file = true;                        // Indicate file has primes
                }
              }
            }

            // Check if there are still primes in the array
            if(current > 0)
            { // There are - so write them to the file
              myFile.seek(myFile.length());           // Go to the end of the file
              for(int i = 0; i < primes.length; i++)
                myFile.writeLong(primes[i]);          // Write the primes
              current = 0;                            // Set free array element index
              file = true;                            // Indicate file has primes
            }

            outputPrimes(numPrimes);                  // Output the primes
          }
          catch(IOException e)
          {
            System.err.println("Exception in main()\n" + e); //Output the error
          }
        }
```

How It Works

The first step is to define the **RandomAccessFile** object for the file. If the file exists, it will be opened for read and write operations. If it doesn't, a new file will be created. You can use a different file path, if you want. We get input from the keyboard using the class **FormattedInput** class that we defined earlier in this chapter, so you will need to make sure the class file for this is in the same directory as this program. By outputting the prompt using the **print()** method, we can get the input value on the same line.

Before we start looking for primes, we need to see how many primes there are in the file. Since a **long** value always occupies eight bytes, we can get the number of primes in the file by dividing the length by eight. If there are primes in the file, we get the next number we want to test by adding two to the last prime we recorded in the file. This will ensure that we only look for new primes. We also need to set the **file** flag and the **current** index appropriately. If there are no primes in the file, we must seed the array, **primes[]**, with the first two prime numbers to kick the process off.

Primes are found in the **for** loop. Note that if the number of primes requested is less than the number on file, the program won't bother to look for any more; it will go straight to the call to the **outputPrimes()** method. If **primeTest()** returns **true**, the current number is stored and the values of **count** and **current** are incremented. Whenever **current** is the same as the length of the array, **primes**, the contents of the array are written to the end of the file. Note how the seek to the end of the file is achieved. You just call the **seek()** method with the file length as the argument. When the array has been written, the index, **current**, is reset to zero so the next prime will be stored in the first element of the array. At this point we also set the **file** flag to **true**, since we are now sure there are primes in the file. At the end of the **for** loop, any primes left in the **primes** array are also written to the file and the **outputPrimes()** method is called to display the requested number of primes.

The program always keeps all the primes in the file, so no time is wasted re-computing primes. Any new primes calculated are always added to the end of the file. The only constraints on the number of primes the program can produce is the amount of disk space you have, and the capacity of a **long** variable.

Storing Objects in a File

The process of storing and retrieving objects in an external file is called **serialization**. Writing an object to a file is referred to as **serializing** the object, and reading an object from a file is called **deserializing** an object. I think you will be surprised at how easy this turns out to be. Perhaps the most impressive aspects of the way serialization is implemented in Java is that you can generally read and write objects of almost any class, including objects of classes that you have defined yourself, without adding any code to the classes involved to support this mechanism. It is all taken care of automatically.

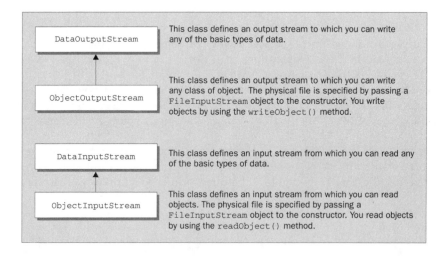

`DataOutputStream`	This class defines an output stream to which you can write any of the basic types of data.
`ObjectOutputStream`	This class defines an output stream to which you can write any class of object. The physical file is specified by passing a `FileInputStream` object to the constructor. You write objects by using the `writeObject()` method.
`DataInputStream`	This class defines an input stream from which you can read any of the basic types of data.
`ObjectInputStream`	This class defines an input stream from which you can read objects. The physical file is specified by passing a `FileInputStream` object to the constructor. You read objects by using the `readObject()` method.

Two classes from the **java.io** package are used for serialization. The output process for objects is managed by an object of the class **ObjectOutputStream**, and input is handled by an object of the class **ObjectInputStream**. These are derived from **DataOutputStream** and **DataInputStream**, respectively, so that they also have the capability to process basic types of data through inherited methods.

Writing an Object to a File

The constructor for the **ObjectOutputStream** class requires a **FileOutputStream** object as an argument that defines the file where you intend to store your objects. You could create an **ObjectOutputStream** object using the file **MyFile** with the following statements:

```
FileOutputStream output = new FileOutputStream("MyFile");
ObjectOutputStream objectOut = new ObjectOutputStream(output);
```

To write an object to the file, **MyFile**, you call the **writeObject()** method for **objectOut** with the object as the argument. Since this method accepts an object of type **Object** as an argument, you can pass an object of any class to the method. There are three basic conditions that have to be met for an object to be written to a stream:

▶ The class must be declared as **public**

▶ The class must implement the **Serializable** interface

▶ The class must have a default constructor—that is, a constructor that requires no arguments.

Implementing the **Serializable** interface is a lot less difficult that it sounds, and we will see how in a moment.

Assuming **myObject** is of a public class that implements **Serializable**, to write **myObject** to the file, you would use the statement:

```
objectOut.writeObject(myObject);
```

This takes care of writing everything to the file that is necessary to enable the object to be reconstituted later in a read operation. This includes information about the class and all its super-classes, as well as the contents and types of the data members of the class. Remarkably, this works even when the data members are themselves class objects. Each independent object you write to the file requires a separate call to the **writeObject()** method, but the objects that are members of an object are taken care of automatically. This is not completely foolproof in that the relationships between the class objects can affect the situation, but for the most part this is all you need to do. We will be using serialization to write quite complex objects to files in Chapter 15.

FYI The **ObjectOutputStream** class also includes methods to enable you to implement your own version of **writeObject()** but this topic is beyond the scope of this book.

As we said at the outset, if you need to, you can also write data of any of the basic types using the methods inherited from **DataOutputStream**. You can mix writing data of the basic types and class objects to the stream. We discussed the methods for writing values of the basic data types to a stream earlier in this chapter, and you apply them in exactly the same way in this context.

Exceptions for Object Serialization

The constructor for an **ObjectOutputStream** object can throw an **IOException** if things go wrong. The **writeObject()** method can also throw the following exceptions:

Exception	Description
InvalidClassException	Thrown when there is something wrong with the class definition for object being written. This might be because the class is not **public**, or the class does not implement a default constructor.
NotSerializableException	Thrown if the object's class, or the class of a data member of the class, does not implement the **Serializable** interface.
IOException	Thrown when a file output error occurs.

The first two exception classes here are sub-classes of **ObjectStreamException**, which is itself a sub-class of **IOException**. If you don't need to catch individual exceptions during object serialization, you can put your code in a **try** block with a **catch** block for **IOException** to take care of all of them.

Implementing the Serializable Interface

To implement the **Serializable** interface for a class, all you need to do is declare that the class implements the interface. No other code is necessary. For example, the following declares a class that implements the interface:

```
public MyClass implements Serializable
{
   // Definition of the class...
}
```

To allow an object of the class to be written to a stream and read back, the default constructor must be included in the class definition, but this is not difficult to implement if it's not there already:

```
public MyClass(){}    // Default constructor
```

There is a small fly in the ointment. All the data members of a class must be either one of the basic data types, or must be objects of a class that is serializable. That will be fine for your own classes, but there are one or two classes that come along with Java that do not implement the **Serializable** interface, and what's more, you can't make them serializable.

The **Graphics** class in the package **java.awt** is an example of such a class—we will see more of this class when we get into programming using windows. All is not lost however. There is an escape route.

Transient Data Members of a Class

If your class has data members that are not serializable, or for one reason or another you don't want to have written to the stream you can declare them as **transient**. For example:

```
public class MyClass implements Serializable
{
  transient protected Graphics g;     // Transient class member

  // Rest of the class definition
}
```

Declaring the data member as **transient** will prevent the **writeObject()** method from attempting to write the data member to the stream. When the class object is read back, it will be created properly, including any members declared as **transient**. They just won't have their values set because they were not written to the stream.

You may want to declare data members that are objects of some of your own classes as **transient**. You would do this when they have a value that is not meaningful out of context—objects that represent the current time, or today's date, for instance. These need to be reconstructed explicitly when the object that contains them is read from the stream.

Reading an Object from a File

Reading back objects from a file is just as easy as writing them. First, you need to create an **ObjectInputStream** object. Then you call the **readObject()** method for that object. This will return an object as type **Object**, so you need to cast it to the appropriate type in order to use it. The **readObject()** method can throw the following exceptions:

Exception	Description
ClassNotFoundException	Thrown if the definition of the class for an object read from the stream is not in the current program.
InvalidClassException	Thrown if there is something wrong with the class for an object. This is commonly caused by changing the definition of a class for an object between writing and reading the file.
StreamCorruptedException	Thrown when control information in the stream is inconsistent.
OptionalDataException	Thrown when basic types of data are read rather than an object.
IOException	Thrown if an error occurred reading the stream.

Clearly, if you do not have a full and accurate class definition for each type of object you want to read from the stream, the read will fail. The last four exception classes are sub-classes of **IOException**, so you can use that as a catch-all if you don't want to catch them individually. However, **ClassNotFoundException** is derived from **Exception**, so you must put a separate **catch** block for this exception in your program, otherwise it will not compile.

For example, if the object in the previous code fragment was of type **MyClass**, you could read it back from the file with the statements:

```
MyClass theObject;      // Store the object here
try
{
  // Create the object input stream for file MyFile
  FileInputStream input = new FileInputStream("MyFile");
  ObjectInputStream objectIn = new ObjectInputStream(input);

  // Deserialize the object
  theObject = (MyClass)objectIn.readObject();
}
catch(IOException e)
{
  System.out.println(e);
}
catch(ClassNotFoundException e)
{
  System.out.println(e);
}
```

Try it out for yourself with a suitable class.

This time we are creating an **ObjectInputStream** object using a **FileInputStream** object corresponding to the file **MyFile**. To deserialize the object, we call the method **readObject()** and cast the object returned to the type **MyClass**. The method **readObject()** can throw **ClassNotFoundException** if the class for the object read from the file is not defined in the current application. Since this is not a sub-class of **IOException** we need a separate catch block for this exception.

For the most part you will know what the class of the object is when you read it back. It is possible that occasionally you won't, in which case you can test it. Of course, you must have definitions for all of the classes that it might be within your program. We could test the object is the code above before storing it in **theObject** as follows:

```
MyClass theObject;
Object temp = objectIn.readObject();
if( temp.getClass().getName().equals("MyClass") )
  theObject = (MyClass) temp;
```

This calls the **getClass()** method for the object (inherited from **Object**) that returns the **Class** object representing the class of the object. Calling the **getName()** method for the **Class** object returns the fully qualified name of the class. If the class name for the object read from the stream is the same as that of **theObject**, we can safely cast it to that type.

Just to make sure that the process of serializing and deserializing objects is clear, we will use it in an example.

Using Object Serialization

Back in Chapter 6 we produced an example that created **PolyLine** objects that contained **Point** objects in a linked list. This is a good basis for demonstrating how effectively serialization takes care of handling objects that are members of objects. We can just modify the class **TryPolyLine** to use serialization.

Try It Out—Serializing a Linked List

1 The classes **PolyLine**, **ListPoint** and **Point** are exactly the same as in Chapter 6 except that we need to implement the **Serializable** interface in **PolyLine** and **Point**, and add a default constructor to each class definition.

```
import java.io.*;

public final class PolyLine implements Serializable
{
  public PolyLine(){}        // Default constructor
  // Class definition as before...
}
```

```
import java.io.*;

public class Point implements Serializable
{
  public Point(){}           // Default constructor
  // Class definition as before...
}

public class ListPoint extends Point
{
  public ListPoint(){}          // Default constructor
  // Class definition as before...
}
```

2 The modified version of the **TryPolyLine** class to write the **PolyLine** objects to a stream looks like this:

```
import java.io.*;

public class TryPolyLine
{
  public static void main(String[] args)
  {
    // Create an array of coordinate pairs
```

```
double[][] coords = { {1., 1.}, {1., 2.}, { 2., 3.},
                      {-3., 5.}, {-5., 1.}, {0., 0.} };

// Create a polyline from the coordinates and display it
PolyLine polygon = new PolyLine(coords);

// Add a point and display the polyline again
polygon.addPoint(10., 10.);

// Create Point objects from the coordinate array
Point[] points = new Point[coords.length];
for(int i = 0; i < points.length; i++)
  points[i] = new Point(coords[i][0],coords[i][1]);

// Use the points to create a new polyline and display it
PolyLine newPoly = new PolyLine(points);
```

```
// Write both polyline objects to the file
try
{
  // Create the object output stream
  ObjectOutputStream objectOut =
             new ObjectOutputStream(
             new BufferedOutputStream(
             new FileOutputStream("c:\\JunkData\\Polygons.bin")));

  objectOut.writeObject(polygon);     // Write first object
  objectOut.writeObject(newPoly);     // Write second object
  objectOut.close();                  // Close the output stream
}
catch(IOException e)
{
  System.out.println(e);
}


// Read the objects back from the file
try
{
  ObjectInputStream objectIn =
             new ObjectInputStream(
             new BufferedInputStream(
             new FileInputStream("c:\\JunkData\\Polygons.bin")));

  PolyLine theLine = (PolyLine)objectIn.readObject();
  theLine.show();                     // Output the first object
  theLine = (PolyLine)objectIn.readObject();
  theLine.show();                     // Output the second object
  objectIn.close();                   // Close the input stream
}
catch(IOException e)
{
```

```
      System.out.println(e);
    }
    catch(ClassNotFoundException e)
    {
      System.out.println(e);
    }
  }
}
```

This produces the output:

```
Polyline points are:
ListPoint 1.0,1.0
ListPoint 1.0,2.0
ListPoint 2.0,3.0
ListPoint -3.0,5.0
ListPoint -5.0,1.0
ListPoint 0.0,0.0
ListPoint 10.0,10.0
Polyline points are:
ListPoint 1.0,1.0
ListPoint 1.0,2.0
ListPoint 2.0,3.0
ListPoint -3.0,5.0
ListPoint -5.0,1.0
ListPoint 0.0,0.0
```

How It Works

We create two different **PolyLine** objects in the same manner as in the original example. You can output the points for these using the **show()** method if you wish. We then create an **ObjectOutputStream** for the file **MyFile** and write each of the **PolyLine** objects to the file using the **writeObject()** method. We then call the **close()** method to close the stream. Note how we don't need to explicitly write the **ListPoint** and **Point** objects to the stream. These are part of the **PolyLine** object so they are taken care of automatically. The same goes for when we read the **PolyLine** objects back. All the subsidiary objects are reconstructed automatically.

To read the file we create an **ObjectInputStream** object for **MyFile**. We then read the first object using the **readObject()** method and store the reference to it in the variable **theObject**. We then output the object read by calling its **show()** method. The same process is repeated for the second **PolyLine** object. It couldn't be simpler really, could it?

Summary

In this chapter we have explored how to use the stream input and output capabilities built into Java. These can be used in console programs or window-based applications in Java, but not in applets under normal circumstances for security reasons. The important points we have seen in this chapter are:

▶ The path to a physical file can be represented by an object of the class **File**

▶ A physical file can also be represented by an object of type **FileDescriptor**

▶ A stream is an abstract representation of a source of serial input, or a destination for serial output

▶ The classes supporting stream operations are contained in the package **java.io**

▶ Two kinds of streams are supported, **byte streams** which contain bytes, and **character streams** where the stream contains characters in the local machine character encoding

▶ No conversion occurs when characters are written to, or read from, a byte stream. Characters are converted from Unicode to the local machine representation of characters when a characters stream is written, and characters are converted back when the character stream is read

▶ Byte input streams are defined by sub-classes of the class **InputStream**, and byte output streams are represented by sub-classes of the class **OutputStream**

▶ Character input streams are defined by sub-classes of **Reader**, and character output streams are defined by sub-classes of the class **Writer**

▶ You cannot append data to a physical file represented by an **OutputStream** object. To do this you must use either a **RandomAccessFile** or a **FileWriter** object

▶ Classes derived from **InputStream** allow you to read a file while those derived from **OutputStream** allow you to write a file. Such classes do not allow you to do both

▶ The filter input and output stream classes can be used to enhance the functionality of the basic input and output stream class objects that represent a physical file

▶ The class **System** in the package **java.lang** defines the member **in**, representing the standard input stream, the keyboard; the member **out**, representing the standard output stream, the screen; and the member **err**, which represents the standard error stream, which is usually also the screen

▶ The **RandomAccessFile** class allows you to both read and write a file

▶ You can access a file randomly using objects of the **RandomAccessFile** class

▶ You can use the **StreamTokenizer** class as a base for reading formatted data from a stream

▶ Object serialization is supported through the **ObjectOutputStream** and **ObjectInputStream** classes

▶ Objects are written to a file by calling the **writeObject()** method for the **ObjectOutputStream** object corresponding to the file

▶ Objects are read from a file by calling the **readObject()** method for the **ObjectInputStream** object corresponding to the file

Exercises

1 Write a program to copy a file that will allow you to enter the paths for both the file to be copied and the new file from the keyboard.

2 Extend the **PrimesFile** example of the chapter, which wrote primes to a file, to optionally display the *n*th prime, when *n* is entered from the keyboard.

3 Extend the program further to output a given number of primes, starting at a given number. For example, output 50 primes starting at the 500th. The previous capabilities should be retained.

4 Write a program using a serial stream to store names in a file, entered as surname followed by first name.

5 Extend the previous program to sort the name file in ascending alphabetical order with the surname sorted first.

Utility Classes

In this chapter we'll look at the most useful components of the package **java.util**, which is something of a general purpose tool kit. Several of the classes that this package contains are often referred to as **container classes**, which you can use to manage data in your programs in various ways. They enable you to deal with situations where you don't know in advance how many items of data you'll need to store, or where you need a little more flexibility in the mechanism for retrieving an item than the indexing mechanism provided by an array gives you.

In this chapter you will learn:

- What the **Enumeration** interface is used for
- What a **Vector** is and how to use **Vector** objects in your programs
- How to manage **Vector** objects so that storing and retrieving elements is type safe
- What a **Stack** is and how you use it
- How you store and retrieve objects in a hash table represented by a **Hashtable** object
- How you can generate hash codes for your own class objects
- How to use the **Observable** class and the **Observer** interface to communicate between objects
- What facilities the **Random** class provides
- How to create and use **Date** objects

Understanding the Utility Classes

The utility classes are primarily a set of tools for storing and managing data in memory in a variety of ways, plus some other odds and ends. If you want an array that automatically expands to accommodate however many objects you throw into it, or you need to be able to store and retrieve an object based on what it is, rather than using an index or a sequence number, then look no further. You get all this and more in the **java.util** package.

We'll be exploring the following capabilities provided by the package:

The **Enumeration** interface	Declares methods for iterating through elements from a set, one at a time.
The **Vector** class	Supports an array-like structure for storing any kind of class object. The number of objects that you can store in a **Vector** object increases automatically when necessary.
The **Stack** class	Supports the storage of any kind of class object in a push down stack.
The **Hashtable** class	Supports the storage of any kind of class object in a hash table, sometimes called a map.
The **Observable** class	Provides a method for signaling other class objects when one class object changes.
The **Observer** interface	Defines a method called by an **Observable** object to signal when an object has changed.
The **Random** class	Defines a more sophisticated random number generator than that provided by the method **Math.random()**.
The **Date** class	Enables you to manipulate date and time information and obtain the current date and time.

We'll start by looking at what the **Enumeration** interface has to offer first, since this pops up in a number of other contexts.

The Enumeration Interface

An **enumeration** is a collection of objects that can be retrieved serially—traveling in one direction through the data. Since an enumeration is intended for one time use, it's usually created on demand by a collection of elements, such as a **Vector** or a **Hashtable**. You just ask the collection to create a new **Enumeration** object whenever you want to iterate through the objects you have stored in that collection.

The **Enumeration** interface only declares two methods:

hasMoreElements()	Returns **true** if more elements are available, and **false** otherwise.
nextElement()	Returns the next object in sequence as type **Object**.

Because the **nextElement()** method returns an object of type **Object**, it can return any type of object and is thus completely general. However, when you retrieve an element, you'll usually want to cast the reference returned to the original type of the object. We will see how you use these methods to retrieve objects when we get into using **Vector** objects.

Vector Storage

The **Vector** class defines a collection of elements of type **Object** that works rather like an array, but with the additional feature that it can grow itself automatically when you need more capacity. Because it stores elements of type **Object**, and **Object** is a superclass of every object, you can store any type of object in a **Vector**. This also means that you can use a single **Vector** object to store objects that are instances of a variety of different classes—this is another advantage the **Vector** class has over arrays. Of course, you'll usually need to have some way to figure out what kind of object you have when you retrieve it from the **Vector**.

This ability to store diverse objects has a downside. It implies that it's very easy for you to store objects in a **Vector** by mistake. You can set up a **Vector** in which you plan to store a particular kind of object, but there's nothing to prevent the storage of some other kind of object in the **Vector**, or signal that this may cause problems. If you need to protect against this kind of error, you must program it yourself. This isn't terribly difficult. As you'll see later in this chapter, all you need to do is package your **Vector** as a private member of a class that you define, and then supply methods to store objects in the **Vector** that will only accept the type that you want.

> *Like arrays, vectors only hold object references, not actual objects. To keep things simple we refer to a **Vector** as holding objects. We'll make the distinction only when it's important, but you should keep in mind that all the storage classes you're about to encounter hold object references.*

Creating a Vector

There are three constructors for a **Vector**. The default constructor creates an empty **Vector** object with the capacity to store up to a default number of objects, and the **Vector** object will increase in size each time you add an element when the **Vector** is full. In Java 1.1, the default capacity of a **Vector** object is ten objects, and the **Vector** object will double in size when you add an object when it is full. For example:

```
Vector transactions = new Vector();      // Create an empty Vector
```

If the default capacity isn't suitable for what you want to do, you can set the initial capacity of a **Vector** explicitly when you create it by using a different constructor. You just specify the capacity you require as an argument of type **int**. For example:

```
Vector transactions = new Vector(100);   // Vector to store 100 objects
```

The **Vector** object we're defining here will store 100 elements initially. It will also double in capacity each time you exceed the current capacity. The process of doubling the capacity of the **Vector** when more space is required can be quite inefficient. For example, if you end up storing 7000 objects in the **Vector** we've just defined, it will actually have space for 12,800 objects. If each object reference requires 4 bytes say, you'll be occupying more than 2 kilobytes of memory unnecessarily.

One way of avoiding this is to specify the amount by which the **Vector** should be incremented as well as the initial capacity when you create the **Vector** object. Both of these arguments to the constructor are of type **int**. For example:

```
Vector transactions = new Vector(100,10);
```

This **Vector** object has an initial capacity of 100, but the capacity will only be increased by 10 elements when more space is required.

Why don't we increment the Vector object by 1 each time then? The reason is that the process of incrementing the capacity takes time. The bigger the vector is, the longer the copy takes and that might impact the program's performance. Besides, in programming Java for desktop computers, you shouldn't concern yourself with memory issues. It's a different story, however, when you're concerned with embedded devices.

The Capacity and Size of a Vector

Although we said at the beginning that a **Vector** works like an array, this isn't strictly true. One significant difference is in the information you can get about the storage space it provides. An array has a single measure, its length, which is the count of the total number of elements it can reference. A vector has two measures relating to the space it provides— the **capacity** and the **size**.

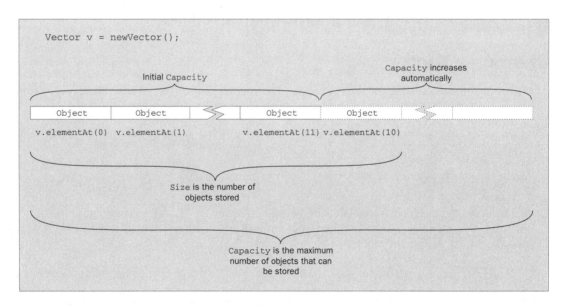

The **capacity** of a **Vector** is the maximum number of objects that it can hold at any given instant. Of course, the capacity can vary over time because when you store an object in a **Vector** object that is full, its capacity will automatically increase. For example, the **Vector** object, **transactions**, that we defined in the last statement above, had an initial capacity of 100. After you've stored 101 objects in it, its capacity will be 110 objects. A vector will typically contain fewer objects than its capacity.

You can obtain the capacity of a **Vector** with the method **capacity()** which returns it as a value of type **int**. For example:

```
int transMax = transactions.capacity();  // Get current capacity
```

If this statement follows the current definition we have for **transactions**, the variable **transMax** will have the value 100.

You can also ensure that a **Vector** has a sufficient capacity for your needs by calling its **ensureCapacity()** method. For example:

```
transactions.ensureCapacity(150);        // Set minimum capacity to 150
```

If the capacity of **transactions** is less than 150, the capacity will be increased to that value. If it's already 150 or greater, it will be unchanged by this statement. The argument you specify for **ensureCapacity()** is of type **int**. There's no return value.

Changing the Size

When you first create a **Vector** object, the elements don't reference anything—they are all **null**. An element will be occupied once you've stored an **object** in it. The number of elements that are occupied by objects in a **Vector** is referred to as the **size** of the **Vector**. The size of a **Vector** clearly can't be greater than the capacity. You can obtain the size of a **Vector** object as a value of type **int** by calling the **size()** method for the object. For example, you could calculate the number of free entries in the **Vector** object, **transactions**, with the statement:

```
int freeCount = transactions.capacity() - transactions.size();
```

You usually increase the size value for a **Vector** indirectly by storing an object in it, but you can also change the size directly by calling a method. Using the method, **setSize()**, you can increase and decrease the size. For example:

```
transactions.setSize(50);                // Set size to 50
```

The size of the **Vector** is set to the argument value (of type **int**). If the **Vector**, **transactions**, has less than fifty elements occupied, the additional elements up to fifty will be filled with **null** references. If it already contains more than fifty objects, all object references in excess of fifty will be discarded. The objects themselves may still be available if other references to them exist.

Looking back to the situation we discussed earlier, we saw how the effects of incrementing the capacity by doubling each time the current capacity was exceeded could waste memory. A **Vector** object provides you with a direct way of dealing with this—the **trimToSize()** method. This just changes the capacity to match the current size. For example:

```
transactions.trimToSize();               // Set capacity to size
```

If the size of the **Vector** is 50 when this statement executes, then the capacity will be too. Of course, you can still add more objects to the **Vector** as it will grow to accommodate them.

377

Storing Objects in a Vector

The simplest way to store an object in a **Vector** is to use the **addElement()** method. For example, to store a transaction in the **transactions Vector**, you could write:

```
transactions.addElement(aTransaction);
```

This will add a reference to the object, **aTransaction**, to the end of the **Vector** object, **transactions**, and increase the *size* of the **Vector** by 1. All the objects that were already stored in the **Vector** remain at their previous index.

You can also store an object at a particular index position in a **Vector**. This index value must be less than or equal to the size of the **Vector**, which implies that this element already contains an object reference or is the next in line to receive one. The index value is the same as for an array—an offset from the first element—so you reference the first element using an index value of zero. For example, to insert the object **aTransaction** as the third entry of **transactions**, you would write:

```
transactions.insertElementAt(aTransaction, 2);
```

The index value specified by the second argument is of type **int**, and it represents the index value for the position of the new object. Thus the new object, **aTransaction**, is inserted in front of the object that previously corresponded to the index value 2, so objects stored in elements with index values equal to or greater than 2, will be shuffled along, and their index values will increase by 1. If you specify an index value argument that is greater than the size of the **Vector**, the method will throw **ArrayIndexOutOfBoundsException**.

To change an element in a vector you use the **setElementAt()** method. This accepts two arguments: the first argument is an object which is the replacement for the element at the index specified by the second argument. To change the third element in the **Vector** object transactions to **theTransaction**, you would write:

```
transactions.setElementAt(theTransaction, 2);
```

If the second argument is negative, or is greater than or equal to the current size of the **Vector**, the method will throw **IndexOutOfBoundsException**.

Retrieving Objects from a Vector

You can retrieve the first element in a **Vector** by using the **firstElement()** method, which returns the object stored as type **Object**. For example:

```
Transaction theTransaction = (Transaction)transactions.firstElement();
```

Note that the explicit cast is essential here. If you don't cast the object returned to the type of the variable that you're using to store it you'll get an error. Of course, this is where an object of an incorrect type in the **Vector** will cause a problem. If the object returned here isn't of type **Transaction**, an exception will be thrown.

You can retrieve the last element in a **Vector** by using the method **lastElement()** in a similar manner.

If you have the index for an element, you can obtain the element at a particular position by using the **elementAt()** method for the **Vector**. For example, the statement,

```
Transaction theTransaction = (Transaction)transactions.elementAt(4);
```

will retrieve the fifth element in the **Vector**, **transactions**.

Accessing Elements through an Enumeration

You can also obtain all the elements in a **Vector** object by using an **Enumeration** object:

```
Enumeration theData = transactions.elements();
```

The method **elements()** returns all the elements in the **Vector** object, **transactions**, as an **Enumeration** object, so you can now process them serially using the methods declared in the **Enumeration** interface. For example, you could now output the elements from **transactions** to the screen with the loop:

```
while(theData.hasMoreElements())
{
  Transaction theTransaction = (Transaction)theData.nextElement();
  System.out.println(theTransaction);
}
```

This loop iterates through all the elements referenced by **theData** one at a time, and outputs each **Transaction** object to the display. When we've retrieved the last element from the **Enumeration**, the method **hasMoreElements()** will return **false** and the loop will end.

Extracting All the Elements from a Vector

A **Vector** provides you with tremendous flexibility of use, in particular the ability to automatically adjust its capacity. Of course, the flexibility you get through using a **Vector** comes at a price. There is always some overhead involved when you're retrieving elements. For this reason, there may be times when you want to get the elements contained in a **Vector** object back as a regular array. The method **copyInto()** will do this for you, but you need to be careful. You must set up the array, of type **Object**, so that it's large enough to hold all the element references from the **Vector**, otherwise the method will throw **IndexOutOfBoundsException**. You would typically use the method **copyInto()** to extract the elements of a **Vector** object, **transactions**, as follows:

```
Object[] data = new Object[transactions.size()];     // Create an array
transactions.copyInto(data);                 // Extract the vector elements
```

By using the **size()** method, we can create the array, **data**, with exactly the number of elements we need. We then pass the array to the method **copyInto()** to fill it with all the elements from **transactions**.

Removing Objects from a Vector

You can remove the reference at a particular index position by calling the
removeElementAt() method with the index position of the object as the argument. For
example,

```
transactions.removeElementAt(3);
```

will remove the fourth reference from **transactions**. The references following this will now
be at index positions that are one less than they were before, so that what was previously
the fifth object reference will now be at index position 3. Of course, the index value that
you specify must be legal for the **Vector** on which you're operating, meaning greater than
or equal to 0 and less than its **size()**, otherwise an exception will be thrown.

Sometimes you'll want to remove a particular reference, rather than the reference at a given
index. If you know what the object is that you want to remove, you can use the
removeElement() method to delete it:

```
boolean deleted = transactions.removeElement(aTransaction);
```

This will search the **Vector**, **transactions**, from the beginning to find the reference to the
object **aTransaction**, and remove its first occurrence. If the object is found and removed,
the method returns **true**, otherwise it returns **false**.

If you want to discard all the elements in a **Vector**, you can use the
removeAllElements() method to empty the **Vector** in one go:

```
transactions.removeAllElements();      // Dump the whole lot
```

With all these ways of removing elements from a **Vector**, there's lots of potential for ending
up with an empty **Vector**. It's often handy to know whether a **Vector** contains elements or
not, particularly if there's been a lot of adding and deleting of elements going on. You can
check whether a **Vector** contains elements or not by using the **isEmpty()** method. This
returns **true** if a **Vector** object has zero **size**, and **false** otherwise.

> Note that a **Vector** may contain only **null** references, but this doesn't mean the size
> will be zero. To empty a **Vector** object you must actually remove the elements, not
> just set the elements to **null**.

Searching a Vector

You can get the index position of an object stored in a **Vector** by passing the object as an
argument to the method **indexOf()**. For example, the statement,

```
int position = transactions.indexOf(aTransaction);
```

will search the **Vector** from the beginning for the object **aTransaction**. The variable **position** will either contain the index of the first reference to the object in **transactions**, or –1 if the object isn't found.

You have another version of the method **indexOf()** available that accepts a second argument which is an index position where the search for the object should begin. The main use for this arises when an object can be referenced more than once in a **Vector**. You can use the method in this situation to recover all occurrences of any particular object, as follows:

```
int position = 0;                          // Search starting index
while(position<transactions.size() )       // Search with a valid index
{
  position = transactions.indexOf(aTransaction, position); // Find next

  if(position ==-1)                        // If object not found...
    break;                                 // ...end the loop

  // Code to process the object in some way...

  ++position;                              // Search from the next element
}
```

The **while** loop will continue as long as the method **indexOf()** returns a valid index value and the index doesn't get incremented beyond the end of the **Vector**.

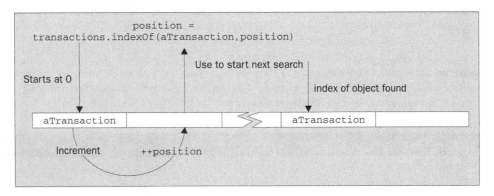

Each iteration will search **transactions** from the element given by the index stored in the variable **position**. When no further references to the object can be found from the position specified by the second argument, the method, **indexOf()**, will return –1 and the **break** will be executed.

Using Vectors

Let's implement a simple example to see how using a **Vector** works out in practice. We will write a program to model a collection of people where we can add the names of the persons that we want in the crowd from the keyboard.

Try It Out—The *Person* **Class**

First we'll define a class to represent a person:

```
public class Person
{
  private String firstName;    // First name of person
  private String surname;      // Second name of person

  // Constructor
  public Person(String firstName, String surname)
  {
    this.firstName = firstName;
    this.surname = surname;
  }

  public String toString()
  {
    return firstName + " " + surname;
  }
}
```

How It Works

The only data members are the **String** members to store the first and second names for a person. By overriding the default implementation of the **toString()** method, provided by the **Object** class, we allow objects of the **Person** class to be used as arguments to the **println()** method for output, since **toString()** will be automatically invoked in this case.

Now we can define a class that will represent a crowd. We could just create a **Vector** object in **main()** but this would mean any type of object could be stored. By defining our own class we can ensure that only **Person** objects can be stored in the **Vector** and in this way make our program less prone to errors.

Try It Out—The *Crowd* **Class**

The class definition representing a crowd is:

```
import java.util.*;

class Crowd
{
  // Person store - only accessible through methods of this class
  private Vector people;

  // Constructors
  public Crowd()
  {
    // Create default Vector object to hold people
```

```
        people = new Vector();
    }

    public Crowd(int numPersons)
    {
      // Create Vector object to hold people with given capacity
      people = new Vector(numPersons);
    }

    // Add a person to the crowd
    public void addPerson(Person someone)
    {
      people.addElement(someone);     // Use the Vector method to add
    }

    // Get first person
    public Person firstPerson()
    {
      return (Person)(people.firstElement());
    }

    // Get number of persons in crowd
    public int size()
    { return people.size(); }

    // Get people store capacity
    public int capacity()
    { return people.capacity(); }

    // Get an enumeration for the crowd
    public Enumeration elements()
    { return people.elements(); }
  }
```

How It Works

We've defined two constructors for the class for illustration purposes, one to create a **Vector** with a default capacity, and the other to create a **Vector** with the capacity given by the argument. Both constructors just call the appropriate **Vector** constructor. You could easily add the ability to provide the capacity increment with a third constructor, if necessary.

By keeping the **Vector** member of the class **private**, we ensure that the only way an object can be added to the **Vector** is by using the **addPerson()** method in the class. Since this method only accepts an argument of type **Person**, we can be sure that it's impossible to store elements of any other type. Of course, if you wanted to allow other specific types to be stored, an object of type **Child** for example, you could either arrange to derive the class **Child** from **Person**, or you could overload the **addPerson()** method to allow an argument of type **Child**.

The remaining methods here are just to show how simple it is to implement the equivalent of the **Vector** methods for our class. In each case they use the **Vector** method to produce the required result.

1 We can now add a class containing a **main()** method to test these classes. We'll call it **TryVector**:

```java
import java.util.*;
import java.io.*;

public class TryVector
{
  public static void main(String[] args)
  {
    Person aPerson;                    // A person object
    Crowd filmCast = new Crowd();

    // Populate the crowd
    for( ; ; )                         // Indefinite loop
    {
      aPerson = readPerson();          // Read in a film star
      if(aPerson == null)              // If null obtained...
        break;                         // We are done...
      filmCast.addPerson(aPerson);     // Otherwise, add to the cast
    }

    // Show who is in the cast
    Enumeration thisLot = filmCast.elements();  // Obtain enumeration

    while(thisLot.hasMoreElements())      // Output all elements
      System.out.println( thisLot.nextElement() );
  }
}
```

2 Note the two **import** statements at the beginning. The first is needed for the **Enumeration** in **main()**. The other is used for the **BufferedReader** and **InputStreamReader** objects in the **readPerson()** method. Add the following method to the **TryVector** class:

```java
// Read a person from the keyboard
static public Person readPerson()
{
  BufferedReader kb = new BufferedReader(
                                        new
InputStreamReader(System.in));
  try
  {
    // Read in the first name and remove blanks front and back
    System.out.println("\nEnter first name, or press Enter to end:");
    String firstName = kb.readLine().trim();

    if(firstName.length() == 0)        // Check for nothing entered
```

```
          return null;                    // If so, we are done...

      // Read in the surname, also trimming blanks
      System.out.println("Enter surname:");
      String surname = kb.readLine().trim();
      return new Person(firstName,surname);
    }
    catch(Exception e)
    {
      System.out.println(e);
      return null;
    }
  }
```

If you've added this method to the **TryVector** class, and placed the source files for the other classes to the same directory, you should be ready to give it a whirl. With a modest film budget, I got the output:

```
Enter first name, or press Enter to end:
Roy
Enter surname:
Rogers

Enter first name, or press Enter to end:
Marilyn
Enter surname:
Monroe

Enter first name, or press Enter to end:
Oliver
Enter surname:
Hardy

Enter first name, or press Enter to end:
Brigitte
Enter surname:
Bardot

Enter first name, or press Enter to end:

Roy Rogers
Marilyn Monroe
Oliver Hardy
Brigitte Bardot
```

How It Works

Here we'll be assembling an all-star cast for a new blockbuster. The method **main()** creates a **Person** variable which will be used as a temporary store for an actor or actress, and a **Crowd** object, **filmCast** to hold the entire cast.

The **for** loop assumes a method **readPerson()** is available which will obtain the necessary information from the keyboard, and return a **Person** object. If nothing is entered from the keyboard **readPerson()** will return **null**. We'll add this method in a moment. The loop continues to add **Person** object to **filmCast** using the **addPerson()** method until **readPerson()** returns **null**, whereupon the break will be executed to end the loop.

We then output the members of the cast by obtaining an **Enumeration**. As you have just seen, this makes the code for listing the members of the cast very simple.

Because we want to read a **String** in **readPerson()**, we need to create a **BufferedReader** object based on the **System.in** object which represents the keyboard. Note how we use the **trim()** method on the **String** object returned by **readLine()** to ensure there are no leading or trailing whitespace characters. The **if** statement takes care of the case where no first name is entered, and **null** is returned.

Sorting Vector Elements

Of course, the output appears in the sequence in which you enter it. If we want to be to be socially correct, we can arrange them in alphabetical order.

Try It Out—Sorting the Stars

1 We can add a method to the **Crowd** class to get them sorted:

```
// Method to sort persons by surname in ascending sequence
public void sort()
{
  int count = size();           // Find the number of persons
  Person spare;                 // Place to store a person
  boolean unsorted = false;     // Indicate whether in order or not

  do                            // Loop until they are sorted
  {
    unsorted = false;           // Assume they are sorted

    // Check the sequence of adjacent elements
    for(int i=0 ; i<count-1 ; i++)
    {
      if( ((Person)people.elementAt(i)).getSurname().compareTo(
                     ((Person)people.elementAt(i+1)).getSurname())>0)
      { // Not in order, so swap elements
        spare = (Person)people.elementAt(i);
        people.setElementAt(people.elementAt(i+1), i);
        people.setElementAt(spare, i+1);
        unsorted = true;        // Signal they are unsorted, go again
      }
    }
  }while(unsorted);
}
```

2 We must now add the `getSurname()` method to the `Person` class definition:

```
public String getSurname()
{
   return surname;
}
```

3 You can now add a statement to the `main()` method in `TryVector`, to sort the cast members. Position it just before the output loop:

```
filmCast.sort();            // Sort out the cast
```

If you run the example with these changes, the cast will be in alphabetical order in the output.

How It Works

This method uses a bubble sort to put the persons in the people `Vector` in ascending alphabetical sequence. The bubble sort isn't the most efficient sort, but its merit is its extreme simplicity. It works by comparing adjacent elements throughout the `Vector` in the `for` loop and when it finds a pair out of order, it swaps them. This process repeats in the `do-while` loop until a pass through the elements occurs with no swaps. The comparison of adjacent elements is done in the `for` loop using the `compareTo()` method for a `String` object. If the surname for an element is greater than that of its successor, the two are swapped using the temporary object, `spare`. When any swap occurs, the `boolean` variable `unsorted` is set to `true` to cause another iteration of the `do-while` loop. If a complete pass through all the elements occurs without the need for a swap, `unsorted` will be left as `false` and the `do-while` loop will end.

To get the object stored at a particular index we use the `elementAt()` method. The object returned from this has to be cast to type `Person` to call the `getSurname()` method for the object.

Stack Storage

A stack is a storage mechanism which works on a last-in first-out basis, often abbreviated to LIFO. Don't confuse this with FIFO, which is first-in first-out, or FIFI, which is a name for a poodle. The operation of a stack is analogous to the plate stack you see in some self-service restaurants. The stack of plates is supported by a spring that allows the stack of plates to sink into a hole in the counter-top so that only the top plate is accessible. The plates come out in the reverse order to the way they went in.

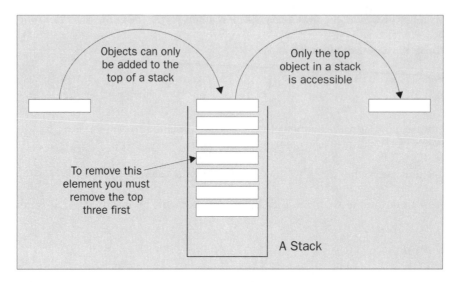

A Stack

A stack in Java doesn't have a spring, but it does have all the facilities of a **Vector** object because the class **Stack** is derived from the class **Vector**. The class adds five methods to those inherited from **Vector**, two of which provide you with the LIFO mechanism, and the other three give you extra capabilities. These methods are:

Method	Description
push(Object anObject)	Pushes a reference to the object, passed as an argument to the method, onto the top of the stack.
pop()	Pops the object reference off the top of the stack and returns it as type **Object**. This removes the reference from the stack. If the stack contains no references when you call this method the **EmptyStackException** will be thrown.
peek()	This method allows you to take a look at the object reference at the top of the stack without popping it off the stack. It returns the reference from the top of the stack as type **Object** without removing it. Like the previous method, this method can throw an **EmptyStackException**.
search(Object anObject)	This will return an **int** value which is the position on the stack of the reference to the object passed as an argument. The reference at the top of the stack is at position 1, the next reference is at position 2 and so on. Note that this is quite different from referencing elements in a **Vector** or an array, where indexes are an offset, so they start at 0. If the object isn't found on the stack, −1 is returned.
empty()	This method returns **true** if the stack is empty, and **false** otherwise.

The only constructor for a **Stack** object is the default constructor. This will call the default constructor for the base class, **Vector**, so you'll always get an initial capacity of 10 objects, but since it's basically a **Vector**, it will grow automatically in the same way.

One possible point of confusion is the relationship between the top of a **Stack** object, and the elements in the underlying **Vector**. Intuitively, you might think that the top of the stack is going to correspond to the first element in the **Vector**, with index 0. If so you would be totally *wrong*! The **push()** method for a **Stack** object is analogous to the **addElement()** for a **Vector** which adds an object to the end of the **Vector**. Thus the top of the **Stack** corresponds to the end of the **Vector**.

Let's try a **Stack** object out in an example so we get a feel for how the methods are used.

Believe it or not, you can use a stack to implement a bubble sort, so we can get some experience pushing and popping persons by modifying the last example to use a **Stack** instead of a **Vector**.

Try It Out—Using a Stack

All the changes are to the class **Crowd**, and they will be as follows:

1 Change the type of the data member **people** in the class **Crowd**, from **Vector** to **Stack**.

```
class Crowd
{
   // Person store - only accessible through methods of this class
   private Stack people;

   // Constructors
   public Crowd()
   {
      // Create default Stack object to hold people
      people = new Stack();
   }
```

2 Delete the **Crowd** constructor that accepts an argument. We don't need this because there's only the default constructor for **Stack** objects.

3 Replace the **sort()** method with a version that uses **Stack** methods.

4 Rename the **TryVector** class to more accurately reflect what the code is trying to show.

With these changes the example should execute exactly the same as before, although, if you're like me, fixing typos is an integral part of the process of change so it won't work straight away.

Sorting Using a Stack

Let's first look at the mechanics of how the sort is going to work as it can be a little confusing. It's a two-step process that we repeat until the **Person** objects on the **people** stack are in alphabetical order. In essence, the first step is to pop objects off the **people** stack and push them onto a new stack which is more ordered than it was before. The second step is to pop them off the new stack and push them back on the **people** stack, again improving the order. Of course, objects pop off a stack in reverse order to the way they were pushed on—LIFO remember? This means the ordering strategy when we pop them off the **people** stack will be the reverse of the strategy used when we pop them off the new stack.

In the first step, we'll take **Person** objects off the **people** stack two at a time, and compare their surnames. The object that's greater in the sort sequence (nearer to Z) will be pushed onto the new stack, and the remaining object saved to compare with the next object that we pop from the **people** stack. This will tend to produce a new stack with the objects ordered from A at the top to Z at the bottom. In the second step we'll push the objects onto the **people** stack with those nearer to A first—towards the bottom of the stack—so we should ultimately end up with the objects in the people **stack** running from Z at the top to A at the bottom. Remember that in **main()** we recover the objects for output using an **Enumeration**. This will deliver the objects starting at the bottom of the stack, which is why we need to produce the Z – A order on the **people** stack.

Try It Out—The Stack Sort Method

Here's the code for the new version of **sort()**:

```
public void sort()
{
  Stack outStack = new Stack();    // Working stack
  boolean sorted = true;           // Sort status indicator
  Person current;                  // Current person off the stack
  Person next;                     // Last person off the stack

  do                               // This loop continues until sorted
  {
    sorted = true;                 // Assume in order
    current = (Person)people.pop(); // Make top object current

    // Process all objects in the people stack
    while(!people.empty())
    {
      next = (Person)people.pop();
      if(current.getSurname().compareTo(next.getSurname())>0)
      {
        outStack.push(current);    // current is nearer Z
        current = next;            // next is new current
      }
      else
      {
```

```
          outStack.push(next);        // push next on the stack
          sorted = false;             // Changed the sequence so not sorted
      }
  }

  outStack.push(current);        // Don't forget the last object

  if(sorted)                     // Are objects in order?
    while(!outStack.empty())     // Yes, so put back in people
      people.push(outStack.pop());
  else
  {                              // No, so re-order as we put back
    current = (Person)outStack.pop();  // Top object is current
    sorted = true;               // Reset sorted flag
    while(!outStack.empty())     // Process all objects in outStack
    {
      next = (Person)outStack.pop();  // Pop next
      if(current.getSurname().compareTo(next.getSurname())<0)
      {
        people.push(current);    // current is nearer A
        current = next;          // next is new current
      }
      else
      {
        people.push(next);       // next is nearer A
        sorted = false;          // Not in order yet
      }
    }
    people.push(current);
  }
}while(!sorted);
}
```

How It Works

The `do-while` loop contains the two steps. Popping persons off the `people` stack is in the first `while` loop; the second step will be one of the two following `while` loops, depending on whether the first step actually got the `Person` objects in order or not. If they are in order on the new stack `outStack`, the flag `sorted` will be `true` so we don't need to do any more comparisons. We just pop and push `Person` objects back to the `people` stack.

If the objects on a stack are already in order, we'll always push the object stored in `current` onto the next stack. If we ever push the object in `next` before `current`, the objects aren't in order, so in this case we set the flag `sorted` to `false`. If we go through all the objects in a stack and always push `current` onto the next stack, `sorted` will be left in its initial `true` state which is set before each `while` loop is executed.

I think you'll agree that using a stack is very simple. You can see that when we transfer the contents of `outStack` to `people`, we can pop from one stack and push onto the other in a single statement. Stacks are a powerful tool in lots of applications. They are often applied in applications that involve syntactical analysis, such as compilers. However, the sort example here is a vehicle for demonstrating how a stack works, not an example of a good sort routine.

Hash Table Storage

A **hash table**, sometimes referred to as a **map**, is a way of storing data that minimizes the need for searching when you want to get an object back. Each object is associated with a key which is used to determine where to store the reference to the object, and both the key and the object are stored in the hash table. Given a key, you can always go more or less directly to the object that has been stored in a hash table based on the key.

In Java, hash tables are implemented by the class **Hashtable**. The keys used to store objects in a **Hashtable** object are objects too, but the object that you use as a key doesn't have to be the same as the object that you're storing—indeed it usually won't be. For example, you could use a **String** object containing a name as a key, for a **Person** object, which would typically contain all kinds of other information in addition to the name. If you know the name for a **Person** object, you can immediately retrieve that object by just supplying the name as the key.

The Hashing Process

It's helpful to understand how the storage mechanism works for a hash table. A **Hashtable** object sets aside an array in which it will store key and object pairs. The index to this array, referred to as a **hash value**, is produced from the key object by a process known as **hashing**. This uses the **hashCode()** method for the object that's used as a key.

Note that each key doesn't have to result in a unique hash value. When two or more different keys produce the same hash value, it's called a collision. The **Hashtable** object is able to deal with collisions by hooking the objects that share the same hash value together in a linked list, as shown below. For the sake of simplicity, the diagram only shows the objects stored in the table, but the key for each object is also stored.

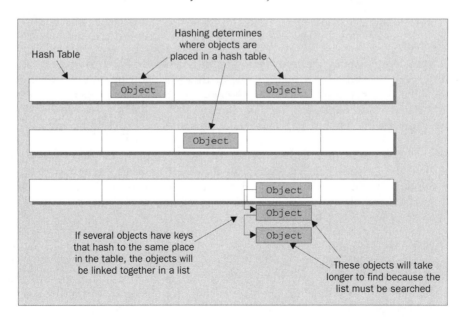

Generally though, the greater the number of unique hash values, the more efficient the operation of the hash table is going to be. When you access one of the objects that share a common hash value, it will involve a serial search of the list of keys corresponding to that hash value. This is illustrated in the diagram. Of course, the price of reducing the possibility of collisions in a hash table is having plenty of empty space in the table.

The class **Object** defines the method **hashCode()** so any object can be used as a key, and it will hash by default, but the method as it is currently implemented in **Object** in Java 1.1 isn't ideal. Since it uses the address where an object is stored to produce the hash value, distinct objects will always produce different hash values. In once sense this is a plus because the more likely it is that a unique hash value will be produced for each key, the more efficient the operation of the hash table is going to be. The huge minus is that objects which use this default behavior and that are distinct, but have identical contents, will produce different hash values. The effect of this is disastrous if you use this default for objects of your own classes that you're using as keys. In this case, an object stored in a hash table can never be retrieved using an object for a key that is distinct from the original key object, even though it may be identical in all other respects. Yet this is precisely what you'll want to do in most cases.

Using your own Class Objects as Keys

For objects of one of your own classes to be usable as keys in a hash table, you must implement two methods in the class: the **equals()** method which accepts an object of the same class as an argument, and returns a **boolean** value; and **hashCode()** which returns the hash value for the object as type **int**. You'll be overriding the versions of these methods that are inherited from the class **Object**.

The **equals()** method is used by methods in the **Hashtable** class to determine when two keys are equal, so your version of this method should return **true** when two different objects are equal keys. This will generally amount to writing the method so that it returns **true** when the data members for the two objects that are used in the **hashCode()** method are identical.

Generating Hash Codes

How you write the **hashCode()** method for your class is up to you. You should aim to return a number of type **int** for an object that has a strong probability of being unique to that object, and the numbers that you produce for several different objects should be as widely distributed across the range of **int** values as possible. A further requirement is that objects that have the same data members must produce the same hash code.

To achieve this you will typically want to combine all the data members in an object to produce the hash code, so the first step is to produce an integer corresponding to each data member. You can then combine these integers to generate the return value by multiplying each of them by a different prime number and then sum the results. This should produce a reasonable distribution of values that have a good probability of being different for different objects. It doesn't matter which prime numbers you use as multipliers, as long as they aren't so large as to cause the result to fall outside the range of type **int**, and you use a different one for each data member.

So how do you get from a data member of a class to an integer? Generating an integer for data members of type **String** is easy: you just call the **hashCode()** method for the member. This has been implemented to produce good hash code values that will be the same for identical strings. You can use integer data members as they are, but floating point data members need a bit of judgment. If they have a small range in integer terms, you need to multiply them by a value that's going to result in a unique integer when they are cast to type **int**. If they have a very large range in integer terms you may need to scale them down.

By way of an example, suppose you intended to use a **Person** object as a key in a hash table, and the class data members were **firstName** and **surname** of type **String**, and **age** of type **int**. You could implement the **hashCode()** method for the class as:

```java
public int hashCode()
{
  return 13*firstName.hashCode() + 17*surname.hashCode() + 19*age;
}
```

Wherever a data member is an object of another class rather than a variable of one of the basic types, you need to implement the **hashCode()** method for that class. You can then use that in the computation of the hash code for the key class.

Creating a Hash Table

You have a choice of three constructors you can use to create a **Hashtable** object:

Constructor	Description
Hashtable()	Creates a hash table with the capacity to store a default number of objects. In Java 1.1 the default capacity is 101 objects and the default load factor (more on the load factor below) is 0.75.
Hashtable(int capacity)	Creates a hash table with the capacity to store the number of objects you specify in the argument, and a default load factor.
Hashtable(int capacity, float loadFactor)	Creates a hash table with the capacity and load factor that you specify.

To create a hash table using the default constructor, you can write something like this:

```java
Hashtable theTable = new Hashtable();
```

The capacity of the hash table is combined with the hash code for the key that you specify in the computation of the index that determines where an object and its key are to be stored. To make this computation produce a good distribution of index values, you should ideally use prime numbers for the capacity of a hash table when you specify it yourself. For example:

```java
Hashtable myTable = new Hashtable(151);
```

This table has a capacity for 151 objects and their keys, although the number of objects stored can never reach the capacity. There must always be spare capacity in a hash table for efficient operation. Too little spare capacity and more keys are likely to generate the same table index, so the more likely it is that the table will be littered with linked lists of objects which are slow to access.

The **load factor** is used to decide when to increase the size of the hash table. When the size of the table reaches a value which is the product of the load factor and the capacity, the capacity will be increased automatically to twice the old capacity plus 1. The default load factor of 0.75 is a good compromise, but if you want to reduce it you could do so using the third constructor:

```
Hashtable aTable = new Hashtable(151, 0.6f);   // 60% load factor
```

This table will work a bit more efficiently than the current default, but at the expense of having more unoccupied space. When ninety objects have been stored, the capacity will be increase to 303, (2*151+1).

Storing and Retrieving Objects

Storing and retrieving objects in a hash table is very simple. There are only two methods involved, **put()** and **get()**:

Method	Description
put(Object key, Object value)	Stores the object **value** in the table using the key specified by the first argument. If an object was previously stored using the same key, it will be returned as type **Object**. The new object, **value**, will replace the previous object that was stored. If no object was stored with this key, **null** is returned. If either of the arguments is **null**, a **NullPointerException** will be thrown.
get(Object key)	Returns the object that was previously stored with the same key as the argument. If no object was previously stored with this key, **null** is returned. Note that the object remains in the table. If the key is **null**, a **NullPointerException** will be thrown.

Any kind of object can be stored in a hash table, since all objects are stored as type **Object**. As with objects stored in a **Vector**, you can cast an object back to its original type when you retrieve it. The same caveats we saw for **Vector** objects, relating to the potential for storing objects of different types, apply to hash tables. If you want to limit the type of object that can be stored, you can use a **Hashtable** object as a member of your own class, and implement its interface **get()** and **put()** methods yourself, to restrict what can be stored.

> *As you can see from the way the **put()** method works, every object in a hash table must have a unique key. Don't confuse the key with the hash code though. Even though all the keys are unique, the hash codes may not be. This will result in several object/key pairs jostling for the same position in the table. This will be taken care of under the covers by linking them together in a list, as we saw earlier.*

You should check that the value returned from the **put()** method is **null**. If it isn't, you are displacing an object that was stored in the table earlier using the same key:

```
String myKey = "Goofy";
Integer theObject = new Integer(12345);

if(aTable.put(myKey, theObject) != null
  System.out.println("Uh-oh, we bounced an object...");
```

Of course, you could throw your own exception here instead of displaying a message.

Note that the **get()** operation will return the object corresponding to a key, but it does not remove it from the table. To retrieve an object and delete it from the table, you must use the **remove()** method. This accepts a key of type **Object** as an argument, and returns the object corresponding to the key:

```
theObject = (Integer)aTable.remove(theKey);
```

If there's no object stored corresponding to **theKey**, **null** will be returned. If **theKey** is **null**, the **remove()** method will throw **NullPointerException**. Note how we have to explicitly cast the object returned from the hash table to the correct class.

Processing all the Elements in a Hash Table

You can obtain an **Enumeration** for either of the objects or the keys in a hash table. The method **elements()** returns an **Enumeration** referencing the objects stored, and the method **keys()** returns an enumeration referencing the keys for those objects. You then have the choice of iterating through the keys, which you can use with the **get()** method to obtain the corresponding objects, so you have both the keys and the objects available to you, or using the **elements()** method and the **Enumeration** returned, when you only want to iterate through the objects.

For example, suppose we've stored objects of type **Person** in a **Hashtable** object, **theTable**, using keys of type **Name**. We could retrieve the keys and the objects with the following code:

```
Enumeration theKeys = theTable.keys();          // Get the keys
Name key;                                        // Store a key
while(theKeys.hasMoreElements())
{
  key = (Name)theKeys.nextElement();             // Get next key
```

```
   // Output the key and the person
   System.out.println("Key: " + key + "\nPerson: " + theTable.get(key));
}
```

Of course, the key object of type **Name** might well be a member of the **Person** object to which it relates, so you might not need both. In this case, you could output just the objects by obtaining an enumeration of them:

```
Enumeration thePersons = theTable.elements();          // Get the persons
while(thePersons.hasMoreElements())
  System.out.println("Person: " + thePersons.nextElement());
```

If you want to remove all the objects references from a **Hashtable** object, you can do it in one go by using the method **clear()**:

```
theTable.clear();                                   // Empty the hash table
```

If you haven't arranged to store the references somewhere else, all the objects that were referenced by the table will become inaccessible, and will ultimately be destroyed.

Other Hash Table Operations

The **Hashtable** class has methods **capacity()** and **size()** to return the current capacity of the table, and the number of objects stored in it. You also have the **isEmpty()** method available which returns **true** if no objects are stored in a **Hashtable** object.

There are two methods which enable you to check whether an object is in a hash table. The method **contains()** returns **true** if the object passed as an argument is referenced at least once in the table. This is determined using the **equals()** method for the object passed as an argument, so if you want this to work properly when you reference objects of your own class, you'll need to have implemented the **equals()** method for your class. The version of **equals()** that's inherited from the class **Object** only returns **true** when both objects are one and the same—that is, the variable you pass as an argument to the method is referring to the same object you invoke the method on. Of course, the same object could be stored several times under different keys, as could different but identical objects. In most practical situations you want different objects with identical data members to be regarded as equal. The method **containsKey()** returns **true** if the key object passed as an argument has been stored along with its associated object. This also involves the use of the **equals()** method for the key class so the same comments apply.

Let's put together an example that stores a variation of the **Person** objects that we stored in a **Vector**. We can change the **Person** class so we get some experience of implementing the **hashCode()** and **equals()** methods for a class.

Try It Out—Using a Hash Table

1 We can redefine the **Person** class as:

```
public class Person
{
  private Name theName;          // Name of person
  // You could add other data members, age, address, etc

  // Constructor
  public Person(String firstName, String surname)
  {
    theName = new Name(firstName, surname);
  }

  // Get the Name member
  public Name getName()
  {
    return theName;
  }

  public String toString()
  {
    return theName.toString();
  }

  // Method to compare two objects for equality
  // The hash table may call this method
  public boolean equals(Object aPerson)
  {
    // Check if aPerson is the same class as this object
    if(!this.getClass().getName().equals(aPerson.getClass().getName()))
      return false;             // It is not, so return false
    else                        // It is, so compare names for equality
      return theName.toString().equals(aPerson.toString());
  }
}
```

2 The **Name** class will need to have an **equals()** method and a **hashCode()** method, as we will use objects of this class as keys to store **Person** objects. We can define the class as:

```
public class Name
{
  private String firstName;    // First name
  private String surname;      // Second name

  // Constructor
  public Name(String firstName, String surname)
  {
```

```
      this.firstName = firstName;
      this.surname = surname;
    }

    // Generate a hash code for an object
    public int hashCode()
    {
      return 7*firstName.hashCode() + 13*surname.hashCode();
    }

    public String toString()
    {
      return firstName + " " + surname;
    }

    public String getFirstName()
    {  return firstName;  }

    public String getSurname()
    {  return surname;  }

    // Overrides method inherited from Object class
    public boolean equals(Object aName)
    {
      // Check if aName is the same class as this object
      if(!this.getClass().getName().equals(aName.getClass().getName()))
        return false;             // It is not return false
      else                        // It is so compare names for equality
        return firstName.equals(((Name)aName).getFirstName()) &&
                          surname.equals(((Name)aName).getSurname());
    }
  }
```

3 All we need now is a class containing **main()** to exercise these classes with a hash
table:

```
import java.util.*;
import java.io.*;

public class TryHashTable
{
  public static void main(String[] args)
  {
    Person aPerson;                          // Working person store
    Hashtable theCast = new Hashtable();   // The hash table

    // Store Persons in the hash table using Name member as key
    for( ; ; )
    {
      aPerson = readPerson();                // Get a person
      if(aPerson == null)                    // If it is null...
```

```
            break;                              // ...we are done
        theCast.put(aPerson.getName(), aPerson);  // Store the person
      }


      // Create an enumeration of the keys in the table
      Enumeration castKeys = theCast.keys();


      // List all the keys
      while(castKeys.hasMoreElements())
        System.out.println(castKeys.nextElement());


      // Check for a particular key
      System.out.println("Table contains Marilyn Monroe? " +
                   theCast.containsKey(new Name("Marilyn", "Monroe")));
      // Check for a particular object
      System.out.println("Table contains Slim Pickens? " +
                   theCast.contains(new Person("Slim", "Pickens")));
      // Check for a particular invalid object
      System.out.println("Table contains Ray Rogers? " +
                   theCast.contains(new Person("Ray", "Rogers")));
    }

    // Method readPerson() to read a person from the keyboard goes here
    // The same as we used with the previous example...
}
```

This is what the example produces with my input:

```
Enter first name, or press Enter to end:
Slim
Enter surname:
Pickens

Enter first name, or press Enter to end:
Marilyn
Enter surname:
Monroe

Enter first name, or press Enter to end:
Roy
Enter surname:
Rogers

Enter first name, or press Enter to end:

Marilyn Monroe
Slim Pickens
Roy Rogers
Table contains Marilyn Monroe? true
Table contains Slim Pickens? true
Table contains Ray Rogers? false
```

How It Works

The **Person** class now stores an object of type **Name**, rather than explicit **String** objects for the first and second names. The **getName()** method makes the **Name** object available externally. You should implement a **toString()** method for your classes as a matter of course, so that objects can be used in output strings and converted automatically.

We've also implemented an **equals()** method that overrides the one inherited from the class **Object**, because some of the **Hashtable** methods can call it. The **equals()** method accepts any object as an argument, so we first need to verify that the variable passed as an argument refers to an object of the same class as the current object. We do this by using the **getClass()** method from the class **Class** that we saw in Chapter 6. We call **getClass()** for the current object and for the argument, and then call the **getName()** member from the class **Class** for each of the objects returned by the **getClass()** calls to get the fully qualified names of the classes as **String** objects. We compare these using the **String** class **equals()** method. If they aren't equal the classes must be different, so we return **false**.

Once we've established that the argument and the current object are of the same class, we can compare the objects for equality. The objects will be equal if their data members are equal, so we use the **String** class **equals()** method to do the work.

The **hashCode()** method in the **Name** class uses the technique we discussed earlier. It combines the hash codes produced by the **hashCode()** method for the objects **firstName** and **surname** by multiplying each by a different prime and adding the results.

The **equals()** method in the **Name** class has essentially the same logic as the version we produced for the class **Person**. Here we need to compare the **firstName** and **surname** data members for the current object and the argument, and if both comparisons return true we return **true** to indicate the **Name** objects are equal.

The test class, **TryHashTable**, just obtains **Person** objects using the **readPerson()** method from the last example, and stores them in a hash table, **theCast**, using the **Name** object for each **Person** object as a key. To retrieve the keys subsequently, we create an enumeration, and then use this to output the keys to the display. We could equally well have output the objects here, or obtained an enumeration of the objects in the table directly by using the **elements()** method.

Lastly, we give the **containsKey()** and **contains()** method in the **Hashtable** object an outing to test the **equals()** methods for our classes.

Observable and Observer Objects

The class **Observable** provides you with a somewhat specialized mechanism for communicating a change in one class object to a number of other class objects. One primary use for this mechanism is in windows programming where you often have one object representing all the data for the application—a text document for instance, or a geometric model of a physical object, and several other objects that represent views of the data that are displayed in separate windows, where each shows a different representation or perhaps a subset of the data. This is referred to as the **document/view architecture** for an application, or sometimes the **model/view architecture**. The document/view terminology is applied to any collection of application data—geometry, bitmaps or whatever. It isn't restricted to what is normally understood by the term 'document'.

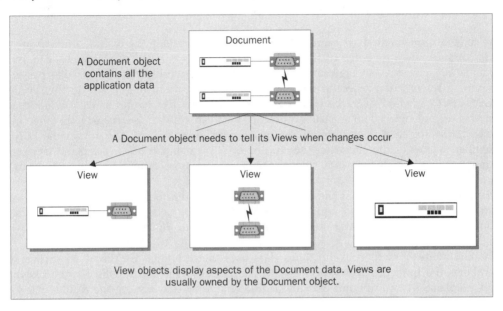

When the document object changes, all the views need to be notified that a change has occurred, since they may well need to update what they display. The document is observable and all the views are observers. This is exactly what the **Observable** class is designed to achieve, used in combination with an interface, **Observer**.

The document/view architecture portrays a many-to-many relationship. A document may have many observers, and a view may observe many documents.

Defining Classes of Observable Objects

You use the **Observable** class in the definition of a class of objects that may be observed. You simply derive the class for objects to be monitored, **Document** say, from the class **Observable**.

Any class that may need to be notified when a **Document** object has been changed, must implement the interface **Observer**. This doesn't in itself cause the observer objects to be notified when a change in an observed object occurs. It just establishes the potential for this to happen, but you need to do something else to link the observers to the observable, which we'll come to in a moment.

The definition of the class for observed objects would be of the form:

```
public class Document extends Observable
{
   // Details of the class definitions
}
```

The class **Document** will inherit methods from the class **Observable** which operate the communications to the observer objects. A class for observers would be defined as:

```
public class View implements Observer
{
   // Method for the interface
   public void update(Observable theObject, Object arg)
   {
      // This method is called when the observed object changes
   }

   // Rest of the class definition...
}
```

The **Observer** interface declares one method, **update()**. It's called when an associated **Observable** object changes, and the **Observable** object is passed as the first argument to the **update()** method. This enables the **View** object to access public methods in the associated **Observable** object, which would be used to access the data to be displayed for example. The second argument passed to **update()** is used to convey additional information to the observer object.

Observable Class Methods

The **Observable** class maintains an internal record of all the **Observer** objects related to the object to be observed. Your class, derived from **Observable**, will inherit the data members that deal with this. Your class of observable objects will also inherit nine methods from the class **Observable**. These are the following:

Method	Description
addObserver(Observer o)	Adds the object passed as an argument to the internal record of observers. Only observer objects in the internal record will be notified when a change in the observable object occurs.
deleteObserver(Observer o)	Deletes the object passed as an argument, from the internal record of observers.
deleteObservers()	Deletes all observers from the internal record of observers.
notifyObservers(Object arg)	Calls the **update()** method for all of the observer objects in the internal record if the current object has been set as changed. The current object is set as changed by calling the **setChanged()** method below. The current object and the argument passed to the **notifyObservers()** method will be passed to the **update()** method for each **Observer** object.

Method	Description
notifyObservers()	Calling this method is equivalent to the previous method with a **null** argument. (See **setChanged()** method below.)
countObservers()	The count of the number of observer objects for the current object is returned as type **int**.
setChanged()	Sets the current object as changed. You must call this method before calling the **notifyObservers()** method.
hasChanged()	Returns **true** if the object has been set as 'changed', and **false** otherwise.
clearChanged()	Resets the changed status of the current object to unchanged.

It's fairly easy to see how these methods are used to manage the relationship between an observable object and its associated observers. An observable object is responsible for adding observer objects to its internal record through the **addObserver()** method. In practice, the observer objects are typically created as objects that are dependent on the observable object and then added to the record, so there's an implied ownership relationship.

This makes sense if you think about what the mechanism is often used for in an application using the document/view architecture. A document has permanence since it represents the data for an application. A view is a transient presentation of some or all of the data in the document, so a **Document** object would naturally create and own its **View** objects. A view will be responsible for managing the interface to the application's user, but the update of the underlying data in the **Document** object would be carried out by methods in the **Document** object, which would then notify other **View** objects that a change has occurred.

Of course, you're in no way limited to using the **Observable** class and the **Observer** interface in the way in which we've described here. You can use it in any context where you want changes that occur in one class object to be communicated to others. We can exercise the process in a silly example.

Try It Out—Observing the Observable

1 We'll first define a class for an object that can exhibit change:

```
import java.util.*;

public class JekyllAndHyde extends Observable
{
  String name = "Dr. Jekyll";

  public void drinkPotion()
  {
    name = "Mr.Hyde";
    setChanged();
```

```
      notifyObservers();
   }

  public String getName()
  {
    return name;
  }
}
```

2 Now we can define the class of person who's looking out for this kind of thing:

```
import java.util.*;

public class Person implements Observer
{
  String name;            // Person's identity
  String says;            // What they say when startled

  // Constructor
  public Person(String name, String says)
  {
    this.name = name;
    this.says = says;
  }

  // Called when observing an object that changes
  public void update(Observable thing, Object o)
  {
    System.out.println("It's " + ((JekyllAndHyde)thing).getName() +
                  "\n" + name + ": " + says);
  }
}
```

3 We can gather a bunch of observers to watch Dr. Jekyll with the following class:

```
// Try out observers
import java.util.*;

public class Horrific
{
  public static void main(String[] args)
  {
    JekyllAndHyde man = new JekyllAndHyde();  // Create Dr. Jekyll

    Observer[] crowd = {
                    new Person("Officer","What's all this then?"),
                    new Person("Eileen Backwards",
                        "Oh, no, it's horrible - those teeth!"),
                    new Person("Phil McCavity",
```

```
                                "I'm your local dentist - here's my card."),
                        new Person("Slim Sagebrush",
                            "What in tarnation's goin' on here?"),
                        new Person("Freaky Weirdo",
                            "Real cool, man. Where can I get that stuff?")};

        // Add the observers
        for(int i = 0; i < crowd.length; i++)
          man.addObserver(crowd[i]);

        man.drinkPotion();                // Dr. Jekyll drinks up
      }
    }
```

If you compile and run this, you should get the output:

```
It's Mr.Hyde
Freaky Weirdo: Real cool, man. Where can I get that stuff?
It's Mr.Hyde
Slim Sagebrush: What in tarnation's goin' on here?
It's Mr.Hyde
Phil McCavity: I'm your local dentist - here's my card.
It's Mr.Hyde
Eileen Backwards: Oh, no, it's horrible - those teeth!
It's Mr.Hyde
Officer: What's all this then?
```

How It Works

JekyllAndHyde is a very simple class with just two methods. The **drinkPotion()** method encourages Dr Jekyll to do his stuff, and the **getName()** method enables anyone who is interested to find out who he is. The class extends the **Observable** class so we can add observers for an object of this class.

The revamped **Person** class implements the **Observer** interface, so an object of this class can observe an observable object. When notified of a change in the object being observed, the **update()** method will be called. Here, it just outputs who the person is, and what they say.

In the **Horrific** class, after defining Dr Jekyll in the variable, **man**, we create an array, **crowd**, of type **Observer** to hold the observers—which are of type **Person**, of course. We can use an array of type **Observer** because the class **Person** implements the **Observer** interface. We pass two arguments to the **Person** class constructor, a name, and a string that is what the person will say when they see a change in Dr Jekyll. We add each of the observers for the object **man** in the **for** loop.

Calling the **drinkPotion()** method for the object, **man**, results in the internal name being changed, the **setChanged()** method being called for the **man** object, and the **notifyObservers()** method that is inherited from the **Observable** class being called. This causes the **update()** method for each of the registered observers to be called which generates the output. If you comment out the **setChanged()** call in the **drinkPotion()** method, and compile and run the program again, you'll get no output. Unless **setChanged()** is called, the observers aren't notified.

We've created an **Observable** class of objects by deriving a class from **Observable**. This will not be practical in many instances because you need to derive your class from another base class. You can easily get around this though. Just add a data member of type **Observable** to your class. You can then use this data member as a surrogate for your class objects. The **Observer** objects will need to be registered with the **Observable** data member, so you'll need a **public** method in your class that will do this. All you then need to do when your class object changes is to call the **setChanged()** and **notifyObservers()** methods for the **Observable** data member. All the **Observer** objects that are registered will then be signaled that your class object has changed.

Generating Random Numbers

The class **Random** enables you to create multiple random number generators that are independent of one another. Each object of the class is a separate random number generator. Any **Random** object can generate pseudorandom numbers of types **int**, **long**, **float** or **double**. These numbers are created using an algorithm that takes a 'seed' and 'grows' a sequence of numbers from it. Initializing the algorithm twice with the same key would produce the same sequence because the algorithm is deterministic.

The integer values generated will be uniformly distributed over the complete range for the type, and the floating point values will be uniformly distributed over the range 0.0 to 1.0 for both types. You can also generate numbers of type **double** with a **Gaussian** distribution (also called the normal distribution) that has a mean of 0.0 and a standard deviation of 1.0. This is the typical bell-shaped curve that represents the probability distribution for many random events.

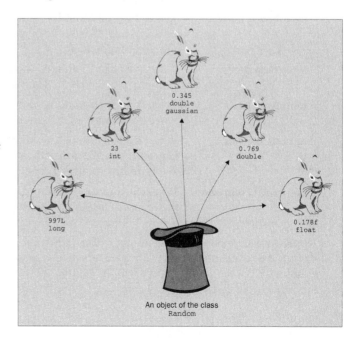

An object of the class
Random

There are two constructors for a **Random** object. The default constructor will create an object that uses the current time from your computer clock as the seed value for generating pseudorandom numbers. The other constructor accepts an argument of type **long** which will be used as the seed.

```
Random lottery = new Random();        // Sequence not repeatable
Random repeatable = new Random(997L);  // Repeatable sequence
```

If you use the default constructor, the sequence of numbers generated will be different each time a program is run, although beware of creating two generators in the same program with the default constructor. The time resolution used is one millisecond, so if you create two objects in successive statements they will usually generate the same sequence because the times used for the starting seed values will be identical. **Random** objects created using the same seed will always produce the same sequence. A major feature of random number generators created using a given seed in Java is that, not only will they always produce the same sequence of pseudorandom numbers from a given seed, but also they will do so even on totally different computers.

Random Operations

The public methods provided by a **Random** object are:

Method	Description
`nextInt()`	Returns a pseudorandom number of type **int**. Values generated will be uniformly distributed across the complete range of values for a number of type **int**.
`nextLong()`	Returns a pseudorandom number of type **long**. Values generated will be uniformly distributed across the complete range of values for a number of type **long**.
`nextFloat()`	Returns a pseudorandom number of type **float**. Values generated will be uniformly distributed across the range **0.0f** to **1.0f**.
`nextDouble()`	Returns a pseudorandom number of type **double**. Values generated will be uniformly distributed across the range 0.0 to 1.0.
`nextGaussian()`	Returns a pseudorandom number of type **double** selected from a Gaussian distribution. Values generated will have a mean of 0.0, and a standard deviation of 1.0.
`setSeed(long seed)`	Resets the random number generator to generate values using the value passed as an argument as a starting seed for the algorithm.

To produce a pseudorandom number of a particular type, you just call the appropriate method for a **Random** object. You can repeat the sequence of numbers generated by a **Random** object that you created with a seed value, by calling the **setSeed()** method with the same seed value as an argument.

We can give the **Random** class an outing with a simple program that simulates throwing a pair of dice. We'll assume you get six throws to try to get a double six.

Try It Out—Using Random Objects

Here's the program:

```
import java.util.Random;
import java.io.IOException;

public class Dice
{
  public static void main(String[] args)
  {
    System.out.println("You have six throws of a pair of dice.\n" +
              "The objective is to get a double six. Here goes...\n");

    Random diceValues = new Random();        // Random number generator
    String[] theThrow = {"First ", "Second ", "Third ",
                    "Fourth ", "Fifth ", "Sixth "};
    int die1 = 0;                            // First die value
    int die2 = 0;                            // Second die value

    for(int i = 0; i < 6; i++)
    {
      die1 = 1 + Math.abs(diceValues.nextInt())%6;  // Number from 1 to 6
      die2 = 1 + Math.abs(diceValues.nextInt())%6;  // Number from 1 to 6
      System.out.println(theThrow[i] + "throw: " + die1 + ", " + die2);

      if(die1 + die2 == 12)                          // Is it double 6?
      {
        System.out.println("    You win!!");          // Yes !!!
        return;
      }
    }
    System.out.println("Sorry, you lost...");
    return;
  }
}
```

How It Works

We use one random number generator here that we create using the default constructor, so it will be seeded with the current time and will produce a different sequence of values each time the program is run. We simulate throwing the dice in the **for** loop. For each throw we need a random number between 1 and 6 for each die. The easiest way to produce this is to use the remainder from dividing the random integer produced by the **diceValues** object by 6, and adding 1. Remember that the pseudorandom integer values that we get from the **nextInt()** method will be uniformly distributed across the whole range of possible values for type **int**, positive and negative. That's why we need to use the **abs()** method from the **Math** class to make sure we end up with a positive die value.

Remember that the odds against a double six are 36:1, so you'll only succeed once on average out of every six times you run the example.

Dates

With the **Date** class you can create an object that represents a given date and time. You have two ways to do this using the following constructors:

Method	Description
Date()	Creates an object based on the current time from your computer clock to the nearest millisecond.
Date(long time)	Creates an object based on the time value in milliseconds since 00:00:00 GMT on January 1st 1970 that is passed as an argument.

With either constructor you create a **Date** object that represents a specific instant in time to the nearest millisecond. Carrying dates around as the number of milliseconds since the dawn of the year 1970 won't grab you as being incredibly user-friendly—but we'll come back to how we can interpret a **Date** object better in a moment. The **Date** class provides three methods for comparing **Date** objects:

Comparison Methods	Description
after(Date earlier)	Returns **true** if the current object represents a date that's later than the date represented by the argument, **earlier**, and **false** otherwise.
before(Date later)	Returns **true** if the current object represents a date that's earlier than the date represented by the argument **later**, and **false** otherwise.
equals(Object aDate)	Returns **true** if the current object and the argument represents the same date and time, and **false** otherwise. This implies that they would both return the same value from **getTime()**.

The **equals()** method returns true if two different **Date** objects represent the same date and time. Since the **hashCode()** method is also implemented for the class, you have all you need to use **Date** objects as keys in a hash table.

Interpreting Date Objects

The **DateFormat** class is an abstract class that you can use to create meaningful **String** representations of **Date** objects. It isn't in the **java.util** package though—it's defined in the package **java.text**. There are four standard representations for the date and the time that are identified by constants defined in the **DateFormat** class. The effects of these will vary in different countries, because the representation for the date and the time will reflect the conventions of those countries. The constants in the **DateFormat** class defining the four formats are:

Date Format	Description
SHORT	A completely numeric representation for a date or a time, such as 2/2/97 or 4:15am.
MEDIUM	A longer representation than **SHORT**, such as 5-Dec-97.
LONG	A longer representation than **MEDIUM**, such as December 5, 1997.
FULL	A comprehensive representation of the date or the time such as Friday, December 5, 1997 AD or 4:45:52 PST where PST is Pacific Standard Time.

A country is defined by a **Locale** object which you can generate from a class constructor that accepts ISO codes for the language and the country. The language codes are defined by ISO-639 and the country codes ISO-3166. You can find the country codes on the Internet at,

http://www.chemie.fu-berlin.de/diverse/doc/ISO_3166.html

and you can find the language codes at,

http://www.ics.uci.edu/pub/ietf/http/related/iso639.txt

For some countries, the easiest way to specify the locale if you don't have the ISO codes on the tip of your tongue, is to use the final **Locale** objects defined within the **Locale** class. In Java 1.1 these are:

UK	**US**	**CANADA**	**FRANCE**	**GERMANY**	**ITALY**
JAPAN	**KOREA**	**CHINA**	**TAIWAN**		

Because the **DateFormat** class is abstract, you can't create objects of the class directly, but you can obtain **DateFormat** objects by using any of the following **static** methods, each of which return a value of type **DateFormat**:

Static Method	Description
getTimeInstance()	Returns a time formatter for the default locale that uses the default style for the time.
getTimeInstance(int timeStyle)	Returns a time formatter for the default locale that uses the style for the time that is specified by the argument.
getTimeInstance(int style, Locale aLocale)	Returns a time formatter for the locale specified by the second argument that uses the style for the time that is specified by the first argument.
getDateInstance()	Returns a date formatter for the default locale that uses the default style for the date.
getDateInstance(int dateStyle)	Returns a date formatter for the default locale that uses the style for the date specified by the argument.

Table Continued on Following Page

Static Method	Description
getDateInstance(int dateStyle, Locale aLocale)	Returns a date formatter for the locale specified by the second argument that uses the style for the date that is specified by the first argument.
getInstance()	Returns a default date and time formatter that uses the **SHORT** style for both the date and the time.
getDateTimeInstance()	Returns a date and time formatter for the default locale that uses the default style for both the date and the time.
getDateTimeInstance(int dateStyle, int timeStyle)	Returns a date and time formatter for the current locale that uses the styles for the date and the time specified by the arguments.
getDateTimeInstance(int dateStyle, timeStyle, Locale aLocale)	Returns a date and time formatter for **aLocale int** with the styles for the date and the time as specified by the first two arguments.

When you've obtained a **DateFormat** object for the country and the style that you want, and the sort of data you want to format—the date or the time or both—you're ready to produce a **String** from the **Date** object. All you need to do is to pass the **Date** object to the **format()** method for the **DateFormat** object. For example:

```
Date today = new Date();    // Object for now - today's date
DateFormat fmt = getDateTimeInstance(Locale.FULL, Locale.US);
String formatted = fmt.format(today);
```

After executing these statements, the **String** variable, **formatted**, will contain a full representation of the date and the time when the **Date** object, **today**, was created.

We can try out some dates and formats in a simple example.

Try It Out—Producing Dates and Times

This example will show the four different date formats for four countries:

```
// Trying date formatting
import java.util.*;
import java.text.*;

public class TryDateFormats
{
  public static void main(String[] args)
  {
    Date today = new Date();
    Locale[] locales = {Locale.US, Locale.UK,
                        Locale.GERMANY, Locale.FRANCE };
```

```
      int[] styles = { DateFormat.FULL,DateFormat.LONG,
                    DateFormat.MEDIUM,DateFormat.SHORT};
   DateFormat fmt;
   String[] styleText = { "FULL", "LONG", "MEDIUM", "SHORT"};

   // Output the date for each locale in four styles
   for(int i = 0; i < locales.length; i++)
   {
     System.out.println("\nThe Date for " +
                     locales[i].getDisplayCountry() + ":");
     for(int j = 0; j < styles.length; j++)
     {
       fmt = DateFormat.getDateInstance(styles[j], locales[i]);
       System.out.println( "\tIn " + styleText[j] +
                        " is " + fmt.format(today));
     }
   }
  }
}
```

When I compiled and ran this it produced the following output:

```
The Date for United States:
        In FULL is Wednesday, April 30, 1997
        In LONG is April 30, 1997
        In MEDIUM is 30-Apr-97
        In SHORT is 4/30/97

The Date for United Kingdom:
        In FULL is Wednesday, 30 April 1997
        In LONG is 30 April, 1997
        In MEDIUM is 30-Apr-97
        In SHORT is 30/04/97

The Date for Germany:
        In FULL is Mittwoch, 30. April 1997
        In LONG is 30. April 1997
        In MEDIUM is 30.4.1997
        In SHORT is 30.4.97

The Date for France:
        In FULL is mercredi, 30 avril 1997
        In LONG is 30 avril 1997
        In MEDIUM is 30 avr 97
        In SHORT is 30/04/97
```

Of course, when you run it the output will be different.

How It Works

The program creates a **Date** object for the current date and time, and an array of **Locale** objects for four countries using values defined in the **Locale** class. It then creates an array of the four possible styles, and another array containing a **String** representation for each style which will be used in the output.

The output is produced in the nested **for** loops. The outer loop iterates over the countries, and the inner loop iterates over the four styles for each country. A **DateFormat** object is created for each combination of style and country, and the **format()** method for the **DateFormat** object is called to produce the formatted date string in the inner call to **println()**.

There are a couple of ways you could change the program. You could initialize the locales array with the expression **DateFormat.getAvailableLocales()**. This will return an array of type **Locale** containing all of the supported locales, but be warned—there are a lot of them. You'll also find that the characters won't display for many countries because your machine doesn't support the country-specific character set. You could also use the method **getTimeInstance()** or **getDateTimeInstance()** instead of **getDateInstance()** to see what sort of output they generate.

Obtaining a Date Object from a String

The **parse()** method for a **DateFormat** object interprets a **String** object passed as an argument as a date and time, and returns a **Date** object corresponding to the date and the time. The **parse()** method will throw a **ParseException** if the **String** object can't be converted to a **Date** object, so you must call it within a **try** block.

The **String** argument to the **parse()** method must correspond to the country and style that you used when you obtained the **DateFormat** object. This makes it a bit tricky to use successfully. For example, the following code will parse the string properly:

```
Date aDate;
DateFormat fmt = DateFormat.getDateInstance(DateFormat.FULL, Locale.US);
try
{
  aDate = fmt.parse("Saturday, July 4, 1998 ");
  System.out.println("The Date string is: " + fmt.format(aDate));
}
catch(ParseException e)
{
  System.out.println(e);
}
```

This works because the string is what would be produced by the locale and style. If you omit the day from the string, or you use the **LONG** style or a different locale, a **ParseException** will be thrown.

Summary

All of the classes in this chapter will be useful sooner or later when you're writing your own Java programs. We'll be applying many of them in examples throughout the remainder of the book.

The important elements we've covered are:

▶ You can use a **Vector** object as a kind of flexible array which expands automatically to accommodate any number of objects stored

▶ The **Stack** class is derived from the **Vector** class and implements a pushdown stack

▶ The **Hashtable** class defines a hash table or map in which objects are stored based on an associated key

▶ An **Enumeration** is an interface for retrieving objects sequentially. An **Enumeration** object allows you to access all the objects it contains serially—but only once. There's no way to go back to the beginning

▶ Objects stored in a **Vector**, a **Stack** or a **Hashtable** can be accessed using **Enumeration**s

▶ Objects of type **Random** can generate pseudorandom numbers of type **int**, **long**, **float** and **double**. The integers are uniformly distributed across the range of the type, **int** or **long**. The floating point numbers are between 0.0 and 1.0. You can also generate numbers of type **double** with a Gaussian distribution with a mean of 0.0 and a standard deviation of 1.0

▶ Classes derived from the **Observable** class can signal changes to classes that implement the **Observer** interface. You define the **Observer** objects that are to be associated with an **Observable** class object by calling the **addObserver()** method. This is primarily intended to be used to implement the document/view architecture for applications in a windowed environment

▶ You can create **Date** objects to represent a date and time that you specify in milliseconds since January 1, 1970, 00:00:00 GMT, or the current date and time from your computer clock

▶ You can use a **DateFormat** object to format the date and time for a **Date** object as a string. The format will be determined by the style and the locale that you specify

Exercises

1 Implement a version of the program to calculate prime numbers that we saw in Chapter 4 to use a **Vector** object instead of an array to store the primes. (Hint— remember the **Integer** class.)

2 Write a program to store a deck of 52 cards on a stack in random sequence using a **Random** class object. You can represent a card as a two character string—**"1C"** for the ace of clubs, **"JD"** for the jack of diamonds, and so on. Output the cards from the stack as four hands of 13 cards.

3 Write a program that uses a hash table to store names, addresses and telephone numbers such that you can enter a name to retrieve a number, and you can enter a number to retrieve the name and address.

4 Extend the previous example using the **Date** class to enable a date to be entered to output the name and address of the individual with that birthday.

5 For the adventurous gambler—use a stack and a **Random** object in a program to simulate a game of Blackjack for one player using two decks of cards.

Threads

In this chapter we'll investigate the facilities Java has to enable you to overlap the execution of segments of a single program. As well as helping to make your programs run more efficiently, this capability is particularly useful when your program is, of necessity, managing several activities concurrently, such as a server program on a network that is communicating with multiple clients.

In this chapter you will learn:

- What a thread is and how you can create threads in your programs
- How to control interactions between threads
- What synchronization means and how to apply it in your code
- What deadlocks are
- How to set thread priorities
- How to create thread groups and specify threads as members of a group
- How to get information about the threads and thread groups in your programs

Understanding Threads

Most programs of any size contain some code segments that are more or less independent of one another, and that could be executed more efficiently if they were overlapped in time. Consider a very simple program that consists of three activities:

- Reads a number of blocks of data from a file
- Performs some calculation on each block of data
- Writes the results of the calculation to another file

You can organize the program as a single sequence of activities. In this case the activities, read file, process, write file, run in sequence, and the sequence is repeated for each block to be read and processed. You can also organize the program so that reading a block from the file is one activity, performing the calculation is a second activity, and writing the results is a third activity. Both of these situations are illustrated below.

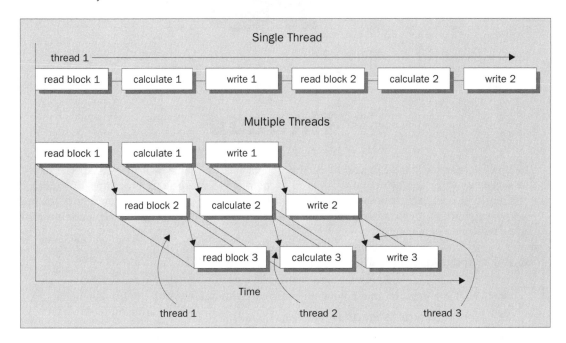

Once a block of data has been read, the computation process can start, and as soon as the computation has been completed, the results can be written out. With the program executing each step in sequence, as shown in the top half of the diagram, the total time for execution will be the sum of the times for each of the individual activities. However, suppose we're able to execute each of the activities independently, as illustrated in the lower half of the diagram. In this case, reading the second block of data can start as soon as the first block has been read, and in theory we can have all three activities executing concurrently. This can have the effect of reducing the total execution time for the program. These three processes that we have identified that run more or less independently of one another—read the file, process the data, and write the results—are called **threads**. Of course, the first example at the top of the diagram has just one thread that does everything in sequence. Every Java program has at least one thread.

However, the three threads in the lower example aren't completely independent of one another. After all, if they were, you might as well make them independent programs. There are practical limitations too—the potential for overlapping these threads will be dependent on the capabilities of your computer, and of your operating system. However, if you can get some overlap in the execution of the threads, the program is going to run faster. There's no magic in using threads though. Your computer has only a finite capacity for executing instructions, and if you have many threads running you may in fact increase the overall execution time because of the overhead implicit in managing the switching of control between threads.

An important consideration when you have a program running multiple threads is that the threads are unlikely to have identical execution times, and if one thread is dependent on another you can't afford to have one overtaking the other—otherwise you'll have chaos. Before you can start calculating in the example in the diagram, you need to be sure that the data block the calculation uses has been read, and before you can write the output, you need to know that the calculation is complete. This necessitates having some means for the threads to communicate with one another.

The way we have shown the threads executing in the previous diagram isn't the only way of organizing the program. You could have three threads, each of which read the file, calculate the results, and write the output, as shown here.

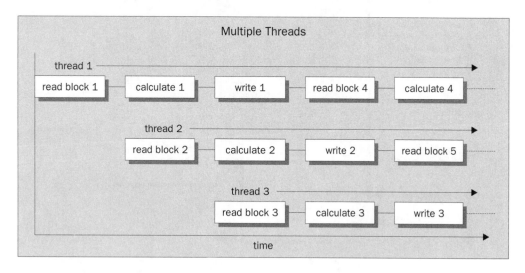

Now there's a different sort of contention between the threads. They are all competing to read the file and write the results, so there needs to be some way of preventing one thread from getting at the input file while another thread is already reading from it. The same goes for the output file. There's another aspect of this arrangement that is different from the previous version. If one thread, *thread1* say, reads a block—*block4* perhaps—that needs a lot of time to compute the results, another thread, *thread2* say, could conceivably read a following block, *block5* maybe, calculate and write the results for *block5*, before *thread1* has written the results for *block4*. If you don't want the results appearing in a different sequence from the input, you would need to do something about this. However, before we delve into the intricacies of making sure our threads don't get knotted, let's first look at how we create a thread.

Creating Threads

Your program always has at least one thread—the one created when the program begins execution. When your program creates a thread, it is in addition to the thread of execution that created it. As you might have guessed, creating a thread involves using an object of a class, and the class you use is **java.lang.Thread**. Each additional thread that your program creates is represented by an object of the class **Thread**, or of a subclass of **Thread**. If your program is to have three additional threads, you will need to create three such objects.

To start the execution of a thread, you call the **start()** method for the **Thread** object. The code that executes in a new thread is always a method called **run()** which is **public**, accepts no arguments, and doesn't return a value. A program that creates three threads is illustrated diagrammatically here.

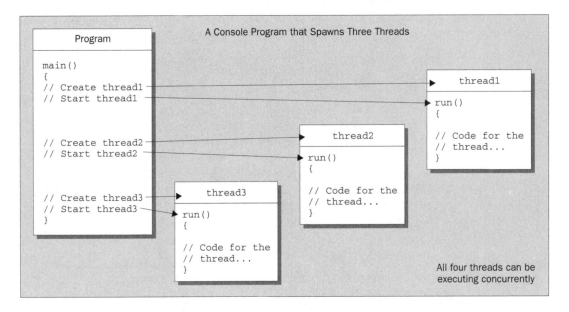

For a thread in your program to do anything, you must implement the method **run()**, as the **run()** method defined in the class **Thread** does nothing. Of course, your implementation of **run()** can call any other methods you want. Our illustration shows **main()** creating all three threads, but, there's no reason why one thread shouldn't create another.

There are two ways in which you can define a class for a thread. One way is to define your class as a subclass of **Thread** and provide a definition of the method **run()** that overrides the superclass method. The other possibility is to define your class as implementing the interface, **Runnable**, which declares the method **run()**, and then creates a **Thread** object in your class when you need to. We need to look at both approaches in a little more detail.

Try It Out—Deriving a Subclass of Thread

We can see how this works by using an example. We'll define a single class, **TryThread**, that we'll derive from **Thread**. Execution starts in the method **main()**:

```java
import java.io.IOException;

public class TryThread extends Thread
{
  private String firstName;                 // Store for first name
  private String secondName;                // Store for second name
  private long aWhile;                       // Delay in milliseconds

  public TryThread(String firstName, String secondName, long delay)
  {
    this.firstName = firstName;             // Store the first name
    this.secondName = secondName;           // Store the second name
    aWhile = delay;                         // Store the delay
    setDaemon(true);                        // Thread is daemon
  }

  public static void main(String[] args)
  {
    // Create three threads
    Thread first = new TryThread("Hopalong ", "Cassidy ", 200L);
    Thread second = new TryThread("Marilyn ", "Monroe ", 300L);
    Thread third = new TryThread("Slim ", "Pickens ", 500L);

    System.out.println("Press Enter when you have had enough...\n");
    first.start();                          // Start the first thread
    second.start();                         // Start the second thread
    third.start();                          // Start the third thread
    try
    {
      System.in.read();                     // Wait until Enter key pressed
      System.out.println("Enter pressed...\n");
      first.stop();                         // Stop the first thread
      second.stop();                        // Stop the second thread
      third.stop();                         // Stop the third thread
    }
    catch (IOException e)                    // Handle IO exception
    {
      System.out.println(e);                // Output the exception
      return;
    }
    return;
  }

  // Method where thread execution will start
  public void run()
  {
    try
    {
      while(true )                                          // Loop indefinitely...
      {
        System.out.print(firstName);                        // Output first name
```

```
        sleep(aWhile);                      // Wait aWhile msec.
        System.out.print(secondName + "\n"); // Output second name
      }
    }
  catch(InterruptedException e)           // Handle thread interruption
  {
    System.out.println(e);                // Output the exception
  }
 }
}
```

If you compile and run the code, you'll see something like this:

```
Press Enter when you have had enough...

Hopalong Marilyn Slim Cassidy
Hopalong Monroe
Marilyn Cassidy
Hopalong Pickens
Slim Cassidy
Hopalong Monroe
Marilyn Cassidy
Hopalong Monroe
Marilyn Cassidy
Hopalong Pickens
Slim Cassidy
Hopalong Monroe
Marilyn
Enter pressed...
```

How It Works

There are three instance variables in our class **TryThread** and these are initialized in the constructor. The two **String** variables hold first and second names, and the variable **aWhile** stores a time period in milliseconds. The constructor for our class, **TryThread()**, will automatically call the default constructor, **Thread()**, for the base class.

Our class containing the method **main()** is derived from **Thread**, and implements **run()**, so objects of this class represent threads. The fact that each object of our class will have a method **main()** is irrelevant—the objects are perfectly good threads. Our method **main()** creates three such objects: **first**, **second** and **third**.

Daemon and User Threads

The call to **setDaemon()** with the argument **true** in the **TryThread** constructor, constructs the **Thread** as a **daemon thread**. A daemon thread is simply a background thread that is subordinate to the thread that creates it, so when the thread that created a daemon thread ends, the daemon thread dies too. In our case, the method **main()** creates the daemon threads so that when **main()** returns, all the threads it has created will also end.

A thread that isn't a daemon thread is called a **user thread**. The diagram below shows two daemon threads and a user thread that are created by the main thread of a program.

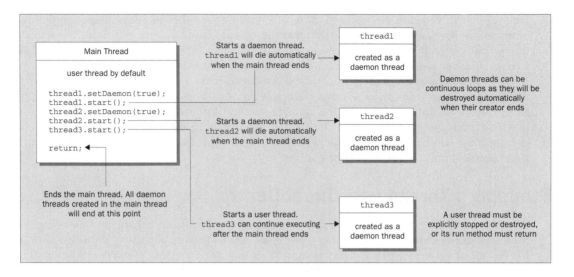

A user thread has a life of its own that isn't dependent on the thread that creates it. It can continue execution after the thread that created it has ended. The default thread that contains **main()** is a user thread, as shown in the diagram, but **thread3** here could continue to execute after **main()** has returned. Threads that run for a finite time can be user threads, but threads that run indefinitely should usually be defined as daemon threads. Note that you can only call **setDaemon()** for a thread before it starts; if you try to do so afterwards, the method will throw an **IllegalThreadStateException** exception.

A thread that is itself created by a daemon thread will be daemon by default.

Creating Thread Objects

In the method **main()**, we create three **Thread** variables that store three different objects of our class **TryThread**. As you can see, each object has an individual name pair as the first two arguments to its constructor, and a different delay value passed as the third argument. Since the output can continue indefinitely, we display a message to explain how to stop it.

Once you've created a thread, it doesn't start executing by itself. You need to set it going. We start the execution of each of the threads represented by the objects, **first**, **second** and **third**, by calling the **start()** method inherited from **Thread**. The **start()** method starts the object's **run()** method executing, then returns to the calling thread. Eventually all three threads are executing in parallel with the original application thread, **main()**.

Implementing the run() Method

The **run()** method contains the code for the thread execution. The code is a single, infinite **while** loop which we put in a **try** block because the method **sleep()**, called in the loop, can throw the exception caught by the **catch** block. The code in the loop outputs the first name, calls the method **sleep()** inherited from **Thread** and then outputs the second name. The **sleep()** method suspends execution of the thread for the number of milliseconds that you specify in the argument. This gives any other threads that have previously been started a chance to execute. This allows the possibility for the output from the three threads being a little jumbled.

Each time a thread calls the method `sleep()`, one of the other waiting threads jumps in. You can see the sequence in which the threads execute from the output. From the names in the output you can deduce that they execute in the sequence `first`, `second`, `third`, `first`, `first`, `second`, `second`, `first`, `first`, `third` and so on. The execution of the `read()` method that is called in `main()` is blocked until you press *Enter*, but all the while the other threads continue executing. The output stops when you press *Enter* because this allows the main thread to continue, and call the `stop()` method for each thread. This method is inherited from the class `Thread`. It has the effect of halting the operation of a thread permanently. After stopping each of the threads it created, the `main()` method then executes a `return` and the program terminates.

Stopping a Thread and ThreadDeath

When you call the `stop()` method for a thread, the thread stops whatever it is doing, and throws a `ThreadDeath` object. You can catch the `ThreadDeath` object by enclosing the code for the thread in a `try` block, and catching it with a `catch` block. However, you shouldn't do so unless you need to do some special clean-up for the thread. If you do need to catch the `ThreadDeath` object, you must rethrow the object in the `catch` block, otherwise the thread will not die.

> *The `ThreadDeath` class is derived from `Error` rather that `Exception`, specifically to avoid a program accidentally catching a `ThreadDeath` object under the umbrella of the `Exception` type, and not rethrowing the object.*

If you need to wait in one thread until another thread dies, you can call the `join()` method for the thread which you expect isn't long for this world. Calling the `join()` method with no arguments, will halt the current thread indefinitely until the specified thread dies:

```
thread1.join();     // Suspend the current thread until thread1 dies
```

You can also pass an `long` value to the `join()` method to specify the number of milliseconds you're prepared to wait for the death of a thread:

```
thread1.join(1000); // Wait up to 1 second for thread1 to die
```

Thread Scheduling

The scheduling of threads depends to some extent on your operating system, but each thread will certainly get a chance to execute when the others are 'asleep', that is, they've called their `sleep()` methods. If your operating system uses pre-emptive multitasking, as Windows 95 does, the program will work without the call to `sleep()` in the `run()` method (you need to remove the `try` and `catch` blocks too, if you remove the `sleep()` call), but if your operating system doesn't schedule in this way, without the `sleep()` call in `run()`, the `first` thread will hog the processor, and will continue indefinitely.

> *The use of the `sleep()` method in the previous example may seem somewhat artificial at first sight, but remember, every thread in your program must relinquish control of the processor from time to time, otherwise implementing the program using threads will just be wasted effort. With a preemptive scheduling operating system such as Windows 95, a thread doesn't necessarily need to give up control voluntarily. Where necessary, control will be forcibly taken from a thread by the operating system at preset intervals, so that other threads of execution can get a turn at using the processor.*

Note that there's another method, `yield()`, defined in the `Thread` class, that gives other threads a chance to execute. You would use this when you just want to allow other threads a look-in if they are waiting, but you don't want to suspend execution of the current thread for a specific period of time. When you call the `sleep()` method for a thread, the thread will not continue for at least the time you have specified as an argument, even if no other threads are waiting. Calling `yield()` will cause the current thread to resume immediately if no threads are waiting.

Implementing the Runnable Interface

An alternative approach to defining the code that runs in a thread involves implementing the interface, `Runnable`, in a class. You'll find that this is generally much more convenient than deriving a class from `Thread` because you can derive your class from a class other than `Thread`, and it can still represent a thread. Because Java only allows a single base class, if you derive your class from `Thread`, it can't inherit functionality from any other class. The interface `Runnable` only declares one method, `run()`, and this is the method that will be executed when the thread is started.

Try It Out—Using the `Runnable` *Interface*

To see how this works in practice, we can write another version of the previous example. We'll call this version of the program `JumbleNames`:

```
import java.io.IOException;

public class JumbleNames implements Runnable
{
  private String firstName;           // Store for first name
  private String secondName;          // Store for second name
  private long aWhile;                // Delay in milliseconds

  // Constructor
  public JumbleNames(String firstName, String secondName, long delay)
  {
    this.firstName = firstName;       // Store the first name
    this.secondName = secondName;     // Store the second name
    aWhile = delay;                   // Store the delay
  }
```

```java
// Method where thread execution will start
public void run()
{
  try
  {
    while(true)                             // Loop indefinitely...
    {
      System.out.print(firstName);          // Output first name
      Thread.sleep(aWhile);                 // Wait aWhile msec.
      System.out.print(secondName+"\n");    // Output second name
    }
  }
  catch(InterruptedException e)             // Handle thread interruption
  {
    System.out.println(e);                  // Output the exception
  }
}

public static void main(String[] args)
{
  // Create three threads
  Thread first = new Thread((Runnable)
                    new JumbleNames("Hopalong ", "Cassidy ", 200L));
  Thread second = new Thread((Runnable)
                    new JumbleNames("Marilyn ", "Monroe ", 300L));
  Thread third = new Thread((Runnable)
                    new JumbleNames("Slim ", "Pickens ", 500L));

  // Set threads as daemon
  first.setDaemon(true);
  second.setDaemon(true);
  third.setDaemon(true);

  System.out.println("Press Enter when you have had enough...\n");
  first.start();                            // Start the first thread
  second.start();                           // Start the second thread
  third.start();                            // Start the third thread
  try
  {
    System.in.read();                       // Wait until Enter key pressed
    System.out.println("Enter pressed...\n");
    first.stop();                           // Stop the first thread
    second.stop();                          // Stop the second thread
    third.stop();                           // Stop the third thread
  }
  catch (IOException e)                      // Handle IO exception
  {
    System.out.println(e);                  // Output the exception
    return;
  }
  return;
}
}
```

How It Works

We have the same data members in this class as we had in the previous example. The constructor is almost the same as previously. We can't call **setDaemon()** in this class constructor because our class isn't derived from **Thread**. Instead, we need to do that after we've created the objects representing the threads in **main()**. The **run()** method implementation is also very similar. Our class doesn't have **sleep()** as a member, but because it's a **public static** member of the class **Thread**, we can call it in our **run()** method by using the class name.

In the method **main()**, we still create a **Thread** object for each thread of execution, but this time we use a constructor that accepts an object of type **Runnable** as an argument. We pass an object of our class **JumbleNames** to it. This is possible because our class implements **Runnable**. The effect of using this constructor is to cause the **run()** method in the **Thread** object to call the **run()** method for the **JumbleNames** object that is passed as an argument, when the thread begins execution.

Thread Names

Threads have a name which, in the case of the **Thread** constructor we're using in the example, will be a default name composed of the string **"Thread*"** with a sequence number appended. If you want to choose your own name for a thread, you can use a **Thread** constructor that accepts a **String** object containing a name for the thread. For example, we could have created the **Thread** object **first**, with the statement:

```
Thread first = new Thread(new JumbleNames("Hopalong ", "Cassidy ", 200L),
                          "firstThread");
```

This would have assigned the name **"firstThread"** to the thread. Note that this name is only used when displaying information about the thread. It has no relation to the name of the **Thread** object, and there's nothing—apart from common sense—to prevent several threads being given the same name. You can obtain the name assigned to a thread by calling the **getName()** method for the **Thread** object. The name of the thread is returned as a **String** object. You can also change the name of a thread by calling the **setName()** method defined in the class **Thread**, and passing a **String** object to it.

Once we've created the three **Thread** objects in the example, we call the **setDaemon()** method for each. The rest of **main()** is the same as in the previous example, and you should get identical output when you run this version of the program.

Managing Threads

In both the examples we've seen in this chapter, the threads are launched and then left to compete for computer resources. Because all three threads compete in an uncontrolled way for the processor, the output from the threads gets muddled up. This isn't normally a desirable feature in a program. In most instances where you use threads, the way in which they execute will need to be managed so that they don't interfere with each other.

Of course, in our examples, the programs are deliberately constructed to release control of the processor part way through outputting a name. While this is very artificial, similar situations can arise in practice, particularly where threads are involved in a repetitive operation. Where two or more threads share a common resource such as a file or a block of memory, you'll need to take steps to ensure that one thread doesn't modify a resource while that resource is still being used by another thread. Having one thread update a record in a file while another thread is part way through retrieving the same record, is a recipe for disaster. One way of managing this sort of situation is to use **synchronization** for the threads involved.

Synchronization

The objective of synchronization is to ensure that, when several threads need access to a single resource, only one thread can access it at any given time. There are two ways in which you can use synchronization to manage your threads of execution:

▶ You can manage code at the method level
▶ You can manage code at the block level

We'll look at how we can use synchronized methods first.

Synchronized Methods

You can make methods for any class object mutually exclusive, by declaring them in the class using the keyword **synchronized**. For example:

```
class MyClass
{
  synchronized public void method1()
  {
    // Code for the method...
  }

  synchronized public void method2()
  {
    // Code for the method...
  }

  public void method3()
  {
    // Code for the method...
  }
}
```

Only one of the synchronized methods in a class object can be executing at any one time. Only when the currently executing synchronized method for an object has ended can another synchronized method start for the same object.

> *Note that there's no limit here on simultaneously executing synchronized methods for two different objects of the same class. It's only concurrent access to any one object that is controlled.*

Of the three methods in **myClass**, two are declared as **synchronized**, so for any object of the class, only one of these methods can be executing at one time. The method that isn't declared as synchronized, **method3()**, can always be executed by a thread, regardless of whether a synchronized method is executing.

It's important to keep clear in your mind the distinction between an object which has instance methods that you declared as **synchronized** in the class definition, and the threads of execution that might use them. A hypothetical relationship between three threads and two objects of the class **myClass** is illustrated in this diagram:

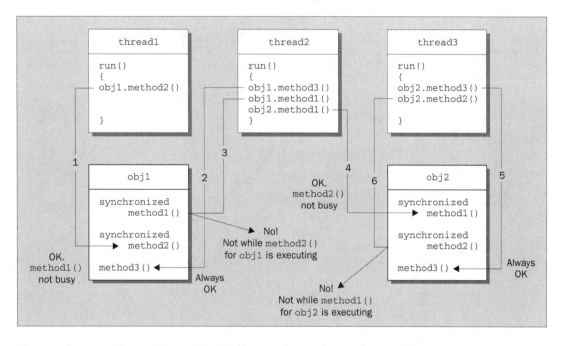

The numbers on the arrows in the diagram indicate the sequence of events. While **method1()** in **obj2** is executing, **method2()** for the same object can't be executed. The synchronization of these two instance methods in an object provides a degree of protection for the object, in that only one synchronized method can be messing with the data in the object at any given time.

However, each object is independent of any other object when it comes to synchronized instance methods. When a thread executes a synchronized method for an object, it is assured exclusive access to the object insofar as the synchronized methods in the object are concerned. Another thread can still call the same method for a different object though. While **method1()** is being executed for **obj1**, this doesn't prevent **method1()** for **obj2** being

431

executed by some other thread. Also, if there's a method in an object that has not been declared as **synchronized**, **method3()** in **obj1** for example, any thread can call that at any time, regardless of the state of any synchronized methods in the object.

If you apply synchronization to **static** methods in a class, only one of the **static** methods in the class can be executing at any point in time.

Using Synchronized Methods

To see how synchronization can be applied in practice, we'll construct a program that provides a simple model of a bank. Our bank is a very young business with only one customer account initially, but we'll have two clerks each working flat out to process transactions against the account, one handling debits and the other handling credits. The objects in our program are illustrated here:

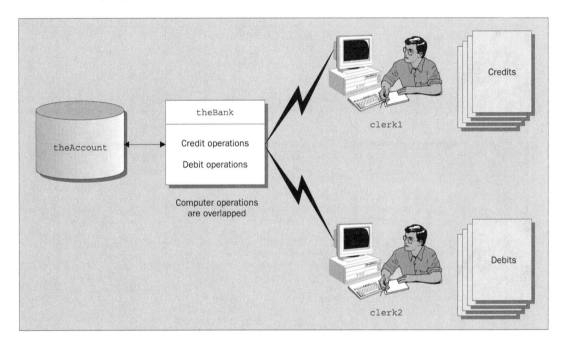

The bank in our model is actually a computer that performs operations on the accounts, and the accounts are stored separately. Each clerk can communicate directly with the bank. We'll be defining four classes in our program: one for the bank computer, one for a clerk, one for an account, and one defining the method **main()** that will determine how it all works.

> *As we develop the code, we won't necessarily get it right first time. This will expose some of the sorts of errors that can arise when you're programming using threads.*

Try It Out—Defining the Bank Classes

1 We can define an account as:

```java
// Defines a customer account
public class Account
{
  private int balance;             // The current account balance

  // Constructor
  public Account(int balance)
  {
    this.balance = balance;        // Set the initial balance
  }

  public int getBalance()
  {
    return balance;                // Return the current balance
  }

  public void setBalance(int balance)
  {
    this.balance = balance;        // Set the current balance
  }
}
```

2 The bank is the agent that will perform the operations on an account. We can define the **Bank** class as:

```java
// Define the bank
class Bank
{
  // Perform a credit operation
  public void credit(Account theAccount, int amount)
  {
    int balance = theAccount.getBalance();   // Get the current balance

    // Checking can take time...
    try
    {
      Thread.sleep(100);
    }
    catch(InterruptedException e)
    {
      System.out.println(e);
    }

    balance += amount;                       // Update the balance...
    theAccount.setBalance(balance);          // ...and put it back
  }
```

```
  // Perform a debit operation
  public void debit(Account theAccount, int amount)
  {
    int balance = theAccount.getBalance();

    // Debits require even more checks...
    try
    {
      Thread.sleep(150);
    }
    catch(InterruptedException e)
    {
      System.out.println(e);
    }

    balance -= amount;                 // Update the balance...
    theAccount.setBalance(balance);    // ...and put it back
  }
}
```

3 A clerk is a rather more complicated animal. He or she retains information about the bank, details of the current transaction, and is capable of initiating debits and credits on an account by communication with the central bank:

```
public class Clerk implements Runnable
{
  Bank theBank;                      // The employer - an electronic marvel

  // Types of transactions
  static final int CREDIT = 1;    // A credit transaction
  static final int DEBIT = 2;     // A debit transaction
  static final int NONE = -1;     // No transaction is in progress

  // Details of the current transaction
  Account theAccount;             // The account
  private int transactionType;    // Type of current transaction
  private int amount = 0;         // Amount for current transaction

  // Constructor
  public Clerk(Bank theBank)
  {
    this.theBank = theBank;         // Who the clerk works for
    transactionType = NONE;         // No transaction initially
  }

  // Process a credit
  public void doCredit(Account theAccount, int amount)
  {
    this.theAccount = theAccount; // Remember the account
    transactionType = CREDIT;       // Set the transaction type
    this.amount = amount;           // Store the amount
  }
```

```
  // Process a debit
  public void doDebit(Account theAccount, int amount)
  {
    this.theAccount = theAccount; // Remember the account
    transactionType = DEBIT;      // Set the transaction type
    this.amount = amount;                 // Store the amount
  }


  // The working clerk...
  public void run()
  {
    while(true)
    {
      if(transactionType == NONE)        // No transaction waiting?
      {
        try
        {
          Thread.sleep(150);             // Then take a break...
        }
        catch(InterruptedException e)
        {
          System.out.println(e);
        }
        continue;                        // Go check for a transaction
      }
      if(transactionType == CREDIT)      // If there is a credit
      {
        theBank.credit(theAccount, amount); // Pass it to the bank
        transactionType = NONE;             // All done
      }
      else
        if(transactionType == DEBIT)     // If there is a debit
        {
          theBank.debit(theAccount, amount); // Pass it to the bank
          transactionType = NONE;            // All done
        }
    }
  }

  // Busy check
  public boolean isBusy()
  {
    return transactionType!=NONE;  // CREDIT or DEBIT means busy
  }
}
```

How It Works

The account class is very simple. It just maintains a record of the amount in the account as balance, and provides methods for retrieving and setting the current balance.

FYI Note that the *set* and *get* accessor methods in `Account` don't need to be synchronized, since Java requires that accessing an `int` asynchronously is done atomically—that is, in one uninterruptable operation.

Our bank model is also very simple. It keeps no records of anything locally as the accounts will be identified separately, and it has just two procedures it can carry out, a credit and a debit to an account. Both of these involve some delay while the standard nameless checks and verifications, that all banks have, are carried out. The delay is simulated by calling the `sleep()` method belonging to the **Thread** class. Of course, during this time, other things in other threads may be going on.

A clerk can remember **theBank**, which is stored when a **Clerk** object is created, and the details of the current transaction being processed. While a transaction is being processed, indicated by **transactionType** containing a value **CREDIT** or **DEBIT**, the **isBusy()** method will return **true**. The details of a transaction are recorded by either the **doCredit()** or the **doDebit()** method. The real work is actually done in the **run()** method. If the transaction type is **NONE**, then there's nothing to do so after sleeping a while, the loop goes around again for another look at the transaction type. When a transaction has been recorded, the appropriate method in **theBank** object is called to carry out a debit or a credit, and the transaction type is reset to **NONE**.

All we need now is the class to drive our model world which we'll call **BankOperation**. This class only requires the method **main()**, but there are quite a lot of things to do in this method so we'll put it together piece by piece.

Try It Out—Defining the Operation of the Bank

1 Here's the basic structure:

```
public class BankOperation
{
  public static void main(String[] args)
  {
    int initialBalance = 500;      // The initial account balance
    int totalCredits = 0;          // Total credits on the account
    int totalDebits =0;            // Total debits on the account
    int transactionCount = 20;     // Number of debits and of credits

    // Create the account, the bank and the clerks...

    // Create the threads for the clerks as daemon, and start them off

    // Generate the transactions of each type and pass to the clerks

    // Wait until both clerks are done
```

```
    // Now output the results
  }
}
```

2 To create the account, the bank object and the clerks, we need to add the following code:

```
// Create the account, the bank and the clerks...
Account account = new Account(initialBalance);    // Create an account
Bank theBank = new Bank();                         // Create a bank
Clerk clerk1 = new Clerk(theBank );        // Create the first clerk
Clerk clerk2 = new Clerk(theBank );        // Create the second clerk
```

3 The next step is to add the code to create the threads for the clerks and start them going:

```
// Create the threads for the clerks as daemon, and start them off
Thread clerk1Thread = new Thread(clerk1);
Thread clerk2Thread = new Thread(clerk2);
clerk1Thread.setDaemon(true);      // Set first as daemon
clerk2Thread.setDaemon(true);      // Set second as daemon
clerk1Thread.start();              // Start the first
clerk2Thread.start();              // Start the second
```

4 The code to generate the transactions looks like a lot, but it is quite repetitive:

```
// Generate transactions of each type and pass to the clerks
for(int i = 1; i <= transactionCount; i++)
{
  // Generate a credit of $50 to $75
  int amount = (int)(50. + 25.*Math.random());
  totalCredits += amount;                     // Keep total credit tally

  // Wait until the first clerk is free
  while(clerk1.isBusy())
    try
    {
      Thread.sleep(25);                       // Busy busy so try later
    }
    catch(InterruptedException e)
    {
      System.out.println(e);
    }

  clerk1.doCredit(account, amount);      // Now do the credit

  // Generate a debit of $30 to $60
  amount = (int)(30. + 30.*Math.random());
  totalDebits += amount;                 // Keep total debit tally
```

```
     // Wait until the second clerk is free
   while(clerk2.isBusy())
     try
     {
       Thread.sleep(25);                    // Busy busy so try later
     }
     catch(InterruptedException e)
     {
       System.out.println(e);
     }

   clerk2.doDebit(account, amount);        // Now do the debit
 }
```

5 Once all the transactions have been processed, we can output the results. However, the clerks could still be busy after we exit from the loop, so we need to wait for both of them to be free before outputting the results. We can do this with a **while** loop:

```
// Wait until both clerks are done
while(clerk1.isBusy() || clerk2.isBusy())
try
{
  Thread.sleep(25);
}
catch(InterruptedException e)
{
  System.out.println(e);
}
```

6 Lastly, we output the results:

```
// Now output the results
System.out.println(
        "Original balance    : $" + initialBalance+"\n" +
        "Total credits       : $" + totalCredits+"\n" +
        "Total debits        : $" + totalDebits+"\n" +
        "Final balance       : $" + account.getBalance() + "\n" +
        "Should be           : $" + (initialBalance + totalCredits -
                                                  totalDebits));
```

How It Works

The variables in the **main()** method that track the total debits and credits, and record the initial account balance, are to help us figure out what has happened after the transactions have been processed. The number of debits and credits to be generated is stored in **transactionCount**, so the total number of transactions will be twice this value. We have added five further blocks of code to perform the functions indicated by the comments, so let's now go through each of them in turn.

The **Account** object is created with the initial balance stored in **initialBalance**. We pass the bank object, **theBank**, to the constructor for each of the **Clerk** objects, so that they can record it.

The **Thread** constructor requires an object of type **Runnable**, so we can just pass the **Clerk** objects in the argument. There's no problem in doing this because the **Clerk** class implements the interface **Runnable**. You can always implicitly cast an object to a type which is any superclass of the object, or any interface that the object class implements.

All the transactions are generated in the **for** loop. The handling of debits is essentially the same as the handling of credits, so we'll only go through the code for the latter in detail. A random amount between $50 and $75 is generated for a credit transaction by using the **static** method **random()** in the standard class **Math**. You'll recall that **random()** returns a **double** value in the range 0.0 to 1.0, so by multiplying this by 25, we get a value between 0.0 and 25.0. We add 50.0 to this and cast the result to type **int** and, hey presto, we have a value between 50 and 75.

Before we pass the transaction to **clerk1**, we must make sure that he or she isn't busy. The **while** loop does this. As long as the **isBusy()** method returns **true**, we continue to call the **sleep()** method for a twenty five millisecond delay, before we go round and check again. When **isBusy()** returns **false**, we call the **doCredit()** method for the clerk and we're done. The **for** loop will run for twenty iterations, so we'll generate twenty random transactions of each type.

The third **while** loop works in the same way as the previous check for a busy clerk—the loop continues if either of the clerks are busy.

Lastly, we just output the original account balance, the totals of credits and debits, and the final balance plus what it should be for comparison. That's all we need in the method **main()**, so we're ready to give it a whirl. Remember that all four classes need to be in the same directory.

Running the Example

As you will have no doubt guessed, we didn't go through all this for nothing, so if you run the example the final balance will be wrong. You should get results something like the following:

```
Original balance   : $500
Total credits      : $1217
Total debits       : $850
Final balance      : $138
Should be          : $867
```

Of course, your results won't be the same as this, but they should be just as wrong. The customer will not be happy. His account balance is seriously out—in the bank's favor of course. The problem is that one operation is retrieving the account balance while another operation is still in the process of amending it. The overlapped operation of the methods in the class **Bank** are the problem.

Try It Out—Synchronizing Methods

We can fix this simply by declaring them as **synchronized**, so you should amend the **Bank** class definition as follows:

```
class Bank
{
  // Perform a credit operation
  synchronized public void credit(Account theAccount, int amount)
  {
    int balance = theAccount.getBalance();   // Get the current balance

    // Checking can take time...
    try
    {
      Thread.sleep(100);
    }
    catch(InterruptedException e)
    {
      System.out.println(e);
    }

    balance += amount;                        // Update the balance...
    theAccount.setBalance(balance);           // ...and put it back
  }

  // Perform a debit operation
  synchronized public void debit(Account theAccount, int amount)
  {
    int balance = theAccount.getBalance();

    // Debits require even more checks...
    try
    {
      Thread.sleep(150);
    }
    catch(InterruptedException e)
    {
      System.out.println(e);
    }

    balance -= amount;                        // Update the balance...
    theAccount.setBalance(balance);           // ...and put it back
  }
}
```

How It Works

Declaring these two methods as **synchronized** will prevent one being executed while the other is still in operation. If you run the example again with this change, the result will be something like:

```
Original balance    : $500
Total credits       : $1201
Total debits        : $931
Final balance       : $770
Should be           : $770
```

The amounts may be different because the transaction amounts are random, but your final balance should be the same as adding the credits to the original balance and subtracting the debits.

As we saw earlier, when you declare methods in a class as **synchronized**, it prevents concurrent execution of such methods within a single object. If you have two or more objects of the same type—two bank objects for example—it doesn't prevent methods from the two objects being run simultaneously. Although this fixes the problem we had, the bank is still relatively inefficient. We can do better, as we shall see.

Synchronizing Statement Blocks

In addition to being able to synchronize methods within a class, you can also specify a statement or a block of code in your program as **synchronized**. This is more powerful, since you specify that the synchronization of the statement or code block relates to any object that you like. When one block that is synchronized with a given object is executing, no other code block that is synchronized to the same object can execute. To synchronize a statement, you just write:

```
synchronized(theObject)
  statement;                    // Synchronized with respect to theObject
```

Any other statements in the program that are synchronized with the same object, **theObject**, can't execute while this statement is executing. Naturally, this applies even when the statement is a call to a method, which may in turn call other methods. Obviously the statement here could equally well be a block of code between braces.

To see precisely how you can use this in practice, let's create a modification of the last example. Suppose we had more than one account. To extend our example to handle more than one account, we just need to make some changes to **main()**. We'll just add one account but modify the code to handle any number.

Try It Out—Handling Multiple Accounts

1 The first modification we need to make is to the definition of the initial balance and the account details:

```
public class BankOperation
{
  public static void main(String[] args)
  {
    int[] initialBalance = {500, 800};  // The initial account balances
    int[] totalCredits = new int[initialBalance.length];  // Total cr's
```

441

```
    int[] totalDebits = new int[initialBalance.length];   // Total db's
    int transactionCount = 20;          // Number of debits and of credits

    // Create the accounts, and initialize total credits and debits
    Account[] accounts = new Account[initialBalance.length];
    for(int i = 0; i < initialBalance.length; i++)
    {
      accounts[i] = new Account(initialBalance[i]); // Create accounts
      totalCredits[i] = totalDebits[i] = 0;
    }

    // Create the bank and the clerks...
    Bank theBank = new Bank();                    // Create a bank
    Clerk clerk1 = new Clerk(theBank );           // Create the first clerk
    Clerk clerk2 = new Clerk(theBank );           // Create the second clerk

    // Create the threads for the clerks as daemon, and start them off

    // Create transactions randomly distributed between the accounts

    // Wait until both clerks are done

    // Now output the results
  }
}
```

The code for creating the bank, the clerks and for creating the threads and starting them, is exactly the same as before. The shaded comments that follow the code indicate the other segments of code in **main()** that we need to modify.

2 The next piece we need to change is the creation and processing of the transactions :

```
// Generate transactions of each type and pass to the clerks
for(int i = 1; i <= transactionCount; i++)
{
  // Generate a credit of $50 to $75
  int amount = (int)(50. + 25.*Math.random());

  // Generate a random account index for credit operation
  int select = ((int)(accounts.length*Math.random()))%accounts.length;
  totalCredits[select] += amount;          // Keep total credit tally

  // Wait until the first clerk is free
  while(clerk1.isBusy())
    try
    {
      Thread.sleep(25);                  // Busy busy so try later
    }
```

```
      catch(InterruptedException e)
      {
        System.out.println(e);
      }
```

```
    clerk1.doCredit(accounts[select], amount);   // Now do the credit
```

```
    // Generate a debit of $30 to $60
    amount = (int)(30.+30.*Math.random());
```

```
    // Generate a random account index for debit operation
    select = ((int)(accounts.length*Math.random()))%accounts.length;
    totalDebits[select] += amount;                // Keep total debit tally
```

```
    // Wait until the second clerk is free
    while(clerk2.isBusy())
      try
      {
        Thread.sleep(25);                        // Busy busy so try later
      }
      catch(InterruptedException e)
      {
        System.out.println(e);
      }
```

```
    clerk2.doDebit(accounts[select], amount);      // Now do the debit
  }
```

3 The last modification to the method **main()** is for outputting the results. We now do this in a loop:

```
for(int i = 0; i < accounts.length; i++)
  System.out.println(
     "Original balance  : $" + initialBalance[i] + "\n" +
     "Total credits     : $" + totalCredits[i] + "\n" +
     "Total debits      : $" + totalDebits[i] + "\n" +
     "Final balance     : $" + accounts[i].getBalance() + "\n" +
     "Should be         : $" + (initialBalance[i] + totalCredits[i] -
                                      totalDebits[i]) + "\n");
```

This is much the same as before except that we now extract values from the arrays we have created. If you run this version it will, of course, work perfectly. A typical set of results are:

```
Original balance  : $500
Total credits     : $713
Total debits      : $491
Final balance     : $722
Should be         : $722
```

```
Original balance    : $800
Total credits       : $480
Total debits        : $384
Final balance       : $896
Should be           : $896
```

How It Works

We now allocate arrays for the initial account balances, the total of credits and debits for each account, and the accounts themselves. The number of initializing values in the **initialBalance[]** array will determine the number of elements in each of the arrays. In the **for** loop, we create each of the accounts with the appropriate initial balance, and initialize the **totalCredits[]** and **totalDebits[]** arrays to zero.

In the modified transactions loop, we select the account from the array for both the debit and the credit transactions by generating a random index value which we store in the variable, **select**. We use the **%** operator to ensure that **select** will never have the value of **accounts.length**. Although the cast to type **int** will round down the **double** value from the expression in parentheses, the result can still be **accounts.length** if the value returned from the **random()** method is exactly 1.0. Using the **%** operator will produce 0 in this case so **select** will have values between **0** and **(accounts.length − 1)**. The index **select** is also used to keep a tally of the total of the transactions of each type.

This is all well and good, but by declaring the methods in the class **Bank** as **synchronized**, we're limiting the program quite significantly. No debit operation of any kind can be carried out while a credit operation is in progress and vice versa. This is unnecessarily restrictive since there's no reason why a credit for one account shouldn't be carried out while a debit for a different account is in progress. What we really want is to just constrain the program to prevent overlapping of operations on the same account, and this is where declaring blocks of code can help.

Let's consider the methods in the class **Bank** once more. What we really want is the code in the methods to be synchronized such that simultaneous processing of the same account is prevented.

Try It Out—Applying synchronized Statement Blocks

We can do this with the following changes:

```
class Bank
{
  // Perform a credit operation
  public void credit(Account theAccount, int amount)
  {
    synchronized(theAccount)
    {
      int balance = theAccount.getBalance();    // Get the current balance
```

```
    // Checking can take time...
    try
    {
      Thread.sleep(100);
    }
    catch(InterruptedException e)
    {
      System.out.println(e);
    }

    balance += amount;                    // Update the balance...
    theAccount.setBalance(balance);       // ...and put it back.
  }
}

// Perform a debit operation
public void debit(Account theAccount, int amount)
{
  synchronized(theAccount)
  {
    int balance = theAccount.getBalance();

    // Debits require even more checks...
    try
    {
      Thread.sleep(150);
    }
    catch(InterruptedException e)
    {
      System.out.println(e);
    }

    balance -= amount;                    // Update the balance...
    theAccount.setBalance(balance);       // ...and put it back.
  }
}
}
```

How It Works

The variable name in parentheses following the keyword **synchronized** specifies the object for which the synchronization applies. Once one synchronized code block is entered with a given account object, no other code block can be entered that has been synchronized with the same object. For example, if the **credit()** method is called with the object **accounts[1]** as an argument, the execution of the method **debit()** with the same object passed to it as an argument will be blocked until the **credit()** method terminates.

The object in a synchronized code block acts rather like a baton in a relay race that serves to synchronize the runners in the team. Only the runner with the baton is allowed to run. The next runner in the team can only run once they get hold of the baton. Of course, in any race there will be several different batons so you can have several sets of runners. In the same way, you can specify several different sets of **synchronized** code blocks in a class, each controlled by a different object. It is important to realize that code blocks that are synchronized with respect to a particular object don't have to be in the same class. They can be anywhere in your program where the appropriate object can be specified.

If you want to verify that we really are overlapping these operations in this example, you can add output statements to the beginning and end of each method in the class **Bank**. Outputting the type of operation, the amount and whether it is the start or end of the transaction will be sufficient to identify them. For example, you could modify the **credit()** method in the **Bank** class to:

```
public void credit(Account theAccount, int amount)
  {
    System.out.println("Start credit of " + amount);
    synchronized(theAccount)
    {
      // Code to process the transaction as before...
    }
    System.out.println("End credit of " + amount);
  }
```

You can modify the **debit()** method in a similar way.

If you want to check that overlapping debits and credits on the same account are inhibited, you can comment out the calculation of the value for **select** for the debit operation in the **for** loop in **main()**. This modification is shown shaded:

```
// Generate a random account index for debit operation
int select = 1;
// select = ((int)(accounts.length*Math.random()))%accounts.length;
totalDebits[select] += amount;                  // Keep total debit tally
```

This will make the debit apply to the same account as the previous credit.

Deadlocks

Since you can synchronize code blocks for a particular object virtually anywhere in your program, there's potential for a particularly nasty kind of bug called a **deadlock**. This involves a mutual interdependence between two threads. This arises when one thread executes some code synchronized on a given object, **theObject** say, and then needs to execute another method that contains code synchronized on another object, **theOtherObject** say. Before this occurs though, a second thread executes some code synchronized to **theOtherObject**, and needs to execute a method containing code synchronized to **theObject**. This situation is illustrated here:

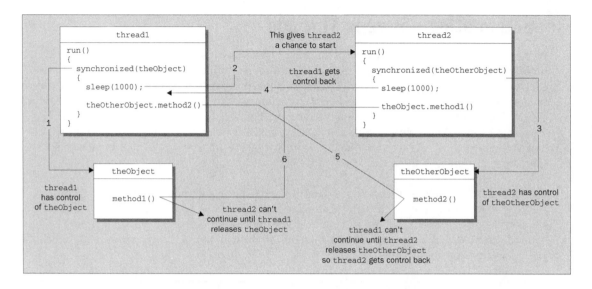

The sequence of events is as follows:

- **thread1** starts first, and synchronizes on **theObject**

- **thread1** then calls **sleep()** so **thread2** can start

- **thread2** starts and synchronizes on **theOtherObject**

- **thread2** then calls **sleep()** allowing **thread1** another go

- **thread1** tries to call **method2()** for **theOtherObject**, but it can't until the block in **thread2** that is synchronized on **theOtherObject** completes execution

- **thread2** gets another go because **thread1** can't proceed, and tries to call **method1()** for **theObject**. This can't proceed until the block in **thread1** that is synchronized on **theObject** completes execution

Neither thread has any possibility of continuing—they are deadlocked. Finding and fixing this sort of problem can be quite difficult, particularly if your program is complicated and has other threads which will continue to execute.

You can create a trivial deadlock in the last example by making the **for** loop in **main()** synchronized to one of the accounts. For example:

```
synchronized(accounts[1])
for(int i = 1; i <= transactionCount; i++)
{
   // code for generating transactions etc...
}
```

A deadlock occurs as soon as a transaction for **accounts[1]** arises because the method in **theBank** object that is called to handle the transaction will be synchronized to the same object, and can't execute until the loop ends. Of course, the loop can't continue until the method in **theBank** object terminates.

Communicating between Threads

We've seen how we can lock methods or code blocks using synchronization to avoid the problems that uncontrolled thread execution can cause. While this gives us a degree of control, we're still introducing inefficiencies into the program. In the last example, there were several occasions where we used a loop to wait for a clerk thread to complete an operation before the current thread could sensibly continue. For example, we couldn't pass a transaction to a **Clerk** object while that object was still busy with the previous transaction. Our solution to this was to use a **while** loop to test the busy status of the **Clerk** object from time to time but there's a better way.

The **Object** class defines the methods, **wait()**, **notify()** and **notifyAll()**, that you can use to provide a more efficient way of dealing with this kind of situation. Since all classes are derived from **Object**, all classes inherit these methods. You must only call these methods from within a **synchronized** method, or from within a synchronized code block. The functions that these methods perform are:

Method	Description
wait()	There are three overloaded versions of this method. This version has no parameters and suspends the current thread until the **notify()** method for the object to which the **wait()** method belongs, is called. Note that when **wait()** is called, it releases the synchronization lock on the object, so another method or code block synchronized on the same object can be called. This will allow other threads to call **wait()** for the same object.
	Since all versions of the **wait()** method can throw an **InterruptedException**, you must call it in a **try** block with a **catch** block for this exception, or indicate that the method calling it throws this exception.
wait(long timeout)	This version suspends the current thread until the number of milliseconds specified by the argument has expired, or until the **notify()** method for the object to which the **wait()** method belongs, is called, if that occurs sooner.
wait(long timeout, int nanos)	This version works in the same way as the previous version, except the time interval is specified by two arguments, the first in milliseconds, and the second in nanoseconds.
notify()	This will restart the thread that has called the **wait()** method for the object to which the **notify()** method belongs. If no threads are waiting, the method does nothing.
notifyAll()	This will restart all threads that have called **wait()** for the object to which the **notifyAll()** method belongs.

Although the action of each of these methods is quite simple, applying them can become very complex. You have the potential for multiple threads to be interacting through several objects with **synchronized** methods and code blocks. We'll just explore the basics by seeing how we can use **wait()** and **notify()** to get rid of a couple of the **while** loops we had in the last example.

Using wait() and notify()

In the **for** loop in **main()**, which generates the transactions and passes them to the **Clerk** objects, we have two **while** loops that call the **isBusy()** method. These were needed so that we don't pass a transaction to a clerk while the clerk is still busy. By altering the **Clerk** class a bit so that it can use **wait()** and **notify()**, we can eliminate the need for these.

Try It Out—Slimming Down the Transactions Loop

1 The code for the **for** loop in **main()** will be modified to:

```
// Generate transactions of each type and pass to the clerks
for(int i = 1; i <= transactionCount; i++)
{
  // Generate a credit of $50 to $75
  int amount = (int)(50. + 25.*Math.random());

  // Generate a random account index
  int select = ((int)(accounts.length*Math.random()))%accounts.length;
  totalCredits[select] += amount;                // Keep total credit tally

  clerk1.doCredit(accounts[select], amount);  // Now do the credit

  // Generate a debit of $30 to $60
  amount = (int)(30. + 30.*Math.random());

  // Generate a random account index
  select = ((int)(accounts.length*Math.random()))%accounts.length;
  totalDebits[select] += amount;                 // Keep total debit tally

  clerk2.doDebit(accounts[select], amount);    // Now do the debit
}
```

This makes it a lot shorter.

2 All we need to do to make the program work without these loops is change the definition of the **Clerk** class. The first modification is to the **doCredit()** and **doDebit()** methods:

```
// Process a credit
synchronized public void doCredit(Account theAccount, int amount)
{
  if(transactionType != NONE)          // Is this object busy?
    try
    {
```

```
        wait();                              // Yes, so wait for notify call
      }
    catch(InterruptedException e)
    {
      System.out.println(e);
    }
  this.theAccount = theAccount;            // Remember the account
  transactionType = CREDIT;                // Set the transaction type
  this.amount = amount;                    // Store the amount
}

// Process a debit
synchronized public void doDebit(Account theAccount, int amount)
{
  if(transactionType != NONE)              // Is this thread busy?
    try
    {
      wait();                              // Yes, so wait for notify call
    }
    catch(InterruptedException e)
    {
      System.out.println(e);
    }
  this.theAccount = theAccount;            // Remember the account
  transactionType = DEBIT;                 // Set the transaction type
  this.amount = amount;                    // Store the amount
}
```

3 The **run()** method also does the processing of the transactions at the moment, but we can't call **notify()** in the **run()** method, since **run()** hasn't been declared as **synchronized**. What's more, we certainly don't want to declare **run()** as **synchronized**, because that would mean when **run()** was executing—which is all the time once the thread has started for a **Clerk** object—we would be prevented from calling the **doDebit()** or **doCredit()** methods.

What we can do is rejig the **run()** method so that we move the bits of code that will call **notify()** into a separate method that we can declare as **synchronized**:

```
// The working clerk...
public void run()
{
  while(true)
  {
    if(transactionType == NONE)
    { // We have no transaction
      try
      {
        Thread.sleep(150);
      }
      catch(InterruptedException e)
      {
```

```
        System.out.println(e);
      }
      continue;              // Go to the next loop iteration
    }
    doTransaction();         // Must be a transaction
  }
}

// Process a transaction
synchronized private void doTransaction()
{
  if(transactionType == CREDIT)
    theBank.credit(theAccount, amount);   // Execute a credit
  else if(transactionType == DEBIT)
    theBank.debit(theAccount, amount);    // Execute a debit
  transactionType = NONE;                 // Reset the transaction type
    notify();                             // Signal waiting thread
}
```

The example will now run without the need for checking whether the **Clerk** objects are busy in the transaction processing loop in **main()**.

4 With a small change to the **isBusy()** method in the **Clerk** class, we can eliminate the need for the **while** loop before we output the results in **main()**:

```
synchronized public void isBusy()
{
  if(transactionType != NONE)    // Is this object busy?
    try
    {
      wait();                    // Yes, so wait for notify call
    }
    catch(InterruptedException e)
    {
      System.out.println(e);
    }
  return;                        // It is free now
}
```

5 The **while** loop in **main()** can be replaced by:

```
// Wait if clerks are busy
clerk1.isBusy();
clerk2.isBusy();
```

How It Works

Each of the methods, **doCredit()** and **doDebit()**, calls the **wait()** method if the value stored in **transactionType** is other than **NONE**, as this means the object is still being used to process a credit or a debit. This will result in the current thread (which is the main thread) being suspended until the **notify()** for the object is called. All we need to decide now, is where we'll call **notify()** to get the thread going again. Of course, when the thread is suspended through calling the **wait()** method, this releases the constraint on other synchronized methods for this object, so any of them can be called by another thread.

After rewriting the **Clerk** class's **run()** method, we have the transaction processing in another **synchronized** method, **doTransaction()**, and we can call **notify()** in this method to allow the main thread to continue when it has been suspended through calling **wait()**.

Because we've declared the **isBusy()** method as **synchronized**, we can call the **wait()** method to suspend the current thread if transactions are still being processed. Since we don't return from the method until the outstanding transaction is complete, we have no need of a **boolean** return value.

Suspending Thread Execution

The **Thread** class has an instance method, **suspend()** which you can use to halt execution of the currently executing thread. This is complemented by another instance method in the **Thread** class, **resume()**, that you call to restart a thread that has been suspended by calling **suspend()**. Calling **resume()** for a thread that is already executing is quite legal and causes no problems. We can see how to use these by applying them to the previous example to eliminate the need to call the **sleep()** method in the **run()** method defined in the class **Clerk**.

Try It Out—Using suspend()

1 In the method **run()** in the class **Clerk**, we want to suspend execution of the current thread when the value stored in the instance variable **transactionType** is **NONE**. To call the **suspend()** method we need access to the object that represents the current thread. So how do we get at it from the **run()** method in the **Clerk** class? We use the **static** method in the **Thread** class, **currentThread()**, as follows:

```
public void run()
{
  while(true)
  {
    if(transactionType == NONE)          // Nothing to do?
      Thread.currentThread().suspend();  // Then suspend the thread
    doTransaction();                     // Must be a transaction
  }
}
```

2 You need to modify the **for** loop that generates transactions to:

```
// Generate transactions of each type and pass to the clerks
for(int i = 1; i <= transactionCount; i++)
{
```

```
// Generate a credit of $50 to $75
int amount = (int)(50. + 25.*Math.random());

// Generate a random account index
int select = ((int)(accounts.length*Math.random()))%accounts.length;
totalCredits[select] += amount;              // Keep total credit tally

clerk1.doCredit(accounts[select], amount);   // Now do the credit
clerk1Thread.resume();                        // Resume thread execution

// Generate a debit of $30 to $60
amount = (int)(30. + 30.*Math.random());

// Generate a random account index
select = ((int)(accounts.length*Math.random()))%accounts.length;
totalDebits[select] += amount;               // Keep total debit tally

clerk2.doDebit(accounts[select], amount);     // Now do the debit
clerk2Thread.resume();                        // Resume thread execution
}
```

How It Works

The **try** block we had in the previous **Clerk** class's **run()** method is replaced by the single shaded statement that calls **suspend()** for the current thread. The method **currentThread()** returns the **Thread** object for the currently executing thread, so we use this to call the **suspend()** method for this object. Execution of this thread will continue with the next statement when the **resume()** method is called for the same **Thread** object. We can do this in **main()**.

In the **main()** method, after we have called **doDebit()** or **doCredit()** for a **Clerk** object, we call **resume()** for the appropriate **Thread** object. This will restart the thread if it is suspended, and have no effect if it is already running.

Thread Priorities

All threads have a priority which determines which thread is executed when several threads are waiting for their turn. The possible values for thread priority are defined in **static** data members of the class **Thread**. These members are of type **int**, and declared as **final**. The maximum thread priority is defined by the member **MAX_PRIORITY** which has the value 10. The minimum priority is **MIN_PRIORITY** defined as 1. The value of the default priority that is assigned to the main thread in a program is **NORM_PRIORITY** which is set to 5. When you create a thread, its priority will be the same as that of the thread that created it.

You can modify the priority of a thread by calling the **setPriority()** method for the **Thread** object. This method accepts an argument of type **int** which defines the new priority for the thread. An **IllegalArgumentException** will be thrown if you specify a priority that is less than **MIN_PRIORITY** or greater than **MAX_PRIORITY**.

453

Of course, if you're going to be messing about with the priorities of the threads in your program, you need to be able to find out the current priority for a thread. You can do this by calling the **getPriority()** method for the **Thread** object. This will return the current priority for the thread as a value of type **int**.

Using Thread Priorities

You could set priorities for the threads by adding statements to **main()** in the last example:

```
clerk1Thread.setPriority(3);     // Credits are a low priority
clerk2Thread.setPriority(8);     // Debits are a high priority
```

You can put these statements following the call to the **start()** method for each of the **Thread** objects for the clerks. However, this won't have much effect in our program since one clerk can't get ahead of the other. This is because each thread only queues one transaction.

In the interests of learning more about how thread priorities affect the execution of your program, let's change the example once again to enable a **Clerk** object to queue transactions. The best way to do this is to use a class **Vector** which we discussed in the previous chapter, so let's change the example to incorporate that.

Try It Out—Setting Thread Priorities

1 First we can define a simple class to define a transaction:

```
class Transaction
{
  private Account theAccount;        // Account for transaction
  private int amount;                // Amount for transaction
  private int type;                  // Type of transaction

  // Constructor
  public Transaction(Account theAccount, int amount, int type)
  {
    this.theAccount = theAccount;    // Store the account
    this.amount = amount;            // Store the amount
    this.type = type;                // Store the transaction type
  }

  public Account getAccount()
  { return theAccount; }             // Return the account

  public int getAmount()
  { return amount; }                 // Return the amount

  public int getType()
  { return type; }                   // Return the transaction type
}
```

2 We can now extend the **Clerk** class to handle **Transaction** objects, and to store transactions in a **Vector** object:

```
import java.util.Vector;

public class Clerk implements Runnable
{
  static final int CREDIT = 1;
  static final int DEBIT = 2;
  Bank theBank;
  private Vector transactions = new Vector(10,2); // Transaction buffer

  public Clerk(Bank theBank )
  {
    this.theBank = theBank;
  }

  public void doCredit(Account theAccount, int amount)
  {
    // Add the transaction to the Vector
    transactions.addElement(new Transaction(theAccount, amount, CREDIT));
  }

  public void doDebit(Account theAccount, int amount)
  {
    transactions.addElement(new Transaction(theAccount, amount, DEBIT));
  }

  public void run()
  {
    while(true)
    {
      if(transactions.isEmpty())
        Thread.currentThread().suspend();    // Suspend thread execution
      else
        doTransaction();                     // Must be a transaction
    }
  }

  // Process a transaction
  synchronized private void doTransaction()
  {
    // Get the first transaction, first in - first out
    Transaction current = (Transaction)transactions.firstElement();

    if(current.getType() == CREDIT)
      theBank.credit(current.getAccount(), current.getAmount());
    else
      theBank.debit(current.getAccount(), current.getAmount());

    transactions.removeElementAt(0);      // Remove the first element
```

```
    if(transactions.isEmpty())           // Any transactions left?
      notify();                          // No, notify we are free
  }

  synchronized public void isBusy()
  {
    if(!transactions.isEmpty())  // Still got transactions to process?
      try
      {
        wait();                          // Yes, so wait for notify call
      catch(InterruptedException e)
      {
        System.out.println(e);
      }
    return;                             // It is free now
  }
}
```

3 If you add an output statement to each of the methods in the **Bank** class, you'll be able to see how the processing of transactions proceeds. For the **credit()** method, you could add the statement:

```
System.out.println("Start credit " + amount);
```

and a similar statement in the **debit()** method.

With the priorities set by the calls to **setPriority()** we saw earlier, the processing of credits should run ahead of the processing of debits although the fact that the time to process a debit is longer than the time for a credit will also have a significant effect. To make the thread priority the determining factor, set the times in the calls to the **sleep()** method in the **Bank** class to the same value. You could then try changing the values for priorities around to see what happens to the sequence in which transactions are processed.

How It Works

The **Transaction** class just stores the three basic values defining a transaction and provides public methods for retrieving the value of these.

We've added the **Vector** object, **transactions**, to the class which has an initial capacity for ten transactions, and will add capacity for two more each time it runs out. We'll call the **isEmpty()** method for the **Vector** to determine whether there's any work to do, so we no longer need the variable **NONE** to tell us when there are no transactions waiting. The **run()** method is much the same as before, except that it now calls **isEmpty()** for the **Vector** to determine when the method **suspend()** should be called for the thread. If **isEmpty()** returns **false**, then **doTransaction()** is called.

The **doTransaction()** method obtains the first object in the **Vector**, so the transactions will be processed in the sequence in which they were added to the **Vector**. The type of the transaction is used to decide which method in **theBank** object should be called to handle it.

When the transaction has been processed, it's deleted from the **Vector** by calling the **removeAt()** method with an index of 0.

Because any number of transactions can be buffered in the **Vector**, we no longer need to declare the **doDebit()** and **doCredit()** methods as **synchronized**. They each just add the transaction to the end of the **Vector**. With the **doTransaction()** and **isBusy()** methods declared as **synchronized**, we have the mechanism to delay outputting the results in the main thread until all transactions have been processed.

Grouping Threads

In a large program, you can have a large number of threads. In this case it's usually convenient to collect related threads together into a group. When you create a group of threads, you can operate on them as a group. For example, you can stop, suspend and resume all the threads in a thread group in one go. Grouping threads also limits the ability of threads in one group to change the priorities of threads in another. A group of threads is represented by an object of the class **ThreadGroup**, and a **ThreadGroup** object can contain other thread groups as well as threads. As you'll see when we get to the practicalities, a thread is created as a member of a thread group by specifying a **ThreadGroup** object as an argument to a **Thread** constructor.

Creating Thread Groups

All threads are members of a thread group by default since the method where the execution of a program starts is in a default thread. When a thread creates a **ThreadGroup** object, unless it is specified otherwise, the thread group it represents will be a member of the thread group that contains the current thread. For example, if you create a **ThreadGroup** object from the main thread with the following statement:

```
ThreadGroup threadGroup1 = new ThreadGroup("threadGroupName1");
```

then **threadGroup1** will also be a member of the default thread group.

> *Note that the **String** passed to the constructor is a name for the thread group, and is mandatory. If you pass a **null** as the argument, the constructor will throw a **NullPointerException**, and, of course, if you omit the argument, the program will not compile.*

In the main thread, you could create a thread in the thread group we have just constructed with the statement:

```
Thread thread2 = new Thread(threadGroup1, threadName2);
```

The first argument to the **Thread** constructor is the **ThreadGroup** object, and the second argument is a **String** object which contains the name of the thread. Perversely, this can be **null** if you don't want to assign a name to the thread.

> *The names for threads and thread groups are purely for convenience when outputting information about a thread or its group. They aren't used in any other way. Don't confuse these names with the names of the variables referencing the* **Thread** *and* **ThreadGroup** *objects, although there's no reason why you can't give a thread or a thread group the same name as the object which it represents.*

Thread Group Hierarchies

As a consequence of the way they are created, thread groups are inevitably arranged in the sort of tree structure that is illustrated here:

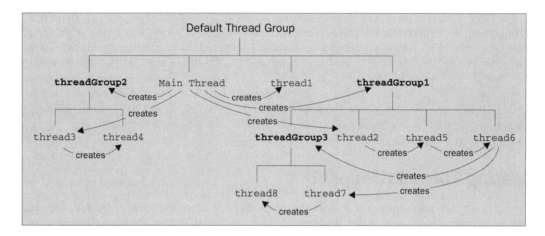

The diagram illustrates an example tree structure of threads and thread groups for a program, and a possible sequence in which the threads and thread groups might have been created. All thread groups in a program will have the default thread group at the top of the tree. This thread group will itself be contained in a thread group with the name **"System"** which contains the Java system that manages your program. The numbers in the names of the threads and thread groups in the diagram indicate the sequence in which they were created. Of course, this structure could have been created in a variety of ways.

The main thread, which is the starting point for execution, generates a thread in the default thread group, as well as two further thread groups. Thread groups are automatically members of the thread group in which they are created, so both thread groups are part of the default thread group. When a thread creates another thread without identifying a **ThreadGroup** object in the constructor, the new thread will be a member of the same thread group as the current thread, so you could deduce that **thread5** and **thread6** were created without specifying a thread group object, whereas **thread2** was created by specifying the **threadGroup1** object in the **Thread** constructor.

Thread Group Operations

So what can you do with threads collected in a thread group that you couldn't do before? Well, the **ThreadGroup** class defines the following methods that operate on all threads that are members of a thread group, or any subgroup of a thread group:

Method	Description
stop()	Stops all threads in the current thread group, and all threads in all subgroups of the current thread group by calling the **stop()** method for each **Thread** object.
suspend()	Suspends all threads in the current thread group, and all threads in all subgroups of the current thread group by calling the **suspend()** method for each **Thread** object.
resume()	Resumes all threads in the current thread group, and all threads in all subgroups of the current thread group by calling the **resume()** method for each **Thread** object.

You can also set a maximum priority for threads in a thread group by calling the **setMaxPriority()** method. This has the interesting property that it doesn't affect threads in the thread group that already have a higher priority. You can use this to ensure that selected threads in a thread group will always have a higher priority than the rest. For example, assuming **thread2** is a member of **threadGroup1**, you could ensure **thread2** always had a higher priority than the other threads in the group with the statements:

```
thread2.setPriority(8);            // thread2 has priority 8
threadGroup1.setMaxPriority(6);    // All others a maximum of 6
```

A thread group can be specified as daemon by calling the **setDaemon()** method:

```
threadGroup1.setDaemon();          // Set thread group as daemon
```

Calling the **setDaemon()** method for a **ThreadGroup** object just ensures that the thread group will be destroyed when all its threads are stopped. This has no effect on the threads in the group. When necessary, you still set an existing thread in this thread group as daemon by calling the **setDaemon()** method for the **Thread** object.

Querying a Thread Group

You can get quite a bit of information about the members of a thread group, and about the thread group itself using methods in the **ThreadGroup** class. The methods that provide information about the members of a thread group are:

Method	Description
`int threadsCount()`	Returns the count of the total number of active threads in this thread group.
`int allThreadsCount()`	Returns the count of the total number of active threads in this thread group, and any subgroup of the current group.
`int groupsCount()`	Returns the count of the total number of active thread groups in this thread group.
`int allGroupsCount()`	Returns the count of the total number of active thread groups in this thread group, or any subgroup of this group.
`Thread[] threads()`	Returns an array containing all the **Thread** objects for the active threads in this thread group.
`Thread[] allThreads()`	Returns an array containing all the **Thread** objects for the active threads in this thread group, or any subgroup of this group.
`ThreadGroup[] groups()`	Returns an array of type **ThreadGroup** containing all the **ThreadGroup** objects for the active thread groups in this thread group.
`ThreadGroup[] allGroups()`	Returns an array of type **ThreadGroup** containing all the **ThreadGroup** objects for the active thread groups in this thread group, or any subgroup of this group.
`int getMaxPriority()`	Returns a value of type **int** that is the maximum priority for any new threads created in the current group.
`list()`	Lists on **System.out** the threads and thread groups by name that are members of the current thread group, and each subgroup of the current group.

You can use the following methods, defined in the **ThreadGroup** class, to obtain information about a thread group:

Method	Description
`String getName()`	Returns a **String** containing the name of the thread group that you specified as an argument in the constructor call.
`ThreadGroup getParent()`	Returns a **ThreadGroup** object that represents the thread group containing the current thread group. If the current thread group has no parent—which is the case for the default thread group—then **null** is returned.
`boolean isDaemon()`	Returns **true** if the thread group is daemon, and false **otherwise**.
`boolean parentOf (ThreadGroup g)`	Returns **true** if the current thread group is identical to the argument, or is a parent of the argument, and **false** otherwise.
`String toString()`	Returns a **String** containing the name and maximum priority for the thread group.

460

You can easily produce a utility method that will list all threads and thread groups from any point in a program.

Try It Out—Getting *Thread* and *ThreadGroup* Information

1 To make this of general use you could make it a **static** method in a separate class:

```
class Utility
{
  public static void listAllThreads()
  {
    // Get the current thread group object
    ThreadGroup next = Thread.currentThread().getThreadGroup();
    ThreadGroup last = next;        // Last non-null thread group
    while (next != null )
    {
      last = next;                  // Save the last non-null object
      next = last.getParent();      // Get its parent
    }
    last.list();                    // List using highest thread group
    return;
  }
}
```

2 Let's add a thread group to our banking example. We can define the **ThreadGroup** object in **main()** just before we define the **Thread** objects. You can amend this bit of code in **main()** to:

```
// Create the threads for the clerks as daemon, and start them off
ThreadGroup theGroup = new ThreadGroup("theGroup");
theGroup.setDaemon(true);
Thread clerk1Thread = new Thread(theGroup, clerk1, "clerk1");
Thread clerk2Thread = new Thread(theGroup, clerk2, "clerk2");
clerk1Thread.setDaemon(true);    // Set first as daemon
clerk2Thread.setDaemon(true);    // Set second as daemon
clerk1Thread.start();            // Start the first
clerk2Thread.start();            // Start the second
clerk1Thread.setPriority(3);     // Credits are a low priority
clerk2Thread.setPriority(8);     // Debits are a high priority
```

3 If you add the source file for the **Utility** class to the directory for the program, you can also add code to **main()** to output information about the program's threads and thread groups. Just put the following statement immediately following the **for** loop that generates transactions:

```
Utility.listAllThreads();        // Get program thread info
```

If you run the program again, in addition to the output that you got before, the program will produce the following output on the program threads:

```
java.lang.ThreadGroup[name=system,maxpri=10]
    Thread[Finalizer thread,1,system]
    java.lang.ThreadGroup[name=main,maxpri=10]
        Thread[main,5,main]
        java.lang.ThreadGroup[name=theGroup,maxpri=10]
            Thread[clerk1,5,theGroup]
            Thread[clerk2,5,theGroup]
```

How It Works

In stage two, after creating the **ThreadGroup** object and setting it as daemon, we create the clerk threads as members of this thread group. The third argument to the **Thread** constructor specifies the name to be used to identify the thread in any **list()** output.

For each thread group in the output, the threads and thread groups that are members are shown indented. As you see, we have three thread groups, a **system** group, the default group **main**, and the group **theGroup** that we created in **main()**. The **system** group contains the **Finalizer** thread which is concerned with destroying objects that are no longer required, and the default thread group, **main**. The thread group **main** contains the thread for **main()**, and the thread group we create in the method **main()**, **theGroup**. This thread group contains the two threads our program explicitly creates, **clerk1** and **clerk2**.

Summary

In this chapter you have learned about threads and how you can create and manage them. We will be using threads from time to time in examples later in this book so be sure you don't move on from here without being comfortable with how you implement your programs to use threads.

The essential points that we have covered in this chapter are:

> Threads are subtasks in a program that can execute in parallel

> A thread is represented by an object of the class **Thread**. Execution of a thread begins with the execution of the **run()** method defined in the class **Thread**

> You define the code to be executed in a thread by implementing the **run()** method in a class derived from **Thread**, or in a class that implements the interface **Runnable**

> A thread specified as **daemon** will cease execution when the thread that created it ends

> A thread that isn't a daemon thread is called a **user thread**. A user thread will not be terminated automatically when the thread that created it ends

> You start execution of a thread by calling the **start()** method for its **Thread** object. You can stop execution of a thread by calling the **stop()** method for its **Thread** object

▶ Methods can be declared as **synchronized**. Only one **synchronized** instance method for an object can execute at any given time. Only one **synchronized** **static** method for a class can execute at one time

▶ A code block can be declared as **synchronized** to an object. Only one synchronized code block for an object can execute at any given time

▶ In a synchronized method or code block, you can call the **wait()** method inherited from the class **Object** to halt execution of a thread. Execution of the thread will continue when the **notify()** method inherited from **Object** is called. The **notify()** method can only be called from a method or code block that is synchronized to the same object as the method or block that contains the **wait()** method that halted the thread

▶ You can call the **suspend()** method for a **Thread** object to suspend execution of a thread. Execution of the thread will continue when the **resume()** method for the **Thread** object is called

▶ Threads can be collected into a group represented by a **ThreadGroup** object

Exercises

1 Modify the last example in the chapter to incorporate an array of clerks, each running in their own thread, and each able to handle both debits and credits.

2 Extend the previous example to incorporate two supervisors for two teams of clerks, where the supervisors each run in their own thread. The supervisor threads should originate transactions and pass them to the clerks they supervise.

3 Modify the previous examples so that the supervisors are in one thread group, and each supervisor thread creates the clerk objects that it supervises and their threads. The clerks for each supervisor should also be in their own thread group. Output the structure of the threads and thread groups for the program.

Creating Windows

In this chapter, we will investigate how to create a window for a Java application and we will take a first look at some of the components we can put together to create a graphical user interface in Java.

You will learn:

- How to create a resizable window
- What components and containers are
- What components are defined by classes in the **java.awt** package
- How you can add components to a window
- How to control the layout of components
- How to create a menu bar for a window
- How to add menus to a menu bar
- How to create a pull-down menu of menu items for each menu on a menu bar
- What a menu shortcut is and how you can add a shortcut for a menu item
- What the restrictions on the capabilities of an applet are
- How to convert an application into an applet

Creating a Window

A basic window in Java is represented by an object of a library class, **Window**. This class is in the package **java.awt**—'awt' being an abbreviation for Abstract Windowing Toolkit. This package supports windows programming. It contains a vast number of classes which cover all aspects of the visual appearance of a window, including all the tools you need to create and manage windows, dialogs, menus, toolbars, mouse operations and so on.

Objects of the class **Window** are hardly ever used directly since borders and a title bar are a fairly basic prerequisite for a window, and this class provides neither. The library class **Frame** is a much more useful class. It is derived from **Window** and defines a top-level resizable window with a title bar, to which you can add menus. You can display a window by creating an object of type **Frame**, calling a method for the object to set the size of the window, and then calling a method to display the window. Let's try that right away.

Try It Out—Framing a Window

Here's the code:

```
import java.awt.*;              // Include the classes for window operations

public class TryWindow
{
  // The window object
  static Frame aWindow = new Frame("This is the Window Title");

  public static void main(String[] args)
  {
    aWindow.setBounds(100, 50, 400, 150);      // Set position and size
    aWindow.setVisible(true);                  // Display the window
  }
}
```

The program will display the window shown:

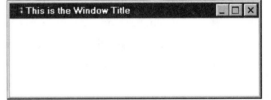

How It Works

The **import** statement adds the definitions for all the classes in the package **java.awt** to our program. This will be virtually standard from now on since most of our programs will be using windows. The object of type **Frame** is created as a **static** member of the class **TryWindow**, so it will be created automatically even though we do not create objects of type **TryWindow**. The argument to the constructor defines the title to be displayed for the window.

The method **main()** calls two methods for **aWindow**. The method **setBounds()** defines the size and position of the window from arguments which correspond to the x and y coordinates of the top-left corner of our application window relative to the top-left corner of the display screen and the width and height of the window in pixels. The screen coordinate system has the origin point, (0, 0), at the top-left corner of the screen, with the positive x-axis running left to right and the positive y-axis from top to bottom. The positive y-axis in screen coordinates is therefore in the opposite direction to the usual Cartesian coordinate system.

466

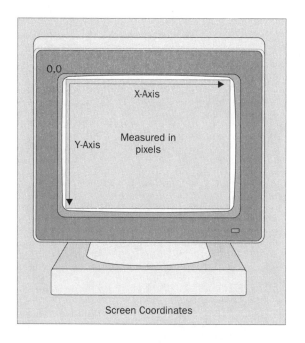

Screen Coordinates

The top-left corner of our application window is at position (100, 50) and, since the window will be 400 pixels wide and 150 pixels high, the bottom right corner will be at position (500, 200). The actual physical width and height will depend on the size of your screen and the display resolution. For a given screen size, the higher your display resolution, the smaller the window will be, simply because the pixels on the screen will be closer together. We will see how Java gets around this potential problem later on in this chapter.

The method **setVisible()** with the argument set to **true**, displays the window on top of any other windows that are currently visible on the screen. If you wanted to hide the window somewhere else in the program, you could just call **setVisible()** again with the argument **false**.

It's a very nice window, but not overly useful. All you can do with it is resize and reshape it. You can drag the borders and you can maximize and minimize it. The close icon doesn't work because our program has no provision for closing the program. You will have to get the operating system to end the task; under Windows 95, switching to the DOS window and pressing *Ctrl-C* will do it. In fact you will have to wait until the next chapter to find out how to make the close icon close the window and the application.

The **setBounds()** method is an inherited member of the **Frame** class. However, its origins don't lie in the class **Window**, instead it goes further back to the **Component** class. The **Component** class defines a lot of different things that you can display including **Window** and **Frame** objects and more besides. Let's take some time to look a little deeper into the super-classes of the class **Frame**, so we get a better feel for the capabilities of the **Frame** class.

Components and Containers

The **Component** class is the grandmother of most of the things you can display in a window-based program. When we refer to a **component**, we mean an object of any class derived from the **Component** class. You can't actually create an object of type **Component** because the **Component** class is **abstract** (a keyword we met in Chapter 6). Part of the class hierarchy with **Component** as a base is shown below. The arrows in the diagram point towards the super-class.

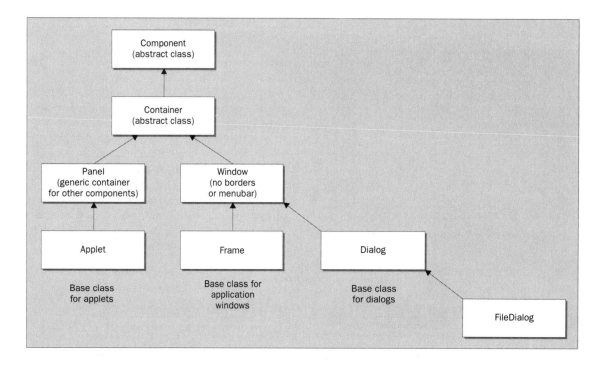

This shows just a few of the sub-classes of **Component**—there are several others which we will look at in a moment. The sub-classes shown here all have the class **Container** as a base, whereas others don't. All the classes derived from **Container** can contain other objects of any of the classes derived from **Component**, and are referred to generically as **containers**. Since the **Container** class is a sub-class of the **Component** class, every container object is a **Component** too, so a container can contain other containers. The exception that proves the rule is the **Window** class and its descendants, which can't be contained. Finally, it's important to note that the **Container** class is an **abstract** class, so you can only create objects that are containers by using one of the sub-classes of **Container**.

FYI

As you can see, the class **Applet**, which is a base class for all applets, is derived from **Component** via the **Container** class, so an applet will inherit the same methods from the **Container** and **Component** classes as the **Window** and **Frame** classes. You should note that the **Applet** class is in the package **java.applet** whereas all the others are in **java.awt**. The package **java.applet** is tiny—it only contains the one class plus three related interfaces.

Differences between Container Components

The basic difference between a **Frame** object and a **Window** object is that a **Frame** object represents the main window for an application, whereas a **Window** object does not—you always need a **Frame** object to create a **Window** object, for example, as a pop-up menu. The

468

constructor for the **Window** class requires a **Frame** object as an argument, and this **Frame** object is usually referred to as the **parent** of the **Window** object. A **Frame** object also has a border, is resizable and has a menu bar built in, to which you can add your own menu. A **Window** object has none of these things.

Since a **Frame** object is the top-level window in an application, its size and location are defined relative to the screen. We shall see how a bit later in this chapter. Since a **Window** object has a **Frame** as a parent, it is usually located relative to its parent.

We will be looking at dialogs later on in Chapter 14, but for the moment, you can see that a dialog is just a specialized type of **Window**. Thus a **Dialog** object will need to have a parent **Frame** object when it is created, just like a **Window** object.

A **Panel** object only has a role as an area in which you place things such as buttons that you will use to control the operation of a program. You can use **Panel** objects in applets and in applications.

Let's summarize how you would typically use the container classes:

Window	This class defines a window with no title bar and no borders. It is not usually used by itself.
Frame	Used as the basic Java application window. An object of this class has a title bar and provision for adding a menu. You can also add other components to it. You will usually sub-class this class to create a window class specific to your application. You can then draw in this window if you want to.
Dialog	Used to define a dialog for inputting data into a program.
FileDialog	Defines a dialog designed specifically for selecting a file.
Panel	This is used to contain and arrange other components. You cannot draw on a panel.
Applet	This is the base class for a Java applet—a program designed to run embedded in a web page. All applets have this class as a base. You can draw in an **Applet** and you can add other components to it too.

Of the six classes here, the **Applet**, **Frame** and **Dialog** classes have the most fundamental roles in your Java programs.

- The **Applet** class is always the base class for an applet. If your program class does not have **Applet** as a base class it cannot run in a web page.

- The **Frame** class is normally the base for the application window in a Java application.

- The **Dialog** class is the base for any dialogs that you need in your program. You usually code the creation of a dialog in response to some menu item in a **Window** object being clicked. However, note that dialogs can be used in both Java applications and applets.

The **Applet**, **Frame** and **Dialog** classes are all containers, since they have **Container** as a base class, and therefore they can contain any kind of component—and they are also all components themselves since they are derived ultimately from the **Component** class.

This is not all there is to components. There is another whole bunch of classes derived from **Component** that do not have **Container** as a base, so let's see what those can do for us.

Components that are not Containers

The other classes that are derived from the **Component** class are shown in the diagram. Objects of these classes are sometimes called **widgets**, the term being a contraction of **wi**ndow ga**dgets**.

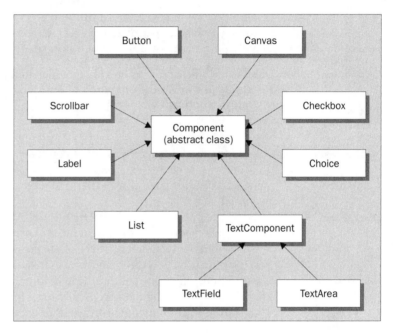

As we said earlier, these classes do not have **Container** as a base class and therefore cannot contain other components. Their sole reason for existence is to be contained in another object. Any of them can be contained within a **Window**, **Frame**, **Dialog**, **Applet** or **Panel** object, that is you can use them in applets and application windows.

> *The **TextComponent** class does not define a component as such. Its purpose is to act as a base class for the **TextField** and **TextArea** classes.*

These components provide you with the following capabilities:

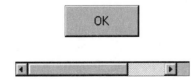

A **Button** object is a labeled button typified by the OK or Cancel button in a dialog.

A **Scrollbar** object provides either a horizontal or vertical scrollbar for scrolling text.

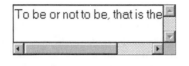

A **TextArea** component can display multiple lines of text that can be either editable or read-only. A **TextArea** object can also have horizontal and vertical scrollbars. It is typically used in a dialog to provide a list of choices, or to allow the text displayed to be edited.

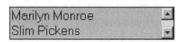

A **Label** object is a single line of read-only text.

A **List** object is a scrollable list of text items.

A **TextField** object displays a single line of editable text.

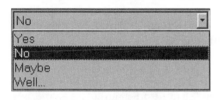

A **Choice** object is a pop-up menu of choices. This is sometimes referred to as a drop-down list box.

A **Checkbox** object is a GUI element that has two states, checked or unchecked. You check or uncheck a checkbox by clicking on it with the mouse.

Java displays these components in a program by calling on the standard representation of the components within the operating system. Therefore the physical appearance of all these components depends on the operating system environment within which your program executes. The examples shown are taken from Windows 95.

Most of these classes define simple user interface elements but the **Canvas** class is a little bit different. You can use the **Canvas** class in two ways. Firstly, you can use it as a base class when you define your own components. Secondly you can draw on a **Canvas** object. It is often a good idea to be able to separate the area in a window where you want to draw things from other areas, and this you can do using a **Canvas** object and a number of **Panel** objects, which would typically contain other components such as buttons. The **Canvas** or **Panel** classes are usually extended for drawing applications. We will be using both in a drawing application that we will be developing throughout the next few chapters, starting towards the end of this chapter.

Rather than go through a laundry list of all the methods for these components, we will introduce them in our examples, as necessary, throughout the rest of the book. Some of them we'll apply when we start to use dialogs in Chapter 14, since dialogs are often used to manage user input, although these components can be also be used in other contexts of course. Having said that, we will now look at the members of the **Component** class, as these are inherited by all of the above component classes.

471

Using Components

As we've seen, the **Frame** class is very important to the implementation of windowing applications. But, to understand what we can do with a **Frame** object, we need to examine what functionality it inherits from the **Component** and **Container** classes. We will look first at the capabilities that are provided by the **Component** class. Remember that all classes derived from **Component** will include this capability, including those we have just described that are not containers.

When a **Component** object is contained within another (which must be a sub-class of the **Container** class, of course), the outer **Component** object is referred to as the **parent**. You can find out what the parent of a **Component** is with the **getParent()** method that is defined in the **Component** class:

Container getParent()   Retrieves the parent of the **Component** object for which this method was called. If there is no parent, **null** is returned.

The return value is of type **Container**, a sub-class of **Component**, because only an object of a sub-class of **Container** can contain other **Component** objects.

Component Attributes

Remember that everything we are discussing here applies to buttons, scrollbars, windows and all the other components that have **Component** as a super-class. The **Component** class defines attributes which record the following information about an object:

▶ The position is stored as (x, y) coordinates. This fixes where the object is in relation to its container in the coordinate system of the container object

▶ The name of the component is stored as a **String** object

▶ The size is recorded as values for the width and the height of the object

▶ The foreground and background color that apply to the object. These color values are used when the object is displayed

▶ The font used by the object when text is displayed

▶ The cursor for the object—this defines the appearance of the cursor when it is over the object

▶ Whether the object is enabled or not—if the component is enabled it is active and can be accessed by the user

▶ Whether the object is visible on the screen or not—if an object is not marked as visible it is not drawn on the screen

▶ Whether the object is 'valid' or not—if an object is not valid, layout of the entities that make up the object has not been determined. This is the case before an object is made visible. You can make a **Container** object invalid by changing its contents. It will then need to be validated before it is displayed correctly

You can only modify the characteristics of a **Component** object by calling its methods or affecting it indirectly in some way, since none of its data members, which store the characteristics are directly accessible—that is, they are **private**. For example, you can change the name of a **Component** object **myWindow** with the statement:

```
myWindow.setName("The Name");
```

If you subsequently want to retrieve the name of an object you can use the **getName()** method which returns the name as a **String** object. For example:

```
String theName = myWindow.getName();
```

The **isVisible()**, **isEnabled()** and **isValid()** methods return **true** if the object is visible, enabled or valid respectively. You can set an object as visible or enabled by passing a value **true** as an argument to the methods **setVisible()** or **setEnabled()**.

Let's see how we can change the size and position of a **Component** object.

The Size and Position of a Component

Position is defined by x and y coordinates of type **int**, while size is defined by the width and the height, also values of type **int**. The size can also be represented as a object of type **Dimension**. The class **Dimension** has two public members of type **int** which are **width** and **height**.

Components have a 'preferred' size which depends on the particular object. For example, the preferred size of a **Button** object is the size that accommodates the label for the button. Note that you will not normally adjust the size of a component unless you are placing it relative to your display screen. A component also has a minimum size. If the space available to it is less than the minimum size, the component will not be displayed. In most cases the size and position of a component are taken care of automatically. We will see the reason for this later in this chapter.

The methods to retrieve or alter the size and position are:

Method	Description
void setBounds(int x, int y, int width, int height)	Sets the position of the **Component** object to the **int** coordinates (**x**, **y**), and the width and height of the object to the values defined by the third and fourth arguments.
void setBounds(Rectangle rect)	Sets the position and size of the **Component** object to be that of the **Rectangle** argument, rect.
void setSize(Dimension d)	Sets the width and height of the **Component** object to the values stored in the members of the object **d**.
Dimension getSize()	Returns the current size of the **Component** object as a **Dimension** object.

Table Continued on Following Page

473

Method	Description
`Point getLocation()`	Returns the position of the **Component** object as an object of type **Point**.
`Rectangle getBounds()`	Returns the position and size of the object as an object of type **Rectangle**.

Another important method that is defined in the **Component** class is **getToolkit()**. This returns an object of type **Toolkit** which contains information about the environment in which your application is running, including the screen size in pixels. You can use the **getToolkit()** method to help you set the size and position of a window on the screen. We can modify the previous example:

Try It Out—Sizing Windows with `Toolkit`

We'll use the **Toolkit** object to display the window in the center of the screen with the width and height set as half of the screen width and height:

```java
import java.awt.*;              // Include the classes for window operations

public class TryWindow
{
  // The window object
  static Frame aWindow = new Frame("This is the Window Title");

  public static void main(String[] args)
  {
    Toolkit theKit = aWindow.getToolkit();        // Get the window toolkit
    Dimension wndSize = theKit.getScreenSize();   // Get screen size

    // Set the position to screen center & size to half screen size
    aWindow.setBounds(wndSize.width/4, wndSize.height/4,    // Position
                      wndSize.width/2, wndSize.height/2);   // Size
    aWindow.show();                                         // Display the window
  }
}
```

If you try this example, you should see the application window centered on your display with a width and height of half that of the screen.

How It Works

The **Toolkit** object, **theKit**, is obtained by calling the **getToolkit()** method for the **Frame** object, **aWindow**. This method is inherited from the **Window** class, so the **Dialog** class can also use this method.

Note that you can't create a **Toolkit** object directly since **Toolkit** is an **abstract** class. The purpose of this class is to connect the windows, buttons, menus and so on, that are defined by classes in **java.awt**, to their specific representations in the environment in which your program is executing.

The **getScreenSize()** method is a member of the **Toolkit** class that returns an object of type **Dimension** containing data members **width** and **height** that hold the number of pixels for the width and height of your display. We use these values to set the coordinates for the position of the window and the width and height of the window through the **setBounds()** method.

Other Toolkit Class Methods

Although **Toolkit** is an **abstract** class, it does have a **static** method you can call to get a **Toolkit** object directly. You can then call the **getScreenSize()** member for this object. The statement to do this would be:

```
Toolkit theKit = Toolkit.getDefaultToolkit();
```

The **Applet** class does not have a **getToolkit()** method but you can use this to get a **Toolkit** object in an applet when you want to know the current screen resolution.

The **getFontList()** method for a **Toolkit** object returns a **String** array that will contain the names of the fonts that are available. We will use this method in Chapter 14 to implement a dialog for the user to choose a font for text display. The **getFontMetrics()** method supplies information about a particular font—we will be looking at how to use this later in this chapter.

Points and Rectangles

Let's digress briefly into the **Point** and **Rectangle** classes before we go on with the **Component** class methods, since they will come up quite often. You will find many of the methods provided by the **Point** and **Rectangle** classes very useful when drawing in a window. Entities that you display in a window will typically have **Rectangle** objects associated with them that define the areas within the window that they occupy. **Point** objects are used in the definition of other geometric entities such as lines and circles, and to specify their position in a window.

> *Note that neither **Point** nor **Rectangle** objects have any physical representation on the screen. They aren't components, they are just abstract geometric entities. If you want to display a rectangle you have to draw it. We will see how to do this in Chapter 13.*

Point Objects

The **Point** class defines a point by two **public** data members of type **int**, **x** and **y**. Let's look at the methods that the class provides.

Try It Out—Playing with `Point` Objects

Try the following code:

```java
import java.awt.*;

public class PlayingPoints
{
  public static void main(String[] args)
  {
    Point aPoint = new Point();                 // Initialize to 0,0
    Point bPoint = new Point(50,25);
    Point cPoint = new Point(bPoint);

    aPoint.move(100,50);                        // Change to position 100,50

    bPoint.x = 110;
    bPoint.y = 70;

    aPoint.translate(10,20);                    // Move by 10 in x and 20 in y
    System.out.println("aPoint is now at: " + aPoint);

    if(aPoint.equals(bPoint))
      System.out.println("aPoint and bPoint are at the same location.");
  }
}
```

If you run the program you should see:

```
aPoint is located at: java.awt.Point[x=0,y=0]
aPoint is now at: java.awt.Point[x=110,y=70]
aPoint and bPoint are at the same location.
```

How It Works

You can see the three constructors that the **Point** class provides in action in the first few lines. We then manipulate the **Point** objects we've instantiated

You can change a **Point** object to a new position with the **move()** method. Alternatively, you can set the values of the **x** and **y** members directly. You can also translate a **Point** object by specified distances in the x and y directions using the **translate()** method.

Lastly, you can compare two **Point** objects using the **equals()** method. This compares the x and y coordinates of the two **Point** objects, and returns **true** if both are equal. The final output statement is executed because the **Point** objects are equal.

Rectangle Objects

The **Rectangle** class defines four **public** data members, all of type **int**. The position of a **Rectangle** object is defined by the members **x** and **y**, and its size is defined by the members **width** and **height**. Since they are all **public** class members, you can retrieve or modify any of these directly, but your code will be a little more readable if you use the methods provided.

You can retrieve or modify the position of a **Rectangle** object using the methods **getPosition()** which returns a **Point** object, and **setPosition()** which requires x and y coordinates of the new position as arguments. You also have **move()** and **translate()** methods which you can apply to a **Rectangle** object, in the same way as the **Point** object.

To retrieve or modify the size of a **Rectangle** object you use the methods **getSize()** which returns a **Dimension** object, and **setSize()** which requires a **Dimension** object specifying the new size as an argument.

There are also several methods that you can use to combine **Rectangle** objects, and to extend a **Rectangle** object to enclose a point. The effect of each of these methods is shown in the following diagram.

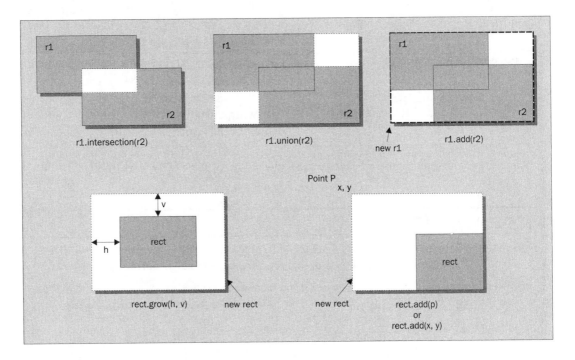

The rectangle that results from each operation is shown dashed. The methods illustrated in the diagram are:

Method	Description
`Rectangle intersection (Rectangle r)`	Returns a `Rectangle` object that is the intersection of the current object and the argument. If the two rectangles do not intersect, the `Rectangle` object returned is at position (0, 0) and the `width` and `height` members are zero so the rectangle is empty.
`Rectangle union (Rectangle r)`	Returns the smallest `Rectangle` object enclosing both the current `Rectangle` object and the `Rectangle` object `r`, passed as an argument.
`void add(Rectangle r)`	Expands the current `Rectangle` object to enclose the argument `Rectangle`.
`void add(Point p)`	Expands the current `Rectangle` object to enclose the `Point` object `p`. The result will be the smallest rectangle that encloses the original rectangle and the point.
`void add(int x, int y)`	Expands the current `Rectangle` object to enclose the point at (`x`, `y`).
`void grow(int h, int v)`	Enlarges the current `Rectangle` object by moving the boundary out from the center by `h` horizontally and `v` vertically.

You can also test and compare `Rectangle` objects in various ways with the following methods:

Method	Description
`boolean isEmpty()`	Returns `true` if the `width` and `height` members of the current `Rectangle` object are zero, and `false` otherwise.
`boolean equals (Object rect)`	Returns `true` if the `Rectangle` object passed as an argument is equal to the current `Rectangle` object, and returns `false` otherwise.
	The two rectangles will be equal if they are at the same position and have the same width and height. If the argument is not a `Rectangle` object, `false` is returned.
`boolean intersects (Rectangle rect)`	Returns `true` if the current `Rectangle` object intersects the `Rectangle` object passed as an argument, and `false` otherwise.
`boolean contains (Point p)`	Returns `true` if the current `Rectangle` object encloses the `Point` argument `p`, and `false` otherwise.

Method	Description
`boolean contains` `(int x, int y)`	Returns **true** if the current **Rectangle** object encloses the point (**x**, **y**), and **false** otherwise.

All of these will be useful when you are dealing with the contents of a Java window. Then you'll be dealing with points and rectangles describing the contents drawn in the window. For example, you might want to enable the user of your program to select some geometric shape from among those displayed on the screen, in order to work with it. You could use the **contains()** method to check whether the point corresponding to the current cursor position is within any of the **Rectangle** objects that enclose each of the circles, lines or whatever is displayed in the window. Then you can decide which of the objects displayed on the screen the user wants to choose.

Visual Characteristics of a Component

The visual appearance of a component is determined by two things, the representation of the component in the underlying operating system that Java calls upon when the component is displayed, and whatever you draw on the component. You can draw on a **Component** object by implementing its **paint()** method. We used this method in Chapter 1 to output the text for our applet. The **paint()** method is called automatically when the component needs to be drawn.

This can be for a variety of reasons—for example, your program requests that the area the component occupies should be redrawn, or the window containing the component is resized. Your implementation of this method must include code to generate whatever you want drawn within the **Component** object. Note that the component itself—the **Button**, or **Frame** or whatever, will be drawn for you. You only need to override the **paint()** method for any additional stuff that you want to draw on it. We will be overriding the **paint()** method in Chapter 13 to draw in a window, so we will leave further discussion of it until then. You can affect the appearance of the basic component though, by calling methods for the object.

The following methods have an effect on the appearance of a **Component** object:

Method	Description
`void setBackground(Color aColor)`	Sets the background color to **aColor**. The background color is the color used for the basic component, as created by the operating system.
`Color getBackground()`	Retrieves the current background color.
`void setForeground(Color bColor)`	Sets the foreground color to **bColor**. The foreground color is the color used for anything appearing on the basic component, such as the label on a button, for example.
`Color getForeground()`	Retrieves the current foreground color.

Table Continued on Following Page

Method	Description
`void setCursor(Cursor aCursor)`	Sets the cursor for the component to **aCursor**. This sets the appearance of the cursor within the area occupied by the **Component** object.
`void setFont(Font aFont)`	Sets the font for the **Component** object.

To be able to make use of these properly we need to understand what **Color** objects are, and we also need to know how we can create **Cursor** and **Font** objects.

Defining Color

A screen color is represented by an object of class **Color**. You define a color value as a combination of the three primary colors, red, green and blue. They are usually expressed in that sequence, and are often referred to as **RGB values**. You can specify the intensity of each primary color to be a value between 0 and 255. If the intensities of all three are 0, you have the color black, and if all three are set to 255 you have white. If just one intensity is positive and the others are zero, you will have a pure primary color; so (0, 100, 0) will be green, for example. We could define variables corresponding to these colors with the statements:

```
Color myBlack = new Color(0,0,0);          // Color black
Color myWhite = new Color(255,255,255);    // Color white
Color myGreen = new Color(0,100,0);        // Color green
```

The three arguments to the constructor correspond to the intensities of the red, green, and blue components of the color respectively. The **Color** class defines a number of standard color constants as **public final static** variables:

```
white          pink           magenta
lightGray      orange         cyan
gray           yellow         blue
darkGray       green
black          black
```

So if we want our window in the previous example to have a pink background, we could add the statement:

```
aWindow.setBackground(Color.pink);
```

When you have created a **Color** object, you can brighten or darken the color by calling the **brighter()** or **darker()** methods which will increase or decrease the intensity of the color components by a predefined factor:

```
thisColor.brighter();          // Brighten the color
thatColor.darker();            // Darken the color
```

The intensities of the component colors will always remain between 0 and 255. When you call **brighter**, and a color component is already at 255, it will remain at that value. The other component intensities will be increased if they are less than 255. In a similar way, the **darker()** method will not change a component intensity if it is zero. The factor used for darkening a color component is 0.7. To brighten a color component the intensity is increased by 1/0.7.

A fundamental point to remember here is that you can only obtain the colors that are available within the computer and the operating system environment on which your Java program is running. If you have a limited range of colors, the **brighter()** and **darker()** methods may appear to have no effect. If your computer supports sixteen colors then although you can create **Color** objects that are supposed to represent all kinds of colors, you will end up with one of your sixteen. If your machine supports 24-bit color and this is supported in your system environment, then everything should be fine and dandy.

You can obtain any of the component intensities by calling **getRed()**, **getGreen()** or **getBlue()** for a **Color** object. A color can also be obtained as a value of type **int** that is a composite of the red, green and blue components of the color represented by a **Color** object. The **getRGB()** method returns this value. You can also create a **Color** object from a single RBG value of type **int**.

To compare two **Color** objects you can use the **equals()** method. For example to compare two color objects **colorA** and **colorB**, you could write:

```
if(colorA.equals(colorB))
   // Do something...
```

The **equals()** method will return **true** if all three components of the two **Color** objects are equal. You could also use the **getRGB()** method to do the same thing:

```
if(colorA.getRGB()==colorB.getRGB())
   // Do something....
```

This just compares the two integer RGB values for equality.

System Colors

The package **java.awt** defines a class **SystemColor** as a sub-class of the **Color** class. The **SystemColor** class encapsulates the standard system colors that are used for various components. The class contains 24 **public**, **final**, **static**, variables of type **SystemColor** that specify the standard system colors used by the operating system. For example, the system colors for a window are referenced by:

window	Defines the background color for a window.
windowText	Defines the text color for a window.
windowBorder	Defines the border color for a window.

You can find the others if you need them by looking at the source code for the **SystemColor** class.

If you want to compare a **SystemColor** value with a **Color** object that you have created, then you must use the **getRGB()** method in the comparison. For example, to see whether **colorA** corresponds to the system background color for a window you would write:

```
if(colorA.getRGB()==SystemColor.window.getRGB())
   // colorA is the window background color...
```

Creating Cursors

An object of the **Cursor** class represents a mouse cursor. The **Cursor** class contains a range of **final static** constants that specify standard cursor types. You use these to select or create a particular cursor. The standard cursor types are:

DEFAULT_CURSOR	N_RESIZE_CURSOR	NE_RESIZE_CURSOR
CROSSHAIR_CURSOR	S_RESIZE_CURSOR	NW_RESIZE_CURSOR
WAIT_CURSOR	E_RESIZE_CURSOR	SE_RESIZE_CURSOR
TEXT_CURSOR	W_RESIZE_CURSOR	SW_RESIZE_CURSOR
HAND_CURSOR		
MOVE_CURSOR		

The resize cursors are the ones you see when resizing a window by dragging its boundaries. Note that these are not like the **Color** constants, which are **Color** objects—these are constants of type **int**, not type **Cursor**.

To create a **Cursor** object representing a text cursor you could write:

```
Cursor myCursor = new Cursor(Cursor.TEXT_CURSOR);
```

Alternatively you can retrieve a cursor of the predefined type using a **static** class method:

```
Cursor myCursor = Cursor.getPredefinedCursor(Cursor.TEXT_CURSOR);
```

This method is particularly useful when you don't want to store the **Cursor** object, but just want to pass it to a method, such as **setCursor()** for a **Component** object.

If you want to see what the standard cursors look like, you could add a cursor to the previous example, along with the pink background:

Try It Out—Color and Cursors

Make the following changes to **TryWindow.java**:

```
import java.awt.*;             // Include the classes for window operations

public class TryWindow
{
  // The window object
  static Frame aWindow = new Frame("This is the Window Title");
```

```
public static void main(String[] args)
{
  Toolkit theKit = aWindow.getToolkit();        // Get the window toolkit
  Dimension wndSize = theKit.getScreenSize();  // Get screen size

  // Set the position to screen center & size to half screen size
  aWindow.setBounds(wndSize.width/4, wndSize.height/4,    // Position
                    wndSize.width/2, wndSize.height/2);  // Size
```

```
  aWindow.setCursor(Cursor.getPredefinedCursor
                                    (Cursor.CROSSHAIR_CURSOR));
  aWindow.setBackground(Color.green);
```

```
  aWindow.show();                                // Display the window
  }
}
```

You can try all the cursors by plugging in each of the standard cursor names in turn. You could also try out a few variations on the background color.

Selecting Fonts

To create a **Font** object you must supply the font name, the style of the font, and the point size. For example, consider the following statement:

```
Font myFont = new Font("Serif", Font.ITALIC, 12);
```

This defines a 12-point Times Roman italic font. The other options you could use for the style are **PLAIN** and **BOLD**. You can specify combined styles by adding them together. If we want **myFont** to be **BOLD** and **ITALIC** we would write the statement as:

```
Font myFont = new Font("Serif", Font.ITALIC + Font.BOLD, 12);
```

You retrieve the style and size of an existing **Font** object by calling its methods **getStyle()** and **getSize()**, both of which return a value of type **int**. You can also check the individual font style for a **Font** object with the methods **isPlain()**, **isBold()**, and **isItalic()**. Each of these methods returns a **boolean** value indicating whether the **Font** object has that style.

Of course, before you create a particular font, you need to know that the font is available on your system. For this you need to retrieve the **Toolkit** object and query it. We could do this for the object **aWindow** as follows:

```
Toolkit theKit = aWindow.getToolkit();
String fontNames[] = theKit.getFontList();  // Get a list of font names
```

The **getFontList()** method returns an array of **String** objects which will be the names of the fonts available on the system. You can then check this list for the font you want to use.

Try It Out—Getting the List of Fonts

This program will output your screen size and resolution, as well as the list of fonts:

```java
import java.awt.*;

public class Sysinfo
{
  public static void main(String[] args)
  {
    Toolkit theKit = Toolkit.getDefaultToolkit();

    System.out.println("\nScreen Resolution: "
                     + theKit.getScreenResolution() + " dots per inch");

    Dimension screenDim = theKit.getScreenSize();
    System.out.println("Screen Size: "
                     + screenDim.width + " by "
                     + screenDim.height + " pixels");

    String myFonts[] = theKit.getFontList();
    System.out.println("\nFonts available on this platform: ");
    for (int i = 0; i < myFonts.length; i++)
      System.out.println(myFonts[i]);

    return;
  }
}
```

On my system I get the following output:

```
Screen Resolution: 96 dots per inch
Screen Size: 1024 by 768 pixels

Fonts available on this platform:
Dialog
SansSerif
Serif
Monospaced
Helvetica
TimesRoman
Courier
DialogInput
ZapfDingbats
```

How It Works

We first get a **Toolkit** object by calling the **static** method **getDefaultToolkit()**—this is the key to the other information. The **getScreenResolution()** returns the number of pixels per inch as a value of type `int`. The `getScreenSize()` method returns a `Dimension` object which specifies the width and height of the screen in pixels. We use the `getFontList()` method that we discussed previously to get a `String` array containing the names of the fonts. After outputting the list of fonts, we call the `beep()` method for the `Toolkit` object to sound a beep for the end of the program.

Font Metrics

Every component has a method `getFontMetrics()` that you can use, surprisingly, to retrieve **font metrics**—the wealth of dimensional data about a font. You pass a `Font` object as an argument to the method, and it returns an object of type `FontMetrics` that you can use to obtain data relating to the particular font. For example, if `aWindow` is a `Frame` object and `myFont` is a `Font` object, you could obtain a `FontMetrics` object corresponding to the font with the statement:

```
FontMetrics metricsTR = aWindow.getFontMetrics(myFont);
```

You can now call any of the following `FontMetrics` methods to get at the basic dimensions for the font:

Method	Description
`int getAscent()`	Returns the **ascent** of the font, which is the distance from the baseline to the top of the majority of the characters in the font. The **baseline** is the line on which the characters rest. Depending on the font, some characters can extend beyond the ascent.
`int getMaxAscent()`	Returns the maximum ascent for the font. No character will exceed this ascent.
`int getDescent()`	Returns the **descent** of the font, which is the distance from the baseline to the bottom of most of the font characters that extend below the base line. Depending on the font, some characters may extend beyond the descent for the font.
`int getMaxDescent()`	Returns the maximum descent of the characters in the font. No character will exceed this descent.
`int getLeading()`	Returns the **leading** for the font, which is the line spacing for the font—that is the spacing between the bottom of one line of text and the top of the next. The term originated when type was actually made of lead, and there was a strip of lead between one line of type and the next when a page was typeset.
`int getHeight()`	Returns the height of the font, which is defined as the sum of the ascent, the descent and the leading.

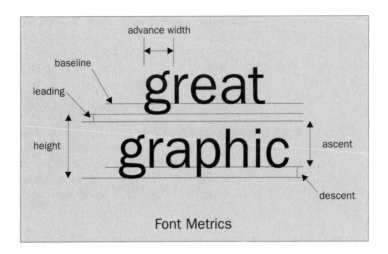

Font Metrics

The diagram shows how the dimensions relate to the font. The **advance width** for a character is the distance from the reference point for the character to the reference point for the next character. The **reference point** for a character is on the base line at the left edge of the character. Each character will have its own advance width which you can obtain by calling a **FontMetrics** method **charWidth()**. For example, you could obtain the advance width for the character **'X'** with the statement:

```
int widthX = metricsTR.charWidth('X');
```

You can also obtain the advance widths for all the characters in the font as an array of type **int** with the method **getWidths()**:

```
int widths[] = metricsTR.getWidths();
```

The numerical value for the character is used to index the array, so you can get the advance width for the character **'X'** with the expression **widths['X']**. If you just want the maximum advance width for the characters in the font, you can call the method **getMaxAdvance()**. Lastly, you can get the total advance width for a **String** object by passing the object to the method **stringWidth()**. The advance width is returned as a value of type **int**.

Although you now know a great deal about how to create and manipulate fonts, you haven't actually created and used a font. We will remedy this when we have learnt a little about using a container.

Using Containers

The **Container** class is the direct base class for the **Window** class and it provides the ability to contain other components. Since the **Container** class is an **abstract** class, you cannot create instances of **Container**. Instead it is objects of the sub-classes, **Window**, **Frame**, **Dialog** and **Panel**, that inherit the ability to contain other components.

> Note that a container cannot contain an object of the class **Window**, or an object of any of the classes derived from **Window**. Any other class derived from **Component** can be contained.

The components within a container are displayed within the area occupied by the container on the display screen. A dialog for example, might contain a **List** object offering some choices, **Checkbox** objects offering other options and **Button** objects enabling the user to end the dialog or enter the selections—and all these components would appear within the boundaries of the dialog. Of course, for the contained components to be visible the container itself must be displayed, as the container effectively 'owns' its components. The container also controls how its embedded components are laid out by means of a **layout manager**. Before we look at what a layout manager is, and how the layout of the components is determined, let's look into the basic methods defined in the **Container** class.

You can find out about the components in a container object by using the following methods defined in the **Container** class:

Method	Description
`int countComponents()`	Returns a count of the number of components contained by the current component
`Component getComponent(int index)`	Returns the component identified by the **index** value. The **index** value is an array index so it must be between 0 and one less than the number of components contained.
`Component[] getComponents()`	Returns an array of the contained components.

If we have a dialog object, **aDialog**, we could iterate through the components in the dialog with the following statements:

```
Component aComponent = null;                          // Stores a Component
int numComponents = aDialog.countComponents();        // Get the count

for(int i = 0; i < numComponents; i++)
{
  aComponent = aDialog.getComponent(i);               // Get the ith component
  // Do something with it...
}
```

This retrieves the components in **aDialog** one at a time in the **for** loop. Alternatively we could retrieve them all at once:

```
Component theComponents[] = aDialog.getComponents(); //Get all components

for(int i = 0; i < numComponents; i++)
{
  // Do something with theComponents[i]...
}
```

Adding Components to a Container

The components stored in a container are recorded in an array within the **Container** object. The array is increased in size when necessary to accommodate as many components as are present. To add a component to a container you use the method **add()**. The **Container** class defines the following four overloaded versions of the **add()** method:

add() Method	Description
Component add(Component c)	Add the component **c** to the end of the list of components stored in the container. The return value is **c**.
Component add(Component c, int index)	Adds the component **c** to the list of components in the container at the position specified by **index**. If **index** is -1, the component is added to the end of the list. If the value of **index** is not -1 it must be less than the number of components in the container, and greater than or equal to 0. The return value is **c**.
Component add(Component c, Object constraints)	Adds the component **c** to the end of the list of components stored in the container. The position of the component relative to the container is subject to the constraints defined by the second parameter. We will see what the constraints are in the next section. The return value is **c**.
Component add(Component c, Object constraints, int index)	Adds the component **c** to the list of components in the container at the position specified by **index**, and position subject to **constraints**. If **index** is -1, the component is added to the end of the list. If the value of **index** is not -1 it must be less than the number of components in the container, and greater than or equal to 0. The return value is **c**.

Before we try out adding components to a container we need to understand what these constraints are, and look at how the layout of components in a container is controlled.

Container Layout Managers

The way that components are arranged in a container is usually determined by an object called a **layout manager**. All containers will have a default layout manager but you can choose a different layout manager for a container. We will be looking at the ones provided in the **java.awt** package, but it is possible to create your own. Creating layout managers is beyond the scope of this book. The layout manager for a container determines the position and size of all the components in the container, so you should not change the size and position of such components yourself.

There are five classes that define different layout managers for a container and they all implement the interface **LayoutManager**, so you can use a variable of type **LayoutManager** to store any of them if necessary. The names of these classes and the basic arrangements that they provide are as follows:

Class	Component Arrangement
FlowLayout	Places components in successive rows in a container, fitting as many on each row as possible, and starting on the next row as soon as a row is full. This works in much the same way as your text processor placing words on a line. Its primary use is for arranging buttons although you can use it with other components. It is the default layout manager for **Panel** and **Applet** objects.
BorderLayout	Places components against any of the four borders of the container and in the center. The component in the center fills the available space. This layout manager is the default for objects of the **Window**, **Frame**, **Dialog**, and **FileDialog** classes.
CardLayout	Places components in a container one on top of the other—like a deck of cards. Only the 'top' component is visible at any one time.
GridLayout	Places components in the container in a rectangular grid with the number of rows and columns that you specify.
GridBagLayout	This also places the components into an arrangement of rows and columns but the rows and columns can vary in length. This is a complicated layout manager with a lot of flexibility in how you control where components are placed in a container.

One question that might occur to you at this point is to ask why we need layout managers at all. Why don't we just place components at some given position in a container? The basic reason is to ensure that the GUI elements for your Java program are displayed properly in every possible Java environment. Layout managers automatically adjust components to fit the space that is available. If you fix the size and position of each of the components, components could run into one another and overlap if the screen area available to your program is reduced.

To set the layout manager of a container, you call the **setLayout()** method for the container. For example, you could change the layout manager for the container object **aWindow** to flow layout with the statements:

```
FlowLayout myFL = new FlowLayout();
aWindow.setLayout(myFL);
```

If you really don't want to use a layout manager, you can remove the default layout manager with the statement:

```
aWindow.setLayout(null);
```

Now you must set the size and position for the components you place in the container. You specify the size and position coordinates relative to the coordinate system for the container.

Let's look at how the layout managers work, and how we can use these layout managers in practice.

Try It Out—Using a Flow Layout Manager

As we said earlier, this layout manager is used primarily to arrange a few components whose relative position is unimportant, so let's implement a **TryFlowLayout** program based on the **TryWindow** example:

```
import java.awt.*;             // Include the classes for window operations

public class TryFlowLayout
{
  // The window object
  static Frame aWindow = new Frame("This is a Flow Layout");

  public static void main(String[] args)
  {
    Toolkit theKit = aWindow.getToolkit();       // Get the window toolkit
    Dimension wndSize = theKit.getScreenSize(); // Get screen size

    // Set the position to screen center & size to half screen size
    aWindow.setBounds(wndSize.width/4, wndSize.height/4,    // Position
                      wndSize.width/2, wndSize.height/2);   // Size

    FlowLayout flow = new FlowLayout();   // Create a layout manager
    aWindow.setLayout(flow);              // Set the container layout mgr

    // Now add six Button components
    for(int i = 1; i <= 6; i++)
      aWindow.add(new Button("Press " + i)); // Add a Button to container

    aWindow.show();                                 // Display the window
  }
}
```

Since it is based on the **TryWindow** class, only the new code is shown shaded. The new code is quite simple. We create a **FlowLayout** object and make this the layout manager for **aWindow** by calling **setLayout()**. We then add six **Button** components to **aWindow** in the loop.

If you compile and run the program you should get a window something like that shown.

The **Button** objects are positioned by the layout manager flow. As you can see, they have been added to the first row in the window, and the row is centered. You can confirm that the row is centered and see how the layout manger automatically spills the components on to the next row once a row is full by reducing the size of the window.

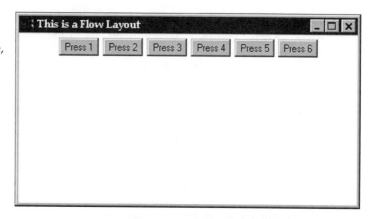

Here the second row is clearly centered. Each button component has been set to its preferred size which comfortably accommodates the text for the label. The centering is determined by the alignment constraint for the layout manger which happens to default to **CENTER**.

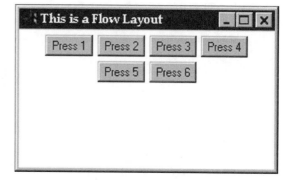

You could also set it to **RIGHT** or **LEFT** by using a different constructor. For example, you could have created the layout manager with the statement:

```
FlowLayout flow = new FlowLayout(FlowLayout.LEFT);
```

The flow layout manager then left-aligns each row of components in the container. If you run the program with this definition for the layout manager and resize the window, it will look as shown here.

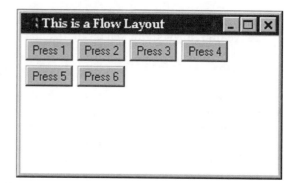

Now the buttons are clearly left-aligned. You could equally well have specified the constraint when you added the component to the container using the constraints parameter in the **add()** method that we saw earlier. Instead of changing the definition of the object **flow**, you could modify the loop to:

```
for(int i = 1; i <= 6; i++)
  aWindow.add(new Button("Press " + i), FlowLayout.LEFT);
```

This would have the same effect as passing the alignment argument to the constructor. The difference here is that the alignment is applied to each component individually.

The flow layout manager in the previous examples applies a default gap between components in a row, and between rows. You can choose values for these gaps by using yet another **FlowLayout** constructor. You can set the horizontal gap to 20 pixels and the vertical gap to 30 pixels with the statement:

```
FlowLayout flow = new FlowLayout(FlowLayout.LEFT, 20, 30);
```

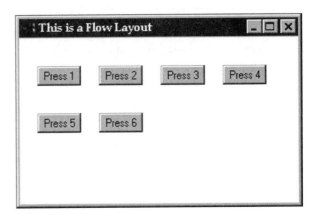

If you run the program with this definition of the layout manager, when you resize the window you will see that the components will be distributed with the spacing specified.

You can also set the gaps between components explicitly by calling the **setHgap()** or the **setVgap()** method. To set the horizontal gap to 35 pixels, you could write:

```
flow.setHgap(35);                      // Set the horizontal gap
```

Don't be misled by this. You can't get differential spacing between components by setting the gap before adding each component to a container. The last values for the gaps between components that you set for a layout manager will apply to all the components in a container. The methods **getHgap()** and **getVgap()** will return the current setting for the horizontal or vertical gap as a value of type **int**.

As we've said, the flow layout manager is the default for applets. You can verify this by adding some buttons to the applet from Chapter 1. You can try out a **Font** object at the same time.

Try It Out—Adding Buttons to an Applet

1 Make the following changes to `MyFirstApplet.java`:

```
import java.applet.Applet;
import java.awt.*;

public class MyFirstApplet extends Applet
{
  public void init()
  {
    for(int i = 1; i <= 6; i++)
    {
      Button button;                                // Stores a button
      add(button = new Button("Press " + i));
      button.setFont(new Font("serif", Font.ITALIC, 14)); // Our own font
    }
  }
  public void paint(Graphics g)
  {
    g.drawString("To climb a ladder, start at the bottom rung", 20, 90);
  }
}
```

2 Recapping Chapter 1, to run the applet, you will need a `.html` file containing:

```
<applet code="MyFirstApplet.class" width=300 height=200>
</applet>
```

This specifies the width and height of the applet—you can use your own values here if you wish. You can save the file as **MyFirstApplet.html**.

3 Once you have compiled the applet source code using **javac**, you can execute it with the **appletviewer** program by entering the following command:

```
C:\>appletviewer MyFirstApplet.html
```

You should see the **AppletViewer** window displaying our applet.

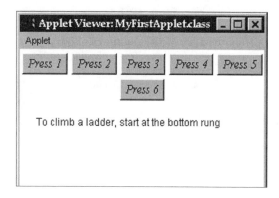

The arrangement of the buttons is the same as we saw in **TryFlowLayout.java**, but here we got the flow layout manager by default. We also have the button labels in our italic font.

How It Works

As we saw in Chapter 1, an applet is executed rather differently from a Java program. The browser (or **appletviewer**) initiates and controls the execution of the applet. Instead of the **main()** method, the browser creates an instance of our applet class, **MyFirstApplet**, and then calls the **init()** method. This method is inherited from the **Applet** class—you will typically override this method to provide your own initialization. The browser also calls the **paint()** method which we have overridden here, as in the original version of the example, to draw whatever is required.

The **import** statement has also been changed to add all the classes in the package **java.awt**, rather than just the **Graphics** class. This is because we need access to the **Button** class.

Using a Border Layout Manager

The border layout manager is intended to place up to five components in a container. Possible positions for components are on any of the four borders of the container and in the center. Only one component can be at each position. If you add a component at a position that is already occupied, the previous component will be displaced. A border is selected by specifying a constraint that can be **NORTH**, **SOUTH**, **EAST**, **WEST** or **CENTER**. These are all **final static** constants defined in the **BorderLayout** class.

You can't specify the constraints in the **BorderLayout** constructor. You specify the position of each component in a container when you add it to the container using the **add()** method. We could modify the previous example to add five buttons in a border layout:

Try It Out—Testing the BorderLayout Manager

Make the following changes to **TryFlowLayout.java** to try out the border layout manager.

```java
import java.awt.*;

public class TryBorderLayout
{
  // The window object
  static Frame aWindow = new Frame("This is a Border Layout");

  public static void main(String[] args)
  {
    Toolkit theKit = aWindow.getToolkit();       // Get the window toolkit
    Dimension wndSize = theKit.getScreenSize();  // Get screen size
```

```
                  // Set the position to screen center & size to half screen size
             aWindow.setBounds(wndSize.width/4, wndSize.height/4,    // Position
                               wndSize.width/2, wndSize.height/2);   // Size
```

```
        // Now add five Button components
        aWindow.add(new Button("EAST "), BorderLayout.EAST);
        aWindow.add(new Button("WEST "), BorderLayout.WEST);
        aWindow.add(new Button("NORTH"), BorderLayout.NORTH);
        aWindow.add(new Button("SOUTH"), BorderLayout.SOUTH);
        aWindow.add(new Button("CENTER"), BorderLayout.CENTER);
```

```
        aWindow.show();                                    // Display the window
    }
  }
```

If you compile and execute the example, you will see the window shown here.

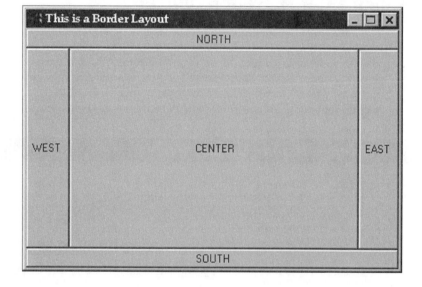

How It Works

The **"NORTH"** and **"SOUTH"** buttons are the full width of the window and the **"EAST"** and **"WEST"** buttons occupy the height remaining unoccupied once the **"NORTH"** and **"SOUTH"** buttons are in place. It always works like this, regardless of the sequence in which you add the buttons—the **"NORTH"** and **"SOUTH"** components occupy the full width of the container. The **"CENTER"** component takes up whatever space is left. If there are no **"NORTH"** and **"SOUTH"** components, the **"EAST"** and **"WEST"** components will extend to the full height of the container.

The width of the **"EAST"** and **"WEST"** buttons is determined by the space required to display the button labels. Similarly, the **"NORTH"** and **"SOUTH"** buttons' width is determined by the height of the characters in the labels for the buttons.

You can alter the spacing between components by passing arguments to the **BorderLayout** constructor—the default gaps are zero. For example, you could set the horizontal gap to 20 pixels and the vertical gap to 30 pixels with the statement:

```
aWindow.setLayout(new BorderLayout(20, 30));
```

Like the flow layout manager, you can also set the gaps individually by calling the methods `setHgap()` and `setVgap()` for the `BorderLayout` object. For example:

```
BorderLayout border = new BorderLayout();   // Construct the object
aWindow.setLayout(border);                  // Set the layout
border.setHgap(20);                         // Set horizontal gap
```

This sets the horizontal gap between the components to 20 pixels and leaves the vertical gap at the default value of zero. You can also retrieve the current values for the gaps with the `getHgap()` and `getVgap()` methods.

Using a Card Layout Manager

The card layout manager generates a stack of components, one on top of the other. The first component that you add to the container will be at the top of the stack, and therefore visible, and the last one will be at the bottom. You can create a `CardLayout` object with the default constructor, `CardLayout()`, or you can specify horizontal and vertical gaps as arguments to the constructor. The gaps in this case are between the edge of the component and the boundary of the container. We can see how this works in an applet:

Try It Out—Dealing Components

Try the following code:

```
import java.applet.Applet;
import java.awt.*;
import java.awt.event.*;         // Classes to handle events

public class TryCardLayout extends Applet
{
  CardLayout card = new CardLayout(50,50);  // Create layout

  public void init()
  {
    setLayout(card);                              // Set card as the layout mgr
    for(int i = 1; i <= 6; i++)
      add(new Button("Press " + i), "Card" + i);  // Add a button
    enableEvents(AWTEvent.MOUSE_EVENT_MASK);      // Enable mouse events
  }

  // Handle mouse events
  public void processMouseEvent(MouseEvent e)
  {
    if(e.getID()==e.MOUSE_CLICKED)
      card.next(this);
    super.processMouseEvent(e);
  }
}
```

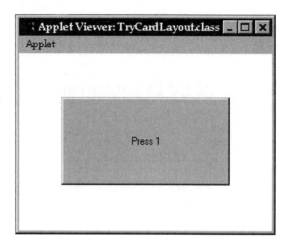

If you run the program the applet should be as shown here. Click in the area around the button—not on the button—and the next button will be displayed.

How It Works

The **CardLayout** object, **card**, is created with horizontal and vertical gaps of fifty pixels. In the **init()** method for our applet, we set **card** as the layout manager and add six buttons to the container. Note that we have two arguments to the **add()** method. Using card layout requires that you identify each component by some **Object**, in this case a **String** object that is passed as the second argument to the **add()** method. We use an arbitrary string for each consisting of the string **"Card"** with the sequence number of the button appended to it.

Next we call the **enableEvents()** method to allow our applet to receive mouse events. This is just to enable you to see that it is possible to flip through the components. We will defer a detailed discussion of events until the next chapter.

It is the method **processMouseEvent()** which calls the **next()** method for the layout when the mouse is clicked. The argument to the **next()** method identifies the container as the **TryCardLayout** object that is created when the applet starts. The **CardLayout** class has other methods that you can use for selecting from the stack of components:

Method	Description
void previous(Container parent)	Selects the previous component in the container, **parent**.
void first(Container parent)	Selects the first component in the container, **parent**.
void last(Container parent)	Selects the last component in the container, **parent**.
void show(Container parent, String name)	Selects the component in the container, **parent**, associated with the **String** object, **name**. This must be one of the **String** objects specified when you called the **add()** method to add components.

Using the **next()** or **previous()** methods you can cycle through the components repeatedly, since the next component after the last is the first, and the component before the first is the last.

Using a Grid Layout Manager

A grid layout manager arranges components in a rectangular grid within the container. You have three constructors for creating **GridLayout** objects:

Constructor	Description
GridLayout()	Creates a grid layout manager that will arrange components in a single row (that is, a single column per component) with no gaps between components.
GridLayout(int rows, int cols)	Creates a grid layout manager that arranges components in a grid with **rows** number of rows and **cols** number of columns, and with no gaps between components.
GridLayout(int rows, int cols, int vgap)	Creates a grid layout manager that arranges **int hgap,** components in a grid with **rows** number of rows and **cols** number of columns, and with horizontal and vertical gaps between components of **hgap** and **vgap** pixels, respectively.

In the second and third constructors shown above, you can specify either the number of rows, or the number of columns as zero (but not both). If you specify the number of rows as zero, the layout manager will provide as many rows in the grid as are necessary to accommodate the number of components you add to the container. Similarly, setting the number of columns as zero indicates an arbitrary number of columns. If you fix both the rows and the columns, and add more components to the container than the grid will accommodate, the number of columns will be increased appropriately.

We can try a grid layout manager out in an application:

Try It Out—Gridlocking Buttons

Make the highlighted changes to **TryWindow.java**.

```
import java.awt.*;              // Include the classes for window operations

public class TryGridLayout
{
  // The window object
  static Frame aWindow = new Frame("This is a Grid Layout");

  public static void main(String[] args)
```

```
  {
    Toolkit theKit = aWindow.getToolkit();        // Get the window
  toolkit
    Dimension wndSize = theKit.getScreenSize();  // Get screen size

    // Set the position to screen center & size to half screen size
    aWindow.setBounds(wndSize.width/4, wndSize.height/4,    // Position
                      wndSize.width/2, wndSize.height/2);   // Size
```

```
    GridLayout grid = new GridLayout(3,4,30,20);
    aWindow.setLayout(grid);                     // Set the container layout mgr

    // Now add ten Button components
    for(int i = 1;  i <= 10;  i++)
      aWindow.add(new Button("Press " + i)); // Add a Button to container
```

```
    aWindow.show();                                        // Display the window
  }
}
```

We create a grid layout manager, grid, for three rows and four columns, and with horizontal and vertical gaps between components of 30 and 20 pixels respectively. With ten buttons in the container, the application will be as shown here.

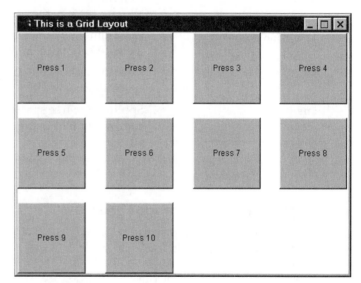

Using a GridBagLayout Manager

The **GridBagLayout** manager is much more flexible than the other layout managers, and consequently rather more complicated to use. The basic mechanism arranges components in a rectangular grid, but the components are not necessarily the same size, and a component can occupy more than one grid position.

Each component in a **GridBagLayout** has its own set of constraints. These are defined by an object of type **GridBagConstraints** that you associate with each component, before you

499

add the component to the container. The location of each component, its relative size and the area it occupies in the grid are all determined by its associated **GridBagConstraints** object.

A **GridBagConstraints** object has no less than eleven public instance variables that you can set to define the constraints for a component. Since they also interact with each other there's more entertainment value here than with a Rubik's cube. Let's first get a rough idea of what these instance variables in a **GridBagConstraints** object do:

Instance Variable	Description
gridx and **gridy**	Determines the position of the component in the container.
gridwidth and **gridheight**	Determines the size of the area occupied by the component in the container.
weightx and **weighty**	Determines how free space is distributed between components in the container.
anchor	Determines where a component is positioned within the area allocated to it in the container.
ipadx and **ipady**	Determines by how much the component size is to be increased above its minimum size.
fill	Determines how the component is to be enlarged to fill the space allocated to it.
insets	Specifies the free space that is to be provided around the component within the space allocated to it in the container.

Well that seems straightforward enough. We can now explore what kinds of values we can set for these and then try them out.

GridBagConstraints Instance Variables

A component will occupy at least one grid position, or **cell**, in a container that uses a **GridBagLayout** object, but it can occupy any rectangular array of cells. The total number of rows and columns, and thus the cell size, in the grid for a container is variable, and determined by the constraints for all of the components in the container. Each component will have a position in the grid plus an area it is allocated defined by a number of horizontal grid positions and a number of vertical grid positions.

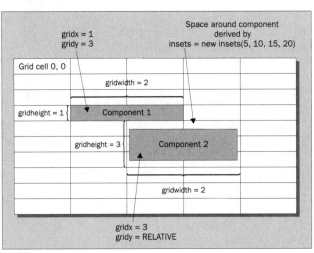

The top-left cell in a layout is at position (0, 0). You define the position of a component by defining where the top-left cell that it occupies is, relative to the grid origin, or relative to the previous component that was added to the container. You specify the position of the top-left cell that a component occupies in the grid by setting values for the following members of the **GridBagConstraints** object:

Type	Variable Name	Purpose
int	**gridx**	Specifies the horizontal position of the top-left cell occupied by the component. You can specify a numerical value where the leftmost grid position is 0, the next is 1 and so on. The default value is **GridBagConstraints.RELATIVE**, a constant which places the top-left grid position for the component in the column immediately to the right of the previous component.
int	**gridy**	Similar to **gridx**, but specifies the vertical position of the top-left cell occupied by the component. So swap row for column in the above description.

You specify the number of cells occupied by a component horizontally and vertically by setting values for the following **GridBagConstraints** instance variables:

Type	Variable Name	Purpose
int	**gridwidth**	Specifies the number of cells that the component occupies horizontally. The default value is 1. If you specify the value as **GridBagConstraints.REMAINDER**, the component will be the last one in the row. If you specify the value as **GridBagConstraints.RELATIVE**, the component will be the penultimate one in the row.
int	**gridheight**	Just as **gridwidth** deals with horizontal cells, so **gridheight** specifies the number of cells that the component occupies vertically.

If the preferred size of the component is less than the display area, you can control how the size of the component is adjusted to fit the display area by setting the following **GridBagConstraints** instance variables:

Type	Variable Name	Purpose
int	**fill**	The value for this variable determines how the size of the component is adjusted in relation to the array of cells it occupies. The default value of **GridBagConstraints.NONE** means that the component is not resized.
		A value of **GridBagConstraints.HORIZONTAL** adjusts the width of the component to fill the display area.

Table Continued on Following Page

Type	Variable Name	Purpose
		A value of **GridBagConstraints.VERTICAL** adjusts the height of the component to fill the display area.
		A value of **GridBagConstraints.BOTH** adjusts the height and the width to completely fill the display area.
Insets	**insets**	This variable stores an object of type **Insets**. The **Insets** class defines the space to be allowed between the edges of the components and boundaries of the display area it occupies. Four parameter values to the class constructor define the top, left side, bottom and right side padding from the edges of the component. The default value is **Insets(0, 0, 0, 0)**.

If you don't intend to expand a component to fill its display area, you may still want to enlarge the component from its minimum size. You can adjust the dimensions of the component by setting the following **GridBagConstraints** instance variables:

Type	Variable Name	Purpose
int	**ipadx**	Defines the number of pixels by which the top and bottom edges of the component are to be expanded. The default value is 0.
int	**ipady**	Defines the number of pixels by which the left and right edges of the component are to be expanded. The default value is 0.

If the component is still smaller than its display area in the container, you can specify whereabouts it is to be placed in relation to its display area by setting a value for the **anchor** instance variable of the **GridBagConstraints** object. Possible values are **NORTH**, **NORTHEAST**, **EAST**, **SOUTHEAST**, **SOUTH**, **SOUTHWEST**, **WEST**, **NORTHWEST**, and **CENTER**, all of which are defined in the **GridBagConstraints** class.

The last **GridBagConstraints** instance variables to consider are **weightx** and **weighty** which are of type **double**. These determine how space in the container is distributed between components in the horizontal and vertical directions. You should always set a value for these as the default of 0 will cause the components to be adjacent to one another in the center of the container. The absolute values for **weightx** and **weighty** are not important. It is the relative values that matter. If you set all the values the same (but not zero), the space for each component will be distributed uniformly. Space is distributed in the proportions defined by the values. For example, if three components in a row have **weightx** values of 1.0, 2.0, and 3.0, the first will get 1/6 of the total in the x direction, the second will get 1/3, and the third will get half. The proportion of the available space that a component gets in the x direction is the **weightx** value for the component divided by the sum of the **weightx** values in the row. The same goes for the **weighty** values for allocating space in the y direction.

Let's start with a simple example of placing two buttons in a window:

Make the following changes to the **TryWindow.java** program to create a window and try out the **GridBagLayout** manager.

```
import java.awt.*;

public class TryGridBagLayout
{
  // The window object
  static Frame aWindow = new Frame("This is a GridBag Layout");

  public static void main(String[] args)
  {
    Toolkit theKit = aWindow.getToolkit();      // Get the window toolkit
    Dimension wndSize = theKit.getScreenSize(); // Get screen size

    // Set the position to screen center & size to half screen size
    aWindow.setBounds(wndSize.width/4, wndSize.height/4,   // Position
                    wndSize.width/2, wndSize.height/2);   // Size

    // Create the layout manager and constraints objects
    GridBagLayout layout = new GridBagLayout();
    GridBagConstraints constraints = new GridBagConstraints();
    aWindow.setLayout(layout);                  // Set the container layout mgr

    // Set constraints and add first button
    constraints.weightx = constraints.weighty = 10.0;
    constraints.fill = constraints.BOTH;                    // Fill the space
    addButton("Press", constraints, layout);               // Add the button

    // Set constraints and add second button
    constraints.gridwidth = constraints.REMAINDER; // Rest of the row
    addButton("GO", constraints, layout);          // Create and add button
    aWindow.show();                                        // Display the window
  }

  static void addButton(String label,
                 GridBagConstraints constraints, GridBagLayout layout)
  {
    Button button = new Button(label);
    layout.setConstraints(button, constraints);
    aWindow.add(button);
  }
}
```

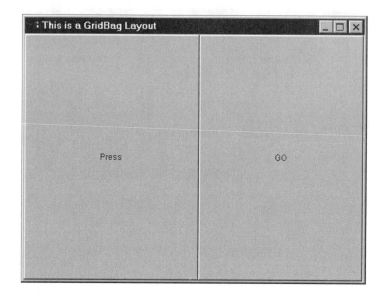

The program window will look like that shown here.

How It Works

Because the process will be the same for every button that we add, we have implemented the helper function **addButton()** which creates **Button** objects, associates the **GridBagConstraints** object with them in the **GridBagLayout** object, and then adds them to the container, **aWindow**.

After creating the layout manager and **GridBagConstraints** objects we set the values for **weightx** and **weighty** to 10.0. A value of 1.0 would be just as good. We set the **fill** constraint to **BOTH** to make the component fill the space it occupies. Note that when the **setConstraints()** method is called to associate the **GridBagConstraints** object with the button object, a copy of the constraints object is stored in the layout—not the object we created. This allows us to change the constraints object and use it for the second button without affecting the constraints for the first.

The buttons are equal in size in the x direction because the **weightx** and **weighty** values are the same for both, and both buttons fill the space available to them because the **fill** constraint is set to **BOTH**. If **fill** was set to **HORIZONTAL** for example, the buttons would be the full width of the grid positions they occupy, but just high enough to accommodate the label, since they would have no preferred size in the y direction.

If we alter the constraints for the second buttons to:

```
// Set constraints and add second button
constraints.weightx = 5.0;                        // Weight half of first
constraints.insets = new Insets(10, 30, 10, 20); // Left 30 & right 20
constraints.gridwidth = constraints.RELATIVE;     // Rest of the row
addButton("GO", constraints, layout);             // Add button to container
```

the application window will be as shown.

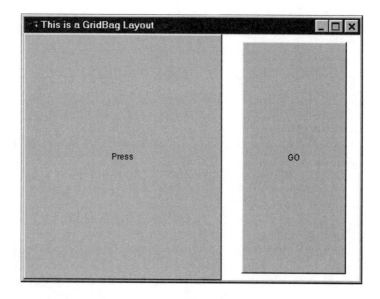

Now the second button occupies one third of the space in the x direction—that is a proportion of 5/(5+10) of the total—and the first button occupies two thirds. Note that the buttons still occupy one grid cell each—the default values for **gridwidth** and **gridheight** of 1 apply—but the **weightx** constraint values have altered the relative sizes of the cells for the two buttons in the x direction. The second button is also inset within the space it has been allocated—ten pixels at the top and bottom and thirty pixels on the left and twenty on the right from the **insets** constraint. You can see that, for a given window size here, the size of a grid position depends on the number of objects. The more components there are, the less space they will each have allocated to them.

Suppose we wanted to add a third button the same width as the **"Press"** button, and immediately below it. We could do that by adding the following code immediately after that for the second button:

```
// Set constraints and add third button
constraints.insets = new Insets(0,0,0,0);      // No insets
constraints.gridx = 0;                          // Begin new row
constraints.gridwidth = 1;                      // Width as "Press"
addButton("Push", constraints, layout);         // Add button to container
```

We reset the **gridx** constraint to zero to put the button at the start of the next row. It has a default **gridwith** of 1 cell, like the others. The window would now look like:

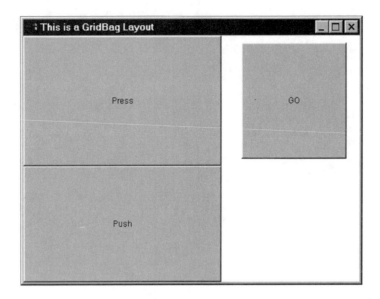

Having seen how it looks now, clearly it would be better if the **"GO"** button were the height of **"Press"** and **"Push"** combined. To arrange them like this, we need to make the height of the **"GO"** button twice that of the other two buttons. The height of the **"Press"** button is 1 by default, so if we make the height of the **"GO"** button 2, and reset the **gridheight** constraint to 1 for the **"Push"** button, we should get the result we want. Modifying the code for the second and third buttons to:

```
// Set constraints and add second button
constraints.weightx = 5.0;                      // Weight half of first
constraints.gridwidth = constraints.REMAINDER;  // Rest of the row
constraints.insets = new Insets(10, 30, 10, 20); // Left & right 30
constraints.gridheight = 2;                      // Height 2x "Press"
addButton("GO", constraints, layout);            // Add button to container

// Set constraints and add third button
constraints.gridx = 0;                           // Begin new row
constraints.gridwidth = 1;                       // Width as "Press"
constraints.gridheight = 1;                      // Height as "Press"
constraints.insets = new Insets(0, 0, 0, 0);     // No insets
addButton("Push", constraints, layout);          // Add button to container
```

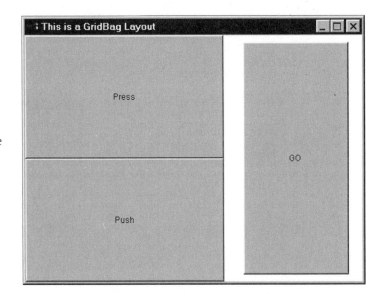

With these code changes, the window will be:

We could also see the effect of padding the components out from their preferred size by altering the button constraints a little:

```
// Create constraints and add first button
constraints.weightx = constraints.weighty =10.0;
constraints.fill = constraints.NONE;
constraints.ipadx = 30;                          / Pad 30 in x
constraints.ipady = 10;                          // Pad 10 in y
addButton("Press", constraints, layout);        // Add button to container

// Set constraints and add second button
constraints.weightx = 5.0;                       // Weight half of first
constraints.fill = constraints.BOTH;             // Expand to fill space
constraints.ipadx = constraints.ipady = 0;       // No padding
constraints.gridwidth = constraints.REMAINDER;   // Rest of the row
constraints.gridheight = 2;                      // Height 2x "Press"
constraints.insets = new Insets(10, 30, 10, 20); // Left 30 & right 20
addButton("GO", constraints, layout);            // Add button to container

// Set constraints and add third button
constraints.gridx = 0;                           // Begin new row
constraints.fill = constraints.NONE;
constraints.ipadx = 30;                          // Pad component in x
constraints.ipady = 10;                          // Pad component in y
constraints.gridwidth = 1;                       // Width as "Press"
constraints.gridheight = 1;                      // Height as "Press"
constraints.insets = new Insets(0, 0, 0, 0);     // No insets
addButton("Push", constraints, layout);          // Add button to container
```

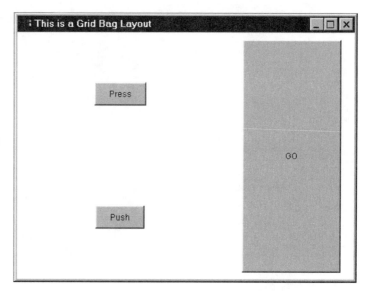

With the constraints for the buttons as above, the window will be as shown here.

Both the Push and the Press button occupy the same space, but because **fill** is set to **NONE**, they are not expanded to fill the space in either direction. The **ipadx** and **ipady** constraints specify by how much the buttons are to be expanded from their preferred size— by thirty pixels on the left and thirty pixels on the right, and by ten pixels on the top and by ten pixels on the bottom. The overall arrangement remains the same.

You need to experiment with using **GridBagLayout** and **GridBagConstraints** to get a good feel for how the layout manager works because you are likely to find yourself using it quite often.

Combining Layout Managers

It may be that for one set of components you might want to use one layout manager, **FlowLayout** for a row of buttons in a toolbar for example, but to place another set of components in a status bar at the bottom of a window you might want to use the facilities provided by a **GridLayout** manager. The way you do this is to arrange the buttons with a **FlowLayout** object in one container, then use another container to arrange the components in the status bar. You can then position both these containers in a window—which is a container of course—using a **BorderLayout** manager.

To see how we can combine layout managers, let's implement a specific example. Suppose we want to add a row of buttons to the top of the application window, and then place the same arrangement of panels that we had in the last example with **GridBagLayout**, in the center of the window. We can do this by creating two **Panel** components—one with buttons arranged using **GridLayout**, and the other with buttons arranged using **GridBagLayout**:

Try It Out—Mixing Layout Managers

To see mixed layout managers in action, we'll make some changes to our ubiquitous test program.

```java
import java.awt.*;

public class TryMixedLayouts
{
  static Frame aWindow = new Frame("This is a Mixed Layout");
  static Panel gridPanel = new Panel();       // Create first panel
  static Panel gbPanel = new Panel();         // Create second panel

  public static void main(String[] args)
  {
    Toolkit theKit = aWindow.getToolkit();      // Get the window toolkit
    Dimension wndSize = theKit.getScreenSize();  // Get screen size

    // Set the position to screen center & size to half screen size
    aWindow.setBounds(wndSize.width/4, wndSize.height/4,   // Position
                      wndSize.width/2, wndSize.height/2);   // Size

    // Arrange the components in the first panel
    GridLayout grid = new GridLayout(1,0);        // Grid of 1 row
    gridPanel.setLayout(grid);                    // Set the panel layout mgr

    for(int i = 1; i <= 6; i++)                   // Add six buttons
      gridPanel.add(new Button("Button " + i));
    aWindow.add(BorderLayout.NORTH, gridPanel); // Add the first panel

    // Arrange the components in the second panel
    GridBagLayout layout = new GridBagLayout();
    GridBagConstraints constraints = new GridBagConstraints();
    gbPanel.setLayout(layout);                    // Set the panel layout mgr

    // Create constraints and add first button
    constraints.weightx = constraints.weighty =10.0;
    constraints.fill = constraints.NONE;
    constraints.ipadx = 30;                       // Pad 30 in x
    constraints.ipady = 10;                       // Pad 10 in y
    addButton("Press", constraints, layout);      // Add button to container

    // Set constraints and add second button
    constraints.weightx = 5.0;                    // Weight half of first
    constraints.fill = constraints.BOTH;          // Expand to fill space
    constraints.ipadx = constraints.ipady = 0; // No padding
```

```
      constraints.gridwidth = constraints.REMAINDER;    // Rest of the row
      constraints.insets = new Insets(10, 30, 10, 20); //Left 30 & right 20
      constraints.gridheight = 2;                          // Height 2x "Press"
      addButton("GO", constraints, layout);        // Add button to container

      // Set constraints and add third button
      constraints.gridx = 0;                         // Begin new row
      constraints.fill = constraints.NONE;
      constraints.ipadx = 30;                        // Pad component in x
      constraints.ipady = 10;                        // Pad component in y
      constraints.gridwidth = 1;                     // Width as "Press"
      constraints.gridheight = 1;                     // Height as "Press"
      constraints.insets = new Insets(0, 0, 0, 0); // No insets
      addButton("Push", constraints, layout);      // Add button to container
      aWindow.add(BorderLayout.CENTER, gbPanel); // Add panel

    aWindow.show();                                         // Display the window
  }

  static void addButton(String label,
                  GridBagConstraints constraints, GridBagLayout layout)
  {
    Button button = new Button(label);
    layout.setConstraints(button, constraints);
    gbPanel.add(button);
  }
}
```

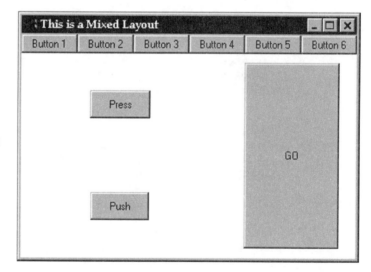

If you run this example, the window should look like that shown here.

How It Works

This shouldn't need much explanation since it just combines two things we have seen before. We use a **GridLayout** object to manage the layout of the first container, **gridPanel**. After adding six buttons to it in the **for** loop, we add the **Panel** object as a component in **aWindow** which has **BorderLayout** as its default layout manager. The **gridPanel** component is positioned in **aWindow** at **NORTH**, against the top border of **aWindow**.

The second **Panel** object, **gbPanel**, uses a **GridBagLayout** manager. We add the same arrangement of buttons to it as in the previous example. We need to modify the helper method, **addButton()**, to add the buttons to **gbPanel** rather than **aWindow**. Once the buttons have been added to the panel, the panel is added as a component to **aWindow** with the position as **CENTER**.

You can use containers as components within containers to whatever depth you wish to get the arrangement you want.

Adding a Menu to a Window

A menu bar and the menu items within it are not components. The classes in the **java.awt** package that enable you to create a menu bar form a separate class hierarchy based on the class **MenuComponent** which is derived from the class that is a base for all Java classes—**Object**.

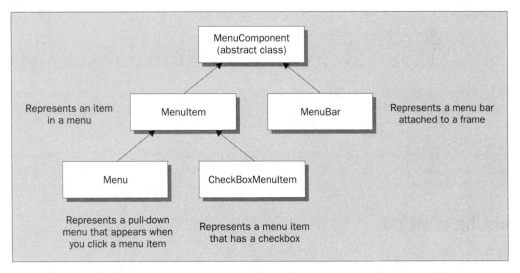

A **MenuBar** object represents the menu bar that is placed at the top of a window. You can add **Menu** or **MenuItem** objects to a **MenuBar** object and these will be displayed on the menu bar. A **Menu** object is a menu item with a label that can display a pull-down menu when it is clicked, whereas a **MenuItem** object represents a simple menu item with a label that results in some program action when it is clicked—such as reading something from a file. Each item on the pull-down menu for an object of type **Menu**, can be an object of type **Menu**, of type **MenuItem** or of type **CheckBoxMenuItem**. A **CheckBoxMenuItem** is a simple menu item with a checkbox associated with it. The checkbox can be checked and unchecked and typically indicates that that menu item was selected last time the pull-down menu was displayed. You can also add separators in a pull-down menu which are simply bars to separate one group of menu items from another.

Creating Menu and MenuItem

To create a **Menu** object you call a **Menu** class constructor and pass a **String** object to it that contains the label for the menu. For example, to create a File menu you would write:

```
Menu fileMenu = new Menu("File");
```

Creating a **MenuItem** object is much the same:

```
MenuItem openMenu = new MenuItem("Open");
```

If you create a **CheckboxMenuItem** object by passing just a **String** argument to the constructor, the object will represent an item that is initially unchecked. For example, you could create an unchecked item with the following statement:

```
CheckboxMenuItem circleItem = new CheckboxMenuItem("Circle");
```

Another constructor for this class allows you to set the check mark by specifying a second argument of type **boolean**. For example:

```
CheckboxMenuItem lineItem = new CheckboxMenuItem("Line", true);
```

This creates an item with the label, **Line**, that will be checked initially. Of course, you can also use this constructor to explicitly specify that you want an item to be unchecked by setting the second argument to **false**.

If you want to use a menu bar in your application window, you must create your window as a **Frame** object, since the **Frame** class incorporates the capability to manage a menu bar. The other container classes do not. Let's see how we can create a menu on a menu bar.

Creating a Menu

To create a window with a menu bar, we will define our own window class as a sub-class of **Frame**. This will be a much more convenient way to manage all the details of the window compared to using a **Frame** object directly. By extending the **Frame** class, we can add our own members that will customize a **Frame** window to our particular needs. We can override the methods defined in the **Frame** class to modify their behavior, if necessary.

We will be adding functionality to this example over several chapters, so create a directory for it with the name **Sketcher**. This program will be a window-based sketching program that will enable you to create sketches using lines, circles, curves and rectangles, and to annotate them with text. By building an example in this way, you will gradually create a much larger Java program than the examples we have seen so far, and you will also gain experience of combining many of the capabilities of **java.awt** and other standard packages in a practical situation.

Try It Out—Building a Menu

1 To start with, we will have two class files in the Sketcher program. The file **Sketcher.java** will contain the method **main()** where execution of the application will start, and the file **SketchFrame.java** will contain the class defining the application window.

We will define a preliminary version of our window class as:

```
// Frame for the Sketcher application
import java.awt.*;

public class SketchFrame extends Frame
{
  MenuBar menuBar = new MenuBar();            // Window menu bar

  // Constructor
  public SketchFrame(String title)
  {
    super(title);                            // Call base constructor
    setMenuBar(menuBar);                      // Add the menu bar to the window

    Menu fileMenu = new Menu("File");         // File menu
    Menu elementMenu = new Menu("Elements");  // Elements menu

    menuBar.add(fileMenu);                    // Add the file menu
    menuBar.add(elementMenu);                 // Add the element menu
  }
}
```

After you have entered this code into a new file, save the file in the **Sketcher** directory as **SketchFrame.java**.

2 Next, you can enter the code for the **Sketcher** class in a separate file:

```
// Sketching application
import java.awt.*;

public class Sketcher
{
  static SketchFrame window;                  // The application window
```

```
   public static void main(String[] args)
   {
     window = new SketchFrame("Sketcher");        // Create the app window
     Toolkit theKit = window.getToolkit();        // Get the window toolkit
     Dimension wndSize = theKit.getScreenSize();  // Get screen size

     // Set the position to screen center & size to half screen size
     window.setBounds(wndSize.width/4, wndSize.height/4,   // Position
                      wndSize.width/2, wndSize.height/2);        // Size

     window.setVisible(true);
   }
 }
```

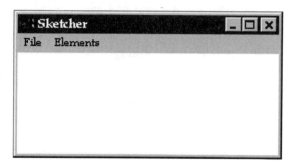

Save this file as **Sketcher.java** in the **Sketcher** directory. If you compile and run **Sketcher** you should see the window shown here.

How It Works

The **Sketcher** class has a **SketchFrame** variable as a data member, which we will use to store the application window object. We must declare this variable as **static** as there will be no instances of the **Sketcher** class around. The variable, **window**, is initialized in the method **main()** that is called when program execution begins. Once the **window** object exists, we set the size of the window based on the screen size in pixels, which we obtain using the **Toolkit** object. This is exactly the same process that we saw earlier in this chapter. Finally, in the method **main()**, we call the **setVisible()** method for the window object with the argument true to display the application window.

In the constructor for the **SketchFrame** class, we pass the title for the window to the super-class constructor. This will create the window with the title bar. We then call the **setMenuBar()** method, inherited from the **Frame** class, to specify **menuBar** as the menu bar for the window. To define the two menus that are to appear on the menu bar, we create one **Menu** object with the label **"File"** and another with the label **"Elements"**—these labels will be displayed on the menu bar. We add the **fileMenu** and **elementMenu** objects to the menu bar by calling the **add()** method for the **menuBar** object.

The instance variable that we have defined in the **SketchFrame** class represents the menu bar. Both the menu items on the menu bar are of type **Menu**, so we need to add pull-down menus to each of them. The File menu will provide the file input, output and print options, and we will eventually use the Elements menu to choose the kind of geometric figure we want to draw. We can add the menu items for these now, developing the menu a bit further.

Adding Items to a Pull-Down Menu

Both the items on the menu bar need a pull-down menu—they can't do anything by themselves because they are of type **Menu**. You use the method **add()** defined in the **Menu** class to add items in a pull-down menu. There are two versions of **add()**. The simplest adds a menu item with the label that you pass as an argument. For example:

```
fileMenu.add("New");                          // Add the menu item "New"
```

This will create a **MenuItem** object with the label **"New"**, and add it to the menu. If you want to operate on the menu item yourself, you can create the **MenuItem** object and then use the second version of the **add()** method to add it:

```
MenuItem newMenu = new MenuItem("New");    // Create the item
fileMenu.add(newMenu);                     // and add it to the menu
```

Because you created the **MenuItem** object explicitly, you can now operate on **newMenu** by calling its methods. Why would you want to do this? For one thing you might want to disable the menu under some circumstances—to render a Save operation inoperative if no file is open for example, and then enable it when a file is active. Or you might want to change the label—if your menu item cycled through a series of options for instance you could make the label reflect the current option. There are other reasons why you would want an explicit menu item which will be apparent in the next chapter when we look at how we deal with the user selecting a menu item.

You can operate on menu items by using the following methods defined in the **MenuItem** class:

Method	Description
void setEnabled(boolean b)	If **b** has the value **true** the menu item is enabled. If **b** has the value **false** the menu item is disabled.
void setLabel(String label)	Sets the menu item label to the string stored in label.
String getLabel()	Returns the current menu item label.

Since the **Menu** class is a sub-class of **MenuItem**, these methods also apply to **Menu** objects.

To add a separator to a pull-down menu you call the **addSeparator()** method for the **Menu** object.

Let's now create the pull down menus for the File and Element menus on the menu bar in the Sketcher application, and try out some of the menu items.

We can change the definition of our **SketchFrame** class to do this:

```java
// Frame for the Sketcher application
import java.awt.*;

public class SketchFrame extends Frame
{
  MenuBar menuBar = new MenuBar();                    // Window menu bar

  // Element menu items
  CheckboxMenuItem lineItem,  rectangleItem, circleItem,
                   curveItem, textItem;
  CheckboxMenuItem redItem, yellowItem, greenItem, blueItem ;

  // Constructor
  public SketchFrame(String title)
  {
    super(title);                           // Call base constructor
    setMenuBar(menuBar);                    // Add the menu bar to the window

    // Construct the file pull down menu
    Menu fileMenu = new Menu("File");       // The File menu bar item
    MenuItem item;
    fileMenu.add("New");                              // Add New item
    fileMenu.add("Open");                             // Add Open item
    fileMenu.add(item = new MenuItem("Close"));       // Add Close item
    fileMenu.addSeparator();
    fileMenu.add(item = new MenuItem("Save"));        // Add Save item
    fileMenu.add(item = new MenuItem("Save As..."));  // Add Save As item
    fileMenu.addSeparator();
    fileMenu.add(item = new MenuItem("Print"));       // Add Print item

    // Construct the Element pull down menu
    Menu  elementMenu = new Menu("Elements"); // Elements menu bar item

    // Construct the Element pull down menu
    lineItem = new CheckboxMenuItem("Line", true);
    rectangleItem = new CheckboxMenuItem("Rectangle", false);
    circleItem = new CheckboxMenuItem("Circle", false);
    curveItem = new CheckboxMenuItem("Curve", false);
    textItem = new CheckboxMenuItem("Text", false);

    redItem = new CheckboxMenuItem("Red", false);
    yellowItem = new CheckboxMenuItem("Yellow", false);
    greenItem = new CheckboxMenuItem("Green", false);
    blueItem = new CheckboxMenuItem("Blue", true);
```

```
    elementMenu.add(lineItem);
    elementMenu.add(rectangleItem);
    elementMenu.add(circleItem);
    elementMenu.add(curveItem);

    elementMenu.addSeparator();

    elementMenu.add(redItem);
    elementMenu.add(yellowItem);
    elementMenu.add(greenItem);
    elementMenu.add(blueItem);
```

```
    menuBar.add(fileMenu);                    // Add the file menu
    menuBar.add(elementMenu);                 // Add the element menu
  }
}
```

If you recompile Sketcher once more, you can run the application again to try out the menus. If you extend the **File** menu, you will see that it has the menu items that we have added.

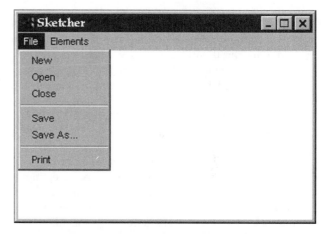

Now if you extend the Elements menu it should appear as shown with the Line and Blue items checked.

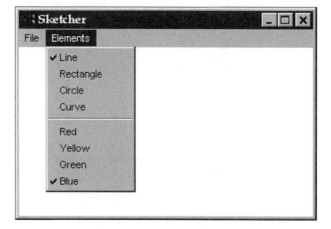

How It Works

We have defined a local **MenuItem** variable, **item**, in the **SketchFrame** class constructor which we use to store some of the **MenuItem** objects that we add to the File menu. The objects are created and stored in the variable **item** in the argument to the **add()** method for **fileMenu**. We could operate on any of the objects stored in **item** if necessary, by adding statements immediately following the call to **add()** for it, and before the variable is reused to store the next **MenuItem** object.

You can see that we don't create the **"New"** and **"Open..."** items explicitly. We just pass the name to the **add()** method and leave it to the **Menu** object to create the item. This is just to illustrate that you can do this. We will want to generate all the items in the file menu explicitly, so amend the code that adds these items to:

```
fileMenu.add(item = new MenuItem("New"));        // Add New item
fileMenu.add(item = new MenuItem("Open"));       // Add Open item
```

The Elements menu items are **CheckboxMenuItem** objects. We use these so that we can indicate the current selection by a check mark. We will make Line the default element type and Blue the default color, so we set both of these as checked by specifying **true** as the second argument to the constructor. The other items will be unchecked initially because we have specified the second argument as **false**. We could have omitted the second argument to set these items unchecked by default, but that means that you need to remember the default in order to determine what is happening. It is much better to set the checks explicitly.

You can see the effect of the **addSeparator()** method in the **Menu** class. It produces the horizontal bar separating the items for selecting an element type from those selecting colors. If you select any of the unchecked items on the Elements pull-down menu, they will be checked automatically and more than one can appear checked. We will add some code in the next chapter to make sure only one item is checked at any given time.

You might want to have the color selection item in an additional pull-down menu. We could do this by changing the code which adds the menu items for Elements as follows:

```
elementMenu.add(lineItem);
elementMenu.add(rectangleItem);
elementMenu.add(circleItem);
elementMenu.add(curveItem);

elementMenu.addSeparator();

Menu colorMenu = new Menu("Color");             // Color sub-menu
colorMenu.add(redItem);
colorMenu.add(yellowItem);
colorMenu.add(greenItem);
colorMenu.add(blueItem);

elementMenu.add(colorMenu);                     // Add the sub-menu

menuBar.add(fileMenu);                          // Add the file menu
```

Now we add a **Menu** object,
colorMenu, to the pull-down menu
for Elements. This has its own pull-
down menu consisting of the color
menu items. The Color item will be
displayed on the Elements menu with
an arrow to show a further pull-
down menu is associated with it. If
you run the application again and
extend the pull-down menus, the
window should be as shown.

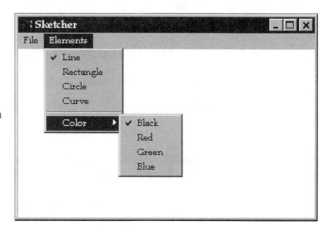

Whether you choose this menu structure or the previous one is a matter of taste. We will
see in the next chapter that the programming necessary to deal with menu selections by the
user is the same in either case.

Adding a Shortcut for a Menu Item

A **shortcut** is a unique key combination that is used to select a menu item direct from the
keyboard. A shortcut is sometimes referred to as a **menu accelerator**. A typical shortcut
would be the *Ctrl* key plus the initial letter of the menu item, so the shortcut for the File/
New menu item might be *Ctrl+N*. A shortcut is represented by an object of the class
MenuShortcut that is defined in the package, **java.awt**. You can only add shortcuts for
plain menu items at the present time. You cannot add shortcuts for **CheckboxMenuItem**
objects.

To create a shortcut, you pass the letter that is to be combined with the *Ctrl* key to form
the shortcut key combination that you want to use, to a **MenuShortcut** class constructor as
type **int**. For example, to create the shortcut that uses the key combination, *Ctrl+N*, you
could write:

```
MenuShortcut newDirect = new MenuShortcut('N');        // Shortcut Ctrl-N
```

You can also create shortcuts that use the *Shift* key, as well as the *Ctrl* key. The
MenuShortcut constructor to do this accepts a second boolean argument which you set as
true to use the *Shift* key. To create the shortcut key combination *Ctrl+Shift+N*, you could
write:

```
MenuShortcut newDirect = new MenuShortcut('N', true);    // Ctrl+Shift+N
```

This can be useful when you have two menu items with the same initial letter. Every
shortcut key combination must be unique, and using the shift key enables you to use the
same initial letter for both.

To add a shortcut to a menu item, you use a **MenuItem** class constructor that accepts a **MenuShortcut** object as a second argument. You can create the New menu item with a shortcut, and add it to the File menu with the statement:

```
fileMenu.add(item = new MenuItem("New", new MenuShortcut('N')));
```

We can add some shortcuts to the menu in the Sketcher application window to see how this works in practice.

Try It Out—Adding Menu Shortcuts

We can add some shortcuts to Sketcher by amending the statements that add the items to the File menu in the **SketchFrame** class constructor:

```
// Frame for the Sketcher application
import java.awt.*;

public SketchFrame(String title)
{
  super(title);                          // Call base constructor
  setMenuBar(menuBar);                   // Add the menu bar to the window

  // Construct the file pull down menu
  Menu fileMenu = new Menu("File");      // The File menu bar item
  MenuItem item;
  fileMenu.add(item = new MenuItem("New",
                    new MenuShortcut('N')));       // Add New item
  fileMenu.add(item = new MenuItem("Open",
                    new MenuShortcut('O')));       // Add Open item
  fileMenu.add(item = new MenuItem("Close",
                     new MenuShortcut('C')));      // Add Close item
  fileMenu.addSeparator();
  fileMenu.add(item = new MenuItem("Save",
                    new MenuShortcut('S')));       // Add Save item
  fileMenu.add(item = new MenuItem("Save As..."));  // Add Save As item
  fileMenu.addSeparator();
  fileMenu.add(item = new MenuItem("Print",
                     new MenuShortcut('P')));      // Add Print item

  // Rest of the constructor as before...
}
```

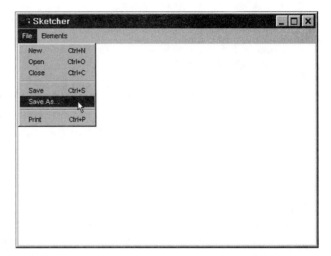

If you save **SketchFrame.java** after you have made the changes, you can recompile Sketcher and run it again. The file menu will now appear as show here.

How It Works

We use the **MenuItem** class constructor that accepts a **MenuShortcut** as a second argument for all the menu items except Save As. You could add one for this too, if you want to, but it must not be the same key combination as that for the Save item.

This just adds the shortcut key combination for each item on the pull-down menu. They don't actually work at the moment but at least they look good. We will add the code to implement the shortcuts in the next chapter.

More on Applets

Applets are a peculiar kind of program as they are only intended to be executed in the context of a **.html** file. This places some rather severe restrictions on what you can do in an applet to protect the environment in which they are executed. Without these restrictions they would be a very direct means for someone to screw up your system—in short, a virus delivery system.

The main limitations on an applet are:

- An applet cannot have any access to files on the local computer
- An applet cannot invoke any other program on the local computer
- An applet cannot communicate with any computer other than the computer from which the **.html** page containing the applet was downloaded

Because they are intended to be shipped over the Internet as part of an **.html** page, applets should be compact. This doesn't mean that they are inevitably simple or unsophisticated. Because they can access the host computer on which they originated they can provide a powerful means of enabling access to files on that host, for example, but they are usually relatively small to allow them to be easily downloaded.

The rather trivial applet we ran in Chapter 1 was:

```
import java.applet.Applet;
import java.awt.Graphics;

public class MyFirstApplet extends Applet
{
  public void paint(Graphics g)
  {
    g.drawString("To climb a ladder, start at the bottom rung", 20, 90);
  }
}
```

You can see that we have **import** statements for the **Applet** class from the package **java.applet**, and the **Graphics** class from the package **java.awt**. We will be seeing a lot more about the **Graphics** class in later chapters. The **paint()** method which we have implemented here to output some text is defined in the class **Component**, so all components have this method. The **paint()** method is used to draw on a component—we will be exploring the detail of how you can implement the **paint()** method to draw on a component in Chapter 13.

Besides the **paint()** method which is called automatically when the applet panel needs to be drawn, the **Applet** class includes the following methods which are all called automatically by the browser or applet viewer that is controlling the applet:

Method	Description
void init()	You implement this method to do any initialization that is necessary for the applet. This method is called once by the browser when the applet starts execution.
void start()	You implement this method to start the processing for the applet. For example, if your applet displayed an animated image, you would start a thread for the animation in this method.
	This method is called immediately after **init()**. It is also called if the user returns to the current **.html** page after leaving it.
void stop()	This method is called when the user moves off the page containing the applet. You implement this to stop any operations that you started in the **start()** method.
void destroy()	This method is called after the **stop()** method when the browser is shut down. In this situation the browser calls the **stop()** method, followed by this method. With it you can release any resources your applet uses that are managed by the local operating system. This includes such things as resources used to display a window.

These are the basic methods you need to implement in the typical applet. We really need some graphics knowledge to go further with implementing an applet, so we will return to the practical application of these methods in Chapter 13.

Converting an Application to an Applet

Subject to the restrictions that we described in the previous section, you can convert an application to an applet relatively easily. You just need to be clear about how each part of program executes. You know that an application is normally started in the method `main()`. The method `main()` is not called for an applet but the method `init()` is, so one thing you need to do is to add an `init()` method to the application class. The other obvious difference is that an applet always extends the `Applet` class.

We could demonstrate how you can convert an application so that it works as an applet as well by changing the definition of the Sketcher class.

Try It Out—Running Sketcher as an Applet

1 You need to modify the contents of `Sketcher.java` so that it contains the following:

```java
// Sketching application
import java.awt.*;
import java.applet.*;

public class Sketcher extends Applet
{
  static Sketcher theApp;                    // The application object
  SketchFrame window;                        // The application window

  public static void main(String[] args)
  {
    theApp = new Sketcher();                 // Create the application object
    theApp.init();                           // ...and initialize it
  }

  // Initialize
  public  void init()
  {
    window = new SketchFrame("Sketcher");      // Create the app window
    Toolkit theKit = window.getToolkit();      // Get the window toolkit
    Dimension wndSize = theKit.getScreenSize(); // Get screen size

    // Set the position to screen center & size to half screen size
    window.setBounds(wndSize.width/4, wndSize.height/4,      // Position
                     wndSize.width/2, wndSize.height/2);      // Size

    window.setVisible(true);
  }
}
```

2 To run Sketcher as an applet, you just need to add an `.html` file to the `Sketcher` directory with the contents:

```
<APPLET code="Sketcher.class" width=300 height=200>
</APPLET>
```

If you recompile the revised version of the `Sketcher` class, you can run it as before, or using `AppletViewer`.

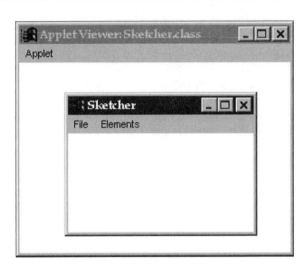

How It Works

The class now extends the class `Applet`, and an `import` statement has been added for the `java.applet` package.

The `init()` method now does most of what the method `main()` did before. The method `main()` now creates an instance of the `Sketcher` class and stores it in the `static` data member `theApp`. The method `main()` then calls the `init()` method for the new `Sketcher` object. The `window` variable no longer needs to be declared as `static` since it is always created in the `init()` method.

The class member, `theApp`, must be declared as `static` for the case when the program is run as an application. When an application starts execution, no `Sketcher` object exists, so the data member, `theApp`, does not exist either. If `theApp` is not declared as `static`, you can only create the `Sketcher` object as a local variable in `main()`.

Even though Sketcher is running as an applet, the application window appears as a detached window from the `AppletViewer` window, and it is still positioned relative to the screen. Of course, when we come to implement the File menu, it will no longer be legal to derive the `Sketcher` class from the `Applet` class since it will contravene the rule that an applet must not access the files on the local machine. All you need to do to provide for this is to remove the `import` statement for `java.applet` and remove `extends Applet` from the `Sketcher` class header line. Everything else can stay as it is.

Summary

In this chapter you have learnt how to create an application window, and how to use containers in the creation of the GUI for a program. We discussed the following important points in this chapter:

- The package **java.awt** provides classes for creating a graphical user interface (GUI)

- A component is an object that is used to form part of the GUI for a program. All components have the class **Component** as a super-class

- A container is a component that can contain other components. A container object is created with a class that is a sub-class of **Container**. The classes **Panel**, **Applet**, **Window**, **Frame**, **Dialog** and **FileDialog** are containers

- The class **Applet** is the base class for an applet. The **Frame** class is a base class for an application window with a title bar, borders and a menu

- The arrangement of components in a container is controlled by a layout manager

- The default layout manager for **Frame** and **Dialog** objects is of type **BorderLayout** and the default layout for an **Applet** object is of type **FlowLayout**

- The **GridBagLayout** provides the most flexible control of the positioning of components in a container. The position of a component in a **GridBagLayout** is controlled by a **GridBagConstraints** object

- A menu bar is represented by a **MenuBar** object. Menu items can be objects of type **Menu**, of type **MenuItem**, or of type **CheckboxMenuItem**

- You associate a pull-down menu with an item of type **Menu**

In the next chapter we will move on to look at events, how we associate program actions with menu items and components within a window, and how we can close a window when the close icon is clicked.

Exercises

1 Create an application with a square window in the center of the screen which is half the height of the screen by deriving your own window class from **Frame**.

2 Add six buttons to the application in the previous example in a vertical column on the left side of the application window.

3 Add a menu bar containing the items File, Edit, Window and Help.

4 Add a pull-down menu for Edit containing the two groups of items of your own choice with a separator between them.

5 Add another item to the Edit pull-down menu which itself has a pull-down menu.

Handling Events

In this chapter you will learn how a window-based application is structured, and how to respond to user actions in an application or an applet. This is the fundamental mechanism you will be using in virtually all of your Java programs. Once you understand how actions are handled in Java, you will be equipped to implement the application-specific code that is necessary to make your program do what you want.

In this chapter you will learn:

▶ What an event is

▶ What an event-driven program is and how it is structured

▶ How events are handled in Java

▶ How events are categorized in Java

▶ How components can handle events

▶ What an event listener is, and how you create one

▶ What an adapter class is and how you can use it to make programming the handling of events easier

Window-Based Programs

Before we get into the programming specifics of window-based programs, we need to understand a little of how such programs are structured, and how they work. There are fundamental differences between the console programs that we have been producing up to now, and a window-based Java program. With a console program, you start the program, and the program code determines the sequences of events. Generally everything is predetermined. You enter data when required and the program will output data when it wants. At any given time, the specific program code to be executed next is usually known.

A window-based program, or an applet come to that, is quite different. The operation of the program is driven by what you do with the GUI. Selecting menu items or buttons using the mouse, or through the keyboard, causes particular actions within the program. At any given moment you have a whole range of possible interactions available to you, each of which will result in a different program action. Until you do something, the specific program code that is to be executed next is not known.

Event-Driven Programs

Your actions when you are using the GUI for a window-based program or an applet—clicking a menu item or a button, moving the mouse, and so on—are first recognized and identified by the operating system. For each action, the operating system determines which of the programs currently running on your computer should know about it, and passes the action on to that program. When you click a mouse button, it is the operating system that registers this and notes the position of the mouse cursor on the screen. It then decides which application owns the window where the cursor was when you pressed the button, and communicates the mouse button press to that program. The signals that a program receives from the operating system as a result of your actions are called **events**.

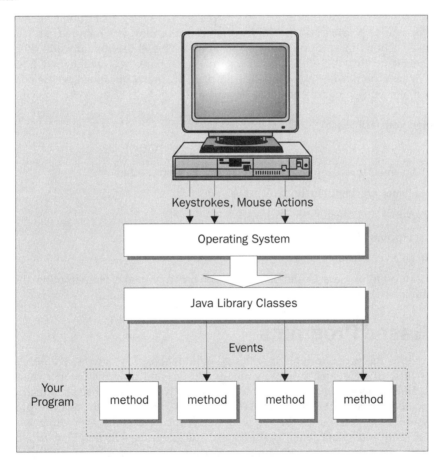

A program is not obliged to respond to any particular event. If you just move the mouse for instance, the program need not include any code to react to that. If it doesn't, the event is quietly disposed of. Each event that the program does recognize is associated with one or more methods, and when the event occurs—when you click a menu item, for example—the particular methods in the program that are associated with that event will be called automatically. A window-based program is called an **event-driven program**, because the sequence of events created as a result of your interaction with the GUI drives and determines what happens in the program.

Events are not limited to window-based applications—they are a quite general concept. Most programs that control or monitor things are event-driven. Any occurrence external to a program such as a switch closing, or a preset temperature being reached, can be registered as an event. In Java you can even create events within your program to signal some other part of the code that something noteworthy has happened. However, we are going to concentrate of the kinds of events that occur when you interact as a user, with a program.

The Event Handling Process

To manage the user's interaction with the components that make up the GUI for a program, we must understand how events are handled in Java. To get an idea of how this works, let's consider a specific example. Don't worry too much about the class names and other details here. Just try to get a feel for how things connect together.

Suppose the user clicks a button in the GUI for your program. The button is the **source** of this event. The event in your program originates in the **Button** object. An event always has a source object. When the button is clicked, it will create a new object that represents and identifies this event—in this case an object of type **ActionEvent**. This object will contain information about the event and its source. Any event that is passed to a Java program will be represented by a particular event object—and this object will be passed as an argument to the method that is to handle the event.

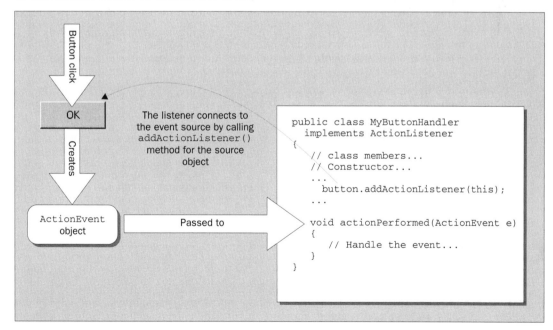

The event object corresponding to the button click will be passed to any **listener** object that has previously registered an interest in this kind of event—a listener object being simply an object that listens for particular events. A listener is also called a **target** for an event. Here, 'passing the event to the listener' just means calling a particular method in the listener object and passing the event object to it as an argument.

So how do you define a listener? You can make the objects of any class listener objects by making the class implement a **listener interface**. There are quite a variety of listener interfaces, to cater for different kinds of events. In the case of our button click, the **ActionListener** interface needs to be implemented to receive the event from the button. The code that is to receive this event object and respond to the event is implemented in a method declared in the listener interface. In our example, the **actionPerformed()** method in the **ActionListener** interface is called when the event occurs, and the event object is passed as an argument. Each kind of listener interface defines particular methods that receive the events that that listener has been designed to deal with.

Of course, just implementing a listener interface doesn't relate the listener object to the event source. You still have to connect the listener to the source, or sources, of the events it is interested in. You register a listener object with a source by calling a particular method in the source object. In this case, we call the **addActionListener()** method for the **Button** object, and pass the listener object as an argument to the method.

This mechanism for handling events using listeners is very flexible, and very efficient, particularly for GUI events. Any number of listeners can receive a particular event. However, a particular event is only passed to the listeners that have registered to receive it, so only interested parties are involved in responding to each event. Since being a listener just requires a suitable interface to be implemented, you can receive and handle events virtually anywhere you like. The way in which events are handled in Java, using listener objects, is referred to as the **delegation event model**. This is because the responsibility for responding to events that originate with a component, such as a button or a menu item, is not handled by the objects that originated the events themselves—but is delegated to separate listener objects.

> *Not all event handling necessarily requires a listener. A component can handle its own events, as we shall see a little later in this chapter.*

Let's now get down to looking at the specifics of what kinds of events we can expect, and the range of listener interfaces that process them.

Event Classes

Clearly, there are lots of different kinds of events to which your program may need to respond—from menus, from buttons, from the mouse, from the keyboard and a number of others. In order to have a structured approach to handling events, these are broken down into subsets. At the topmost level, there are two broad categories of events in Java:

▶ **Low-level Events**—these are events that arise from the keyboard or from the mouse, or events associated with operations on a window such as reducing it to an icon or closing it. The meaning of a low-level event is something like 'the mouse was moved on this component', 'this window has been closed' or 'this key was pressed'.

▶ **Semantic Events**—these are specific component-related events such as clicking a button to cause some program action, or adjusting a scrollbar. They originate, and you interpret them, in the context of the GUI you have created for your program. The meaning of a semantic event is typically something like 'the OK button was pressed' or 'the Save menu item was selected'. Each kind of component, a button or a menu item for example, can generate a particular kind of semantic event.

These two categories can seem to be a bit confusing as they overlap in a way. If you click a button, you create a semantic event object—that's the **ActionEvent** we had in the example we just discussed. The click also produces a low-level event object in the form of a mouse click on that component. In fact it produces more than one mouse event as we shall see. All of these events are perfectly valid. Whether your program handles the low-level events or the semantic event, or possibly both kinds of event, depends on what you want to do.

All events relating to the GUI for a program are represent by classes defined in the package **java.awt.event**. This package also defines the listener interfaces for the various kinds of events that can occur in this context.

Low-Level Event Classes

There are four kinds of low-level events that you can elect to handle in your programs. They are represented by the following classes in the **java.awt.event** package:

Event	Description
FocusEvent	Objects of this class represent events that originate when a component gains or loses focus. Any component can create these events.
MouseEvent	Objects of this class represent events that result from user actions with the mouse such as moving the mouse or pressing a mouse key.
KeyEvent	Objects of this class represent events that arise from pressing keys on the keyboard.
WindowEvent	Objects of this class represent events that relate to a window, such as activating or deactivating a window, reducing a window to its icon or closing a window. These events relate to objects of the **Window** class or any sub-class of **Window**.

Just so that you know, this is not an exhaustive list of all of the low-level event classes. It is a list of the ones you need to know about. For example, there is the **PaintEvent** class which is concerned with the internals of how components get painted on the screen. There is also another low-level event class, **ContainerEvent**, which defines events relating to a container such as adding or removing components. You can ignore this class as these events are handled automatically.

Each of these classes defines methods that enable you to analyze the event. For a **MouseEvent** object, for example, you can get the coordinates of the cursor when the event occurred. These low-level event classes also inherit methods from their super-classes, and are related in the manner shown in the diagram:

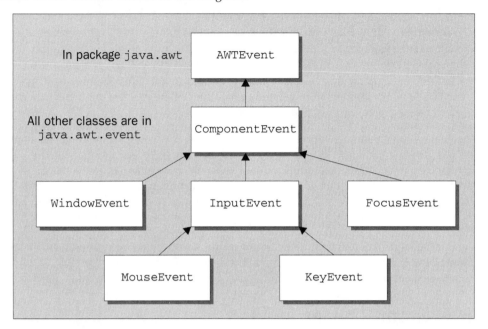

The class **AWTEvent** is itself a subclass of **java.util.EventObject**. The **EventObject** class implements the **Serializable** interface, so all objects of the event classes in the diagram are serializable. It also defines a method **getSource()** which returns the object that is the source of an event as type **Object**. This method will be inherited by all the event classes shown.

The class **AWTEvent** defines **public** variables with **final** values that identify the various kinds of events. These variables are named consistently in the form of the event name in capital letters, followed by _**MASK**. The variables identifying the low-level events we are interested in are:

MOUSE_EVENT_MASK	**MOUSE_MOTION_EVENT_MASK**
KEY_EVENT_MASK	**FOCUS_EVENT_MASK**
WINDOW_EVENT_MASK	

There are two variables covering mouse events. This is to separate the mouse button events from the mouse movement events. As we will see there are two listener interfaces for mouse events covering the two categories of events identified by **MOUSE_EVENT_MASK** and **MOUSE_MOTION_EVENT_MASK**.

FYI There are also event masks for component events that are represented by objects of the class `ComponentEvent`, and for container events. These events occur when a component is moved or resized, or a component is added to a container, for example. You won't need to get involved in these events at all because they are all taken care of automatically, as we noted earlier.

You can use the variables identifying event masks to enable a particular group of events in a component object. You call the **enableEvents()** method for the component, and pass the variable for the events you want enabled as an argument. However, you *only* do this when you are not using a listener. Registering a listener automatically enables the events that the listener wants to hear, so you don't need to call the **enableEvents()** method. The circumstance when you would do this is when you want an object to handle some of its own events.

Making a Window Handle its own Events

An example of where you might want to call **enableEvents()** exists in our **SketchFrame** class in the Sketcher program. We can make the close icon work in the program by handling the event associated with it within the window object itself, without using a listener object.

Try It Out—Closing a Window

We need to modify the **SketchFrame** class definition from the previous chapter as follows:

```
// Frame for Sketcher application
import java.awt.*;
import java.awt.event.*;

public class SketchFrame extends Frame
{
  MenuBar menubar = new MenuBar();           // Window menu bar

  // Element menu items
  CheckboxMenuItem lineItem,  rectangleItem, circleItem, curveItem,
           textItem;

  // Color menu items
  CheckboxMenuItem redItem, yellowItem, greenItem, blueItem;

  // Constructor
  public SketchFrame(String title)
  {
    super(title);                    // Call base constructor
    setMenuBar(menubar);             // Add the menu bar to the window
```

```java
// Construct the file pull down menu
Menu fileMenu = new Menu("File");     // The File menu bar item
MenuItem item;
fileMenu.add(item = new MenuItem("New",
                new MenuShortcut('N')));          // Add New item
fileMenu.add(item = new MenuItem("Open",
                 new MenuShortcut('O')));         // Add Open item
fileMenu.add(item = new MenuItem("Close",
                  new MenuShortcut('C')));        // Add Close item
fileMenu.addSeparator();
fileMenu.add(item = new MenuItem("Save",
                new MenuShortcut('S')));          // Add Save item
fileMenu.add(item = new MenuItem("Save As..."));  // Add Save as item
fileMenu.addSeparator();
fileMenu.add(item = new MenuItem("Print",
                new MenuShortcut('P')));          // Add Print item

// Construct the Element pull down menu
Menu  elementMenu = new Menu("Elements"); // Elements menu bar item
lineItem = new CheckboxMenuItem("Line", true);
rectangleItem = new CheckboxMenuItem("Rectangle", false);
circleItem = new CheckboxMenuItem("Circle", false);
curveItem = new CheckboxMenuItem("Curve", false);
textItem = new CheckboxMenuItem("Text", false);

// Add the element type menu items
elementMenu.add(lineItem);
elementMenu.add(rectangleItem);
elementMenu.add(circleItem);
elementMenu.add(curveItem);
elementMenu.add(textItem);
elementMenu.addSeparator();

// Construct the Color item pull down menu
Menu colorMenu = new Menu("Color");      // Color sub-menu item
redItem = new CheckboxMenuItem("Red", false);
yellowItem = new CheckboxMenuItem("Yellow", false);
greenItem = new CheckboxMenuItem("Green", false);
blueItem = new CheckboxMenuItem("Blue", true);

// Add the color menu items
colorMenu.add(redItem);
colorMenu.add(yellowItem);
colorMenu.add(greenItem);
colorMenu.add(blueItem);

elementMenu.add(colorMenu);                      // Add the color sub-menu

menubar.add(fileMenu);                           // Add the file menu
menubar.add(elementMenu);                        // Add the element menu
```

```
      enableEvents(AWTEvent.WINDOW_EVENT_MASK);  // Enable window events
    }

    // Handle window events
    protected void processWindowEvent(WindowEvent e)
    {
      if (e.getID() == WindowEvent.WINDOW_CLOSING)
      {
        dispose();                      // Release resources
        System.exit(0);                 // Exit the program
      }
      super.processWindowEvent(e);      // Pass on the event
    }
  }
```

When you compile **SketchFrame** and run **Sketcher**, you'll now be able to close the window and exit the program gracefully.

How It Works

The **import** statement makes the **java.awt.event** package and its various event classes available to the class file. We call **enableEvents()** in the constructor with **WINDOW_EVENT_MASK** as the argument to enable window events. This enables all the window events which are identified by a set of **event IDs** defined by the following variables in the **WindowEvent** class:

Event ID	Description
WINDOW_OPENED	The event that occurs the first time a window is made visible.
WINDOW_CLOSING	The event that occurs as a result of the close icon being selected or Close being selected from the window's system menu. Under Windows 95, the system menu pops up if you click on the icon at the left-hand end of the title bar.
WINDOW_CLOSED	The event that occurs when the window has been closed.
WINDOW_ACTIVATED	The event that occurs when the window is activated—for example, by clicking on it when it is deactivated.
WINDOW_DEACTIVATED	The event that occurs when the window is deactivated—by clicking on another window, for example.
WINDOW_ICONIFIED	The event that occurs when the window is minimized and reduced to an icon.
WINDOW_DEICONIFIED	The event that occurs when the window is maximized and restored from an icon.

Any of these events occurring will result in the **processWindowEvent()** method that we have added to the class being called. Our version of the method overrides the base class method which is responsible for passing the event to any listeners that have been registered.

The argument of type **WindowEvent** that is passed to the method identifies the particular event that occurs. To obtain the ID of the event, we call the **getID()** method for the event object **e**, and compare the ID returned to the **WINDOW_CLOSING** event ID. If the event is **WINDOW_CLOSING**, we call the **dispose()** method for the window to close the window and release the system resources it is using. We then call the **exit()** method defined in the class **System** to close the application.

> *The **getID()** method is defined in the class **AWTEvent** which is a super-class of all the AWT event classes, so all event objects have this method.*

In our **SketchFrame** class, the **dispose()** method is inherited from the class **Frame**. It releases all the resources for the object including those for all components owned by the object. Note that calling the **dispose()** method doesn't affect the window object in our program. It just tells the operating system that the resources used to display the window and the components it contains are no longer required. The window object is still around together with its components, so you could call its methods or even open it again.

> *Note that we call the **processWindowEvent()** method in the super-class if it is not the closing event. This is most important as this allows the event to be passed on to any listeners that have been registered for these events. If we don't call **processWindowEvent()** for the super-class, any events that we do not handle will be lost, because the base class method is normally responsible for passing the event to the listeners that have been registered to receive it.*

Enabling Other Low-Level Events

The **enableEvents()** method is inherited from the **Component** class. This means that any component can elect to handle its own events. You just call **enableEvents()** method for the component and pass an argument defining the events you want the component to handle. If you want to enable more than one type of event for a component, you just combine the event masks from **AWTEvent** that we saw earlier by ORing them together. To make our window handle mouse events as well as window events, you could write:

```
enableEvents(AWTEvent.WINDOW_EVENT_MASK|AWTEvent.MOUSE_EVENT_MASK);
```

Of course, you must now implement **processMouseEvent()** for the class. Like the **processWindowEvent()** method, this method is **protected** and has **void** as a return type. It passes the event as an argument of type **MouseEvent**. The set of event handling methods that you can override to handle component events are:

Event Handling Methods	Description
processEvent(AWTEvent e)	This method is called for any events that are enabled for the component.
processFocusEvent(FocusEvent e)	This method will be called for focus events if they are enabled for the component.

536

Event Handling Methods	Description
`processKeyEvent(KeyEvent e)`	This method will be called for key events if they are enabled for the component.
`processMouseEvent(MouseEvent e)`	This method will be called for mouse button events if they are enabled for the component.
`processMouseMotionEvent(MouseEvent e)`	This method will be called for mouse move and drag events if they are enabled for the component.

These are all **protected** methods that have a return type of **void**. The method `processWindowEvent()` is only available for **Window**, **Frame**, **Dialog** and **FileDialog** objects so don't try to enable window events on other components.

Although it was very convenient to handle the window closing event in the SketchFrame class by implementing processWindowEvent(), as a general rule you should use listeners to handle events. Using listeners is the recommended approach to handling events in the majority of circumstances, since separating the event handling from the object that originated the event results in a simpler code structure, and is less error prone.

Low-Level Event Listeners

To create a class that defines an event listener, your class must implement a listener interface. All event listener interfaces extend the interface **java.util.EventListener**. This interface does not declare any methods though, since it is just used to identify an interface as an event listener interface. It also allows a variable of type **EventListener** to store any kind of event listener object.

There are five low-level event listener interfaces corresponding to the five event masks that are of interest to us that we saw earlier. These declare the following methods:

Listener Interfaces	Defined Methods	Description
`WindowListener`	`windowOpened(WindowEvent e)`	Called the first time the window is opened.
	`windowClosing(WindowEvent e)`	Called when the system menu <u>C</u>lose item or the window close icon is selected.
	`windowClosed(WindowEvent e)`	Called when the window has been closed.

Table Continued on Following Page

Listener Interfaces	Defined Methods	Description
	`windowActivated(WindowEvent e)`	Called when the window is activated—by clicking on it, for example.
	`windowDeactivated(WindowEvent e)`	Called when a window is deactivated—by clicking on another window, for example.
	`windowIconified(WindowEvent e)`	Called when a window is minimized and reduced to an icon.
	`windowDeiconified(WindowEvent e)`	Called when a window is maximized from an icon.
`MouseListener`	`mouseClicked(MouseEvent e)`	Called when a mouse button is clicked on a component—the button is pressed and released.
	`mousePressed(MouseEvent e)`	Called when a mouse button is pressed on a component.
	`mouseReleased(MouseEvent e)`	Called when a mouse button is pressed on a component.
	`mouseEntered(MouseEvent e)`	Called when the mouse enters the area occupied by a component.
	`mouseExited(MouseEvent e)`	Called when the mouse enters the area occupied by a component.
`MouseMotionListener`	`mouseMoved(MouseEvent e)`	Called when the mouse is moved within a component.
	`mouseDragged(MouseEvent e)`	Called when the mouse is moved within a component while a mouse button is held down.
`KeyListener`	`keyTyped(KeyEvent e)`	Called when a key on the keyboard is pressed then released.
	`keyPressed(KeyEvent e)`	Called when a key on the keyboard is pressed.

Listener Interfaces	Defined Methods	Description
	keyReleased(KeyEvent e)	Called when a key on the keyboard is released.
FocusListener	focusGained(FocusEvent e)	Called when a compo nent gains the keyboard focus.
	focusLost(FocusEvent e)	Called when a component loses the keyboard focus.

There is a method declared in the **WindowListener** interface corresponding to each of the event IDs that are defined in the **WindowEvent** class that we saw earlier. If you deduced from this that the methods in the other listener interface correspond to event IDs for the other event classes, you are right. All the IDs for mouse events are defined in the **MouseEvent** class. These are:

MOUSE_CLICKED	**MOUSE_PRESSED**	**MOUSE_RELEASED**
MOUSE_ENTERED	**MOUSE_EXITED**	
MOUSE_MOVED	**MOUSE_DRAGGED**	

The event IDs defined in the **KeyEvent** class are:

KEY_TYPED	**KEY_PRESSED**	**KEY_RELEASED**

Those defined in the **FocusEvent** class are:

FOCUS_GAINED	**FOCUS_LOST**

To implement a listener for a particular event type you just need to implement the interface methods. We could handle the window events for our **SketchFrame** class by making the application class the listener for window events.

Try It Out—Implementing a Low-Level Event Listener

First delete the call to the **enableEvents()** method in the **SketchFrame()** constructor. Then delete the definition of the **processWindowEvent()** method from the class definition. Now we can modify the **Sketcher** class so that it is a listener for window events:

```
// Sketching application
import java.awt.*;
import java.awt.event.*;
```

539

```java
public class Sketcher implements WindowListener
{
  static Sketcher theApp;      // The application object
  SketchFrame window;          // The document view

  public static void main(String[] args)
  {
    theApp = new Sketcher();                  // Create the application object
    theApp.init();                            // ...and initialize it
  }

  // Initialization of the application
  public void init()
  {
    window = new SketchFrame("Sketcher");       // Create the app window
    Toolkit theKit = window.getToolkit();       // Get the window toolkit
    Dimension wndSize = theKit.getScreenSize(); // Get screen size

    // Set the position to screen center & size to 2/3 screen size
    window.setBounds(wndSize.width/6, wndSize.height/6,       // Position
                     2*wndSize.width/3, 2*wndSize.height/3);  // Size

    window.addWindowListener(this);           // theApp as window listener
    window.setVisible(true);                  // Display the window
    window.requestFocus();                    // Request the focus
  }

  // Handler for window closing event
  public void windowClosing(WindowEvent e)
  {
    if(e.getID() == WindowEvent.WINDOW_CLOSING)
    {
      window.dispose();          // Release the window resources
      System.exit(0);            // End the application
    }
  }

  // Listener interface functions we must implement - but don't need
  public void windowOpened(WindowEvent e) {}
  public void windowClosed(WindowEvent e) {}
  public void windowIconified(WindowEvent e) {}
  public void windowDeiconified(WindowEvent e) {}
  public void windowActivated(WindowEvent e) {}
  public void windowDeactivated(WindowEvent e) {}
}
```

If you run the Sketcher program again, you will see it works just as before, but now the close operation is being handled by the **Sketcher** class object.

How It Works

A couple of minor unrelated changes have been made here. The class no longer implements **Applet**, because some of the things we will add eventually are not consistent with Sketcher being run as an applet. The size of the window has also been increased to two thirds of the screen size. This will be a rather more convenient size for the application window since we will be adding more to it before the end of this chapter.

The **import** statement for the package **java.awt.event** is essential here because we need access to the **WindowListener** interface. The **Sketcher** class definition now implements the **WindowListener** interface which means we must implement all seven methods declared in the interface. Only the **windowClosing()** method has any content here—all the rest are empty because we don't need to use them. The **windowClosing()** method does the same as the **processWindowEvent()** method that we implemented for the previous version of the **SketchFrame** class, but here we don't need to pass the event on. This is only necessary when you handle events within the object that originates them, in order to allow any listeners the chance to receive the events. Here, if there were other listeners around for our window events they would automatically receive the event.

We register the application object as the listener for the **window** object by calling **addWindowListener()** for that object in the **init()** method. The argument to **addWindowListener()** is the listener object that is to receive window events. Here it is the variable **this**—which references the application object. If we had other listener objects that we wanted to register to receive this event, we would just need to add more calls to the **addWindowListener()** method—one call for each listener.

Having to implement six methods that we don't need is rather tedious. We have a way to get around this though—by using an inner class (which we met in Chapter 5), and what is called an **adapter class**, to define a listener.

Using Adapter Classes

An **adapter class** is a term for a class that implements a listener interface with methods that have no content. You can derive your own listener class from the adapter classes that are provided with the AWT, and just implement the methods that you are interested in. The other empty methods will be inherited from the adapter class so you don't have to worry about them. There is an adapter class for each of the low-level listener interfaces:

FocusAdapter	KeyAdapter
MouseAdapter	MouseMotionAdapter
WindowAdapter	

They each implement all of the methods in the correspondingly named listener interface.

To handle the window closing event for the Sketcher application, we could derive our own class from the **WindowAdapter** class and just implement the **windowClosing()** method. We can also make it an inner class for the class **Sketcher**, so we don't need to put it in a separate file.

Try It Out—Implementing an Adapter Class

The version of the **Sketcher** class to implement this will be as follows, with changes to the previous version highlighted:

```
// Sketching application
import java.awt.*;
import java.awt.event.*;

public class Sketcher
{
  static Sketcher theApp;    // The application object
  SketchFrame window;        // The document view

public static void main(String[] args)
  {
    theApp = new Sketcher();            // Create the application object
    theApp.init();                      // ...and initialize it
  }

  // Initialization of the application
  public void init()
  {
    window = new SketchFrame("Sketcher");
    Toolkit theKit = window.getToolkit();       // Get the window toolkit
    Dimension wndSize = theKit.getScreenSize(); // Get screen size

    // Set the position to screen center & size to 2/3 screen size
    window.setBounds(wndSize.width/6, wndSize.height/6,      // Position
                     2*wndSize.width/3, 2*wndSize.height/3); // Size

    window.addWindowListener(new WindowHandler()); // Add window listener
    window.setVisible(true);                        // Display the window
    window.requestFocus();                          // Request the focus
  }

  // Handler class for window events
  class WindowHandler extends WindowAdapter
  {
    // Handler for window closing event
    public void windowClosing(WindowEvent e)
    {
      if (e.getID() == WindowEvent.WINDOW_CLOSING)
      {
        window.dispose();        // Release the window resources
        System.exit(0);          // End the application
      }
    }
  }
}
```

How It Works

As the **Sketcher** class is no longer the listener for **window**, it does not need to implement the **WindowListener** interface. The **WindowHandler** class is the listener class for window events. Because the **WindowHandler** class is an inner class to the **Sketcher** class, it has access to all the members of the class, so calling the **dispose()** method for the **window** object is straightforward—we just access the **window** member of the top-level class. The **WindowAdapter** object that is the listener for the **window** object is created in the argument to the **addWindowListener()** method for **window**. We don't need an explicit variable to contain it. It will be stored in a data member of the **window** class object. This data member is inherited from the **Window** super-class for our **SketchFrame** class.

 *An easy mistake to make when you are using adapter classes is to misspell the name of the method that you are implementing the event—typically by using the wrong case for a letter. In this case you won't be overriding the adapter class method at all, you will be adding a new method. Your code will compile perfectly well but your program will not handle any events. They will all be passed to the method in the adapter class with the name your method should have—which does nothing of course. This can be a bit mystifying until you realize where the problem is.*

Clearly we have not finished with low-level events yet. We will return to handling more low-level events in the next chapter when we begin to add drawing code to the Sketcher program. In the meantime, let's start looking into how we can manage semantic events.

Semantic Events

As we said earlier, semantic events are events relating to operations on the components in the GUI for your program. If you select a menu item or click on a button, a semantic event is generated. There are three classes that represent semantic events, and they are all derived from the **AWTEvent** class, as shown in the diagram.

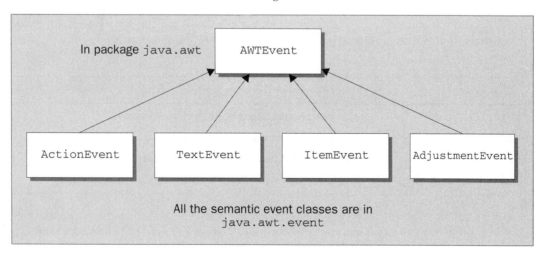

Different kinds of components can produce different kinds of semantic event. The events that can be produced by the various components are:

Event Type	Produced by Objects of Type
ActionEvent	Button
	List
	MenuItem
	TextField
TextEvent	TextArea
	TextField
ItemEvent	Checkbox
	CheckboxMenuItem
	Choice
	List
AdjustmentEvent	Scrollbar

Only a **List** object can produce two different semantic events. For all the others, the component only produces one kind of event. In the AWT, the **AdjustmentEvent** type is unique to **Scrollbar** objects.

Of course, any class you derive from these classes to define customized components can be the source for the event that the base class generates. If you define your own class for buttons, **MyFancyButton** say, your class will have **Button** as a base class, inherit all of the methods from the **Button** class, and objects of your class will originate events of type **ActionEvent**.

Each of the component classes in the table defines a method that you can override in your derived class when you want your objects of your component class to handle their own events. The method name will correspond to the type of event the component can create, and there are four possible methods corresponding to the four kinds of semantic event, as follows:

Event Type	Event Handling Method
ActionEvent	processActionEvent(ActionEvent e)
TextEvent	processTextEvent(TextEvent e)
ItemEvent	processItemEvent(ItemEvent e)
AdjustmentEvent	processAdjustmentEvent(AdjustmentEvent e)

As you can see, each of these methods expects to receive an object of the appropriate event type as an argument—**ActionEvent**, **TextEvent**, **ItemEvent** and **AdjustmentEvent** respectively. They are all defined in the component classes as **protected**, and they all have a **void** return type.

Just as we saw with low-level events, if you want your component object to handle its own events, you need to call **enableEvents()** for the component and pass the mask variable identifying the event to the method. The class **AWTEvent** defines three public mask variables that identify semantic events:

ACTION_EVENT_MASK   **ITEM_EVENT_MASK**   **ADJUSTMENT_EVENT_MASK**

However, most of the time, it is more convenient and more flexible to handle semantic events using listeners, so we'll delve into the listener interfaces for semantic events next.

Semantic Event Listeners

We have a listener interface defined for each of the semantic event types, and they each declare a single method:

Listener Interface	Method
ActionListener	**void actionPerformed(ActionEvent e)**
ItemListener	**void itemStateChanged(ItemEvent e)**
AdjustmentListener	**void adjustmentValueChanged(AdjustmentEvent e)**

Since each semantic event listener interface declares only one method, there are no adapter classes defined for semantic events. They were only there for the low-level events because of the number of methods involved in each listener interface. To define your semantic event listener objects, you just define a class that implements the appropriate listener interface. We can try that out by implementing a simple applet now, and then see how we can deal with semantic events in a more complicated context by adding to the Sketcher program later.

Semantic Event Handling in Applets

Event handling in an applet is exactly the same as in an application, but we ought to see it for ourselves. An applet does not usually have a window or a menu bar although you can add a window as we saw in the previous chapter, when we ran Sketcher as an applet. They often have buttons though, so let's see how we would handle events for buttons in an applet. We can create an applet with buttons that handle their own events, and buttons that have listeners so we can see both in action in the same program.

To make this example more interesting, we'll throw in the possibility of monetary gain. That's interesting to almost everybody. Let's suppose we want to have an applet to create random entries for a lottery. The requirement is to generate six different random numbers between 1 and 49. It would also be nice to be able to change a single number if you don't like it, so we will add that capability as well. If your local lottery is not like this, you should be able to adapt the applet to fit your requirements easily enough.

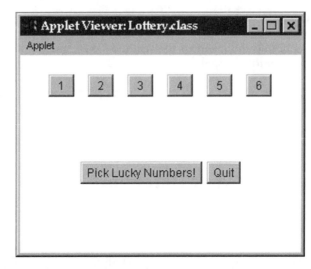

By displaying the six selected numbers on buttons, we can provide for changing one of the choices by processing the action event for that button Thus clicking a button will provide another number. We will also need a couple of control buttons, one to make a new selection, and another to quit the applet. Here's how the applet will look when running under **AppletViewer**:

We can outline the broad structure of the code for the applet as follows:

```
// Applet to generate lottery entries
import java.applet.*;
import java.awt.*;
import java.awt.event.*;

public class Lottery extends Applet
{
  // An array of custom buttons for the selected numbers
  Selection[] luckyNumbers = {new Selection(1), new Selection(2),
                              new Selection(3), new Selection(4),
                              new Selection(5), new Selection(6)};

  // Initialize the applet
  public void init()
  {
    // Set up the lucky numbers buttons...

    // Set up the control buttons...
  }

  // Custom button showing lottery selection
  class Selection extends Button
  {
    // Constructor
    public Selection(int value)
    {
      // Create the button with the value...
    }
```

```
      // Handle selection button event
      public void processActionEvent(ActionEvent e)
      {
        // Change the current selection value to a new selection...
      }

      // Details of the rest of the selection class definition...
    }

    // Class defining a handler for a control button
    class HandleControlButton implements ActionListener
    {
      // Details of the handler class definition...
    }
  }
```

How It Works

The applet class is called **Lottery** and it contains two inner classes, **Selection** and **HandleControlButton**. The **Selection** class will provide a custom button that will show a number as its label. We can make an object of the **Selection** class handle its own action events, and as we said at the outset, an event for a selection will change the label of the button to a different value. Of course, we will need to make sure this doesn't duplicate any of the values for the other buttons. The control buttons will use listeners to handle their action events. Only the button creating the set of lucky numbers will require serious effort. The other control button will just quit the applet.

The **Lottery** class has an array of **Selection** objects as a data member—we can have arrays of components just like arrays of any other kind of object. Since the **Selection** buttons will all be the same, it's very convenient to create them as an array, and having an array of components will enable us to set them up in a loop. Since the buttons need some kind of valid label, we arbitrarily give them the numbers 1 to 6 initially which we pass as an argument to the constructor.

Let's implement the **init()** method for the **Lottery** class first, as this sets up the **Selection** buttons and the rest of the applet.

Try It Out—Initializing the Applet

1   In the class outline we identified two tasks for the **init()** method, setting up the lucky number buttons which are contained in the **luckyNumbers** array, and setting up the two control buttons. Here's the code to do that:

```
// Initialize the applet
public void init()
{
  setLayout(new GridLayout(0,1));  // Set the layout for the applet
```

```
        // Set up the panel to hold the lucky number buttons
        Panel buttonPane = new Panel();   // Add the pane containing numbers
        buttonPane.setLayout(new FlowLayout(FlowLayout.CENTER, 15, 20));

        // Add the numbers buttons
        for(int i = 0; i < luckyNumbers.length; i++)
          buttonPane.add(luckyNumbers[i]);

        // Add the pane containing control buttons
        Panel controlPane = new Panel();
        controlPane.setLayout(new FlowLayout(FlowLayout.CENTER, 5, 10));
        add(buttonPane);

        // Add the two control buttons
        Button button;                 // A button variable
        controlPane.add(button = new Button("Pick Lucky Numbers!"));
        button.addActionListener(new HandleControlButton(PICK_LUCKY_NUMBERS));
        controlPane.add(button = new Button("Quit"));
        button.addActionListener(new HandleControlButton(QUIT));
        add(controlPane);
      }
```

2 We use the variables `PICK_LUCKY_NUMBERS` and `QUIT` as IDs for the control buttons so we must define these. You can add the following statements to the `Lottery` class after the definition of the `luckyNumbers` array:

```
final public int PICK_LUCKY_NUMBERS = 1;    // Select button ID
final public int QUIT               = 2;    // Quit button ID
```

How It Works

The first step is to define the layout manager for the applet. We specify it as a grid layout with one column, since we need to add two panels one above the other. The top panel will contain the lucky number buttons and the bottom panel will contain the control buttons.

The `buttonPane` panel which contains the lucky number buttons has a `FlowLayout` object as its layout manager with the buttons centered and with horizontal and vertical gaps of fifteen and twenty pixels respectively. We add the buttons defined in the `luckyNumbers` array in the `for` loop. Since these buttons are going to handle their own events, we don't need to worry about action listeners for them.

The `controlPane` panel also has a `FlowLayout` object as its layout manager. Each of the buttons has an action listener object of type `HandleControlButton`.

Having the two IDs as data members of the `Lottery` class will make them directly available to the `ControlButtonHandler` class where we will need them in the constructor and the `actionPerformed()` method.

Let's now add the inner class, `Selection`, that defines the lucky number buttons. Each button will need to store the value shown on the label, so the class will need a data member for this purpose. The class will also need a constructor, a method to set the value for the button to a new value and a method to compare the current value for a button to a given value. We need to be able to set the value for a button for two reasons—we will set up the six selections in the listener for the select control button, and we want to reset the value for a button to change it individually. The method to compare the value set for a button to a given integer will enable us to exclude a number that was already assigned to a button in the process of generating the button values. We will also need to implement the **processActionEvent()** method to handle the action events for the button, as the buttons are going to handle their own events.

Try It Out—Defining the Selection Buttons

1 Here's the basic code for the class definition excluding the detail of **processActionEvent()**:

```
// Custom button showing lottery selection
class Selection extends Button
{
    int value;                      // Value for the selection button

    // Constructor
    Selection(int value)
    {
        super(" " + value + " ");  // Call base constructor and set the label
        this.value = value;         // Save the value
        enableEvents(AWTEvent.ACTION_EVENT_MASK);  // enable action events
    }

    // Set the value for the selection
    public void setValue(int value)
    {
        setLabel(" " + value + " ");        // Set value as the button label
        this.value = value;                 // Save the value
    }

    // Check the value for the selection
    boolean hasValue(int possible)
    {
        return value==possible;    // Return true if equals current value
    }

    // Handle selection button event
    public void processActionEvent(ActionEvent e)
    {
        // Change this selection to a new selection...
        super.processActionEvent(e); // Pass the event on
    }
}
```

2 We can implement the details of the `processActionEvent()` method to randomly generate the labels for the `Selection` buttons, the labels being the lucky numbers of course:

```
// Handle selection button event
public void processActionEvent(ActionEvent e)
{
    // Change this selection to a new selection
    int[] numbers = new int[43];              // Array of possible values

    // Set up array excluding the 6 current selections
    int index = 0;                            // Index to the numbers array
    for(int i = 1; i <= 49; i++)
        if(!currentSelection(i))
            numbers[index++] = i;

    // Set the value as a random selection from the numbers array
    setValue(numbers[((int)(numbers.length*Math.random()))
                %numbers.length]);
    super.processActionEvent(e);              // Pass the event on
}
```

3 To complete the action event handling process we must add a definition for the `currentSelection()` method to the `Selection` class:

```
// Check the current choices
boolean currentSelection(int possible)
{
    for(int i = 0; i < luckyNumbers.length; i++) // For each button
        if(luckyNumbers[i].hasValue(possible))    // check against possible
            return true;                          // Return true for any =
    return false;                                 // Otherwise return false
}
```

How It Works

The constructor calls the base class constructor to set the initial label for the button. It also stores the value of type **int** passed as an argument and enables action events for the class so that the `processActionEvent()` method will be called. The `setValue()` method updates the value for a selection button with the value passed as an argument. The `setLabel()` method which is inherited from the base class is used to update the label for the button, and the value is store in the data member, **value**. The `hasValue()` method just returns **true** if the argument value is equal to the current value stored in the data member **value**, and **false** otherwise.

The `processActionEvent()` method has a bit more meat to it. To change the selection to a new selection, it must create a new random value for the button from the numbers 1 to 49, but exclude any of the numbers currently assigned to the six buttons. We don't want to duplicate any of the other button values, and we also want the new number to be different from the old one. For this reason we will arrange to pick from the numbers that we haven't already chosen.

550

The **numbers** array will store the 43 values from which we will select the new value—the original 49 possible numbers, less the six already used in the present button values. The **for** loop copies the 43 values from 1 to 49 that exclude those already assigned to existing buttons. The **currentSelection()** method will return **true** if the argument value is the same as the value assigned to any of the buttons, and **false** otherwise. We only increment index for the **numbers** array after we copy a value into it.

After the **numbers** array has been set up, we choose a random index value between 1 and 43 for the numbers array with the expression:

```
((int)(numbers.length*Math.random()))%numbers.length
```

Let's make sure we understand how this works. Starting with the innermost parentheses, we multiply together:

- The random value of type **double** between 0.0 and 1.0 that is returned by the **random()** method
- The length of the **numbers** array, which is 43

This will result in a random value of type double between 0.0 and 43.0. By casting this to **int** we arrive at a random integer between 0 and 43. The integers between 0 and 42 are more or less equally probable, and the number 43 only arises when the value returned by the method **random()** is exactly 1.0. We don't want this value to occur, as the maximum legal index to the **numbers** array is 42 so we use the **%** operator to get the integer value modulo 43. Thus 43 will become 0 and all the other possible values will be left as they are. This result is used to index the **numbers** array and the value stored is passed to the **setValue()** method for the current object.

In the **currentSelection()** method, we just work through the array of **Selection** objects, **luckyNumbers**, comparing each value with the **possible** argument using the **hasValue()** method. If any button has the same value as **possible** the method returns **true**, otherwise it return **false**.

The listener object for the control buttons, as defined by the inner class **HandleControlButton**, will make a selection of six numbers when the select button is clicked. This is really the heart of the applet. We can implement that next:

Try It Out—Defining the Control Button Handler Class

1 We can start by putting most of the class definition together, but we will deal with the process for generating the six random numbers separately:

```
class HandleControlButton implements ActionListener
{
    int buttonID;                           // ID for the button

    // Constructor
    public HandleControlButton(int buttonID)
```

```
  {
    this.buttonID = buttonID;                    // Store the button ID
  }

  // Handle button click
  public void actionPerformed(ActionEvent e)
  {
    switch(buttonID)
    {
      case PICK_LUCKY_NUMBERS:
        int[] numbers = getSixNumbers();         // Get six random numbers
        for(int i = 0; i < numbers.length; i++)
          luckyNumbers[i].setValue(numbers[i]);  // Set the button values
        break;
      case QUIT:
        System.exit(0);                          // Close the applet
    }
  }

  // Generate 6 number between 1 and 49
  int[] getSixNumbers()
  {
    // Generate the six numbers and return as an array...
  }
}
```

2 To complete the whole thing, all we need is the implementation of the
  `getSixNumbers()` method:

```
// Generate 6 number between 1 and 49
int[] getSixNumbers()
{
  int[] numbers = new int[6];   // Store for the six numbers returned
  int[] values = new int[49];   // Store for the numbers to choose from

  // Set up the initial array of choices
  for(int i = 0; i < values.length; i++)
    values[i] = i + 1;          // Values are from 1 to 49

  int[] possibles = values;     // Array to store possible choices

  for(int i = 0; i < numbers.length; i++)
  {
    numbers[i] =
    possibles[((int)(possibles.length*Math.random()))%possibles.length];
    possibles = new int[values.length - 1];
    int index = 0;
    for(int j = 0; j < values.length; j++)
      if(values[j] != numbers[i])
        possibles[index++] = values[j];
    values = possibles;
  }
```

```
    return numbers;
}
```

3 We are ready to start generating lottery entries. If you compile the **Lottery.java** file you can run the applet using **AppletViewer**. You will need an **.html** file of course. The following contents for the file will do the job:

```
<APPLET code="Lottery.class" width=300 height=200>
</APPLET>
```

You can adjust the width and height values to suit your monitor resolution if necessary.

The applet should produce a selection each time you click the left control button, as show here.

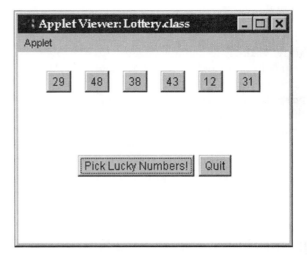

Clicking on any of the selection buttons will generate an action event that will cause a new value to be created for the button. This enables you to replace any selection that you know to be unlucky with an alternative.

> *A depressing aspect of entering a lottery is the fact that the original selection of the numbers 1 to 6 is just as likely to win as any other set. However, it is unwise to enter this particular set. Even if you win you will have to share the prize with thousands of statisticians and other clever dicks who also choose 1 to 6 as their entry. Undoubtedly, anyone who profits from using this applet will have immense feelings of gratitude and indebtedness towards the author, who will not be offended in the slightest by any offers of a portion of any success, however large.*

How It Works

The class works using a very similar technique to that we've used previously. Each listener object stores a unique ID that identifies the button which originates the action events. The IDs were defined in the **Lottery** class, and the constructor here just stored the ID passed as an argument. A **HandleControlButton** object will always execute statements corresponding to either the first or the second case of the **switch** statement in the **actionPerformed()**

method, depending on the button to which the object relates. The listener object for the Quit button always executes the statement corresponding to the second case, which terminates the applet. The listener object for the select button executes the statements for the first case in the **switch**. This calls the method **getSixNumbers()** which returns an array of six different random integer values between 1 and 49. These are used to set up the values and thus the label for the selection buttons in the **for** loop.

It's a little tricky to generate several random numbers and guarantee they are all different. The way we achieve this is to first set up an initial array of possible choices, **values**, and pick a random element from this array by generating a random index to it. We then create a new array from the original array, but with the element that was chosen omitted. This new array is then the basis for the next choice. We just do this six times to get the six random values.

The six random values will be stored in the array **numbers**. The first **for** loop set up the array, **values**, to contain integers from 1 to 49. The second **for** loop generates the six values to be stored in the array, **numbers**. At the outset, the array variable, **possibles**, references the same array as the array variable, **values**. We pick an element from the array **possibles** by generating a random index value between 0 and one less than the length of the array. The expression to do this is essentially the same as we saw earlier in the **processActionEvent()** method in the **Selection** class definition. The element value is stored in the numbers array, and a new **possibles** array is created with a length that is one less than the previous array. The elements from the array values are then copied to the new **possibles** array, but omitting the element that was selected. The **values** variable is then set to reference the new **possibles** array, ready for the next selection to be made on the next loop iteration. What fun!

Handling Low-Level and Semantic Events

We said earlier in this chapter that a component generates both low-level and semantic events, and you could handle both if you want. We can demonstrate this quite easily with a small extension to the Lottery applet. Suppose we want to change the cursor to a hand cursor when it is over one of the selection buttons. This would be a good cue that you can select these buttons individually. We can do this by adding a mouse listener for each button.

Try It Out—A Mouse Listener for the Selection Buttons

1 There are many ways in which you can define the listener class. We will define it as a separate class, called **HandleMouse**. Here's the class definition:

```
// Mouse event handler for a selection button
import java.awt.*;
import java.awt.event.*;

class MouseHandler extends MouseAdapter
{
  Cursor handCursor = new Cursor(Cursor.HAND_CURSOR);
  Cursor defaultCursor = new Cursor(Cursor.DEFAULT_CURSOR);
```

```
   // Handle mouse entering the selection button
   public void mouseEntered(MouseEvent e)
   {
     e.getComponent().setCursor(handCursor);      //Switch to hand cursor
   }

   // Handle mouse exiting the selection button
   public void mouseExited(MouseEvent e)
   {
     e.getComponent().setCursor(defaultCursor); //Change to default cursor
   }
 }
```

2   All we need to do to expedite this is to add mouse listeners for each of the six selection buttons. We can do this by changing the loop in the **init()** method for the applet to add the listeners:

```
// Add the numbers buttons
for(int i = 0; i < luckyNumbers.length; i++)
{
  luckyNumbers[i].addMouseListener(new MouseHandler());
  buttonPane.add(luckyNumbers[i]);
}
```

How It Works

The **mouseEntered()** method will be called when the mouse enters the area of the component that the listener is registered with, and we then change the cursor for the component to a hand cursor. When the cursor is moved out of the area occupied by the component, the **mouseExited()** method is called, and we restore the default cursor.

There is just one extra statement in **init()** which adds a listener for each selection button, plus the braces for the loop block of course. If you recompile the applet and run it again, a hand cursor should appear whenever the mouse is over the selection buttons.

Semantic Event Listeners in an Application

The immediate candidate for implementing semantic event listeners in the Sketcher program is to support the operation of the menu bar in the class **SketchFrame**. When we click on an item in one of the pull-down menus, a semantic event will be generated which we can then use to cause the appropriate program action. However, this is starting to get application specific. We need a brief diversion into a bit more of how our Sketcher program is going to be structured before we jump into handling the menus.

The Document/View Architecture

We need to develop an idea of how we are going to manage the data for a sketch in the Sketcher program because this will affect where and how we handle events. We already have a class that defines an application window, **SketchFrame**, but this class would not be a very sensible place to store the underlying data that defines a sketch. For one thing, we will want to save a sketch in a file, and serialization is the easiest way to do that. If we are going to use serialization to store a sketch, we won't want all the stuff in the members of the **SketchFrame** class muddled up with the data relating to the sketch we have created. For another, it will make the program easier to implement if we separate out the basic data defining a sketch from the definition of the GUI.

Ideally, we should manage the sketch data in a class designed specifically for that purpose. Such a class is often referred to as a **document class**, with the class representing the displayed document as the **view class**. This is not the only way of implementing the things we want in the Sketcher program, but it's quite a good way. A document class does not necessarily contain what you might immediately think of as a document—although it can. A document class contains any kind of data that defines the kind of object the application is concerned with. You can then have different views presenting the same document data in different ways. A word processing application would have document objects that contain text for example, so this really would be a document in the normal sense. In most word processing packages you have a variety of ways in which you can view the document. On the other hand, a document class in an image application would contain image data. Different views of the document in this case might present the image at different scales.

Our document object will contain a mixture of text and graphics that will go to make up a sketch. We will call our document class **SketchDoc** and the document view class **SketchView**, although we won't be adding the view to the program until the next chapter. The diagram illustrates the relationships between the classes we will have in Sketcher.

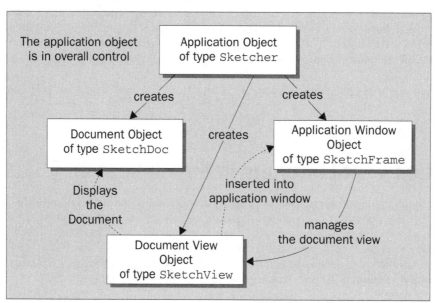

The application object has overall responsibility for managing links between the other objects involved in the program. Any object that has access to the application object will be able to communicate with any other object as long as the application class has methods to make each of the objects available.

Note that **SketchFrame** is not the view class—it defines the application window. When we create a **SketchView** object in the next chapter, we will arrange to insert the **Sketchview** object into the **SketchFrame** object, and manage it using the layout manager in **SketchFrame**. By defining the view class separately from the application class, we separate the view of the document from the menus and other components we use to interact with the program. One benefit of this is that the area in which we display the document has its own coordinate system, independent of that of the application window.

Because some of the actions for the menus in **SketchFrame** relate specifically to the document—setting the type of element to be created next for instance—it will be advantageous to add a skeleton, or 'dummy', document class to the Sketcher application at this point, even though we won't be creating any data items for what will be displayed until the next chapter. Defining the class now will enable us to make some of the listeners for semantic events operate on the document object.

Implementing a Basic Document/View Architecture

Over the next few pages, we're going to implement a basic document/view architecture for the Sketcher application, which will stand us in good stead for the next three chapters. At the same time we'll be adding plenty of functionality to the **SketchFrame** class to prepare it to respond to events. There is quite a lot of work in this, so of necessity, this process is going to take quite a few pages and involve incremental updates to a number of files. Therefore the Try It Out headings will not necessarily reflect compilable stages in the program's extension, but will be used to explain sections of source code.

Try It Out—Updating the `Sketcher` and `SketchFrame` Classes

1 The **Sketcher** class represents the application object, and it already creates a **SketchFrame** object which is the application window. We can now update the **Sketcher** class to create a document object in addition to the application window:

```
// Sketching application
import java.awt.*;
import java.awt.event.*;

public class Sketcher
{
  static Sketcher theApp;      // The application object
  SketchFrame window;          // The document view
  SketchDoc sketch;            // The document object

  // Initialization of the application
  public void init()
  {
    sketch = new SketchDoc(this);                    // Define the document
    window = new SketchFrame("Sketcher", this);      // Create the app window
    Toolkit theKit = window.getToolkit();            // Get the window toolkit
    Dimension wndSize = theKit.getScreenSize();      // Get screen size
```

```
       // Set the position to screen center & size to 2/3 screen size
       window.setBounds(wndSize.width/6, wndSize.height/6,       // Position
                    2*wndSize.width/3, 2*wndSize.height/3);   // Size

       window.addWindowListener(new WindowHandler()); // Add window listener
       window.setVisible(true);                        // Display the window
       window.requestFocus();                          // Request the focus
    }

    public static void main(String[] args)
    {
       theApp = new Sketcher();              // Create the application object
       theApp.init();                        // ...and initialize it
    }

    // Get the document object
    public SketchDoc getDocument()
    { return sketch; }

    // Handler class for window events
    class WindowHandler extends WindowAdapter
    {
       // Class definition as before...
    }
}
```

2 Next, we extend **SketchFrame.java** which we defined in the previous chapter. We won't show all the old code, otherwise it becomes too unwieldy. We will show just enough for you to see how the new or modified code that is shown shaded, fits with the old. Here's the amended definition of **SketchFrame**:

```
// Frame for Sketcher application
import java.awt.*;

public SketchFrame extends Frame
{
    Sketcher theApp;                            // The application object
    MenuBar menubar = new MenuBar();            // Window menu bar

    // Element menu items
    CheckboxMenuItem lineItem, rectangleItem, circleItem, curveItem,
                textItem;

    // Color menu items
    CheckboxMenuItem redItem, yellowItem, greenItem, blueItem ;

    // Constructor
    public SketchFrame(String title, Sketcher theApp)
    {
       super(title);                        // Call base constructor
       this.theApp = theApp;                // Store the application object
       setMenuBar(menubar);                 // Add the menu bar to the window
```

```
     // Construct the menus as before...
   }
}
```

How It Works

We have added the instance variable, **sketch**, to the application object which will store the document for the application. The document object, of type **SketchDoc**, is created in the **init()** method for the application object. The application object is passed to the constructor for **SketchDoc**, so the document object will be able to communicate with it. This will be necessary when we want the document to add its view to the application object window for instance.

> *Don't confuse the application window and the view. The application window (the SketchFrame class in our example) will provide the means of controlling the application through its menus and other facilities we will add. The view will just display the document. However, the document view will be displayed within the application window, as we will see later.*

Note that we also pass the application object as a second argument to the **SketchFrame** constructor when we create the application window. We need to amend the **SketchFrame** class to provide for storing the application object and update the constructor to take care of it. This will allow the application window to get information from the document object when necessary, by calling the **getDocument()** method we have added to the application class.

In **SketchFrame**, the variable **theApp** stores the reference to the application object that is passed as the second argument to the constructor. When we need to get access to the document from this class, we can just call the **getDocument()** method.

Try It Out—Defining a Dummy Document Class

1 Here's the definition for the basic document class:

```java
// Class defining the sketch document
import java.awt.*;

public class SketchDoc implements Constants
{
  protected Sketcher theApp;                 // The application object
  protected Color elementColor;              // Current element color
  protected int elementType;                 // Current element type

  public SketchDoc(Sketcher theApp)
  {
    this.theApp = theApp;                     // Store the document object
    elementColor = DEFAULT_ELEMENT_COLOR;     // Initial element color
    elementType = DEFAULT_ELEMENT_TYPE;       // Initial element type
  }
```

```java
  // Get the current element type
  public int getElementType()
  {
    return elementType;
  }

  // Set the current element type
  public void setElementType(int elementType)
  {
    this.elementType = elementType;
  }

  // Get the current element color
  public Color getElementColor()
  {
    return new Color(elementColor.getRGB());
  }

  // Set the current element color
  public void setElementColor(Color elementColor)
  {
    this.elementColor = new Color(elementColor.getRGB());
  }
}
```

2 Our initial definition for the **Constants** interface we've implemented above, needs to include definitions for the integer values that represent the various element types the program will create, plus the **DEFAULT_ELEMENT_COLOR** and **DEFAULT_ELEMENT_TYPE** variables. Save the following lines of code in a file called **Constants.java**:

```java
// Defines application wide constants
import java.awt.*;

public interface Constants
{
  // Element type definitions
  int LINE      = 101;
  int RECTANGLE = 102;
  int CIRCLE    = 103;
  int CURVE     = 104;
  int TEXT      = 105;

  // Initial conditions
  int DEFAULT_ELEMENT_TYPE = LINE;
  Color DEFAULT_ELEMENT_COLOR = Color.blue;
}
```

3 Now that we have defined variables for the standard element types in Sketcher, and what the initial element type and color are going to be, we can go back and modify the creation of the Element menu items in the **SketchFrame** class to automatically set the initial check marks to correspond with the defaults. **SketchFrame** will now need to implement the **Constants** interface to get access to the standard values, so change the class definition to:

```
public class SketchFrame extends Frame implements Constants
{
    // Class definition as before...

    // Constructor
    public SketchFrame(String title, Sketcher theApp)
    {
        // Constructor code as before...

        // Construct the file pull down menu as before...

        // Construct the Element pull down menu
        Menu  elementMenu = new Menu("Elements"); // Elements menu bar item
        lineItem = new CheckboxMenuItem("Line",
                            DEFAULT_ELEMENT_TYPE==LINE);
        rectangleItem = new CheckboxMenuItem("Rectangle",
                            DEFAULT_ELEMENT_TYPE==RECTANGLE);
        circleItem = new CheckboxMenuItem("Circle",
                            DEFAULT_ELEMENT_TYPE==CIRCLE);
        curveItem = new CheckboxMenuItem("Curve",
                            DEFAULT_ELEMENT_TYPE==CURVE);
        textItem = new CheckboxMenuItem("Text",
                            DEFAULT_ELEMENT_TYPE==TEXT);

        // Add the element type items as before...

        // Construct the Color item pull down menu
        Menu colorMenu = new Menu("Color");      // Color sub-menu item
        redItem = new CheckboxMenuItem("Red",
                            DEFAULT_ELEMENT_COLOR.equals(Color.red));
        yellowItem = new CheckboxMenuItem("Yellow",
                            DEFAULT_ELEMENT_COLOR.equals(Color.yellow));
        greenItem = new CheckboxMenuItem("Green",
                            DEFAULT_ELEMENT_COLOR.equals(Color.green));
        blueItem = new CheckboxMenuItem("Blue",
                            DEFAULT_ELEMENT_COLOR.equals(Color.blue));

        // Rest of the constructor as before...
    }

    // rest of the class definition as before...
}
```

How It Works

The **SketchDoc** class has three data members storing the application object, the current element color and the color element type. We will represent each type of element that the program can create by a different value of type **int**. Similarly, the color of an element will be represented by a value of type **Color**. The constructor initializes all three data members. The reference to the application object is passed as an argument to the constructor, and the initial values for the other two data members are defined by the variables **DEFAULT_ELEMENT_TYPE** and **DEFAULT_ELEMENT_COLOR**—we will see where these come from in a moment. The application object will be the link to the other classes, since it originates each of them.

The reason for using variables for current element type and color, is so that these can be set using the **Element** menu. When the user of the Sketcher program picks an element type or a color from the menu, this will need to be recorded in the document object. When we get to create an element, we will always create an element of the current type and color. So you will draw red circles for example, and if you then want to draw green circles, you just select the Green item from the menu. We have defined *get* and *set* methods for the **elementType** and **elementColor** variables. Clearly the menu-item listeners will need to set these values, and other parts of the program will need access to them.

Note how we create new **Color** objects in the **getElementColor()** and **setElementColor()** methods. We create new **Color** objects in both cases. The **getRGB()** method returns an **int** value which contains the components of red, green and blue in the color, and we pass this to the **Color** constructor. Remember that objects are passed by reference. If we don't create new **Color** objects here, the **Color** object referenced by the **elementColor** variable will be shared with the method that calls the *get* or *set* method. This allows the object to which the **elementColor** variable refers, to be changed 'silently' by modifying the object directly elsewhere. In our case we will be using standard colors defined by values that are **final**, so it can't happen. However, if we were to change the program at a later date to use colors that are not standard, it could happen. It's a good idea generally to keep in mind the potential effects of creating shared objects, especially when implementing *get* and *set* methods.

The **Constants** interface will be the repository for all the standard values of various kinds that we need across the program. Whenever one of our classes needs to access some of the application constants, we can just make it implement the **Constants** interface to make all our standard values available. Remember that data members that you define in an interface are **public**, **static**, and **final**, by definition, so it is an ideal place to keep all your constants values.

The values for the element types are completely arbitrary. You could choose a different set of numbers if you want, the only prerequisite being that they should all be different. The **DEFAULT_ELEMENT_TYPE** variable is defined by one of the standard types—**LINE** in this case. By having these definitions in just one place, and implementing constants whenever we need access to these in a class, it makes it very easy to change the program to work with different defaults. If you wanted **CIRCLE** to be the default element type, you just need to change the definition here to fix it for the entire program.

There are three changes to the **SketchFrame** class definition—the class implements the **Constants** interface that we just defined, we have modified the creation of the element type menu items, and we have modified the statements creating the color menu items. The check is set for each type menu item by passing a **boolean** expression that compares the type for the menu item with the default type. Only one menu item will have **true** as the second argument to the constructor—the one corresponding to the default type. The color menu items are much the same. Note that we must use the **equals()** method in the **Color** class here though. Using the **==** operator would be a serious mistake, since this would compare the object references, not the objects themselves. It would work by accident in this case, since we are only using constant **Color** objects defined in the class. If we changed the program to use arbitrary colors that we created our own objects for, it would not work. Using the **==** operator to compare two different objects that represented the same color would always result in **false**.

We are now about ready to add listeners for the items in the **Element** menu.

Defining Element Type Item Listeners

We will define the listener classes for the **Element** menu items as separate classes, and make them update the variables in the document object when an item in the pull-down menu is selected. We will define two listener classes, one for the element type items, and one for the element color items. Why two separate classes? Primarily because an element type and an element color are values of quite different types, so we need to treat them differently.

As soon as we have defined the first listener class for handling the element type menu items, we will modify the **SketchFrame** class to create and register the listeners. Then we will move on to deal with the element color menu items. That way, you will be able to see how the listeners are created and registered, while the listener class implementation is still fresh in your mind.

Try It Out-Implementing a Listener Class for the Element Type Menu

Here is the definition of the class for handling the element type items:

```
// Element menu command handler class
import java.awt.event.*;

class ElementCommand implements ItemListener
{
  int itemID;              // ID for the menu item handled
  SketchDoc sketch;        // The document object

  // Constructor for item listener
  public ElementCommand(int itemID, SketchDoc sketch)
  {
    this.itemID = itemID;    // Save the menu item ID
```

```
      this.sketch = sketch;    // Store the document
   }

   // Handle element menu item state changed
   public void itemStateChanged(ItemEvent e)
   {
     sketch.setElementType(itemID);  // Store new element type
   }
 }
```

How It Works

The listener objects defined by this class relate to **CheckboxMenuItem** object events, so the class needs to implement the **ItemListener** event interface. To access this interface, we must have an **import** statement for the **java.awt.event** package.

Since we want the listener objects to update the document object, we have assumed that a reference to the document object is passed to the constructor. We can use the reference to the document object to call any of its public methods—in particular its **setElementType()** method. Of course, here we need to share the document object with the calling program—not create a new one, so pass-by-reference is doing exactly what we want.

The constructor initializes two data members in the class, the reference to the document and a variable **itemID** which will store the ID for the type of element to which the menu relates. This will be one of the standard values for the element types that we defined in the **Constants** interface. When we create a listener for the Line menu item, for example, we will pass the value **LINE** to the constructor. By this means, each listener object knows implicitly what type of element is being chosen when an event occurs. None of the standard element types are referred to explicitly in the **ElementCommand** class, so it doesn't need to implement the **Constants** interface.

When a menu item event occurs, the **itemStateChanged()** method is called automatically with an argument of type **ItemEvent** passed as an argument—remember that this is the method declared in the **ItemListener** interface. We will create a separate listener object for each menu item, so the **itemStateChanged()** method doesn't need to analyze the **ItemEvent** object. It just calls the **setElementType()** method for the document object with the **itemID** as the argument. This will set the **elementType** variable in the document object to the element type corresponding to the menu item that was selected.

Using Element Type Item Listeners

We will create the listeners for the element type items and register them with the menu item objects in the constructor for the **SketchFrame** class.

Try It Out—Adding the Element Type Listeners to *SketchFrame*

We need to modify the code for the **SketchFrame** class definition as follows:

```java
// Frame for Sketcher application
import java.awt.*;
import java.awt.event.*;

public class SketchFrame extends Frame implements Constants
{
  Sketcher theApp;                      // The application object
  SketchDoc sketch;                     // The document object
  MenuBar menuBar = new MenuBar();      // Window menu bar

  // Element menu items
  CheckboxMenuItem lineItem, rectangleItem, circleItem,
                   curveItem, textItem;

  // Color menu items
  CheckboxMenuItem redItem, yellowItem, greenItem, blueItem;

  // Constructor
  public SketchFrame(String title, Sketcher theApp)
  {
    super(title);                       // Call base constructor
    this.theApp = theApp;               // Store the application object
    sketch = theApp.getDocument();      // Get the document object
    setMenuBar(menuBar);                // Add the menu bar to the window

    // Construct the file pull down menu
    Menu fileMenu = new Menu("File");   // The File menu bar item
    MenuItem item;
    fileMenu.add(item = new MenuItem("New",
                  new MenuShortcut('N')));        // Add New item
    fileMenu.add(item = new MenuItem("Open",
                  new MenuShortcut('O')));        // Add Open item
    fileMenu.add(item = new MenuItem("Close",
                   new MenuShortcut('C')));       // Add Close item
    fileMenu.addSeparator();
    fileMenu.add(item = new MenuItem("Save",
                  new MenuShortcut('S')));        // Add Save item
    fileMenu.add(item = new MenuItem("Save As..."));  // Add Save As item
    fileMenu.addSeparator();
    fileMenu.add(item = new MenuItem("Print",
                  new MenuShortcut('P')));        // Add Print item

    // Construct the Element pull-down menu as before...

    // Add the element menu listeners
    lineItem.addItemListener(new ElementCommand(LINE, sketch));
    rectangleItem.addItemListener(new ElementCommand(RECTANGLE, sketch));
    circleItem.addItemListener(new ElementCommand(CIRCLE, sketch));
    curveItem.addItemListener(new ElementCommand(CURVE, sketch));
    textItem.addItemListener(new ElementCommand(TEXT, sketch));
```

```
        // Add the element type items as before...

        // Construct the Color item pull down menu as before...

        elementMenu.add(colorMenu);             // Add the sub-menu

        menuBar.add(fileMenu);                  // Add the file menu
        menuBar.add(elementMenu);               // Add the element menu
    }
}
```

How It Works

Rather than have lots of calls to **getDocument()** to obtain a reference to the document object, we have added a data member, **sketch**, to store the reference which we initialize in the constructor. This will make our code a bit more efficient and reduces the amount we need to type in.

The additions to the original code add the listeners of type **ElementCommand** for the element type menu items. A listener is added for a **CheckboxMenuItem** object by calling its **addListener()** method and passing the listener object to it. Each menu item has its own individual listener object, and we pass the element type for the menu item as the first argument to the constructor for the listener. The second argument is the reference to the document, **sketch**, which we initialized at the beginning of the **SketchFrame** class constructor. That's all we need for the element type item listeners. Let's look at the color item listeners.

Try It Out—Defining Color Item Listeners

1 The definition of a class defining a color menu item listener is very similar to the class we created for the type listeners:

```
// Color sub-menu handler class
import java.awt.*;
import java.awt.event.*;

class ColorCommand implements ItemListener
{
  Color itemColor;                      // Color for the item handled
  SketchDoc sketch;

  // Constructor for item listener
  public ColorCommand(Color itemColor, SketchDoc sketch)
  {
    this.itemColor = new Color(itemColor.getRGB()); //Save the item color
    this.sketch = sketch;                           //Store the document
  }

  // Handle element menu item state changed
  public void itemStateChanged(ItemEvent e)
```

```
    {
       sketch.setElementColor(itemColor);  // Store new element color
    }
  }
```

2 Add the following code to the **SketchFrame** constructor:

```
// Constructor
public SketchFrame(String title, Sketcher theApp)
{
  // Construct the file pull down menu

  // Construct the Element pull down menu as before...

  // Add the element menu listeners as before...

  // Add the element type items as before...

  // Construct the Color item pull down menu as before...

  // Add the color menu listeners
  redItem.addItemListener(new ColorCommand(Color.red, sketch));
  yellowItem.addItemListener(new ColorCommand(Color.yellow, sketch));
  greenItem.addItemListener(new ColorCommand(Color.green, sketch));
  blueItem.addItemListener(new ColorCommand(Color.blue, sketch));

  // Add the color menu items as before...

  elementMenu.add(colorMenu);              // Add the sub-menu

  menuBar.add(fileMenu);                    // Add the file menu
  menuBar.add(elementMenu);                 // Add the element menu
}
```

This is a good point to try the listeners out. You can recompile Sketcher at this point and run it. The element type menu items should now work with the check mark being set for whichever is the current element type, and similarly for the color menu items. The effect is shown here.

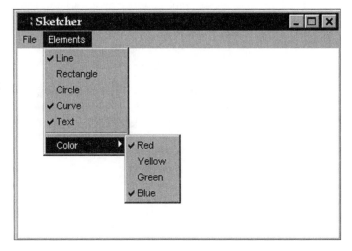

The listeners are working fine, but not quite as we wanted. The problem is that the check marks are not being reset when we change the element type. This is not a problem with the listeners, it's a problem with needing to manage the setting of the check marks. We set them up correctly in the `SketchFrame` class constructor, but each time we select a new item, the old one is not being reset. We need to add some code to reset them each time we change the element type or color.

How It Works

`ColorCommand` has a data member storing the color corresponding to the menu item to which the listener applies. In this case, because we have a `Color` object, we create a new object identical to the `Color` object passed as an argument for the reasons we discussed earlier.

The `itemStateChanged()` method, declared in the `ItemListener` interface, is called when a color menu item event occurs. It just calls the `setElementColor()` method for the document object to set the color appropriately. All we need to do to activate the color menu listeners is to create and register them in the `SketchFrame` class constructor.

There are just four extra lines of coded after the comment, one to register each `ColorCommand` listener object. Each listener object is created and passed directly to the `addItemListener()` method for the corresponding menu item. That's it. When you click an element menu item, someone will be listening.

We can accommodate this requirement quite easily by adding methods to the `SketchFrame` class to set the menu item check marks for element type or element color, so that only one menu item within each group is checked. One method will deal with the type menu items, the other with the color menu items. We can then call the appropriate one from the `setElementType()` and `setElementColor()` methods in the `SketchDoc` class.

Try It Out—Checking Just One Type or Color in the Menu

1 To deal with the type menu items, add the following method to the `SketchFrame` class definition:

```
// Set element type menu check marks
public void setTypeMenuChecks(int elementType)
{
  lineItem.setState(LINE==elementType);
  rectangleItem.setState(RECTANGLE==elementType);
  circleItem.setState(CIRCLE==elementType);
  curveItem.setState(CURVE==elementType);
  textItem.setState(TEXT==elementType);
}
```

2 Now you can also add a very similar method to the **SketchFrame** class to handle the color menu item checks:

```
// Set color check marks
public void setColorMenuChecks(Color elementColor)
{
  redItem.setState(elementColor.equals(Color.red));
  yellowItem.setState(elementColor.equals(Color.yellow));
  greenItem.setState(elementColor.equals(Color.green));
  blueItem.setState(elementColor.equals(Color.blue));
}
```

3 The next thing we need to do is to modify the **setElementType()** method in the **SketchDoc** class, but we only have the application object as the means of communication. We need access to the application window object to call the **setTypeMenuChecks()** method that we just defined. To make this possible, we can add a method to **Sketcher.java** which will return a reference to the application window:

```
// Get the application window
public SketchFrame getAppWindow()
{
  return window;
}
```

4 Now we can modify the **setElementType()** method in **SketchDoc** to use this to set the element type menu item checks:

```
// Set the current element type
public void setElementType(int elementType)
{
  this.elementType = elementType;
  theApp.getAppWindow().setTypeMenuChecks(elementType);
}
```

5 And we can do the same thing for the **setElementColor()** method in **SketchDoc**:

```
// Set the current element color
public void setElementColor(Color elementColor)
{
  this.elementColor = new Color(elementColor.getRGB());
  theApp.getAppWindow().setColorMenuChecks(elementColor);
}
```

If you recompile and run Sketcher again, you should now see that the menu checks are set correctly.

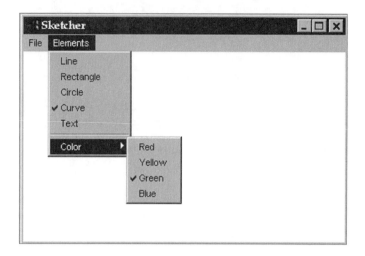

How It Works

We have added two methods that are responsible for setting the Element menu item checks. In the **setTypeMenuChecks()** method in the **SketchFrame** class, we set the check mark for every type menu item by calling its **setState()** method. If the argument is **true**, the check mark will be set, and if it's **false**, it won't be. We use the same arguments that we originally used to set the check marks for the items in the **SketchFrame** constructor, so it will work the same way here too. Only the item corresponding to the current element type will be checked. All the others will be set as unchecked. The **setColorMenuChecks()** works in exactly the same way.

The **getAppWindow()** method in **Sketcher** just returns the **SketchFrame** object that was created in the **init()** method of the application object. This provides the key to calling any of the **SketchFrame** object's public methods. Any class that has a reference to the application object will be able to access the methods to operate on the application window in the same way.

One additional line of code in the **SketchDoc**'s **setElementType()** method does it. We first call the **getAppWindow()** method to get the application window object, and then call the **setTypeMenuChecks()** method for the window object with the current element type as an argument. This will reset all the element type menu check marks correctly. The **setElementColor()** method follows exactly the same procedure to set the color menu item checks. It calls the **getAppWindow()** method for the application object, and uses the reference to the **SketchFrame** object that is returned to call the **setColorMenuChecks()** method for the application window.

It may seem like that we have added a lot of code here, so let's step back and look at the logic of what's going on. It's illustrated in the diagram below.

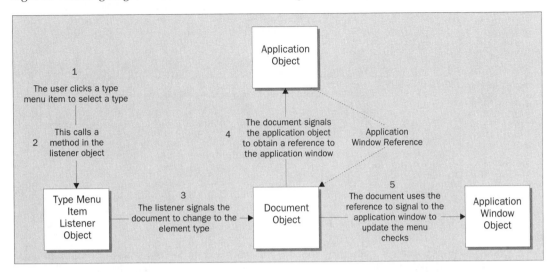

Selecting a menu item results in communications between four objects in our program, and involves the five step sequence shown in the diagram. When you click on an Element menu item with the mouse, the **itemStateChanged()** method in the listener registered for that menu item is called. This signals to the document object to change the default element type by calling its **setElementType()** or **setElementColor()** method. The document object then records the change and calls the **getAppWindow()** method in the application object to get a reference to the application window. Using this reference, the document object signals to the application window to update the relevant menu items—by calling either the **setTypeMenuChecks()** or the **setColorMenuChecks()** method. It's not really difficult, is it?

Now that we have a basic idea of how to handle menu items, we could improve the Sketcher GUI and get some experience of handling events for other components by adding a toolbar to the program.

Adding a Toolbar

A toolbar is a bar below the menu bar containing a row of buttons, usually providing a more direct route to menu options. We could add a toolbar for the Elements menu items so you could change the color or the type of an element just by clicking a button. Just so that you know where we are heading, the kind of toolbar we will end up with ultimately is shown next.

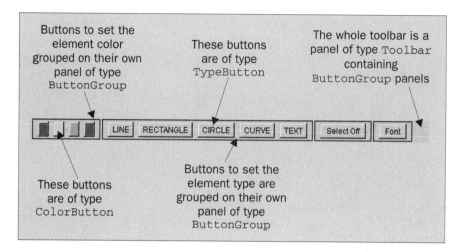

Buttons to set the element color grouped on their own panel of type `ButtonGroup`

These buttons are of type `TypeButton`

The whole toolbar is a panel of type `Toolbar` containing `ButtonGroup` panels

| LINE | RECTANGLE | CIRCLE | CURVE | TEXT | Select Off | Font |

These buttons are of type `ColorButton`

Buttons to set the element type are grouped on their own panel of type `ButtonGroup`

So how are we going to put this toolbar together?

A good starting point for gathering components together is to use a **Panel** object as a base, as shown in the illustration. The toolbar itself, by a leap of the imagination, will be a class called **Toolbar** derived from the component class, **Panel**. Each group of related buttons is on its own panel that we will add to the **Toolbar** panel. The panels containing the groups of buttons will be called **ButtonGroup**, and will also have **Panel** as a base class. The color buttons and the type buttons will each be defined by their own class derived from the **Button** class we saw in the previous chapter. We will call these classes **ColorButton** and **TypeButton** respectively. By creating a class for the buttons in a group, we can make the button objects handle their own events. The other buttons we will add later on, so ignore them for now. Let's start by mapping out the outline of the **Toolbar** class definition:

Try It Out—The `Toolbar` Class Definition

Save the following as **Toolbar.java**.

```
// Class defining a toolbar
import java.awt.*;

class Toolbar extends Panel implements Constants
{
  Sketcher theApp;                                // Reference to the app
  ButtonGroup colorGroup = new ButtonGroup();  // Group to select color
  ButtonGroup typeGroup = new ButtonGroup();   // Group to select type

  // Constructor
  public Toolbar(Sketcher theApp)
  {
    this.theApp = theApp;                         // Store the app reference
    // Rest of constructor implementation...
  }
```

```
    // Inner class defining a group of toolbar buttons
    class ButtonGroup extends Panel
    {
      // Constructor
      public ButtonGroup()
      {
         // Constructor implementation..
      }
    }

    // Inner class defining a color button
    class ColorButton extends Button
    {
       // Definition of a color button...
    }

    // Inner class defining a type button
    class TypeButton extends Button
    {
       // Definition of a type button...
    }
  }
```

How It Works

The **java.awt** package provides the definitions for the **Panel** and **Button** classes we are using here. Note that the **Toolbar** class implements our interface, **Constants**. This will provide access to the values we need to represent standard element types and colors. The **Toolbar** class contains three inner classes; the **ButtonGroup** class to define a group of buttons, and the **ColorButton** and **TypeButton** classes which define the buttons in the first two groups we are going to add. The **Toolbar** class has data members that define the buttons groups for selecting the element color and type, and a data member to store a reference to the application object. We will need this to get at the document and application window class methods.

Because the button and button group classes are inner classes to the **Toolbar** class, they will have direct access to the application object stored in the **Toolbar** object, so getting the document or the menus' update when a button is clicked will be easy.

Let's work from the bottom up, and start by defining the detail of the button class definitions.

Try It Out—Defining the Toolbar Button Classes

1   The type buttons will need to know what element type they set—a simple way to arrange this is to use a data member to store a type that is passed to the constructor.

We can define the class **TypeButton** as:

```
// Inner class defining a type button
class TypeButton extends Button
{
  int elementType;                          // Type for this button
  public TypeButton(int elementType)
  {
    String text;
    switch(elementType)     // Select the button label for the type
    {
      case LINE:       text = "LINE";       break;
      case RECTANGLE:  text = "RECTANGLE";  break;
      case CIRCLE:     text = "CIRCLE";     break;
      case CURVE:      text = "CURVE";      break;
      case TEXT:       text = "TEXT";       break;
      default:         text = "ERROR";      break;
    }
    setLabel(text);                                // Set the button label
    this.elementType = elementType;                // Store the type
    enableEvents(AWTEvent.ACTION_EVENT_MASK); // Enable action events
  }

  // Handle action events for the button
  protected void processActionEvent(ActionEvent e)
  {
    // Update the type in the document
    theApp.getDocument().setElementType(elementType);
    super.processActionEvent(e);                    // Pass the event on
  }
}
```

We need to remember to add an extra **import** statement to the **Toolbar** class, for the **java.awt.event** package, since we're using the **ActionEvent** class in the argument to the **processActionEvent()** method.

2 For the color buttons we can color each button in the element color that it selects, rather than just setting the button label. This, in fact, turns out to be slightly easier to implement. Here's the definition of the inner class **ColorButton**:

```
// Inner class defining a color button
class ColorButton extends Button
{
  Color elementColor;                             // Color for this button

  // Constructor
  public ColorButton(Color elementColor)
  {
    super(" ");                                    // Blank button label

    // Store the button color
    this.elementColor = new Color(elementColor.getRGB());
    setBackground(elementColor);              // Color the button background
```

```
        enableEvents(AWTEvent.ACTION_EVENT_MASK);
      }

      // Handle action events for this button
      protected void processActionEvent(ActionEvent e)
      {
        // Set element color in the document
        theApp.getDocument().setElementColor(elementColor);
        super.processActionEvent(e);              // Pass the event on
      }
    }
```

How It Works

The **TypeButton** constructor does three things:

- It sets the label for the button based on the element type passed as an argument

- It stores the element type for use when an event occurs

- It enables the object to handle its own action events

The **switch** statement selects the appropriate string for the button label, based on the parameter, **elementType**. This is set for the button by passing the string as an argument to the **setLabel()** method that is inherited from the super-class, **Button**. The element types are available through the top-level class, **Toolbar**, implementing the **Constants** interface that defines them.

After storing the **elementType** argument value in the data member of the same name, we enable the handling of action events within the **TypeButton** object by calling **enableEvents()** with the argument **AWTEvent.ACTION_EVENT_MASK**. When an action event occurs for a button, its **processActionEvent()** method will be called.

Our implementation of **processActionEvent()** just calls the **setElementType()** method for the document object that is obtained from the application object to set the type. This will automatically update the menu checks because we arranged for this to happen when we implemented the menu item event listeners. It then calls the **processActionEvent()** method for the super-class to pass the event on. This ensures that if we were to add other listeners for a button, they too could receive the same event.

The **ColorButton** class has a data member to store the color passed in the constructor. This is the color that the particular **ColorButton** will set in the document when it is clicked. To color the button, we just call the **setBackground()** method, which, in our class, is inherited from the **Button** class. We then enable action events for the object, as with the **TypeButton** class. The **processActionEvent()** method also works in the same way as in the **TypeButton** class. It calls the **setElementColor()** method for the document to set the color, and this method takes car of updating the menu check marks.

That's the button classes to set the color and type defined. We can move on to defining a button group.

Try It Out—Defining a Button Group Class

At this point we don't need a lot to define the **ButtonGroup** class. Here it is:

```java
// Inner class defining a group of toolbar buttons
class ButtonGroup extends Panel
{
  public ButtonGroup()
  {
    setLayout(new FlowLayout(FlowLayout.CENTER,8,3));
    setBackground(Color.lightGray);
  }
}
```

How It Works

This sets the layout as **FlowLayout**, with the buttons it contains positioned at the center of the panel. The second and third arguments to the **FlowLayout** class constructor specify the horizontal and vertical gaps around the buttons. We will add buttons to a **GroupButton** panel using the **add()** method that is inherited from the **Panel** class.

The only method we need for now is the **Toolbar** constructor.

Try It Out—Defining the Toolbar Class

1 The **Toolbar** class constructor will create the **ButtonGroup** objects, add the buttons to them, and then add the **ButtonGroup** objects to the **Toolbar**. We can implement this with the following code:

```java
// Class defining a toolbar
import java.awt.*;
import java.awt.event.*;

class Toolbar extends Panel implements Constants
{
  Sketcher theApp;                                  // Reference to the app
  ButtonGroup colorGroup = new ButtonGroup();  // Group to select color
  ButtonGroup typeGroup = new ButtonGroup();   // Group to select type

  // Constructor
  public Toolbar(Sketcher theApp)
  {
    this.theApp = theApp;                           // Store the app reference

    setLayout(new FlowLayout(FlowLayout.LEFT,5,2)); // Set flow layout
    setBackground(Color.lightGray);                 // Set the background color

    // Add the element color button group
    colorGroup.add(new ColorButton(Color.red));
    colorGroup.add(new ColorButton(Color.yellow));
```

```
        colorGroup.add(new ColorButton(Color.green));
        colorGroup.add(new ColorButton(Color.blue));
        add(colorGroup);

        // Add the element type button group
        typeGroup.add(new TypeButton(LINE));
        typeGroup.add(new TypeButton(RECTANGLE));
        typeGroup.add(new TypeButton(CIRCLE));
        typeGroup.add(new TypeButton(CURVE));
        typeGroup.add(new TypeButton(TEXT));
        add(typeGroup);
    }

    // Inner class defining a group of toolbar buttons as before...

    // Inner class defining a color button as before...

    // Inner class defining a type button as before...

}
```

That's the basic **Toolbar** defined, believe it or not. To use it, we just need to add it to the application window.

2 To add the toolbar to the application window, we need an extra data member in the **SketchFrame** class, and a small addition to the **SketchFrame** class constructor:

```
// Frame for Sketcher application
import java.awt.*;
import java.awt.event.*;

public class SketchFrame extends Frame implements Constants
{
    Sketcher theApp;                     // The application object
    SketchDoc sketch;                    // The document object
    MenuBar menubar = new MenuBar();     // Window menu bar
    Toolbar toolbar;                     // Window tool bar

    // Element menu items
    CheckboxMenuItem lineItem, rectangleItem, circleItem, curveItem,
                textItem;

    // Color menu items
    CheckboxMenuItem redItem, yellowItem, greenItem, blueItem;

    // Constructor
    public SketchFrame(String title, Sketcher theApp)
    {
        super(title);                    // Call base constructor
        this.theApp = theApp;            // Store the application object
        sketch = theApp.getDocument();   // Get the document object
        setMenuBar(menubar);             // Add the menu bar to the window
```

```
    toolbar = new Toolbar(theApp);        // Create the toolbar
    add(toolbar, BorderLayout.NORTH);     // Place it at the top

  // Rest of the constructor as before...
  }

  // The methods to set the menu check marks, as before...

}
```

You need to compile the **Toolbar.java** and recompile **SketchFrame.java**. You can then run Sketcher once again, and the application window should be as shown below—but with the color buttons in color.

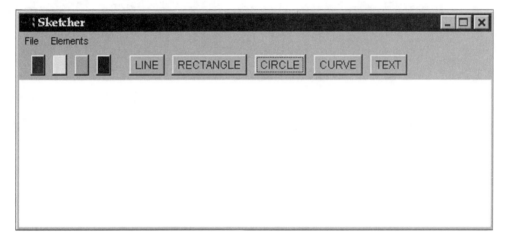

If you click on any of the buttons, you can verify that the appropriate selection is being made by extending the Elements pull-down menu. The item check mark should be set for the button you clicked. You can see how the size of each button is automatically adjusted to accommodate the text for the button label.

It would be nice to make the division between the menu bar and the toolbar a bit clearer. The button groups need to be better identified in some way. We will be addressing both of these requirements in the next chapter.

How It Works

The constructor isn't too taxing. The **import** statement is there to add the definitions for the **ActionEvent** class that we use in the button classes. The **Toolbar** constructor has a statement specifying the layout for the toolbar panel as **FlowLayout**, with the **ButtonGroup** panels that we will add positioned to the left. The gaps around the **ButtonGroup** panels are specified as five pixels vertically, and two pixels horizontally. If you don't like this spacing, you can always change it.

The next block of new code creates the **ColorButton** objects for each of the element colors, and adds them to the **ButtonGroup** object, **colorGroup**, which is defined as an initialized data member of the **Toolbar** class. The following statement block creates and adds the **TypeButton** objects to the **typeGroup** panel. Since each button is handling its own action event, we don't need to add any listeners, and we don't need to store the button objects explicitly in the **Toolbar** class.

In **SketchFrame**, the data member to store the **Toolbar** object is not essential at this point. We could equally well create it and add it to the application window in the **SketchFrame** constructor, but we will need it later on when we add other buttons to the toolbar, so adding it now will save some amendments later. The two lines we have added to the constructor create the **Toolbar** object, pass a reference to it to the application object and add the **toolbar** object to the application window. By specifying the second argument to the **add()** method as **BorderLayout.NORTH**, we ensure it is positioned at the top of the window underneath the menu bar. Now we have added it to the application window, the toolbar is ready for a trial run.

Handling Key Events

You will recall from the previous chapter that shortcuts are a key combination that you enter to select a particular menu item. To support menu shortcuts you must handle key events. Let's understand a little more about what happens when you press a key on the keyboard.

We saw earlier in this chapter that the **KeyListener** interface defines three methods which are called automatically for keyboard events. They are **keyPressed()**, which is called when you press a key, **keyReleased()** which is called when you release a key, and **keyTyped()** which is called after you release a key that actually enters a character. The **keyTyped()** method will not be called for functions keys or control keys.

Each of the methods declared in the **KeyListener** interface will be passed a **KeyEvent** object as an argument. The **KeyEvent** object will contain the following methods that provide information about the key that caused the event:

Method	Description
getKeyCode()	Returns a code of type **int** that identifies which key was pressed or released. We will look at the possible codes that can be returned in a moment.
getKeyChar()	Returns that character corresponding to the key that was pressed as type **char**. If there is no character corresponding to the key, a value of type **KeyEvent.CHAR_UNDEFINED** will be returned.
getKeyText()	Returns an object of type **String** that describes the key originating the event. For example **"F1"** or **"Q"**.

Table Continued on Following Page

Method	Description
`getKeyModifiersText()`	Returns a **String** object that describes any modifier keys that were pressed when the event originated. For example, **"Shift"** or **"Ctrl+Shift"**.
`isActionKey()`	Returns **true** if the key causing the event was an action key such as a function key.

There are a large number of codes identifying keys defined in the **KeyEvent** class as static data members of type **int**. They are all prefixed with the sequence VK_. The numeric keys are identified by constants with the names **VK_0**, **VK_1**, through **VK_9**. The letter keys are identified by constants **VK_A** through **VK_Z**. There are also constants defining the other character keys. For example, **VK_PERIOD**, **VK_COMMA**, **VK_PAGEDOWN**, **VK_EQUALS, VK_QUOTE**, **VK_OPEN_BRACKET** and so on. The function keys are identified by the constants **VK_F1** through **VK_F12**. No key code is defined for a **KEY_TYPED** event—they are only defined for **KeyEvent** objects passed to the **keyPressed()** or **keyReleased()** methods. If you call **getKeyCode()** for the **KeyEvent** object passed to the **key_Typed()** method, the value **KeyEvent.VK_UNDEFINED** will be returned. You can get the character for the key though, by calling **getKeyChar()** for the event object.

Don't be misled into thinking that getting keyboard input into a window-based program is going to be some kind of nightmare. You don't need to worry about any of this in that context. You use components such as **TextField** objects for that. This is just for analyzing key strokes when you need to handle keyboard events individually—when you want to implement shortcuts for instance.

To implement the shortcuts in the Sketcher program, we need to add a key listener that will determine whether the key pressed represents a shortcut, and if it does, initiate the appropriate action for the menu item corresponding to the shortcut.

Try It Out—Supporting Menu Shortcuts

1　We can add a class defining a key listener for the application window in Sketcher as an inner class to the **SketchFrame** class:

```
class KeyHandler extends KeyAdapter
{
  // Handle the key pressed event
  public void keyPressed(KeyEvent e)
  {
    if(e.getModifiers()==Event.CTRL_MASK)  // Verify Ctrl key pressed
    {
      // Get the shortcut for the key, then the item for the shortcut
      MenuShortcut s = new MenuShortcut(e.getKeyCode());
      MenuItem item = menuBar.getShortcutMenuItem(s);
```

```
        // If there is an item for the shortcut, dispatch an event for it
        if(item!=null)
        item.dispatchEvent(newActionEvent(item,ActionEvent.ACTION_PERFORMED,
                    item.getActionCommand()));
    }
  }
}
```

2 The only other things we need to do to enable shortcuts in Sketcher is to add an import statement at the beginning of `SketchFrame.java` for the `java.awt.event` package, and to add a `KeyHandler` listener for the `SketchFrame` object that is the application window. You can do this by adding one statement at the end of the `SketchFrame` constructor:

```
addKeyListener(new KeyHandler());     // Add the key listener
```

How It Works

We only need to implement the `keyPressed()` method, so we derive our listener class, `KeyHandler`, from the `KeyAdapter` class. The implementation to handle shortcuts is surprisingly simple.

The first step is to establish that the *Ctrl* key was pressed. This is done by calling the `getModifiers()` method for the event passed to the `keyPressed()` method and comparing the return value with `Event.CTRL_MASK` which is the modifier that is set when the *Ctrl* key is down. The `Event` class in the package `java.awt` also defines the modifier values `SHIFT_MASK` and `ALT_MASK` which are set when the *Shift* key or the *Alt* key are pressed. If we had defined any shortcuts in Sketcher using the *Shift* key, of course we would need to look for the modifier corresponding to this, as well.

If the *Ctrl* key is pressed, the key entry could be a shortcut for one of the items in the menu. We therefore create a `MenuShortcut` object from the event's key code, a combination of the key that was pressed and the *Ctrl* key. The key code is returned by the `getKeyCode()` method of the `KeyEvent` object, `e`. Once we have the shortcut corresponding to the keys pressed, we use the handy little method `getShortcutMenuItem()` defined in the `MenuBar` class to return the menu item in a `MenuItem` object that matches the shortcut passed as an argument. If no menu item matches the shortcut, `null` is returned.

Entering a menu shortcut should be equivalent to selecting the corresponding menu item. We could implement whole chunk of code to handle the events for the menu items, but it would be much better if we could create an event for the menu item corresponding to the shortcut. Then the code that we will add to handle menu item events would take care of it. That's exactly what the program does.

The classes that define menu items inherit a method, `dispatchEvent()`, which allows you to initiate an event to a menu item object. The event object is passed to the method as an argument. The `Component` class defines the same method, so you can create events for any component just by calling the `dispatchEvent()` method for it. This means that you can translate an event for one component into an event for another. This is ideal when events for both components should result in the same program action.

So, to respond to a shortcut key being pressed for the File menu items, we need to create an **ActionEvent** object, and pass it to the **dispatchEvent()** method for the menu item. Note that this is different from the **CheckboxMenuItem** objects on the Element menu—they generated **ItemEvent** objects. To create an **ActionEvent** for the item corresponding to the shortcut, we call the constructor for the **ActionEvent** class with the expression:

```
new ActionEvent(item,
                ActionEvent.ACTION_PERFORMED,
                item.getActionCommand())
```

There are three arguments for the constructor. The first is the source of the event. Since this parameter is type object you can pass any kind of object as an argument. This would be useful if the event handling for the menu item needed to know where the event came from. This information is stored in the **ActionEvent** object. We don't care here, so we just pass the item object since we don't look at this in the item event handler anyway. The second argument is an **int** value specifying the event type. What we have specified, **ACTION_PERFORMED**, is the only choice in this case. The third argument is a **String** object that identifies the command corresponding to the event. We just pass on the command string for the menu item. We don't use this information in handling the menu item event in any case.

To dispatch the event we call the **dispatchEvent()** method for the menu item with the statement:

```
item.dispatchEvent(new ActionEvent(item,
                   ActionEvent.ACTION_PERFORMED,
item.getActionCommand())));
```

From the event handling point of view, this event will seem just the same as if the user selected the menu item. The action listener for the menu item will take care of processing the event in the normal way.

We will be adding the listeners for the File menu items later in the book. In fact we won't get to do that until Chapter 15. If you can't wait that long and you want to verify that the shortcuts really are working, you can add listeners for each of the menu items with shortcuts, which simply outputs a suitable message using the **println()** method. Just add the listener object immediately after the creation of the menu item in the **SketchFrame** constructor, where you can use the **item** variable to call the method to add the listener. Note that menu clicks are action events, not item events, so you must use the **addActionListener()** method to add them.

Summary

In this chapter you have learnt how to handle events in your applications and in your applets. Events are fundamental to all window-based applications, as well as most applets, so you will be applying the techniques from this chapter throughout the rest of the book.

The most important points we have discussed in this chapter are:

▶ A user interaction generates an event in the context of a component.

▶ There are two categories of events associated with a component: **low-level events** from the mouse or keyboard, or window system events such as opening or closing a window, and **semantic events** which represent component actions such as pressing a button or selecting a menu item.

▶ Both low-level and semantic events can arise simultaneously.

▶ An event for a component can be handled by the component object itself, or by a separate object that implements a listener interface corresponding to the event type.

▶ A component that is to handle its own events does so by calling its **enableEvents()** method and implementing the class method to process the kind of event that has been enabled.

▶ A listener object is connected to a component's events by registering itself using the **addListener()** method for that component.

▶ A listener interface for low-level events requires several event handling methods to be implemented.

▶ A listener interface for semantic events declares a single event handling method.

▶ An adapter class is a class that defines a set of empty methods for a low-level event interface. You can derive your own class defining a low-level event listener by deriving your class from an adapter class, and just implementing the event handling methods you are interested in.

▶ Events in applications and in applets are handled in exactly the same way.

▶ You can create events for a component or a menu item by passing an event object to the **dispatchEvent()** method for the component or menu item object.

Exercises

1 Implement a listener to handle the File | Exit menu item in the Sketcher application.

2 Modify the lottery applet to present the six numbers selected in ascending sequence.

3 Replace the action listener for the selection buttons in the Lottery applet with a mouse listener, and use the **mousePressed()** method to update the selection with a new value.

4 Modify the Lottery applet to implement the mouse listener for a selection button as an inner class to the **Lottery** class.

5 Modify the Lottery applet to implement the mouse listener for a selection button as an inner class to the **Selection** class.

6 Change the Lottery applet to handle the **MOUSE_ENTERED** and **MOUSE_EXITED** events within the **Selection** button object.

Drawing in a Window

In this chapter we will look at how you can draw with Java, both in an applet and in an application. We will investigate how we can combine the event-handling capability we learned about in the previous chapter with the drawing facilities we'll explore in this chapter, to implement an interactive graphical user interface.

By the end of this chapter you will have learned:

- What components you can draw on
- How coordinates are defined for a component
- How you implement drawing on a component
- How to structure the components in a window for drawing
- What kinds of shapes you can draw on a component
- How you can add a status bar to a window
- How you can implement mouse listener methods to enable interactive drawing operations

Coordinate Systems in Components

In Chapter 11, we saw how your computer screen has a coordinate system that is used to define the position and size of a window. We also saw how we can add components to a container with their position established within the container by a layout manager. The position of each component within a container is defined by the layout manager in terms of a coordinate system that is specific to the container. This coordinate system is analogous to the screen coordinate system. The origin is at the top-left corner of the container, with the positive x-axis running horizontally from left to right, and the positive y-axis running from top to bottom. The positions of buttons in a **Window** or a **Frame** object are specified as a pair of (x, y) pixel coordinates, relative to the origin at the top-left corner of the container object on the screen. Below you can see the coordinate system for the Sketcher application window.

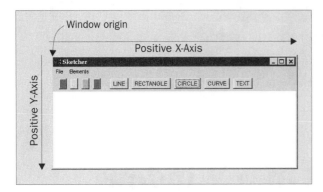

It's not just containers and windows that have their own coordinate system either. **Button** objects too each have their own system, as do **Panel** and **Canvas** objects. In fact, *every* component has its own coordinate system.

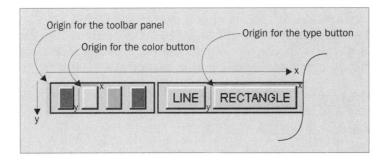

It's clear that a container needs a coordinate system—it's necessary in order to specify the positions of the components it contains, but why are there coordinate systems for components that aren't containers? One reason is so that you can draw on them. Another reason is to define where the mouse cursor is in relation to a component. These two aspects of the use of components are quite closely related in practice, as we shall see in this chapter.

Drawing on a Component

Let's get an idea of how we can draw on a component. We can add some temporary code to the Sketcher application to illustrate how it works. We'll draw something on the application window, the **SketchFrame** object. The **Component** class defines the method **paint()**, which is called when the object needs to be drawn. This can occur when the component size changes, or if the component was obscured and becomes visible again for instance. We can override the **paint()** method in the **SketchFrame** class to draw on the application window.

Try It Out—Painting on a Window

Add the following implementation of the method to the **SketchFrame** class:

```
public void paint(Graphics g)
{
  g.drawRect(50, 50, 150, 100);           // Draw a rectangle
  g.drawString("A nice rectangle", 60, 100);   // Draw some text
}
```

If you recompile the file **SketchFrame.java** and run Sketcher, you can see what the **paint()** method produces. You should see the window shown here.

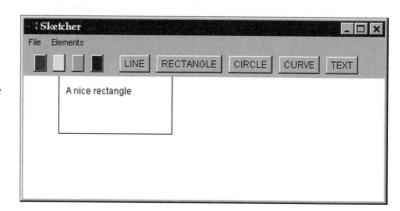

How It Works

We'll come back to the **Graphics** class, which is the type of the argument to the **paint()** method, in a moment. For now we'll just say it provides all the methods you need for drawing on a component. Here we call the **drawRect()** method to draw a rectangle. The first two arguments are the x and y coordinates of the top-left corner of the rectangle to be drawn, relative to the origin of the component—in this case the application window. The third and fourth arguments are the width and height of the rectangle respectively. We have seen the **drawString()** method before. This draws the string specified as the first argument at the position determined by the second and third argument—which are the x and y coordinates of the bottom-left corner of the first letter of the string.

As you can see, the rectangle is partially obscured by the toolbar. This is because we are drawing relative to the window origin which is the top-left corner, so the bottom edge of the menu bar must be more than 50 pixels down the window. This is one reason why it's generally not such a good idea to draw directly in a window. Later in this chapter we'll define a class **SketchView** which will contain a view of the document, and add the **SketchView** object to the application window. The **SketchView** object will have its own origin so the things we draw will not be obscured by the menu bar or the toolbar. This also allows us to dissociate the coordinate system for what we display in the view from all the other stuff that appears in the application window.

If you want to try moving the rectangle down a bit, try increasing the second argument of the **drawRect()** method to 100 say. You'll need to change the y coordinate for the position of the text as well if you want it to sit comfortably in the rectangle.

The key to drawing on a component is in the **Graphics** class, so let's examine that a little more closely.

The Graphics Class

An object of the **Graphics** class defines what is called a **graphics context**, which encapsulates what you're drawing on, and provides methods that you use to implement and manage the drawing process. The graphics context not only contains information about the component you're drawing on, but also encapsulates the **context** in which the drawing is taking place—the screen, or a printer for example. Don't confuse the graphics context with the component though. The graphics context is the means by which you draw on a component—a bit like the spray can a graffiti artist might use to color the blank face of a wall. When you're done drawing on a component, you can, and should, chuck the graphics context away—as the graffiti artist might dispose of the can once he's finished his work if for any reason he thinks that it might compromise his position in the eyes of the law. The component remains complete with your graffiti.

It may appear strange to you at first to find that **Graphics** is an **abstract** class, so you can't create objects of the class directly. The reason for this is that a **Graphics** object only has significance in relation to a particular component—the thing that you'll be drawing on—so it has no meaning by itself. Therefore a **Graphics** object is always obtained from a component. You can do this by calling the **getGraphics()** method that every component inherits from the **Component** class. This returns an object of type **Graphics** specific to the component. However, quite a lot of the time—and in the **paint()** method, in particular—the **Graphics** object is provided as an object passed to the method. Of course, this will be the **Graphics** object for the component that owns the **paint()** method, and it will have been obtained behind the scenes, as it were, so you don't have to obtain it yourself.

The Drawing Process

We've already said that the coordinate system used to draw on a component has its origin at the top-left corner of the component and the positive axes running from left to right and from top to bottom. We've also said that the unit of measure is a pixel. However, the coordinate positions don't represent the pixels on your screen—they lie *in between* the pixels.

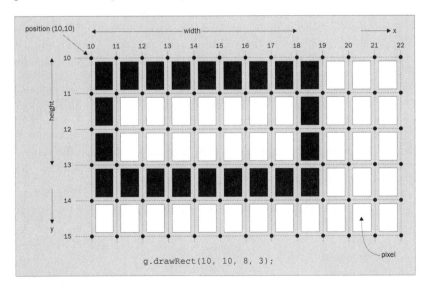

g.drawRect(10, 10, 8, 3);

The diagram shows an array of pixels as the black and white rectangles, relative to the coordinate positions represented by the circular black dots that lie between the pixels. When you draw, a shape is produced by traversing the pixels below, and to the right of the coordinate positions you use to specify the shape. This applies to lines, rectangles, circles or whatever shape you are drawing.

Here, a rectangle produced by the **drawRect()** method is shown by the pixels that are black. The first two arguments specify the x and y coordinates of the top-left corner of the rectangle as (10, 10). The next two arguments specify the width and height of the rectangle as 8 and 3 respectively. You can see that the rectangle produced is actually nine pixels wide—one pixel wider than the width value, 8, passed as the third argument to the method. The height of the rectangle is also one pixel more than the height value, 3, passed as the fourth argument to the method. It's important to understand and remember this. We'll often need to specify the rectangular area enclosing a shape—when we want to redraw the shape when we change it, for example—and we must be careful to define this area correctly. For the rectangle in the diagram, the area enclosing it is at position (10, 10), with a width of nine pixels and a height of four pixels.

Understanding the Drawing Process

We can understand the drawing process better by applying it in a practical context. We could emphasize the button groupings on the toolbar in Sketcher by drawing rectangles around them.

We can add the **paint()** method to our **Toolbar** class definition in Sketcher, and draw rectangles around each group of buttons. One way to do this is to implement a **draw()** method for the inner class, **ButtonGroup**, that will draw a rectangle around it, and then call this method from the **paint()** method for the **Toolbar** class.

Try It Out—Grouping Buttons

1 Here's the code for the **paint()** method for the **Toolbar** class:

```
// Paint the toolbar
public void paint(Graphics g)
{
  g.setColor(Color.darkGray);     // Set the drawing color
  colorGroup.draw(g);             // Draw round the color button group
  typeGroup.draw(g);              // Draw round the type button group
}
```

This sets the drawing color to dark gray and calls the **draw**() method for each of the **ButtonGroup** objects on the toolbar. The graphics context for the **Toolbar** object is passed to the **ButtonGroup** objects' **draw()** methods, so all drawing is done within the coordinate system for the toolbar.

2 With this in mind, we can implement the **draw()** method in the inner class **ButtonGroup** as:

```
// Inner class defining a group of toolbar buttons
class ButtonGroup extends Panel
{
    // Inner class definition as before...

    // Draw a rectangle around the button group
    public void draw(Graphics g)
    {
        Rectangle bounds = getBounds();        // Get object bounds
        g.drawRect(bounds.x - 1, bounds.y - 1,
                   bounds.width + 1, bounds.height + 1);
    }
}
```

If you recompile **Toolbar.java**, and run Sketcher again, the application window should now look as shown here.

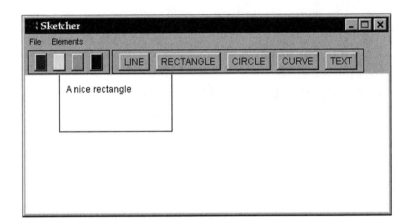

We can now see the button grouping quite clearly with the rectangle around them.

How It Works

The **getBounds()** method for the **ButtonGroup** component returns the rectangle bounding the object in the toolbar coordinate system. We must subtract 1 from the x and y coordinates of the top-left corner of the **bounds** rectangle, to arrive at the top-left corner for the rectangle we want to draw. This is because drawing is below, and to the right of the coordinate position. If we don't adjust the top-left corner in this way, the lines at the top and side of the rectangle will not show because they will be obscured by the **ButtonGroup** object itself, as that will be drawn on top of the toolbar. Since we have to move the top-left corner up and to the left by one pixel, we must increase the width and height to accommodate this, and to prevent the bottom and right sides of the rectangle being hidden under the **ButtonGroup** object.

We could also have produced a similar effect by implementing the **paint()** method for the inner **ButtonGroup** class.

Try It Out—An Alternative Way to Draw a Rectangle around Button Groups

1 First delete the `paint()` method from the `Toolbar` class, as well as the `draw()` method from the `ButtonGroup` class.

2 Now add the following `paint()` method to the `ButtonGroup` class:

```
// Paint the button group
public void paint(Graphics g)
{
  Dimension size = getSize();
  g.drawRect(0, 0, size.width-1, size.height-1);
}
```

If you recompile the **Toolbar** class and run Sketcher again, the application window should look like this:

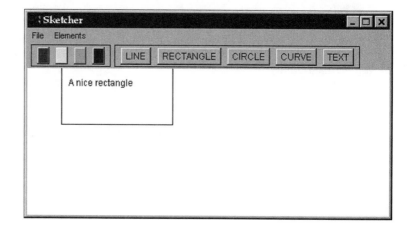

How It Works

This time we're drawing in the coordinate system of the **ButtonGroup** object. The top-left corner of the button group is at position (0, 0), and the **getSize()** method returns a **Dimension** object specifying the height and width. We must draw the rectangle within the boundaries of the **ButtonGroup** object—anything you attempt to draw outside will be **clipped**, which means it will not be drawn. Because the drawing process is below and to the right of the coordinate positions that we specify, we must subtract one from the width and height of the button group to ensure the bottom and right side of the rectangle lie inside the boundaries of the object.

It's almost the same as the previous example, but not quite. On the screen you should be able to see that the rectangles around the groups of buttons are now slightly smaller because they are drawn inside the **ButtonGroup** objects. Try omitting the adjustment of the width and height by −1. You'll see that the bottom and right sides of each rectangle no longer appear. Because they lie outside the objects they are clipped. On balance drawing the rectangle in the **paint()** method for the **ButtonGroup** class is preferable. This keeps the button group objects self-contained so that they are responsible for their own appearance. However many button groups we add to the toolbar, they will each draw their own outline automatically. The code is simpler and neater too.

Changing the Drawing Color

The rectangle drawn in the **paint()** method in the **SketchFrame** class, as well as the rectangles we've just been drawing, appear in black. Black is the default drawing color but you can change this. The drawing color is specified by a **Color** object that you pass as an argument to the **setColor()** method for the graphics context object.

For example, we could draw the rectangle in red and the text in blue by modifying the **paint()** method in **SketchFrame** to:

```
public void paint(Graphics g)
{
    g.setColor(Color.red);                  // Set red drawing color
    g.drawRect(50, 50, 150, 100);           // Draw a rectangle
    g.setColor(Color.blue);                 // Set blue drawing color
    g.drawString("A nice rectangle", 60, 100);   // Draw some text
}
```

Of course, you can also create your own **Color** objects and use those to set the drawing color. You could also retrieve the element color from the **SketchDoc** object, and use that as the element color:

```
public void paint(Graphics g)
{
    g.setColor(sketch.getElementColor());   // Set current element color
    g.drawRect(50, 50, 150, 100);           // Draw a rectangle
    g.drawString("A nice rectangle",60, 100 ); // Draw some text
}
```

Here we set the drawing color as the **Color** object returned by the **getElementColor()** method for the sketch object—the document for Sketcher. When you select a different color using the toolbar buttons or the menu nothing happens. The reason is that the **paint()** method is only called when something happens that requires the component to be repainted. We'll see later that you can program this, but for now you can cause the **paint()** method to be called by resizing the application window. The rectangle and the text will then be drawn in the current color set in the document.

We saw in Chapter 11 that the background color for a component is set by calling the **setBackground()** method for the component. Remember that this doesn't involve the graphics context. To draw on a green background in Sketcher, you can add one statement to the beginning of the **paint()** method for **SketchFrame**:

```
setBackground(Color.green);                 // Set the background green
```

You will then get the rectangle and the text drawn in the current element color on a green background. Of course, if you set the current color to green, the rectangle and text will be invisible.

It may be that in a complicated sequence of drawing operations, you need to find out what the current drawing color is. When you need to do this, you just call the `getColor()` method for the graphics context. This method returns a `Color` object corresponding to the current drawing color set in the graphics context.

Methods for Drawing

We've already seen how to draw rectangles, but there are quite a few other methods in the `Graphics` class that draw shapes and there are methods for filling shapes too. We also have other methods besides `drawString()` for drawing text. All the draw methods have a `void` return type.

Let's divide the methods that draw shapes into two groups. We can look first at shapes consisting of straight lines, such as the rectangle we've already seen, then we can investigate the methods that draw curves of various kinds. We'll then explore how we can fill shapes and complete the set by looking at methods for drawing text.

Shapes Based on Lines

Let's step back to the simplest possible figure we can draw: a line. You draw a line by calling the `drawLine()` method. For example, to draw a line from the point (10, 20) to the point (50, 60) you would write:

```
g.drawLine(10, 20, 50, 60);                  // Draw a line
```

The first two arguments are the x and y coordinates of the starting point for the line, and the last two arguments are the coordinates of the end point. Remember that the line will be drawn by coloring pixels in the current color below and to the right of the coordinate positions that you use to define the line.

We could try out the `drawLine()` method in the context of enhancing the Sketcher program a little.

Creating a Status Bar

One limitation of the Sketcher program, as it stands, is that you have no direct feedback on what current element type and color have been selected. You could look at the pull-down menu to see which item is checked, but we can do better than that. A window status bar is a common, and very convenient way of displaying the status of various application parameters. A status bar has one or more areas where information is displayed that are often referred to as **panes**. We will use the `drawLine()` method to highlight each pane in the status bar. We'll add a status bar at the bottom of the application window that will have two panes to show the current element type and color. We can start by defining a `Statusbar` class that will represent the status bar in the application window.

The `Statusbar` object will be a panel that we add to the bottom of the application window which is defined by the `SketchFrame` class in Sketcher. The `Panel` class is an appropriate base class for the `Statusbar` class, since we can add components to it. We can define a pane by an inner class we'll call `StatusPane`. We'll need two `StatusPane` objects within the `Statusbar` panel, one to display the current element type and the other to display the current color.

Try It Out—Defining a Status Bar Class

Here's an initial stab at the definition for the **Statusbar** class:

```java
// Class defining a status bar
import java.awt.*;

class Statusbar extends Panel implements Constants
{
  StatusPane colorPane = new StatusPane("BLUE");
  StatusPane typePane = new StatusPane("LINE");

  // Constructor
  public Statusbar()
  {
    setLayout(new FlowLayout(FlowLayout.LEFT, 10, 3));
    setBackground(Color.lightGray);
    setColorPane(DEFAULT_ELEMENT_COLOR);
    setTypePane(DEFAULT_ELEMENT_TYPE);
    add(colorPane);                       // Add color pane to status bar
    add(typePane);                        // Add type pane to status bar
  }

  // Set color pane label
  public void setColorPane(Color color)
  {
    // Set the text for the color pane...
  }

  // Set type pane label
  public void setTypePane(int elementType)
  {
    // Set the text for the type pane...
  }

  // Paint the staus bar
  public void paint(Graphics g)
  {
    colorPane.draw(g);   // Draw color pane outline
    typePane.draw(g);    // Draw type pane outline
  }

  // Inner class defining a status bar pane
  class StatusPane extends Label
  {
    // Constructor
     public StatusPane(String text)
     {
       // Code to construct a status pane..
     }

     public void draw(Graphics g)
```

```
        {
          // Draw the pane outline...
        }

        // Rest of the definition of the inner class ...
      }
    }
```

How It Works

Since the **Statusbar** class implements our **Constants** interface, all the variables that represent possible element types and colors are available. This preliminary version of **Statusbar** has two data members of type **StatusPane**, which will be the panes showing the current color and element type. The initial information to be displayed by a **StatusPane** object is passed to the constructor as a **String** object. In the **Statusbar** constructor we update the text for each pane by calling the **setColorPane()** and **setTypePane()** methods. These ensure that initially the **StatusPane**s display the default color and type that we've defined for the application. One or other of these methods will be called whenever it is necessary to update the status bar. We'll complete the definitions for **setColorPane()** and **setTypePane()** when we've defined the detail of the **StatusPane** class.

The **Statusbar** panel has a **FlowLayout** manager which is set in the constructor. The panes in the status bar need only display a small amount of text, so we've derived the **StatusPane** class from the **Label** class—so a pane for the status bar will be a specialized kind of **Label**. The **StatusPane** objects will be left-justified when they are added to the status bar, as a result of the first argument to the **setLayout()** method call in the **Statusbar** constructor. The layout manager will leave a ten-pixel gap between successive panes in the status bar.

The **paint()** method for the **Statusbar** class just calls the **draw()** method for each of the **StatusPane** objects. The **draw()** method in the **StatusPane** class will draw the outline of the pane to highlight it.

Before we develop the full detail of the **Statusbar** class definition, we should put the detailed definition of the inner class, **StatusPane**, together. To maintain a tidy appearance, we should ensure that all the panes in the status bar are the same height. To achieve this we can fix the font for every pane by storing a fixed font in the **StatusPane** class. The **StatusPane** class will need to have a method to change the **String** displayed.

Try It Out—Defining Status Bar Panes

Here's a more developed version of the **StatusPane** class:

```
// Class defining a status bar pane
class StatusPane extends Label
{
  Font paneFont = new Font("Serif", Font.PLAIN, 10);
```

```java
    public StatusPane(String text)
    {
      setBackground(Color.lightGray);     // Set background color
      setFont(paneFont);                  // Set the fixed font
      setAlignment(CENTER);               // Center the pane text
      setLabel(text);                     // Set the text in the pane
    }

    // Set the pane label
    void setLabel(String text)
    {
      // String buffer with 12 blanks - pane holds total of 14 characters
      StringBuffer string = new StringBuffer("            "); // 12 blanks

      // Make sure text contains no more than 12 characters
      if(text.length() > 12)
        text = text.substring(0,11);

      // Create string of 14 characters starting with two spaces
      // Set string length
      string.setLength(string.length()-text.length());
      text = "  "+text+string;    // 2 spaces + text + spaces up to 14 chars

      setText(text);                      // Set the composite string
    }

    public void draw(Graphics g)
    {
      // Draw the pane as recessed...
    }
  }
```

How It Works

The only data member is the **Font** object, **font**. We've defined the font for a pane as standard 10-point Serif. In the constructor we set the background color to light gray and we set the standard font. We also set the alignment of the text as centered by calling the inherited method **setAlignment()**, and passing the value **CENTER** to it, which is also defined in the base class, **Label**. Lastly, in the constructor we set the text for the pane by calling the **setLabel()** method.

If we can maintain a fixed width for each pane, it will avoid the size of the pane jumping around when we change the text displayed. We can do this by fixing the length of the string that is displayed at fourteen characters, say, and then padding whatever text is to be displayed with spaces to make up the length. The choice of fourteen is determined by adding a few spaces at the beginning and the end of the maximum length string we want to display, which is **"Rectangle"**.

We pad out the text with spaces in the **setLabel()** method. To do this, we create a string consisting of two spaces, followed by the required text, followed by as many spaces as necessary to have a total of fourteen characters in the string. We first set up a

StringBuffer object, **string**, containing twelve blank characters which we'll truncate to the number of spaces we want to add at the end. It shouldn't happen, but just to be on the safe side we check that the string, **text**, has no more than 12 characters, and if it has, we create a new **String** object from the first 12 characters and use that. To truncate **string**, we call its **setLength()** method with the argument as the difference between the original length, and the length of the string, **text**. To set the text we call the inherited method, **setText()** with the composite string we've constructed.

Try It Out—Outlining the Status Bar Panes

To complete the **StatusPane** class we need a definition for the **draw()** method which will outline a pane:

```
// Draw pane as recessed
public void draw(Graphics g)
{
  Rectangle bounds = getBounds();          // Get pane bounds
  g.setColor(Color.darkGray);              // Set top and left side color
  g.drawLine(bounds.x - 1, bounds.y - 1,   // Draw top
          bounds.x + bounds.width + 1, bounds.y - 1);
  g.drawLine(bounds.x - 1, bounds.y - 1,   // Draw left side
          bounds.x - 1, bounds.y + bounds.height + 1);

  g.setColor(Color.white);          // Set bottom and right side color
  g.drawLine(bounds.x - 1, bounds.y + bounds.height + 1, //Draw bottom
          bounds.x + bounds.width + 1, bounds.y + bounds.height + 1);
  g.drawLine(bounds.x + bounds.width + 1, bounds.y - 1, //Draw right side
          bounds.x + bounds.width + 1, bounds.y + bounds.height + 1);
}
```

How It Works

The **getBounds()** method will return a bound rectangle for the pane in the **Statusbar** object coordinate system. We want to draw the outline of the pane on the status bar, so we draw a rectangle consisting of four lines that is one pixel bigger all round than the rectangle returned by the **getBounds()** method for the pane. The rectangle we draw must be a bit bigger than the **StatusPane** object, otherwise the lines will be hidden behind the pane.

To create the illusion of a pane being recessed into the status bar, we draw the top and left side in dark gray, and the bottom and right side in white. This gives the impression that the status bar is lit from the top-left, so the top and left side are in shadow while the bottom and right side are in the light. If you want to display the panes as raised, just reverse the use of the colors—white for the top and left, and dark gray for the bottom and right.

To complete the **Statusbar** class we must implement the **setColorPane()** and **setTypePane()** methods using the **setLabel()** method we've defined for the **StatusPane** class.

Try It Out—Updating the Panes

1 We can code the **setColorPane()** method as:

```
// Set color pane label
public void setColorPane(Color color)
{
  String text;                              // Text for the color pane
  if(color.equals(Color.red))
    text = "RED";
  else if(color.equals(Color.yellow))
    text = "YELLOW";
  else if(color.equals(Color.green))
    text = "GREEN";
  else if(color.equals(Color.blue))
    text = "BLUE";
  else
    text = "ERROR";
  colorPane.setLabel(text);                 // Set the pane text
}
```

2 In the code for the **setTypePane()** method we can use a **switch** rather than **if**s to test the parameter value because it is of type **int**:

```
// Set type pane label
public void setTypePane(int elementType)
{
  String text;          // Text for the type pane
  switch(elementType)
  {
    case LINE:
      text = "LINE";
      break;
    case RECTANGLE:
      text = "RECTANGLE";
      break;
    case CIRCLE:
      text = "CIRCLE";
      break;
    case CURVE:
      text = "CURVE";
      break;
    case TEXT:
      text = "TEXT";
      break;
    default:
      text = "ERROR";
      break;
  }
  typePane.setLabel(text);  // Set the pane text
}
```

How It Works

This code is quite simple. The text to be displayed is selected in the series of **if-else** statements. They each compare the color passed as an argument with the standard colors we use in Sketcher and set the text accordingly. The last **else** should never be reached, but it will be obvious if it is.

All we need now is to implement the status bar in the **SketchFrame** class. For this we must add a data member that defines the status bar, add the status bar to the window in the class constructor and extend the **setTypeMenuChecks()** and **setColorMenuChecks()** methods to update the status bar whenever the element type or color is altered.

Try It Out—The Status Bar in Action

1 You can add the following statement to the **SketchFrame** class to define the status bar as a data member:

```
Statusbar statusbar = new Statusbar();     // Window status bar
```

2 We create **statusbar** as a data member so that it can be accessed throughout the class definition. You need to add one statement to the end of the **SketchFrame** class constructor:

```
public SketchFrame(String title, Sketcher theApp)
{
  // Constructor code as before

  add(statusbar, BorderLayout.SOUTH);      // Add the status bar
}
```

This adds the status bar to the bottom of the application window.

3 To update the status bar when the element type changes, you can add one statement to the **setTypeMenuChecks()** method:

```
public void setTypeMenuChecks(int elementType)
{
  // Code as before for this method...

  statusbar.setTypePane(elementType);      // Update the type pane
}
```

The type pane is updated by calling the **setTypePane()** method for the status bar and passing the current element type to it as an argument.

4 We can add a similar statement to the **setColorMenuChecks()** method to update the color pane:

```
   public void setColorMenuChecks(Color elementColor)
   {
     // Code as before for this method...
```

```
     statusbar.setColorPane(elementColor);    // Update the color pane
   }
```

If you now recompile the **SketchFrame** class, and run Sketcher again, you'll see the status bar in the application.

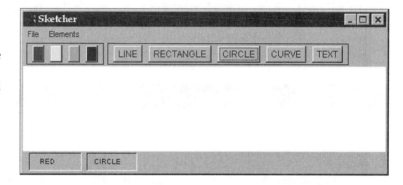

As you change the element type and color, the status bar will be updated automatically. To obtain the window shown here, the **paint()** method we added earlier was deleted from the **SketchFrame** class. You can leave it in for the time being as we'll be using it again in a modified form in this chapter to demonstrate some other drawing operations.

Drawing Polylines

A shape consisting of an arbitrary number of connected line segments is called a **polyline**. The method that will draw a polyline is **drawPolyline()**. It requires three arguments to be specified. The first argument is an **int** array of x coordinates for the defining points, the second argument is an **int** array of y coordinates for the defining points, and the last argument is the count of the number of points. Lines are drawn between successive points defined by pairs of corresponding elements in the arrays specified as the first and second arguments to the method.

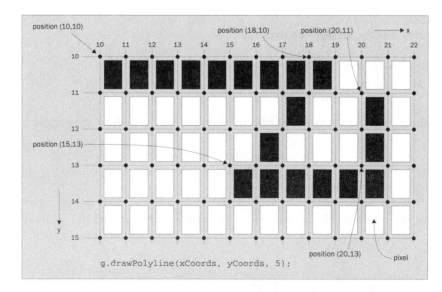

The diagram shows a polyline drawn by the following statements:

```
int[] xCoords = { 10, 18, 15, 20, 20 };        // Define x coordinates
int[] yCoords = { 10, 10, 13, 13, 11 };        // Define y coordinates
g.drawPolyline(xCoords, yCoords, 5);           // Draw the polyline
```

We have five points defining four lines. You can see how the lines are each drawn by coloring the sequence of pixels below and to the right of a line joining the defining points. In practice you would be better off specifying the third argument as **xCoords.length** rather than as an explicit integer, as this avoids any possibility of an error here.

Drawing Polygons

A closed shape, defined by a series of connected lines, is a polygon, and you can draw a polygon using the **drawPolygon()** method. The three arguments for this method are the same as for the previous method—an array of x coordinates and an array of y coordinates to define the points, plus the count of the number of points.

We can use the **drawPolygon()** method to draw a rectangle that is the same size as the rectangle that we created in the **paint()** method for the **SketchFrame** class, but starting at the point (50, 100) so it isn't obscured by the toolbar:

```
int[] xCoords = {  50, 200, 200,  50,  50 };        // Define x coordinates
int[] yCoords = { 100, 100, 200, 200, 100 };        // Define y coordinates
g.drawPolygon(xCoords, yCoords, xCoords.length);    // Draw the polygon
```

We have five points defining the four sides of the polygon. These are defined in the sequence top, right side, bottom, left side. You can see that we're defining a closed figure here because the last pair of coordinates are identical to the first. However, the **drawPolygon()** method will always draw a closed figure. If the last point is different from the first, the method will add a line connecting the last point to the first. This means we can draw the rectangle with just four points:

```
int[] xCoords = {  50, 200, 200,  50 };             // Define x coordinates
int[] yCoords = { 100, 100, 200, 200 };             // Define y coordinates
g.drawPolygon(xCoords, yCoords, xCoords.length);    // Draw the polygon
```

You can try this out by putting this code in place of the **drawRect()** method call in the **paint()** method for the **SketchFrame** class.

There's an overloaded version of the **drawPolygon()** method that accepts an argument of type **Polygon**. The **Polygon** class is defined in the package **java.awt**. As well as the default constructor which creates an empty polygon, there's a constructor that accepts three arguments: an **int** array of x coordinates, an **int** array of y coordinates and an **int** value that is the count of the number of points. These arguments are the same as those used in the previous version of the **drawPolygon()** method so instead of that **drawPolygon()** method call, you could first create a **Polygon** object with the statement:

```
Polygon poly = new Polygon(xCoords, yCoords, xCoords.length);
```

You could then draw the polygon with the statement:

```
g.drawPolygon(poly);
```

The advantage of creating a separate **Polygon** object is that you can operate on it using methods defined by the **Polygon** class:

Method	Description
void addPoint(int x, int y)	Adds the new point (**x**, **y**) to the end of the list of points defining the polygon.
Rectangle getBounds()	Returns the rectangle bounding the polygon.
boolean contains(int x, int y)	Returns **true** if the point (**x**, **y**) lies inside the polygon, and **false** otherwise.
boolean contains(Point p)	Returns **true** if the point **p** lies inside the polygon, and **false** otherwise.
void translate(int xIncr, int yIncr)	Moves the polygon a distance **xIncr** in the x direction, and **yIncr** in the y direction.

We could use a **Polygon** object to draw an array of stars in Sketcher.

Try It Out—Drawing an Array of Stars

Here's the code for the **SketchFrame** class **paint()** method:

```
public void paint(Graphics g)
{
  // Create the polygon
  int[] xCoords = { 75,  70,  50,  70,  75,  80, 100,  80 };
  int[] yCoords = {100, 120, 125, 130, 150, 130, 125, 120 };
  Polygon poly = new Polygon(xCoords, yCoords, xCoords.length);

  int rowCount = 3;                    // Number of rows
  int colCount = 7;                    // Number of columns
  for(int i = 0; i < rowCount; i++)
  {
    for(int j = 0; j < colCount; j++)
    {
      g.drawPolygon(poly);             // Draw the polygon
      poly.translate(60, 0);           // Move to next column
    }
    // Move to first column of next row
    poly.translate(-60*colCount, 60);
  }
}
```

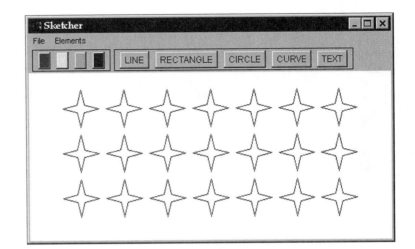

When you run Sketcher
you'll see:

How It Works

The code draws three rows of stars with seven stars in each row. The gap between successive rows and columns is sixty pixels. The outer **for** loop is for the rows, and the inner **for** loop draws a star at each column position in the row. In the inner loop, we move the **Polygon** object, **poly**, sixty pixels in x direction using the **translate()** method for the object. When the inner loop ends, the **poly** object will have been moved a total of **60*rowCount** pixels to the right, so we move it to the left by this distance and down by sixty pixels to start the next row.

Because we reuse the **Polygon** object by moving it about, we can use the same code to create any number of rows and columns of stars, just by changing the values of **rowCount** and **colCount**.

Drawing Rectangles

We already know how to draw basic rectangles but the **Graphics** class has two other methods for drawing rectangles. You can draw a rectangle with a three dimensional appearance with the **draw3DRect()** method. This has one extra argument over the **drawRectangle()** method which is a **boolean** value which you set to **true** if you want the rectangle to appear raised, and **false** if you want it to look recessed. To draw the previous rectangle we produced with **drawPolygon()** as a raised rectangle, you would write:

```
g.draw3DRect(50, 100, 150, 100, true);        // Draw a raised rectangle
```

The first two arguments are the coordinates of the top-left corner of the rectangle, and the third and fourth arguments are the width and height respectively. You can try this out by plugging this statement into the **paint()** method for **SketchFrame** and running Sketcher again.

603

The recessed 3D effect is created in the same way as we used in the status bar implementation for Sketcher, by drawing the top and left side in a darker color than the bottom and right, and the raised effect is produced by drawing the top and left lighter than the bottom and right. The effectiveness of the 3D effect is dependent on the current color because the method adjusts the current color to get the lighter or darker color required. If the current color is very dark or very light, there may not be enough color difference between the light and dark sides of the rectangle to make a difference. Try setting different drawing colors to see how it works. The 3D effect is also affected by the background color, and if you want to create a 3D rectangle you may find it just as easy to draw the rectangle yourself using the `drawLine()` method as we did for the status bar. Then you can use your own choice of colors for the lines.

You can draw a rectangle with rounded corners with the `drawRoundedRect()` method. In addition to the basic four arguments to define a rectangle, there are two more for this method, the width of the arc in the corners in pixels, and the height of the arc. To get circular corners you should specify the width and height of the arc as the same value. With different values for the width and height, the corner arc will be elliptic. Here's how you can draw the previous rectangle with circular corners with a radius of twenty pixels:

```
g.drawRoundRect(50, 100, 150, 100, 20, 20);  // Draw a round rectangle
```

You could draw a rectangle with elliptic corners that is the same size but positioned 200 pixels to the right with the following statement:

```
g.drawRoundRect(250, 100, 150, 100, 50, 30); // Draw a round rectangle
```

If you plug these statements into the `paint()` method for `SketchFrame`, the Sketcher program will draw the rectangles shown here.

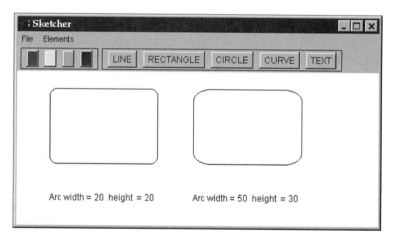

The annotations below the rectangles were produced by a couple of `drawString()` method calls that were added in the `paint()` method:

```
        g.drawString("Arc width = 20   height  = 20", 50, 250);
        g.drawString("Arc width = 50   height  = 30", 250, 250);
```

The y coordinates have been chosen to position the text below the corresponding rectangle, and the x coordinates align the first character of each string with the left side of the rectangle above it.

Curved Shapes

The **Graphics** class has two methods that draw curves, one for closed curves and another for open curves where the ends aren't joined. The **drawOval()** methods draws a closed curve that is an oval (more technically an ellipse) defined by a rectangle that bounds it. When you make the width and height of the defining rectangle equal you'll draw a circle. The **drawOval()** method requires four arguments. The first two are the x and y coordinates of the rectangle defining the curve and the last two are the width and height of the rectangle.

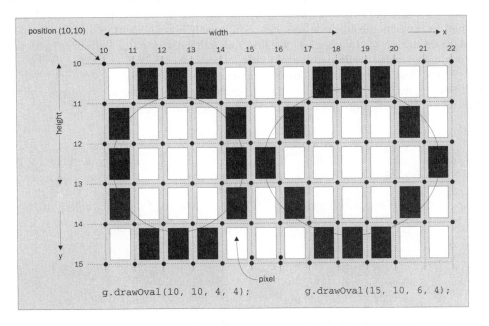

The diagram illustrates two examples of using the **drawOval()** method—albeit on a very small scale. On the left a circle is produced because the width and height values for the defining rectangle are the same. On the right an ellipse is produced. Note how in each case the curve is one pixel wider and higher that the width and height of the rectangle defining the curve.

You could try out the **drawOval()** method with shapes of a more practical size than those in the diagram:

```
        g.drawOval(50,100, 99, 99);        // Draw a circle with radius of 50
        g.drawOval(200,100, 199, 99);      // Draw an ellipse
```

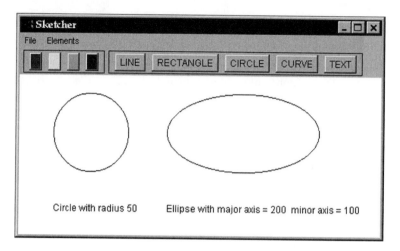

If you put these statements in the **SketchFrame** class **paint()** method, they will draw the shapes shown here.

The **drawArc()** method draws an open curve, so the ends aren't connected. The curve is a segment of the same sort of curve that the **drawOval()** method produces, and the curve is defined by a rectangle in the same way. You specify the segment of the curve that you want to be drawn by two angles, the first indicating the start of the curve, and the second the angle subtended by the arc—or in other words the angle through which the arc is drawn. The first four arguments to the **drawArc()** method are the same as those for the **drawOval()** method—they specify the rectangle—but there also are two more of type **int** that define the start angle and the arc angle in degrees.

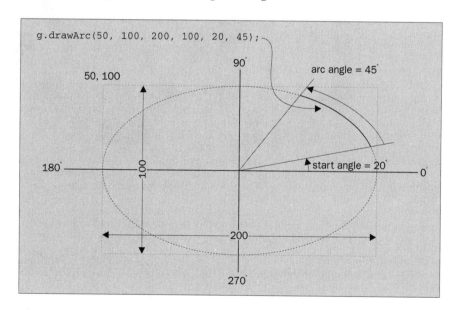

Curves are drawn counter-clockwise from the horizontal, so positive angles are measured in the same sense, as indicated by the arrows for the angles in the diagram. The diagram shows the segment of the ellipse drawn by the statement:

```
g.drawArc(50, 100, 200, 100, 20, 45);
```

If you put this in the **paint()** method for **SketchFrame**, along with the statement,

```
g.drawString("g.drawArc(50, 100, 200, 100, 20, 45);", 50, 200);
```

you should get the arc
displayed as well as the
statement that produced
it, as shown here:

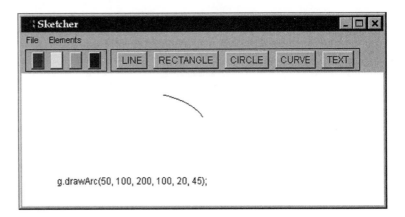

Either, or both, the start angle and the arc angle can be specified as negative. A negative start angle is measured clockwise from the horizontal. A negative arc angle is also measured clockwise. You can draw the same curve as shown above with the statement:

```
g.drawArc(50, 100, 200, 100, -340, 45);
```

This just draws the arc counter-clockwise through 45° from the position 340° clockwise from the horizontal—so the start position is the same as previously and we get the same arc. Below you can see the arcs produced by various combinations of negative and positive angles.

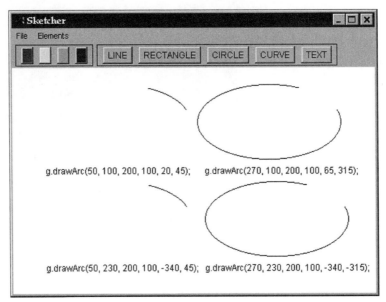

Filling Shapes

There are methods to produce shapes that are filled with the current color, corresponding to each of the methods we have seen for drawing closed shapes. They each have a name that is prefixed with **fill** in place of **draw**.

Filling Rectangles

The methods for producing filled rectangles are:

```
fillRect(int x, int y, int width, int height)
fillRoundRect(int x, int y, int width, int height, int arcWidth,
              int arcHeight)
```

The arguments to these methods are exactly the same as those of the corresponding draw methods, so we won't go over them again. The following version of the **paint()** method in **SketchFrame** will display two filled rectangles:

```
public void paint(Graphics g)
{
  g.setColor(Color.red);
  g.fillRect(50, 100, 200, 100);
  g.drawString("g.fillRect(50, 100, 200, 100);", 50, 220);

  g.setColor(Color.blue);
  g.fillRoundRect(270, 100, 200, 100, 30, 20);
  g.drawString("g.fillRoundRect(270, 100, 200, 100, 30, 20);", 270, 220);
}
```

This should display the screen shown here, but with rather more color.

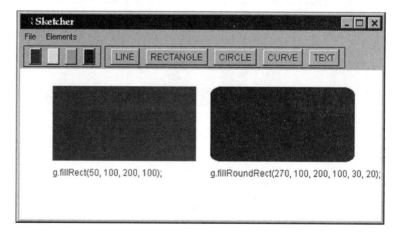

If we were following the sequence we went through for the unfilled entities, we would look at filled polygons next, but since they've an added complication, let's take ovals and arcs now and come back to polygons afterwards.

Filling Ovals and Arcs

The `fillOval()` method works in much the same way and the arguments are the same as for the `drawOval()` method so we won't elaborate this further. The `fillArc()` method is interesting though because it fills a pie-shaped area, so you can use it to create pie charts, among other things. We could write a method to produce a pie chart from an arbitrary number of samples.

Let's assume we want our method to accept an `int` array of samples, and produce a pie chart showing the relative proportions of the samples. The method will need to accept the array of samples, a `Point` object defining the top-left corner of the pie, an `int` value for the width and height of the pie and a `Graphics` object.

Try It Out—Creating a Pie Chart

1 Here's how it could be implemented in its basic form:

```
// Method to display a pie chart
public void drawPie(int[] samples, Point position, int pieSize,
                                                    Graphics g)
{
  // Colors for pie segments
  Color[] colors = { Color.red, Color.yellow,
                     Color.green, Color.blue };

  // Get the total of all the samples
  int total = 0;
  for(int i = 0; i < samples.length; i++)
    total += samples[i];

  int arcAngle = 0;      // Arc angle for a pie segment
  int startAngle = 0;    // Start angle for a pie segment

  // Draw the pie
  for(int i = 0; i < samples.length; i++)
  {
    g.setColor(colors[i%colors.length]);           // Set the segment color
    arcAngle = i ==(samples.length - 1)?
      360-startAngle : (360*samples[i])/total;   // Get the segment angle
    g.fillArc(position.x, position.y, pieSize, pieSize,
              startAngle, arcAngle);
    startAngle += arcAngle;                        // Update the start angle
  }
}
```

2 Add the `drawPie()` method to the `SketchFrame` class, and change the `paint()` method to:

```
public void paint(Graphics g)
{
```

609

```
    int[] samples = { 100, 30, 50, 75  };          // Pie samples
    drawPie(samples, new Point( 50, 100), 200, g);   // Draw the pie
}
```

With just four samples
this produces the pie chart
shown here. You could try
it with more.

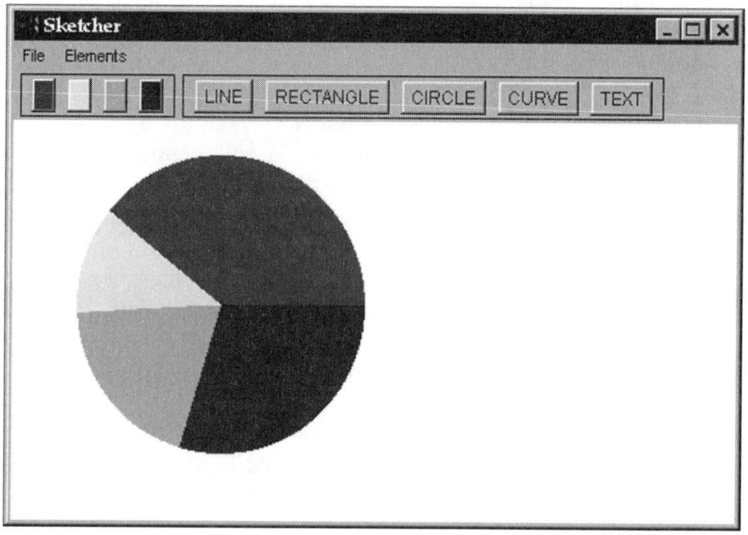

How It Works

We have defined four colors to color the segments of the pie. The first step is to calculate
the total of all the samples as we'll calculate the arc angle for each segment as a fraction of
360° by dividing each sample by the total and multiplying by 360. In the loop that draws
the segments, we set the color by calling the **setColor()** method for **g** with the argument
as an element from our colors array. The array index of **i%colors.length** will cycle
through the legal indices for colors repeatedly, as many times as necessary.

To draw each segment we need a start angle and an arc angle. The start angle for the first
segment is 0, and the start angle for successive segments is produced by adding the arc
angle for the previous segment. The arc angle is basically given by the expression
(360*samples[i])/total, but it's possible that rounding errors could accumulate in the
calculation of the arc angle. If this occurred we could get an untidy looking gap between
the last and the first segment. To obviate this possibility we use the conditional operator to
make sure that the last segment occupies the whole of whatever angle is left in the pie.

There are some improvements you could make to the **drawPie()** method. At the moment it
doesn't check that all the samples are positive, and it should. If the number of samples
modulo the number of colors is 1, then two adjacent segments—the first and the last—will
have the same color. It would also be nice to have names for the samples, and to draw
them on the corresponding segments.

An Applet to Draw Pie Charts

We can also use a version of the `drawPie()` method in an applet and get some practice with using layout managers in combination. Our applet will have an upper panel where we either enter input data or display a pie chart from the input, and a lower panel with three control buttons, to create the pie chart, select input mode or quit the applet. The way in which the components are placed in the containers, and how the containers combine, is illustrated here:

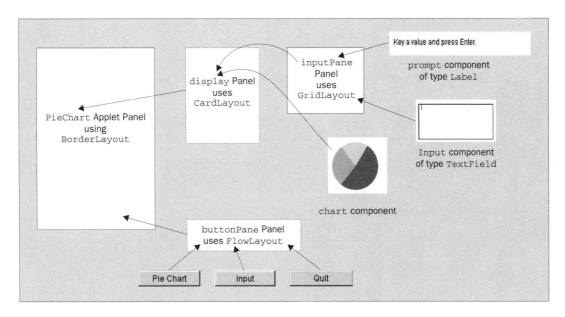

The applet panel will use **BorderLayout** to position two panels, a **Panel** object **display** positioned as **BorderLayout.CENTER** and **buttonPane** containing the three buttons positioned as **BorderLayout.SOUTH**, with the buttons arranged using **FlowLayout**. The display panel will use **CardLayout** to overlay the pie chart object on another **Panel** object, **inputPane**, which will receive the sample values to be displayed as a pie chart. The **inputPane** panel contains two components, a **Label** component called **prompt**, and below it a **TextField** component called, **input**, to receive the input. These are arranged in the **inputPane** panel using **GridLayout**.

Try It Out—Coding the Pie Chart Applet

Here's the initial outline coding for the **PieChart** class:

```
// Applet to create a pie chart
import java.awt.*;
import java.awt.event.*;
import java.applet.*;
```

```java
public class PieChart extends Applet
{
  final int CHART = 101;                      // ID for chart button
  final int INPUT = 102;                      // ID for input button
  final int QUIT  = 103;                      // ID for chart quit

  int[] samples = new int[20];                // Array of samples
  int count = 0;                              // Count of samples

  // Display panel to hold pie chart and input panel
  Panel display = new Panel();
  CardLayout card = new CardLayout(25,25);    // Layout for display
  Chart chart = new Chart();                  // Pie chart component
  TextField input = new TextField(10);        // Input component

  // Prompt messages
  String message = "Key a value and press Enter.                    ";
  String invalid = "Invalid input. Key another value and press Enter ";

  Label prompt = new Label(message);          // Input prompt component

  // Initialize the applet
  public void init()
  {
    setLayout(new BorderLayout());     // Layout for the applet

    // Create the panel containing control buttons...

    // Create the input panel...

    // Set up the panel holding input panel and pie chart canvas...
  }

  // Definition of the Pie Chart object
  class Chart extends Canvas
  {
    // Details of the inner class definition...
  }

  // Handler for button press
  class ButtonHandler implements ActionListener
  {
    // Details of the inner class definition...
  }

  // Handle input from text field
  class InputHandler implements ActionListener
  {
    // Details of the inner class definition...
  }
}
```

How It Works

The data members of the class **PieChart** are those that we'll need to access in the inner classes. There are three IDs defined for the buttons we'll add to the **buttonPane**. We'll use these IDs in the inner class **ButtonHandler**, which will define listener objects for the buttons. Next we define the **Panel** object, **display**, that will hold both the pie chart and another **Panel** object containing the input **TextField** component. The **CardLayout** object, **card**, is for use with **display** to overlay the pie chart and the panel containing the input component. We have two **String** objects that are the messages to be displayed in the **prompt** label.

The **PieChart** class has three inner classes—a class defining a **Chart** object, a class **ButtonHandler** to define listeners for the buttons and a class **InputHandler** to define a listener for the **TextField** object input. We need to define the **Chart** class based on the **Canvas** class because we'll want to draw the pie chart. Remember—we can't draw on a **Panel** object.

Try It Out—Initializing the Applet

The **init()** method has three tasks, as indicated by the comments. The details of the **init()** method to accomplish them are:

```
// Initialize the applet
public void init()
{
  setLayout(new BorderLayout());      // Layout for the applet
```

```
  // Create the panel containing control buttons
  Panel buttonPane = new Panel();    // Panel for control buttons
  Button button;                      // Store for a button
  buttonPane.add(button = new Button("Pie Chart"));
  button.addActionListener(new ButtonHandler(CHART));
  buttonPane.add(button = new Button("Input"));
  button.addActionListener(new ButtonHandler(INPUT));
  buttonPane.add(button = new Button("Quit"));
  button.addActionListener(new ButtonHandler(QUIT));
  add(buttonPane, BorderLayout.SOUTH); // Add the panel to the applet
```

```
  // Create the input panel
  Panel inputPane = new Panel();             // Panel for input component
  inputPane.setLayout(new GridLayout(0,1)); // layout for input
  TextField input = new TextField(10);       // Input component
  input.addActionListener(new InputHandler()); // Listener for input
  inputPane.add(prompt);                     // Add the prompt
  inputPane.add(input);                      // Add the input component
```

```
  // Set up the panel holding input panel and pie chart canvas
  display.setLayout(card);                   // Panels overlaid
  display.add(chart, "Chart");               // Add the pie chart
  display.add(inputPane, "InputPane");       // Add the input panel
```

613

```
      add(display, BorderLayout.CENTER);        // Add the display panel
      card.show(display, "InputPane");          // Display input pane
      input.requestFocus();                     // Get the focus
   }
```

How It Works

The first block of code here creates the **buttonPane** object, and creates and adds the three control buttons. Each button has its own listener object of type **ButtonHandler**. The **buttonPane** panel is placed at the bottom of the applet panel by specifying its constraint as **BorderLayout.SOUTH**.

The second block of code creates the **inputPane** object and adds the **Label** object **prompt**, and the **TextField** object **input** to it. The panel **inputPane** uses a **GridLayout** with a single column of positions—this is determined by the arguments to the constructor, 0 for the number of rows which specifies any number, and 1 for the number of columns. The **TextField** component has a listener defined of type **InputHandler** which will process the input. The action event will arise when the *Enter* key is pressed while the **TextField** component has the focus.

The third block specifies the layout for the **display** panel as **card**, and adds the **chart** and **inputPane** objects to the **display** panel. The **display** panel is then added to the center of the applet panel. Lastly, the **inputPane** panel is placed at the top in the **CardLayout** by calling the **show()** method for the **card** object. The first argument is the container, **display**, and the second argument is the **String**, **"InputPane"**, which we associated with the **inputPane** object when we added it to the **display** panel.

Try It Out—Defining the *Chart* **Class**

We can define the inner class, **Chart**, as:

```
// Definition of the Pie Chart object
class Chart extends Canvas
{
  public void paint(Graphics g)
  {
    if(count > 0)
    {
      Dimension size = chart.getSize();    // Get the size

      // Draw the chart to fill the minimum of width & height
      drawPie(new Point(0, 0), Math.min(size.width,size.height), g);
    }
  }

  // Method to draw a pie chart
  public void drawPie( Point position, int pieSize, Graphics g)
  {
    // Colors for pie segments
```

```
      Color[] colors = {Color.red, Color.yellow, Color.green, Color.blue};

      // Get the total of all the samples
      int total = 0;
      for(int i = 0; i < count; i++)
        total += samples[i];

      int arcAngle = 0;                       // Arc angle for a pie segment
      int startAngle = 0;                     // Start angle for a pie segment

      // Draw the pie
      for(int i = 0; i < count; i++)
      {
        g.setColor(colors[i%colors.length]);       // Set the segment color
        arcAngle = i==(count-1)?
          360-startAngle : (360*samples[i])/total; // Get the segment angle
        g.fillArc(position.x, position.y, pieSize, pieSize,
                                              startAngle, arcAngle);
        startAngle += arcAngle;                     // Update the start angle
      }
    }
  }
```

How It Works

The **paint()** method calls the **drawPie()** method as long as there's at least one sample. The **drawPie()** method is essentially the same as we used in the Sketcher modification. Just the parameter list has been changed to access the **samples[]** array directly, and we use **count** for the number of samples, not the length of the **samples[]** array.

Try It Out—Defining the Class for a Button Listener

The **HandleButton** class that defines listeners for the buttons is structured in much the same way as button listener classes we've seen before, using an ID to identify the button:

```
// Handler for button press
class ButtonHandler implements ActionListener
{
  int buttonID;                              // ID for the button

  // Constructor
  public ButtonHandler(int buttonID)
  {
    this.buttonID = buttonID;                // Store the button ID
  }
```

615

```
  // Handle a button press event
  public void actionPerformed(ActionEvent e)
  {
    switch(buttonID)
    {
      case INPUT:
        count = 0;                              // Reset sample count
        card.show(display, "InputPane");        // Display input pane
        prompt.transferFocus();                 // Focus to input
        break;
      case CHART:
        prompt.setText(message);                // Reset in case invalid last
        card.show(display, "Chart");            // Show the chart
        chart.repaint();                        // Draw the chart
        break;
      case QUIT:
        System.exit(0);                         // Exit
        break;
    }
  }
}
```

How It Works

Each listener stores the ID of the button to which it applies. The processing of the action events for each button is separated out in the **actionPerformed()** method based on the **buttonID** value using a **switch** statement.

The **QUIT** button is the simplest to deal with. When the **QUIT** button is pressed, we just call **exit()** for the **System** class to terminate the applet.

When the **INPUT** button is pressed, we initiate a new cycle of accepting values for input samples, so we reset the count value to zero and display the **inputPane** panel which contains the **TextField** component **input**. By calling the **transferFocus()** method for the **prompt** component, we ensure that the focus is always transferred to the **input** component so you can enter data immediately. The **transferFocus()** method is defined in the **Component** class so that it is inherited in all the subclasses of **Component** and therefore available for every component. Its effect is to transfer the focus to the next component in its container, if the current component has the focus.

When the **CHART** button is pressed, we want to display a pie chart from the samples that have been entered. The first step is to reset the message in the prompt component. This covers the possibility that the last sample entered was invalid, causing an error prompt to be displayed. We'll see how this works in a moment when we define the **InputHandler** class. To display the pie chart, we call the **show()** method for the layout manager, **card**, to display the chart object rather than the **inputPane** panel. The call **repaint()** for the **chart** object actually causes the pie chart to be drawn, but by a somewhat indirect mechanism, which we need to understand in a little more detail.

Repainting a Component

Calling **repaint()** for a component generates a request for the **update()** method for the component to be called as soon as possible. The **update()** method is passed a **Graphics** object of the component, to allow the component to be repainted. The default implementation of the **update()** method first fills the whole of the component area with the background color to erase whatever was drawn on the component previously. It then calls the **paint()** method for the component which you normally implement to draw whatever you need on the component. For the chart object, our **paint()** method draws the pie chart.

Having the **update()** method fill the background for the chart object is fine in this case, but this isn't so in every situation. Repainting the background for the whole area of a component is quite time consuming, particularly if the component covers a large area on your display screen, and there are situations—when your program is animating an image for instance—where you don't want the background to be repainted because it causes flicker. In these cases you can override the default version of the **update()** to just call the **paint()** method.

There's also more to the **repaint()** method than our use of it here. There are four different overloaded versions of it. They all have a **void** return type and cause the **update()** method for the component to be called. The four versions of **repaint()** work as follows:

repaint() Method	Description
repaint()	Requests that the **update()** method for the component is called as soon as possible to repaint the whole of the component.
repaint(long msecs)	Requests that the **update()** method for the component is called within **msecs** milliseconds.
repaint(int x, int y, int width, int height)	Requests that the **update()** method for the component is called as soon as possible to repaint the rectangular area of the component specified by the arguments. The position of the rectangle is (**x**, **y**) and the width and height are specified by the last two arguments.
repaint(long msecs, int x, int y, int width, int height)	Requests that the **update()** method for the component is called within **msecs** milliseconds to repaint the rectangular area of the component specified by the last four arguments.

Note that in each case the result of calling **repaint()** is a *request* for **update()** to be called—there's no guarantee that **update()** will be called each time you call the **repaint()** method. If your program calls **repaint()** several times in quick succession, the requests may be combined into a single call for **update()**. When this occurs, and you have specified the rectangles that are to be updated in the **repaint()** calls, they will be combined into a single area for the **update()** method call.

1 The last bit that we must add to the code for our applet is the class defining the listener for the **TextField** object, **input**:

```
// Handle input from text field
class InputHandler implements ActionListener
{
  // Handle Enter key press
  public void actionPerformed(ActionEvent e)
  {
    if(count == samples.length)  // If the samples array is full
      return;                    // Ignore this input

    TextField input = (TextField)(e.getSource());
    try
    { // Convert input text to integer
      int value = Integer.parseInt(input.getText());
      samples[count++] = value;        // Store value in samples array
      input.setText("");               // Reset the input area
      prompt.setText(message);         // Reset the message
    }
    catch(NumberFormatException nfe)   // Invalid input
    {
      prompt.setText(invalid );        // Display error message
      input.setText("");               // Reset input
    }
  }
}
```

2 After you've compiled **PieChart.java** you can create a file **PieChart.html** containing:

```
<APPLET code="PieChart.class" width=300 height=200>
</APPLET>
```

You can then run the applet with **AppletViewer PieChart.html**. And input up to 20 integer samples pressing *Enter* after each one. When you've entered all your sample values and want to have the pie chart displayed, just click on the Pie Chart button.

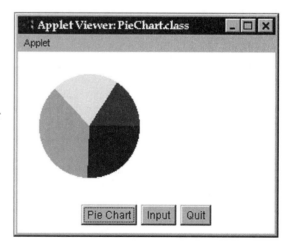

If you want to enter a new set of samples for another pie chart, you can click on the Input button. The Quit button will close the applet.

The **actionPerformed()** method is called when the *Enter* key is pressed at the end of inputting a sample value. The **getText()** method for the **TextField** component returns the **String** that was entered, and this is passed to the **parseInt()** method in the class **Integer** to convert the type to the **int** value it represents. If the input text contains an invalid character, the **parseInt()** method will throw a **NumberFormatException**, so we need to add a **catch** block after the **try** block to take care of this. Note that we store the result from **parseInt()** in a temporary variable, **value**. If you store the result directly in the **samples[]** array, you'll get erroneous values stored even when an exception is thrown. By storing the value in the **samples[]** array in the next statement we avoid this possibility. Note that we update the **count** variable in the same statement that stores the value in the **samples[]** array. Once the value has been stored successfully, we reset the input field and display the **message** string in **prompt** in case the previous entry was in error and the **invalid** string was displayed.

In the **catch** block we display the **invalid** message in the **Label** object, **prompt**. This will be reset when the *Enter* key is pressed for the next correct input value, or in the **CHART** button handler if you press that button immediately after an erroneous input. The **catch** block also resets the input field.

Filling Polygons

After that slight detour and equipped with a bit more knowledge, we're now ready to look at filling polygons. We can fill a closed polygon with the **fillPolygon()** method.

Try It Out—Coloring in the Stars

You can modify the **paint()** method for the **SketchFrame** class that we implemented earlier in this chapter to draw polygons to see how the fill operation works:

```
public void paint(Graphics g)
{
  // Create the polygon
  int[] xCoords = { 75,  70,  50,  70,  75,  80, 100,  80 };
  int[] yCoords = {100, 120, 125, 130, 150, 130, 125, 120 };
  Polygon poly = new Polygon(xCoords, yCoords, xCoords.length);

  g.setColor(Color.red);

  int rowCount = 3;                    // Number of rows
  int colCount = 7;                    // Number of columns
  for(int i = 0; i < rowCount; i++)
  {
    for(int j = 0; j < colCount; j++)
    {
      g.fillPolygon(poly);             // Draw the filled polygon
```

```
    poly.translate(60, 0);            // Move to next column
  }
  // Move to first column of next row
  poly.translate(-60*colCount, 60);
 }
}
```

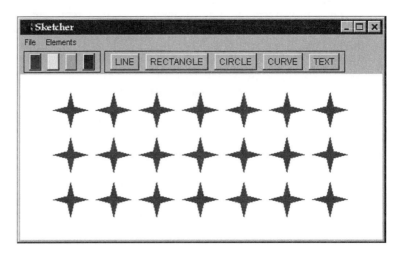

There's one additional statement to set the color for the fill operation to **Color.red**, and the **drawPolygon()** method call, is replaced by a call to **fillPolygon()**. The output is much the same as before except that the polygons are filled in the current color.

This example is quite straightforward, but a slight complication may arise with filling polygons in that, not only can the polygon be non-convex, as is the case with our example, but also the lines defining the border of a polygon can intersect. In this situation, the question of what is the inside the polygon arises, since that is the bit that needs to be colored. This question is neatly sidestepped by defining a rule by which the fill process is carried out—called the **alternating fill rule**.

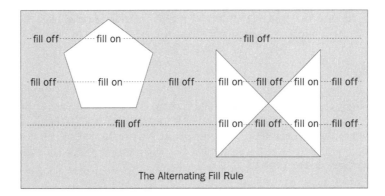

The Alternating Fill Rule

The mechanism is simple and is illustrated in the diagram with a convex shape on the left and a shape with intersecting boundaries on the right. The fill process works along scan lines from left to right. When a scan line crosses the boundary of a shape, the fill color is switched on. Crossing another boundary line switches the fill color off. The fill color alternates between on and off each time a boundary is crossed. After crossing an odd number of boundaries, fill is on, and after crossing an even number of boundaries, fill is off.

You can see this in action by moving the left point of the stars in the previous example by modifying the coordinates in the **paint()** method to:

```
int[] xCoords = { 75,  70,  95,  70,  75,  80, 100,  80 };
int[] yCoords = {100, 120, 100, 130, 150, 130, 125, 120 };
```

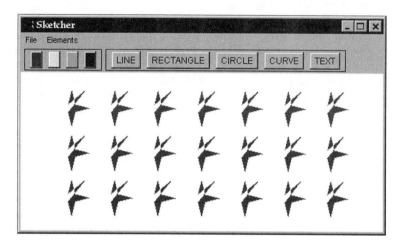

Here's the result of moving the left point of the star. If you visualize the scan lines running from left to right, you should be able to see how this produces the fill pattern that it does.

Drawing Text

The methods in the **Graphics** class that draw text all draw in the current font and color. The font is set by the **setFont()** method which requires an argument of type **Font**. There's also a complementary method, **getFont()** which returns the current font as an object of type **Font**. Besides the **drawString()** method which we've already used on several occasions, the **Graphics** class defines two other methods that draw text. They are very similar to one another:

Method	Description
drawBytes(byte data[], int offset, int length, int x, int y)	This method draws **length** characters from the array **data** starting at the index position **offset** in the array at the position **x,y**. The method creates a **String** object internally from the elements of the array of type **byte**.
drawChars(char data[], int offset, int length, int x, int y)	This method works exactly the same way as **drawBytes()** except the characters to be drawn are supplied in an array of type **char**.

Drawing Using the Mouse

In this section we'll apply several of the techniques from this chapter and the previous chapter to extend the capability of our Sketcher program. At this point you can remove the **paint()** method and the **drawPie()** method from the **SketchFrame** class in Sketcher as we no longer need them.

We've drawn shapes so far using data that's internal to the program. In our Sketcher program we want to be able to draw shapes using the mouse. We want the process to be as natural as possible, so we'll implement a mechanism that allows you to draw by pressing the left mouse button (button 1) and dragging the cursor to draw the current type of shape. So for a line, for instance, the point where you depress the mouse button will be the start point for the line, and the point where you release the button will be the end point.

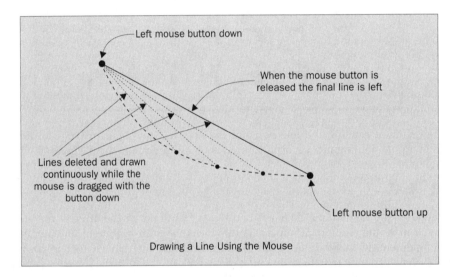

Drawing a Line Using the Mouse

As you drag the mouse with the button down, we'll display the line as it looks at that point, so the line will be displayed dynamically all the time the mouse cursor is being dragged and the left button remains pressed. This process is called **rubber-banding**.

Before we start worrying about how we're going to do this, we must consider how we are going to represent shapes in the Sketcher program, as ultimately we want to be able to store them in the document object.

Defining Shapes

When shapes are created in Sketcher, we'll have no idea of the sequence of shape types that will occur. This is determined totally by the person using the program to produce a sketch. We'll therefore need to be able to draw shapes and perform other operations on them without knowing what they are. Polymorphism can help us in this situation.

We can start by defining a base class, **Element**, from which we'll derive the classes defining specific types of shapes. The **Element** class will have data members that are common to all types of shapes, and we can put the methods that we want to execute polymorphically in this class too. The **draw()** method is a typical example of such a method. All we'll need to do is make sure that each shape class that is derived from the **Element** class has its own implementation of the **draw()** method. We'll then be able to use a variable of type **Element** to hold a reference to a shape object, and use that to call any of the methods that are to be executed in this way.

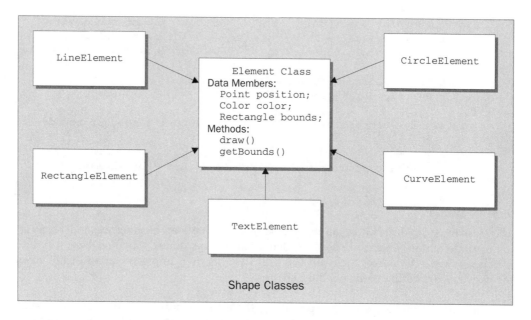

We'll be defining the five classes shown in the diagram with the **Element** class as a base. They provide objects that represent lines, rectangles, circles, freehand curves and blocks of text. These classes will all inherit the data members that we define for the **Element** class. We can now define the **Element** class. Note that this won't be the final version, as we'll be adding more functionality in later chapters.

The Element Class Definition

Every shape will need a reference point that determines its position, and a color for the shape, so we should include these in the **Element** class. To draw a shape we'll also need a method, **draw()**, to enable a shape to draw itself. When we need to redraw a shape, we don't necessarily want to redraw the whole area of the sketch. In these situations, if we know the area that is occupied by a shape, we can arrange to draw just that portion of the sketch. To accommodate this we can include a **bounds** object defining the rectangle that the shape occupies, and a method to obtain access to it. We can define all these as members of the base class since they will be common to all shapes.

Here's the initial definition of the **Element** class:

```
// Abstract base class for shape definition classes
import java.awt.*;

public abstract class Element
{
  protected Point position;         // Position of the element
  protected Color color;            // Color of the element
  protected Rectangle bounds;       // Rectangle bounding the element

  // Get the bounding rectangle for an element
  public Rectangle getBounds()
  {
    return new Rectangle(bounds);   // Return a copy of bounds
  }

  public abstract void draw(Graphics g); // Draw the element
}
```

How It Works

The class must be declared as **abstract** because we have an abstract method, **draw()**, in the class definition. There's no sensible definition for the **draw()** method here so we declare it as **abstract**. Of course, each subclass will have its own implementation of the **draw()** method that draws the corresponding shape.

The three data members are self-explanatory: the element position is defined by a **Point** object, **position**, the color is defined by a **Color** object, **color**, and the **Rectangle** object, **bounds**, defines the area occupied by a shape. The **getBounds()** method returns a **Rectangle** object that is a copy of the rectangle object stored in the class. We don't return a reference to the original **bounds** object because this would expose the object to the risk of being modified externally. We'll initialize the **bounds** data member in the constructor for each shape subclass.

We'll develop the classes that represent specific shapes in Sketcher during the implementation of the processes that draw them.

Storing Shapes in the Document

Even though we haven't defined the classes for the shapes that Sketcher will create, we can implement the mechanism for storing them in the **SketchDoc** class. We'll be storing all of them as objects of type **Element**. We can use a **Vector** object to hold an arbitrary number of **Element** objects, since a **Vector** can store any kind of object, and will automatically expand its capacity when necessary.

Try It Out—Storing Shapes

1 The **Vector** class is defined in the package **java.util**, so we must add an **import** statement for it to the beginning of the **SketchDoc.java** file:

```
import java.util.*;
```

2 Add the following definition to **SketchDoc** at the end of the statements defining the data members of the class:

```
protected Vector sketchElements = new Vector(30,5);  // Sketch elements
```

This defines a **Vector** object with an initial capacity to store thirty objects, and it will increase its capacity when necessary in increments of five objects.

3 To make the **Vector** object more secure, we'll add our own methods to the **SketchDoc** class to add and delete elements. These methods will only work with objects of type **Element**. If we were to allow the **addElement()** method for the **Vector** object to be used directly, any kind of element could be added to the vector. We can code the method to add an element as:

```
// Add an element to the document
public void addElement(Element element)
{
   sketchElements.addElement(element);        // Add the element
}
```

4 The definition of the method to delete an element will be:

```
// Remove an element from the document
public void removeElement(Element element)
{
   sketchElements.removeElement(element);     // Delete the element
}
```

How It Works

The **addElement()** method above just calls the **addElement()** method for the **Vector**, **sketchElements**. The **addElement()** method in the **Vector** class will accept any kind of object, because the parameter type is **Object**. Our method, **addElement()**, will only accept objects of type **Element**, which includes objects of the classes derived from the **Element** class. The **removeElement()** method is similar.

Since we know how the shapes are going to be stored in the document, and we also know that every shape object will have a **draw()** method that will draw it, we can implement a **draw()** method for the whole document.

Add the following method definition to the **SketchDoc** class:

```
// Draw the document
public void draw(Graphics g)
{
  for(Enumeration elmnts = sketchElements.elements();
                                   elmnts.hasMoreElements(); )
    ((Element)(elmnts.nextElement())).draw(g);        // Draw each element
}
```

How It Works

We use a **for** loop to iterate through the elements in the **Vector, sketchElements**. This may look a bit strange but it's quite simple. The first expression for the **for** loop:

```
Enumeration elmnts = sketchElements.elements()
```

sets the initial condition—this is executed just once. It obtains an **Enumeration** object for the elements stored in **sketchElements**. The second expression is:

```
elmnts.hasMoreElements()
```

This will return **true** as long as there are more elements in the **Enumeration, elmnts**, so as long as this is the case, the loop will continue. When the **hasMoreElements()** method returns **false**, the loop will end.

The loop statement obtains the next element from the **Enumeration, elmnts**, by calling its **nextElement()** method. The object returned will be of type **Object**, so we must cast it to type **Element** to enable the **draw()** method for the shape to be called. The power of polymorphism will ensure that the specific **draw()** method for whatever kind of shape is stored will be called for each element. You may be wondering at this point where this drawing is taking place. The **Graphics** object, **g**, that is passed to the **draw()** method in **SketchDoc**, and then passed on to each shape's **draw()** method is the graphics context for the component on which the shapes will be drawn—and we'll define that next.

Now would be a good time to recompile **SketchDoc** to make sure there are no typos in the code you've entered.

The Drawing Surface

We already know that we don't want to draw directly on the application window, defined as a **SketchFrame** object, because the origin of the window is behind the menu bar. It will give us a great deal more flexibility if we create a separate component on which we can draw, and add that to the **SketchFrame** object. This will be the view object associated with the **SketchDoc** object. Of the component classes we've seen, a **Canvas** object looks like a good candidate because it is a very simple component with no added decorations or features and we can draw on it. We can derive a class **SketchView** from **Canvas** which will define the component object on which we'll draw the document.

Try It Out—Defining the `SketchView` Class

The initial definition of the **SketchView** class is as follows:

```java
// Defines a document view
import java.awt.*;

public class SketchView extends Canvas implements Constants
{
  SketchDoc sketch;          // The parent document

  // Constructor
  public SketchView(SketchDoc sketch)
  {
    this.sketch = sketch;
  }

  // Draw the sketch
  public void paint(Graphics g)
  {
    sketch.draw(g);          // Draw the document
  }
}
```

The only data member is the document object, **sketch**. This is passed to the constructor when a **SketchView** object is created. The view will need access to that in order to be able to draw it when required, in the **paint()** method. Drawing the document now becomes extremely simple. We just call the **draw()** method for the **sketch** object, and pass the **Graphics** object, **g**, to it. This will draw the entire document, whatever it contains.

We now need to define a drawing surface object in Sketcher, tie it in to the document, and add it to the application window.

Try It Out—Implementing the Drawing Surface

1 We'll create the **SketchView** object in the **init()** method of the **Sketcher** class after we've created the document object. First add a data member to the **Sketcher** class with the statement:

```java
SketchView view;                                    // The document view
```

2 You can put this immediately following the other data members in the class. Now you can modify the **init()** method as follows:

```java
// Initialization of the application
public void init()
{
  sketch = new SketchDoc(this);                     // Define the document
```

```
        // Create the view and add it to the document
        sketch.addView(view = new SketchView(sketch));

    window = new SketchFrame("Sketcher", this);  // Create the app window
    window.addView(view);                          // Add the document view
    Toolkit theKit = window.getToolkit();          // Get the window toolkit
    Dimension wndSize = theKit.getScreenSize();   // Get screen size

    // Set the position to screen center & size to half screen size
    window.setBounds(wndSize.width/6, wndSize.height/6,      // Position
                     2*wndSize.width/3, 2*wndSize.height/3);  // Size
    window.addWindowListener(new WindowHandler()); // Add window listener
    window.setVisible(true);                        // Display the window
    window.requestFocus();                          // Request the focus
    }
```

How It Works

We create a **SketchView** object and pass the **sketch** object to its constructor in the argument to the method **addView()** which we'll implement in the **SketchDoc** class. The document will need access to the view during the shape creation process. We could add a method to the **Sketcher** class to retrieve the **view** object, and then obtain a reference to it when we need to, but storing it locally will be faster, and we don't want to slow up mouse handling methods if we can avoid it. We also pass the object **view** to the **addView()** method that we'll implement for the application window class, **SketchFrame**. This is to allow the view to be displayed in the application window.

Try It Out—Connecting *SketchView* to the Other Classes

1   The **addView()** method in the **SketchDoc** class should be implemented as:

```
// Add a document view
public void addView(SketchView view)
{
  this.view = view;                        // Store the view reference
}
```

2   Of course, we must also add the data member, **view**, to the document class with the statement. You can add this after the existing data member declarations in the **SketchDoc** class:

```
protected SketchView view;                 // The document view
```

3   The implementation of the **addView()** method for the **SketchFrame** class will be:

```
// Add the document view to the window
public void addView(SketchView view)
```

```
{
    add(view, BorderLayout.CENTER);  // Add the view to the window
}
```

How It Works

This adds the **SketchView** object, which is passed to the method, to the center of the window. This will make it occupy the whole of the central area of the application window bounded by the toolbar at the top and the status bar at the bottom.

We've finished adding a document view to Sketcher, so recompile everything you've changed and run the program again. It won't look any different, but you'll know that it still works. Now we're ready to write the code that will enable us to create a sketch.

Drawing Lines

Because the drawing operations are accomplished using the mouse, we must implement the process for creating elements within the methods that will handle the mouse events. The mouse events we're interested in will originate in the **SketchView** object because that's where we'll be drawing shapes, but where should we put the listener classes for them? We have quite a few options—we could define them as independent classes, we could put them in the **Sketcher** class, we could put them in the **SketchFrame** class, we could put them in the **SketchView** class or we could put them in the document class **SketchDoc**. Since we'll be using the listeners for mouse events to create elements to be stored in the document, the last option looks like the best choice.

Handling MouseEvents

Drawing a line interactively will involve us in handling three different kinds of mouse event, so let's summarize what they are, and what we need to do when they occur:

Event	Action
Left Button (button 1) Pressed	Save the cursor position as the starting point for the line. We'll store this in a data member, **elementPosition**, of the document class, **SketchDoc**. This will be of type **Point**.
Mouse Dragged	Store the current cursor position in a data member, **endPoint**, in the **SketchDoc** class. Erase any previously drawn temporary line, and draw a new temporary line from the starting point, **elementPosition**, to the current cursor position stored in **endPoint**. We'll store the temporary line in a data member, **tempElement**, of the document class. This will be of type **Element**, so it will hold a reference to any kind of shape object.
Left Button (button 1) Released	If there's a shape reference stored in **tempElement**, store it in the document, and draw it.

You'll remember from the previous chapter that there are two mouse listener interfaces: **MouseListener** which has methods to handle events that occur when the mouse buttons are pressed or released; and **MouseMotionListener** which has methods to handle events that arise when the mouse is moved. We need to implement both of these listener interfaces so we'll add two inner classes to the **SketchDoc** class. Because the variables **elementPosition**, and **tempElement** need to be accessible in both the listener classes, we define them as members of the document class rather than as members of one of the listener classes. We'll also use the variable **endPoint** in the document class, so that can be a member of **SketchDoc** too.

Try It Out—Handling Mouse Button Events

1   Add the following three statements to the **SketchDoc** class definition, at the end of the statements defining the other data members:

```
protected Element tempElement = null;      // Temporary element
protected Point elementPosition = null;    // Temporary element position
protected Point endPoint = null;           // Temporary element end point
```

2   We'll derive our classes from the adapter classes that implement the listener interfaces. Let's start with a class to handle the button press and release, which we'll derive from the **MouseAdapter** class. You should add the following inner class definition within the **SketchDoc** class definition:

```
// Handler class for mouse button press
class MouseButtonHandler extends MouseAdapter
{
  // Mouse button pressed handler
  public void mousePressed(MouseEvent e)
  {
    if(e.getModifiers()==InputEvent.BUTTON1_MASK)   // Button 1 down?
    {
      elementPosition = e.getPoint();               // Save cursor position
      tempG = e.getComponent().getGraphics();       // Get graphics context
    }
  }

  // Mouse button released handler
  public void mouseReleased(MouseEvent e)
  {
    if(tempG!=null)                        // If there is a graphics context...
    {
      tempG.dispose();                     // ...release context resources
      tempG = null;                        // Reset the reference
    }
```

```
      if(tempElement!=null)                // If we have an element
      {
        addElement(tempElement);           // ...add it to the document
        Rectangle bounds = tempElement.getBounds();

        // Repaint the view area occupied by the element
        view.repaint(bounds.x, bounds.y, bounds.width, bounds.height);
        tempElement = null;                // Reset temporary
      }
    }
  }
```

3 Of course, we need the definition of the adapter class available in the
      SketchDoc.java file, so add the **import** statement for the package **java.awt.event**
      to the file:

```
import java.awt.event.*;
```

4 Add the following statement after the **endPoint** member definition:

```
protected Graphics tempG;                        // Context for temporary element
```

> *A reminder about a potential error in using adapter classes—be sure to spell the
> method names correctly. If you don't, your method won't get called, the base
> class member will. The base class method does nothing so your code won't work
> as you expect—but there will be no warning or error messages about this
> because your code will be perfectly legal—though quite wrong.*

How It Works

Here we're implementing two of the five methods defined in the **MouseAdapter** class. In
the **mousePressed()** method, we first check that button 1 was pressed by comparing the
modifier returned by the **getModifiers()** method for the event object with the
BUTTON1_MASK value defined in the **InputEvent** class. There's a modifier for each of the
three possible buttons, so to test for the other two buttons you use **BUTTON2_MASK** or
BUTTON3_MASK.

At the time of writing, there's a bug in java.awt in that the BUTTON1_MASK **never
gets set**. It should be fixed by the time you read this, but if it isn't you can change
the if to:

```
if(e.getModifiers()!=InputEvent.BUTTON2_MASK &&
   e.getModifiers()!=InputEvent.BUTTON3_MASK)
```

This just checks that neither button 2 nor button 3 were pressed, so it must be
button 1.

If button 1 was pressed, we get the current cursor position by calling the **getPoint()** method for the event object, **e**. The cursor position when the button was pressed is returned as a **Point** object in the coordinate system of the component to which the listener is registered with—in our case it will be the **SketchView** object. We also get a reference to the component for which the event occurred by calling the **getComponent()** method for the event object, and then we use this to obtain a graphics context object for the component. We'll need this when we create the temporary element and draw it. This will be when we handle the **MOUSE_DRAGGED** event in the other mouse listener class that we'll define shortly. By getting the graphics context here, we can reuse it when the mouse is being dragged, rather than retrieving a new context every time the mouse is dragged. This is a much more efficient approach because there can be a lot of **MOUSE_DRAGGED** events to handle. We need to add a member to **SketchDoc** to store the graphics context though, and this we do in the fourth stage above.

When the button is released, the line creation process is complete—although we have yet to implement the bit that actually creates the line when the mouse is dragged with the button down. Releasing the button will cause the **mouseReleased()** method to be called. The first thing the **mouseReleased()** method does is to call **dispose()** for the graphics context stored in **tempG** and reset the variable back to **null**. It's important to do this when you're finished with a **Graphics** object that you obtained yourself, otherwise you may run out of resources, and your computer may stop working altogether.

If a line was created, a reference to it will be stored in **tempElement** so **tempElement** will be non-**null**. We add the line to the document by calling the **addElement()** method that we implemented a little earlier in this chapter. This will store the reference to the element in the **Vector** object, **sketchElements**. We then call the **getBounds()** method that we defined in the **Element** class to obtain the rectangle in the view that is occupied by the line. We use this rectangle in the call to the **repaint()** method to draw just this area— rather than the whole of the view.

To handle the mouse button events for the view we need to create a **MouseButtonHandler** object, and register it as a listener for the view.

Try It Out—Adding *SketchView* as a Mouse Event Listener

We could do this at a variety of places in the Sketcher program, in the **addView()** method in the **SketchDoc** class for example, or the method with the same name in **SketchFrame**. We can also do it in the constructor for **SketchView**, so let's try that:

```
public SketchView(SketchDoc sketch)
{
    this.sketch = sketch;
    addMouseListener(sketch.new MouseButtonHandler());
}
```

How It Works

Because **MouseButtonHandler** is an inner class of **SketchDoc**, we must qualify the call to the constructor with the name of the document object, **sketch**. This is necessary because you can only create instances of inner classes in the context of an object of the top-level class. We pass the **MouseButtonHandler** object that we create to the **addMouseListener()** method for the **SketchView** component to register it as a listener.

At this point we need to implement the method in the **MouseMotionListener** interface that handles **MOUSE_DRAGGED** events to complete the process for drawing a line. The code for this method must delete any existing temporary element stored in **tempElement**, create a line from the cursor position that we stored in **elementPosition** to the current cursor position and store a reference to it in **tempElement**, and draw the new line. This deleting and redrawing of the line, or whatever other element is being created, has to happen while the mouse is being dragged. If we are to get the effect of rubber-banding the element, it must be *fast*. We can make it fast by using a special drawing mode, so before we start writing the code to handle **MOUSE_DRAGGED** events, let's understand a little more about how things get drawn in Java.

Graphics Drawing Modes

There are actually two drawing modes available when you draw on a component. Up to now we've been using the default drawing mode, referred to as **paint mode**. In paint mode, pixels in the current drawing color overwrite the background so the pixels in the background color are replaced. The alternative drawing mode is called **XOR mode** or eXclusive **OR** mode. This mode is set by calling the method **setXORMode()** for the **Graphics** object you're using to draw, and passing a color as an argument. You'll usually pass the background color to the **setXORMode()** method.

The color of the pixels that you draw in XOR mode depends on what color they were before. The color is produced by combining the current drawing color with the original color of the pixels. If the background pixels are the color that you passed to the **setXORMode()** method, drawing will be in the current color. If the pixels are already the current color, drawing will be in the color that you passed to the **setXORMode()** method. Thus the XOR mode enables you to alternate between the current color and the color that you specified.

You will almost certainly have realized by now that the XOR mode provides a very fast way of erasing a shape that you have drawn. To erase a shape you just need to draw over it again to change it to the background color. It will then be invisible. We'll use this mechanism to erase the previous shape each time we create a new one in the method that will handle the **MOUSE_DRAGGED** event.

Try It Out—Setting the XOR Mode in *SketchDoc*

To make this possible we must set the XOR mode, and the convenient place to do this is in the **mousePressed()** method in the inner class, **MouseButtonHandler**, that we added to the **SketchDoc** class:

```
public void mousePressed(MouseEvent e)
{
  if(e.getModifiers()==InputEvent.BUTTON1_MASK)      // Button 1 down?
  {
    elementPosition = e.getPoint();                  // Save cursor position
    tempG = e.getComponent().getGraphics();          // Get graphics context

    // Get the background color and set XOR mode
    tempG.setXORMode(e.getComponent().getBackground());
  }
}
```

How It Works

We obtain a reference to the component we're drawing on by calling the **getComponent()** method for the **MouseEvent** object, **e**. We then use this reference to obtain the background color for the component we're drawing on by calling its **getBackground()** method. We pass this color to the **setXORMode()** method. As a result, the first time we draw a shape it will be drawn in the current color. When we draw it a second time, it will be drawn in the background color and will therefore disappear.

Note that if you pass a color that is not the background color to the **setXORMode()** method, the color of a shape will still alternate when you draw it repeatedly, but you won't get the shape disappearing of course.

Handling Mouse Motion Events

When the handler for the **MOUSE_DRAGGED** event is called, the **mousePressed()** method will already have been called, so the **Graphics** object **tempG** will contain a reference to the graphics context for the view, and the XOR mode will have been set. All we need to do is take care of creating the shape and dealing with the erase/redraw process for it.

Try It Out—Creating the Shape

1   We'll define another inner class to **SketchDoc**, and call it **MouseMoveHandler**. We'll derive it from the adapter class **MouseMotionAdapter**:

```
// Handler class for mouse motion events
class MouseMoveHandler extends MouseMotionAdapter
{
  // Handle mouse dragging
  public void mouseDragged(MouseEvent e)
  {
    endPoint = e.getPoint();            // Get current cursor position
    if(tempElement!=null)               // For previous element
      tempElement.draw(tempG);          // ... redraw to erase
```

```
      tempElement = createElement();        // Now create new element
      if(tempElement!=null)
        tempElement.draw(tempG);            // ... and draw it
    }
  }
```

2 We mustn't forget to register a mouse motion listener for the view, so add a statement to the **SketchView** class constructor to do this:

```
public SketchView(SketchDoc sketch)
{
  this.sketch = sketch;
  addMouseListener(sketch.new MouseButtonHandler());
  addMouseMotionListener(sketch.new MouseMoveHandler());
}
```

3 The **createElement()** method in the **SketchDoc** class needs to be able to create a variety of elements, not just lines. Here's an initial version of the code for it:

```
// Create an element of the current type and color
protected Element createElement()
{
  switch(elementType)
  {
    case LINE:
      return new LineElement(elementPosition, endPoint, elementColor);
    case RECTANGLE:
      // Create a rectangle
    case CIRCLE:
      // Create a circle
    case CURVE:
      // Create a curve
  }
  return null;
}
```

How It Works

We only need to implement the **mouseDragged()** method here. For the moment, we aren't interested in the other method, **mouseMoved()**, that is included in the adapter class. We first squirrel away the current cursor position in the variable **endPoint** in the **Sketchdoc** class. Before we create a new line to the current cursor position, we must check whether we have previously created a line. If we have, **tempElement** will not be **null**, in which case we draw the element again by calling its **draw()** method with the graphics context, **tempG**, as an argument. This will restore the line to the background color so it will be invisible.

We then create the new line by calling a method in the **SketchDoc** class, **createElement()**. Creating the new line will use the start point already stored in the **mousePressed()** method, and the end point recorded in the current call of the **mouseDragged()** method. We'll put the **createElement()** method together in a moment, when we'll make sure that it returns the line as an object of type **Element**. Here, we store the object returned by **createElement()** in the variable **tempElement**. The final step is to use the reference stored in **tempElement** to call the **draw()** method for the line, and pass the graphics context, **tempG**, to it, but only after verifying that we didn't get a **null** returned from **createElement()**. If another **MOUSE_DRAGGED** event occurs, the reference to the line that we have just drawn will be used in the **mouseDragged()** method to redraw it in the background color and effectively erase it.

The **MouseMoveHandler** object that we create is registered as a listener by passing it to the **addMouseMotionListener()** method for the **SketchView** object.

In the **createElement()** method, we have a **switch** statement that selects the particular kind of element that we want to create, based on the value stored in the variable **elementType**. This is set through the Element menu or by selecting an element type using the toolbar. The **TEXT** element is notable by its absence here. This isn't an oversight. Drawing text is rather different from drawing geometric shapes—you have to enter the text for one thing—so we'll need to deal with this separately in the next chapter. For the **LINE** element, we call the constructor for the **LineElement** class, so we need to add a file containing the definition for that class to the Sketcher directory.

Try It Out—Defining the LineElement Class

If we add a definition for the **LineElement** class, we should be in a position to draw lines interactively in Sketcher. The class will contain two methods, a constructor, and the **draw()** method to draw a line. Here's the code for the class:

```
// Class to represent a line
import java.awt.*;

public class LineElement extends Element
{
  // Line is drawn from the position of the line to the end
  protected int xIncr;        // X increment from position to end
  protected int yIncr;        // Y increment from position to end

  // Constructor
  public LineElement (Point position, Point endPoint, Color color)
  {
    this.position = new Point(position);     // Store the position
    this.color = new Color(color.getRGB());  // Store the color
    xIncr = endPoint.x-position.x;           // Store the x increment
    yIncr = endPoint.y-position.y;           // Store the y increment

    // Create the rectangle bounding the element
    bounds = new Rectangle(
              Math.min(position.x, endPoint.x),
              Math.min(position.y, endPoint.y),     // top left
              Math.abs(position.x-endPoint.x)+1,
```

```
                         Math.abs(position.y-endPoint.y)+1);  // x & y dimensions
    }

    // Draw a line
    public void draw(Graphics g)
    {
      g.setColor(color);                                    // Set the color
      g.drawLine(position.x, position.y,                    // Start point
              position.x+xIncr, position.y+yIncr);          // end point

    }
  }
```

How It Works

The first two arguments to the constructor are the start and end points of the line as `Point` objects. The third argument is the color. The constructor stores the start point in the data member, `position`, that is inherited from the base class, and the color in the data member `color` that is also inherited from the `Element` class. We'll represent a line by the start point stored in `position` and a pair of x and y increments to the start point to define the end point. These increments will be stored in the data members `xIncr` and `yIncr` respectively. We could just store the end point explicitly, but by defining the line relative to the point stored in `position`, we make it very easy to move a line. Moving a line represented in this way is accomplished by modifying `position` only—the end point will be taken care of automatically. We'll define all our geometric elements in this way so that any of them can be moved just by changing the reference point. The increments for the end point are calculated in the constructor by taking the difference between the x and y coordinates for the start and end points passed as arguments.

We must take care in calculating **bounds**, the rectangle that bounds the line. We need to be conscious of the fact that the start point isn't necessarily the top-left corner of the rectangle—indeed, the top-left corner may not be either of the defining points.

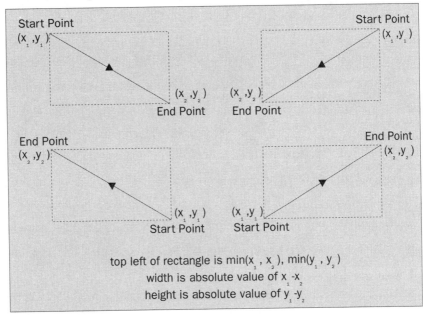

There are four possible configurations that can arise, as the diagram shows. The coordinates for the top-left corner of the bounding rectangle for the line are calculated as the minimum x and minimum y coordinates from the start and end points of the line. The width and height are obtained from the difference between the x coordinates and the difference between the y coordinates respectively. We must take the absolute values of the differences using the **abs()** method from the **Math** class to ensure the width and height are positive. We must also add one pixel to the width and the height because of the way lines are drawn, below and to the right of the defining points. If we don't make sure that we produce the bounding rectangles consistently, we'll have problems if we want to operate on the rectangles—to combine them, for instance.

The **draw()** method is very simple. After setting the color, it calls the **drawLine()** method for the **Graphics** object, **g**, to draw the line. If you compile and run Sketcher, you should now be able to draw lines.

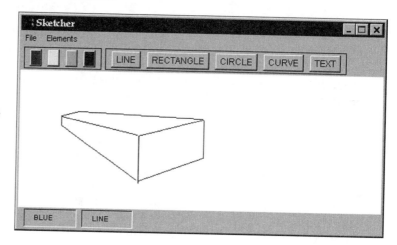

You can drag the end point to wherever you want as long as you keep the left mouse button pressed, and the line will stretch and move to connect to the cursor position. Releasing the button fixes the line.

Drawing Rectangles

This is going to be a piece of cake. All we need is the definition for the **RectangleElement** class, and a modification to the **createElement()** method in the **SketchDoc** class and we're there. The code we've already written that takes care of the mouse button and dragging events will work for rectangles just as it is.

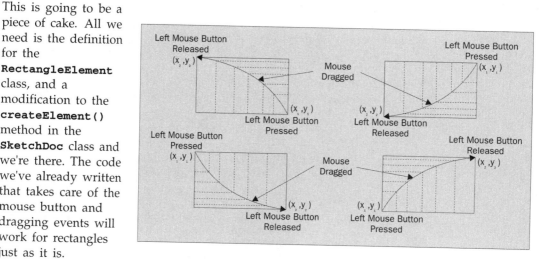

The interactive mechanism that we'll implement for drawing a rectangle will be similar to that for a line. The point where the left mouse button is pressed will be the first point of a diagonal, and the point where the button is released will be the end of the diagonal. As the mouse is dragged we'll rubber-band the rectangle by repeatedly drawing a new rectangle and deleting the old one as the mouse is dragged. The diagram shows the four possible orientations of the mouse path as it is dragged in relation to the rectangle drawn. The top-left corner will have coordinates that are the minimum x and the minimum y from the points at the ends of the diagonal. The width will be the absolute value of the difference between the x coordinates for the two ends, and the height will be the absolute value of the difference between the y coordinates.

Try It Out—The `RectangleElement` Class

1 Here's the definition of the class for a rectangle object:

```
// Class defining a rectangle element
import java.awt.*;

public class RectangleElement extends Element
{
  // Rectangle is drawn with position as top left
  protected int width;          // Width of the rectangle
  protected int height;         // Height of the rectangle

  // Constructor creates a rectangle from opposite corners
  public RectangleElement (Point startPoint, Point endPoint, Color color)
  {
    this.color = new Color(color.getRGB());          // Store the color

    // Store top left point
    position = new Point(Math.min(startPoint.x, endPoint.x),
                         Math.min(startPoint.y, endPoint.y));

    width = Math.abs(startPoint.x-endPoint.x);        // Get width
    height = Math.abs(startPoint.y-endPoint.y);       // Get height

    // Calculate the bounds for the rectangle
    bounds = new Rectangle(position, new Dimension(width+1, height+1));
  }

  // Draw a rectangle
  public void draw(Graphics g)
  {
    g.setColor(color);
    g.drawRect(position.x, position.y, width, height);
  }
}
```

2 The modification to the **createElement()** method in the **SketchDoc** class is also trivial:

```
protected Element createElement()
{
  switch(elementType)
  {
    case LINE:
      return new LineElement(elementPosition, endPoint, elementColor);
    case RECTANGLE:
      return new RectangleElement(elementPosition,
                                      endPoint, elementColor);
    case CIRCLE:
      // Create a circle
    case CURVE:
      // Create a curve
  }
  return null;
}
```

How It Works

The rectangle is defined by its top-left corner stored in the data member position inherited from the **Element** class, and its width and height. We use the **min()** method from the **Math** class that calculates the minimum of two values in the computation of the top-left corner. The **abs()** function from the **Math** class is used to obtain positive values for the width and height. The **bounds** rectangle is easy to create. It's at the same position as the rectangle itself, but with a width and height that is one pixel larger.

The **draw()** method is trivial. It sets the color and uses the **drawRect()** method for the **Graphics** object, **g**, to draw the rectangle.

When the variable **elementType** is set to **RECTANGLE** (as defined in the **Constants** interface), we create a new **RectangleElement** object using the cursor position that was saved by the mouse event handlers, and the color stored in **elementColor**, and return it.

If you recompile **SketchDoc.java**, and run Sketcher, you should be able to draw rectangles.

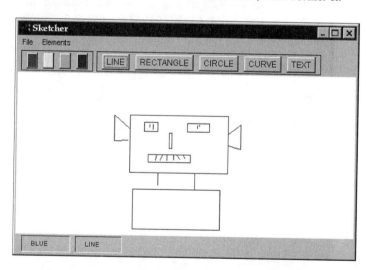

The impressive piece of artwork in the screen shown was produced using just rectangles and a few lines.

Drawing Circles

The most natural mechanism for drawing a circle is to make the point where the mouse button was pressed the center, and the point where the mouse button is released the end of the radius—that is, on the circumference. We'll need to do a little calculation for this.

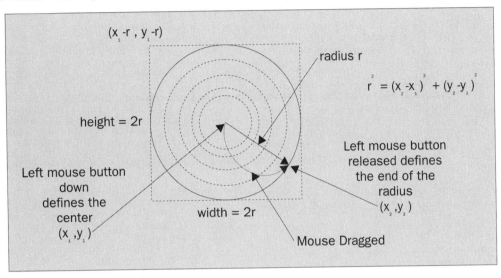

The diagram illustrates the drawing mechanism. Circles will be drawn dynamically as the mouse is dragged, with the cursor position being on the circumference of the circle. Using Pythagoras' theorem, we can calculate the radius from the point at the center and the point on the circumference. We can then calculate the top-left point and the height and width of the rectangle bounding the circle from the center point and the radius.

Try It Out—Adding Circles

1 Here's how this is applied in the definition of the `CircleElement` class:

```
// Class defining a circle element
import java.awt.*;

public class CircleElement extends Element
{
  // Drawn with position as center & circum on the circle
  protected int radius;    // Radius of the circle

  // Constructor
  public CircleElement (Point center, Point circum, Color color)
  {
    position = new Point(center);              // Store the center
```

```
      this.color = new Color(color.getRGB());            // Store the color

   // Calculate the radius
   radius = (int)Math.sqrt((center.x-circum.x)*(center.x-circum.x)+
                         (center.y-circum.y)*(center.y-circum.y));

   // Create the rectangle bounding the element
   bounds = new Rectangle(center.x-radius, center.y-radius,  // top left
                       2*radius+1, 2*radius+1);       // width & height
 }

 // Draw a circle
 public void draw(Graphics g)
 {
   g.setColor(color);
   g.drawOval(position.x-radius, position.y-radius, 2*radius, 2*radius);
 }
}
```

2 If we amend the `createElement()` method in the `SketchDoc` class we will be ready to draw circles:

```
protected Element createElement()
{
  switch(elementType)
  {
    case LINE:
      return new LineElement(elementPosition, endPoint, elementColor);
    case RECTANGLE:
      return new RectangleElement(elementPosition, endPoint,
elementColor);
    case CIRCLE:
      return new CircleElement(elementPosition, endPoint, elementColor);
    case CURVE:
      // Create a curve
  }
  return null;
}
```

How It Works

You should be able to see how the code is derived from the diagram. We store the center of the circle in the variable position inherited from the base class, and calculate the radius from the center point and the point on the circumference using methods from the **Math** class. The class has a data member, **radius**, to store this value. We then create the rectangle bounding the circle which is one pixel wider and higher than the rectangle that defines the circle. We draw the circle using the **drawOval()** method for the **Graphics** object **g**. Like shelling peas, isn't it?

If you recompile the **SketchDoc** class, your Sketcher program will be equipped to draw circles as well as lines and rectangles.

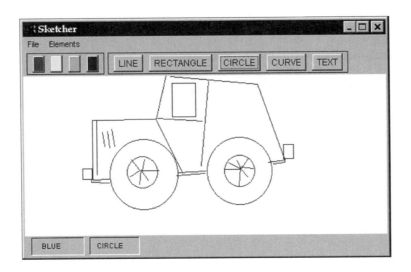

Drawing Curves

Curves are a bit trickier to deal with than the other shapes. We want to be able to create a freehand curve by dragging the mouse, so as the cursor moves, the curve extends—it isn't necessary to create a new curve. This will need to be reflected in how we define the **CurveElement** class, and we'll also need to treat a curve as a special case in the **mousePressed()** and **mouseDragged()** methods. Let's first consider how the process of drawing a curve is going to work, and define the **CurveElement** class based on that.

A curve is going to be represented by a series of connected line segments, but we don't know ahead of time how many there are going to be—as long as the mouse is being dragged we'll be collecting more points. This gives us a hint as to the approach we could adopt to creating a curve.

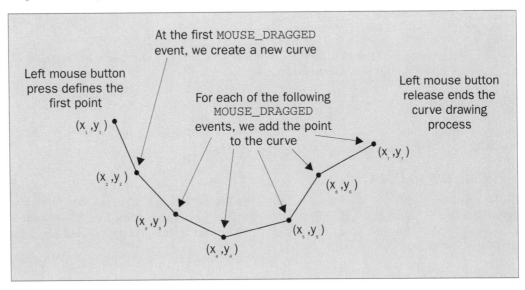

If we construct a curve as soon as we have two points, which is when we receive the first **MOUSE_DRAGGED** event, we can extend the initial curve by calling a method to add another point for each of the subsequent **MOUSE_DRAGGED** events.

Try It Out—A CurveElement Class

This means that the **CurveElement** class will need at least three methods: a constructor, a method to add a segment to the curve and, of course, a **draw()** method so the outline of the **CurveElement** class is going to be:

```
// Class defining a curve element
import java.awt.*;

public class CurveElement extends Element
{
  // Data members defining the curve...

  // Constructor
  public CurveElement(Point firstPoint, Point secondPoint, Color color)
  {
    this.color = new Color(color.getRGB());// Store the color
    position = new Point(firstPoint);        // Store the curve position
    // Create the curve...
  }

  // Add a segment to the curve
  public void addSegment(Point newPoint)
  {
    // Code to add a segment to the curve...
  }

  // Draw a curve
  public void draw(Graphics g)
  {
    g.setColor(color);                              // Set the color
    // Code to draw the curve...
  }
}
```

Before we can define the detail here we must decide how we're going to store the data defining the curve.

Storing the Curve Data

To be consistent with the other shapes we're creating in Sketcher, a curve's position should be defined by the **Point** object stored in the variable **position** defined in the **Element** class—this will be the first point of the curve. The other defining points should be defined as relative positions.

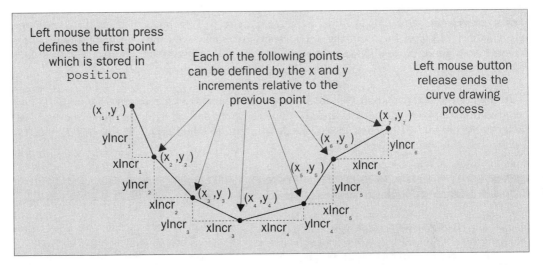

All we need is a mechanism for storing the increments. We could use a **Vector**, but let's be adventurous and use it as an opportunity to hone our Java coding skills. We'll create our own linked list.

We'll create an inner class, **SegmentList** to the **CurveElement** class that defines a linked list. The list elements we'll define by a class, **SegmentNode**, which will be an inner class to the **SegmentList** class, so we'll have an inner class with an inner class.

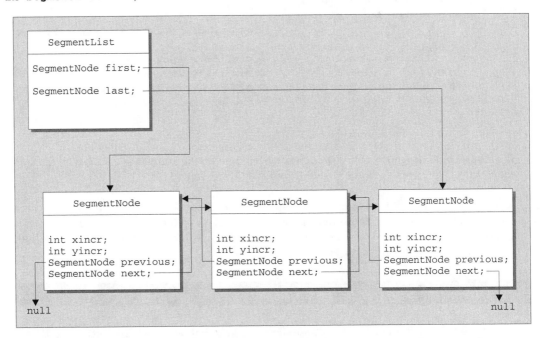

Each **SegmentNode** object will store an x increment and a y increment that are to be applied to the coordinates of the previous point to obtain the current point. Each **SegmentNode** object will also contain a reference to the previous **SegmentNode** object in sequence, plus a reference to the next **SegmentNode** object in sequence—for the first one in

645

a list **previous** will be **null** and for the last, **next** will be **null**. This will make it possible to go through the elements in the list forwards or backwards by working through to the sequence of **next** or **previous** references. We don't need both possibilities for a curve but we'll implement it anyway so you see how the complete linked list works.

The **SegmentList** class will contain just two data members: a reference to the first **SegmentNode** object in the list, and a reference to the last. It will also have methods to add a node to the end of the list, to get the first or the last node, and to get the next or the previous node from a given node.

Try It Out—The SegmentNode Class

The **SegmentNode** class will only need a constructor, so let's define that class first:

```
// Class to define a node in a list of points
class SegmentNode
{
  int xIncr;              // X increment
  int yIncr;              // Y increment
  SegmentNode previous;   // Previous node
  SegmentNode next;       // Next node

  // Create a segment list node
  public SegmentNode(int xIncr, int yIncr,
                                 SegmentNode previous, SegmentNode next)
  {
    this.xIncr = xIncr;            // Store the x increment
    this.yIncr = yIncr;            // Store the y increment
    this.previous = previous;      // Store the reference to the previous node
    this.next = next;             // Store the reference to the next node
  }
}
```

The **SegmentNode** constructor just stores the values for the four data members—the coordinate increments, and the forward and backward references.

Now we can define the **SegmentList** class which will contain **SegmentNode** as an inner class. Remember too that **SegmentList** is an inner class of the **CurveElement** class. The **SegmentList** class represents the linked list, and so will have methods to traverse the list and provide the necessary housekeeping.

Try It Out—The SegmentList Class

1 Here's the definition for the **SegmentList** class that we need to store curve data:

```
// Class to define a linked list of segments
class SegmentList
{
  private SegmentNode first;   // reference to first node
  private SegmentNode last;    // reference to last node

  // Constructor
  public SegmentList(int xIncr, int yIncr)
  {
    first = new SegmentNode(xIncr, yIncr, null , null);
    last = first;
  }

  // Add a segment
  public void addTail(int xIncr, int yIncr)
  {
    // Create new node
    SegmentNode newNode = new SegmentNode(xIncr, yIncr, last, null);

    last.next = newNode;          // the new one is next for the old last
    last = newNode;               // Set the new one as last
  }

  // Get the first node
  public SegmentNode getFirst()
  {
    return first;
  }

  // Get the next node
  public SegmentNode getNext(SegmentNode current)
  {
    return current==null ? null:current.next;
  }
```

```
// Class to define a node in a list of points
class SegmentNode
{
   // Definition of the SegmentNode class...
}
}
```

2 That's all we need for the purposes of handling curve segments, but if you wanted to round out the **SegmentList** class, you could add a method to get the last node:

```
// Get the last node
public SegmentNode getLast()
{
  return last;
}
```

647

3 Given the last node, you might want to iterate through the nodes in the list backwards using a **getPrevious()** method:

```
// Get the previous node
public SegmentNode getPrevious(SegmentNode current)
{
   return current==null ? null:current.previous;
}
```

4 You might also want to be able to add to the beginning of the list of segments:

```
public void addHead(int xIncr, int yIncr)
{
   // Create new node
   SegmentNode newNode = new SegmentNode(xIncr, yIncr, null, first);

   first.previous = newNode;   // New node is previous for the old first
   first = newNode;            // Set the new one as first
}
```

How It Works

The constructor always creates a **SegmentList** object with one **SegmentNode** object that contains the coordinate increments passed as arguments. These will be the increments from the first point stored in **position** to the point at which the first **MOUSE_DRAGGED** event occurs. Both **previous** and **next** will be **null** because there are no other nodes. The **first** and the **last** data members will both reference the same **SegmentNode** object since there's only one.

Subsequent segments are added to the list by calling the **addTail()** method. This creates a new **SegmentNode** object containing the coordinate increments, with the **previous** data member referencing the object referred to by the **last** variable in the **SegmentList** object, and the **next** data member as **null**. The new **SegmentNode** object is now the last, so a reference to it is stored in the **last** member of **SegmentList**.

We'll need to iterate through the segment list when we draw the curve, so we must be able to get hold of the first node. The method **getFirst()** returns the first node in the list. Once we have the first node, the **getNext()** method will provide access to all the following nodes. The method returns the reference stored in the **next** member of the node passed as an argument. For the last node, this reference will be **null**, so we can use that to detect when we reach the end of the list.

We've implemented everything we need to store the data defining a curve. We can now implement the methods in the **CurveElement** class.

Try It Out—Completing the Curve Class

1 We'll need two data members in the class, one to store a reference to the **SegmentList** object, and the other to store the last point that was added to the curve. We need to remember the last point so that we can calculate the increments when the next point comes along. Let's complete the constructor first:

```java
// Class defining a curve element
import java.awt.*;

public class CurveElement extends Element
{
  private Point lastPoint;            // Last curve point
  private SegmentList segments;       // List of curve segment increments

  // Constructor
  public CurveElement(Point firstPoint, Point secondPoint, Color color)
  {
    this.color = new Color(color.getRGB());   // Store the color
    position = new Point(firstPoint);         // Set the curve position
    lastPoint = secondPoint;                  // Save last defining point

    // Create the segment list object with one segment
    segments = new SegmentList(secondPoint.x-firstPoint.x,
                               secondPoint.y-firstPoint.y);

    // Calculate the bounding rectangle for the curve
    bounds = new Rectangle(Math.min(firstPoint.x, secondPoint.x), //left
                           Math.min(firstPoint.y, secondPoint.y), //top
                  Math.abs(firstPoint.x-secondPoint.x)+1,    //width
                  Math.abs(firstPoint.y-secondPoint.y)+1); //height
  }

  // Add a segment to the curve
  public void addSegment(Point newPoint)
  {
    // Code to add a segment to a curve
  }

  // Draw a curve
  public void draw(Graphics g)
  {
    // Code to draw a curve...
  }

  // Class to define a linked list of segments   class SegmentList
  class SegmentList
```

```
  {
    // Definition of the inner class Segment list...

    // Class to define a node in a list of points
    class SegmentNode
    {
      // Definition of the inner inner class SegmentNode...
    }
  }
}
```

2 The method to add a segment to the curve is complicated by the need to adjust the bounding rectangle to enclose the new segment:

```
// Add a segment to the curve
public void addSegment(Point newPoint)
{
  segments.addTail(newPoint.x-lastPoint.x,   // Add a segment
                   newPoint.y-lastPoint.y);
  lastPoint = newPoint;                       // New point is the last
  bounds.add(newPoint);            // Add the point to the bound rectangle

  // Adjust the width and height if necessary
  if(bounds.x+bounds.width==newPoint.x)    // If point is on right edge
    bounds.width++;                        // ...adjust width
  if(bounds.y+bounds.height==newPoint.y)   // If point is on bottom edge
    bounds.height++;                       // ...adjust height
}
```

3 Drawing the curve involves iterating through the segment list:

```
// Draw a curve
public void draw(Graphics g)
{
  g.setColor(color);                               // Set the color

  Point from = new Point(position);                // Draw from point
  Point to = new Point(position);                  // Draw to point

  // Get first segment
  SegmentList.SegmentNode segment = segments.getFirst();

  while(segment!=null)                             // Iterate through the list
  {
    // Draw the line segment
    to.translate(segment.xIncr, segment.yIncr);   // Set the to point
    g.drawLine(from.x, from.y, to.x, to.y);       // Draw the segment
    from = new Point(to);                         // from is old to
```

```
        segment = segments.getNext(segment);          // Get next segment
    }
}
```

How It Works

After storing the color and the reference point for the curve, we store the end point of the first segment, which is in **secondPoint** in the data member **lastPoint**. The **SegmentList** object is created from the increments for the x and y coordinates from **firstPoint** to **secondPoint**. The bounding rectangle is calculated in the same way as for a **LineElement** object—the top-left is the minimum x and y from the two defining points, and the width and height are the absolute values of the differences between the pair of x coordinates and the pair of y coordinates.

Adding the segment is simple. The increments from the previous point, stored in **lastPoint**, and the new point are used to add a new segment to the list, and the new point is stored in **lastPoint**. The method **add()** for the **Rectangle** object, **bounds**, adds the new point to the rectangle, but we have to go the extra mile to deal with the situation when the new point is on the right or bottom edge of the rectangle. In these cases we need to take account of the fact that the drawing process draws pixels below and to the right of the coordinates given. This means making the **width** or **height** for **bounds** one pixel greater.

We set up two **Point** variables: **from** to hold the first point in a segment, and **to** to hold the second point. Both are initialized to the reference point for the curve stored in **position**. We iterate through the segment list in the **while** loop. We use the **translate()** method in the **Point** class to move the **to** point by the increments in the current segment. We then draw the line from the **from** point to the **to** point. The next **from** point is the current **to** point, but writing,

```
from = to;        // Wrong!!!
```

would be a serious mistake. The problem is that you don't get a new point, you just store a reference to **to** in **from**. When you change **to** on the next iteration, **from** will refer to the modified **to** point.

At the end of each iteration, we get the next segment by calling the **getNext()** method for the **SegmentList** object, **segments**. This will be used to increment the **to** point on the next iteration. When **getNext()** returns **null**, the loop ends.

Try It Out—Updating the Mouse Event Handling Methods

1   The mouse listener classes that are defined as inner classes to the **SketchDoc** class need to be updated. We have to fix the **mousePressed()** method in the **MouseButtonHandler** class so that it doesn't turn on **XOR** drawing mode when the element type is a **CURVE**:

```
public void mousePressed(MouseEvent e)
{
  if(e.getModifiers()==InputEvent.BUTTON1_MASK)
  {
    elementPosition = e.getPoint();            // Save cursor position
    tempG = e.getComponent().getGraphics();    // Get graphics context

    if(elementType!=CURVE)          // If it is not a curve set XOR mode
      tempG.setXORMode(e.getComponent().getBackground());
  }
}
```

Now we only set **XOR** drawing mode if the element type is not **CURVE**.

2 The **mouseDragged()** method in the **MouseMoveHandler** class must handle curve elements as a special case. For the first event we want to create a **CurveElement** object and draw it, and for subsequent events we want to add a segment to the curve:

```
public void mouseDragged(MouseEvent e)
{
  endPoint = e.getPoint();              // Get current cursor position

  if(elementType==CURVE)
  { // Special process for a curve
    if(tempElement==null)                       // If there is no curve
      tempElement = createElement();            // ...create one
    else                               // Otherwise add a curve segment
      ((CurveElement)tempElement).addSegment(endPoint);

    tempElement.draw(tempG);                    // Draw the curve
  }
  else
  {
    if(tempElement!=null)              // For previous element
      tempElement.draw(tempG);        // ...redraw to erase

    tempElement = createElement();    // Now create new element
    if(tempElement!=null)
      tempElement.draw(tempG);              // ... and draw it
  }
}
```

3 Of course, we must update the **createElement()** method in the **SketchDoc** class to call the **CurveElement** constructor for the **CURVE** element type:

```
  protected Element createElement()
  {
    switch(elementType)
    {
      case LINE:
        return new LineElement(elementPosition, endPoint, elementColor);
      case RECTANGLE:
        return new RectangleElement(elementPosition, endPoint,
                                                     elementColor);
      case CIRCLE:
        return new CircleElement(elementPosition, endPoint, elementColor);
      case CURVE:
        return new CurveElement(elementPosition, endPoint, elementColor);
    }
    return null;
  }
```

How It Works

In the **mouseDragged()** method, we determine if the current element type is **CURVE** in the first **if**. If **tempElement** is **null**, this must be the first **MOUSE_DRAGGED** event for the curve so we create a new **CurveElement** object by calling **createElement()**. Otherwise we call the **addSegment()** method for the **CurveElement** object reference in **tempElement**. In either case we draw the curve. If it's not a curve, the code is as we had before.

Now you're ready to give curves a whirl. Compile the **CurveElement** class, recompile the **SketchDoc** class, then spend an hour or two getting rid of the typos and Sketcher is go for really fancy sketches.

There's some fabricated text here. In the next chapter we'll add a rather more sophisticated facility for adding text to a sketch.

Managing the Classes

You may not have been counting, but we've accumulated fourteen class files in the Sketcher program, and we'll add a few more in subsequent chapters. It's a good time to give some thought to how we can manage our program files a little better. A program of any size really needs to have its source files divided up into packages containing the definitions of related class files. We can create our own packages for the Sketcher program.

The most obvious candidates for a package at this point are the shape classes plus their base class, **Element**. These form a strongly related group that we could put in a package we could call **Elements**. The first step is to create an **Elements** directory as a subdirectory of the **Sketcher** directory. You can then move the files **Element.java**, **LineElement.java**, **RectangleElement.java**, **CircleElement.java** and **CurveElement.java** into it. You need to delete all the **.class** files corresponding to these **.java** files from the **Sketcher** directory.

Each class that is a member of a package must have a **package** statement to identify the package that it belongs to, so add the following statement to the beginning of each of the files that you've moved to the **Elements** directory:

```
package Elements;
```

The only file that contains references to the members of the **Elements** package is **SketchDoc.java**, so to allow the shape classes to be referenced by their unqualified names, we must add an **import** statement to the beginning of this file:

```
import Elements.*;
```

This imports all the classes defined in the **Elements** package. Having done that you just need to recompile the **SketchDoc** class file and the compiler will compile the classes in the **Elements** package as well. When that is done, the program should run as before.

Summary

In this chapter you have learned how to draw on components and how you can use mouse listeners to implement a drawing interface. The important points we have covered in this chapter are:

- A graphics object defines a **Graphics** context for a component that represents the drawing surface of the component
- You draw on a component by calling methods for a **Graphics** object
- The coordinate system for drawing on a component has the origin in the top-left corner of the component with the positive x axis from left to right, and the positive y axis from top to bottom

▶ You normally draw on a component by implementing its **paint()** method. The **paint()** method is passed a **Graphics** object that is the graphics context for the component. The **paint()** method is called whenever the component needs to be redrawn

▶ You can't create a **Graphics** object. If you want to draw on a component outside the **paint()** method, you can obtain a **Graphics** object for the component by calling its **getGraphics()** method

▶ There are two drawing modes that you can use. The default mode is **paint mode**, where drawing overwrites the background pixels with pixels of the current color. The other mode is **XOR mode** where the current color is combined with the background color. This is typically used to alternate between the current color and a color passed to the **setXORMode()** method

▶ The **Graphics** class defines methods for drawing outline shapes as well as filled shapes

Exercises

1 Add the code to the Sketcher program to support drawing an ellipse.

2 Modify the Sketcher program to include a button for switching fill mode on and off, and add a toolbar pane to show whether fill is on or off.

3 Extend the classes defining rectangles, circles and ellipses to support filled shapes.

4 Extend the curve class to support filled shapes (you'll need to draw the curve as a polygon).

5 Implement an applet to display colors. The applet should display two buttons for each of the primary colors red, green and blue, one to increase the intensity of the color and the other to decrease it. The color which is a composite of the red, green and blue intensities should be displayed in the applet.

Extending the GUI

In this chapter we will investigate how we can create dialogs, and how we can use them to communicate with the user, and to manage input. Another GUI capability we will be exploring is pop-up menus and we will be applying these to enhance the Sketcher application. We will also looking at how we can use scrollbars for varying data values as well as scrolling a window. All of this will give you a lot more practice in implementing event listeners.

In this chapter you will learn:

- How to create a dialog
- What a modal dialog is and how it differs from a modeless dialog
- How to create a message box dialog
- How you can use components in a dialog to receive input
- What a pop-up menu is
- What a context menu is and how you can implement context menus
- How to create and manage scrollbars
- How to implement a scrolling window

Using Dialogs

A dialog is a window that is displayed within the context of another window—its parent. As we saw in Chapter 11, dialogs are defined by the **Dialog** class in the **java.awt** package, and a **Dialog** object is a specialized sort of **Window**. A **Dialog** object will typically contain one or more components which display some information or allow data to be entered, plus some buttons for selecting dialog options, including closing the dialog. Below is a dialog that we will create later in this chapter. This dialog will enable you to enter the text for a text element in Sketcher.

This dialog will be displayed when you have set the element type to **TEXT**, and you click on a location in the sketch where you want the text to appear. Dialogs are usually created as a response to a user action such as clicking the mouse, as in this case, or selecting a menu item or toolbar button, although they can be displayed spontaneously to display warning or advisory messages when unusual situations arise during program execution.

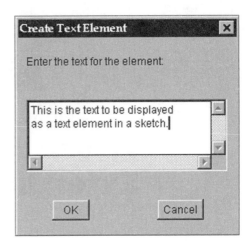

Modal and Modeless Dialogs

There are two different kinds of dialog that you can create, and they have distinct operating characteristics. You have a choice of creating either a **modal dialog** or a **modeless dialog**. When you display a modal dialog, by selecting a menu item or a button typically, it inhibits operations with any other windows in the application until you close the dialog. The example of a dialog which creates a text element, that appears above, is a modal dialog. The user will enter some text, and then click on the OK button to close the dialog and enter the text into the program. Modal dialogs that manage input will normally have at least two buttons, an OK button that you use to accept whatever input has been entered and then close the dialog, and a Cancel button to just close the dialog and abort the entry of the data.

A modeless dialog on the other hand can be left on the screen for as long as you want, since it does not block interaction with other windows in the application. You can switch back and forth between using the dialog and using any other application windows that are displayed. However, in most cases you don't want to do this. It is usually more convenient when more than one window is required to use a regular window rather than a modeless dialog. For this reason, modal dialogs are much more common.

Whether you create a modal or a modeless dialog is determined either by an argument to a dialog class constructor, or by which constructor you choose, since two of them create modeless dialogs by default. There's a choice of four constructors for a **Dialog** object:

Constructor	Description
`Dialog(Frame parent)`	Always creates a modeless dialog with an empty title bar that is initially invisible. The argument, **parent**, identifies the parent window for the dialog.
`Dialog(Frame parent, String title)`	Always creates a modeless dialog that is initially invisible with **title** as the title bar. The argument, **parent**, identifies the parent window for the dialog.

Constructor	Description
`Dialog(Frame parent, boolean modal)`	Creates a dialog with an empty title bar, and which is initially invisible. The argument, `parent`, identifies the parent window for the dialog. If the value of `modal` is `true`, the dialog will be modal, if it is `false` the dialog will be modeless.
`Dialog(Frame parent, String title, boolean modal)`	Creates a dialog that is initially invisible, and with `title` as the title bar. The argument, `parent`, identifies the parent window for the dialog. If the value of `modal` is `true`, the dialog will be modal, if it is `false` the dialog will be modeless.

> Note that you must always specify a parent *Frame* window when you create a *Dialog* object. If the value of *parent* is *null*, the constructor will throw an *IllegalArgumentException*.

After you have created a `Dialog` object, you can change the kind of dialog window it will produce from modal to modeless, or vice versa, by calling the `setModal()` method for the object. If you specify the argument to the method as `true`, the dialog will be modal, and a `false` argument will make it modeless. You can also check whether a `Dialog` object is modal or not. The `isModal()` method for the object will return `true` if it represents a modal dialog, and `false` otherwise.

The dialog window will be displayed when you call the `setVisible()` method for the `Dialog` object with the argument `true`. This method is inherited from the `Component` class via the `Container` and `Window` classes. If you call `setVisible()` with the argument `false`, the dialog window is removed from the screen. Once you have displayed a modal dialog window, the user cannot interact with any of the other application windows until you call `setVisible()` for the dialog object with the argument `false`, so you typically do this in the event handler which is called to close the dialog. Note that the `setVisible()` method only affects the visibility of the dialog. You still have a perfectly good `Dialog` object so that when you want to display the dialog again, you just call its `setVisible()` method with an argument set to `true`.

To set or change the title bar for a dialog, you just pass a `String` object to the `setTitle()` method for the `Dialog` object. If you want to know what the current title for a dialog is, you can call the `getTitle()` method which will return a `String` object containing the title bar string.

Dialog windows are resizable by default, so you can normally change the size of a dialog window by dragging its boundaries. If you don't want to allow a dialog window to be resized, you can inhibit this by calling the `setResizable()` for the `Dialog` object with the argument as `false`. An argument value of `true` re-enables the resizing capability.

A Simple Modal Dialog

The simplest kind of dialog is one which just displays some information. We could see how this works by adding a Help menu with an About menu item, and then displaying an About dialog to provide information about the application.

Rather than just create a specific About dialog, we could derive a more generic **MessageBox** class from **Dialog** that will display a modal dialog with any title bar and message that we want. We can then use it to display an About box, or any other message if the need arises. Let's first define the **MessageBox** class, and then use it in support of a Help | About menu option.

Try It Out—Defining the *MessageBox* Class

The constructor for our **MessageBox** class will need to accept three arguments—the parent **Frame** object, a **String** object defining what should appear on the title bar and a **String** object for the message we want to display. We will only need one button in the dialog window, an OK button to close the dialog. We can make the whole thing self-contained by making the **MessageBox** class the action listener for the button.

Here's the class definition:

```
// Class defining a general purpose message box
import java.awt.*;
import java.awt.event.*;

class MessageBox extends Dialog implements ActionListener
{
  // Constructor
  public MessageBox(Frame frame, String title, String messageString)
  {
    super(frame, title, true);    // Create modal dialog

    // Position the dialog in the parent window
    Rectangle bounds = frame.getBounds();
    setLocation(bounds.x + bounds.width/3, bounds.y + bounds.height/3);

    // Set up panel to display the message
    Panel messagePane = new Panel();             // Create the message panel
    Label message = new Label(messageString);    // Label to hold message
    messagePane.add(message);                    // Add the label
    add(messagePane, BorderLayout.CENTER);       // Add the pane centrally

    // Create the dialog buttons
    Panel buttonPane = new Panel();              // Create the panel for buttons
    Button button = new Button("  OK  ");        // The OK button
    buttonPane.add(button);                      // Add the button to the pane
    button.addActionListener(this);              // Add the button listener
    add(buttonPane, BorderLayout.SOUTH);         // Add the button at the bottom
```

```
      pack();                                 // Pack the dialog window
  }

  // Handle button events
  public void actionPerformed(ActionEvent e)
  {
    setVisible(false);                        // Hide the dialog
  }
}
```

How It Works

The constructor first calls the base **Dialog** class constructor to create a modal dialog with the title bar given by the **title** argument. It then defines the position of the dialog relative to the position of the frame.

> *When we create an instance of this class in the Sketcher program a little later in this chapter, we will specify the **SketchFrame** object as the parent for the dialog. Although the **SketchFrame** object will be the parent of the **MessageBox** dialog, it does not contain it. A parent is not the same as a container. The parent relationship between windows implies a lifetime dependency. When the **SketchFrame** object is destroyed, the **MessageBox** object will be too, because it is a child of the **SketchFrame** object. This does not just apply to **Frame** and **Dialog** objects—any **Window** object can have another **Window** object as a parent.*

The **MessageBox** window is positioned in screen coordinates—relative to the top-left corner of the screen. Thus to position the dialog appropriately, we set the coordinates of the top-left corner of the dialog as one third of the distance across the width of the application window, and one third of the distance down from the top-left corner of the application window.

Because the **Dialog** class is a sub-class of **Window**, our **MessageBox** dialog object will have **BorderLayout** as the default layout manager. The dialog contains two **Panel** objects that are created in the constructor, one to hold a **Label** object for the message that is passed to the constructor, and the other to hold the OK button that will close the dialog. The **messagePane** object is added so that it fills the center of the dialog window. The **buttonPane** position is specified as **BorderLayout.SOUTH**, so it will be at the bottom of the dialog window. Both **Panel** objects have a **FlowLayout** manager by default. The **MessageBox** object is the listener for the OK button so, in the **addActionListener()** method call for the button, we pass the **this** variable.

The **pack()** method is inherited from the **Window** class. This method packs the components in the window, setting the window to a size to accommodate the components it contains.

The **actionPerformed()** method will be called when the OK button is selected. This just hides the dialog window by calling the **setVisible()** method for the **MessageBox** object so the dialog window will disappear from the screen.

To add a Help Menu with an About item to our Sketcher application, we must add some code to the **SketchFrame** class constructor.

Try It Out—Creating an About Menu Item

1 First, we add a data member to the `SketchFrame` class to hold the `MessageBox` object for the About dialog:

```
MessageBox aboutBox;                      // Dialog for About menu item
```

You can add this line to the `SketchFrame` class definition immediately following the statement defining the `statusbar` variable.

2 We will need an action listener for the About menu item. Since all the event handler needs to do is to show the `aboutBox` dialog, we can make the `SketchFrame` object the listener for this menu item. Modify the class definition so that the class implements the `ActionListener` interface:

```
public class SketchFrame extends Frame
                              implements Constants, ActionListener
```

3 The changes to the constructor to add the Help menu will be:

```
public SketchFrame(String title, Sketcher theApp)
{
  super(title);                       // Call base constructor
  this.theApp = theApp;               // Store the application object
  sketch = theApp.getDocument();      // Get the document object
  setMenuBar(menuBar);                // Add the menu bar to the window

  toolbar = new Toolbar(theApp);      // Create the toolbar
  add(toolbar, BorderLayout.NORTH);   // Place it at the top

  // Construct the file pull down menu...

  // Construct the Element pull down menu...

  // Construct the Help pull down menu
  Menu helpMenu = new Menu("Help");      // The Help menu bar item
  helpMenu.add(item = new MenuItem("About"));
  item.addActionListener(this);          // Make the frame the listener

  menuBar.add(fileMenu);                 // Add the file menu
  menuBar.add(elementMenu);              // Add the element menu
  menuBar.add(helpMenu);                 // Add the help menu

  addKeyListener(new KeyHandler());      // Add the key handler

  add(statusbar, BorderLayout.SOUTH);    // Add the status bar
  pack();                                // Pack the window
}
```

4 Lastly, we need to implement is the method in the **SketchFrame** class to handle the About menu item's events:

```
// Handle About menu events
public void actionPerformed(ActionEvent e)
{
  if(aboutBox==null)
    // Create dialog for About menu item
    aboutBox = new MessageBox(this, "About Sketcher",
              "Sketcher Program for Beginning Java ©Ivor Horton 1997");

  aboutBox.setVisible(true);      // Show the dialog
}
```

5 Of course, the dialog will occupy system resources once the **MessageBox** object has been created. To release these resources, you call the **dispose()** method for the object. Since we keep the object for the life of the application window, a good place to release the resources would be in the **finalize()** method for the **SketchFrame** class:

```
// Clean-up when the frame window is destroyed
protected void finalize()
{
  if(aboutBox != null)
    aboutBox.dispose();                  // Release the dialog box resources
}
```

You can now compile **MessageBox.java** and recompile **SketchFrame.java** to try out our smart new dialog.

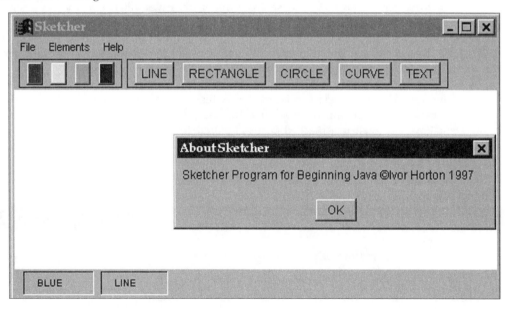

The dialog pops up when you select the About item in the Help menu. Until you select the OK button in the About Sketcher dialog, you can't interact with the application window at all since we created this as a modal dialog. By changing the argument in the call to the parent constructor in the **MessageBox** constructor, you can make it modeless and see how that works. This kind of dialog is usually modal though.

If you resize the application window before you display the About dialog, you will see that its position of the dialog relative to the application window is adjusted accordingly.

How It Works

This is stuff that should be very familiar by now. We create a **Menu** object for the Help item on the menu bar, and add a **MenuItem** object which is the About menu item. We then call the **addActionListener()** method for the **MenuItem** object to make the **SketchFrame** object the listener for the item. Finally we add the **helpMenu** object to the **menubar** object.

The dialog that we want to display will always display the same message, so there is no point to creating and destroying it each time we want to display it. We have arranged that we only create it once in the event handler, when **aboutBox** is **null**, which will be the first time the **actionPerformed()** method is called. On all other occasions we just reuse the **MessageBox** object and make the dialog visible by calling its **setVisible()** method. The OK button handler in the **MessageBox** class will make it invisible when the button is clicked.

Using a Dialog to Create Text Elements

A dialog is the obvious way to create text elements in the Sketcher program where we need a mechanism for entering the text. You saw the dialog that we will use at the beginning of this chapter. It will provide us with a good practical context in which to try out some more components. It has a **TextArea** component into which you can enter the text, plus an OK button and a Cancel button. There is also a **Label** above the **TextArea** as a prompt for the entry of the text.

We can define this dialog as a class **TextDialog** which will have **Dialog** as the super-class. We can also make it self-contained by adding an inner class to define the handlers for button events. We can then use the text that is entered to create the **TextElement** object and add it to the document externally. With this approach, when the dialog is closed, we will need to verify that the OK button was pressed and some text was entered so that we avoid trying to create a new element when no text is available.

Try It Out—Defining the *TextDialog* Class

1 We can define an outline of the **TextDialog** class first, and then add the detail of the class definition afterwards:

```
// Class defining the text element creation dialog
import java.awt.*;
import java.awt.event.*;
```

```java
import java.util.*;

class TextDialog extends Dialog implements Constants
{
  TextArea textArea;                       // Receives text input
  String[] text;                           // Stores input as multi-line

  public TextDialog(SketchFrame window)
  {
    super(window,"Create Text Element", true);    // Create modal dialog

    // Code to set the dialog window position...

    // Code to create the dialog button panel...

    // Code to create the dialog text entry panel..

    enableEvents(AWTEvent.WINDOW_EVENT_MASK); // Deal with the close icon
    addFocusListener(new FocusHandler()); // Add a handler for the focus
  }

  // Handle dialog closing event
  protected  void processWindowEvent(WindowEvent e)
  {
    if(e.getID()==WindowEvent.WINDOW_CLOSING)
    {
      requestFocus();                        // Focus to the dialog window
      setVisible(false);                     // Close the window
    }
    super.processWindowEvent(e);             // Pass on the event
  }

  // Get the multi-line text input
  public String[] getText()
  {
    return text;
  }

  // Class defining button handlers
  class ButtonHandler implements ActionListener
  {
    int buttonID;                           // ID for button

    // Constructor
    public ButtonHandler(int buttonID)
    {
      this.buttonID = buttonID;             // Save the button ID
    }

    // Handle button press
    public void actionPerformed(ActionEvent e)
```

665

```
  {
    requestFocus();                        // Focus to the dialog window
    if(buttonID==OK)
    {
      // Code to store the text and hide the dialog...
    }
    else
    {
      // Code to set text to null and hide the dialog...
    }
  }
}

// Handle dialog focus events
class FocusHandler extends FocusAdapter
{
  public void focusGained(FocusEvent e)
  {
    textArea.requestFocus();
  }
}  // End of FocusHandler class definition
}
```

2 Note that the **TextDialog** class implements the **Constants** interface. This is because we will define standard IDs for the OK button and the Cancel button in this interface. Add the following statements to the **Constants.java** file:

```
import java.awt.*;
public interface Constants
{
  // Element type definitions as before...

  // Button IDs
  int OK     = 501;
  int CANCEL = 502;

  // File menu IDs as before...
}
```

How It Works

The **import** statements add the package **java.util**, as well as the **java.awt** and **java.awt.event** packages to the **TextDialog** class, because we will be using a class from **java.util** to help us analyze the text that is entered.

The constructor needs access to the application window object, because that will be the parent **Frame** object for the dialog. We will locate the dialog window within the application window in the same way as we located the **MessageBox** dialog. We add two panels to the dialog, one to hold the buttons and the other to contain the **TextArea** component and a **Label** object displaying a prompt. Since the **Dialog** class is derived ultimately from the

Window class, the default layout manager will be **BorderLayout**. We have two lines of code at the end of the constructor, one to enable window events so that the close icon will work, and the other to add a focus listener.

In the **processWindowEvent()** method we want to handle the **WINDOW_CLOSING** event that corresponds to the close icon being selected. To make sure that the dialog window has the focus, rather than one of the components in the window, we call **requestFocus()**. This method is inherited from the **Component** class, so you can request the focus for any component. For the method to be effective, the component must be visible on the screen. Calling **requestFocus()** for the dialog window ensures that the focus transfers back to the parent window properly when we close the dialog. To close the dialog window we just call the **setVisible()** method with the argument **false**. Note that we also call **requestFocus()** in the **actionPerformed()** method in the **ButtonHandler** class for the same reason.

The **FocusHandler** class which implements the **FocusListener** interface is an inner class that appears at the end of the **TextDialog** class definition. The **FocusListener** declares one method, **focusGained()**, which will be called when the dialog window opens. This provides an opportunity to make sure the **textArea** component gets the focus when the dialog window opens. To do this the method calls **requestFocus()** for the **textArea** object. Since we transfer the focus to the **textArea** component as soon as the dialog opens, you can key in the text straight away.

The **getText()** method will enable us to retrieve any text that was entered in the dialog, from other parts of Sketcher. The text input will be stored in the **text[]** array that is a member of the **TextDialog** class by the action listener for the OK button.

Now we can get down to implementing the constructor for the class.

Try It Out—The TextDialog Class Constructor

1 Since the constructor will be quite long, let's deal with the code piecemeal. First we can add the code to position the dialog window within the parent frame:

```java
public TextDialog(SketchFrame window)
{
  super(window,"Create Text Element", true);    // Create modal dialog

  // Set the dialog window position
  Rectangle bounds = window.getBounds();
  setLocation(bounds.x + bounds.width/3, bounds.y + bounds.height/3);

  // Code to create the dialog button panel...

  // Code to create the dialog text entry panel..

  enableEvents(AWTEvent.WINDOW_EVENT_MASK); // Deal with the close icon
  addFocusListener(new FocusHandler());    // Add a handler for the focus
}
```

2 We can add the button panel next. In order to position the buttons 'nicely', we will use a **GridBagLayout** manager for the **Panel** object:

```
public TextDialog(SketchFrame window)
{
    super(window,"Create Text Element", true);   // Create modal dialog

    // Code to set the dialog window position...

    // Create panel holding the dialog buttons
    Panel buttonPane = new Panel();                   // Create the button panel
    GridBagLayout gbLayout = new GridBagLayout();// Button pane Layout
    buttonPane.setLayout(gbLayout);                   // Set the layout

    // Define the constraints for buttons
    GridBagConstraints constraints = new GridBagConstraints();
    constraints.weightx = 1.0;
    constraints.weighty = 1.0;
    constraints.fill = GridBagConstraints.NONE;
    constraints.insets = new Insets(15, 10, 15, 10);  // Spacing
    Button button = new Button("  OK  ");             // OK button
    gbLayout.setConstraints(button, constraints);
    buttonPane.add(button);                           // Add the OK button
    button.addActionListener(new ButtonHandler(OK));
    constraints.gridwidth = GridBagConstraints.REMAINDER;
    gbLayout.setConstraints(button = new Button("Cancel"), constraints);
    buttonPane.add(button);                           // Add the Cancel button
    button.addActionListener(new ButtonHandler(CANCEL));
    add(buttonPane, BorderLayout.SOUTH);              // Add the button panel

    // Code to create the dialog text entry panel..

    enableEvents(AWTEvent.WINDOW_EVENT_MASK); // Deal with the close icon
    addFocusListener(new FocusHandler());     // Add a handler for the focus
}
```

3 The **Panel** to hold the **TextArea** object is next. In order to allow multiple lines of text to be entered, we will equip the **TextArea** object with scrollbars. The code which will do this is as follows:

```
public TextDialog(SketchFrame window)
{
    super(window,"Create Text Element", true);   // Create modal dialog

    // Code to set the dialog window position...

    // Code to create the dialog button panel...

    // Create the text entry control
    Panel textEntryPane = new Panel();
```

```
        gbLayout = new GridBagLayout();
        textEntryPane.setLayout(gbLayout);

        // Add the prompt label
        Label label = new Label("Enter the text for the element:");
        constraints.anchor = GridBagConstraints.WEST;     // Anchor to the left
        gbLayout.setConstraints(label, constraints);
        textEntryPane.add(label);                         // Add the label to the pane

        // Add the text input component
        textArea = new TextArea("", 4, 30, TextArea.SCROLLBARS_BOTH);
        gbLayout.setConstraints(textArea, constraints);
        textEntryPane.add(textArea);                 // Add input area to the pane
        add(textEntryPane, BorderLayout.CENTER); // Center the text entry pane
        pack();                                   // Pack the window
```

```
      enableEvents(AWTEvent.WINDOW_EVENT_MASK); // Deal with the close icon
      addFocusListener(new FocusHandler());     // Add a handler for the focus
  }
```

How It Works

The first section has just the same code as we used to position the **MessageBox** dialog. We set the position of the dialog window one third of the distance across and down the parent **Frame** window.

Next, we first create the **buttonPane** object, its layout manager object, **gbLayout** and call **setLayout()** for **buttonPane** to register the layout manager object. We set up the layout constraints, using the **GridBagConstraints** class to create the **constraints** object. We set **weightx** and **weighty** to 1.0, and this will apply to both buttons so they have equal weighting. We don't want the buttons to fill their grid positions so we set the **fill** constraint to **NONE**. The **insets** constraint is defined to give a reasonable spacing around each button. The OK button is created and added to **buttonPane**, and its action listener is defined with the ID, **OK**, from the **Constants** interface, and registered with the button object. We reuse the variable **button** to add the Cancel button to **buttonPane**. Finally we add **buttonPane** to the bottom of the dialog window—this is easy since the **TextDialog** class has **BorderLayout** as the default layout manager.

Again we use a **GridBagLayout** manager for the **Panel** object for flexibility in positioning the components. The first component added to the **textPane Panel** is a **Label** object showing a prompt. The **Label** object, **label**, is added with the **anchor** constraint set to **WEST** to left-justify the prompt. The **TextArea** object is created to display four lines of text, each thirty characters long. The first argument to the constructor is the initial contents—here it is an empty string. The last argument specifies that we want both a vertical and a horizontal scrollbar. Alternative values you could use for this argument are **SCROLLBARS_VERTICAL**, **SCROLLBARS_HORIZONTAL** and **SCROLLBARS_NONE**. When we have added the **textArea** object to the **textEntryPane**, we add the **textEntryPane** to the dialog window so that it occupies the center. Lastly, we pack the window so that its size adjusts to fit the components.

The only serious work that the handler class has to do is to extract the text from the **textArea** object, and separate each line of text into a separate **String** object. We will carry out the latter operation in a separate class method.

Try It Out—Defining the ButtonHandler Inner Class

1 Here's the basic code we need to add to the inner class definition:

```
// Handler for text dialog buttons
class ButtonHandler implements ActionListener
{
  int buttonID;                          // ID for button

  public ButtonHandler(int buttonID)
  {
    this.buttonID = buttonID;       // Save the button ID
  }

  // Handle button press
  public void actionPerformed(ActionEvent e)
  {
    requestFocus();                              // Focus to the dialog window
    if(buttonID==OK)
    {
      text = extractLines(textArea.getText());     // Retrieve the text
      setVisible(false);                           // Hide the dialog
    }
    else
    {
      text = null;                                 // No input
      setVisible(false);                           // Hide the dialog
    }
  }
  // Separate lines of input text into an array
  String[] extractLines(String text)
  {
    // Code to extract lines of text...
  }
}
```

2 To separate out the lines of text, we can implement the **extractLines()** method using the **StringTokenizer** class from the **java.util** package:

```
// Separate lines of input text into an array
String[] extractLines(String text)
{
  if(text.length()==0)                    // If there is no text
    return null;                          // Return null
```

```
   // Create a tokenizer object for a string
   StringTokenizer st = new StringTokenizer(text, "\n");

   int index=0;                           // Index for storing substrings

   String[] subStr = new String[st.countTokens()]; // Array for substrings

   while (st.hasMoreTokens())             // While there are more substrings
     subStr[index++] = st.nextToken();    // Store the next substring
   return subStr;                         // Return the array of sub-strings
 }
```

How It Works

In the **actionPerformed()** method, if the button ID is **OK** we call the **extractLines()** method to separate each line of text into an element of the **String** array text that is a member of the **TextDialog** class. We then call **setVisible()** to hide the dialog window. For the Cancel button, we just set the variable **text** to **null** because there is no input, and then we hide the dialog.

In Chapter 4, we did exactly what the **extractLines()** method does the hard way—in the interests of getting some experience in manipulating strings. It's a whole lot easier with the aid of the **StringTokenizer** class from the **java.util** package since this class is designed to do exactly what we want to do here. A **StringTokenizer** object breaks a given string up into sub-strings—or tokens, where each sub-string is separated from the next by any character or sequence of characters that you specify. The **StringTokenizer** class implements the **Enumeration** interface and uses the methods that this interface declares to implement string-specific methods for extracting sub-strings.

The **extractLines()** method first checks that there is some text by checking the length of the parameter, **text**—if the length is zero we return **null**. If **text** does contain characters we create a **StringTokenizer** object, **st**. The constructor that we use to create **st** has two arguments of type **String**: the string to be broken up, **text**, and a string containing the set of separator characters, which in our case contains just one character, **"\n"**. This can, however, be anything you want. The **countTokens()** method for **st** returns the number of sub-strings in the string to be tokenized, so we use this to specify the size of the array, **subStr[]**, that we will use to store the sub-strings. We extract the sub-strings into the **subStr[]** array in the **while** loop. The **hasMoreTokens()** method, which you can compare with the **hasMoreElements()** method for an **Enumeration**, returns **true** as long as there are still tokens to be extracted, so at the end of the string it will return **false** and end the loop. The **nextToken()** method, which compares with **nextElement()** for an **Enumeration**, returns the next sub-string, which we store in the array using the variable, **index**, to select the array element. The variable **index** is incremented after the sub-string is stored, so that it will be set to the index for the next vacant array element, ready for the next iteration. Simple really, isn't it?

There are two other constructors defined in the **StringTokenizer** class that you may find useful:

671

Method	Description
`StringTokenizer(String str)`	Creates an object to tokenize the string, **str**, that assumes the separator can be any of the follwing—a space, a newline, a tab or a carriage return.
`StringTokenizer(String str, String delim, boolean returnTokens)`	Creates an object to tokenize the string, **str**, that assumes the separator can be any of the characters in the string, **delim**. If the third argument is **true** the separators will also be return as tokens.

The **StringTokenizer** class also defines a version of **nextToken()** which accepts a **String** argument defining a new set of delimiters to determine where the sub-string to be extracted ends, so you can use this to change the separator characters as you go along.

Before we can use the **TextDialog** class to help us create text elements, we must define the **TextElement** class.

Try It Out—Defining a Text Element

1 The **TextElement** class needs to be in the **Elements** package, so we have a package statement at the beginning of the file, and we must save **TextElement.java** in the **Elements** directory.

A **TextElement** object is a little odd in that it requires information from the graphics context of the view in order to calculate the bounds for the element. This is because we need a **Graphics** object for the view to obtain the height of the font characters and the width of the block of text. For this reason the constructor will need to be passed a **SketchView** object. The outline definition of the class will be:

```java
// Class defining a text element
package Elements;

import SketchView;
import java.awt.*;

public class TextElement extends Element
{
  String[] text;                        // Store multiple text lines
  int height;                           // Height of a text line
  Font font;                            // The font for the text

  // Constructor
  public TextElement(SketchView view, Point position,
                     String[] text, Font font, Color color)
  {
    this.text = text;                                   // Store the text
    this.font = new Font(font.getName(),
             font.getStyle(), font.getSize()); // Store the font
```

```
      this.position = new Point(position);           // Store the position
      this.color = new Color(color.getRGB());        // Store the color

      // Code to calculate bounds...
    }

    // Draw a text element
    public void draw(Graphics g)
    {
      // Code to draw a text element...
    }
}
```

2 To calculate the rectangle bounding the text element we must work out the rectangle occupied by the block of text drawn using the font specified. The code to do this is as follows:

```
public TextElement(SketchView view, Point position,
                   String[] text, Font font, Color color)
{
  this.text = text;                                 // Store the text
  this.font = new Font(font.getName(),
             font.getStyle(), font.getSize());      // Store the font
  this.position = new Point(position);              // Store the position
  this.color = new Color(color.getRGB());           // Store the color

  // Calculate bounds
  Graphics g = view.getGraphics();
  FontMetrics fm = g.getFontMetrics(font);
  height = fm.getHeight();

  // Text block height is height x number of lines
  int totalHeight = text.length*height;

  // Calculate the width as the width of the longest line
  int width = 0;
  for(int i = 0; i < text.length; i++)
    // Get maximum width
    width = Math.max(width, fm.stringWidth(text[i]));

  // Create rectangle - text reference point is on the baseline
  bounds = new Rectangle(position.x, position.y - fm.getMaxAscent(),
                    width + 1, totalHeight + 1);
  g.dispose();                                 // Release context resources
}
```

3 To draw a text element we must draw each line of text separately, because the **drawString()** method can only draw on a single line:

```
// Draw a text element
public void draw(Graphics g)
```

```
{
    g.setColor(color);
    g.setFont(font);                          // Set the font
    int x = position.x;                       // Get initial x position
    int y = position.y;                       // Get initial y position
    for(int i = 0; i < text.length; i++)
        g.drawString(text[i], x, y + i*height);   // Draw the text line
}
```

How It Works

The constructor has five parameters, a reference to the document view the position of the text element, the text the element should contain, the font to be used for the text and the color of the text. The text and the font are stored in data members of the current class, and the position and the color are stored in data members inherited from the base class. The only other method defined in the class is the **draw()** method.

Note that we must add an **import** statement to add the **SketchView** class definition to the file. Because we have defined this class in the package, **Elements**, the **SketchView** class is not directly accessible, since it is in the **Sketcher** directory. The alternative to the **import** statement would be to use the fully qualified name for the **SketchView** class including the full path when we use it in the parameter list to the constructor, which is clearly not a good idea.

The Constructor for a Text Element

The **Graphics** object, **g**, for the view enables us to get the font metrics object **fm**. By calling the **getHeight()** method for **fm** we obtain the overall height of the font—in other words the spacing from one line of text to the next. The overall height of the text block is going to be the value of **height** multiplied by the number of lines of text—which is given by the length of the array, **text[]**.

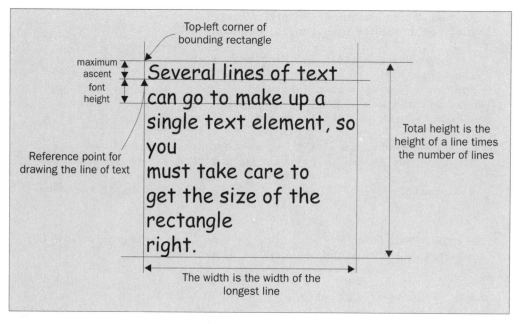

The width of the block of text will be the width of the longest text line. We obtain this value by getting the width of each line of text by calling the **stringWidth()** method for each element of the array, **text[]**. Using the **max()** method from the **Math** class in the **for** loop, we get the largest of these width values.

Since the reference point for a line of text is on the baseline, we must define the top of the rectangle enclosing the text as a distance above the point, **position**, that corresponds to the maximum ascent of the font characters. This distance is returned by the **getMaxAscent()** method for the **FontMetrics** object, **fm**. Didn't you just know that all that stuff about fonts in Chapter 11 was going to turn out to be useful sooner or later? The width and height of the rectangle are one pixel larger than the width and height we calculated for the text to ensure the text is fully inside the rectangle.

Drawing a Text Element

The text lines are drawn in the **for** loop, after we have set the font and the color in the graphics context. Each line after the first has its y-coordinate incremented by **height**. This moves the reference point down the distance that is required between lines for the font.

We can now use the **TextDialog** to help us create text elements.

Try It Out—Creating Text Elements

1 We will create text elements in the **mousePressed()** handler method in the **MouseButtonHandler** inner class to the document class, **SketchDoc**. We will need an extra data member in the **SketchDoc** class to store the current font, so add the following statement at the end of the statements for the existing data members:

```
protected Graphics tempG;              // Context for temporary element
protected Font font = new Font("Times Roman", Font.PLAIN, 10);

public SketchDoc(Sketcher theApp)
{
  ...
```

This defines the default font to be used for **TextElement** objects. We will add the capability to choose different fonts a little later in this chapter.

2 To create text elements we will need to treat the situation where the **elementType** variable has the value **TEXT** as a special case. To do this, we can modify the **mousePressed()** method as follows:

```
public void mousePressed(MouseEvent e)
{
  if(e.getModifiers()==InputEvent.BUTTON1_MASK)
  {
    elementPosition = e.getPoint();                  // Save cursor position
    if(elementType==TEXT)
```

```
    {
      TextDialog textDlg = new TextDialog(theApp.getAppWindow());
      textDlg.setVisible(true);                  // Display the dialog

      // When we return to here the dialog has been closed
      String[] text = textDlg.getText(); // Get the text from the dialog
      textDlg.dispose();                         // Release the dialog resources

      if(text!=null)
      { // If we get some text then create an element
        TextElement textElement = new TextElement(view, elementPosition,
                                      text, font, elementColor);
        addElement(textElement);       // Add the element to the document
        Rectangle bounds = textElement.getBounds();  // Get the bounds
        view.repaint(bounds.x, bounds.y, bounds.width, bounds.height);
      }
    }
    else
    {
      tempG = e.getComponent().getGraphics();     // Get graphics context
      if(elementType!=CURVE)         // If it is not a curve...set XOR mode
        tempG.setXORMode(e.getComponent().getBackground());
    }
  }
}
```

How It Works

The original code which set XOR mode except when we are drawing a curve is now in the **else** clause of the **if** statement we have added to check the element type for **TEXT**. If we are to create a text element, we instantiate a **TextDialog** object and display it by calling its **setVisible()** method with the argument **true**. Because the dialog is modal, the code following the **setVisible()** call will not be executed until the dialog is closed. This could be by selecting either of the buttons. We retrieve a reference to the text array that is stored in the dialog by calling the **getText()** method. If **null** is returned then either the Cancel button was pressed, or no text had been entered when the OK button was pressed. In either case we do nothing. Note that after we retrieve the text from the dialog object, **textDlg**, we call its **dispose()** method, inherited from the **Window** class. This disposes of the dialog window and releases the system resources that it was using.

If variable text is not **null** we use it to create a **TextElement** at the current cursor position, and with the current font and color. We add this element to the document by passing it to the **addElement()** method. Finally we get the bounding rectangle for the element and use this to get the region of the view occupied by the new element redrawn.

Testing the TextDialog Class

All you need to do now is compile the new classes and recompile the old ones we have changed. To open the text dialog, select the TEXT button and click in the view where you want the text to appear.

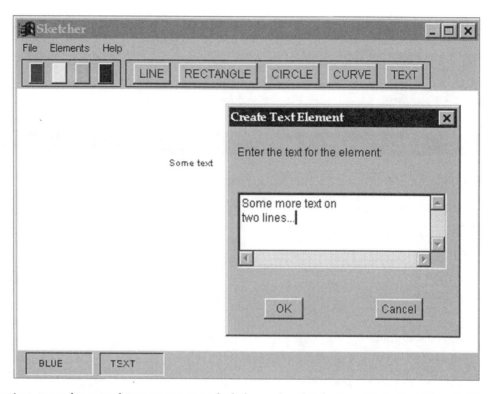

You just type the text that you want and click on the OK button. Note that the scrollbars on the **TextArea** object are inactive initially. Although we specified that the **TextArea** object should have four lines of thirty characters, and this is the amount you can see within the component—you can add as much as you want. Try adding longer lines, and more than four lines. The scrollbars will come into operation automatically when you enter more text than can be seen directly in the component.

A Font Selection Dialog

A font dialog will enable us to change the font for text elements to any of those available on the system. It will also give us a chance to see how we get at and process the fonts that are available, and learn yet more about how we can use components in a dialog. Let's first establish what our font dialog will do.

We want to be able to choose the font name from those available on the system, the style of the font and the point size. The dialog will therefore need to obtain a list of the fonts available and display them in a component. It will also need a component to allow the point size to be selected, and it must provide a means whereby the style can be chosen.

We can use **Choice** components to display the font names, and to list the point sizes, and we can provide check boxes for the choice of styles. The fact that we have three possible styles **ITALIC**, **BOLD** and **PLAIN**, is a bit misleading because we don't need to provide three possible choices. These three boil down to two choices for font styles, either **BOLD** or not, and either **ITALIC** or not, as the **PLAIN** style means *not* **BOLD** and *not* **ITALIC**. That covers the provision for choosing a font. The dialog will be modal and it will need an OK button and a Cancel button to close it.

We can start by defining the **FontDialog** class with its data members and its constructor, and come back to the question of listeners when we have done that.

Try It Out—A FontDialog Class

1 Here's the code for the outline of the class:

```
// Class to define a dialog to choose a font
import java.awt.*;
import java.awt.event.*;

class FontDialog extends Dialog implements Constants
{
  SketchDoc sketch;              // Reference to the document
  String fontName= null;         // Font name
  int fontStyle ;                // Font style - Plain,Bold,Italic
  int fontSize;                  // Font point size

  // Constructor
  public FontDialog(Sketcher theApp)
  {
    // Code to initialize the data members...

    // Code to create buttons and the button Panel...

    // Code to create the data input panel ...

    // Code to create the font choice and add it to the input panel...

    // Code to create the font size choice
    //  and add it to the input panel...

    // Code to create the font style check boxes
    //  and add them to the input panel...
  }
}
```

2 The code to initialize the data members within the **FontDialog** constructor of the font dialog is easy:

```
public FontDialog(Sketcher theApp)
{
  // Call the base constructor to create a modal dialog
  super(theApp.getAppWindow(), "Font Selection", true);

  sketch = theApp.getDocument();          // Store the document reference
```

```
// Set dialog position a third down and across the app window
Rectangle bounds = theApp.getAppWindow().getBounds();  // Frame bounds
setLocation(bounds.x + bounds.width/3, bounds.y + bounds.height/3);

Font font = sketch.getFont();                  // Get the current font
fontName = font.getName();                     // Set current as default
fontStyle = font.getStyle();                   // ...style
fontSize = font.getSize();                     // ...and size
```

```
// Plus the code for the rest of the constructor...
}
```

3 The `getFont()` method does not exist at the moment, so while we have it in mind, open the **SketchDoc.java** file and add a definition for it to the **SketchDoc** class:

```
// Get the document font
public Font getFont()
{
  return font;
}
```

4 Next we can add the code to the constructor that will create the button panel that we will place at the bottom of the dialog using the default **BorderLayout** manager:

```
public FontDialog(Sketcher theApp)
{
  // Initialization as before...
```

```
// Create the dialog button panel
Panel buttonPane = new Panel();      // Create the panel to hold buttons
GridBagLayout gbLayout = new GridBagLayout();   // Create the layout
buttonPane.setLayout(gbLayout);                 // Set the layout

// Define the initial constraints
GridBagConstraints constraints = new GridBagConstraints();
constraints.weightx = 1.0;
constraints.weighty = 1.0;
constraints.insets = new Insets(5, 10, 5, 10);
constraints.fill = GridBagConstraints.NONE;
constraints.gridwidth = 1;

// Create and add the buttons to the buttonPane
Button button;                                  // Store a button
gbLayout.setConstraints(button = new Button("  OK  "), constraints);
buttonPane.add(button);                         // Add the OK button
button.addActionListener(new ButtonHandler(OK)); // OK listener
constraints.gridwidth = GridBagConstraints.REMAINDER;
gbLayout.setConstraints(button = new Button("Cancel"), constraints);
buttonPane.add(button);                         // Add the Cancel button
button.addActionListener(new ButtonHandler(CANCEL)); // Cancel listener
```

```
    add(buttonPane, BorderLayout.SOUTH);    // Add the button pane to dialog

  // Plus the code for the rest of the constructor...
  }
```

5 We can now add a panel to contain the components that will receive input. We will have a **Choice** object for the font names, a **Choice** object for the point size of the font and a couple of **Checkbox** objects for selecting the font style. We will add the code to create the panel and add the component to deal with font names first:

```
public FontDialog(Sketcher theApp)
{
  // Initialization as before...

  // Button panel code as before...

  // Set up the data input panel
  Panel dataPane = new Panel();    // Create the data entry panel
  gbLayout = new GridBagLayout(); // Create the layout
  dataPane.setLayout(gbLayout);    // Set the layout
  constraints.gridwidth = 3;
  constraints.anchor = GridBagConstraints.WEST;

  // Add the font choice label
  Label label = new Label("Choose a font");
  gbLayout.setConstraints(label, constraints);
  dataPane.add(label);

  // Set up font list choice component
  Toolkit theKit = getToolkit();                     // Get the dialog toolkit
  String[] fontList = theKit.getFontList();          // Get available fonts
  Choice chooseFont = new Choice();                  // Create choice of fonts
  for(int i = 0; i < fontList.length; i++)
    chooseFont.addItem(fontList[i]);                 // Add font name
  chooseFont.select(fontName);                       // Select current font
  chooseFont.addItemListener(new FontListener()); // Add font listener

  // Add the font list choice
  constraints.gridwidth = GridBagConstraints.REMAINDER;
  gbLayout.setConstraints(chooseFont, constraints);
  dataPane.add(chooseFont);
```

```
  // Plus the code for the rest of the constructor...
  }
```

6 The next two components we want to add to the **dataPane** are the **Label** object supplying prompt for the point size input and the **Choice** object to provide the range of point sizes. The code to do that is as follows:

```
public FontDialog(Sketcher theApp)
{
  // Initialization as before...
```

```
// Button panel code as before...

// Set up the data input panel as before...

// The font name choice as before...
```

```
// Set up the size label
label = new Label("Choose point size");         // Prompt for point size
constraints.gridwidth = 1;
gbLayout.setConstraints(label, constraints);
dataPane.add(label);                            // Add the prompt

// Set up the size choice
String[] sizeList = { "8", "10", "12", "14", "16", "18", "20", "22",
                      "24"};
Choice chooseSize = new Choice();
for(int i = 0; i < sizeList.length; i++)
  chooseSize.addItem(sizeList[i]);              // Add size
chooseSize.select(Integer.toString(fontSize));  // Default selection
chooseSize.addItemListener(new SizeListener()); // Add size listener

// Add the size list choice
constraints.gridwidth = GridBagConstraints.REMAINDER;
gbLayout.setConstraints(chooseSize, constraints);
dataPane.add(chooseSize);
```

```
    // Plus the code for the rest of the constructor...
  }
```

7 The last row in the **dataPane** will be occupied by the check boxes used to select the font style. The code to add these is as follows:

```
public FontDialog(Sketcher theApp)
{
  // Initialization as before...

  // Button panel code as before...

  // Set up the data input panel as before...

  // The font name choice as before...

  // The font size choice as before...
```

```
// Set up style options
Checkbox boldBox = new Checkbox("Bold", (fontStyle & Font.BOLD) > 0);
boldBox.addItemListener(new StyleListener(Font.BOLD));
Checkbox italicBox = new Checkbox("Italic", (fontStyle&Font.ITALIC)>0);
italicBox.addItemListener(new StyleListener(Font.ITALIC));

// Add style options
```

```
        constraints.gridwidth = 1;
        gbLayout.setConstraints(italicBox, constraints);
        dataPane.add(italicBox);
        constraints.gridwidth = GridBagConstraints.REMAINDER;
        gbLayout.setConstraints(boldBox, constraints);
        dataPane.add(boldBox);

        add(dataPane, BorderLayout.CENTER);
        pack();
    }
```

How It Works

Ideally the dialog should operate in a self-contained way. This will mean that the font stored in the document object will be automatically updated by the dialog when the OK button is pressed. To do this the dialog will need a reference to the document object. Of course, the dialog will also need a reference to the **SketchFrame** object that represents the application window, since this will be the parent **Frame** object for the dialog. The simplest way to provide access to both of these is to pass a reference to the application object, **theApp**, to the dialog constructor. This object, of class **Sketcher**, has methods we can use to get both the references we require in the font dialog.

The FontDialog Constructor

We save the reference to the document in the **sketch** data member because we will want to use it to update the font in the document in the OK button handler. We set the position of the dialog relative to the top-left corner of the application window—a third of the way down and a third of the distance across. We then get a reference to the current document font by calling the **getFont()** method for the **sketch** object, and save the details of it in data members of the dialog. We will be updating these in the event handlers for the various input components we will add to the dialog.

Adding the Buttons

It looks like quite a chunk of code but it's very easy and you have seen it all before. The **buttonPane** panel uses a **GridBagLayout** manager with the constraints set the way we have seen previously for placing buttons. We create and add the OK and Cancel buttons and provide them both with a listener of type **ButtonHandler**. We will add **ButtonHandler** as an inner class to the **FontDialog** class a little later on. When the buttons have been added, we add the **buttonPane** to the bottom of the dialog window using the default **BorderLayout** manager.

Adding the Font Name Choice

We use the **GridBagLayout** manager for the **dataPane** panel. By setting the **anchor** constraint to **WEST**, we will position components left-justified in the **Panel** object. The first component that we add is a **Label** object, **label**, which will display a prompt for the font name choice component.

Before we can set up the font names choice component we must get hold the fonts that are available. Since the dialog is a window, we can call its **getToolkit()** method to obtain a

Toolkit object. The **getFontList()** method for the **Toolkit** object returns a **String** array containing the names of all the fonts that are available. The **Choice** object, **chooseFont**, will provide the means to choose a font name. The font names are added to the component in the **for** loop. Each name from the array, **fontList[]** is passed to the **addItem()** method for the **chooseFont** object. These will be displayed in a drop-down list by the component. By passing the current font to the **select()** method for the **Choice** object, we ensure that this will be the default selection in the list. The listener for the **chooseFont** object is of type **FontListener**. We will add **FontListener** as an inner class to **FontDialog**. The **chooseFont** component is added to the **dataPane** panel with the **gridwidth** constraint set to **REMAINDER**. This will place the component to the right of the previous **label** component which displays the prompt. The next component that we add will begin a new row in the layout.

Adding the Font Size Choice

The **Label** object here is similar to the previous one. Since we are starting a new row in the layout, we must set the **gridwidth** constraint back to 1 before adding it to the panel. The range of point sizes is set up in the **String** array **sizeList[]**. Why don't we set up the size values as integers? For the simple reason that the **Choice** component requires **String** objects as items. We will convert the chosen point size back to an integer value before we use it in the event handler for the component.

The listener for the **Choice** component is of type **SizeListener**, so we will need yet another inner class to define it. Each of the items in the choice list are added in the way you have seen with the previous **Choice** component—using the **addItem()** method. The current font point size is set as the default selection in the list by passing it to the **select()** method for the **chooseSize** object. Of course, it must be a **String** object, so we convert it using the **toString()** method in the **Integer** class. To make the **chooseSize** component fill up the rest of the row, we set the **gridwidth** constraint to **REMAINDER**.

Adding Font Style Selection

This is the last block of code in the constructor. Two **Checkbox** components are created— **boldBox** which will select the **BOLD** style when it is checked, and **italicBox** which will select the **ITALIC** style when it is checked. They both have a listener of type **StyleListener**, so we will add one more inner class to the **FontDialog** class to define this kind of listener.

We must set the **gridwidth** constraint back to 1 again to start a new row in the layout. We then add both **Checkbox** components in the same row. The last step is to add the **dataPane** panel centered in the dialog window before calling **pack()** to set the size of the **FontDialog** to accommodate the components it contains.

Defining the Font Dialog Listeners

We have four inner classes to add to the **FontDialog** class to define the listeners for the various components receiving input, and the dialog buttons. The inner class to define button listeners is the easiest because we have seen this on several occasions, so let's add that first.

Try It Out—Defining the `ButtonHandler` Class

1 This will work exactly as we have seen previously. A class object will store the ID of the button for which it is listening. You can add the following definition of the `ButtonHandler` inner class to the `FontDialog` class:

```java
// Class defining listener for text dialog button events
class ButtonHandler implements ActionListener
{
  int buttonID;                                  // ID for button

  // Constructor
  public ButtonHandler(int buttonID)
  {
    this.buttonID = buttonID;                    // Save the button ID
  }

  // Handle button press
  public void actionPerformed(ActionEvent e)
  {
    requestFocus();                              // Focus to the dialog window
    // If  the OK was pressed, update the document
    if(buttonID == OK)
      sketch.setFont(new Font(fontName, fontStyle, fontSize));

    setVisible(false);                           // Hide the dialog anyway
  }
}
```

2 The `setFont()` method is another method that doesn't yet exist, so open the `SketchDoc.java` file once again and add the following definition to the class:

```java
// Set the document font
public void setFont(Font font)
{
  this.font = font;
}
```

How It Works

The constructor just saves the button ID that it receives as an argument. Since the `actionPerformed()` method always calls the `requestFocus()` method for the dialog object first, focus is always returned to the window before the dialog closes. If the OK button was pressed, the `actionPerformed()` method constructs a font from the font name, point size and style, that are stored in the dialog, and passes it to the `SketchDoc` object, `sketch`, using the `setFont()` method.

Back in the `actionPerformed()` method in the `ButtonHandler` class, the `setVisible()` method is called with the argument **false** to hide the dialog if either button was pressed. Of course, for the Cancel button that's all it does.

A **StyleListener** object deals with changes to the font style. This class must implement the **ItemListener** interface because **Checkbox** components generate events of type **ItemEvent**. Checking or unchecking a **Checkbox** component will generate an **ItemEvent**, and cause the **itemStateChanged()** method for the registered listener object to be called.

Try It Out—Defining the *StyleListener Class*

Add the following definition for the **StyleListener** inner class to the **FontDialog** class:

```
// Class defining listener for font style selection events
class StyleListener implements ItemListener
{
  int style;      // Font style for the listener

  // Constructor
  public StyleListener(int style)
  {
    this.style = style;
  }

  // Handler for font style selection events
  public void itemStateChanged(ItemEvent e)
  {
    if(e.getStateChange() == ItemEvent.SELECTED)
      fontStyle |= style;      // Set the style
    else
      fontStyle &= ~style;     // Reset the style
  }
}
```

How It Works

An object of this class will listen for events concerned with checking or unchecking the **BOLD** check box, or the **ITALIC** check box, and in each case the object will store the applicable font style in its data member, **style**. When a check box that is unchecked is checked, the **getStateChange()** method for the **ItemEvent** object passed to the method, **itemStateChanged()**, will return the **SELECTED** value defined in the **ItemEvent** class. If a checked check box is unchecked, the **UNSELECTED** value is returned by **getStateChange()**. When **SELECTED** is returned, we want to set the style to the style for the listener, so we OR the style stored in the listener with the current style stored in the dialog. This is necessary to preserve the other style if it is set, **BOLD** for example if this is an **ITALIC** listener, or vice versa. You will remember from Chapter 2 that OR is used to set flags, and you AND the NOT of a flag to remove it.

If **getStateChange()** does not return **SELECTED**, it must be because the check box has been unchecked, so we AND the NOT of the style stored in the listener with the style in the dialog to reset it. The result of all this is that whenever you check or uncheck either of the check boxes in the font dialog, the **style** member of the dialog will be updated.

A **FontListener** object deals with events that arise from the **Choice** component in the font dialog that allows a new font name to be selected. This also generates events of type **ItemEvent**, so the class defining the listener must implement the ItemListener interface.

Try It Out—Defining the *FontListener Class*

Add the following inner class definition to the **FontDialog** class:

```
// Class defining listener for font choice events
class FontListener implements ItemListener
{
  // Handle font selection event
  public void itemStateChanged(ItemEvent e)
  {
    fontName = (String)e.getItem();
  }
}
```

How It Works

This turns out to be very simple. We don't even need to define a constructor—the default constructor will be fine. All the **itemStateChanged()** method does is to call the **getItem()** method for the event object, **e**. This method will return the item that was selected in the **Choice** object as type **Object**. We stored the font names as **String** objects in the component, so we cast the reference returned to type **String** before storing it in the **fontName** member of the **FontDialog** object. Thus, each time you select a font name from the drop-down list in the component, the **fontName** member of the dialog will be updated.

The **SizeListener** class will define the listener object for the **Choice** component that provides a selection of point sizes for you to choose from. This is also very simple.

Try It Out—Defining the *SizeListener Class*

Add the following inner class definition to the **FontDialog** class definition:

```
// Class defining listener for font size events
class SizeListener implements ItemListener
{
  // Handle font size selection event
  public void itemStateChanged(ItemEvent e)
  {
    fontSize = Integer.parseInt((String)e.getItem());
  }
}
```

How It Works

This works in a similar way to the previous listener, but we want the item in the list that is selected to end up as type **int**. We achieve this in two stages. The **getItem()** method for the event returns the item that was selected as type **Object**. We cast this to type **String**, and then pass it as an argument to the `parseInt()` method that is defined in the `Integer` class. This will return the `int` value that is equivalent to the digits in the `String` object and this is stored in the `fontSize` member of the dialog. This listener will update the value in `fontSize` each time you choose a new size.

The `parseInt()` method will throw a `NumberFormatException` if the argument does not contain characters that define an integer, so if there is any doubt about the `String` you are converting—if the `String` was keyed in for instance—then you should put the method call in a `try` block and catch the exception.

Try It Out—Using the Font Dialog

1 We can add a button to the toolbar to open the font dialog. We just need to define a `FontButton` class that handles its own events and add an extra `buttonGroup` object in the constructor containing a `FontButton` button. First of all, add the following data member to our `Toolbar` class:

```
ButtonGroup fontGroup = new ButtonGroup();   // Group to select a font
```

2 Next we can modify the constructor for the `Toolbar` class:

```
public Toolbar(Sketcher theApp)
{
  this.theApp = theApp;                       // Store the app reference
  setLayout(new FlowLayout(FlowLayout.LEFT,5,2));  // Set flow layout
  setBackground(Color.lightGray);

  // Code to add the element color button group as before...

  // Code to add the element type button group as before...

  // Add the font button in its own group
  fontGroup.add(new FontButton());          // Create and add the button
  add(fontGroup);                           // Add the group to the toolbar
}
```

3 All we need now is the `FontButton` class definition. We can add this as an inner class to the `Toolbar` class. The `FontButton` class definition will be:

```
// Font selection button
class FontButton extends Button
{
  // Constructor
  public FontButton()
  {
    setLabel(" FONT ");                     // Set the button label
    enableEvents(AWTEvent.ACTION_EVENT_MASK);
  }
```

```
    // Handle font button press
    protected void processActionEvent(ActionEvent e)
    {
      FontDialog dialog = new FontDialog(theApp);
      dialog.setVisible(true);          // Make dialog visible
      dialog.dispose();                 // Release the dialog resources
    }
  }
```

If you compile **FontDialog.java** and recompile **Toolbar.java** and **SketchDoc.java**, you will be ready to run Sketcher again to try out the font dialog.

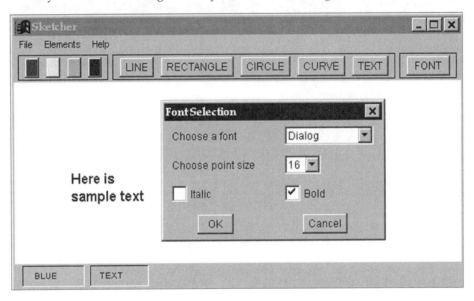

How It Works

The first stage defines the **ButtonGroup** object that will contain the **FONT** button. Remember that we defined the **ButtonGroup** class so that objects will be automatically highlighted by drawing a rectangle around them.

Next we create a **FontButton** object for the **fontGroup** that we defined as a member of the **Toolbar** class, and then add the **fontGroup** object to the **Toolbar**.

Lastly, the constructor sets the label for the button, and enables action events for the class. When the button is pressed the **processActionEvent()** method will be called. This will create a **FontDialog** object and display the dialog it represents. When the dialog window closes, the **setVisible()** method will return control to the **processActionEvent()** method, and the **dispose()** method for the dialog object will be called to release any system resources acquired by the dialog window.

Our font dialog works OK but it could do with some improvement. First of all the close icon at the top right of the dialog window doesn't work, and we don't know what the font looks like when we change it. Let's fix both of these deficiencies.

Try It Out—Enhancing the Font Dialog

1 Depending on your screen size and resolution, you may find that the initial application window is not large enough initially to display the FONT button. We can fix this by changing the `init()` method in the `Sketcher` class so that it always adjusts the size of the application window to accommodate the toolbar. You can modify the `init()` method as follows:

```
public void init()
{
  sketch = new SketchDoc(this);                   // Define the document
  sketch.addView(view = new SketchView(sketch));
  window = new SketchFrame("Sketcher", this);  // Create the app window
  window.addView(view);               // Add the document view
  Toolkit theKit = window.getToolkit();        // Get the window toolkit
  Dimension wndSize = theKit.getScreenSize();  // Get screen size

  //Set the position to screen center & size to at least half screen size
  Dimension prefSize = window.getPreferredSize();   // Get preferred size
  window.setBounds(wndSize.width/6, wndSize.height/6,        // Position
             Math.max(prefSize.width, 2*wndSize.width/3), // Width
             2*wndSize.height/3);                          // Height

  window.addWindowListener(new WindowHandler());  // Add window listener
  window.setVisible(true);                        // Display the window
  window.requestFocus();                          // Request the focus
}
```

2 To make the close icon work, we can make the dialog class handle its own window events, then close the dialog in the `processWindowEvent()` method before the class. First you need to add one line to the end of the code in the `FontDialog` constructor:

```
enableEvents(AWTEvent.WINDOW_EVENT_MASK);
```

3 This will enable window events for the dialog to be directed to the `processWindowEvent()` method in the class. We can implement this as:

```
// Handle dialog closing event
protected void processWindowEvent(WindowEvent e)
{
  requestFound();                             // Focus to the dialog window
  if(e.getID()==WindowEvent.WINDOW_CLOSING)   // For window closing event
    setVisible(false);                        // ... hide the dialog
  super.processWindowEvent(e);                // Pass on the event
}
```

4 A preview of the font is rather easy to add to the `FontDialog` class. First we will add members to the `FontDialog` class to store a `TextArea` component and a `String` object that it will display as sample text. Add the following lines to the end of the data member definitions in the class:

```
String sampleText = "This is a sample of the font";
TextArea fontSample;              // Will show a sample of the current font
```

5 Next we will modify the `FontDialog` constructor to add the `fontSample` component to the end of the `dataPane` so that it displays the sample string stored in the data member, `sampleText`, in the current font. This code goes just before we add the `dataPane` to the dialog in the constructor:

```
public FontDialog(Sketcher theApp)
{
  // Initialize and create the button and data panels as before...

  // Add the display for a sample of the current font
  constraints.fill = GridBagConstraints.HORIZONTAL;
  fontSample = new TextArea(sampleText,1, 30, TextArea.SCROLLBARS_NONE);
  fontSample.setFont(font);                    // Set current font
  constraints.gridwidth = GridBagConstraints.REMAINDER;
  gbLayout.setConstraints(fontSample,constraints);
  dataPane.add(fontSample);                    // Add to the data pane

  add(dataPane, BorderLayout.CENTER);
  pack();
  enableEvents(AWTEvent.WINDOW_EVENT_MASK);
}
```

6 We will want to update the `TextArea` component each time the font name, the font size or the font style is changed, so we must alter the methods that deal with these events in the inner classes. All the changes are quite minor.

Here's the modified version of the method in the `FontListener` class:

```
// Handle font selection event
public void itemStateChanged(ItemEvent e)
{
  fontName = (String)e.getItem();
  fontSample.setFont(new Font(fontName, fontStyle, fontSize));
}
```

7 We add the same line of code to the other methods handling input component events in the font dialog. We need to change the method in the `SizeListener` class to:

```
// Handle font size selection event
public void itemStateChanged(ItemEvent e)
{
  fontSize = Integer.parseInt((String)e.getItem());
  fontSample.setFont(new Font(fontName, fontStyle, fontSize));
}
```

8 And the method in the **StyleListener** class becomes:

```
// Handler for font style selection events
public void itemStateChanged(ItemEvent e)
{
  System.out.println("Style change event "+ e.getStateChange());
  if(e.getStateChange()==ItemEvent.SELECTED)
    fontStyle |= style;      // Set the style
  else
    fontStyle &= ~style;     // Reset the style
  fontSample.setFont(new Font(fontName, fontStyle, fontSize));
}
```

That's it. You can recompile **FontDialog.java** and try the Sketcher application again.

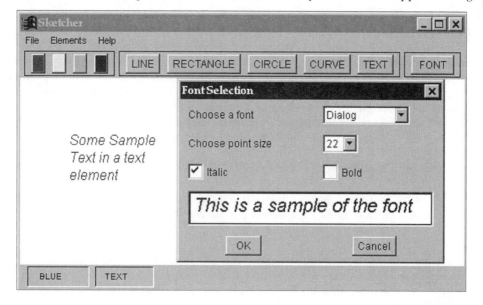

Now we get positive confirmation of what the font looks like, before we commit to using it. Each time you change some aspect of the font, the sample text changes to reflect the new font. Isn't that pretty?

How It Works

The code to set the initial size of the application window has been changed so that it is always at least two-thirds the width of the screen, but is adjusted to the width of the toolbar if the preferred width of the toolbar is larger. The size of the toolbar is obtained by calling its **getPreferredSize()** method which returns the size as a **Dimension** object. This has data members **width** and **height** which contain the preferred width and height of the toolbar in pixels.

The second and third stages just hide the dialog window when the **WINDOW_CLOSING** event occurs, allowing control to return to the point where the dialog was displayed—the **FontButton** class handler we added to the **Toolbar** class. In case there are listeners registered for window events we pass the event on—there aren't in our case but it's good practice.

691

Displaying a Sample of the Font

The advantage of using a **TextArea** component is that you can enter your own text to see what that looks like in the current font, as well as viewing the sample text that is displayed. We want the **TextArea** component to be the width of the dialog, so we set the fill constraint to **HORIZONTAL**. The **TextArea** object is created with the sample text, and has one row of thirty characters. It is created with no scrollbars because we don't need addition lines of text or more characters per line. When the constraints are set, we just add the **fontSample** component to the **dataPane** panel.

In the modified listener classes, we simply reset the font in the **fontSample** component to the new font defined using the selected font name. The sample text will now appear in the new font.

Pop-Up Menus

The **java.awt** package defines a class **PopupMenu** that represents a menu that you can pop-up at any position within a component, but usually at the current mouse cursor position. A pop-up menu is typically displayed when a mouse button is pressed. There are two constructors in the **PopupMenu** class, one that you pass a **String** object to that defines a name for the menu, and a default constructor that defines a menu without a name. If you specify a name for a pop-up menu with a statement such as:

```
generalPopup = new PopupMenu("General");
```

the name is only for identification purposes—it is not displayed when the menu is popped up. This is different from a menu on a menu bar where the string you pass to the constructor is what appears on the menu bar.

To populate a pop-up menu with menu items, you add **MenuItem** objects or **CheckboxMenuItem** objects, just as you would with a menu on a menu bar. Handling the events for the menu items is also an identical process to that which you have seen already for regular menu items.

A pop-up menu must have a parent component. The component class defines the **add()** method which accepts a **PopupMenu** object as an argument. You display a pop-up within the coordinate system of its parent component, by calling the **show()** method for the **PopupMenu** object. The method requires three arguments to be specified, a reference to the parent component for the pop-up, and the x and y coordinates where the menu is to be displayed, relative to the origin of the parent. For example:

```
generalPopup.show(view, xCoord, yCoord);
```

This displays the pop-up at position (**xCoord**, **yCoord**) in the coordinate system for the component, **view**. It assumes that the object, **generalPopup**, has been added to the container, **view**, using the **add()** method for the component **view**.

A pop-up menu is often implemented as a context menu. A context menu is a pop-up menu that appears when you press a mouse button—usually the right mouse button—and which displays a different set of menu items depending on the context—that is, what is under the cursor. We will now look more closely at how this works, and how we could implement a context menu capability in Sketcher.

Implementing a Context Menu

As a context menu displays a different menu when the right mouse button is clicked depending on the context, it follows that the program needs to know what is under the cursor at the time the mouse button is pressed. Let's take the specific instance of the view in Sketcher. We could define two contexts for the cursor—one when an element is under the cursor, and another when there is no element under the cursor. In the first context, we could display a pop-up menu of a general nature—the same menu items as in the **Elements** menu on the menu bar, say—while, in the second, we could have a special pop-up menu that is particularly applicable to an element—with menu items to delete the element, or move it, for example. For the context menu to be really useful, the user also needs to know which element is under the cursor before they pop-up the context menu, otherwise they can't be sure to which element the pop-up menu is referring. What we need is some visual feedback when an element is under the cursor—highlighting the element under the cursor by changing its color, for instance.

Try It Out—Highlighting an Element

1 To highlight an element, we will draw it in magenta rather than its normal color. Every element will need a **boolean** variable to indicate whether it is highlighted or not. This variable will be used to determine which color should be used in the **draw()** method. We can add this variable as a data member of the **Element** class:

```
protected boolean highlighted = false;          // Highlight flag
```

You can add this line immediately following the statements for the other data members in the **Element** class definition. The variable **highlighted** will be inherited by all of the sub-classes of **Element**.

2 We can also add the method to set the **highlighted** flag to the **Element** class:

```
// Set or reset highlight color
public void setHighlight(boolean highlighted)
{
  this.highlighted = highlighted;
}
```

3 To implement highlighting, you need to change one line in the **draw()** method for each of the sub-classes of **Element**—that is, **LineElement**, **CircleElement**, **CurveElement**, **RectangleElement** and **TextElement**. The line to change is the one that sets the drawing color—it's the first line in each of the **draw()** methods. You should change it to:

```
g.setColor(highlighted?Color.magenta:color);
```

693

How It Works

The **setSelectMode()** method accepts a **boolean** value as an argument and stores it in the data member, **highlighted**. When you want an element to be highlighted, you just call this method with the argument as **true**. To switch highlighting off for an element, you call this method with the argument **false**.

Previously, the **setColor()** statement just set the color stored in the data member, **color**, as the drawing color. Now, if highlighted is **true**, the color will be set to magenta, and if highlighted is **false**, the color stored in the data member, **color**, will be used.

To make use of this to provide the visual feedback necessary for a user-friendly implementation of the context menu, we need to determine at all times what is under the cursor. This means we must track and analyze all mouse moves.

Tracking Mouse Moves

Whenever the mouse is moved, the **mouseMoved()** method in the **MouseMotionListener** interface is called. We can therefore track mouse moves by implementing this method in the **MoveHandler** class that is an inner class to the **SketchDoc** class. Before we get into that, we need to decide what we mean by an element being under the cursor, and how we are going to find out to which element, if any, this applies.

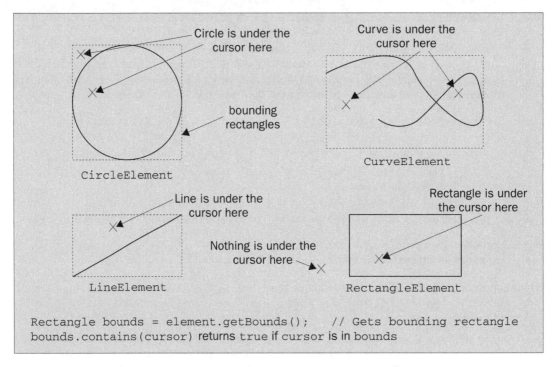

It's not going to be too difficult. We can arbitrarily decide that an element is under the cursor when the cursor position is inside the bounding rectangle for an element. This is not too precise a method, but it has the great attraction that it avoids all the math involved in determining the shortest distance from a point to a circle or an arbitrary curve. Electing to add all that complexity will not help us to understand the principles here, so we will stick with the simple approach.

So what is going to be the methodology for finding the element under the cursor? Whenever the mouse is moved, we can just search through the bounding rectangles for each of the elements in the document until we find one that encloses the current cursor position. We will then arrange for this element to be highlighted. If we get right through all the elements in the document without finding a bounding rectangle that encloses the cursor, there isn't one.

To record a reference to the element that is under the cursor, we will add a data member to the **SketchDoc** class of type **Element**. If there isn't an element under the cursor, we will make sure this data member is **null**.

Try It Out—Referring to Elements

1 Add the following statement following the statements declaring the other data members in the **SketchDoc** class definition:

```
protected Element highlightElement;                // Highlighted element
```

2 The **mouseMoved()** method is going to be called very frequently, so we need to make sure it executes as fast as possible. This means that for any given set of conditions, we execute the minimum amount of code. Here's the implementation of the **mouseMoved()** method in the **MouseMoveHandler** class in **SketchDoc**:

```
// Handle mouse moves
public void mouseMoved(MouseEvent e)
{
  Point currentCursor = e.getPoint();   // Get current cursor position
  Graphics localG = null;               // Store for graphics context
  Element element = null;               // Stores an element

  // Go through all elements until one is found under the cursor
  for(Enumeration elmnts = sketchElements.elements();
                  elmnts.hasMoreElements(); )
  {
    element = (Element)(elmnts.nextElement());        // Get an element
    if(element.getBounds().contains(currentCursor))   // Under the cursor?
    {
      if(element==highlightElement)                // If its already highlighted
        return;                                    // we are done

      localG = e.getComponent().getGraphics(); // Get graphics context

      if(highlightElement!=null)                 // If an element is highlighted
      {
        highlightElement.setHighlight(false); // Unhighlight it and
        highlightElement.draw(localG);         // draw it normal color
      }
```

```
            element.setHighlight(true);    // Set highlight for new element
            highlightElement = element;    // Store new highlighted element
            element.draw(localG);          // Draw it highlighted
            localG.dispose();              // Release graphic context resources
            return;
        }
    }
    // Here there is no element under the cursor so...
    if(highlightElement!=null)                 // If an element is highlighted
    {
      localG = e.getComponent().getGraphics(); // Get graphics context
      highlightElement.setHighlight(false);    // ... reset it
      highlightElement.draw(localG);           // Redraw the element
      highlightElement = null;                 // No element highlighted
      localG.dispose();                  // Release graphic context resources
    }
  }
```

To check that highlighting works, recompile **SketchDoc.java** and all the classes in the
Elements package and run Sketcher again. If you draw a few elements, you should see
them change color as the cursor moves over them.

How It Works

It's quite a lot of code, so let's work through it step by step. The first statement saves the
current cursor position in the local variable, **currentCursor**. The next two statements create
a **Graphics** variable, **localG**, and declare a variable, **element**, that we will use to store
each element that we retrieve from the document. The variable, **localG** will be used to
hold a graphics context for the document view when we need to draw an element—to
highlight or un-highlight it.

The **for** loop uses an **Enumeration** to iterate through the elements in the document—you
have seen how this works previously. In the loop, we obtain the bounding rectangle for
each element by calling its **getBounds()** method, and then call the **contains()** method for
the rectangle that is returned. This will return **true** if the rectangle encloses the point,
currentCursor, that is passed as an argument. When we find an element under the cursor,
it is quite possible that the element is already highlighted because the element was found
last time the **mouseMoved()** method was called. This will occur when you move the cursor
within the rectangle bounding an element. In this case we don't need to do anything, so we
return from the method.

If the element found is not the same as last time, we obtain a graphics context for the view
since we definitely need it—at least to draw the new element we have found under the
cursor in the highlight color. We then check that the variable **highlightElement** is not
null—it will be **null** if the cursor just entered the rectangle for an element and previously
none was highlighted. If **highlightElement** is not **null** we must un-highlight the old
element before we highlight the new one. To do this we call its **setHighlight()** method
with the argument **false**, and call its **draw()** method. We don't need to involve the
paint() method for the view here since we are simply drawing over an element that is
already displayed. To highlight the new element, we call its **setHighlight()** method with

the argument **true**, store a reference to the element in **highlightElement**, and call its **draw()** method to get it drawn in the highlight color. We then release the graphics context resources by calling the **dispose()** method for **localG** and return.

The next block of code in the method is executed if we exit the **for** loop because no element is under the cursor. In this case we must check if there was an element highlighted last time around. If there was, we un-highlight it, redraw it in its normal color, and reset **highlightElement** to **null**.

Disabling Highlighting

Depending on the speed of your processor, you may find that having highlighting as a permanent feature of the Sketcher application is a tad inconvenient because it slows things up too much. In this case you can add the capability to switch highlighting on and off. Of course, when highlighting is off, you won't be able to get at the popup menu for an element—you will only get the general pop-up.

Try It Out—Adding a Select Mode

1 To provide for switching highlighting you can add a **boolean** data member, **selectMode**, to the **SketchDoc** class with a default value of **true**.

```
protected boolean selectMode = true;  // Select mode flag
```

2 Inevitably, you will need a couple of methods that get and set the **selectMode** flag. To get the select mode flag, the method will be:

```
// Get select mode
public boolean getSelectMode()
{
  return selectMode;
}
```

3 To set the select mode we can write—probably in our sleep by now:

```
// Set select mode
public void setSelectMode(boolean selectMode)
{
  this.selectMode = selectMode;
}
```

4 Then you add an **if** to the beginning of the **mouseMoved()** method in the inner class, **MouseMoveHandler** plus braces around the code that does the highlighting, as follows:

```
public void mouseMoved(MouseEvent e)
{
  Point currentCursor = e.getPoint();  // Get current cursor position
  if(selectMode)                        // If select mode is on
  {
```

```
     // All the code we had before for the highlight operation...
    }
  }
```

5 Now all you require is a button on the toolbar—in its own group of course, that will switch select mode on and off. Add a data member for the button group to the **Toolbar** class :

```
ButtonGroup selectGroup = new ButtonGroup();//Group to switch select mode
```

6 Then add the button to the group and add the group to the toolbar by inserting the following statements at the end of the **Toolbar** class constructor:

```
selectGroup.add(new SelectButton());
add(selectGroup);
```

7 The only other thing we need is an inner class to the **Toolbar** class that defines the **SelectButton** type and handles its own action events.

You can adjust the label for the button according to whether the select mode is on or off—although which way round you set it is a matter of taste. If you want the button to say what it does, you make the button label Select On when select mode is off, and vice versa. If you want the button label to reflect the current status, just set the label to Select On when select mode is on.

The code for the inner class, **SelectButton** to do the latter is:

```
// Select mode button
class SelectButton extends Button
{
  public SelectButton()
  {
   setLabel(theApp.getDocument().getSelectMode()?"selectOn":"selectOff");
    enableEvents(AWTEvent.ACTION_EVENT_MASK);
  }

  protected void processActionEvent(ActionEvent e)
  {
    // Get the new select mode - the inverse of the previous mode
    boolean selectMode = !theApp.getDocument().getSelectMode();
    setLabel(selectMode?"selectOn":"selectOff");  // Set the button label
    theApp.getDocument().setSelectMode(selectMode);//Set mode in document
    super.processActionEvent(e);                   // Pass the event on
  }
}
```

If you recompile the source code for the **Toolbar** and **SketchDoc** classes, you will be able to switch highlighting on and off by clicking the new toolbar button on the right.

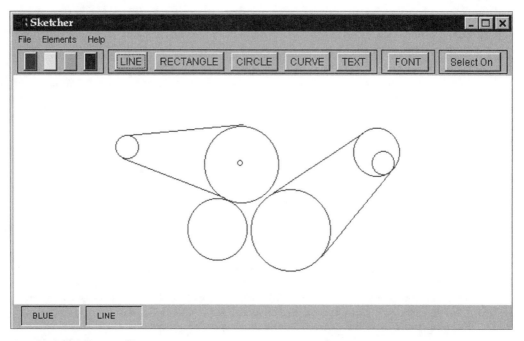

With highlighting fully operational we can put the context menus together.

Defining the Context Menus

We could define the context menus almost anywhere, but since the **SketchView** class is relatively uncluttered, and they will be displayed within the coordinate system of the document view, let's add the code for them there.

We will be defining two context menus;

▶ A general pop-up menu—Displayed when there is nothing under the cursor when the right mouse button is pressed

▶ A pop-up specific to operations on an element—Displayed when the right mouse button is pressed if an element has been detected at the cursor position and is highlighted

Try It Out—Creating Context Menus

1 We can start off by adding two data members of type **PopupMenu**, plus the **CheckboxMenuItems** for the general pop-up menu:

```
// Pop-up menus
PopupMenu elementPopup;    // Element pop-up
PopupMenu generalPopup;    // General pop-up
```

```
// System pop-up items
CheckboxMenuItem lineItem, rectangleItem, circleItem, curveItem, textItem;
CheckboxMenuItem redItem, yellowItem, greenItem, blueItem ;
```

2   We will assemble the context menus in the `SketchView` constructor. We can add the
code for the general pop-up first:

```
// Constructor
public SketchView(SketchDoc sketch)
{
  this.sketch = sketch;
  addMouseListener(sketch.new MouseButtonHandler());
  addMouseMotionListener(sketch.new MouseMoveHandler());
```

```
  // Create the general pop-up
  generalPopup = new PopupMenu("General");

  // Create the element items for the general pop-up
  MenuItem item;
  int elementType = sketch.getElementType();          // Get element type
  lineItem = new CheckboxMenuItem("Line", LINE==elementType);
  rectangleItem = new CheckboxMenuItem("Rectangle",
                                                RECTANGLE==elementType);
  circleItem = new CheckboxMenuItem("Circle", CIRCLE==elementType);
  curveItem = new CheckboxMenuItem("Curve", CURVE==elementType);
  textItem = new CheckboxMenuItem("Text", TEXT==elementType);

  // Create the color sub-menu & items for the general pop-up
  Color elementColor = sketch.getElementColor();  // Get element color
  Menu colorMenu = new Menu("Color");              // Color sub-menu item
  redItem = new CheckboxMenuItem("Red", elementColor.equals(Color.red));
  yellowItem = new CheckboxMenuItem("Yellow",
                                       elementColor.equals(Color.yellow));
  greenItem = new CheckboxMenuItem("Green",
                                        elementColor.equals(Color.green));
  blueItem = new CheckboxMenuItem("Blue",
                                        elementColor.equals(Color.blue));

  // Add the general pop-up listeners
  lineItem.addItemListener(new ElementCommand(LINE, sketch));
  rectangleItem.addItemListener(new ElementCommand(RECTANGLE, sketch));
  circleItem.addItemListener(new ElementCommand(CIRCLE, sketch));
  curveItem.addItemListener(new ElementCommand(CURVE, sketch));
  textItem.addItemListener(new ElementCommand(TEXT, sketch));
  redItem.addItemListener(new ColorCommand(Color.red, sketch));
  yellowItem.addItemListener(new ColorCommand(Color.yellow, sketch));
  greenItem.addItemListener(new ColorCommand(Color.green, sketch));
  blueItem.addItemListener(new ColorCommand(Color.blue, sketch));
```

```
      colorMenu.add(redItem);
      colorMenu.add(yellowItem);
      colorMenu.add(greenItem);
      colorMenu.add(blueItem);

      generalPopup.add(lineItem);
      generalPopup.add(rectangleItem);
      generalPopup.add(circleItem);
      generalPopup.add(curveItem);
      generalPopup.add(textItem);
      generalPopup.addSeparator();
      generalPopup.add(colorMenu);

      add(generalPopup);                    // Add to the  view

      // Code to create and assemble the element pop-up...
   }
```

The general pop-up is exactly the same as the Elements menu on the menu bar using the same types of event handlers so we won't go through the detail again.

3   We must also arrange to update the checks for the items here when the items in the main menu are changed. We can add a method to **SketchView** to update the type item check marks:

```
// Set general pop-up element check marks
public void setTypeMenuChecks(int elementType)
{
  lineItem.setState(LINE==elementType);
  rectangleItem.setState(RECTANGLE==elementType);
  circleItem.setState(CIRCLE==elementType);
  curveItem.setState(CURVE==elementType);
  textItem.setState(TEXT==elementType);
}
```

This updates the type menu items in the context menu in precisely the same way as we used for the **Elements** menu items.

4   We need a similar method to update the element color items in the pop-up:

```
// Set general pop-up color check marks
public void setColorMenuChecks(Color elementColor)
{
  redItem.setState(elementColor.equals(Color.red));
  yellowItem.setState(elementColor.equals(Color.yellow));
  greenItem.setState(elementColor.equals(Color.green));
  blueItem.setState(elementColor.equals(Color.blue));
}
```

5 If we call these methods from the methods in the **SketchDoc** class that update the data members that store the current element type and color, then all the menu updating will be taken care of. You need to add one line to the end of the **setElementType()** method:

```
public void setElementType(int elementType)
{
  this.elementType = elementType;
  theApp.getAppWindow().setTypeMenuChecks(elementType);
  view.setTypeMenuChecks(elementType);
}
```

6 And one line to the **setElementColor()** method in the **SketchDoc** class:

```
public void setElementColor(Color elementColor)
{
  this.elementColor = new Color(elementColor.getRGB());
  theApp.getAppWindow().setColorMenuChecks(elementColor);
  view.setColorMenuChecks(elementColor);
}
```

7 Next we can add the code to the **SketchView** class constructor to create the **elementPopup** context menu:

```
// Constructor
public SketchView(SketchDoc sketch)
{
  this.sketch = sketch;
  addMouseListener(sketch.new MouseButtonHandler());
  addMouseMotionListener(sketch.new MouseMoveHandler());

  // Code to create and assemble the general pop-up as before...

  // Create the element pop-up
  elementPopup = new PopupMenu("Element");

  // Add the items to the element pop-up
  elementPopup.add(item = new MenuItem("Move"));
  item.addActionListener(sketch.new MoveHandler());    // Move listener
  elementPopup.add(item = new MenuItem("Delete"));
  item.addActionListener(sketch.new DeleteHandler()); // Delete listener
  elementPopup.add(item = new MenuItem("Send to Back"));
  item.addActionListener(sketch.new SendToBackHandler());

  add(elementPopup);                      // Add to the view
}
```

8 We will be displaying the context menus from a method in the **MouseButtonHandler** class that has **SketchDoc** as its top-level class, so we will add methods to the **SketchView** that provide a reference to each of the pop-ups. To provide access to the general pop-up we can add the method:

```
// Get the general pop-up menu
public PopupMenu getGeneralPopup()
{
  return generalPopup;
}
```

9 We will add a similar method that returns a reference to the element pop-up:

```
// Get the element pop-up menu
public PopupMenu getElementPopup()
{
  return elementPopup;
}
```

How It Works

The `elementPopup` has three menu items. The first two have obvious uses, one will move the highlighted element, and the other will delete the highlighted element. The third item on the `elementPopup` menu, Send to Back, will deal with the situation where the rectangle of one element completely encloses that of another, and the outer element appears earlier in the sequence of elements than the inner element. In this case it will be impossible for you to select the enclosed element, because the enclosing element will always be detected and highlighted first. The Send to Back item will enable you to move the outer element to the end of the sequence—which will allow the enclosed element to be highlighted as it will precede the outer element in the sequence. Each item in the `elementPopup` menu has a new handler type, so we will be adding inner classes to the `SketchDoc` class to define these.

> Note that you must add both the `PopupMenu` objects to the `SketchView` object. Pop-up menus need a parent component in order to be displayed as we saw earlier. If you don't add a pop-up to its parent, your program will throw `NullPointerException` when you call the `show()` method to display the pop-up.

When we want to display one or other of these pop-ups in the `MouseButtonHandler` class, we will call the appropriate method in `SketchView` to obtain a reference to the menu, and then use that to call its `show()` method.

Displaying a Context Menu

The convention for which mouse button is used to display a pop-up varies between different operating systems. If you code your handler to respond to a particular button being used, you tie your program into the particular operating systems that use that button and it won't work on others. The `MouseEvent` class defines a method `isPopupTrigger()` which returns `true` if the button that is used to trigger context menus is clicked—whichever button it happens to be in the environment in which your program is executing. However, to use this method we must implement the `mouseReleased()` method to display the appropriate context menu, as the trigger is not set at the time the `mousePressed()` method is called.

Try It Out—Adding to the `mouseReleased` *Event*

1 First we need to add another data member to the **SketchDoc** class to remember where the cursor was when the context menu is displayed:

```
protected Point startCursor = null;        // Cursor position for a pop-up
```

We will use this in the move operation that starts when the Move menu item in the element pop-up is selected. By remembering where the cursor was when we started out, we can provide for the possibility of undoing the move.

2 The new code to display the context menus goes at the beginning of the **mouseReleased()** method:

```
public void mouseReleased(MouseEvent e)
{
  if(e.isPopupTrigger())
  { // Pop-up trigger set
    startCursor = e.getPoint();            // Get the cursor position
    if(highlightElement==null)
    { // Pop the element pop-up
      view.getGeneralPopup().show(e.getComponent(), StartCurrsor.x,
                  StartCursor.y);
    }
    else
    { // Pop the general pop-up
      view.getElementPopup().show(e.getComponent(), StartCursor.x,
                  StartCursor.y);
    }
    return;                     // Context menu displayed so we are done
  }

  if(tempG!=null)                       // If there is a graphics context...
  {
    tempG.dispose();                    // ... release context resources
    tempG = null;                       // Reset the reference
  }

  if(tempElement!=null)                 // If we have an element
  {
    addElement(tempElement);            // ... add it to the document
    Rectangle bounds = tempElement.getBounds();

    // Repaint the view area occupied by the element
    view.repaint(bounds.x, bounds.y, bounds.width, bounds.height);
    tempElement = null;                 // Reset temporary
  }
}
```

How It Works

We check for the pop-up trigger before the existing code that deals with the button release when we are creating an element, so that there is no possibility of interference between the two operations that this method handles. You need to think carefully about the sequence of events when using **mousePressed()** and **mouseReleased()** together, as it is all too easy for subtle problems to occur here.

If the **isPopupTrigger()** returns **true**, then we display a context menu. We use the **highlightElement** member of **SketchDoc** to select which menu to display. If this variable is **null**, then there is no element under the cursor so we display the general pop-up menu. If it is not **null**, there is an element highlighted so we display the element pop-up. You can see that we obtain a reference to the component that originated the event by calling the **getComponent()** method, and pass the reference to the **show()** method for the **PopupMenu** object. This technique is typically used where the listener object may be listening for events in more than one view for example. Here we only have one view, so we could have specified the variable **view** for the first argument to the **show()** method directly. The position of the cursor is obtained by calling the **getPoint()** method for the event object, and the coordinates are used to position the context menu in the view.

The general context menu items are already taken care of by the listeners we have already defined. We must define the inner classes to the **SketchDoc** class for the new listeners that listen for the events originating in the element context menu. We will deal with the easiest one first—the send-to-back operation.

Try It Out—The Send-to-Back Operation

The **actionPerformed()** method in this listener class has the job of removing the highlighted element from wherever it is in the document, and then adding it back at the end. This is very easy using the methods we already have in the **SketchDoc** class for operating on the **sketchElements** member. Here's the definition of the listener class:

```
// Handler for Send to Back pop-up item
class SendToBackHandler implements ActionListener
{
  // Handle Send to Back element command
  public void actionPerformed(ActionEvent e)
  {
    if(highlightElement!=null)
    { // Remove the element & add it to the end
      sketchElements.removeElement(highlightElement);
      sketchElements.addElement(highlightElement);
    }
  }
}
```

How It Works

This uses the `removeElement()` method in `SketchDoc` to remove the highlighted element, and then calls the `addElement()` method to put it back—it will be automatically added to the end of the elements in the `sketchElements` vector. We don't need to worry about redrawing the element as it has not been changed in any way.

The delete operation is almost as easy, but we do need to redraw the area the element occupied after it has been removed from the document.

Try It Out—Delete Operations

To delete an element, we remove it from the vector, `sketchElements`, and then redraw the rectangle it occupied to remove it from the view. We can implement this as follows:

```
// Handler for Delete pop-up item
class DeleteHandler implements ActionListener
{
  // Handle delete element command
  public void actionPerformed(ActionEvent e)
  {
    if(highlightElement!=null)
    {
      // Delete highlighted element from the document
      sketchElements.removeElement(highlightElement);

      // Redraw the area occupied by the highlighted element
      Rectangle bounds = highlightElement.getBounds(); // Get bounds
      view.repaint(bounds.x, bounds.y, bounds. width, bounds.height);

      highlightElement = null;                      // No element highlighted
    }
  }
}
```

How It Works

To remove the element, we call the `removeElement()` method in `SketchDoc` that we implemented earlier. It is important to reset the `highlightElement` variable to `null` since the object it references no longer exists so far as the document is concerned and you want it to be destroyed. An object won't be destroyed as long as you still have a reference to it around somewhere.

The last bit is the move operation which will require a bit more effort on our part. An element move operation is going to be processed in the `mouseMoved()` method in the `MouseMotionHandler` class. We will 'glue' the highlighted element to the cursor, so that it follows the movement of the cursor as you move the mouse around. Pressing the left button will fix the position and end the move operation. Pressing the right button will abort the move and return the element to its original position. The move operation will involve code in the **mousePressed()**, the **mouseReleased()** and the **mouseMoved()** methods in the inner classes of **SketchDoc**.

Try It Out—Move Operations

1 To make this all work we will need an indicator in the **SketchDoc** class that a move operation is in progress and somewhere to store the cursor position as the mouse is moved, so add the following definitions at the end of the existing data members in the class:

```
protected boolean moveMode = false;          // Move mode flag
protected Point lastMovePoint = null;        // Stores last move origin
```

When a move operation is initiated, we will set the **moveMode** flag to **true** and the **lastMovePoint** to the point that was saved in **startCursor** when the context menu was displayed.

2 We will do this in the event listener for the Move menu item that we will implement as an inner class to **SketchDoc**:

```
// Handler for Move pop-up item
class MoveHandler implements ActionListener
{
  // Handle move element command
  public void actionPerformed(ActionEvent e)
  {
    if(highlightElement!=null)
    {
      moveMode = true;                 // Move mode on
      lastMovePoint = startCursor;     // Initial cursor position
    }
  }
}
```

3 To move an element, we can add a method to the **Element** class that will translate the reference point for the element a distance in x and a distance in y. Since all our elements are drawn relative to the reference point, this one method will work for all element types. Add the following method to the **Element** class in the **Elements** package:

```
// Move the element
public void move(int xDistance, int yDistance)
{
  position.translate(xDistance, yDistance); // Move the position
  bounds.translate(xDistance, yDistance);   // Move the bound rectangle
}
```

4   The code we need to add to the **mouseMoved()** method in **SketchDoc** to do this is as follows:

```
public void mouseMoved(MouseEvent e)
{
  Point currentCursor = e.getPoint();  // Get current cursor postion
  if(moveMode)
  {
    // Get the bounding rectangle before the move, then move the element
    Rectangle bounds = highlightElement.getBounds();
    highlightElement.move(currentCursor.x - lastMovePoint.x,
                          currentCursor.y - lastMovePoint.y);
    lastMovePoint = currentCursor;          // Save the last cursor position

    // Combine old and new rectangles and repaint
    bounds = bounds.union(highlightElement.getBounds());
    view.repaint(bounds.x, bounds.y, bounds.width, bounds.height);
    return;
  }

  // Code to handle highlighting as before...
}
```

5   A move operation ends when you press the left mouse button. This leaves the highlighted element in the last position it was moved to, and switches the **moveMode** off. The code to do this goes in the **mousePressed()** handler, in **SketchDoc**'s **MouseButtonHandler** class:

```
public void mousePressed(MouseEvent e)
{
  if(e.getModifiers()==InputEvent.BUTTON1_MASK)
  {
    if(moveMode)
    { // Accept move
      moveMode = false;
      return;
    }

    // Code to handle creating an element as before...
  }
}
```

6   To abort the move operation, you can add the following code to the **mouseReleased()** method:

```
public void mouseReleased(MouseEvent e)
{
  if(moveMode)
  { // Abort move so move element back to original position
    // Get the bounding rectangle before the move, then move the element
    Rectangle bounds = highlightElement.getBounds();
    highlightElement.move(startCursor.x-lastMovePoint.x,
                          startCursor.y-lastMovePoint.y);

    highlightElement.setHighlight(false);    // Un-highlight the element

    // Combine old and new rectangles and repaint
    bounds = bounds.union(highlightElement.getBounds());
    view.repaint(bounds.x, bounds.y, bounds.width, bounds.height);
    highlightElement = null;
    moveMode = false;
    return;
  }

  // Code to handle context menus as before...
}
```

How It Works

All the event handler does is set **moveMode** to **true** and set the last move point the same as the initial cursor position. The real work will be done elsewhere in the mouse handling methods. The check for a non-**null** reference in **highlightElement** is somewhat belt-and-braces here, since we should only display the menu if this is already the case. However, what should be the case and what is the case are not always the same in programming.

Moving an Element

Taking the trouble to define all the elements relative to a reference point really pays off here. To move any element is just two lines of code. We call the **translate()** method for the **Point** object, **position**, to move the reference point the distances specified by the arguments. We then move the bounds rectangle using the **translate()** method defined in the **Rectangle** class.

Let's review the process we will be implementing to make a move. All the moving of the highlighted element will be managed in the **mouseMoved()** method in the **MouseMotionHandler** class.

709

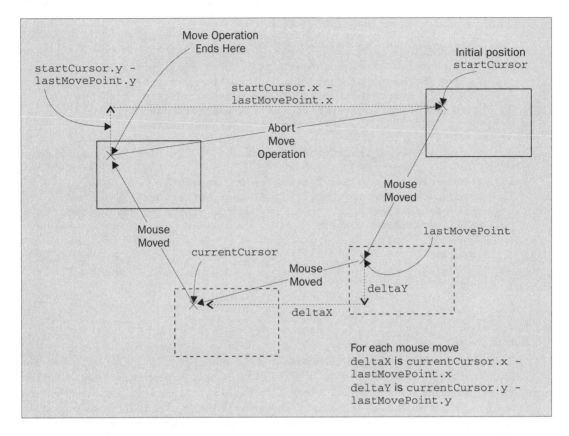

Each move will be from the previous cursor position stored in **lastMovePoint**, to the current cursor position when the **MOUSE_MOVED** event occurred. The current cursor position will be obtained by calling the **getPoint()** method for the event object. Once each mouse move has been processed, the final cursor position will then be stored in the variable **lastMovePoint**, ready for the next event. Since we move the element the distance between successive cursor positions, to move it back to its original position is simply a move from the last cursor position to the starting cursor position.

In the **mouseMoved()** method, we have to get the bounding rectangle for the highlighted element before we move it. We combine this rectangle with its bounding rectangle after we have moved it and redraw the resulting rectangle. We move the highlighted element by calling the **move()** method that we implemented a moment ago. The arguments are the x and y increments from the previous position stored in **lastMovePoint** and the current cursor position. When the move is complete, we save the current cursor position in **lastMovePoint**. Each time this method is called, the highlighted element is moved the distance between successive cursor positions.

Completing a Move Operation

The extra code in **mousePressed()** is inserted at the beginning of the **if** block that is executed when the left mouse button is pressed. All it does is check for **moveMode** being

true, and, if it is, set it to **false** and return. The highlighted element is already in its new position, and it remains highlighted since that's where the cursor is. If it is not **moveMode**, the code we had before is executed.

Aborting a Move Operation

We have to be careful about how we deal with aborting a move, since it involves using the right mouse button which is often used as the pop-up trigger—it is in Windows 95 for example. We must prevent the context menu being displayed if we are aborting a move operation, so we will use the **MOUSE_RELEASED** event to trigger canceling the move operation. The last diagram showed that all we need to do to cancel a move is to move the highlighted element from where it is, the distance from the current cursor position in **lastMovePoint** back to the point that we stored in **startCursor**.

We inserted the new code immediately preceding the code that was already there. If it is not in move mode, the old code will be executed. The process here is very similar to the process in the **mouseMoved()** method. The only differences are that we must remove highlighting from the element since it will not be at the cursor position in general, we must set **highlightElement** to **null**, and we must switch off move mode. The move itself and redrawing the element back in its original position is essentially the same.

Testing the Context Menus

Recompile all the stuff we have changed and try the new context menus. Having a move capability gives you much more precision in position elements relative to one another, so there should be a massive leap forward in the quality of your artwork.

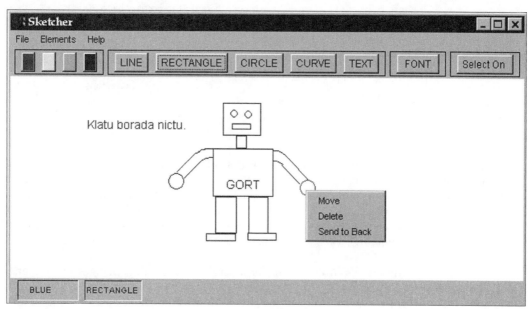

The Delete option is also an invaluable addition in that you can erase your mistakes. Draw a few elements superimposed and see how the Send to Back facility can enable you to highlight any of the elements. For those in the know, the screen shows how to prevent the world being destroyed.

Using Scrollbars

A scrollbar is most commonly used for scrolling text in a window, but it can be applied to varying just about anything you like. The slider on the scrollbar is associated with a value within a given range that you define. At one end of a scrollbar—the left end of a horizontal scrollbar or the top end of a vertical scrollbar, the slider will correspond to the minimum value, and at the opposite end it will correspond to the maximum value.

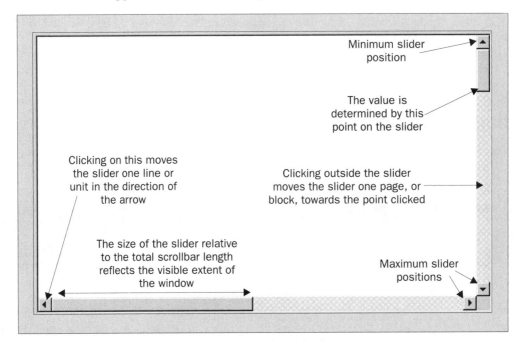

The illustration shows a horizontal and a vertical scrollbar, bordering a display area within a window. Although the scrollbars shown in the illustration appear to have a relationship to the area they bound, this is only the case if you program it—although in some instances, such as the **TextArea** object that we used in the text dialog, the work has been done for you. What happens when a scrollbar slider is moved is entirely up to you. For example, it could scroll text in a window, vary a color value or even alter the shape of a curve.

When you click on the arrows at either end of a scrollbar, the value changes by one line, although what 'a line' means is up to you. In the case of a vertical scrollbar controlling text, it almost certainly will mean one line. If you are using a scrollbar to control some other kind of parameter—a color, for instance—you will define the meaning of a line to suit the context. The same goes for a page. A line increment is more generally called a **unit increment**, and a page is referred to as a **block increment**.

Creating Scrollbars

You have a choice of three constructors to create a **Scrollbar** object:

Constructor	Description
`Scrollbar()`	Creates a vertical scrollbar with a range of values from 0 to 100, with an initial value of 0 and with an initial size for the slider of 10. When you use a scrollbar to scroll a window the size of the slider relative to the total range should represent the visible area in the window, as is illustrated on the horizontal scrollbar in the previous diagram.
`Scrollbar(int orientation)`	Create a scrollbar with the orientation that you specify—it can be either **Scrollbar.VERTICAL** or **Scrollbar.HORIZONTAL**. The range and slider size are the same as those for the previous constructor.
`Scrollbar(int orientation, int value, int visible, int minimum, int maximum)`	Creates a scrollbar with the parameters you specify. The initial value is **value**, the slider size is specified by **visible**, the **minimum** and **maximum** parameters define the range of values. Obviously **maximum** should be greater than **minimum**, **value** should be greater than or equal to **minimum** and less than or equal to **maximum** minus **visible**, and the **visible** value should be greater than 1 and less than the difference between **minimum** and **maximum**.

Note that none of the constructors set the values for a line or a page. You use class methods to change these when necessary.

Operations with Scrollbars

By default, a line increment will be 1 and a page increment will be 10. You can set these to your own values by passing the value you require to the **setUnitIncrement()** or **setBlockIncrement()** method for the **Scrollbar** object. You can override any of the values that you specify in the constructor by using the following methods:

Constructor	Description
`setOrientation (int orientation)`	Sets the orientation depending on the argument value, which can be either **Scrollbar.VERTICAL** or **Scrollbar.HORIZONTAL**.
`setValue(int value)`	Sets the value for the **Scrollbar** object. If the new value is below the minimum or above the maximum, it is set to the minimum or maximum for the scrollbar.

Table Continued on Following Page

Constructor	Description
`setValues(int value, int minimum, int visible, int maximum)`	Sets all four values and checks that `value` and `visible` are consistent with `minimum` and `maximum`. Any inconsistencies are removed by adjusting `value` or `visible`.
`setVisibleAmount (int visible)`	Sets `visible` and adjusts the slider's size for consistency, if necessary.
`setMinimum(int minimum)`	Sets a new `minimum` and adjusts `value` and `visible`, if necessary, for consistency.
`setMaximum(int maximum)`	Sets a new `maximum` and adjusts `value` and `visible`, if necessary, for consistency.

There are *get* methods corresponding to each of the *set* methods above, which return the appropriate value for the `Scrollbar` object.

Scrollbar Events

`Scrollbar` objects create unique events of type `AdjustmentEvent`. To handle scrollbar events, you must implement the `AdjustmentListener` interface that declares the method `adjustmentValueChanged()` which receives the `AdjustmentEvent` object as an argument.

When an event occurs, you can obtain the current value for the `Scrollbar` object by calling the `getValue()` method for the `AdjustmentEvent` object. The event object also has a method `getAdjustmentType()` which returns an `int` value that specifies what kind of action caused the event. It will be one of the following values defined in the `Scrollbar` class:

`AdjustmentEvent` Constant	Description
`UNIT_INCREMENT`	An increment by one unit, or line.
`UNIT_DECREMENT`	A decrement by one unit, or line.
`BLOCK_INCREMENT`	An increment by one block, or page.
`BLOCK_DECREMENT`	A decrement by one block, or page.
`TRACK`	An absolute tracking adjustment caused by moving the slider.

If you need to, you can also get hold of a reference to the `Scrollbar` object that originated the event by calling the `getAdjustable()` method for the `AdjustmentEvent` object. This returns a reference of type `Adjustable`—`Adjustable` being the interface implemented by the `Scrollbar` class.

That's enough theory. What we need now is a bit of practice.

Using Scrollbars to Mix Colors

We can try out scrollbars in an applet that will enable you to set the level of the red, green and blue color components, and display the resulting color. We will use a scrollbar to control the level of each primary color.

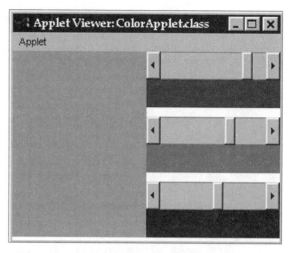

For this to work effectively you need to be able to display at least 16-bit color values, and if you have 24-bit color capability that will be even better. If you can display only 256 colors you won't be able to see much variation in the colors as you move the sliders. Each scrollbar has an area below it that shows the current color for that component. The area on the left shows the color that is the composite of the three primary color values. Adjusting any of the sliders should vary the color below it, and the composite color on the left—subject to you having at least a 16-bit color capability.

We will define the combination of a scrollbar plus the color display beneath it in an inner class to the applet class we will call `ColorControl`. The `ColorControl` class will handle its own scrollbar events so it will implement the `AdjustmentListener` interface.

Try It Out—Defining the `ColorApplet` *Class*

1 Let's start by defining the outline of the applet class, and add the detail of the class methods and the inner class incrementally:

```
// Applet to display colors
import java.applet.*;
import java.awt.*;
import java.awt.event.*;

public class ColorApplet extends Applet
{
   // Color IDs to identify the ColorControl objects
   protected final int RED   = 101,
                       GREEN = 102,
                       BLUE  = 103;

   Canvas colorDisplay;                          // Shows the composite color
```

```
    ColorControl redControl = new ColorControl(RED);     // Red control
    ColorControl greenControl = new ColorControl(GREEN); // Green control
    ColorControl blueControl = new ColorControl(BLUE);   // Blue control

    // Initialize the applet
    public void init()
    {
      // Set up the display panel and the color controls...
    }

    // Set color display
    public void setColorDisplay()
    {
      // Set the composite color as background color to colorDisplay...
    }

    // Inner class defining RGB controls
    class ColorControl extends Panel implements AdjustmentListener
    {
      // Inner class definition...
    }
}
```

2   The applet will contain the **Canvas** object, **colorDisplay** on the left and a **Panel**
object containing three **ColorControl** objects on the right. We can use a **GridLayout**
manager with one row for the applet, and a **GridLayout** manager with one column
for the panel containing the color controls. The code to set this up will go in the
constructor:

```
// Initialize the applet
public void init()
{
    setLayout(new GridLayout(1, 0, 0, 0));           // Single row grid
    Panel controlPane = new Panel();                 // Holds the controls
    controlPane.setLayout(new GridLayout(0, 1, 0, 10)); // Single column
    controlPane.add(redControl);                     // Add the control for red
    controlPane.add(greenControl);                   // Add the control for green
    controlPane.add(blueControl);                    // Add the control for blue
    colorDisplay = new Canvas();
    setColorDisplay();                               // Set the composite color
    add(colorDisplay);                               // Add the color display
    add(controlPane);                                // Add the control panel
}
```

3   The **setColorDisplay()** method sets the composite color as the background color for
colorDisplay:

```
// Set color display
public void setColorDisplay()
{
```

```
           // Composite color from the component colors in the controls
           colorDisplay.setBackground(new Color(redControl.getColorValue(),
                                                 greenControl.getColorValue(),
                                                 blueControl.getColorValue()));
  }
```

How It Works

The `ColorControl` objects will be differentiated by an integer color ID that will be passed to the constructor and stored in the `ColorControl` object. The screen illustration showed that each color control has a scrollbar for adjusting the color. You can see from the `ColorControl` class that it is a specialization of the `Panel` class, and that it implements the `AdjustmentListener` interface, to handle its own scrollbar events. The `colorDisplay` object will show the composite color in the left-hand part of the applet. We will set the background color for this object by the `setColorDisplay()` method.

The layout manager for the applet has no gaps specified so the `controlPane` object and the `colorDisplay` object will touch, and completely fill the applet. The layout manager for `controlPane` has a vertical gap of ten pixels to separate the color controls from one another.

In the `setColorDisplay()` method, we retrieve the value for each component color from the corresponding `ColorControl` object by calling its `getColorValue()` method. These values are passed as arguments to the `Color` class constructor to create the composite color. Finally we pass the new `Color` object that we have created to the `setBackground()` method for `colorDisplay`.

All we need now is the definition for a `ColorControl` object.

Try It Out—Defining a Color Control

1   We will start with the outline of the `ColorControl` class, which is an inner class to `ColorApplet`, and then add the detail code for the class methods:

```
// Inner class defining RGB controls
class ColorControl extends Panel implements AdjustmentListener
{
  int colorID;                        // ID for the color
  int colorValue = 128;               // Initial color intensity
  Scrollbar colorBar;                 // Controls the primary color intensity
  Canvas colorSample = new Canvas();  // Displays the color

  // Constructor
  public ColorControl(int colorID)
  {
    // Code to initialize the object...
  }
```

```
  // Handler for scrollbar adjustment event
  public void adjustmentValueChanged(AdjustmentEvent e)
  {
    // Code to handle the adjustment event...
  }


  // Set the sample color
  public void setColor()
  {
    // Code to set the component color display...
  }

  public int getColorValue()
  {
    return colorValue;
  }
}
```

2 The constructor has to create the **Scrollbar** object and put it together with the **colorSample** object:

```
// Constructor
public ColorControl(int colorID)
{
  this.colorID = colorID;
  GridLayout layout = new GridLayout(0, 1, 0, 0);
  setLayout(layout);
  colorBar = new Scrollbar(Scrollbar.HORIZONTAL,
                           128,              // Initial value
                           25,               // Slider size
                           0,                // Minimum value
                           275);             // Maximum value
  colorBar.setUnitIncrement(5);             // Unit is 5
  colorBar.setBlockIncrement(25);           // Block is 25
  colorBar.addAdjustmentListener(this);     // This object listens
  add(colorBar);
  setColor();
  add(colorSample);
}
```

3 The background color for the **colorSample** object is set by calling the **setColor()** method, that we can implement as follows:

```
// Set the sample color
public void setColor()
{
  // Set the component color display
  colorSample.setBackground(new Color(colorID==RED?colorValue:0,
                                      colorID==GREEN?colorValue:0,
                                      colorID==BLUE?colorValue:0));
}
```

4 An event for the **Scrollbar** member of the current **ColorControl** object will cause the **adjustmentValueChanged()** method to be called. We must implement this so that it updates the color in the control, and updates the color in the **colorDisplay** member of the top-level class:

```
// Handler for scrollbar adjustment event
public void adjustmentValueChanged(AdjustmentEvent e)
{
    colorValue = e.getValue();          // Retrieve the current value
    setColor();                         // Update the control
    setColorDisplay();                  // Update the composite color
}
```

How It Works

Each **ColorControl** object will manage the intensity of one of the primary colors, red, green or blue, that make up the composite color we will display in the **colorDisplay** object. Each **ColorControl** object has three data members, a color ID to identify the primary color to which an object relates, a color intensity with an initial value of 128—remember that each color value can be between 0 and 255, a **Scrollbar** object which controls the color intensity, and a **Canvas** object to display the color.

In the constructor, we use a **GridLayout** manager with a single column to position the **colorSample** object below the **colorBar** object. We want the range of values for the **Scrollbar** object to be from 0 to 255, so we adjust the maximum to allow for the size of the slider and the unit increment value of 5 that we set using the **setUnitIncrement()** method. We also set the block increment to be 25. After adding the current **ColorControl** object as a listener for the scrollbar we add the scrollbar and the **colorSample** object.

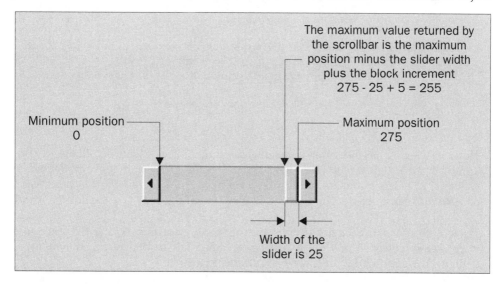

The current color value stored in the **colorValue** member only applies to one of the three arguments to the **Color** constructor in the **setColor()** method. Which one it is depends on the **colorID** value for the current object. We use conditional operators to select each of the argument values. The value will be applied to the `Color` constructor argument corresponding to the value of `colorID`, and the other two argument values will be 0.

The `adjustmentValueChanged()` method is very simple. The value obtained from the `Scrollbar` object is stored in the `colorValue` member of the current control object. The primary color corresponding to this is displayed in the control, and a new composite color is set by calling the `setColorDisplay()` method in the top-level class.

That's all there is to it.

Creating a Larger Document

Although scrollbars are not difficult, unbelievably Java makes them even easier in the context of scrolling a window. Let's see how that works by adding a bit more functionality to Sketcher.

Drawing within the confines of the view area provided within the Sketcher application window is quite a serious limitation. We really need a much larger area for Sketcher to be of any practical use. We can create a larger area by fixing the size of the `SketchView` object in the constructor. All we need to do is to call the `setSize()` method for the object to specify the width and height of the view in pixels.

Try It Out—Expanding SketchView

1 You can add the following code to the beginning of the constructor to do this:

```
public SketchView(SketchDoc sketch)
{
    // Set the size of the view in inches from screen pixels per inch
    int pixelsPerInch = getToolkit().getScreenResolution();
    setSize(11*pixelsPerInch,17*pixelsPerInch);  //Set size to 11x17 inches

    // Rest of the code for the constructor as before...
}
```

2 Now we need some means of managing the larger sheet—some scrollbars to pan around it for instance. The class `ScrollPane` in the `java.awt` package defines a container that has scrollbars built in. All we need to do is to add the document view to a `ScrollPane` object, then add the `ScrollPane` object to the application window.

We will need a data member in the `SketchFrame` class to hold the reference to the `ScrollPane` object so add the following statement at the end of the statements defining the existing data members of `SketchFrame`:

```
ScrollPane drawArea = null;              // The area to contain the view
```

3 At the moment, the view is added to the application window in the `addView()` method, so that would be the appropriate place to add the `drawArea` object with the view inserted into it:

```
// Add the document view to the window
public void addView(SketchView view)
{
    drawArea = new ScrollPane();              // Create a new draw area
    drawArea.add(view);                        // Add the view to the draw area
    add(drawArea, BorderLayout.CENTER);        // Add the draw area to the window
}
```

Believe it or not, that's all we need to do to have a scrolling drawing area.

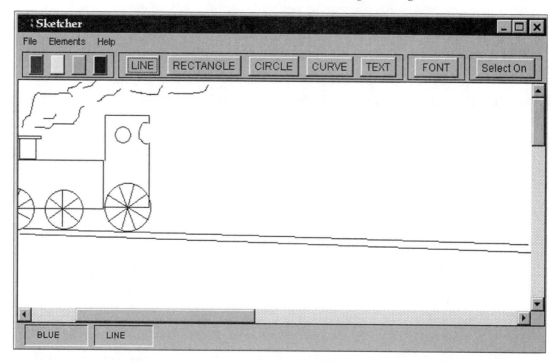

We can now draw over an area much larger than the window area, and move around the sketch using the scrollbars. This now raises the question of how we get the sketch out on paper, seeing as how we can no longer view all of it at one time, but you will have to wait until the next chapter for that.

How It Works

Ideally we want to know how big our drawing sheet is going to be in some sensible units such as inches, not pixels which are dependent on the size and resolution of the monitor. We can do this by obtaining the number of screen pixels per inch in a call to the `getScreenResolution()` method of the `Toolkit` object for the view. We multiply the value obtained by the dimensions we want for the drawing sheet in inches. Here it is 11x17 inches which is A3 size, but you can make it larger if you want.

In `addView()`, instead of adding the view directly into the `SketchFrame` object, we create the `ScrollPane` object, add the `view` object to that, and then add the `drawArea` object to the application window. The scrollbars in the `ScrollPane` object are automatically set to manage the dimensions of the view. The range for the horizontal scrollbar will be from zero to the width of the view, and that of the vertical scrollbar from zero to the height of the view.

Summary

In this chapter you have learnt how to use dialogs to manage data input. You have also learned how to implement context menus which can bring a professional feel to the GUI in your applications. You have applied scrollbars to varying data values as well as scrolling a window so you should be in a position to use them in whatever context you need.

The important points we have covered in this chapter are:

- ▶ A dialog is a window that is always owned by a parent window
- ▶ A modal dialog blocks input from other windows in the same application as long as it is displayed
- ▶ A modeless dialog does not block input to other windows. You can switch the focus between a modeless dialog and other windows in the application whenever necessary
- ▶ A pop-up menu is a menu that can be displayed at any point within the coordinate system of a component
- ▶ A context menu is a pop-up menu that is specific to what lies at the point where the menu is displayed—so the contents of the menu depends on the context
- ▶ A context is usually displayed as a result of a right mouse button click
- ▶ You can create scrollbars with either a vertical or a horizontal orientation
- ▶ A scrollbar has a value associated with it that depends on the position of the slider. The value always lies between the maximum and minimum values that have been set for the scrollbar
- ▶ A scrollbar has an associated unit value, which is the amount that the value is changed up or down whenever either of the arrows at the ends of the scrollbar is clicked
- ▶ The size of the slider for a scrollbar should correspond to the visible area in a window, when the scrollbar is being used to scroll a window
- ▶ The `ScrollPane` class defines a container with built in scrollbars for scrolling a component that has been added to the `ScrollPane` object

Exercises

1 Implement a dialog initiated from a toolbar button to select the current element color.

2 Add a menu item to the Element context menu to display information about the element at the cursor in a dialog—what it is and its basic defining data.

3 Display a special context menu when the cursor is over a TEXT object that provides a menu option to edit the text through a dialog.

4 Implement an applet that displays a filled circle with a radius controlled by a horizontal scrollbar.

5 Add a vertical scrollbar to the previous applet and modify its operation so that the width and height are controlled by the appropriate scrollbar.

Filing and Printing Documents

In this chapter we will explore serializing and printing documents in an application, and add these as the finishing touches to our Sketcher program. These capabilities are not available in an untrusted applet for security reasons, so everything we will cover here only applies to applications and trusted applets (for more information on these, see Appendix B). Although we have already covered serialization in Chapter 8, you will find that there is quite a difference between understanding how the basic methods for object input and output work, and applying them in a practical context.

In this chapter you will learn:

- How to use the **FileDialog** class
- How to save a document object in a file
- How to implement the Save As menu mechanism
- How to open a document stored in a file and integrate it into the application
- How to create a new document and integrate it into the application
- How to track when a document has changed
- How to ensure that the current document is saved before the application is closed or a new document is loaded
- How printing in Java works
- How you obtain a graphics context for a page to be printed
- How to change the origin for output and set the clip rectangle
- How to implement multi-page printing for a document object.

Serializing the Document

Our Sketcher program can only be considered to be a practical application if we can save sketch documents in a file, and retrieve them later—in other words we need to implement serialization for a sketch document and use that to make the File menu work.

We have seen how to serialize objects, way back in Chapter 8. All we need to do to serialize a sketch document in our Sketcher program, is to apply what we learned then. Of course, there are a few more classes lying around that make up a document, but it will be remarkably easy, considering the potential complexity of a sketch—I promise!

Of course, saving a sketch on disk and reading it back from a file implies supporting the File menu, and that will be significantly more work than implementing serialization for the document. Before we get into that, there is a more fundamental point we should address— our document doesn't have a name. We should at least make provision for assigning a file name to a document, and maybe display the document name in the title bar of the application window.

Try It Out—Assigning a Document Name

1   If a document is going to have a name, we need to provide for storing it somewhere, so add the following data member to the **SketchDoc** class definition:

```
protected String sketchName;                    // The document file name
```

2   We can initialize this in the **SketchDoc** class constructor:

```
public SketchDoc(Sketcher theApp)
{
   this.theApp = theApp;                      // Store the document object
   elementType = DEFAULT_ELEMENT_TYPE;        // Set default element type
   elementColor = DEFAULT_ELEMENT_COLOR;      // Set default element color
   sketchName = DEFAULT_FILE_NAME;            // File name for the sketch
}
```

3   We can define the value of **DEFAULT_NAME** in **Constants.java** by adding the following line to the interface definition:

```
String DEFAULT_FILE_NAME = "Untitled.ske";
```

I have chosen the extension **.ske** for Sketcher files, but you can choose something different if you wish.

4   We will also need a way to set the name for the document—at least when we write the document to a file. We can add a method to the **SketchDoc** class to set the name for the document:

```
// Set the file name for the document
public void setName(String sketchName)
{
  this.sketchName = sketchName;
}
```

We can use this to set the name from anywhere in the program.

5   We are also likely to want to retrieve the name, to display it on the title bar of the application window for instance, so we should add a complementary **getName()** method as well:

```
// Get the file name for the document
public String getName()
{
  return sketchName;
}
```

6   To display the document name on the title bar of the application window, we need to make a couple of small changes to the **Sketcher** class definition. First, add a data member that defines the basic title that should appear:

```
String title = "Sketcher";   // The application title
```

7   We can amend the creation of the **SketchFrame** object in the **init()** method of the **Sketcher** class to append the document name to the basic title to form the string to appear in the title bar:

```
// Create the application window
window = new SketchFrame(title + ":  " + sketch.getName(), this);
```

This will construct the window object with the title bar containing the basic application title and the document name separated by a colon and two spaces.

If you recompile Sketcher and run it, you should now see the document title displayed in the title bar.

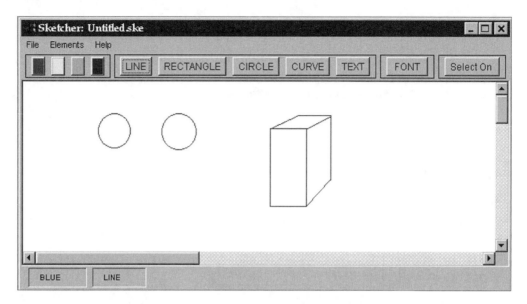

We now have a name assigned to the document, but there's another point to consider when we have the capability to store a sketch. When we close the application, we should have a means of checking whether the document needs to be saved. Otherwise it will be all too easy to close Sketcher and lose the brilliant sketch that you have just spent three hours crafting. This is not difficult. We just need to record the fact that the document has changed.

Try It Out—Recording Document Changes

1 To provide the means of recording whether a document has been changed or not, we can add a **boolean** data member to the **SketchDoc** class that we will set to **true** when the document changes, and to **false** when it is not changed—which is when it has just been saved in a file. Add the following data member definition to the class:

```
protected boolean isChanged = false;          // Document changed flag
```

The flag is **false** initially because the document is empty and therefore unchanged by definition.

2 There are three ways in which we can change a document—by adding an element, by deleting an element and by moving an element. The first two are easy to take care of, since both of these are handled by methods in the **SketchDoc** class. You need to add one line to the **addElement()** method:

```
public void addElement(Element element)
{
  sketchElements.addElement(element);       // Add the element
  isChanged = true;                          // Mark the document as changed
}
```

3 And exactly the same line of code to the **removeElement()** method:

```
public void removeElement(Element element)
{
  sketchElements.removeElement(element);   // Delete the element
  isChanged = true;                        // Mark the document as changed
}
```

When either of these methods is called, the **isChanged** flag will be set to **true**.

4 The operation of moving an element is completed by pressing the left mouse button, so we must set the **isChanged** flag in the **mousePressed()** method in the **MouseButtonHandler** class:

```
public void mousePressed(MouseEvent e)
{
  if(e.getModifiers()==InputEvent.BUTTON1_MASK)
  {
    if(moveMode)
    { // Accept move
      moveMode = false;
      isChanged = true;             // Set changed flag
      return;
    }
    // Rest of the method as before...
  }
}
```

This now sets the flag to **true** when a move is completed.

5 The only other thing we must consider is the File menu operations themselves. When we save a document, we will want to reset the **isChanged** flag back to false, and we require a method in **SketchDoc** to do this:

```
// Set the document changed flag
public void setChanged(boolean flag)
{
  isChanged = flag;
}
```

With this method you can set the flag whichever way you want by passing **true** or **false** as an argument.

6 When we deal with closing the application, we will want to interrogate the **isChanged** flag to see whether we should save the document or not, so we should add a method to the **SketchDoc** class that will return the value of the flag as well:

```
// Get the document changed flag
boolean isChanged()
```

```
{
  return isChanged;
}
```

 You may have noticed that we have used the same name for the method as we used for the flag. This is quite legal and Java has no problem distinguishing the two things. It's not a good idea to do this on an extensive basis though as it can make the code confusing. It was included here to demonstrate that it works. The name getChanged() **would be a better choice in practice.**

That's just about all the odds and ends we need. We can now press ahead with serializing the document.

Implementing the Serializable Interface

As I hope you still remember, the fundamental step in making objects serializable is to implement the **Serializable** interface in every class that defines objects we want written to a file. We need a methodical approach here, so how about top-down—starting with the **SketchDoc** class.

Try It Out—Serializing SketchDoc

1 This is where we get a great deal from astonishingly little effort. To implement serialization for the **SketchDoc** class, you must first modify the class definition header to:

```
public class SketchDoc implements Constants, Serializable
```

This just adds the **Serializable** interface, in addition to the **Constants** interface that is already implemented by the class.

2 The **Serializable** interface is defined in the package **java.io** so we need to add an **import** statement to the beginning of the **SketchDoc.java** file:

```
import java.io.*;
```

The **Serializable** interface declares no methods—so that's it!

Is that enough to serialize a sketch document? Not quite. For a class to be serializable, all its data members must be serializable or declared as **transient**, so we must trawl through the data elements of the **SketchDoc** class, and if any of these are our own classes, we must make sure they either implement the **Serializable** interface, or are declared as **transient**. We won't need to consume vast quantities of fish to do that though.

Data members that we declare as **transient** are those that we don't want to be written to the file Let's consider first what types of data members these might be. It is important to understand what is happening when we read a document back from a file in this context. The connections between the four principle classes in the application are as shown.

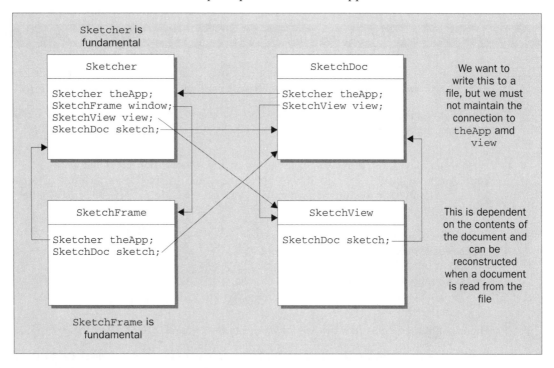

It has developed into quite a complicated set of classes hasn't it? It could be simplified. For example, we could keep references to the four classes in the **Sketcher** class and just record a reference to the **Sketcher** object in each of the other three classes. The price we would pay for this is that we would need to call a method in the **Sketcher** object from these three classes whenever we want to access either of the other two. There would be a performance penalty for this but probably not a serious one. But there are more fundamental issues.

To understand where the potential problems lie, let's assume we have written a **SketchDoc** object to the file. A little later, we run Sketcher again, and read the object back. Of course, the Sketcher program we are running already exists, so it has a specific **Sketcher** object (and other objects of course). If the **SketchDoc** object was serialized to include the data member **theApp**, this will refer to a *different* **Sketcher** object—which no longer exists. If we serialized the **Sketcher** class as well, it will exist when we read the document, but we will end up with *two* **Sketcher** objects—the one that was created when the program started, plus the one that we read from the file. The way to eliminate all this confusion and potential mayhem is to make sure that we declare all the data members in the document class that store links to other classes as **transient**. We can then reconstruct these links once we have read the document back.

There is also another difficulty. The menu items for the Element menu have listeners that are objects of a class that contain references to the old document class. These won't connect to the new **SketchDoc** object at all—they will still be linked to the old document. We will come back to how we can solve this problem later, let's look now at what we can do about the data members of the **SketchDoc** class.

Try It Out—Transient Data Members of the Document Class

1 From the diagram you can see that there are two data members we want to declare as **transient**, **theApp** and **view**. Modify the declarations for these in **SketchDoc** to:

```
transient protected Sketcher theApp;      // The application object
transient protected SketchView view;      // The document view
```

2 We already have the ability to set the view in the **SketchDoc** class using the **addView()** method, but we will also need to be able to set the application object after we have retrieved a document from a file. We can provide for this by adding the following method:

```
// Set the application object
public void setApp(Sketcher theApp)
{
   this.theApp = theApp;
}
```

3 There is another data member we must declare as **transient**:

```
transient protected Graphics tempG;     // Context for temporary element
```

> *The* **Graphics** *class is abstract and* **Graphics** *class objects are not serializable. You must always obtain a* **Graphics** *object from a component when you need one so we must declare the* **tempG** *member of* **SketchDoc** *as* **transient***.*

4 **Vector** objects are serializable but the **Vector** object in the **SketchDoc** class contains our shape objects so we must make all of our shape classes in the **Elements** package implement the **Serializable** interface. We can do this by modifying the header in the base class definition:

```
import java.awt.*;
import java.io.*;

public abstract class Element implements Serializable
{
   // Class definition as before...
}
```

5 Does that cover all the shape classes? After all the implementation of the **Serializable** interface will be inherited in the sub-classes of **Element**? Well, almost, but the **CurveElement** class has an inner class that we want to serialize, and that won't be affected by implementing the **Serializable** interface in the **Element** class. In fact we must implement the interface in the inner class, and in the inner class of the inner class, as follows:

```
// Class defining a curve element
package Elements;
import java.awt.*;
import java.io.*;

public class CurveElement extends Element
{
  // Implementation of the class as before...

  // Class to define a linked list of segments
  class SegmentList implements Serializable
  {
    // Implementation of the inner class as before...

    // Class to define a node in a list of points
    class SegmentNode implements Serializable
    {
      // Implementation of the inner class to the inner class as before...

    }
  }
}
```

None of the internals of the classes here need to be changed. You just add the **Serializable** interface to each class definition, and add the **import** statement for the **java.io** package to the beginning of the file.

That does it. We have done all that is necessary to implement serialization for the **SketchDoc** class. We can turn our attention to supporting the File menu where we will put serialization into operation.

Supporting the File Menu

To support the menu items in the File menu, we must add listeners for each of them. Since most of the activity is concerned with file operations, we will define the listener class as an inner class to the **Sketcher** class. We can manage the links between all the classes relatively easily from the **Sketcher** class. We can make this listener class handle the events for any of the items in the File menu.

Try It Out—A File Menu Listener

1 Let's add the outline of the class and add the detail later when we look at how we will deal with events from the individual menu items:

```
// Listener class for File menu items
class FileMenuHandler implements ActionListener
```

```
{
  int itemID;            // Identifies file menu item
  String fileName;       // Document name

  // Constructor
  public FileMenuHandler(int itemID)
  {
    this.itemID = itemID;
  }

  // Handle file menu item
  public void actionPerformed(ActionEvent e)
  {
    fileName = sketch.getName();    // File name for current document
    switch(itemID)
    {
      case SAVE:
        // Handle Save menu item event...
        break;
      case SAVE_AS:
       // Handle Save As menu item event...
        break;
      case OPEN:
        // Handle Open menu item event...
         break;
      case NEW:
        // Handle New menu item event...
        break;
      case CLOSE:
        // Handle Close menu item event...
       break;
      case PRINT:
        // Handle Print menu item event...
        break;
    }
  }
}
```

2 Of course, we need to define the IDs that identify the menu items somewhere, and
our **Constants** interface is a natural choice, so add the following definitions to the
interface definition in **Constants.java**:

```
// File menu IDs
int NEW     = 601;
int OPEN    = 602;
int CLOSE   = 603;
int SAVE    = 604;
int SAVE_AS = 605;
int PRINT   = 606;
```

3 To make these available in the **Sketcher** class we can make the class implement the **Constants** interface by changing the class definition to:

```
public class Sketcher implements Constants
```

4 When you have saved the **Sketcher** class file with these modifications we can add the listeners for the File menu items. To do this we must amend the **SketchFrame** class constructor, because that's where the menus are assembled. Here's the code you need to add for the listeners:

```
public SketchFrame(String title, Sketcher theApp)
{
  super(title);                          // Call base constructor
  this.theApp = theApp;                  // Store the application object
  sketch = theApp.getDocument();         // Get the document object
  setMenuBar(menubar);                   // Add the menu bar to the window

  toolbar = new Toolbar(theApp);         // Create the toolbar
  add(toolbar, BorderLayout.NORTH);      // Place it at the top

  // Construct the file pull down menu
  Menu fileMenu = new Menu("File");       // The File menu bar item
  MenuItem item;
  fileMenu.add(item = new MenuItem("New", new MenuShortcut('N')));
  // New listener
  item.addActionListener(theApp.new FileMenuHandler(NEW));
  fileMenu.add(item = new MenuItem("Open", new MenuShortcut('O')));
  // Open listener
  item.addActionListener(theApp.new FileMenuHandler(OPEN));
  fileMenu.add(item = new MenuItem("Close", new MenuShortcut('C')));
  // Close listener
  item.addActionListener(theApp.new FileMenuHandler(CLOSE));
  fileMenu.addSeparator();
  fileMenu.add(item = new MenuItem("Save", new MenuShortcut('S')));
  // Save listener
  item.addActionListener(theApp.new FileMenuHandler(SAVE));
  fileMenu.add(item = new MenuItem("Save As..."));
  // SaveAs listener
  item.addActionListener(theApp.new FileMenuHandler(SAVE_AS));
  fileMenu.addSeparator();
  fileMenu.add(item = new MenuItem("Print", new MenuShortcut('P')));
  // Print listener
  item.addActionListener(theApp.new FileMenuHandler(PRINT));

  // Rest of the code for the constructor, as before...
}
```

How It Works

This works using the same mechanism we have used several times before—an ID in the class identifies the menu item to which the listener object applies, and the **actionedPerformed()** method uses this ID to switch to the appropriate code for the event. Before the **switch** statement we retrieve the document name ready for use if we save the document. There is a **case** label corresponding to each of the items in the File menu. We can now work through adding a block of code to support the function required for each menu item.

In the modified **SketchFrame** constructor, after each statement adding a menu item to the File menu, we have added a call to the **addActionListener()** for the item. The argument passed to the constructor for each listener object will select the appropriate code in the method that will be handling the events for these items.

We can now start implementing the support for the menu items in the File menu. A very powerful aid here is provided by the **FileDialog** class, that is designed specifically for use in file input/output operations.

File Dialogs

There is a specialized version of the **Dialog** class, **FileDialog**, available in the **java.awt** package. This provides precisely the capability we need when we are storing or retrieving documents. It does almost all of the work in that it has built-in facilities for browsing the directories in your system. The sort of dialog that you can create with a **FileDialog** object is shown below, in this case it's one of the Windows 95 common dialogs.

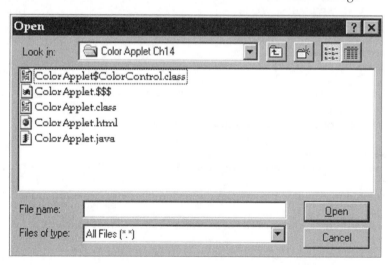

The title bar is set when the dialog is created, but all the rest of the stuff that appears in the dialog window come for free. All the buttons are fully supported so not only can you browse the directories in your system, you can create new directories too. A file dialog doesn't actually read the file, or write the file away though—for the simple reason that it has no idea what you want written to the file, or where the data is to go when you read a file. You have to program the input and output operations yourself.

Since **FileDialog** is a specialization of the **Dialog** class, it inherits all the methods we saw in the previous chapter for the **Dialog** class. Like the basic dialog, a **FileDialog** must have a parent **Frame** object. File dialogs are always modal—there is no option for a modeless file dialog. There are three constructors you can use to create a **FileDialog** object:

Constructor	Description
FileDialog(Frame parent)	Creates a file dialog for loading a file with **parent** as the parent **Frame** object. The title bar for the dialog will be empty but you can set it later using the **setTitle()** method inherited from the **Window** class.
FileDialog(Frame parent, String title)	Creates a file dialog for loading a file with **parent** as the parent **Frame** object, and with the string, **title**, displayed in the title bar.
FileDialog(Frame parent, String title, int mode)	Creates a file dialog for loading a file with **parent** as the parent **Frame** object, and with the string, **title**, displayed in the title bar. The third argument can be specified as either **LOAD** for a dialog to load a file, or **SAVE** to create a dialog to save a file. **LOAD** and **SAVE** are defined in the **FileDialog** class.

You can set the mode for a **FileDialog** object to **LOAD** or **SAVE** before you display it by calling its **setMode()** method, and passing the mode you want as an argument. This means you can create a single **FileDialog** object which you can then keep around and reuse for either loading or saving operations.

When you want to save a file, you will usually want the name of the file displayed in the File name: box in the dialog window when it opens. You can do this by calling the **setFile()** method for the **FileDialog** object before you display the dialog, and pass a **String** object containing the file name to the method. Of course, the file name can be edited in the dialog window, so you will want to know what it is after the dialog closes. You just call the **getFile()** method for the **FileDialog** object which will return a **String** object containing the file name.

By default, a file dialog will display the files in the current directory. You can select a specific directory by passing a **String** object specifying the directory to the **setDirectory()** method for the **FileDialog** object. Equally, after the dialog closes you can retrieve the directory by calling the **getDirectory()** method. In general you will need to obtain the directory for use when you are creating a **File** object before writing the file.

> *At the time of writing it is not possible to set the title bar in a **FileDialog** window under Windows 95. Neither passing a title argument to the constructor, nor calling the **setTitle()** method for the **FileDialog** object have any effect—the **LOAD** dialog window always has the title Open, and the **SAVE** dialog always has the title Save As. However, on the assumption that this will be fixed at some time, we will write the code in this chapter as though **FileDialog** objects work as described.*

Let's see how the file dialog works in practice. We will start with Save since you can't open a file until you have saved one.

File Save Operations

The Save menu item shouldn't just save the document in a file. The current file name in the document affects the situation quite significantly. If the file name is the default name that we set initially in the **SketchDoc** constructor, we should give the user a chance to enter a new file name. Otherwise, it is highly probable that another file that happens to have the default file name will be overwritten when you don't want it to be. The default file name is intended to be a placeholder for the real file name, and the user should choose a file name when they save the file. On the other hand, if the file name has already been changed, this means that it has been saved previously and assigned a new name, so it is reasonable to overwrite the previous version automatically.

Try It Out—Implementing the *Save Menu Item*

1 We can conclude that if the file name recorded in the document is still the default, we should display a **SAVE** file dialog to allow the name to be changed. Otherwise we just write the document with its current name. Here's the code we must insert in the **switch** statement in the **actionPerformed()** method of the **FileHandler** inner class:

```
public void actionPerformed(ActionEvent e)
{
  String fileName = sketch.getName();   // File name for current document
  switch(itemID)
  {
    case SAVE:
      if(fileName.equals(DEFAULT_FILE_NAME))
        runSaveDialog("File Save Dialog");     // Display the save dialog
      else
        saveDocument(sketch.getDirectory(), fileName); // Just write the
                                                       // sketch
      break;   // Rest of the code for the switch...
    // Code for the rest of the switch...
  }
}
```

2 We can implement the **runSaveDialog()** method in the **Sketcher** class as:

```
// Run the Save file dialog
protected void runSaveDialog(String dlgTitle)
{
  String fileName = sketch.getName();     // get current document name
  FileDialog saveDialog = new FileDialog(window, dlgTitle,
                                     FileDialog.SAVE);
  saveDialog.setFile(fileName);              // Set the current document name
  if(!fileName.equals(DEFAULT_FILE_NAME))       // If its not default name
```

```
      saveDialog.setDirectory(sketch.getDirectory()); // Set the directory
   saveDialog.show();                       // Display the dialog
   fileName = saveDialog.getFile();         // Get the file name

   if(fileName!=null)
   {
     sketch.setName(fileName);              // Update document name
     String directory = saveDialog.getDirectory();
     sketch.setDirectory(directory); // Save the directory in the document
     window.setTitle(title + ": " + fileName); // Update window title
     saveDocument(directory, fileName);     // Save the document
   }
   saveDialog.dispose();                    // Release the resources
}
```

3   To store the directory string in the **SketchDoc** class, you can add the following data member definition after the other in the class definition:

```
protected String directory = null;          // Directory for this document
```

4   We also need to add standard form *get* and *set* methods for this variable. The *get* method definition will be:

```
// Get the directory where the document is stored
public String getDirectory()
{
  return directory;
}
```

5   The *set* method definition is:

```
// Set the directory for the document
public void setDirectory(String directory)
{
  this.directory = directory;
}
```

How It Works

The **if** statement checks the name retrieved from the document object and stored in the class data member, **fileName**. If it is still the default name, we want to display a dialog that will permit the file name and the current directory to be modified if necessary. If the name in the document is not the default, the document must have been saved previously, so we can save it directly using the current file name and directory that will be retrieved from the document in the **saveDocument()** method. We will come back to the implementation of this method later.

There are two reasons for hiving off segments of code into separate methods as we are doing with runSaveDialog(). Firstly it helps make the code more readable because it is in smaller, more comprehensible units. Secondly, some of the other menu items will be able to use the functionality in these methods, so we reduce the overall size of the code.

In **runSaveDialog()**, after retrieving the current file name stored in the document, we create a **FileDialog** object with the **SAVE** mode set, and pass the **String** object received as a parameter to define the contents of the title bar for the dialog window. The reason for passing the title as an argument is that we will want a different title for the dialog window when we use it in the Save As menu processing code. The current name of the document is passed to the dialog object next, and then we check if the file name is still the default. If it isn't, we know that the directory will have been saved in the document, so we can set the directory for the dialog too, before displaying the dialog window.

The statement following the call to **show()** will be executed when the dialog is closed, by selecting the OK button or the Cancel button, or clicking the close icon for the dialog window. The **getFile()** method retrieves a **String** object from the dialog that will contain the file name if the OK button was pressed, and **null** otherwise.

If **fileName** is not **null**, the OK button was pressed so we do want to save the document. After setting the new name in the document we retrieve the directory for use in the save operation. We save the directory in the document for use if the Save menu is selected again later for this document—this will happen in the **else** clause of the **if** statement back in the **SAVE** case of the **switch** statement. We must add the mechanics for saving the directory in the document to the **SketchDoc** class in a moment, as well as a method for retrieving it.

To make sure the application window reflects the current document name, we set the window title using the name we have retrieved from the dialog. Finally, to save the document, we call the **saveDocument()** method which we will implement writing to the file. This has the directory and the file name that we get from the dialog as arguments.

Let's save the document next.

Try It Out—Saving the Document

We can implement the **saveDocument()** method in the **Sketcher** class—it doesn't need to be a member of the **FileHandler** class. The save operation will be a direct application of what we learned in Chapter 8 about how we write objects to a file. We must remember that file operations throw exceptions, so the code must go in a **try** block. You can implement the method as follows:

```
// Save the document
protected void saveDocument(String directory, String fileName)
{
  try
```

```
      {
         FileOutputStream output = new FileOutputStream(
                                        new File(directory, fileName));
         ObjectOutputStream objectOut = new ObjectOutputStream(output);
         objectOut.writeObject(sketch);         // Write the document
         sketch.setChanged(false);              // Reset document changed flag
      }
      catch(IOException eOutput)
      {
         MessageBox ioErrorBox = new MessageBox(window, "File Write Error",
                                             eOutput.toString());
         ioErrorBox.show();
         ioErrorBox.dispose();                  // Release resources
      }
   }
```

*Don't forget to add an **import** statement for the **java.io** package to the **Sketcher** class.*

If you recompile Sketcher, you should be ready to save your first sketch—so make it a good one.

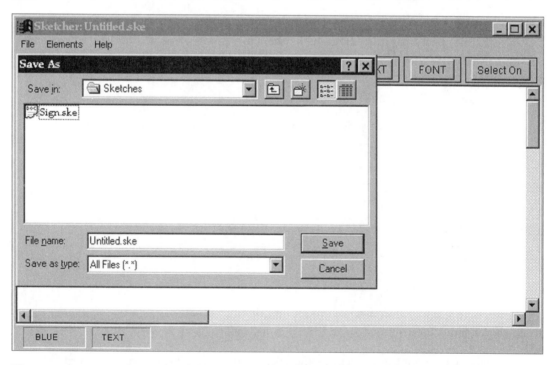

The sample screen shows the default title bar in the dialog—hopefully your version will have the correct title bar set. That's a major step forward for the Sketcher application. I hope you agree that it was remarkably easy to implement. You can now save any sketch in a file, regardless of its complexity.

How It Works

From the directory and file name that are passed to the method, we create a **File** object which is passed to the **OutputFileStream** constructor. From the **OutputFileStream** object, we create an **ObjectOutputStream** object which is used for outputting objects to the file stream. To write the document to the file, we just pass the reference to the document stored in the **sketch** member of the **Sketcher** class to the **writeObject()** method of **objectOut**. If the write operation is successful, we set the **isChanged** flag in the document to **false**. This will allow the application to be closed without prompting to save the document, as long as no further changes are made.

The **catch** block will catch any exceptions thrown by the output operation. We use our **MessageBox** class to create and display a dialog showing information about the error. The dialog window title bar will indicate that it is a file write error, and the message will provide detailed information about the error.

We can implement the Save As menu item next, as its operation is very similar to that of the Save process.

Try It Out—File Save-As Operations

In responding to the Save As menu item, we always want to display a dialog to save the file, so it's basically the same as the Save process, but without the **else** clause that is executed when the document has the default name. Of course, we need a different title in the dialog window. The code for this will be:

```
public void actionPerformed(ActionEvent e)
{
  String fileName = sketch.getName();   // File name for current document
  switch(itemID)
  {
    case SAVE:
      // Code for Save operation, as before...
      break;
    case SAVE_AS:
      runSaveDialog("File Save As Dialog");
      break;
    // Code for the rest of the switch...
  }
}
```

There's nothing new here. We are simply reusing the code we put in the **runSaveDialog()** method for the Save As dialog.

Let's look at how we can implement the operation for the Open menu item next.

File Open Operations

Supporting the File|Open operation is a little more complicated than Save. We have to consider the current document first of all. Does it need to be saved? If it does, we must deal with that before we can read a new document from the file. When we get to the point of reading a document from the file, some more complications arise. We must detach the existing document and its view from the application, and connect the new document and its view to the application. However, we can make good use of some of the code we have already.

Try It Out—Implementing the Open Menu Item

We can implement it like this:

```
public void actionPerformed(ActionEvent e)
{
  String fileName = sketch.getName();    // File name for current document
  switch(itemID)
  {
    case SAVE:
      // Code for Save operation, as before...
      break;
    case SAVE_AS:
      // Code for Save As operation as before...
      break;
    case OPEN:
      view.setEnabled(false);         // Disable the view
      checkForSave(fileName);         // Save current document if necessary

      // Display open file dialog
      FileDialog openDialog = new FileDialog(window, "File Open Dialog");
      openDialog.show();
      fileName = openDialog.getFile();

      // If OK button was pressed, fileName should not be null
      if(fileName!=null)
        loadDocument(openDialog.getDirectory(), fileName);
      else
        view.setEnabled(true);      // No document load - so re-enable view
      openDialog.dispose();            // Release resources
      break;

    // Code for the rest of the switch...
  }
}
```

How It Works

The code here involves replacing the current document and its view, so to avoid any accidental mouse events being originated for the current view while this is going on, we call **setEnabled()** for the view object with the argument **false** to disable the view. This will prevent any interaction with the old view.

To check whether the document needs to be saved, we call another magic method, that we will add shortly, the **checkForSave()** method. This will take care of checking whether the current document should be saved. Once that is complete, we need to obtain the file name and directory for the document that is to be read from the file, so we create a **FileDialog** object which has the default **LOAD** mode, and display it.

After the dialog window closes we get the file name that was entered and save it in the **fileName** member of the **FileHandler** class. If this is not **null** we pass the directory from the dialog and the file name as arguments to the **loadDocument()** method, which we will implement to take care of everything that is necessary to read the document from the file and integrate it into the application. If **fileName** is **null**, the user has aborted the Open operation, so we must restore interaction with the old view by calling the **setEnabled()** method for it with the argument, **true**. Finally we release the resources for the dialog.

Checking for Save

We will implement the **checkForSave()** method as a member of the **Sketcher** class—then we can use it any where in the **Sketcher** class or its inner classes. This method will check the **isChanged** flag in the document, and if the flag is **true**, it will display a prompt dialog asking whether the document should be saved. The **PromptDialog** class is a new modal dialog class that we will add after we have sorted this method out. It will display the dialog shown here.

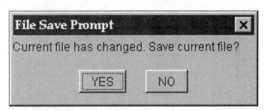

Try It Out—Prompting the User to Save a Sketch

1 If the YES button in the prompt dialog is pressed, we want to go through our standard Save routine. If not, we have nothing else to do because the user has elected not to save the current sketch. Here's the code for that:

```
// Check for save
protected void checkForSave(String fileName)
{
  if(sketch.isChanged())
  { // Prompt to save current document
    PromptDialog prompt = new PromptDialog(window);
    prompt.show();                            // Display the dialog

    if(prompt.isYES())                        // YES button pressed?
      if(fileName.equals(DEFAULT_FILE_NAME))  // Name is default?
```

```
        runSaveDialog("File Save Dialog");       // Then use Save dialog
      else       // save the document with current name
        saveDocument(sketch.getDirectory(), fileName);
    prompt.dispose();                            // Release dialog resources
  }
}
```

2 The `PromptDialog` class is very simple—most of the code is adding the components to the dialog window. Here's the class definition:

```
// Class defining a file save prompt dialog
import java.awt.*;
import java.awt.event.*;

class PromptDialog extends Dialog implements ActionListener
{
  boolean YES = false;          // YES button pressed flag
  String yesLabel = "  YES  ";  // Label for OK button

  // Constructor
  public PromptDialog(Frame frame)
  {
    super(frame, true);                // Create modal dialog
    setTitle("File Save Prompt");

    // Position the dialog in the parent frame
    Rectangle bounds = frame.getBounds();
    setLocation(bounds.x+bounds.width/3, bounds.y+bounds.height/3);

    add(new Label("Current file has changed. Save current file?"),
                                        BorderLayout.CENTER);

    // Create the dialog button pane
    Panel buttonPane = new Panel();                // Create the panel
    buttonPane.setLayout(new FlowLayout(FlowLayout.CENTER,20,10));

    // Create and add the buttons to the button pane
    Button button;                                 // Store a button
    buttonPane.add(button = new Button(yesLabel)); // Create & add OK
    button.addActionListener(this);                // Add a listener
    buttonPane.add(button = new Button("  NO  ")); // Create & add NO
                                                   // button
    button.addActionListener(this);                // Add a listener
    add(buttonPane, BorderLayout.SOUTH);           // Add button panel
    pack();
  }

  // YES check
  boolean isYES()
```

```
  {
    return YES;                      // Return the YES button flag
  }

  // Handle button events
  public void actionPerformed(ActionEvent e)
  {
    if(e.getActionCommand().equals(yesLabel))
      YES = true;                    // YES button pressed
    setVisible(false);               // Hide the dialog window
  }
}
```

You should save this as **PromptDialog.java** in the **Sketcher** directory. If you feel there are too many files in this directory now, you can create another package and put the dialog classes in it.

How It Works

If the **isChanged()** method returns **true**, we create a **PromptDialog** object and display the dialog window. The **isYES()** method for the dialog object will return **true** if the YES button was pressed, and **false** otherwise. In the former case, we check the file name for the document and call the **runSaveDialog()** method if it is still the default, and just call the **saveDocument()** method if it has been saved previously. Lastly we release the resources for the **PromptDialog** object.

The dialog window contains a **Label** component showing the prompt text, and two buttons, YES and NO. The **boolean** variable **YES** is used to indicate whether the YES button was pressed. Its default value is **false**, so if you exit using the close-window icon or the NO button, it will be **false**. The **PromptDialog** object is the listener for both the buttons it contains so their events are received by the **actionPerformed()** method in the class. This just sets the **YES** flag to **true** if it was the YES button that was pressed—the **getActionCommand()** method for the event object returns the label for the button that was pressed. Regardless of which button was pressed, the **actionPerformed()** method calls **setVisible()** to hide the dialog window and return to the point following the call to its **show()** method.

Try It Out—Opening a Document

The **loadDocument()** method in the **Sketcher** class is the core of the Open operation. Reading the document object from the file is the easiest bit. It's just a question of applying what we learned in Chapter 8:

```
// Load a document from file
protected void loadDocument(String directory, String fileName)
{
  if(fileName!=null)
  // Read the sketch back from the file
```

```
    try
    {
      // Create the file stream and the object stream
      FileInputStream input = new FileInputStream
                                        (newFile(directory,fileName));
      ObjectInputStream objectIn = new ObjectInputStream(input);

      sketch = (SketchDoc)objectIn.readObject();     // Read the document
      sketch.setChanged(false);                 // Set a document as unchanged

      // Code to create a view and attach the document and its view...
    }
    catch(IOException eInput)
    {
      MessageBox ioErrorBox = new MessageBox(window, "File Read Error",
                                        eInput.toString());
      ioErrorBox.show();
      ioErrorBox.dispose();
    }
    catch(ClassNotFoundException eNoClass)
    {
      MessageBox noClassErrorBox = new MessageBox(window,
                        "File Read Error", "Incompatible file format.");
      noClassErrorBox.show();
      noClassErrorBox.dispose();
    }
  }
```

How It Works

After making sure that the **fileName** reference passed to the method is not **null**, we create a **FileInputStream** object from a **File** object that is based on the directory and **fileName** passed as arguments. The **FileInputStream** object is then used to create the **ObjectInputStream** object, **objectIn**. We read the document object from the object input stream by calling the **readObject()** method for **objectIn**. The object that is returned is of type **Object**, so we cast this to type **SketchDoc** before storing it in the **sketch** member of the **Sketcher** class.

Note that we need two **catch** blocks because we can get two kinds of exception thrown by the **readObject()** method. The first kind is a regular input error that can occur with any read operation. The second kind of exception, **ClassNotFoundException**, arises if the file does not contain data in the correct format and sequence. This exception will be thrown if you make changes to the data members of the class for the object being read, after the object was originally written to the file. Then the class defined in your program will not match the class information stored in the file.

After the code in the **try** block has been executed, the application object will contain a reference to the new document object—the old document having been cut adrift. However, the new document will not have a valid reference to the application or view object, and the application window will still contain the view for the old document object. Further, the listeners for the **Element** menu items in the application window will also refer to the old document so some work on the **SketchFrame** class is necessary.

Try It Out—Updating Menu Listeners in the Application Window

1   At the moment the `SketchFrame` class constructor does not retain references to the listeners for the `Element` menu items. We need to change that. We will need to replace the listeners for these menu items with new listener objects that reference the new document. First we will add some data members to the `SketchFrame` class to store the listeners:

```
// Element type listeners
ElementCommand lineListener, rectangleListener, circleListener,
                          curveListener, textListener;


// Element color listeners
ColorCommand redListener, yellowListener, greenListener, blueListener;
```

2   We now need to set these in the constructor. If we add another method to create and add these listeners, we can use it in the constructor, and then reuse it when we add a new document. Add the following method to the `SketchFrame` class:

```
// Add element menu listeners
public void addElementMenuListeners()
{
  // Add the type menu listeners
  lineItem.addItemListener(lineListener = new ElementCommand(LINE,
                              sketch));
  rectangleItem.addItemListener(rectangleListener = new ElementCommand
                              (RECTANGLE, sketch));
  circleItem.addItemListener(circleListener = new ElementCommand
                              (CIRCLE, sketch));
  curveItem.addItemListener(curveListener = new ElementCommand
                              (CURVE, sketch));
  textItem.addItemListener(textListener = new ElementCommand
                              (TEXT, sketch));

  // Add the color menu listeners
  redItem.addItemListener(redListener = new ColorCommand(Color.red,
                              sketch));
  yellowItem.addItemListener(yellowListener = new ColorCommand
                              (Color.yellow, sketch));
  greenItem.addItemListener(greenListener = new ColorCommand
                              (Color.green, sketch));
  blueItem.addItemListener(blueListener = new ColorCommand
                              (Color.blue, sketch));
}
```

This is almost identical to the code we had in the constructor to add these listeners, except that the objects are stored in the data members we declared for the purpose.

3   We can now alter the constructor to call this method to add the listeners:

```
public SketchFrame(String title, Sketcher theApp)
{
  super(title);                      // Call base constructor
  this.theApp = theApp;              // Store the application object
  sketch = theApp.getDocument();     // Get the document object
  setMenuBar(menubar);               // Add the menu bar to the window

  toolbar = new Toolbar(theApp);     // Create the toolbar
  add(toolbar, BorderLayout.NORTH);  // Place it at the top

  // Code to construct the file pull down menu as before...

  // Code to construct the Element pull down menu as before...

  // Code to add the element type items as before...

  // Code to construct the Color item pull down menu as before...

  // Code to add the color menu items as before...

  addElementMenuListeners();    // Add listeners for Element menu items
  elementMenu.add(colorMenu);   // Add the sub-menu

  // Code to construct the Help pull down menu as before...

  menubar.add(fileMenu);             // Add the file menu
  menubar.add(elementMenu);          // Add the element menu
  menubar.add(helpMenu);             // Add the help menu

  addKeyListener(new KeyHandler());  // Add the key handler

  add(statusbar, BorderLayout.SOUTH); // Add the status bar
  pack();
}
```

The code that added the listeners for the type and color menu items has been removed, and one new line of code to call the method we just added has been inserted just before the statement that adds the **colorMenu** object to the element menu.

4 When we want to replace the **Element** menu listeners we will need to remove all the old listeners before we add the new ones. We can add a method to **SketchFrame** to do this:

```
// Remove element menu listeners
public void removeElementMenuListeners()
{
  // Remove the type menu listeners
  lineItem.removeItemListener(lineListener);
  rectangleItem.removeItemListener(rectangleListener);
  circleItem.removeItemListener(circleListener);
  curveItem.removeItemListener(curveListener);
  textItem.removeItemListener(textListener);
```

```
      // Remove the color menu listeners
      redItem.removeItemListener(redListener);
      yellowItem.removeItemListener(yellowListener);
      greenItem.removeItemListener(greenListener);
      blueItem.removeItemListener(blueListener);
   }
```

5 The present implementation of the **addView()** method in the **SketchFrame** class was designed to add the view in the **ScrollPane** component. We need to amend this method to enable a view to be replaced with a new one. It's quite a simple change that we need to make:

```
// Add the document view to the window
public void addView(SketchView view)
{
  if(drawArea!=null)                 // If we have a draw area
  {
    drawArea.removeAll();            // Remove its components
    remove(drawArea);                // Remove it from the window
  }
  drawArea = new ScrollPane();            // Create a new draw area
  drawArea.add(view);                     // Add the view to the draw area
  add(drawArea, BorderLayout.CENTER);     // Add the draw area to the window
}
```

6 We can add a method to insert a reference to the new document into the application window object. This will do three things—it will store the new document reference in the **SketchDoc** member, **sketch**; it will replace the **Element** menu listeners and it will set the **Element** menu checks to correspond the element type and color in the new document.

Add the following definition of the method to the **SketchFrame** class:

```
// Insert a new document into the application window
public void insertNewDocument(SketchDoc sketch)
{
  this.sketch = sketch;                          // Store  the new document

  // Insert listeners from the new document
  removeElementMenuListeners();
  addElementMenuListeners();

  // Set menu checks as the new document
  setTypeMenuChecks(sketch.getElementType());
  setColorMenuChecks(sketch.getElementColor());
}
```

With the other methods we have added, this becomes very easy. The menu check marks are set by calling the methods we already have for this purpose.

7 We can now go back to completing the `loadDocument()` method in the `Sketcher` class to call the method we have just written. The code to insert the document after it has been read from the file is as follows:

```
// Load a document from file
protected void loadDocument(String directory, String fileName)
{
  if(fileName!=null)
  // Read the sketch back from the file
  try
  {
    // Create the file stream and the object stream and read the new
    // document..

    // Create a view and attach the document and its view
    sketch.addView(view = new SketchView(sketch)); // Create & add the
                                                                view
    sketch.setApp(this);              // Set the app in the document
    window.addView(view);             // Add the view to the app window
    window.insertNewDocument(sketch); // Insert document into app window
    window.setTitle(title + ": " + fileName);// Set the app window title
    window.validate();                // Validate the app window
  }
  catch(/* Exceptions to be caught */)
  {
    // Code to handle exceptions
  }
}
```

That completes the code to make the File|Open menu item work. You can recompile Sketcher and give it a whirl.

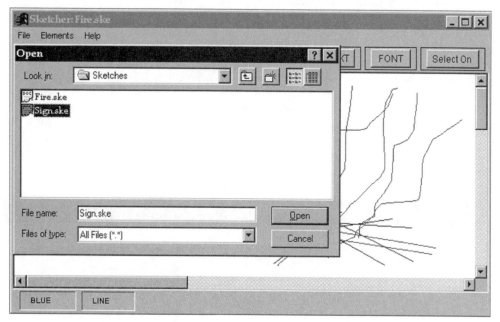

How It Works

Removing a listener from a **CheckboxMenuItem** object is very easy. You just call the **removeItemListener()** for the menu item, passing a reference to the listener that you want removed as an argument. Although we have not used the capability, you can add multiple listeners for events so it is necessary to specify the listener that is to be removed to the **removeItemListener()** method.

Adding a New View in the Application Window

The first time the method is called, the **drawArea** member of the **SketchFrame** class will be **null**, because the method is called as part of the process of initializing the application. On subsequent occasions, it will be called to insert a new document view, so in these cases **drawArea** will not be **null**, and the two statements in the **if** block will be executed. The **removeAll()** method in **ScrollPane** is inherited from the **Container** class, and it removes all components that have been added to the object. After removing the old **view** object, we remove the current the **ScrollPane** object from the application window, so that we can add a new one containing the new document view.

Inserting a New Document into the Application Window

The first step in creating a view in **loadDocument()** adds a new view to the document and stores a reference to it in the **view** member of the application object. The **SketchView** object sets up the context menus itself, using the new document object, so all that is self-contained and we don't need to worry about it. Next we pass a reference to the current application object to the document to set the link back to the application from the document correctly. This is done by calling the **setApp()** method that we added to the **SketchDoc** class earlier in this chapter. The **loadDocument()** method is in the **Sketcher** class so the **this** variable refers to the current application object.

Calling the **addView()** method for the window object inserts the view corresponding to the document we have read from file into the application window. We then call **insertNewDocument()** for the window object to insert the document and update the Element menu items. Finally we reset the title bar in the application window to reflect the new document name, and call **validate()** for the **window** object. This last call is essential—it performs a new layout for the components in the **window** object. Without this call, the new document view will not be displayed correctly.

We can now save sketches in a file and restore them, and we have reasonable protection from accidental loss of our work. We can provide the mechanism for starting with a clean sheet next. The File | New operation is rather like the File | Open operation—except that we will create the new document rather than read it from a file. Apart from that, the logic will be the virtually the same.

Try It Out—File New Operations

1   The code we need to add in the **actionPerformed()** method in the **Sketcher** class is almost trivial:

```
  public void actionPerformed(ActionEvent e)
  {
    String fileName = sketch.getName();   // File name for current document
    switch(itemID)
    {
      case SAVE:
        // Code for Save operation, as before...
        break;
      case SAVE_AS:
        // Code for Save As operation as before...
        break;
      case OPEN:
        // Code for Open operation as before...
        break;
      case NEW:
        view.setEnabled(false);        // Disable the view
        checkForSave(fileName);        // Save current document if necessary
        makeNewDocument();             // Make a new document
        break;                         // Code for the rest of the switch...
      // Code for the rest of the switch...
    }
  }
```

2 The code for **makeNewDocument()** is as follows:

```
// Create new document
protected void makeNewDocument()
{
  // Create the new document & insert it in  the application
  sketch = new SketchDoc(theApp);                    // Create the document
  sketch.addView(view = new SketchView(sketch)); // Create & add view
  window.addView(view);                        // Add new view to the app window
  window.insertNewDocument(sketch);     // Insert document into app window
  window.setTitle(title + ": " + sketch.getName()); // Set the app window
                                                     // title
  window.validate();                         // Validate the app window
}
```

How It Works

The view is disabled to inhibit accidental interaction while we are displaying and hiding the Save dialog, should that be necessary. The **checkForSave()** will display the dialog if the **isChanged** flag in the current document is **true**. The last step is to call the **makeNewDocument()** method, which we have added to the **Sketcher** class definition. As you see, this is the same as the code for **loadDocument()** except that we create a new **SketchDoc** object rather that reading a file. Because the new document will already have its **isChanged** flag set to **false**, we don't need to call the **setChanged()** method here.

We can now move on to implementing the Close menu item.

Try It Out—Supporting Close

1 When File | Close is selected, we want to check whether the current document should be saved, and then close the application. We have most of the code to do this already. All we need is the code for the **case** statement in the **actionPerformed()** method:

```
public void actionPerformed(ActionEvent e)
{
  String fileName = sketch.getName();   // File name for current document
  switch(itemID)
  {
    case SAVE:
      // Code for Save operation, as before...
      break;
    case SAVE_AS:
      // Code for Save As operation as before...
      break;
    case OPEN:
      // Code for Open operation as before...
      break;
    case NEW:
      // Code for New operation as before...
      break;
    case CLOSE:
      checkForSave(fileName);  // Save the current document if necessary
      System.exit(0);                     // Exit the application
      break;
    // Code for the rest of the switch...
  }
}
```

2 There is another event we need to consider. At the moment, the close icon for the application window just closes the application down without checking anything. We need to change this so it doesn't bail out without checking if the current document needs to be saved. We can change the **windowClosing()** method in the **WindowHandler** class that has **Sketcher** as its top-level class:

```
public void windowClosing(WindowEvent e)
{
  if (e.getID() == WindowEvent.WINDOW_CLOSING)
  {
    checkForSave(sketch.getName()); // Save current document if necessary
    window.dispose();                        // Release window resources
    System.exit(0);                          // Exit the application
  }
}
```

How It Works

You can see how this works—it just calls the **checkForSave()** method that will deal with saving the current document if necessary, and then calls the **exit()** method in the **System**

class to end the application. And all that's required in the
WindowHandler.windowClosing() method is to call the **checkForSave()** method. That
takes care of everything.

To make the File menu fully operational, we must add support for the Print menu item. It's
a little complicated, but doesn't involve a great deal of code.

Printing in Java

Printing in most environments is a messy business—inevitably so, because you must worry
about tedious details such as the size of a page, margin sizes and how many pages you are
going to need for your output. The way through this is to take it one step at a time. The
starting point for us is handling events from the File I Print menu item.

We can add the code to deal with events from the File | Print menu item very easily.
Just add the following code to the **actionPerformed()** method in the **FileHandler**
inner class:

```
public void actionPerformed(ActionEvent e)
{
  String fileName = sketch.getName();   // File name for current document
  switch(itemID)
  {
    case SAVE:
      // Code for Save operation, as before...
      break;
    case SAVE_AS:
      // Code for Save As operation as before...
      break;
    case OPEN:
      // Code for Open operation as before...
      break;
    case NEW:
      // Code for New operation as before...
      break;
    case CLOSE:
      // Code for Close operation as before...
      break;
    case PRINT:
      printDocument(fileName);
      break;
  }
}
```

Now all it takes to make printing work in our application is to implement the
printDocument() method. This will make use of a class in the **java.awt** package that is
specific to printing.

Creating a PrintJob Object

Printing in Java can be done through an object of type **PrintJob**. The **PrintJob** object is your interface to the printing support in the operating system on your computer. You can't create a **PrintJob** object directly—you must get one from a **Toolkit** object.

FYI As we've seen over the last few chapters, the Toolkit object is your connection to the underlying environment in which your Java program is running.

All you need to do to obtain a **PrintJob** object is to get a **Toolkit** object, and then call the **getPrintJob()** method for the **Toolkit** object. We will be adding the **printDocument()** method to the **Sketcher** class to print a document.

Try It Out—Getting a PrintJob

1 We can kick off the definition of **printDocument()** by getting a **PrintJob** object from the **Toolkit** object for the document view. We can do this with the statements:

```
// Print the current document
protected void printDocument(String fileName)
{
  Toolkit theKit = view.getToolkit(); // Get toolkit for the view
  PrintJob print = theKit.getPrintJob(window, "Printing sketch", null);

  // Plus the rest of the code for the method...
}
```

2 This presupposes that we have the method **getView()** in the variable **sketch**. You can add the following code to **SketchDoc** for this:

```
public SketchView getView()
{
  return view;
}
```

How It Works

The first argument to the **getPrintJob()** method must be a **Frame** object, so we can pass the **window** object to it. The method requires a **Frame** object because when you call the **getPrintJob()** method, it will start the printing process in the operating system environment, and this will typically involve displaying a dialog. The dialog will be displayed with the **Frame** object as its parent. The second argument to the **getPrintJob()** method is a **String** object that is simply a title for the print job. The third argument is a **Properties** object.

The `Properties` **class is defined in the package** `java.util`, **and objects of this class can represent a list of properties of any kind. A property is simply a key that identifies what the property is, plus a value. We won't be using properties for printing, so the argument is** `null` **here.**

It is possible that the **getPrintJob()** method won't return a **PrintJob** object—it may return **null** if the printing process does not start for some reason. We must therefore check for a **null** return from the method, but what should we do about it? We could just display a message box but there will be other possible errors during printing, so here's a chance to throw our very own exception.

Try It Out—Throwing Your Own *PrintExceptions*

1   Before we can throw anything of our own in Java, we must decide on a suitable missile. To this end we will define our own exception class, which, after a great deal of cogitation, we will call **PrintException**. The definition of an exception class must extend the **Throwable** class.

We can define our exception class as:

```
// Class to define a printing exception
public class PrintException extends Throwable
{
  // Constructors
  public PrintException()
  {  super("Error while printing."); }       // Default constructor

  public PrintException(String s)
  {
    super(s);                                 // Call the base class constructor
  }
}
```

2   We can use this class immediately, in the **printDocument()** method:

```
// Print the current document
protected void printDocument(String fileName) throws PrintException
{
  Toolkit theKit = view.getToolkit();  // Get toolkit for the view
  PrintJob print = theKit.getPrintJob(window, "Printing sketch", null);
  if(print ==null)
    // Print operation failed
    throw new PrintException("No print job object created.");

  // Plus the rest of the code for the method...
}
```

3 For the **Sketcher** class to compile, we must put the call to the **printDocument()** method in a **try** block, and catch any **PrintException** objects that are thrown. You need to modify the code that deals with the **PRINT** case in the **actionPerformed()** method to:

```
public void actionPerformed(ActionEvent e)
{
  String fileName = sketch.getName();   // File name for current document
  switch(itemID)
  {
    case SAVE:
      // Code for Save operation, as before...
      break;
    case SAVE_AS:
      // Code for Save As operation as before...
      break;
    case OPEN:
      // Code for Open operation as before...
      break;
    case NEW:
      // Code for New operation as before...
      break;
    case CLOSE:
      // Code for Close operation as before...
      break;
    case PRINT:
      try
      {
        printDocument(fileName);
      }
      catch(PrintException ePrint)
      {
        MessageBox printErrorBox = new MessageBox(window, "Print Error",
                                  ePrint.toString());
        printErrorBox.show();
      }
      break;
  }
}
```

How It Works

You can save **PrintException.java** in the Sketcher directory. The class has two constructors—a default constructor that passes a standard string to the base class constructor, and a constructor that accepts a **String** argument that is passed on to the base class constructor. We can use the default constructor when we don't know exactly what caused the error, and the other constructor when we have more information about the problem. The **String** object is accessible when a **PrintException** is caught by calling the **toString()** method for the exception object.

Of course we must declare that the **printDocument()** method can throw a
PrintException—the method won't compile if we don't. If the **PrintJob** object is **null** we
throw a **PrintException** with a string that records the reason for the exception.

We have put the **printDocument()** method call in a **try** block, followed by a **catch** block
to handle **PrintException** objects. All we do, if one is thrown, is display the message in a
message box using our **MessageBox** dialog class.

We can try this out now. If you recompile Sketcher you can run the program and try
printing a document.

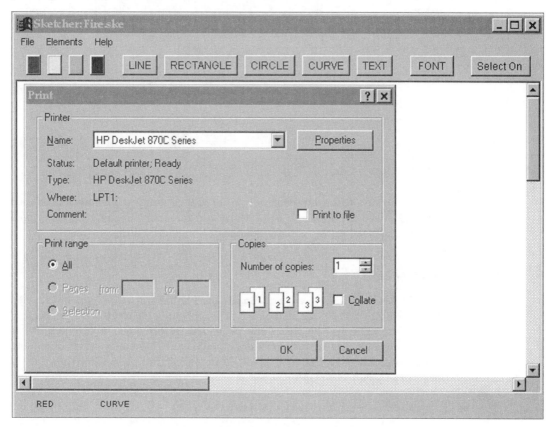

When you select Print on the File menu, the **printDocument()** method is called and the
getPrintJob() method displays the dialog for your printing process. I have an HP DeskJet
printer so I get the dialog above.

We haven't yet implemented any printing—but the exit from the print dialog will determine
whether or not a **PrintJob** object is returned. If you select the OK button you get an object
returned, if you select Cancel, **null** will be returned, so we will throw our very first
PrintException.

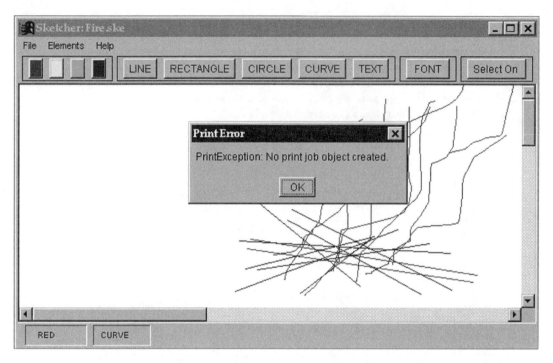

Since we can't print anyway at the moment, select the Cancel button. The **PrintException** gets thrown so you will see the message box displaying the error message. Let's get back to the printing process and develop the **printDocument()** method a little further.

Using a PrintJob Object

The **PrintJob** object has a method, **getPageDimension()**, that provides you with information about the size of the page that you will be printing. It returns a **Dimension** object that contains the width and height of the page. This information is essential, because it is up to you to figure out how to print the document—and to arrange what document information is to go on each page that you print. You can get the page size from the **PrintJob** object, **print**, with the statement:

```
Dimension pageSize = print.getPageDimension();        // Get the page size
```

The width and height information is obtained from the print manager in the operating system environment, but conveniently, they are returned in units of screen pixels. This means that they are in the same units as the **Graphics** object that is the graphics context for the screen. Since these are the units that our element **draw()** methods use, we will be able to apply these directly to print the document.

If it wasn't implemented this way, we would have the horrific job of figuring out how to draw the document in completely different units from those that we use to display the document. Darn clever, those people at JavaSoft!

There is another method defined in the **PrintJob** class, **getPageResolution()**, that returns the resolution for a page in pixels-per-inch when it is printed—although it is not guaranteed that this will be the same resolution that your printer uses—although it usually will be. You can use this to relate screen resolution to the resolution at which the printing will be done. However, you *don't* use this for calculating positions on a page, or to specify margin sizes, since all these things will be done in units of screen pixels.

The page size returned by the **getPageDimension()** method is for the paper's complete size, so you will want to allow for some margins on each side of the paper, and top and bottom.

Try It Out—Sizing the Paper

Lets add some code to the **printDocument()** method to determine how big the margins are in screen pixels, and to figure out how big the residual print area is on a page. We will provide for 1 inch margins top and bottom, and a ¾ inch margin either side. Here's the code you can add to do that:

```
protected void printDocument(String fileName) throws PrintException
{
  Toolkit theKit = view.getToolkit();   // Get toolkit for the view
  PrintJob print = theKit.getPrintJob(window, "Printing sketch", null);
  if(print ==null)
    // Print op failed
    throw new PrintException("No print job object created.");

  Dimension pageSize = print.getPageDimension();     // Get the page size

  // Calculate margin sizes - should be screen units, not print units
  int pixelsPerInch = theKit.getScreenResolution();   // Get screen
                                                       // resolution
  int topMargin = pixelsPerInch;             // 1 inch top and bottom margin
  int sideMargin = (3*pixelsPerInch)/4;           // 3/4 inch side margins

  // Define size of page print area
  Dimension printArea = new Dimension(pageSize.width-2*sideMargin,//width
                            pageSize.height-2*topMargin);//Height

  // Plus the rest of the code for the method...
}
```

How It Works

After we have stored the overall page size in the variable **pageSize**, we work out what the margin sizes are in screen pixels. The **getScreenResolution()** method in the **Toolkit** class returns the number of screen pixels in an inch, so all we have to do is multiply this value by the size of each margin in inches. Since there are two side margins and a margin top and bottom, we get the printing area on a page by subtracting twice the corresponding margin size from the overall width and height of a page. We store the width and height of the printing area in the **Dimension** object, **printArea**.

Unless you have a really big printer, we are into multi-page printing to print a document in Sketcher. Therefore we need to work out how big the document actually is, and how many pages it will take to print it.

Calculating the Document Size

The document's size isn't necessarily the size of the view that we assigned in the **SketchView** constructor. This may contain a lot of empty space. If your minimalist sketch consists of a small rectangle you can accommodate that on a single page—you won't want to print several empty pages to cover the whole area of the view. We need to compute the size of the rectangle actually occupied by elements that we have drawn. Then, given that we know the size of a page, we can work out how many pages the whole document will occupy. The total size of the sketch is not difficult to obtain. The diagram illustrates how we can get the overall extent of three elements, a **CircleElement**, a **TextElement** and a **CurveElement** from their bounding rectangles.

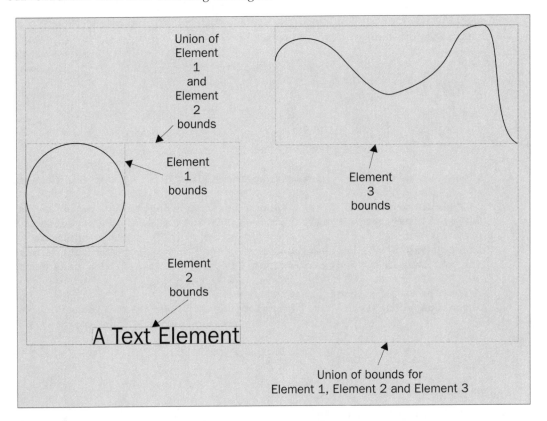

All we need to do is to combine the bounding rectangles for the elements to produce a single rectangle that contains all the elements. The **union()** method in the **Rectangle** class increases the size of the rectangle for which it is called, so that it additionally contains the

Rectangle object that is passed as an argument. Therefore we can use the **union()** method to combine the bounds for the first element with that of the second to produce a rectangle enclosing both, and then use the same method to combine the resultant rectangle with the bounds for the third to produce a rectangle enclosing all three. Clearly this process can be applied to any number of elements.

Try It Out—Sizing the Document

We can add a method to the **SketchDoc** class to do exactly this:

```
// Get the total document size
public Rectangle getExtent()
{
  // Get enumeration for document
  Enumeration elmnts = sketchElements.elements();

  // Get bounds for first element
  Rectangle extent = ((Element)(elmnts.nextElement())).getBounds();

  // Add the bounds for each element
  while(elmnts.hasMoreElements())
    extent = extent.union(((Element)(elmnts.nextElement())).getBounds());
  return extent;         // Return total extent
}
```

How It Works

Using the enumeration object, **elmnts**, we iterate through all of the elements in the document. The **Rectangle** variable, **extent**, is initialized with the bounding rectangle for the first element. The bounding rectangles for each of the other elements in the documents are combined with **extent**. The variable, **extent**, will ultimately reference a **Rectangle** object that encloses all of the elements in the document.

We can use this method to work out how many pages we need.

Getting the Page Count for a Document

To work out how many pages a printed version of a document will require, we will tile the document extent with the printing area for a page, starting at the top-left corner of the document extent. We should make this as general as possible, in case we want to increase the size of the document later. You won't want to go rummaging around the code to print the document every time you change the size of the view. The diagram below illustrates the situation where eight pages are needed to print the entire document.

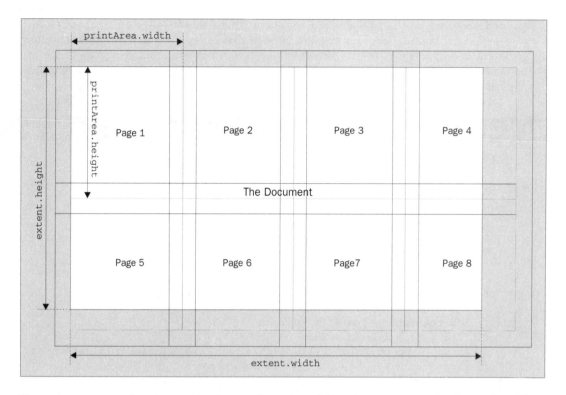

The printing area of each page is shown dashed, and the document area is shown in white. You should be able to see that we can get the number of pages across the document—in a row—by dividing the width of the document extent by the width of the printing area on a page, and rounding up to the nearest whole number of pages. Similarly, we can get the number of rows of pages by dividing the height of the document extent by the height of the printing area on a page, and rounding up to the nearest whole number.

Try It Out—Counting the Pages

We can add the code to the **printDocument()** method to do this as follows:

```
protected void printDocument(String fileName) throws PrintException
{
  Toolkit theKit = view.getToolkit();   // Get toolkit for
                                        the view
  PrintJob print = theKit.getPrintJob(window, "Printing sketch", null);
  if(print ==null)
    throw new PrintException("No print job object created."); // Print op
                                                              // failed

  Dimension pageSize = print.getPageDimension();   // Get the page size

  // Calculate margin sizes - should be screen units, not print units
  int pixelsPerInch = theKit.getScreenResolution();   // Get screen
                                                      // resolution
```

```
    int topMargin = pixelsPerInch;              // 1 inch top and bottom margin
    int sideMargin = (3*pixelsPerInch)/4;          // 3/4 inch side margins

    // Define size of page print area
    Dimension printArea = new Dimension(pageSize.width-2*sideMargin,
    //width
     pageSize.height-2*topMargin);
     // Height
```

```
    // Calculate the number of pages for the document
    Rectangle extent = sketch.getExtent(); // Get the total document extent

    // Get the number of pages across and down the document
    int hCount = (int)Math.ceil(((double)extent.width)/printArea.width);
     // Across
    int vCount = (int)Math.ceil(((double)extent.height)/printArea.height);
     // Down
```

```
    // Plus the rest of the code for the method...
  }
```

How It Works

To get the document extent, we call the method that we added to the **SketchDoc** class. The division of the document width by the print area width is done in floating point because we want to round the result up to the next highest integer value. If we left it as integer arithmetic it would be rounded down, as you know. To round up, we pass the result to the **ceil()** function in the **Math** class. This returns a value of type **double** that is the next whole number that is greater than, or equal to, the value of the argument. We must cast the result to **int** before storing it in the variable, **hCount**, which records the number of pages across the document—that is, in a row. If we don't put an explicit cast, the compiler will complain, because there is a potential for losing information when casting from **double** to **int** and the compiler will only insert automatic casts when this is not the case. The number of rows of pages to tile the complete document is calculated using essentially the same process, and the result is stored in the local variable, **vCount**.

Printing a Single Page

The process of printing a page involves using an object of type **Graphics** just as we have used to draw on the screen—but here the **Graphics** object is the graphics context for a printed page. Because it is of type **Graphics**, it has all the methods for outputting text and drawing shapes that we have already seen and used, but of course, the output is directed to the printer. You can obtain a graphics context for the printer attached to your computer by calling the **getGraphics()** method for the **PrintJob** object. For example, the statement:

```
    Graphics printG = print.getGraphics();       // Get print context for page
```

returns a **Graphics** object that is the graphics context for a single page. You can't reuse it for another page. Each time you want to print a new page, you must throw away the old **Graphics** object and obtain a new one. To print on the page you just call the appropriate methods for the **Graphics** object. All the **draw()** method for the elements in Sketcher already use these methods, so you can print the document on a page just by calling the **draw()** method for the **SketchDoc** object. However, a document is potentially larger than one page, so we need to sort out how we are going to chop the document up into as many pages as are required to print the whole thing.

Multi-Page Printing

We have assembled most of the data that we need to be able to print the document. We now need to understand how we are going to print the pages necessary to cover the entire document. This will involve manipulating two things:

> The **origin** in the graphics context we are using for printing—this is the reference point from which all the coordinates that you use in drawing are measured

> The **clip rectangle** that determines what gets printed

A clip rectangle is a special rectangle defined for a graphics context. Anything drawn inside the rectangle will be output to the device—the printer or the screen or whatever the context applies to—and anything drawn outside the rectangle will be clipped, which means it isn't output. You can set the clip rectangle to whatever you want by calling the method **setClip()** for the **Graphics** object. For example, you can set the clip rectangle for the **Graphics** object, **g**, with the following statement:

```
g.setClip(x, y, width, height);              // Set the clip rectangle
```

This defines a clip rectangle with its top-left corner at position (**x**, **y**) and with the width and height as specified by the third and fourth arguments. Anything within the region bounded by **x** on the left and **x + width** on the right, and **y** at the top, and **y + height** at the bottom will be output. Anything outside this region will be clipped. For example, if you draw a line that crossed the edge of the clip rectangle, the part of the line that is inside will be visible, and the part that is outside will not.

Coordinates for shapes that you draw in a graphics context are relative to the origin for the context. The origin in a graphics context is a point at position (0, 0) by default, but you can change it. This can be a bit confusing—at least it always seems so to me—so I will endeavor to explain exactly what is going on. To change the origin you just call the **translate()** method for the **Graphics** object. The method requires two arguments to be specified, the x and y coordinates relative to the present origin where the new origin should be. All subsequent draw operations will be relative to the new origin. Changing the origin does not affect anything that you have drawn already, and it does not affect the clip rectangle. Of course, after you have changed the origin, the coordinates in a new call to **setClip()** will be relative to the new origin.

The following diagram shows a graphic context used with and without calling the **translate()** method.

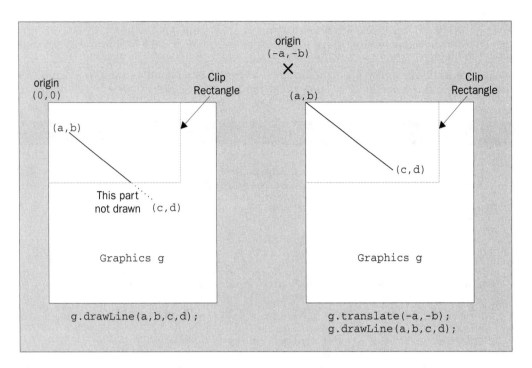

In both cases we draw a line from the point (a, b) to the point (c, d). The dashed rectangle is the clip rectangle, so the portion of the line that lies outside this on the left is not drawn. In the example on the right, we call the **translate()** method for the **Graphics** object, **g**, to move the context origin to the point (-a, -b). As a result, the same call to the **drawLine()** method draws a line from the top-left corner of the clip rectangle to the point (c, d)—the whole line has been effectively shifted by –a in x and by -b in y. As a result, the point (a, b) now appears at the point that was originally (0, 0) but is, of course, (a, b)—otherwise where would our line start?

So one way of envisaging how you can use the **translate()** method is that, if you want the point **(a, b)** in drawing coordinates to be where the current origin is, call the **translate()** method with arguments -a and -b.

By setting the clip rectangle and moving the origin appropriately in the graphics context before we call the **draw()** method for the document object, we can print each of the pages for a document.

The Printing Process

The origin for printing in a **Graphics** object for a page is the top-left corner of the page, so our technique for printing all the pages will be to adjust the origin so that it corresponds to the top-left corner of each page to be printed, and then set the clip rectangle to correspond to the print area for that page.

We will print the document by row—that is, we will print all the pages in the first row, then the pages in the next row and so on, until we have printed all the rows. Remember, from our discussion earlier there will be **vCount** rows, and **hCount** pages in a row, so the basic logic is going to involve a nested loop with the outer loop running through **vCount** iterations and the inner loop running through **hCount** iterations.

Try It Out—Printing Each Page

Here's the code we need to add to the **printDocument()** method to do this—it follows on directly after the code we have already put in the method:

```java
protected void printDocument(String fileName) throws PrintException
{
  // All the code that we added earlier...

    int xOrg;                        // x origin position
    int yOrg = extent.y - topMargin; // y origin position

    Graphics printG = null;          // Print device context

    for(int i = 0; i < vCount; i++)
    {
      xOrg = extent.x-sideMargin;    // x origin position for 1st page in row
      for(int j = 0; j < hCount; j++)
      {
        printG = print.getGraphics();        // Get print context for page
        if(printG==null)
          // Print context failed - throw exception
          throw new PrintException("Failed to create print context.");

        // Print the page
        printG.translate(-xOrg, -yOrg);      // Translate the origin

        // Set clip rectangle to print area
        printG.setClip(xOrg + sideMargin, yOrg + topMargin,
                                  printArea.width, printArea.height);

        sketch.draw(printG);         // Draw the sketch

        printG.dispose();            // Release context resources
        xOrg += printArea.width;     // Move x origin by print area width
      }
      yOrg += printArea.height;      // Move y origin by print area height
    }
    print.end();                     // End the print job
}
```

How It Works

Before we enter the nested loop, we declare a variable **xOrg**, to hold the x coordinate of the origin in the graphics context, and we define a variable, **yOrg**, to hold the y coordinate for the origin initialized to the top of the document extent, less the top margin dimension. The diagram shows the position of the first page in relation to the document.

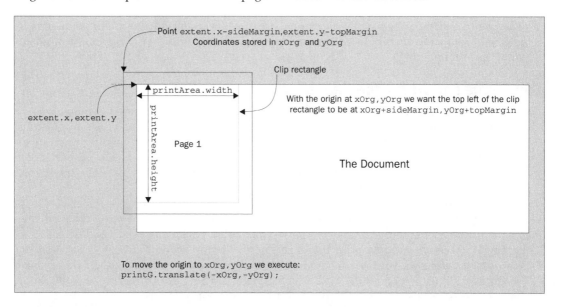

The initial value of **xOrg** is set in the outer loop because we want it to be reset to this value at the beginning of each row. In the inner loop we get a graphics context for a page by calling the **getGraphics()** method for the **PrintJob** object. If this fails we throw another **PrintException** which will be caught in the **actionPerformed()** method for the **FileHandler** object. We get a new **Graphics** object for each page to be printed.

Once we have the **Graphics** object, we call the **translate()** method to move the origin. This will make the top-left corner of the area of the document we want to print map to the top-left corner of the print area on the page. We then set the clip rectangle inset from (**xOrg**, **yOrg**) by the margin sizes, and with the width and height corresponding to the print area on the page. To print the page we call the **draw()** method for the document object, **sketch**. Although this can potentially draw the entire document, everything outside the clip rectangle will be suppressed.

At the end of each iteration in the inner loop, we release the resources for the graphics context because we are done with it. We will obtain a new one for the next page on the next iteration. We also increment **xOrg** by the width of the **printArea** so that **xOrg** and **yOrg** will be set to the coordinates of the next page in the row. The distance between each page in a row and its successor is always the width of the print area.

At the end of the inner loop, which will be when **hCount** pages have been printed, the value of **yOrg** is incremented by the height of the print area on the page to move down to the next row. The distance between each row and the next is always the height of the print area. At the beginning of the next iteration of the outer loop, the value of **xOrg** is reset to the position at the beginning of a row, and then the inner loop takes care of printing all the pages in the next row.

The statement which is executed once the nested loop finishes, calls the **end()** method for the **PrintJob** object. This terminates the print job and does any necessary cleanup.

The code we have added here will print the entire document but how will we assemble the pages? If you drop them you will never know what sequence they were in. We need to add some page numbering

Numbering and Titling the Pages

As well as numbering the pages, it would be good to have some record of what was printed, so we will add a title as well. We could add simple sequential-page numbering, but since a document may be several rows of pages, we perhaps should number them in the form *row_number.page_number*. This will enable you to decide whether your 12 pages of output are 4 rows of 3 pages, 6 rows of 2 pages or one of the other possible arrangements.

We will use the file name as the title, and print the title and the page number at the top of each page. We can print the title for each page immediately after we have obtained the graphics context for the page and before we mess about with the origin and set the clip rectangle. Since we want to print the page title in the top margin area, it is essential that we print it before we set the clip rectangle to the print area on the page. At this point the origin is at (0, 0), we know the width of the page and the size of the top margin, so all we have to do is to position the title in the center of the top margin.

Try It Out—Headers and Footers

Here's the additional code we need:

```java
protected void printDocument(String fileName) throws PrintException
{
  // All the code that we added earlier...
  int xOrg;                        // x origin position
  int yOrg = extent.y-topMargin;   // y origin position
  Graphics printG = null;          // Print device context

  String pageTitle = null;         // Page title
  int titleWidth = 0;              // Page title width
  int titleHeight = 0;             // Page title height
  Font titleFont = new Font("Times Roman", Font.BOLD, 14);

  for(int i=0 ; i<vCount ; i++)
  {
    xOrg = extent.x-sideMargin;  // x origin position for 1st page in row
    for(int j=0 ; j<hCount ; j++)
    {
      printG = print.getGraphics();          // Get print context for page
      if(printG==null)
        // Print context failed - throw exception
        throw new PrintException("Failed to create print context.");
```

```
        // Print the page title
        pageTitle = fileName + "  " + (i+1) + "." + (j+1); //Make the title
        printG.setFont(titleFont);
        FontMetrics fm = printG.getFontMetrics(titleFont); // Get font
                                                           // metrics
        titleWidth = fm.stringWidth(pageTitle);       // Get title width
        titleHeight = fm.getHeight();                 // Get title height
        printG.drawString(pageTitle, (pageSize.width-titleWidth)/2,
                                           (topMargin+titleHeight)/2 );
```

```
      // Print the page
      printG.translate(-xOrg , -yOrg);              // Translate the origin

      // Set clip rectangle to print area
      printG.setClip(xOrg+sideMargin,yOrg+topMargin,
      printArea.width,printArea.height);

      sketch.draw(printG);              // Draw the sketch

      printG.dispose();                 // Release context resources
      xOrg += printArea.width;          // Move x origin by print area width
    }
    yOrg += printArea.height;        // Move y origin by print area height
  }
  print.end();                       // End the print job
}
```

How It Works

After we declare some working variables, we define a **Font** object for the title. We need to do this because we want to figure out the size of the title text so that we can center the title. We form the text for the title by appending the page number to the file name for the document. The page number is row number plus 1, followed by a period, followed by the column number plus 1. We then set the font in the graphics context by calling **setFont()**. To get the size of the text we obtain a **FontMetrics** object from the **Graphics** object. We use the dimension returned by the **stringWidth()** and **stringHeight()** methods for the object **fm**, to position the text centrally within the top margin. This means that the mid-point of the text string should be halfway across the width of the page, and mid-way between the top and bottom of the top margin.

Once the page title has been printed, we then adjust the origin and the clip rectangle as before to print the part of the document that belongs on the current page. With these additions to the **printDocument()** method, you have implemented full multi-page printing that will handle a document of any size.

Summary

In this chapter you have added full support for the **File** menu to the Sketcher application, for both document storage and retrieval, and for printing. You should find that the techniques that you have used here are readily applicable in other Java applications. The approach to saving and restoring a document object is not usually dependent on the kind of data it contains, and the approach to printing a document is basically the same as you have seen here. Of course, if your application is a word processor, you will have a little more work to do taking care that each page contains a whole number of lines—so that you don't split a line of text between one page and the next.

The important points we have covered in this chapter are:

▶ With a document/view application architecture, you must consider carefully how the document is linked to the application when you are implementing file input/output operations

▶ A printing operation is initiated by creating a **PrintJob** object. This object is also used to manage the printing process

▶ Methods for a **PrintJob** object can provide you with the dimensions of the page, the resolution applicable to the printing operation in pixels-per-inch, and a **Graphics** object that is a graphics context for the page

▶ You print a page by calling methods for the **Graphics** object obtained from the **PrintJob** object

▶ The units applicable when you are drawing on a page are screen units—pixels-per-inch

▶ You can change the origin in a graphics context by calling the **translate()** method for the **Graphics** object

▶ You can set the clip rectangle within a graphics context by calling the **setClip()** member of the **Graphics** object

▶ To end the printing process you must call the **end()** method for the **PrintJob** object

Exercises

1 Change the Sketcher program so that the File menu reuses a **FileDialog** object, rather than creating a new one each time a document is saved or opened.

2 Modify the Sketcher program to print the title at the top of the page and the page number at the bottom.

3 Implement a dialog for printing that will enable margins to be set by the user. Make the dialog show either default margin sizes, or the last margin sizes that were set.

4 Modify the **printDocument()** method so the boundary of the document area on each page is outlined with a solid line.

5 Extend the previous example so that the outline on each page is a dashed line.

Networking

Networking is about connecting computers so that they can communicate. One of the most powerful features of Java is its networking capabilities which are built into the class library. All the classes supporting networking are in the package **java.net**. This chapter will introduce you to the basic ideas involved in programs that handle network communications, and illustrate these with some simple examples.

> *To run all these examples your computer will need to have TCP/IP installed, an IP address assigned, access to the Internet and, if you use a dial-up connection, the dial-up software must be active.*

In this chapter we will look at:

- What is involved in communications between computers on a network
- What IP addresses and port numbers are
- What a URL is and how you can define URLs in your programs
- The different types of sockets you can use to connect to a network
- How data can be transmitted without connecting directly to the destination
- What client/server communication means and how it works
- Some examples of networking with Java

Networks

A computer network, as I'm sure you know, is a whole bunch of computers—well, at least two—connected together by means of telephone lines, fiber optic cables, satellite links or indeed anything that allows one computer to pass information to another. The archetypal network is the Internet (although strictly speaking that is a network of networks), with some tens of millions of computers currently attached to it, and still growing at a remarkable rate.

Computers on the Internet come in all sorts of different shapes and sizes, supplied by a diverse variety of manufacturers, and many of these computers will have incompatible hardware architectures, and run quite different operating systems. The way they manage to communicate happily is by standardizing three things:

- How computers are uniquely identified on the network
- How files are identified on the network
- The ways in which they can talk to one another

Let's look into these three things in a bit more detail.

Identifying Network Computers

TCP/IP is the open standard set of protocols that form the basis of the Internet as well as many local networks. On a network supporting TCP/IP, every computer is identified by an Internet Protocol address, or IP address—which is a unique number within the network. A network computer will have at least one IP address, but it can have several. All IP addresses consist of four numbers separated by periods. This form of address is sometimes called the **dotted quad format**. An example of an IP address is **204.160.241.99**. This is a network-unique number that identifies a particular computer (like an address for a building: every building has a unique address defined by its country, city, street and house number). All four components of the IP address are always less than 256, so the maximum number of IP addresses on the Internet at the moment is 4,294,967,296. This seems like a lot, but the IP addresses are being consumed at a phenomenal rate, largely due to the need to group IP addresses into networks, so work is in hand to produce a new form of IP address that will many more addresses—in excess of 10^{38}.

An IP address is not a very convenient way for people to refer to a computer on a network. A much friendlier way to identify a computer is by using a **host name**, sometimes also referred to as a **domain name**. A host name is just a text string consisting of names separated by periods such as **java.sun.com** or **wrox.com**. Host names also have to be unique on a network, and will always be associated with an underlying IP address. This oversimplifies somewhat, since a domain name can actually refer to a group of computers. The domain name identifies the domain name server that provides information about, and links to, the services provided by the group of computers.

Java has a class, **InetAddress**, that defines objects that encapsulate IP addresses. It doesn't have any public constructors though, so you can't create **InetAddress** objects directly. You can obtain them by calling static methods defined in the **InetAddress** class. To get an **InetAddress** object for a particular IP address, you need to know the IP address already, or the domain name corresponding to the IP address. You can then get the **InetAddress** object for the computer by calling the **getByName()** method, as follows:

```
InetAddress addr = InetAddress.getByName("java.sun.com");
```

If the computer has several IP addresses, you can obtain objects for all of them with the statement:

```
InetAddress[] addr = InetAddress.getAllByName(domain);
```

The **getAllByName()** method is another static method defined in the class **InetAddress** that returns an array of type **InetAddress[]**.

Obtaining InetAddress Objects

Once you have an **InetAddress** object you can get the domain name by calling its **getHostName()** method, and you can get the IP address by calling its **getHostAddress()** method. Let's try that out in an example.

Try It Out—Using a Host Name to Get the IP Address

This example will dial out to your Internet service provider and obtain the IP address identified by the host name in the program—the Wrox Press web site. This will only work if your dial connection software is active. Here's the code:

```java
// Get objects encapsulating IP addresses
import java.net.*;

class GetIPAddress
{
  public static void main(String[] args)
  {
    String domain = "wrox.com";              // Domain name for computer
    try
    {
      // Get objects for all the IP addresses
      InetAddress[] addr = InetAddress.getAllByName(domain);

      // Output the domain name and IP address for each object
      for(int i = 0; i < addr.length; i++)
        System.out.println("Domain name: " + addr[i].getHostName() +
                           " IP Address:" + addr[i].getHostAddress());

    }
    catch (UnknownHostException e)
    {
      System.out.println(e);
    }
  }
}
```

This produces the output:

```
Domain name: wrox.com IP Address:204.148.170.2
```

How It Works

The **String** object, **domain**, is initialized with the name for the Wrox Press web site computer. In the **try** block, we call the static **getAllByName()** method in the class **InetAddress** to retrieve an array of **InetAddress** objects for the domain name. We then output the domain name and the IP address for each object returned—there is only one in this case.

The **getAllByName()** method can throw a **UnknownHostException** if the name we supply is not recognized, so we must put the code in a **try** block and catch the exception.

Getting Your Own IP Address

You can obtain an **InetAddress** object for the local machine by calling the static method, **getLocalHost()** in the **InetAddress** class:

```
InetAddress addr = InetAddress.getLocalHost();
```

Although, there is clearly no need to dial out to get the **InetAddress** object for the local machine, the method can still throw the **UnknownHostException**, since the local machine may not have an IP address. For this reason you must place the call to it in a **try** block. Once you have the **InetAddress** object for your machine, you can then retrieve the IP address by calling the **getHostAddress()** method, as we did in the last example.

You could try this out in an example as well.

Try It Out—Getting Your Own IP Address

Here's the code—it is very simple:

```java
// Get objects encapsulating IP addresses
import java.net.*;

class GetLocalIPAddress
{
  public static void main(String[] args)
  {
    try
    {
      InetAddress addr = InetAddress.getLocalHost();
      System.out.println("Domain name: " + addr.getHostName() +
                          " IP Address:" + addr.getHostAddress());
    }
    catch (UnknownHostException e)
    {
      System.out.println(e);
    }
  }
}
```

On my machine, I get the output:

```
Domain name: P200Pro IP Address:193.130.244.181
```

On your machine you will get whatever name you have assigned to the machine, plus the IP address. This is almost identical to the previous example. The only significant difference is that we call the `getLocalHost()` method to obtain the `InetAddress` object.

Identifying Files on a Network

Files on a network are identified by a Uniform Resource Locator, or URL. A URL is a relatively straightforward extension of normal way of identifying a file by the path followed by the file name. It just has some extra bits to identify the computer that contains the file, and how you should communicate with the computer to get at the file. A URL is made up of four pieces of information:

Protocol	Domain Name	Port Number	Path and File Name
`http://`	`wrox.com`	`:80`	`/index.html`
`ftp://`	`java.sun.com`		

▶ The protocol identifies the particular communications method that is to be used to get at the file. **HTTP** is the **H**yper**T**ext **T**ransfer **P**rotocol used on the World Wide Web, **FTP** is the **F**ile **T**ransfer **P**rotocol, and there are others (we'll see one in the next chapter)

▶ The domain name identifies the computer uniquely. The last name identifies the kind of organization that owns the computer. For instance, a domain name ending in `.com` is a commercial organization in the USA such as Wrox Press or Sun, `.co.uk` is a UK company, `.edu` is an educational establishment in the USA, `.ac.uk` is an academic or research organization in the UK and `.gov` is a government or other public body. These are just a few examples. There are lots of others

▶ A port is just a number identifying a particular service on a computer. A computer can have several ports—each providing a different service. You don't usually need to specify the port number in a URL because a standard port number, that is typically associated with a particular protocol, will be assigned by default. The port number for the `http` protocol is 80 for example, and the port number for `ftp` is 21

Because the domain name is part of the reference to a file, every file in a network has a unique URL. As long as you know the URL for a file you want on the Internet, and the machine containing it is connected and active, you can go straight to it. A URL can reference any kind of 'resource' on the Internet such as a web page, a directory, a single file, an image or anything else you can find out there.

The URL Class

You have a class that encapsulates URLs—the **URL** class. This is not just a way to represent a URL as an object; it is a great deal more than that. A **URL** object provides with the tools to get at it and read it, wherever it is on the network. You can create a **URL** object from a string specifying the URL, for example:

```
URL sourceURL = new URL("http://www.wrox.com/");
```

This defines a **URL** object corresponding to the home page on the Wrox Press web site. You can also define a **URL** object by supplying a constructor with separate values for the protocol, the host name and the file name. The web site defined by the domain name **"www.ncsa.uiuc.edu"** contains a page that explains what a URL is. The file path and name for the page is **"/demoweb/url-primer.html"**. You could define a **URL** object for this page with the statement:

```
URL sourceURL = new URL("http",                      // Protocol
                        "www.ncsa.uiuc.edu" ,        // Host name
                        "/demoweb/url-primer.html");  // File
```

This uses the default port number for the protocol. You just need to supply the protocol, the domain name and the file path as **String** objects:

There is an alternative constructor defined in the **URL** class where you specify the port number as type **int**, and the other arguments as type **String**:

```
URL sourceURL = new URL("http",                      // Protocol
                        "www.ncsa.uiuc.edu" ,        // Host name
                        80,                           // Port number
                        "/demoweb/url-primer.html");  // File
```

The value of 80 for the port number is the standard port number for **http**. The value of -1 for the port name selects the default port number for the protocol, which avoids the possibility of getting it wrong. If you explicitly specify the port name and you get it wrong, a **MalformedURLException** will be thrown. This exception will also be thrown if the URL is not correct for some other reason.

Once you have a **URL** object, you can get the components of the URL by calling the **getProtocol()**, the **getHost()**, the **getPort()** and the **getFile()** methods for the object. The **getPort()** method returns the port number as type **int**, and the other methods return objects of type **String**.

The **URL** class also implements an **equals()** method that you can use to compare two **URL** objects. The expression **URL1.equals(URL2)** will return **true** if **URL1** and **URL2** represent the same file.

Perhaps the most useful method in the **URL** class is the **openStream()** method. This returns an object of type **InputStream** which you can use to read the file represented by the URL. We could try this out by reading the file referenced by the **sourceURL** object we created in the code fragment above.

Try It Out—Reading a URL

On my machine, this example will connect to my Internet service provider to access the URL because of the way my computer is set up, but you may need to be connected to your ISP first. When the program closes, the connection will still be open, so you will need to close it manually. Here's the program to read a URL:

> *The program assumes that the directory **JunkData** that we used in Chapter 8 is still on your C: drive. If it isn't, you can add it, or better still add the code to check that the directory is there, and if it isn't then create it.*

```java
import java.net.*;
import java.io.*;

class ReadURL
{
  public static void main(String[] args)
  {
    try
    {
      // Define a URL
      URL sourceURL = new URL(
                    "http://www.ncsa.uiuc.edu/demoweb/url-primer.html");

      // Get a character input stream for the URL
      BufferedReader in = new BufferedReader(
                          new InputStreamReader(
                              sourceURL.openStream()));

      // Create the stream for the output file
      PrintWriter out =  new PrintWriter(
                          new BufferedWriter(
                          new FileWriter(
                          new File("C:\\JunkData\\netdata.html"))));

      System.out.println("Reading the file " + sourceURL.getFile() +
                        " on the host " + sourceURL.getHost() +
                        " using " + sourceURL.getProtocol());

      // Read  the URL and write it to a file
      String buffer;                            // Buffer to store lines
      while(!(null==(buffer=in.readLine())))
        out.println(buffer);

      in.close();                               // Close the input stream
      out.close();                              // Close the output file
    }
    catch(MalformedURLException e)
    {
      System.out.println("Failed to create URL:\n" + e);
```

```
      }
      catch(IOException e)
      {
        System.out.println("File error:\n" + e);
      }
    }
  }
```

This produces the output:

```
Reading the file /demoweb/url-primer.html on the host www.ncsa.uiuc.edu
using http
```

It will also write the contents of the URL to the file **netdata.html**.

How It Works

The object **sourceURL** is created directly from the URL string. Because the constructor can throw a **MalformedURLException**—if you type the URL string incorrectly, for example—we have a **catch** block for this exception following the **try** block. Note that this exception is derived from **IOException** so the **catch** block for this must precede the **catch** block for **IOException**.

By calling the **openStream()** method for the **URL** object, we obtain a stream that we can pass to the **InputStreamReader** constructor. A character reader will automatically take care of converting characters from the stream to Unicode. From the **InputStreamReader** we create a **BufferedReader** object so input from the stream will be buffered in memory.

The file is a sizable html file, so rather than writing it to the screen, we write it to a file in the **JunkData** directory that we used in Chapter 8. You will then be able to view the file using your web browser. Once we have the **BufferedReader** object for the URL, the reading of the URL and writing the local file follows the sort of process you have already seen in Chapter 8. We just use the **readLine()** method to read a line at a time from the URL into the string buffer, and we use the **println()** method to transfer the contents of buffer to the local file.

The URLEncoder Class

You don't create objects of this class. This class contains a single static utility method that converts a string into a MIME format called **'x-www-form-urlencoded'** format :

```
public static String encode(String s)
```

The output of the conversion is:

▶ The ASCII characters **a** through **z**, **A** through **Z**, and **0** through **9** remain the same

▶ Space characters are converted to plus signs, **+**

▶ Other characters (including the **+** sign) are converted to the hexadecimal representation of the lower 8-bits of the characters. The notation used for each character is **%XY** where **XY** are the two-digits of the hexadecimal representation.

Thus the statement:

```
String mimeStr = URLEncoder("Hallo Jack! How are you?");
```

will result in reference to the string **"Hallo+Jack%21+How+are+you%3F"** being stored in **mimeStr**. Data encoded in this way avoids the use of spaces and special characters. This is used when the protocol used to transfer data along the way can corrupt information because of disparities between the character sets used on different systems.

If you've ever filled in a form (e.g. a search engine's query) on a WWW browser, you might have seen that the data you typed in was sent to the HTTP server encoded in this manner.

The URLConnection Class

Objects of the **URLConnection** class represent a communications link between your program and a URL. You can use instances of the **URLConnection** class to read from and write to the resource represented by a URL. You can't create objects of the **URLConnection** class directly though. You must first create a **URL** object, and then obtain a **URLConnection** object representing the link to the URL. You do this by calling the **openConnection()** method for the **URL** object:

```
URLConnection connection = sourceURL.openConnection();
```

The object, connection, is not actually connected to the URL at this point. To establish the connection, you call its **connect()** method:

```
connection.connect();
```

Now that we have established a connection, the **URLConnection** object can provide an **InputStream** object that you can use to read the contents of the URL:

```
InputStream in = connection.getInputStream();
```

This will throw an **IOException** if an error occurs creating the input stream.

You can find the content length of the URL by calling the **getContentLength()** method for the **URLConnection** object:

```
int contentLength = connection.getContentLength();
```

If a connection has not been established when you call this method, it will call the **connect()** method anyway. If the content length is unknown, -1 will be returned.

There is a lot more to the **URLConnection** class, but that is beyond the scope of this book. We shall just try it out on a simple program that will read the contents of a URL.

To read the content of a file on a web server you can use a **URL** class object to obtain an object of the **URLConnection** class as we saw, and then read from the input stream obtained from the **URLConnection** object. Here's how to do it:

```java
import java.net.*;
import java.io.*;

class DownloadFile
{
  public static void main(String[] args)
  {
    byte byteBuffer[];
    int bytesRead = 0;

    byteBuffer = new byte[4096];

    try
    {
      // Establish a connection
      URL sourceURL = new URL(args[0]);
      URLConnection connection = sourceURL.openConnection();
      connection.connect();

        // if the file does not exist, the following will throw an
        //exception:
      InputStream in = connection.getInputStream();

        // Read it
      bytesRead = in.read(byteBuffer);
    }
    catch(Exception ex)
    {
      System.out.println("Couldn't open the specified file");
      System.exit(1);
    }

    // Print content to screen
    System.out.println("contents of " + args[0] + " :\n" +
                        new String(byteBuffer, 0, bytesRead));
  }
}
```

This class reads the content of the file as a stream of bytes, regardless of its actual content. To run the program you enter the program name, **DownloadFile**, followed by a string specifying the URL of the file you want to read.

How It Works

From the string entered on the command line, we create a **URL** object. We use this object to obtain a **URLConnection** object representing a link to the URL. To establish the connection to the URL, we call the **connect()** method for the **URLConnection** object. The **getInputStream()** method returns an **InputStream** object that we use to read data from the URL into the array, **byteBuffer**. We write the data received in the **byteBuffer** array to the screen.

Communications on a Network

We have already implemented a program for network communications. That last two examples went out on the network, talked to the computer holding the file specified by the URL, and read it back to the local machine. We were hardly in control though. We didn't see any of the outgoing communications in our code. There's got to be more to it. So how does your program communicate with the remote web site?

There are four layers of software involved in this, sitting on top of the hardware that connects to the network. For most people, the hardware is a modem attached to their PC. The diagram shows the software on your computer that is active when your computer is talking to a server on the Internet.

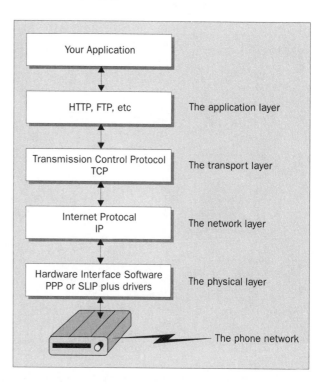

In the physical layer **PPP** is Point to Point Protocol, and **SLIP** stands for Serial Line Interface Protocol. PPP is a standard protocol that is the default for the Microsoft Dial-Up adapter under Windows 95. SLIP is an older standard protocol used by some Unix systems. If your computer is connected to a local area network, then the physical layer is likely to be Ethernet. The diagram is simplified in the sense that there will also be some software to deal with dialing the service provider—the machine that you attach to when you access the Internet.

On the server machine there will also be the same four intervening layers of software. Of course, the physical layer will correspond with whatever hardware actually interfaces to the Internet, but the software for network layer, the transport layer and the application layer will be essentially the same. Each layer defines a standard interface to the layer with which it communicates, and deals with the data in a standard way. The data that is passed between layers also has a standard structure.

There are two different types of data connection which your computer can use to talk to a network—connection-oriented protocols such as the **Transmission Control Protocol** (TCP) and connectionless protocols such as the **Datagram Protocol** (UDP).

Client/Server Applications

Client/Server applications use TCP and this is the way your computer communicates over the Internet. The `ReadURL` example was an instance of a client/server connection. Your computer was the client—the one requesting and receiving the service, and the machine holding the file specified by the URL was the server—the one providing the service.

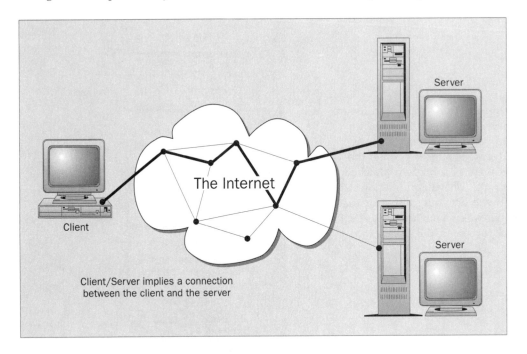

There are three characteristics of this dialog that are important. Firstly, that it was a dialog—your machine was communicating directly with a specific computer on the network. There was an active connection between the two machines. Other machines were involved en route—each piece of information that passed between the two machines was passed along a chain of machines between your machine, the client, and the server, but the dialog was specific to those two. Secondly, the communication of the data was ordered—it was received in the same sequence that it was sent. Thirdly, each chunk of data was verified as received correctly by one machine before another chunk was sent, so the accuracy of the data was guaranteed.

UDP Mode

It is also possible for a machine to send data to another machine on a network without having an active connection—that is, there is no direct dialog between the two machines. This is the User Datagram Protocol for transferring data on a network.

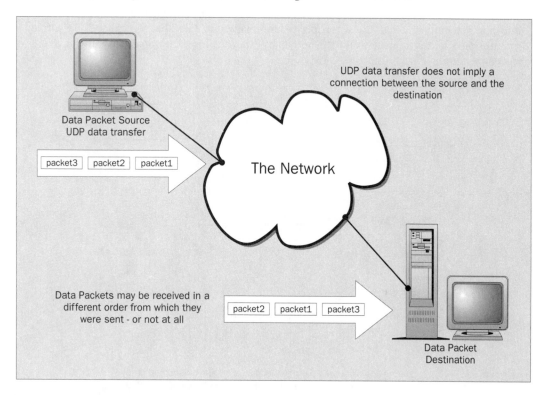

Your machine can package a chunk of data up into a packet, put a label on it that identifies the machine that should receive it, and toss it to the adjacent machine on the network. That machine will then cast around to figure out where to send the data next, based on the address—just like the snail mail service. If the machine doesn't know where the destination is, it will just pass the data onto a default router for onward transmission. Again, just like the snail mail service in many places, there is no guarantee at all that it will actually end up at its destination. There is, however, a difference. By definition the UDP protocol can discard packets, but the postal service isn't supposed to. If you are sending a lot of data, you would normally package it up in a number of chunks, and you would send each chunk separately. Assuming these arrive at the destination, there is no guarantee that they will arrive in the same sequence that they were sent.

Peer-to-Peer Communications

Peer-to-peer communications is a client/server mode connection where both parties can be, but are not necessarily, both client and server. Peer-to-peer communication is a networking concept. It doesn't reflect the status of the participants in any way. For example, on one end there could be a simple temperature gauge, and on the other end a complex environmental control system. Of course the temperature gauge needs to be fairly intelligent—some mercury in a glass tube just won't hack it. The two parties in a peer-to-peer connection are considered peers because both ends use simple sockets.

A very common use of a peer-to-peer connection is for file and printer sharing between machines. Each resource that is designated as shared on one machine can be accessed by another machine that has the appropriate authorization. File sharing can be via a fixed connection such as a local in-house network, Ethernet for example, or it can be over a dial-up connection.

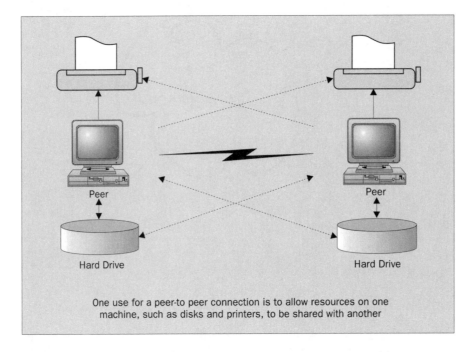

One use for a peer-to peer connection is to allow resources on one machine, such as disks and printers, to be shared with another

Java supports network communications using **sockets**. It has stream sockets for managing direct communications between two machines on a network—this can be a client/server connection or a peer-to-peer connection, and datagram sockets for sending data on a wing and a prayer.

What are Sockets?

A socket is an abstraction that represents a terminal for communications between processes across a network. Sockets are used to support both the networking protocols we've just met:

- ▶ Sockets can be used for an active communication between two specific computers on a network, where they establish a connection-oriented service
- ▶ Sockets can also be used for connectionless communication. When a socket is used for connectionless data transmission, the data is sent out on the network with a specified destination, but with no established connection with the intended

recipient—this is the UDP mode we discussed just a moment ago. A socket for UDP mode can also receive data without being connected to a source. The socket just waits for some data to turn up

Socket implementation is provided by the host operating system. Java provides classes that encapsulate the system's socket implementation on the machine where your program executes. These classes are defined in the package **java.net**.

> *Most socket communication systems in most operating systems are implementations of the socket interface known as Berkley Sockets. This networking interface was first introduced in a version of the UNIX operating system named BSD UNIX (Berkeley Software Distribution UNIX). Java 1.1 socket classes support most of the BSD socket features.*

Every socket has two characteristics that identify it, the IP address of the computer the socket resides in, and a port number. There are often several network-based services provided by a single computer. These could include FTP, HTTP, electronic mail and others. As we saw earlier, each of the services is assigned a well known port number—an address inside the computer (like an apartment number in a building) that everyone knows of—and everyone who wishes to use a service connects to the port for that service.

The port numbers are only allocated for software convenience, and have no deeper meaning. Ports with numbers below 1024 are assigned by the Internet Assigned Numbers Authority (IANA), and are not available for use by 'normal' programs. You should use port numbers above 1024 for your own applications (and it's better to avoid 1234 and other 'obvious' numbers otherwise your application is likely to collide with others). The largest port number is 65,535.

Connectionless Interfaces to a Network

A datagram socket provides a connectionless interface to a network. It is encapsulated by the **DatagramSocket** class. A datagram socket sends information to a destination on the network, in chunks that are called datagram packets. A datagram packet is encapsulated by the **DatagramPacket** class.

In a connectionless interface to a network, such as UDP, an application only needs to open a socket and send the data. To receive data, an application needs to open a socket and bind it to the port to which it wishes to listen. The discrete packets that are sent may arrive out of order (that is, if packet A was transmitted before packet B, there is no guarantee that A will be received before B). It is also possible that incoming datagram packets may be lost, but you will never get a corrupted packet.

Datagram packets contain the data that is to be sent, as well as the identity of the destination for the data. They are routed by the computers and other network devices (hubs, bridges, routers etc.) on the path from the source computer to the target. Each packet is routed independently of any others, and different packets may be routed differently—that's how the packets can get out of sequence.

Datagram sockets are appropriate when you don't mind losing a packet now and then, and you know how to deal with packets arriving out of sequence. Because datagram sockets implement a send-and-forget protocol, they are faster than stream sockets. If your application can use this kind of socket, it probably should. An example of such an application is a central time synchronization facility for a network. Each computer maintains the time locally, but every now and then it will receive a time packet to make sure that it's synchronized with some central computer. It then adjusts its local time accordingly. The time synchronization algorithm can compensate for losing a packet now and then, so it is not concerned if the odd packet doesn't turn up.

The DatagramSocket Class

This class encapsulates a socket used for sending and receiving datagram packets. Since the routing information is contained in the packets themselves, the constructors are not concerned with the destination for the data at all. You can create a **DatagramSocket** object with the default constructor:

```
DatagramSocket socket = new DatagramSocket();
```

This creates a datagram socket that attaches to any available port on the host computer. You would use this to create a sending socket, since you don't care what port is used in this case.

A receiving socket needs to use a specific fixed port, since the source of the data must know the port number of the destination. To create a receiving datagram socket, you could use the following constructor:

```
DatagramSocket socket = new DatagramSocket(portNumber);
```

The port number is an argument of type **int**. This could also be used to send data of course—all the sockets are bi-directional. You can also create a **DatagramSocket** object from a port number and an IP address:

```
DatagramSocket socket = new DatagramSocket(portNumber, address);
```

Here, the second argument is an object of type **InetAddress**.

You can get the port number for a socket by calling its **getPort()** method:

```
int portNumber = getLocalPort();
```

This returns the port number used by the socket as a value of type **int**. You might use this to check on the port number for a socket that you created using the default constructor. You can also get an **InetAddress** object encapsulating the IP address by calling the **getLocalAddress()** method.

To send data you call the **send()** method for the **DatagramSocket** object, and pass the **DatagramPacket** object to be sent as an argument:

```
try
{
  socket.send(packet);                   // Send a packet
}
catch(IOException e)
{
  System.out.println("Error sending packet: " + e);
}
```

As we indicated earlier, the packet will contain the data plus the IP address and the port number of the destination for the data. An input error will result in an **IOException** being thrown.

To receive data you call the **receive()** method for the **DatagramSocket** object:

```
try
{
  socket.receive(packet);                // Receive a packet
}
catch(IOException e)
{
  System.out.println("Error sending packet: " + e);
}
```

This method blocks until a packet is received. This could be indefinite if no one is sending anything to you, so you might want to limit the amount of time that the method waits for input. You do this by calling the **setSoTimeout()** method for the **DatagramSocket** object, before you call the **receive()** method:

```
socket.setSoTimeout(1000);              // Receive to wait 1 second for input
```

The argument is the maximum time in milliseconds that the **receive()** method should wait to receive a packet. If you specify the time as zero, the **receive()** method will wait indefinitely. The **setSoTimeout()** method will throw a **SocketException** if an error occurs, so you should put the call in a **try** block. This exception is derived from **IOException**, so you need to put the **catch** block for it before any **catch** block for the more general **IOException**. The **receive()** method will throw an **InterruptedIOException** if the wait time expires before a packet is received, so you must catch this exception for the **receive()** method call, too:

```
try
{
  socket.setSoTimeout(1000);            // Receive to wait 1 second for input
  socket.receive(packet);              // Receive a packet
}
catch(SocketException e)
{
  System.out.println("Socket error: " + e);
```

```
  }
  catch(InterruptedIOException e)
  {
    System.out.println("Receive timed out: " + e);
  }
  catch(IOException e)
  {
    System.out.println("Error sending packet: " + e);
  }
```

If an **InterruptedIOException** occurs, the socket is still valid, so you can still use it. You could put the **try** block and the **catch** block in a loop to have several goes at receiving a packet:

```
try
{
  socket.setSoTimeout(1000);          // Receive to wait 1 second for input

  // Try six receive() operations
  for int(int i = 0; i < 5; i++)
  {
    try
    {
      socket.receive(packet);                 // Receive a packet
    }
    catch(InterruptedIOException e)
    {
      System.out.println("Receive timed out: " + e);
    }
    // Do something before trying again...
  }
}
catch(SocketException e)
{
  System.out.println("Socket error: " + e);
}
catch(IOException e)
{
  System.out.println("Error sending packet: " + e);
}
```

If you need to find out how long the **receive()** method will wait for a packet, you can call the **getSoTimeout()** method for the socket. The **getSoTimeout()** method can also throw a **SocketException**, so you should put it in a **try** block:

```
try
{
  int waitTime = socket.getSoTimeout; // Get the maximum wait time
}
catch(SocketException e)
```

```
{
    System.out.println("Socket error: " + e);
}
```

When you are finished with a **DatagramSocket** object, you can close the socket by calling its **close()** method.

```
socket.close();                      // Close the socket
```

This closes the socket and frees up the port that it was connected to. Let's unveil the secrets of the **DatagramPacket** class next.

The DatagramPacket Class

This class encapsulates a datagram packet, either incoming or outgoing. Each packet is routed from the sender to the receiver based solely on information contained within that packet. There are two constructors for **DatagramPacket** objects, one for packets that you receive, and one for packets that you intend to send. To create a **DatagramPacket** object to contain a received packet, you would write:

```
byte[] inBuffer = new byte[length];
DatagramPacket packet = new DatagramPacket(inBuffer, packetLength);
```

This constructor creates a **DatagramPacket** for receiving packets of **packetLength** bytes. The first argument is a byte array to receive the data. The second argument, **packetLength**, must not be greater than the number of elements of **inBuffer[]**. You would pass this object to the **receive()** method for a **DatagramSocket**. The array **inBuffer[]** will contain the datagram that is received.

To create a **DatagramPacket** object to be sent, you write:

```
DatagramPacket packet = new DatagramPacket(outBuffer,  // Type byte[]
                                          packetLength, // Type int
                                          destination,  // Type InetAddress
                                          portNumber)   // Type int
```

This constructor creates a **DatagramPacket** that contains the first **packetLength** bytes of **outBuffer[]** that are to be sent to the specified port number, **portNumber** on the host identified by the **InetAddress** object, **destination**. The **packetLength** argument must be less than or equal to **outBuffer.length**. To send the packet, you pass the object to the **send()** method for a **DatagramSocket** object.

If you want to know where a packet came from, you call the **getAddress()** method for the **DatagramPacket** object that you received. This method returns an object of type **InetAddress** encapsulating the IP address of the machine that sent the packet. You can get the port number by calling the **getPort()** method for the **DatagramPacket** object. You can also call these methods for a packet that you are sending and obtain the **InetAddress** object and the port number for the local computer.

You can also obtain the data contained in the packet by calling the **getData()** method:

```
byte[] packetData = packet.getData();
```

The data is returned as an array of type **byte**.

You can set the address for a **DatagramPacket** object by calling its **setAddress()** method and passing an **InetAddress** object as an argument. The **setPort()** method will set the port number. The port number is passed to the method as type **int**. You can use these for setting the destination of a packet you intend to send, or possibly for rerouting a packet you have received to another destination.

You can set the data in a packet by calling the **setData()** method, and passing an array of type **byte[]** that contains the data. The **setLength()** method will set the length of the data to be sent—you specify the length as an argument of type **int**.

Stream Sockets

Stream sockets are the end points of a communications link between two programs that are typically on two separate computers on a network (although we will produce an example where both ends are on the same computer—saves you rushing out to buy another machine in order to run the example). Stream sockets would be used for an HTTP connection for example. Both of the computers that are talking to one another will each have a socket that identifies the connection to the other.

Stream sockets are appropriate for applications that require guaranteed delivery of information. Most applications fall into this category:

- Terminal session applications
- File transfer applications
- Mail applications
- and many more

Streams sockets are slower than datagram sockets. One of the reasons for this is that the sender needs confirmation that each block of data it sent arrived safely so each packet is checked. If an error occurs, the sender will go back and resend the packet that was not received correctly.

To communicate over the network the two parties must establish a connection. First, a listening socket is bound to a specific network address, then another socket is connected to the listening socket. Once the sockets on both sides are connected the parties can engage in communication. A new socket is needed for every session. This means that, not only do you need a new socket for every computer you wish to communicate with, but that you also require several sockets to communicate with multiple services on a single computer.

Stream sockets provide the sequenced and reliable flow of data that we referred to earlier when we discussed network communications. What goes in one end comes out the other, and it comes out in the same order as it went in. One kind of stream socket is a client socket that is used to connect to a server. The client socket identifies the connection to the server machine, and on the server machine there needs to be a similar socket that identifies the client. However, there is a slight complication at the server end, because the client knows all about the server, but the server knows nothing of the client. Let's look at client sockets first, and then come back to the server end.

Client Sockets

A client socket on your computer is represented by an object of the **Socket** class. You can create a client socket from the domain name for the computer that you want to talk to, and the port number for the service on that computer you want. For example:

```
Socket sock = new Socket("wrox.com", 80);
```

Alternatively, you can use an **InetAddress** object to create a **Socket** object:

```
InetAddress wroxIP = InetAddress.getByName("wrox.com");
Socket sock = new Socket(wroxIP, 80);
```

If your computer has several ports active, you may want to create a **Socket** object that binds to a particular port. In this case you can use another **Socket** constructor, as follows:

```
InetAddress wroxIP = InetAddress.getByName("wrox.com");
Socket sock = new Socket(wroxIP, 80, InetAddress.getLocalHost(), 80);
```

The first two arguments are the **InetAddress** object and port for the remote machine service, and the second two are the **InetAddress** object for the local machine and the port number to be used. All three **Socket** constructors can throw an **IOException** if an error occurs.

So now we have a client socket, what can we do with it? We can get some incredibly interesting information for a start.

- You can get the **InetAddress** object and the port number for the remote host by calling the methods **getInetAddress()** and **getPort()** methods for the **Socket** object

- The **getLocalAddress()** and **getLocalPort()** methods will supply the same information for the local computer

- The real meat though is provided by the **getInputStream()** and **getOutputStream()** classes. These return an **InputStream** object and an **OutputStream** object respectively, that you can use to communicate with the remote host computer. Once you have the **InputStream** and **OutputStream** object for the **Socket** object, communicating with the remote computer is just the regular stream I/O stuff we saw in Chapter 8

We can create a client program for use with a server that we will put together a little later in this chapter. The client program will involve two classes, one containing the method **main()** that will establish a connection to a server and send messages to it, and another that defines a separate thread to receive input from the server.

Try It Out—Creating a Client

1 Here's the outline of the first class where execution starts with comments to show what it will do:

```
// Implements a client
import java.net.*;
import java.io.*;

class LocalClient
{
  static BufferedWriter socketOut;                    // Socket output stream

  public static void main(String[] args)
  {
    // Create a keyboard input stream....
    // Create a new socket and obtain its output stream...
    // Create a thread to read from the server and start it...

    // Send user information to the server
    // Get the user's input  and send to the server until bye entered...
    // When bye is entered stop the listening thread...
    // Close the streams
  }
}
```

2 We can implement the method **main()** with the following code:

```
public static void main(String[] args)
{
  Socket socket;                    // The socket to the server
  String  stringToSend;             // Message to send to server
  ClientListenThread receiveThread;  // Thread to receive from server

  // Create an input stream for the keyboard
  BufferedReader keyboard  = new BufferedReader(  // Keyboard stream
                     new FileReader(FileDescriptor.in));

  try
  {
    // Create a new socket and obtain its output stream
    socket = new Socket(InetAddress.getLocalHost(), 1997);
    socketOut = new BufferedWriter(              // Socket output stream
            new OutputStreamWriter(socket.getOutputStream()));
```

```java
                // Create the thread to receive data from the server
                receiveThread = new ClientListenThread(socket);

                receiveThread.start();                    // Start the receive thread

                // Send user information to the server
                System.out.print("Enter your name: ");    // Prompt for name
                stringToSend = keyboard.readLine();        // Read the name
                send(stringToSend);                        // Send the name
                stringToSend = "";                         // Reset string

                // Send the user's input to the server until bye entered
                while(!stringToSend.equals("bye"))
                {
                  stringToSend = keyboard.readLine();      // Read message
                  send(stringToSend);                      // Send message
                }

                // Terminate the session - stop the listening thread
                receiveThread.stop();                 // Stop the thread
                try
                { // Wait for the listening thread to stop
                  Thread.currentThread().sleep(500);
                }
                catch(InterruptedException e) { }
              }
              catch(IOException e)
              {
                System.err.println("Error while writing : " + e);
                System.err.flush();
              }
              finally
              {
                try
                {
                  socketOut.close();                 // Close socket output stream
                  keyboard.close();                  // Close keyboard input stream
                }
                catch(IOException e) { }
              }
            }
```

3 The method to send messages to the server is as follows:

```java
          // Send a message
          private static void send(String msg)
          {
            try
            {
              socketOut.write(msg);                      // Send the text
              socketOut.newLine();                       // Send a newline character
```

```
      socketOut.flush();                    // Flush the stream buffer
  }
  catch(IOException e)
  {
    System.err.println("Error writing in send: " + e);
  }
}
```

4 The outline of the class to define the receive thread for the client is as follows:

```
// Thread to handle input to the client from the server
import java.io.*;
import java.net.*;

class ClientListenThread extends Thread
{
  private BufferedReader socketIn;              // Socket input stream
  private Socket socket;                        // The socket

  public ClientListenThread(Socket socket)
  {
    // Store the socket reference and create a socket input stream...
  }

  public void run()
  {
    // Loop reading input from the socket stream and output to the screen
  }
}
```

5 The constructor for `ClientListenThread` is quite simple—it just stores the reference to the socket and creates an input stream for it. The code for it will be:

```
public ClientListenThread(Socket socket)
{
  this.socket = socket;                  // Store the socket reference
  try
  {
    socketIn  = new BufferedReader(    // Socket input stream
                new InputStreamReader(socket.getInputStream()));
  }
  catch(IOException e)
  {
    System.err.println("Error while constructing " +
                        "ClientListenThread :\n" + e );
    System.exit(1);
  }
}
```

The creation of the socket input stream must be in a **try** block because the **getInputStream()** method for the **Socket** object can throw an **IOException**.

6 The **run()** method for the thread is quite long, but only because of the exceptions that we must plan on catching. Here's the code:

```
public void run()
{
  String input;
  try
  {
    while(true) // This thread is stopped from the outside
    {
      // Wait for incoming message then output it to the screen
      input = socketIn.readLine();
      System.out.println("SERVER>" + input );
    }
  }
  catch(ThreadDeath td)
  { // The thread was stopped by the main thread
    System.out.println("Connection closed!");
    throw td;
  }
  catch(IOException e)
  {
    System.err.println("Error while reading : " + e);
  }
  finally
  {
    try
    {
      socketIn.close();                 // Close socket input stream
      socket.close();                   // Close the socket
    }
    catch(IOException e) { }
  }
}
```

How It Works

The data member **socketOut** is **static** because we want an instance of the variable to be created, even though there are no objects of type **LocalClient**. We have it as a class variable because will be adding another method that needs access to it, besides the method, **main()**.

In **main()**, we first create a **keyboard** stream for user input that is to be sent to the server. The stream is created from the **FileDescriptor** object, **in**, which is a static member of the **FileDescriptor** class.

The program is supposed to run on the local machine, so we create a socket to connect to the machine defined by the local IP address which is returned by the static `getLocalHost()` method in the `InetAddress` class. If we fail to obtain a `Socket` object—if the server isn't active, for example—an `IOException` will be thrown by the constructor. Once we have the `Socket` object, we create a `BufferedWriter` stream so we can send messages to the server.

Next we create a thread to handle input from the server which we start immediately. This will run asynchronously from the current thread in `main()`, which will take care of input from the keyboard, and the transmission of the keyboard input to the server. After sending the user name to the server in `main()`, we read messages from the keyboard and send them to the server in the `while` loop. The loop will continue until `"bye"` is entered to end the dialog. When the loop ends, we stop the receive thread, and after waiting 500 milliseconds to give the receive thread time to close down, we close the socket input stream and the keyboard stream.

The `send()` method is very simple. We write the `String` that is passed to the method to the socket output stream, followed by a newline. The newline is important because the server will use the `readLine()` method to read input from the stream for a client—which requires a newline to terminate input. To get the data sent immediately, we call `flush()` for the output stream. If we don't do this, messages will pile up in the stream until the buffer is full, and they will all be sent together. It won't exactly be a dialog in that case.

The `run()` method will be called when the `start()` method for the thread is called in `main()`. The bit that does the work is in the indefinite `while` loop. Each line that is read from the server is output to the screen. Each line of output is prefixed so that it is easy to identify as input from the server. The `ThreadDeath` exception will be thrown when the `stop()` method for the thread is called in `main()`. All we do is output a message and re-throw the exception. The `catch` block for `IOException` will catch errors reading the input stream. The `finally` block will close the input stream and the socket.

Of course, we can't do anything with the client program until we have a server, so let's take a look at how we can create a server.

Server Sockets

There are two problems to be addressed at the server end of a client/server communication. The first is; how does the server create a socket to connect to the client, when the server knows nothing about the client? The second is; how does the server manage to talk to multiple clients?

The solution to both of these problems is a special kind of socket called a server socket, which just listens for clients who want to connect to it. Server sockets are bound to a specific port on the host machine. That's how a client can connect to the server—it connects to the port that the server socket uses. A server socket doesn't handle any data transfer operations itself. When a client turns up, the server socket creates another socket—a regular client socket, hands over the responsibility for communicating with the client to the new socket, and then goes back to listening for a new client.

A server socket is represented by an object of the **ServerSocket** class. Obviously, since a server socket is just waiting for clients to turn up, there is no remote machine involved in defining an object to represent it. You can define a **ServerSocket** object by just specifying the port number that it is to use. For example:

```
ServerSocket serveSock = new ServerSocket(1997);
```

The port number is just a value of type **int**. Clients that want to talk to this server will need to specify this port number for their socket connection. It is possible that a server may get a lot of clients wanting to talk to it. As clients come in to connect to a server, they are placed in a queue. You can set the size of the backlog queue for a **ServerSocket** object by creating it with a constructor that accepts a second argument defining the length of the backlog queue. For example:

```
ServerSocket serveSock = new ServerSocket(1997, 20);
```

This **ServerSocket** object will only allow up to twenty clients to be waiting to connect to the server socket. A client can only communicate with the server when it has been accepted by the server. Once the queue of waiting clients is full, further clients will be rejected, and they will not be able to connect.

If the server machine has several IP addresses, you can use a **ServerSocket** constructor that will accept an **InetAddress** object as a third argument beyond the two in the last example, to specify the address to be used for the server socket.

If you need to get the IP address or the port number for a **ServerSocket** object, you can call its **getInetAddress()** method which returns an **InetAddress** object, or its **getLocalPort()** method which returns the port number as type **int**. When you are finished with the **ServerSocket** object and want to shut it down, you call the **close()** method for the object.

Accepting a Client Connection

A client can connect to a **ServerSocket** once you have called the **accept()** method for the **ServerSocket** object. This method returns a **Socket** object that will communicate with the client. So you might call this method with a statement such as:

```
Socket newClient = serverSock.accept();
```

This method blocks until a client requests connection to the server, so you would put this statement after everything else that needs to be done to prepare for connecting to a client. Once the method returns a connection, it is up to you to initiate a thread and pass the **newClient** object across to it to handle the communications. The **ServerSocket** cannot accept another client until you call the **accept()** method again. The **accept()** method will throw an **IOException** if an error occurs.

If you don't want the **accept()** method to block indefinitely—because your program wants to do other things besides listening for possible clients, for example—you can limit the amount of time the method will wait for a client. You just call the `setSoTimeout()` method for the `ServerSocket` object with an argument of type `int` that specifies the maximum time to wait in milliseconds. For example:

```
serverSock.setSoTimeout(1000);    // Only wait one second for a client
```

If this statement is executed before you call the `accept()` method and if no client request is received for one second, the method will throw an `InterruptedIOException`. The `ServerSocket` object is still valid though, so you can go back and call the `accept()` method again after handling the exception and doing whatever you want to do. If you have set a timeout interval, and you want to reset it so that the `accept()` method will wait indefinitely for a client, you just call the `setSoTimeout()` method with a zero argument.

We now have enough to put together a server of our own. This server will be designed to run on the local machine, along with the clients it is servicing. Your machine will need to have TCP/IP operational, and an IP address defined for it.

Our server will simulate an electronic advisor that you can customize however you want. There will be two classes in our server program. One will start the server and listen for new clients. The other will define a thread that communicates with a client. The main thread will create a separate thread to handle the dialog with each new client.

Try It Out—Creating a Server

1 Here's the outline of the main `LocalServer` class, indicating what it will do:

```
// Implements a local server
import java.net.*;
import java.io.*;

public class LocalServer
{
  public static void main(String[] args)
  {
    // Create a server socket and wait for clients...
    // Create a thread to talk to each new client and start it...
    // If there no clients for one minute close the program...
  }
}
```

2 We only need to implement a `main()` method. It looks like a lot of code but the `catch` blocks for exceptions and the `finally` block make up half of it:

```
public static void main(String[] args)
{
  ServerSocket serverSocket = null;        // Server socket
  Socket clientSocket;                     // Socket for client
  ClientThread talkToClient;               // Thread for client dialog
```

```java
    int noClients = 0;                            // No client period count

    try
    {
      serverSocket = new ServerSocket(1997);      // Create the server socket
      System.out.println("Server is " +
                         serverSocket.getInetAddress().getHostName() +
                         " On port number " + serverSocket.getLocalPort());
      System.out.println("Local Server is up and waiting " +
                         "for connections...");
      while(true)
      { // Listen for clients
        serverSocket.setSoTimeout(10000);            // Set maximum wait time
        try
        {
          clientSocket = serverSocket.accept();      // Accept a client
          System.out.println("SERVER: Contacted by " +
                             clientSocket.getInetAddress());

          // Create a thread for the new client
          talkToClient = new ClientThread(clientSocket); // Create it
          talkToClient.start();                        // Start it
          noClients = 0;                               // Reset period count
        }
        catch(InterruptedIOException e)
        { // We get here if accept() times out
          if(ClientThread.haveNoClients() && (++noClients==6))
            break;                                // Exit if 6 successive timeouts
        }
      }
    }
    catch(IOException e)
    {
      System.err.println("ERROR IN SERVER : " + e);
    }
    finally
    { // Last action before exiting
      try
      {
        serverSocket.close();                        // Close the server socket
      }
      catch(IOException e) { }
    }
    // We get to here if the server times out
    System.out.println("Server timed out - no clients for 1 minute !");
  }
```

How It Works

In the main **try** block, we create the server socket, **serverSocket**. We then have an indefinite **while** loop in which we set the maximum wait period for a client to ten seconds, and the call **accept()** for the server socket to wait for a client. If a client turns up, the **accept()** method returns a reference to a **Socket** object that connects to the client—if no client turns up within the timeout period, it throws an **InterruptedIOException**.

When a client arrives, we create a **ClientThread** object to which we pass the new socket, and start the thread. This thread will then talk independently to the new client, so we can go back to waiting for another client.

Note that the **catch** block for the **InterruptedIOException** is inside the **while** loop. When an **InterruptedIOException** is thrown, the code in the **catch** block checks whether there are any clients and whether this is the sixth period with no clients. The **ClientThread** class will have a static method, **haveNoClients()**, which will return **true** if no clients are connected. On the sixth period without clients, corresponding to one minute because the timeout period is 10 seconds, the **break** exits the **while** loop so we stop listening for more clients. The period with no clients only gets incremented while there are no clients. If a client arrives the count is reset to zero so the process of counting periods without clients starts over again. An input/output error on the server socket will also end the **while** loop.

When we exit the while loop, the **println()** statement is executed, followed by the **finally** block which closes the server socket.

The **ClientThread** class will have a number of static data members and methods dealing with tracking and identifying clients, plus a number of instance variables and methods dealing with the communications with an individual client. Let's look at the static class members first. We need to keep track of how many clients there are, so we will give each client a unique integer ID, and record in the clients in a **Hashtable** object.

Try It Out—Managing Client Communications

1 Here's the class definition with the static stuff:

```
// Implements server thread to talk to a client
import java.net.*;
import java.io.*;
import java.util.*;

class ClientThread extends Thread implements Replies
{
  static Hashtable clientMap = new Hashtable();    // Stores clients
  static long IDSource = 0;                          // Base for IDs

  // Supply a new client ID
  static synchronized long newID()
```

```
    {
      return ++IDSource;                              // Increment base value
    }

    // Add a new client
    static synchronized void addClient(long id, ClientThread client)
    {
      clientMap.put(new Long(id), client);            // Store client in map
    }

    // Delete a client
    static synchronized void removeClient(long id)
    {
      clientMap.remove(new Long(id));                 // Remove client from map
    }

    // Broadcast a message to all but the current client
    static synchronized void broadcastMessage(long ID, String msg)
    { // Go through all the clients
      for(Enumeration e = clientMap.elements(); e.hasMoreElements(); )
      {
        ClientThread aClient = (ClientThread)e.nextElement();
        if(aClient.getID()!=ID)
          aClient.send(msg);          // Send message except for this client
      }
    }

    // Get the number of clients
    static synchronized int getClientCount()
    {
      return clientMap.size();
    }

    // Test for presence of clients
    public static synchronized boolean haveNoClients()
    {
      return clientMap.isEmpty();
    }

    // Plus the instance members of the class...
  }
```

We will add the interface, **Replies**, in a moment—it will just contain a **String** array, **replies[]**, of possible replies to clients.

2 Let's add the instance members to the **ClientThread** class now. The class will have three instance variables:

```
Socket socket;                          // Socket connecting to client
BufferedWriter socketOut;               // Output stream for socket
long ID;                                // ID for client
```

Each client will have it's own set of these variables.

3 The socket and the ID are initialized in the constructor for a `ClientThread` object, which is as follows:

```
public ClientThread(Socket clientSocket)
{
  ID = newID();                         // Get a client ID
  socket = clientSocket;                // Store the client socket
}
```

4 The `run()` method does most of the work in talking to a client. The code for it assumes there is also a `send()` method that will send a message to the client. We can code the `run()` method as:

```
public void run()
{
  BufferedReader socketIn = null;       // Socket input stream
  String  inString = " ";               // Input from client
  String clientName = "Nemo";           // Client name
  int clientCount = getClientCount();   // Number of clients
  try
  {
    addClient(ID, this);                          // Add the client
    socketIn = new BufferedReader(                // Socket input stream
            new InputStreamReader(socket.getInputStream()));
    socketOut = new BufferedWriter(               // Socket output stream
              new OutputStreamWriter(socket.getOutputStream()));
    clientName = socketIn.readLine();             // Get client name

    // Send greetings and connection count to the new client
    send("SERVER : Hello " + clientName +
        ", This is your electronic shrink here");
    send("SERVER : There "+(clientCount==1?"is ":"are ") + clientCount +
        " client"+(clientCount==1?"":"s")+
        " being counseled at the moment.");
    send("SERVER : What seems to be the trouble?");

    // Tell everyone we have a new client
    broadcastMessage(ID, clientName + " has joined us." );

    // Talk with the client
    while(true)
    {
      if((inString = socketIn.readLine())!=null) // Get input
      {
```

```
            if(inString.equals("bye"))          // Is it bye?
               break;                            // Yes, so quit loop

            send(replies                         // Reply to client
                [((int)(replies.length*Math.random()))%replies.length]);
         }
      }

      // Tell everyone the client is leaving
      broadcastMessage(ID, clientName + " disconnected.");
   }
   catch(EOFException e)
   { // Socket unexpectedly closed on the other side
     System.err.println( clientName + " closed socket");
   }
   catch(IOException e)
   { // Error reading client input
      System.err.println("ERROR: While reading from " +
                           clientName + " : " + e);
   }
   finally
   {
     try
     {
       removeClient(ID);                 // Delete the client
       socketIn.close();                 // Close the socket input stream
       socketOut.close();                // Close the socket output stream
       socket.close();                   // Close the socket
     }
     catch(IOException e){}
   }
}
```

5 The **send()** method that sends messages to the current client is as follows:

```
private synchronized void send(String msg)
{
  try
  {
    socketOut.write(msg);             // Send the message text to the client
    socketOut.newLine();             // Send newline to end the message
    socketOut.flush();               // Flush the output buffer
  }
  catch(IOException e)
  {
    System.err.println("ERROR: Could not send data: " + e);
  }
}
```

6 The **broadcastMessage()** method needs to obtain the ID for each **ClientThread** object. This is provided by the **getID()** method:

```
// Get the client ID
public long getID()
{
  return ID;                                // Return the client ID
}
```

This just returns the ID stored in the instance variable, **ID**. That completes the definition of the **ClientThread** class.

7 The last piece of code we need for the server is the definition of the **Replies** interface:

```
public interface Replies
{
  String[] replies = {
                      "My bill for $300 will be in the mail today.",
                      "Well, you don't say.",
                      "Well I never.",
                      "Mustn't grumble though, eh?",
                      "Never mind, eh?",
                      "I see.",
                      "You're right about that, that's for sure.",
                      "What a shame.",
                      Try and calm down.",
                   "Pull yourself together now - you're a grown person.",
                      "Well, you are a miserable devil, and no mistake."
                        };
}
```

You can now run the server, and then start some clients. Don't forget you only have one minute to get the first client started. I ran it with two clients. The output from the server was:

```
Server is P200PRO          On port number 1997
Local Server is up and waiting for connections...
SERVER: Contacted by 193.130.244.181/193.130.244.181
SERVER: Contacted by 193.130.244.181/193.130.244.181
Server timed out - no clients for 1 minute !
```

Here's the dialog with the first client

```
Enter your name: Todd
SERVER>Hello Todd, This is your electronic shrink here
SERVER>There is 1 user being counseled at the moment.
SERVER>What seems to be the trouble?
My head hurts
SERVER>My bill for $300 will be in the mail today.
And I feel sick
SERVER >Mustn't grumble though, eh?
SERVER >Alexa has joined us.
```

```
I feel very unhappy
SERVER >Pull yourself together now - you're a grown person.
Why won't you help me?
SERVER >Try and calm down.
OK
SERVER >Well I never.
bye
Connection closed!
```

The dialog with the other concurrent client was as follows:

```
Enter your name: Alexa
SERVER>Hello Alexa, This is your electronic shrink here
SERVER>There are 2 users being counseled at the moment.
SERVER>What seems to be the trouble?
Everybody hates me
SERVER>What a shame.
I'm all alone
SERVER>My bill for $300 will be in the mail today.
I can't afford it
SERVER>Well I never.
bye
Connection closed!
```

How It Works

Note that all the static methods in **ClientThread** are declared as synchronized. This is to prevent the possibility of two methods being executed concurrently. We don't want to have one method updating the **Hashtable** object while another method is using it.

Each client will be identified by an integer ID that is created by the **newID()** method. All it does is increment the static variable **IDSource**, and return its value, so IDs will be 1, 2, 3 and so on. Clients are stored in the **Hashtable** object, **clientMap**. We have static methods **addClient()** and **removeClient()** to add and remove clients from **clientMap**. The **haveNoClients()** method just calls the **isEmpty()** method for the **Hashtable** object which returns **true** if there are no keys stored. The **getClientCount()** method is equally simple—it just calls the **size()** method for the **Hashtable** object. The **broadcastMessage()** method sends a message to all of the clients, except for the one originating the message. This method is also static and synchronized because it accesses the **Hashtable** object. Again, we don't want the hash table updated while we are iterating through it to send a message to the clients. The **for** loop controls the process of going through all the entries in the hash table by obtaining an **Enumeration** for it, and using that to control when the **for** loop ends. The condition expression in the **for** loop will be **true** as long as there are more elements in the enumeration.

In the **run()** method, after adding the new client to the hash table, we create input and output streams for the socket. We then send some initial messages to the client, and broadcast to all the other clients that the new client has joined. Communications with the client takes place in the indefinite **while** loop. This reads a line of input from the client, and sends a random reply from the array **replies[]** defined in the **Replies** interface. If the client enters **"bye"**, we terminate the loop. The other clients are then notified that the client is leaving. Lastly, the **finally** block will remove the client from the hash table, close the input and output streams, and close the socket.

If the socket gets closed at the client end, an **EOFException** will be thrown so we will end the dialog. An error reading input from the client will also end the communication.

We declare the **send()** method as **synchronized** to prevent the **send()** method for a given client object being called while it is still being executed. This potential arises because one client may broadcast a message while another client is in the midst of sending a message. All the method does is to send the string, **msg**, that is received as an argument, to the client, followed by a newline to terminate the message. The **flush()** method is called for the output stream to ensure that the message is sent immediately. The output operation may throw an **IOException**, so we have put the code in a **try** block, followed by a **catch** block to deal with the exception.

The **Replies** interface just defines an array of **String** objects that are the possible replies from the server to the client. You can put whatever you want in here. The server will select them at random from whatever strings you put in the array.

To summarize, the server waits for clients to connect to the server socket. As each client connects, the server creates a new thread to communicate with the client, and that runs independently while the server continues to listen for clients. If six successive periods occur where no client attempts to connect, and there are no clients connected, the server shuts down automatically.

Summary

In this chapter we have dipped briefly into Java's networking capabilities. We have discussed sockets and looked at UDP, and we have seen how client/server communication works. You have also seen some examples of networking in practice.

The important points we have covered in this chapter are:

- A computer on a network is identified by one or more IP addresses
- A connection to a computer on a network is to a port number for a particular IP address
- A service provided by a computer is identified by an IP address, the protocol to be used (TCP or UDP), and a port number
- Files and documents on a network are referenced by a Uniform Resource Locator, or URL. A URL is encapsulated by the **URL** class
- Java uses sockets to communicate with a network
- Objects of the class **DatagramSocket** are used for UDP data transmission

▶ The **ServerSocket** class encapsulates the socket that is used by a server to listen for clients

▶ The **Socket** class encapsulates an ordinary socket. The transmission of data, between a client and a server, is managed by an object of type **Socket**. The **ServerSocket** object will create a **Socket** object for each client that is attached.

Exercises

1 Create a program to accept a URL from the keyboard, and then retrieve the file reference by that URL and store it locally. The program should continue retrieving documents until a suitable 'end' string is entered.

2 Create a server program that will echo the data received from a client back to the client.

3 Create a server program that will broadcast the data received from a client to all the clients attached to the server.

Talking to Databases

In the next two chapters, we're going to look at how Java programs can interface with relational databases, using classes that come with the JDK.

First of all we will look at the basic ideas behind databases and how they store data. This leads naturally onto a discussion of SQL, the language used by relational databases to both define and query data. Only then do we introduce the Java Database Connectivity (JDBC) class library, which provides a standard way for establishing and maintaining a Java program's connection to a database, during which time the two can talk SQL to their heart's content.

In this first chapter, we'll take a whirlwind tour of databasing concepts, SQL and JDBC. We'll cover:

- ▶ What databases are
- ▶ Introducing SQL
- ▶ The rationale behind JDBC
- ▶ Writing your first JDBC program
- ▶ Introducing key elements of the JDBC API

JDBC Concepts and Terminology

The first versions of the Java Development Kit did not provide any facilities for standard database access. In order to remedy this, JavaSoft introduced the Java Database Connectivity (JDBC) library. JDBC was designed by JavaSoft as an object-oriented, Java-based API for database access—a standard to which Java developers and database vendors could adhere.

> *That it is based on other standard program-database interfaces should come as no surprise, but knowledge of these standards isn't necessary to use JDBC. However, if you've programmed database access before, you should be able to draw on this experience.*

The library is implemented in the **java.sql** package. It is a set of classes and interfaces that provide a uniform API for access to a broad range of databases.

FYI

Before we get started on learning about databases and JDBC, it's worth while setting up a couple of programs.

Firstly, we need a sample database and a suitable JDBC driver for our code to use. The database is called **technical_library**, and is a list of technical books and related information. This is provided as an Access database with the sample code available from the Wrox web site.

If you have a database other than Access, and the correct driver already set up (something I'm afraid I'll have to leave to you), you can use a small Java class, **build_tables**, also included with the book's code, to create the sample database's tables. Simply run:

```
java build_tables buildlibrary_access.sql
```

or

```
java build_tables buildlibrary_msql.sql
```

if you're using the mSQL database. Note that these programs take a little time to run.

This is something of a chicken-and-egg situation, but try these text files on other databases as you need, and then edit them to set the correct functionality for that particular database. For example, the version for mSQL doesn't use String-like variables, but instead assigns fixed-length character arrays. Knowledge of how this works is not assumed in the rest of the chapter, so if you have no luck, try reading on and then re-reading the driver and database documentation.

Having got a suitable database and JDBC driver installed, you can try running the **InteractiveSQL** program, which we'll be using in this chapter to show how to send commands to a database. We'll build the application at the end of this chapter, when its workings should be plain.

To start, we need to look at basic database terminology. Firstly, just what is **data access**? Data access is the process of retrieving or manipulating data in an application which is taken from a remote or local **data source**. Data sources come in a variety of different forms. Common examples of a datasource are:

- Remote relational database on a server, for example, SQL Server
- Local relational database, for example, Personal Oracle
- Text file on a local computer
- Spreadsheet

> Mainframe/midrange host

> On-line information service (Dow Jones, etc.)

JDBC is, by definition, an interface to relational data sources. While it is conceivable that non-relational sources may be accessible through JDBC, we will be concentrating on relational databases in this chapter and the next. Fortunately the structure of relational databases is logical and fairly easy to learn.

The following figure uses an example database to illustrate some key concepts.

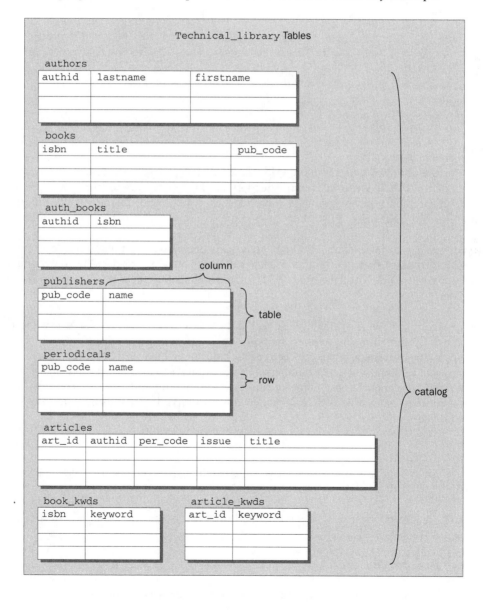

Table

Tables, like **authors** in the above figure, are the primary database construct that you'll be dealing with. Any time that you define, create, update or delete data, you will do so within the context of a table. When you create a table within a database, you are creating a 'template' for a grid. In relational parlance, tables specifically refer to a collection of rows conforming to the specifications of the corresponding columns.

> *According to E. F. Codd's relational rules, tables are a collection of relationships expressed as one or more unordered rows without duplicated rows and without repeating groups.*
>
> *If the data source that you're using is relational (or somewhat relational), it probably uses the term 'table' to refer to the primary storage unit. The data source doesn't have to be relational—it could just as easily be a text file, in which case "table" refers to a file. The only requirement is that the data source is represented within a relational context.*

Column

Think for a minute of a rectangular grid of cells. The grid has a number of columns and a number of rows. You write in column headers at the top of each column, and decide what sort of information you are going to have in each column. So, in the previous figure, the column named **lastname** illustrates one of three columns defined for the **authors** table.

Depending on the data source, columns may also be known as 'fields'. By deciding on the type of information that is going into each column, you are also deciding on the **data type** of each column (SQL has data types that correspond to the basic Java data types—we'll list them later).

It's important that columns have consistent data types and semantics for every piece of data stored. Each column is defined to represent a specific piece of information. For example, in the **authors** table, the **lastname** column, which is defined as a text field, will only be used to store text—not numbers. The column's semantics must be preserved too— the column represents the last name of authors. You would not use this column to store an author's hobbies or favorite movie. If you wanted to record that information, you'd need to create new columns.

Row

Again, if you visualize the table as a two-dimensional spreadsheet, **rows** are the collection of data elements that make up an entity. Some data sources refer to a row as a **record**.

So the figure illustrates a row of data in the **authors** table. An example row from that table would look like this:

20	Celko	Joe

with the data for columns **authid**, **lastname** and **firstname** columns.

Catalog

In general, the **catalog** refers to the database system tables. System tables are similar to tables used by your application, except instead of storing application information, they are used to store information about the databases, tables, and the composition of those tables. The catalog can be queried to find out what tables are available from a data source, what columns are defined for a given table, and so forth.

In the figure, 'catalog' refers to the entire `technical_library` database.

Depending on the particular database to which you're connected, the catalog can contain more detailed information, including security details, foreign keys and stored procedures.

The column values that uniquely identify a row make up the primary key. Rows may also contain values that refer to key values in different tables. For example, the `auth_books` table contains a column `author_id` whose value is the primary key for a row in the `authors` table. When a table contains columns that are key columns for another table, values in those columns are referred to as foreign keys.

Procedures

If you're not already familiar with procedures, you'll get an introduction here, and learn how to use them later in Chapter 18.

Many database servers are capable of executing pre-built scripts, as well as SQL statements. These server-based scripts are called by the application, and are executed by the database server. They are frequently referred to as **stored procedures**, or just **procedures.**

Metadata

Metadata, or data about data, is the information that describes the database, tables and anything else relating to the database. Most of the metadata available through JDBC is analogous to the 'dictionary' or 'catalog' of a database. Metadata isn't limited to this information, however. Metadata can also include security information, product information and the terminology used by the database.

Normalization

Relational database theory includes some basic guidelines for designing records and tables. These rules of normalization are intended to help avoid problems with databases, including data inconsistencies and update anomalies. The **normal forms** are models that conform to specific rules. Here is a quick look at 'unnormalized' data, followed by an explanation of the five normal forms.

Unnormalized Data	Unnormalized data has no consistency in record structure from one record to the next. There aren't a consistent number of fields in each record, and the data contained within fields may vary in semantics from one record to the next. Data contained within fields may not be **atomic**—that is, the field may contain multiple, decomposable bits of information, such as a field that contains a street address, city, state and zipcode.
First Normal Form	Data that is in first normal form has a consistent logical 'shape'. Every record contains exactly the same number of fields—it's at least tabular. Note that first normal form is the 'minimum bid' for working with relational databases—data with varying numbers of fields is outside the domain of relational theory.
Second Normal Form	Data in second normal form conforms to the requirements of first normal form, and also introduces a relationship between the key and non-key fields. Non-key fields provide information that is wholly dependent on the key value(s) and nothing but the key value(s).

Second normal form is violated if fields are dependent on a part of the key but not the whole key. That's a subtle point, but here's an example. Suppose that the **auth_books** table in the last figure was instead structured as illustrated in the following figure:

Restructured auth_books table window
second normal form

auth_books

isbn	authid	auth_email	pub_date

The **auth_books** table maintains the relationships between books and their authors. This table has two key parts—**isbn** and **authid**. The table illustrated above violates second normal form because it contains fields that are dependent on a key part but not on the entire key. In fact, it contains two such violations: **auth_email** is dependent on **authid**, and **pub_date** is dependent on **isbn**, but neither **auth_email** nor **pub_date** are a function of the entire key.

Third Normal Form	Data in third normal form conforms to second normal form, and does not contain any fields that are dependent on other non-key fields. Suppose that the **books** table were restructured as shown below:

**Restructured books table violates
third normal form**

books

isbn	title	pub_code	pub_name

The **isbn** column is the key to the **books** table. The table illustrated above violates third normal form because the **pub_name** column, a non-key column, is dependent on **pub_code**, another non-key column.

Fourth Normal Form

Data in fourth normal form must first satisfy the criteria for third normal form. Fourth normal form is concerned with multi-valued facts, which can be in the form of many-to-many relationships (such as authors to books), or many-to-one relationships (such as books to publishers). Data in fourth normal form contains no more than one multi-valued fact about an entity. For example, suppose that we wanted to keep track of two sets of multi-valued facts about authors—books and hobbies. An author may have contributed to more than one book, and may have more than one hobby. These two many-to-many relationships might be stored in a table similar to the one illustrated below:

**Table violates fourth
normal form**

auth_info

authid	isbn	hobby

The **auth_info** table illustrated above demonstrates a violation of fourth normal form. This table contains more than one multi-value fact describing the key. To correct this design error, each multi-value fact should be split into its own table.

Fifth Normal Form

Fifth normal form, like fourth normal form, is concerned with multivalued data. Data that is in fifth normal form must first be in fourth normal form. In addition, data that complies with fifth normal form contains no multivalue data that can be broken down into smaller pieces without information loss. For example, consider the following table:

```
                        Table violates fifth
                           normal form

   auth_books
   | authid | isbn | title |
   |        |      |       |
   |        |      |       |
   |        |      |       |
```

This table contains multi-valued facts—the **isbn** and the **title**. This still conforms to fourth normal form, since the title is dependent on the ISBN. This information, however, could be decomposed into another table without losing information. By creating another table for books, and referencing the book title through this table, we make our table conform to fifth normal form, as shown in the original database figure.

Introducing SQL

Structured Query Language (SQL) has developed, through a series of incarnations, as an interactive, declarative language supporting E.F. Codd's relational model. It has emerged from *de facto* status, with considerable support from a broad range of vendors and a broad variety of platforms, to international acceptance as an official standard for relational database access. Chief amongst the reasons for the acceptance of SQL as *the* relational query language was the move towards client/server architectures that began in the late 1980's.

FYI

> Not all versions and dialects of SQL are created equal, however. As each vendor has incorporated SQL into products, extensions to the grammar have often been added. That was convenient for the database vendors but tough for anyone else trying to work with more than one database vendor. In order to ensure SQL's place as a standard for database access, organizations like ISO and ANSI have worked with the industry to develop standards for SQL. The current ISO operating standard is SQL-92, to which JDBC adheres.
>
> SQL is different from other programming languages that you may be familiar with, in that it is declarative, not procedural. In other words, you don't use SQL to define complex processes, but rather use SQL to define and manipulate data.
>
> If you need more information about using SQL, you may want to check out *Instant SQL* by Joe Celko (ISBN 1-874416-50-8), published by Wrox Press.

The first thing that strikes you about SQL is that it is very readable, if that is, you can read English. The way that each query is structured reads like a sentence. The syntax is easy to learn, and the constructs and concepts are very easy to grasp. Secondly, with SQL you always issue commands. You send the command to the database and the database either returns the required data, or performs the required action.

Let's look at an example. I need to store information about a group of people inside a database. How would I go about defining the tables I need?

The example database shown in the earlier figure is a technical library database. In it we want to keep track of books, magazine articles, their authors and their publishers.

Try It Out—Designing a Table for an Example Database

1 The first step in designing tables is to decide what information you want to capture. Then, using the normalization rules, you design tables around that information.

I want to keep track of the following things:

Books

Articles

Authors

Publishers

2 Next, I define the information that I want for each of these:

Books	ISBN Book title Author(s) Publisher
Articles	Author Title Periodical it was published in Issue of publication
Authors	Last name First name Books published Articles published
Publishers	Publisher code Name

3 I'll start out with a table to keep track of authors. I'll call this table **authors**, and describe the columns that I want for this table:

Column Heading	Description
authid	Unique identifier, since more than one author can have the same name
lastname	Family name
firstname	First name
address1	Address line one
address2	Address line two
city	City
state_prov	State or province
postcode	Zip or postal code
country	Country
phone	Contact phone number
fax	Fax number
email	Email address

4 We need to assign a data type to each column heading in order for the program to be able to pass this information to the database engine, and have the engine store it.

So, let's look at some example SQL data types:

SQL Data Type	Description
CHAR	Fixed length string of characters
VARCHAR	Variable length string of characters
BOOLEAN	Logical value—**true** or **false**
SMALLINT	Small integer value, from -127 to +127
INTEGER	Larger integer value, from -32767 to +32767
FLOAT	Floating point
CURRENCY	Stores monetary values
DOUBLE	Higher precision floating point
DATE	Date
TIME	Time
DATETIME	Date and time
RAW	Raw binary data (can be used to store objects in a streamed binary format)

5 Using these data types we can assign data types for each column in the table:

Column Name	Data Type
authid	INTEGER
lastname	VARCHAR
firstname	VARCHAR
address1	VARCHAR
address2	VARCHAR
city	VARCHAR
state_prov	VARCHAR
postcode	VARCHAR
country	VARCHAR
phone	VARCHAR
fax	VARCHAR
email	VARCHAR

How It Works

The names that we have given each field tell us something about the information that will be stored in that field, but they don't tell the computer what type of information has been stored, or how to store it. While we are interested in the information stored in the columns, all the database engine wants to know about is the *type* of the information.

You probably noticed that a column labeled **authid** has been placed at the top of the list of columns in the **authors** table. This is to give each record a unique identifier so that an individual record can easily be retrieved. Think of the nightmare you'd have if you were managing books and journals for a large university library and you had ten authors named John Smith. Each time you wanted to retrieve information about John Smith, you would get ten authors in your list, and not have any easy way of distinguishing between. It's essential to give each record a unique identifier, and use this as the author's ID.

Most of the data in the **authors** table is string information, so the **VARCHAR** data type was chosen to allow as much or as little text information to be stored in that field as necessary.

> *Not all databases support **VARCHAR**, including the mSQL database. In such cases, you will have to define these fields as **CHAR** type, and estimate the maximum number of characters these fields will require.*

The next requirement is to be able to store information about books. There are two ways that this can be achieved. Firstly, we could store the data in the **authors** table using extra columns. If we were to store books in the **authors** table, we would perhaps add two columns—**title** and **publisher**, but this would only allow us to store a limited amount of information about books written by a particular author. Remember, each author has only one record in the **authors** table, but authors will frequently write more than one book or article. Alternatively, we can store books in a separate table, and this is the better way.

Try It Out—Designing another Table

1 This could easily be done by creating a table with the following information:

Column Heading	Description
isbn	ISBN is a globally unique identifier for a book
title	Title of the book
pub_code	Code identifying the publisher of the book

2 Let us look at some possible data type assignments for our **books** table.

Column Heading	Description
isbn	VARCHAR
title	VARCHAR
pub_code	CHAR(8)

How It Works

The **books** table allows us to record each book by its ISBN, its title and publisher. It will enable us to associate books with authors, and later we'll also be able to associate the book with publisher information as well.

Designing an Intersection Table

For each record in the **books** table, we store:

▶ A unique identifier—the ISBN

▶ The title of the book

▶ A code identifying the publisher

Notice, however, that we haven't included any information about the author. This isn't an oversight. Since more than one author can be involved in the writing of a book and an author can be involved in the writing of more than one book, we need to add some more information that links an author with a book. It is not difficult to see that we could create this link by using the **isbn** (the book identifier) and the **authid**. If we create a table with these two pieces of information, we can add a record in this table for each combination of authors and books they authored or co-authored. This table is simple enough—it merely contains a column for the author identifier and the ISBN. The data types must match the corresponding columns in the **authors** and **books** tables:

Column heading	Data Type
authid	INTEGER
isbn	VARCHAR

Now that we've decided on the design of the tables, how do we use SQL to create them and add information to them?

SQL Commands

SQL commands are more commonly known as 'statements' and fall neatly into two groups:

- Data Definition Language (DDL)
- Data Manipulation Language (DML)—DML can be further divided into two groups:

    select statements—Statements that return a set of results

    everything else—Statements that don't return a set of results.

In order to create our tables in the above example, we would have used DDL, which defines a syntax for commands such as 'Create Table' and 'Create Unique Index'. We would use it to define the structure of the database.

A typical DDL statement might look like:

```
CREATE TABLE authors (
  authid INT NOT NULL PRIMARY KEY,
  lastname CHAR(25),
  firstname CHAR(15),
  address1 CHAR(25),
  address2 CHAR(25),
  city CHAR(25),
  state_prov CHAR(25),
  postcode CHAR(10),
  country CHAR(15),
  phone CHAR(20),
  fax CHAR(20),
  email CHAR(25));
```

which is not so dissimilar to the data type assignments described above. Note, however, that in this SQL statement, I've used fixed length **CHAR** fields rather than **VARCHAR** types. The clause **NOT NULL PRIMARY KEY** tells the database two things. Firstly, don't allow any row in this column of the table to contain a **null** value. This means that every row in the table will always contain a valid value in this column. Secondly, it tells the database to create a unique index on the **authid** column. This ensures that there will be no more than one row with any given author ID. This also greatly assists the database when searching through and ordering records. Think how difficult it would be to search for an entry in an encyclopedia without an index in one of the volumes. This is the same principle on which database indexes work.

Now that we have a table created, we need to put data into the table. The SQL **insert** statement does exactly that.

825

Insert Statements

There are three basic parts to an **insert statement**:

> ▶ Define the target table for inserting data
> ▶ Define the columns that will have values assigned
> ▶ Define the values for those columns

An insert statement begins with the keywords **insert into** , followed by the name of target table:

```
insert into authors
```

There follows a list of columns that will receive values. The columns are enclosed in parentheses:

```
(authid, lastname, firstname, email)
```

Lastly, the keyword **values** follows with the column values in parentheses:

```
values (99, 'Phillips', 'Ron', 'ronp@happykitty.com')
```

The complete **insert** statement is:

```
insert into authors (authid, lastname, firstname, email)
        values (99, 'Phillips', 'Ron', 'ronp@happykitty.com')
```

The result of executing this statement is a new row inserted into the **authors** table. This statement does not fill in values for every column in the table, however. The SQL database will supply a **null** value where no values were supplied by the **insert** statement. If we had attempted to insert a row without a value for **authid**, the database would have reported an error, since the table was created with the **authid** column specified as **not null**.

A variation on the **insert** statement can be used when all column values are being filled by the statement. When no columns are specified, SQL assumes that the values following the **values** keyword correspond to each column in the order that they were specified when the table was created. For example, you could add a row to the books table with the following statement:

```
insert into books (isbn, title, pub_code)
  values ('1874416680', 'Beginning Linux Programming', 'WROX')
```

but since the books column contains only the three columns, the following statement has exactly the same results:

```
insert into books
  values ('1874416680', 'Beginning Linux Programming', 'WROX')
```

826

Now, let us look at a basic **select** statement, as this will give a starting point for getting some data back from a database we prepared earlier.

Select Statements

There are four parts to a SQL select statement:

- ▶ Defining what you want
- ▶ Defining where you want to get it from
- ▶ Defining the conditions for retrieval—joining tables, and record filtering
- ▶ Defining the order in which you want to see the data.

So, how do you define what you want? The first keyword in the select statement, is unsurprisingly, **select**. This tells the database that we intend to get some data back in the form of a resultset, or a relation. Think of a resultset as a table of data—with a fixed number of columns and a number of rows—essentially some subset of data from a database table.

The next identifier allow us to define what we want to see—it allows us to specify which columns we want to retrieve and have as our table headers. We specify each column name as part of a comma-separated list.

So our sample statement so far looks like:

```
select firstname, lastname, authid
```

We now have to specify which table we want to retrieve the data from. When creating a table, there is nothing to stop the developer giving similar column names to each table, so we must ensure that there are no ambiguities when selecting similar column names from two tables.

We specify the table or tables that we wish to retrieve data from, in a **from clause**. This clause immediately follows the select clause. A from clause is specified by the keyword **from**, and then a comma-separated list of tables that you wish to access:

```
from authors
```

Giving:

```
select firstname, lastname, authid from authors
```

This is a complete statement that will retrieve the name, surname and author ID for each row in the **authors** table.

When a resultset is retrieved from the database, each resultset column has a label. This is usually derived from the column names in the select clause. It is possible to provide aliases for the column names. Column aliases are specified by keywords appearing after the column names in the select clause. For example:

```
select firstname, lastname, authid author_identifier
      from authors
```

would alias the **authid** as **author_identifier**.

A **select** statement can also return calculated columns based on operations performed on the table columns. Here's an example:

```
select (firstname + ' ' + lastname) fullname, authid
      from authors
```

Suppose I wanted to limit the rows returned to only include authors that reside within the UK. In order to accomplish that, I would add a **where** clause. Where clauses are used to filter rows. For example, to get a list of authors in the UK:

```
select lastname, firstname from authors
   where country = 'UK'
```

Multiple criteria can be specified in a **where** clause. For example, I might want to get a list of authors in the UK for whom I don't have an email address on record:

```
select lastname, firstname, phone from authors
   where country = 'UK'
      and email is null
```

Note the construction of the **where** clause—there are two conditions that a row is required to satisfy before it will be returned. Firstly, the **country** field must contain a value that is equal to the string value **UK**, and the **email** field must be **null**.

One final example of a **select** statement: a table join. I want to see a list of all authors and the books they have authored, so let us see if we can design a statement that will return this information:

```
select a.lastname, a.firstname, b.title
   from authors a, books b, auth_books ab
   where a.authid = ab.authid
      and b.isbn = ab.isbn
```

The table join appears in the first line of the where clause—we specify the condition for each row that the **authid** columns of the **authors** table and the **auth_books** table must be equal. We also specify that the **isbn** column of **books** and **auth_books** must be equal. Notice also, one small addition to the statement.

If you remember, we were able to alias column names by specifying another keyword after each table identifier, or expression. We are now aliasing the table names, as can be seen in the from clause. The **authors** table is aliased as **a**, the **books** table is aliased as **b** and the **auth_books** table is aliased as **ab**. Back in the **select** statement, the column names are 'qualified' with the aliases of each table. This is the way that column name ambiguities are removed. If we did not have a qualifier in front of the **authid** column, the database engine would have no way of knowing which column was required.

Update Statements

Update statements provide a way of modifying existing data in a table. Update statements are constructed in a similar way to **select** statements. You first start with the **update** keyword, followed by the name of the table you wish to modify:

```
update authors
```

You then specify the **set** keyword, and the data members you wish to modify, with their new values:

```
set lastname='Burk'
```

Finally, the **where** clause is used to filter the records that we wish to update. An update statement cannot be performed across a table join, so the **where** clause is not used to specify a join of this type.

```
where authid = 27
```

The full statement:

```
update authors set lastname='Burk' where authid = 27
```

will update the author record to reflect a change in last name for the author with the id 27.

Update statements do not return a resultset; they merely modify data in the database.

Delete Statements

Delete statements provide a way of deleting particular rows from tables in a database. Delete statements consist of the **delete** keyword, a **from** clause and a **where** clause. For example:

```
delete from books where isbn = '0131259075'
```

deletes the record in the books table with the ISBN value '0131259075'. In the case of the **books** table, there can only be one row with this value, since its primary key is the ISBN. If a similar **delete** statement were executed against the **auth_books** table, however, it would delete all rows with the matching ISBN value.

By now you should understand:

> ▶ The way SQL is constructed
> ▶ How to read SQL statements
> ▶ How to construct basic SQL statements

829

You can expect SQL statements to work with relational databases that adhere to ANSI standards, although each database probably also implements its own extensions to SQL and has slightly differing functionality. Be sure to understand the functionality of the SQL that is used by the underlying database, as this will affect the way you use JDBC to write your Java applications.

The JDBC Package

The JDBC library was designed as an interface for executing SQL statements, and not as a high-level abstraction layer for data access. So, although it wasn't designed to automatically map Java classes to rows in a database, it allows large scale applications to be written to the JDBC interface without worrying too much about which database will be deployed with the application. The application is well insulated from vendor-specific issues, and so the application doesn't have to be reengineered for specific databases. This also ties in with JavaSoft's commitment to platform independent Java code, though more on how this is achieved in JDBC later.

So, from the user's point of view, the Java application looks something like this:

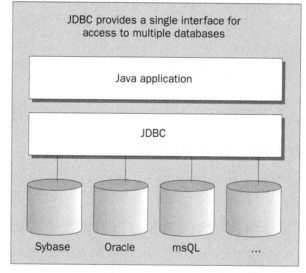

JDBC manages this by having an implementation of the JDBC interface for each specific database—a driver. This handles the mapping of Java program calls to JDBC classes to the database API. We'll learn more about this later on.

Relating JDBC to ODBC

One of the fundamental principles of JDBC's design was to make it practical to build JDBC drivers based on other database APIs. To this end, JDBC was designed specifically with an existing standard, ODBC, in mind. There is a very close and deliberate mapping between the JDBC architecture and API, and their ODBC counterparts. They share some important conceptual components:

▶ Driver Manager   Loads database drivers, and manages the connections between the application and the driver.

▶ Driver   Translates API calls into operations for a specific data source.

▶ Connection   A session between an application and a driver.

▶ Statement   A SQL statement to perform a query or update operation.

▶ Metadata   Information about returned data, the database and the driver.

▶ Result Set   Logical set of columns and rows of data returned by executing a statement.

JDBC Basics

Assuming you have followed the instructions given at the start of the chapter, and have the requisite sample databases and database drivers installed on your machine, we are ready to look at the essential JDBC program, which has the following basic steps:

▶ Import the necessary classes

▶ Load the JDBC driver

▶ Identify the data source

▶ Allocate a **Connection** object

▶ Allocate a **Statement** object

▶ Execute a query using the **Statement** object

▶ Retrieve data from the returned **ResultSet** object

▶ Close the **ResultSet**

▶ Close the **Statement** object

▶ Close the **Connection** object

First we'd better take a quick look at what some of these terms mean.

The JDBC architecture is based on a collection of Java interfaces and classes that together enable the developer to establish sessions to data sources, create and execute SQL statements and retrieve data. These are summarized in the figure below:

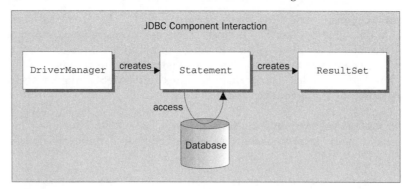

DriverManager

All work with the JDBC classes begins with the **DriverManager** class. The **DriverManager** is responsible for loading JDBC drivers and for establishing connections to the data sources accessed through the JDBC drivers. The **DriverManager** can also be used to determine which drivers are loaded, as well as register or unregister drivers 'on the fly'.

The **DriverManager** provides **static**, factory methods for creating objects implementing the **Connection** interface. As the name implies, factory methods are responsible for creating new objects on demand. When you need a new connection to a JDBC driver, you don't create the new object yourself—you ask the **DriverManager** to do it for you.

You can think of the **DriverManager** class as having a role like the maître d' of a restaurant. The maître d' is responsible for greeting you and finding you a table and a waiter. He's also responsible for managing all of the restaurant staff. Once you're seated, though, as far as you're concerned, he pretty much disappears.

Connection

The **Connection** class represents a session with a specific data source. In order to create and execute SQL statements, you must first have a **Connection** object. It establishes a connection to the data source, and allocates **Statement** objects, which are used to define and execute specific SQL queries. The **Connection** object can also be used to query the data source for information that defines the data (metadata), including available tables, capabilities and so on.

Statement

The **Statement** object allocated by the **Connection** object implements the **Statement** interface. When a **Statement** object is created, it provides a workspace for creating an SQL query, executing it, and retrieving returned results. JDBC provides three kinds of **Statement** objects: **Statement**, **PreparedStatement** and **CallableStatement**.

Statement objects are created by calling the **createStatement()** method of a valid **Connection** object. Once created, **Statement** objects are executed by calling the **executeQuery()** method of the **Statement** object, which is passed a **String** containing the text of the SQL query.

PreparedStatement objects differ from **Statement** objects in that the SQL statement is pre-compiled, and has placeholders for runtime parameters. **PreparedStatement** objects are very useful when a statement will be executed multiple times (for example, adding new rows to a table) or it is not convenient to create a single string that contains the entire SQL statement. I'll present examples later in this chapter that illustrate equivalent SQL statements implemented as both **Statement** and **PreparedStatement** objects.

Finally, the **CallableStatement** object is used for calling procedures on the database. As we saw earlier, many database servers have the ability to execute procedures on the server.

This allows you to define business logic and rules at the server level, rather than relying on applications to replicate and enforce those rules. This is where the real power of client/ server computing comes into play.

ResultSet

Results are returned in the form of an object implementing the **ResultSet** interface. From the **ResultSet** object, you can retrieve the value of columns by name or by position, and determine information about columns such as the number of columns returned, the data types of columns and so forth.

The JDBC API provides access to metadata, not only for the **Connection** object, but also for the **ResultSet** object. The JDBC API provides a **ResultSetMetaData** object that lets you peek into the data behind the **ResultSet** object. If you plan on providing interactive browsing facilities in your JDBC applications, you'll find this particularly useful.

Together, these classes and interfaces make up the bulk of the JDBC components that you will be working with. Let's now put them into action with a simple code example.

Try It Out—Our First Example

The following source code illustrates a minimal JDBC program that creates a **Connection** object.

```java
import java.sql.*;

public class MakingTheConnection
{
  public static void main(String[] args)
  {
    // Load the driver
    try
    {
      // Load the driver class
      Class.forName("sun.jdbc.odbc.JdbcOdbcDriver");

      // This defines the data source for the driver
      String sourceURL = new String("jdbc:odbc:technical_library");

      // Create connection through the DriverManager
      Connection databaseConnection =
                          DriverManager.getConnection(sourceURL);
    }
    catch(ClassNotFoundException cnfe)
    {
      System.out.println(cnfe);
    }
```

```
      catch(SQLException sqle)
      {
        System.out.println(sqle);
      }
    }
  }
```

How It Works

The first step to creating a JDBC program is to import the necessary classes and interfaces for the JDBC library. Those classes are found in the **java.sql** package.

Next, the code ensures that the JDBC driver class required by your program is loaded. This will guarantee that any initialization that the JDBC driver must do will be handled before your code actually uses the driver. The simplest way to do this is to explicitly load the class using the **forName()** method of the **Class** class, as illustrated above. The **forName()** method is passed the name of the class that implements the JDBC driver. Note that the **forName()** method can throw a **ClassNotFoundException**, which must be caught.

> *In the examples we show in this chapter—we'll be using the JDBC-ODBC driver—**sun.jdbc.odbc.JdbcOdbcDriver**—to access an Access database, **technical_library.mdb**. We covered how to create the **technical_library** database using **build_tables** at the start of the chapter.*

Explicitly loading the driver class ensures that the Java interpreter's class loader loads the class. When the driver class is loaded, Java will look to find out if the driver class has a **static** method. If it does, it will call the **static** method immediately after the class is loaded. That allows the driver to implement any required initialization code (for example, loading a dynamic link library if the driver uses native methods) in a way that it is guaranteed to get called before any other method.

 FYI Alternatively, the driver name can be specified in the **System** property **Sql.Drivers**, in which case the **DriverManager** will automatically load the JDBC driver.

If you have read the previous chapter, you're already familiar with Uniform Resource Locators (URLs). A URL describes an electronic resource, such as a World Wide Web page, a file on an FTP server, in a manner that uniquely identifies that resource.

URLs play a central role in networked application development in Java. JDBC uses URLs to identify drivers and datasources. JDBC URLs have the format:

```
jdbc:<subprotocol>://<data source identifier>
```

The scheme **jdbc** indicates that the URL refers to a JDBC data source. The sub-protocol identifies which JDBC driver to use. For example, the JDBC-ODBC bridge uses the driver identifier **odbc**, and the mSQL JDBC driver uses the driver identifier **msql**.

The JDBC driver dictates the format of the data source identifier. In our example above, the JDBC-ODBC bridge simply uses the ODBC datasource name. In order to use the ODBC driver with the **technical_library** ODBC datasource, you would create a URL with the format:

```
jdbc:odbc:technical_library
```

The next step to getting data to or from database is to create a **Connection** object. The **Connection** object essentially establishes a context in which you can create and execute statements. Since the data source in this chapter's examples doesn't require a user name or password, the simplest form of the **getConnection()** method can be used.

Most JDBC methods handle errors by throwing an exception of the type **SQLException**, and the **getConnection()** method of the **DriverManager** class does exactly that. Note that the code fragment above is bracketed with a **try-catch** clause that traps the **SQLException** exception. In the next chapter, you will learn more sophisticated error handling techniques, but for this example, a simple message will be printed to the console in the event of a problem loading the JDBC driver or creating a **Connection** to the data source.

More on DriverManager

As we've seen, the **DriverManager** class manages the JDBC drivers that are available and have registered with the manager (reported for work, as it were). It also matches up your request for a data source in the form of an URL with the appropriate driver, which in turn provides you with a connection.

Creating a connection is by far the most common use of the **DriverManager** class. In our previous example, we saw the following minimal code:

```
// create Connection through the DriverManager
Connection databaseConnection = DriverManager.getConnection(sourceURL);
```

There are three overloaded **getConnection()** methods in the **DriverManager** class. If the database requires a user name and password, the second form of the **getConnection()** method can be used:

```
databaseConnection = DriverManager.getConnection(sourceURL,
                                        "myusername",
                                        "mypassword");
```

In some cases, however, the user name and password may not be all the information required to establish a connection. In order to accommodate those situations, the **DriverManager** class provides another **getConnection()** method that accepts a **Properties** object as a parameter.

The **Properties** class, defined in the **java.util** package, associates names with values. More precisely, the **Properties** object stores key/value pairs where a key is supplied as a **String** and the value can be any valid object.

835

The **Properties** object should contain, minimally, a value for **"user"** and a value for **"password"**. JDBC drivers will define the keys for other required values.

The code fragment below illustrates creation of a connection for the mSQL JDBC driver. Note that the **Properties** class is imported from the **java.util** package, and we've added another **catch** clause to trap a **NullPointerException**, which may be thrown by the **put()** method for the **Properties** object.

```
import java.util.Properties;

// ...

String driverName = "imaginary.sql.iMsqlDriver";
String sourceURL =
                "jdbc:msql://zorak.happykitty.com:4333/technical_library";

try
{
  Class.forName (driverName);
  Properties prop = new Properties();
  prop.put("user","myusername");
  prop.put("password","mypassword");
  databaseConnection = DriverManager.getConnection(sourceURL, prop);
}
catch(ClassNotFoundException cnfe)
{
  System.out.println("Error loading " + driverName);
}
catch(SQLException sqle)
{
  System.out.println(sqle);
}
catch(NullPointerException npe)
{
  System.out.println("Bad object passed to Properties");
}
```

While this pretty much covers everything that most developers will ever do with the **DriverManager** class, there are other methods that may be useful. We will take a look at these next.

LogStream

The **DriverManager** class provides a pair of access methods for the **PrintStream** object that is used by the **DriverManager** class and all drivers. This allows you to set, or reroute, the **PrintStream** that the driver uses to log information. The two access methods are:

```
public static void setLogStream(PrintStream out)
public static PrintStream getLogStream()
```

The **LogStream** can be disabled by setting the **PrintStream** to **null**.

Examining the log can be pretty interesting. While it will never make the best seller list, if you want to find out what's going on behind the scenes, take a look at the information that gets generated by the JDBC-ODBC driver. You'll get a very good look at how that driver works.

Your application can print to the **LogStream** using the **DriverManager**'s **println()** method

```
public static void println(String message)
```

This method is typically used by JDBC drivers, but it may prove useful for debugging or logging database-related errors or events.

Login Timeout

The **DriverManager** class provides a pair of access methods for the login timeout period. These allow you to specify a timeout period (in seconds) that limits the time that a driver spends logging into the database. The two access methods are:

```
public static void setLoginTimeout(int seconds)
public static int getLoginTimeout()
```

Specifying a non-default timeout period can be useful for troubleshooting applications that are having difficulty connecting to a remote database server. For example, if my application is trying to connect to a very busy server, my applications may appear to have hung. I can tell the **DriverManager** to fail the connection attempt by specifying a timeout period. The code fragment below tells the **DriverManager** to fail the login attempt after 60 seconds:

```
String driverName = "imaginary.sql.iMsqlDriver";
String sourceURL =
            "jdbc:msql://zorak.happykitty.com:4333/technical_library";

try
{
  Class.forName (driverName);
  Properties prop = new Properties();
  prop.put("user","myusername");
  prop.put("password","mypassword");

   // fail after 60 seconds
  DriverManager.setLoginTimeout(60);

  databaseConnection = DriverManager.getConnection(sourceURL, prop);
}
catch(ClassNotFoundException cnfe)
{
```

```
      System.out.println("Error loading " + driverName);
   }
   catch(SQLException sqle)
   {
      System.out.println(sqle);
   }
   catch(NullPointerException npe)
   {
      System.out.println("Bad object passed to Properties");
   }
```

More on Drivers

As we said earlier, a major design consideration behind JDBC was that Java applications that retrieve and manipulate data should be able to access different data sources at runtime. In Java, functionality is **linked** into the application at compile time, in order that references to the data access functions can be resolved and an executable built. This means that a single library must be available to the application developer to link into their application to provide access to any data source. Any further code required to access the data source must be made available at runtime and can be specified as a parameter within the application. The library that is linked into the application at compile time is the **driver manager** and the code that is dynamically included at runtime is a **driver**. As JDBC developers you will get used to using:

```
import java.sql.*;
```

Java is a late binding language, which means that all the actual code used to execute the program is linked at runtime. It is, however, necessary to inform the compiler of its location at compile-time, to ensure that the references can be resolved before the program executes.

When the **DriverManager** class has been linked, or imported, into the application, it is then possible to connect to a data source using a particular driver. Driver implementations come in four flavors:

- JDBC-ODBC bridge driver
- Native API partly-Java
- Net protocol all-Java client
- Native protocol all-Java

Understanding how drivers are built, and their limitations, may affect your application development decisions.

JDBC-ODBC Bridge Driver

The JDBC-ODBC bridge, which is included with the JDK 1.1, enables Java applications to access data through drivers written to the ODBC standard. The driver bridge is very useful for accessing data in data sources for which no pure JDBC drivers exist.

The bridge works by translating the JDBC methods into ODBC function calls. It has the advantage of working with a huge number of ODBC drivers, but it only works under the Windows and Solaris operating systems.

Native API/Partly Java Driver

This classification of driver is quite similar to the bridge driver. It consists of Java code that accesses data through native methods—typically calls to a particular vendor library. Like the bridge driver, this class of driver is convenient when a C data access library already exists, but it isn't usually very portable across platforms.

Net Protocol All Java Client

This class of driver is implemented as 'middleware', with the client driver completely implemented in Java. This client driver communicates with a separate middleware component (usually through TCP/IP) which translates requests into database access calls. This form of driver is an extension of the previous class, with the Java and native API separated into separate client and proxy processes.

Native Protocol All Java

This class of driver communicates directly to the database server using the server's native protocol. Unlike the previous driver type, there is no translation step that converts the Java-initiated request into some other form. The client talks directly to the server.

There are a number of JDBC drivers available. The best source of up-to-date information about JDBC drivers is from the JavaSoft JDBC drivers page on their Web site: `http://splash.javasoft.com/jdbc/jdbc.drivers.html`

Using the JDBC library for programming applications, the only time that you'll probably come in contact with the **Driver** object is when you install it. Your applications need not ever interact directly with the **Driver** itself. The **DriverManager** class actually takes care of communicating with the **Driver**. When you call the **getConnection()** method of the **DriverManager** class, it iterates through the drivers that are registered with the **DriverManager**, and ask each one in turn if it can handle the URL that you've passed it. When a driver can satisfy the connection defined by the URL, that driver creates a **Connection** object, which is passed back to the application by way of the **DriverManager**.

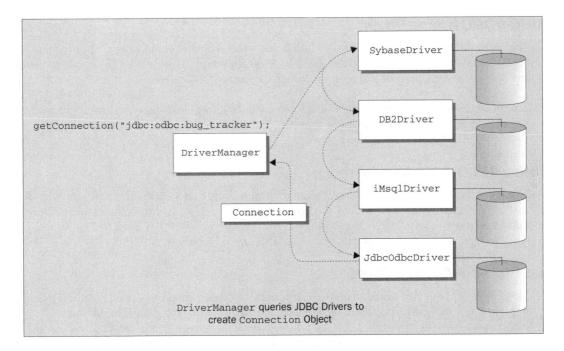

DriverManager queries JDBC Drivers to
create Connection Object

There are occasions, however, that you may want to query a specific driver for information, such as its version number, or whether it is JDBC-compliant or not. For example, you may know that a particular feature of a driver wasn't incorporated until version 2.1. You can query the driver to get the version so your program can handle an earlier version intelligently.

In order to get the **Driver** object, you call the **getDriver()** method of the **DriverManager** class, passing it the URL of the data source. If the **DriverManager** finds a driver that can accommodate the data source, a reference to the driver is returned. The code fragment below illustrates testing the version of a JDBC driver.

```java
int verMajor, verMinor;
int verPreferredMajor, verPreferredMinor;

verPreferredMajor = 1;
verPreferredMinor = 1;

String sourceURL = "jdbc:odbc:bug_tracker";

Driver theDriver = DriverManager.getDriver(sourceURL);

verMajor = theDriver.getMajorVersion();
verMinor = theDriver.getMinorVersion();

if ((verMajor >= verPreferredMajor) && (verMinor >= verPreferredMinor))
   System.out.println("Version " + verMajor + "." + verMinor + " found");
else
```

```
System.out.println("Required version of driver (" +
                    verPreferredMajor + "." +
                    verPreferredMinor + ") not found");
```

Identifying Datasources

At it's most basic level, the syntax of the URL is:

```
<scheme>:<scheme-specific-part>
```

The **scheme**, or access method, identifies how programs access a resource. In most cases, you can think of the scheme being synonymous with the 'protocol'. The format of the remainder of the URL depends on the scheme. The Internet standard document RFC1738 specifies the format:

```
protocol://<user>:<password>@<host>:<port>/<url-path>
```

of which the user, password and port are optional. The following table lists some common URL schemes.

Scheme	Description	URL format
`http`	Hypertext transfer protocol	`http://host:port/path`
`ftp`	File transfer protocol	`ftp://user:password@host/path;type=<type>`
`news`	USENET news protocol	`news:<newsgroupname>`
`file`	File	`file://host/path`

The mSQL JDBC driver requires more information in order to establish a connection to the database. The mSQL driver requires a host name, a port number and a database name, and so it defines the data source identifier as:

```
//<host>:<port>/<database name>
```

In order to access the **technical_library** database on the host **zorak.happykitty.com** using the TCP/IP port 4333, create your URL as:

```
jdbc:msql://zorak.happykitty.com:4333/technical_library
```

Using the Connection

The **Connection** class itself will most typically be used for creating **Statement** objects, but can also be used for querying a database's catalog and transaction characteristics.

The JDBC API provides a rich set of methods for accessing database metadata. The JDBC **Connection** class has a **getMetaData()** method that allows you a substantial look into the information behind the database. Depending on the database driver, it's pretty easy to create browsing programs that allow the user to interactively explore the contents of a database. We'll see how shortly.

Let's now proceed to do something useful with the **Connection** object we've created.

Try It Out—Creating a Statement

Using the **MakingTheConnection** class, add the shaded lines below:

```java
import java.sql.*;

public class MakingAStatement
{
  public static void main(String[] args)
  {
    // Load the driver
    try
    {
      // Load the driver class
      Class.forName("sun.jdbc.odbc.JdbcOdbcDriver");

      // This defines the data source for the driver
      String sourceURL = new String("jdbc:odbc:technical_library");

      // Create connection through the DriverManager
      Connection databaseConnection =
                          DriverManager.getConnection(sourceURL);

      Statement myStatement = databaseConnection.createStatement();

      ResultSet authorResults = myStatement.executeQuery(
                      "select lastname, firstname from authors");
    }
    catch(ClassNotFoundException cnfe)
    {
      System.out.println(cnfe);
    }
    catch(SQLException sqle)
    {
      System.out.println(sqle);
    }
  }
}
```

How It Works

Once the connection has been established, the next step is to have the **Connection** object allocate a **Statement** object. The **Statement** object enables you to execute a static SQL statement and retrieve results. To create a **Statement**, simply call the **createStatement()** method of the **Connection** object.

Once the **Statement** has been created, a SQL query can be executed by simply specifying the SQL query as a string passed to the **executeQuery()** method of the **Statement** object.

The **executeQuery()** method returns an object that implements the **ResultSet** interface. As the name implies, the **ResultSet** interface enables you to get information that was found by the query. You can think of the **ResultSet** interface as providing row-at-a-time access to a virtual table of results. The **ResultSet** object provides an internal **cursor**, or logical pointer to the current row, to keep track of its current row. When the **ResultSet** is first returned, the cursor is positioned just before the first row of data.

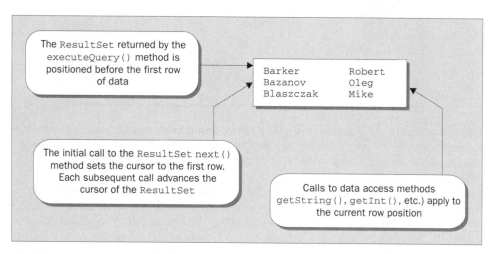

The ResultSet returned by the executeQuery() method is positioned before the first row of data

Barker   Robert
Bazanov   Oleg
Blaszczak   Mike

The initial call to the ResultSet next() method sets the cursor to the first row. Each subsequent call advances the cursor of the ResultSet

Calls to data access methods getString(), getInt(), etc.) apply to the current row position

After executing the query and before any column data can be accessed, the row position needs to be advanced by calling the **next()** method. The **next()** method returns a **boolean** value that indicates if the **ResultSet** is positioned at a valid row (**true**), or that there are no more rows (**false**).

When the **ResultSet** is positioned at a valid row, the **ResultSet** can be queried for specific column values. The **ResultSet** interface provides a set of column retrieval methods that return specific data types.

Retrieving Data by Column Position

Columns can be referenced by position or by column name. For example, suppose that you've executed the following SQL statement:

```
select lastname, firstname from authors order by lastname
```

This statement will return a set of rows consisting of two columns:

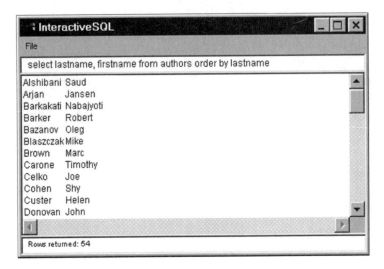

When this information is returned by JDBC in a **ResultSet** object, you can access each row's column data by either specifying the column number (with the first column numbered 1, the second 2 and so forth) or by specifying the table column's name.

If you know the column ordering, as in the case of a pre-compiled SQL statement, using the column position is slightly faster than using the column name to retrieve column data (since there is no additional overhead in matching a column name to a particular column position). It can also be more convenient to refer to columns in an expression, using their position. The **ResultSet** provides methods for retrieving data from specific columns. For example:

```
String authorID = authorResults.getString(1);
```

returns a **String** object for the first column at the current **ResultSet** row position.

Retrieving Data by Column Name

There may be situations where you don't necessarily know the column ordering. For example, if you executed the statement:

```
select * from authors
```

the order of returned columns will be determined by the database. There is no guarantee that the table hasn't been modified with additional columns, and certainly no guarantee that identical tables on different databases will return columns in the same order. For these cases, the JDBC **ResultSet** API still allows you retrieve data by column name. The **ResultSet** provides methods for retrieving data from specific columns by column name. For example

```
String authorID = authorResults.getString("authid");
```

returns a **String** object for the **authid** column at the current **ResultSet** row position.

The Essential JDBC Program

We now have all the pieces to make up the essential JDBC program, which initializes the environment, allocates **Connection** and **Statement** objects, and retrieves data by both position and column name.

Try It Out—Putting It All Together

1 First import the necessary classes:

```
import java.sql.*;
```

2 Now define the application class, the variables and the **main()** function. The **main()** function will make the query.

```
public class EssentialJDBC
{
  ResultSet authorResults;
  Connection databaseConnection;
  Statement myStatement;
  String sourceURL;
  String queryIdAndName;
  String queryWildcard;

  public static void main (String[] args)
  {
    EssentialJDBC SQLExample;
    SQLExample = new EssentialJDBC();

    SQLExample.getStatementResultsByColumnPosition();
    SQLExample.getStatementResultsByColumnName();
  }
```

3 Next we write the constructor for the class.

> *The data source is identified with an URL in the form,*
> **jdbc:driver_name:datasource**. *The datasource identifier format is defined by the driver. In the case of the JDBC-ODBC bridge, the data source is the ODBC source name.*

```
public EssentialJDBC()
{
  String authorID;
  String authorName;

  sourceURL = "jdbc:odbc:technical_library";
  queryIdAndName = " select authid, lastname, firstname from authors";
  queryWildcard = " select * from authors";
```

```
try
{
   Class.forName("sun.jdbc.odbc.JdbcOdbcDriver");
   databaseConnection = DriverManager.getConnection(sourceURL);
}
catch(SQLException sqle)
{
   System.out.println("Error creating connection");
}
catch(ClassNotFoundException cnfe)
{
   System.out.println(cnfe.toString());
}
}
```

4 We will also write a `finalize()` method which will close the connection automatically when the garbage collector comes for the **EssentialJDBC** object. This ensures that whatever happens in the program, the connection will always be closed gracefully. Notice that this method tests the value of the connection to avoid trying to close a **null** connection.

```
public void finalize() throws Throwable
{
  if(databaseConnection != null)
    databaseConnection.close();
}
```

5 Next we code the `getStatementResultsByColumnPosition()` method, creating the **Statement** object from the **Connection** object, and sending the SQL query to get a result set back. The cursor is initially positioned just before the first row. The **next()** method is executed to position cursor at the first row.

```
void getStatementResultsByColumnPosition()
{
   String authorID;
   String authorLastName;
   String authorFirstName;

   try
   {
      Statement myStatement = databaseConnection.createStatement();
      ResultSet authorResults = myStatement.executeQuery(queryIdAndName);
      int row = 0;
      boolean more = authorResults.next ();
```

6 While there are still rows available in the result set, we go ahead and retrieve the **authid, lastname** and **firstname** columns from the result set. The returned columns, their data type and their order are known at compile time. Therefore, we can retrieve the columns by number and gain a performance advantage.

Then, we retrieve the ID and the name as strings using the position. Note that the first position is one, the second two and so forth.

```
while (more)
{
  row++;

  authorID = authorResults.getString(1);
  authorLastName = authorResults.getString(2);
  authorFirstName = authorResults.getString(3);
  System.out.println("Row " + Integer.toString(row) + ") "
                     + authorID + " " + authorLastName + " , "
                     + authorFirstName);

  more = authorResults.next ();
}
// Close the result set
authorResults.close();
}
```

7 This **SQLException** handler doesn't provide very elegant error handling for this program, since it will handle an error at any point in the program and stop it. It is required, however, by the JDBC methods. Later examples will illustrate more complete and robust error handling.

```
catch (SQLException ex)
{
    System.out.println ("\nSQLException------------------\n");
    System.out.println ("SQLState: " + ex.getSQLState ());
    System.out.println ("Message :  " + ex.getMessage ());
}
}
```

8 Much the same applies to the **getStatementResultsByColumnName()** method:

```
void getStatementResultsByColumnName()
{
  String authorID;
  String authorLastName;
  String authorFirstName;

  try
  {
    Statement myStatement = databaseConnection.createStatement();
    ResultSet authorResults =
                        myStatement.executeQuery(queryWildcard);
    int row = 0;
    boolean more = authorResults.next ();

    while (more)
```

```
      {
        row++;
        authorID = authorResults.getString("authid");
        authorLastName = authorResults.getString("lastname");
        authorFirstName = authorResults.getString("firstname");
        System.out.println("Row " + Integer.toString(row) + ") "
                           + authorID + " " + authorLastName + " , "
                           + authorFirstName);
        more = authorResults.next ();
      }
      authorResults.close();
    }
    catch (SQLException sqle)
    {
      System.out.println ("\nSQLException-------------------\n");
      System.out.println ("SQLState: " + sqle.getSQLState ());
      System.out.println ("Message :  " + sqle.getMessage ());
    }
  }
}
```

Running this code produces the following results:

```
Row 1)  1 Gross                    , Christian
Row 2)  2 Roche                    , Kevin
Row 3)  3 Tracy                    , Michael
Row 4)  4 Horton                   , Ivor
Row 5)  5 Cohen                    , Shy
Row 6)  6 Gonzalez                 , Andres
Row 7)  7 Hammil                   , Kerry
Row 8)  8 Mitchell                 , Tom
Row 9)  9 Rodrigues                , Larry
Row 10) 10 Matthew                  , Neil
Row 11) 11 Stones                   , Richard
...
Row 1)  1 Gross                    , Christian
Row 2)  2 Roche                    , Kevin
Row 3)  3 Tracy                    , Michael
Row 4)  4 Horton                   , Ivor
Row 5)  5 Cohen                    , Shy
Row 6)  6 Gonzalez                 , Andres
Row 7)  7 Hammil                   , Kerry
Row 8)  8 Mitchell                 , Tom
Row 9)  9 Rodrigues                , Larry
Row 10) 10 Matthew                  , Neil
Row 11) 11 Stones                   , Richard
...
```

How It Works

The **EssentialJDBC** class provides a **main()** method to declare and allocate an **EssentialJDBC** object by calling the class constructor. It then calls the **getStatementResultsByColumnPosition()** and the **getStatementResultsByColumnName()** methods of the new object.

The constructor initializes member variables, and loads the **JdbcOdbcDriver** class. Next it creates a **Connection** object by calling the static **getConnection()** method of the **DriverManager** class.

The bulk of the work, however, occurs within the **getStatementResultsByColumnPosition()** and **getStatementResultsByColumnName()**. These methods do exactly what the names imply: both create a **Statement** object and execute a SQL query. The difference between the two methods is how they retrieve the returned data.

The **getStatementResultsByColumnPosition()** method executes a SQL query where the column names are specified, and the column ordering of the returned results are determined by that SQL query. This query is executed by calling the **executeQuery()** method of the **Statement** object. This method returns the data in a **ResultSet** object. Since the column ordering is known ahead of time, we can retrieve data by column position. The current row position of the **ResultSet** is advanced, and for each valid row, the column data is retrieved as strings and printed to the console. Finally, the **ResultSet** and the **Statement** object are closed. Note that the garbage collection of Java will handle this automatically, but calling **close()** explicitly ensures that those resources will be cleaned up immediately.

The **getStatementResultsByColumnName()** method functions almost identically to the **getStatementResultsByColumnPosition()** except for a couple of differences. The SQL statement executed by the **Statement** in this method executes a wildcard **select**, so the column ordering isn't known ahead of time—the column ordering is entirely up to the database itself. For that reason, this method uses explicit column names to retrieve the data from the **ResultSet**. Like the previous method, the column data is retrieved as strings and printed to the console for each row returned. Finally, the **ResultSet** and the **Statement** objects are closed.

More on ResultSet

When a **Statement** executes SQL that returns values, those values are returned in the form of an object implementing the **ResultSet** interface. You'll often hear of the **ResultSet** referred to as an object—this is shorthand for referring to the object implementing that interface.

The **ResultSet** defines an interface that presents returned values in a logical table format. The **ResultSet** interface provides methods for retrieving column data as Java types. The methods listed below illustrate the data retrieval methods. The **ResultSet** provides a method form of each of these methods, as you saw earlier, for accessing columns either by column position or column name.

```
getAsciiStream()        getTimestamp()          getTime()
getBoolean()            getBinaryStream()       getBignum()
getDate()               getBytes()              getByte()
getInt()                getFloat()              getDouble()
getShort()              getObject()             getLong()
getString()
```

ResultSetMetaData

The **ResultSet** object also provides access to information about the columns themselves in the form of the **ResultSetMetaData** object.

Consider, for example, that you want to execute the SQL query:

```
select authid, lastname, firstname from authors
```

to get the set of author IDs, their last name and first name from the **authors** table.

That query, if executed, produces a **ResultSet** whose contents look like this:

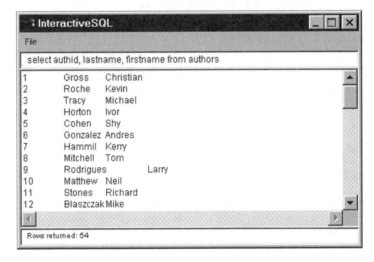

This is the raw data that the query produced, but there is additional information about this data that will be meaningful. For example, we'll probably want to know, for each column, what the data type is, what caption for each column of data should be used, and how many characters wide the data will be. The figure below illustrates the relationship between the **ResultSet** data and its metadata.

850

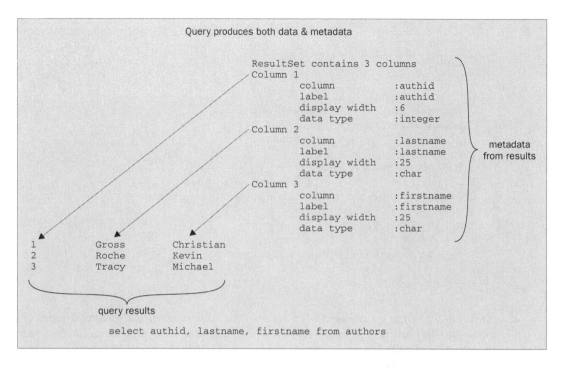

The **ResultSetMetaData** object can be obtained by calling the **getMetaData()** method of a valid **ResultSet**.

Using a PreparedStatement Object

The next example will perform two identical SQL **select** statement using both **Statement** and a **PreparedStatement** objects. For each of these, the results will be displayed along with metadata.

Try It Out—Statements and Metadata

1 First import the necessary classes. Then define the **StatementTest** class and its member data. Define the class entry point **main()**, which will instantiate an **StatementTest** object, and then call the methods **doStatement()** and **doPreparedStatement()** for that object.

```
import java.sql.*;

public class StatementTest
{
  Connection databaseConnection;
  String driverName;
  String sourceURL;
```

```
public static void main(String[] args)
{
  StatementTest SQLExample;

  try
  {
    SQLExample = new StatementTest();
    SQLExample.doStatement();
    SQLExample.doPreparedStatement();
  }
  catch(SQLException sqle)
  {
    System.out.println("SQL Exception: " + sqle);
  }
  catch(ClassNotFoundException cnfe)
  {
    System.out.println(cnfe.toString());
  }
}
```

2 Next we define the **StatementTest** constructor. This constructor assigns the driver name and the source URL that defines where the data will come from. It then loads the driver and calls the static **getConnection()** method of the **DriverManager** to establish the database connection.

```
public StatementTest() throws SQLException, ClassNotFoundException
{
  driverName = "sun.jdbc.odbc.JdbcOdbcDriver";
  sourceURL = "jdbc:odbc:technical_library";

  Class.forName (driverName);
  databaseConnection = DriverManager.getConnection(sourceURL);
}
```

3 Define the **doStatement()** method. This method is a revision of how we create and execute a **Statement**. The resulting **ResultSet** object is returned by the **executeQuery()** method of the **Statement**, and is passed to the **showResults()** method of the **StatementTest** class to print out the results information.

```
public void doStatement() throws SQLException
{
  Statement myStatement = databaseConnection.createStatement();
  ResultSet myResults = myStatement.executeQuery(
                  "select authid, lastname, firstname from authors");

  showResults(myResults);
}
```

4 Define the **doPreparedStatement()** method. This method demonstrates how a
PreparedStatement is created and executed.

```
public void doPreparedStatement() throws SQLException
{
    PreparedStatement myStatement = databaseConnection.prepareStatement(
                    "select authid, lastname, firstname from authors");
    ResultSet myResults = myStatement.executeQuery();
    showResults(myResults);
}
```

5 Define the **showResults()** method. This method is passed a **ResultSet** object, from
which it extracts both data and metadata. Notice that the first thing this method does
is retrieve the **ResultSetMetaData** object, from which it determines the number of
columns returned. It then loops through and retrieves each column value as a string
and prints it out.

After the data is printed, it then extracts information about each column, which it
displays.

```
public void showResults(ResultSet myResults) throws SQLException
{
    int n;

    // Retrieve ResultSetMetaData object from ResultSet
    ResultSetMetaData myResultMetadata = myResults.getMetaData();
    // How many columns were returned?
    int numColumns = myResultMetadata.getColumnCount();

    System.out.println("------------Query Results---------------");
    // Loop through the ResultSet and get data
    while(myResults.next())
    {
        for (n = 1; n <= numColumns; n++)
            System.out.print(myResults.getString(n) + "\t");
        System.out.print("\n");
    }

    System.out.println("\n\n----------Query Metadata---------------");
    System.out.println("ResultSet contains " + numColumns + " columns");
    for (n = 1; n <= numColumns; n++)
    {
        System.out.println("Column " + n);
        // Print the column name
        System.out.println("\tcolumn\t\t:" +
                                        myResultMetadata.getColumnName(n));
        // Print the label name
        System.out.println("\tlabel\t\t:" +
                                        myResultMetadata.getColumnLabel(n));
        // Print the column's display size
```

```
        System.out.println("\tdisplay width\t:" +
                            myResultMetadata.getColumnDisplaySize(n) +
                            " characters");
    // Print the column's type
    System.out.println("\tdata type:\t:" +
                            myResultMetadata.getColumnTypeName(n));
    }
}
```

6   The **finalize()** method cleans up the database connection when the program finishes.

```
public void finalize() throws Throwable
{
  if(databaseConnection != null)
    databaseConnection.close();
}
}
```

When you run **StatementTest.class**, you should get the following results twice:

```
-------------Query Results----------------
1        Gross                     Christian
2        Roche                     Kevin
3        Tracy                     Michael
4        Horton                    Ivor
...
52       Pompeii                   John
53       Brown                     Marc
54       Woelk                     Darrel


----------Query Metadata----------------
ResultSet contains 3 columns
Column 1
        column          :authid
        label           :authid
        display width   :11 characters
        data type:      :LONG
Column 2
        column          :lastname
        label           :lastname
        display width   :25 characters
        data type:      :CHAR
Column 3
        column          :firstname
        label           :firstname
        display width   :15 characters
        data type:      :CHAR
```

How It Works

What we've done in this example is taken concepts that you've seen in this chapter and the previous one, and put them together into a functioning program.

The program creates and executes both a **Statement** and a **PreparedStatement** object, which should produce identical results. In this case, there were no parameters for the **PreparedStatement** (not to worry—you'll have more than enough **PreparedStatement** objects in the next chapter!). And since the results were identical, the **ResultSetMetaData** is identical for the two executed SQL statements as well.

Notice that all of the exception handling for this example is handled within **main()**. Each of the other methods that might generate exceptions declares those exceptions in their **throws** clause. If an exception occurs within those methods, the method will simply throw that exception back to the calling routine—**main()**.

The InteractiveSQL Tool

The InteractiveSQL tool is a simple front end to the JDBC API. It provides a means of executing SQL statements, and a display area for viewing results. This tool is pretty basic in terms of functionality, but comes in handy for testing SQL statements. You can always add extensions to this utility as you become more familiar with JDBC.

Functional Requirements

Our requirements for the InteractiveSQL tool are pretty simple:

- Enable the user to enter and execute a SQL command
- Display the result set from a SQL query
- Enable the user to save the results to a text file
- Enable the user to clear the results viewer
- Display error information where appropriate

Application Strategy

The figure below is a basic sketch of the user interface for the InteractiveSQL tool. The text field provides an entry area for typing in the SQL statement, and will be implemented using a **TextField**. The results display provides a scrollable area for the results of the executed SQL command. This will be implemented using a simple **TextArea** object. A status line, implemented as a **Label**, provides the user with the number of rows returned from the query, or the text of any **SQLException** objects generated by the query.

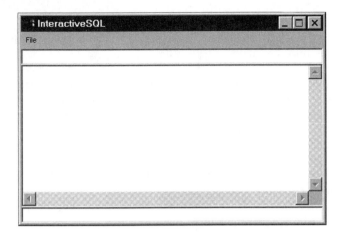

We'll provide a menu that will execute the query entered on the command line, save the results out to a file and clear the result's display area. The menu structure will be:

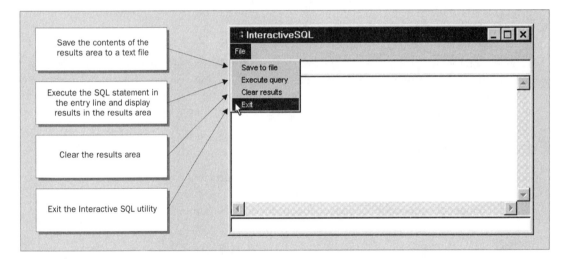

Here's the code for the primary class for this application.

Try It Out—Constructing the `InteractiveSQL` Class

The class **InteractiveSQL** is derived from the **Frame** class, and forms the foundation for the application. Its constructor is responsible for loading the JDBC driver class, creating a connection, and creating the user interface.

```java
import java.awt.*;

public class InteractiveSQL extends Frame
{
  public static String itemSave = "Save to file";
  public static String itemExec = "Execute query";
  public static String itemClear = "Clear results";
```

```
public static String itemExit = "Exit";

TextField command;
TextArea results;
TextField status;
MenuBar theMenu;
Menu menuFile;
MenuItem menuSaveToFile;
MenuItem menuExec;
MenuItem menuClearResults;
MenuItem menuExit;

public static void main(String[] args)
{
  InteractiveSQL theApp;

  theApp = new InteractiveSQL("guest", "guest",
                              "jdbc:odbc:technical_library",
                              "sun.jdbc.odbc.JdbcOdbcDriver");
  theApp.show();
};

public InteractiveSQL(String user, String password,
                      String url, String driver)
{
  super("InteractiveSQL");
  this.setBounds(new Rectangle(0, 0, 400, 300));

  this.setLayout(new BorderLayout());
  command = new TextField();
  this.add(command, "North");

  results = new TextArea();
  this.add(results, "Center");

  status = new TextField();
  this.add(status, "South");

  theMenu = new MenuBar();
  menuFile = new Menu("File");

  menuSaveToFile = new MenuItem(itemSave);
  menuExec = new MenuItem(itemExec);
  menuClearResults = new MenuItem(itemClear);
  menuExit = new MenuItem(itemExit);

  menuFile.add(menuSaveToFile);
  menuFile.add(menuExec);
  menuFile.add(menuClearResults);
  menuFile.add(menuExit);
  theMenu.add(menuFile);
  this.setMenuBar(theMenu);
```

```
        this.show();
    }
}
```

So far, so good. Try running the application and you should wind up with an application interface that looks like that shown earlier.

How It Works

The constructor is passed the parameters required to load the appropriate driver and create a **Connection**. The first executable statement in this constructor calls the constructor for the **Frame** class, passing it a default caption. The constructor then creates and arranges the user interface components.

Animating the Interface

Notice that, in the **main()** method, we pass hard coded parameters to the constructor for the **InteractiveSQL** class. Let's make this a bit more usable and get the values for the user name, password, database URL and JDBC driver from the command line.

Try It Out—Command Line Parameters

Change the **main()** method:

```
public static void main(String[] args)
{
    String user, password, url, driver;

    // Set default values for the command line args
    user = new String("guest");
    password = new String("guest");
    url = new String("jdbc:odbc:technical_library");
    driver = new String("sun.jdbc.odbc.JdbcOdbcDriver");

    switch(args.length)
    {
        case 4:
            driver = args[3];
            // Fall through to the next case
        case 3:
            password = args[2];
            // Fall through to the next case
        case 2:
            user = args[1];
            // Fall through to the next case
        case 1:
            url = args[0];
    }
```

```
        InteractiveSQL theApp =
                        new InteractiveSQL(user, password, url, driver);
    }
```

How It Works

This enables you to optionally specify the JDBC URL, the user name and password, and the JDBC driver on the command line. The mechanism that handles the optional parameters is pretty simple. Check out the **switch** statement which tests the number of parameters that were specified on the command line. If one parameter was passed, it's interpreted as the JDBC URL. If two parameters were passed, the second parameter is used as the user name. There are no **break** statements, so control drops through to the next case.

Next, we need event handling logic for the menus. Add the following code inside the **InteractiveSQL** class.

Try It Out—Events in InteractiveSQL

1 First, we need to add the interface declaration to the class definition. This class will implement the **ActionListener** interface to handle menu events.

We also need to import the necessary packages to use Java's AWT event, JDBC and stream classes.

```
import java.awt.*;
import java.awt.event.;
import java.sql.*;
import java.io.*;

public class InteractiveSQL extends Frame implements ActionListener
```

2 Add the class member variable for the JDBC **Connection** object. Add this declaration to the other class member declarations just before the **main()** method

```
Connection databaseConnection;
```

3 Add the following code to the class constructor. This code should follow the code that creates the menu item instances. This code will 'hook up' the menu items to the **actionPerformed()** method defined by the **ActionListener** interface. That method will be implemented next.

```
menuSaveToFile.addActionListener(this);
menuExec.addActionListener(this);
menuClearResults.addActionListener(this);
menuExit.addActionListener(this);
```

4 Add the `actionPerformed()` method. This method will get the command string, which is the menu item text, and use that value to determine which item was selected.

```java
public void actionPerformed(ActionEvent ae)
{
  String cmd = ae.getActionCommand();
  if(cmd.equalsIgnoreCase(itemSave))
    selectedSave();
  else if(cmd.equalsIgnoreCase(itemExec))
    selectedExecute();
  else if(cmd.equalsIgnoreCase(itemExit))
    System.exit(0);
  else if(cmd.equalsIgnoreCase(itemClear))
    results.setText("");
}
```

5 Add the `selectedSave()` method, called by selecting the File | Save Results menu. This method creates a `FileDialog` object that prompts the user for a filename to save the contents of the `Results TextArea` as a `FileWriter` object is created using the filename, and a `PrintWriter` object created from the `FileWriter`. With the `PrintWriter` object, we can simply `println()` the contents to the stream, and close it.

```java
public void selectedSave()
{
  // Get a file name, open the file, and write out
  // the contents of the list box
  try
  {
    FileDialog fdlg = new FileDialog(this, "Save results");
    fdlg.show();

    String filename = fdlg.getFile();
    FileWriter fw = new FileWriter(filename);
    PrintWriter pw = new PrintWriter(fw);
    pw.println(results.getText());
    fw.close();
  }
  catch (IOException ioe)
  {
    System.out.println(ioe);
  }
}
```

6 We need to obtain the `Connection` class object. Add the following code to the end of the constructor

```java
try
{
  Class.forName(driver);
```

```
      databaseConnection = DriverManager.getConnection(url, user, password);
   }
   catch(ClassNotFoundException cnfe)
   {
      System.out.println(cnfe);
   }
   catch(SQLException sqle)
   {
      System.out.println(sqle);
   }
```

7 Finally, you add the JDBC code that responds to the Execute Query menu item being selected.

```
public void selectedExecute()
{
   String theQuery = command.getText();
   int numRows = 0;
   int thisCol;

   try
   {
      Statement queryStatement = databaseConnection.createStatement();
      ResultSet theResults = queryStatement.executeQuery(theQuery);
      ResultSetMetaData rsmeta = theResults.getMetaData();

      int numColumns = rsmeta.getColumnCount();
      String resultsText = new String("");

      // if there is anything in the results, we'll append to it.
      if (results.getText().length() > 0)
        resultsText = results.getText().concat("\n");

      while(theResults.next())
      {
        numRows++;
        for (thisCol = 1; thisCol <= numColumns; thisCol++)
          resultsText = resultsText.concat(
                           theResults.getString(thisCol).trim() + "\t");
        resultsText = resultsText.concat("\n");
      }
      results.setText(resultsText);

      status.setFont(new Font("Arial", Font.PLAIN, 10));
      status.setText("Rows returned: " + numRows);
   }
   catch(SQLException sqle)
   {
      status.setFont(new Font("Arial", Font.BOLD, 10));
     status.setText(sqle.toString());
   }
}
```

Compile and run the application, and remember the command line parameters: `<URL>`
`<user id> <password> <driver>`. For example, try:

```
java InteractiveSQL jdbc:odbc:technical_library
```

and then execute the SQL query below:

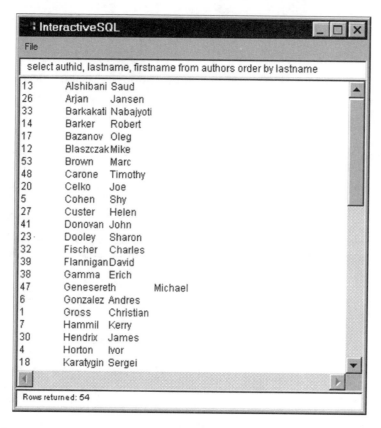

How It Works

Most of the interesting stuff in the InteractiveSQL application happens in the
`selectedExecute()` method. The SQL query text that is executed is the text value in the
`command TextField`. We then need to create a `Statement`. The `Connection` to the
database has already been created in the constructor and stored in the
`databaseConnection` member variable, so you can call the `createStatement()` method
of that object.

The SQL query string is passed to the `executeQuery()` method of the newly created
`Statement` object, and a `ResultSet` object is returned.

We looked at the `ResultSetMetaData` object in the last example. Since we don't know
ahead of time how many columns will be returned by a query, the `ResultSetMetaData`
object obtained from the `ResultSet` is used to find out how many columns were returned.

The **while** loop simply goes through each row, and extracts each column value. Notice that even though columns may be of other types, they are all being retrieved here as a **String**. The **ResultSet** will perform the conversion just by asking for the data as a **String**, and in this way the program avoids the additional step of converting values to strings so they can be displayed.

The **String**s are concatenated to a buffer, with each column value separated with a tab character, **"\t"**, and each row separated with a newline character, **"\n"**. When there are no more rows to read, the text value of the **Results TextArea** is then set to the value of the buffer.

If it all runs without exception, the text of the **TextField status** is set to indicate the number of rows read. You might be wondering why the font is changed just prior to setting the status text. That's because of the **catch** block for **SQLException**. The exception handler prints the text of the exception to the status area, and sets the font to Arial bold to draw the user's eye to the status line. The next time a statement is executed without problems, the font style is returned to Arial plain.

You now have a simple but useful tool for executing SQL statements through JDBC.

Summary

In this chapter you've been introduced to JDBC programming, and seen it in action. Briefly, the fundamental components of JDBC are:

▶ **DriverManager**   Manages loading of JDBC drivers and connections to client applications

▶ **Connection**   Provides a connection to a specific data source

▶ **Statement**   Provides a context for executing SQL statements

▶ **ResultSet**   Provides a means for accessing data returned from an executed **Statement**

The essential JDBC program has the following basic structure:

▶ Import the necessary classes
▶ Load the JDBC driver
▶ Identify the data source
▶ Allocate a **Connection** object
▶ Allocate a **Statement** object
▶ Execute a query using the **Statement** object
▶ Retrieve data from the returned **ResultSet** object
▶ Close the **ResultSet**

> Close the **Statement** object

> Close the **Connection** object

In the next chapter we'll look more closely at what these and other database terms mean.

Exercises

1 Write a class that displays all authors in the **technical_library** database with last names starting with the letters A through H.

2 Write a class that lists all books and the authors for that book. (Hint: you will need a SQL join and the **author_books** table.)

3 How would you write a class that allowed the user to specify which database to use?

The JDBC in Action

The last chapter introduced you to some of the detail of the JDBC API. In this chapter we're going to put that API to work. We'll:

▶ Look at the mapping between SQL and Java data types

▶ Start laying out a foundation for data access by introducing a strategy for mapping relational data onto Java objects

▶ Take another look at the JDBC **Statement** and **PreparedStatement** interfaces. The objective here is to give you the skills to extend the SQL-Java mapping to include full create, read, update and delete capabilities in your Java programs

▶ Learn more about the **ResultSet** object

▶ Look at the help you can get from the **SQLException** class

Data Types and JDBC

In all of the examples so far, all of the data extracted from a result set was retrieved as a **String**. You'll certainly need to get other types of data, and as you saw earlier, the **ResultSet** provides a number of methods for retrieving different data types. But first, we need to look at the SQL data types.

Mapping between Java and SQL Data Types

The SQL-92 standard defines a set of data types that don't map one-for-one with those in Java. As you write applications that move data from SQL to Java and back, you'll need to understand how JDBC manages that mapping. That is, you need to know the appropriate Java data type to represent a given SQL data type, and vice versa.

When you're retrieving data from a JDBC data source, the **ResultSet** implementation will map the SQL data onto Java data types. The table below illustrates the SQL-to-Java mappings:

SQL Data Type	Java Data Type
CHAR	String
VARCHAR	String
LONGVARCHAR	String
NUMERIC	java.math.BigDecimal
DECIMAL	java.math.BigDecimal
BIT	boolean
TINYINT	byte
SMALLINT	short
INTEGER	int
BIGINT	long
REAL	float
FLOAT	double
DOUBLE	double
BINARY	byte[]
VARBINARY	byte[]
LONGVARBINARY	byte[]
DATE	java.sql.Date
TIME	java.sql.Time
TIMESTAMP	java.sql.Timestamp

Conversely, when you are relating Java-to-SQL data types, the following mappings apply:

Java Data Type	SQL Data Type
String	VARCHAR, LONGVARCHAR
java.math.BigDecimal	NUMERIC
boolean	BIT
byte	TINYINT
short	SMALLINT
int	INTEGER
long	BIGINT
float	REAL
double	DOUBLE
byte[]	VARBINARY, LONGVARBINARY
java.sql.Date	DATE
java.sql.Time	TIME
java.sql.Timestamp	TIMESTAMP

*Note that some databases, such as Oracle 7, implement **INTEGER** data types as **NUMERIC**. When accessing **INTEGER** elements through the JDBC, it is important to associate the JDBC data type with the internal data type actually stored in the database.*

Mapping Relational Data onto Java Objects

In the previous chapter, we learned how to get the basic data from the JDBC **ResultSet** object. So far, though, we haven't been concerned with the whys and wherefores of creating Java classes that are instantiated by a relational back end. That's what we will focus on now, and in the process, you'll get some more experience with the **Statement** and **ResultSet** interfaces.

Here's the basic problem: the way that information is handled at the object level is usually different from the way that data is stored in a relational database. In the world of objects, the underlying principle is to make those objects exhibit the same characteristics (information and behavior) as their real-world counterparts—in other words, objects function at the level of the conceptual model. Relational databases, on the other hand, work at the data model level. As you saw in the previous chapter, relational databases store information using normalized forms, where conceptual objects like invoices and customers can be decomposed into a number of tables. So how do you deal with the problem of mapping objects to relational data models?

Sometimes there is a straight-forward relationship between the columns in a table and the member variables in an object. In that case, the mapping task consists simply of matching the data types of the database with those of Java. The following figure shows this simple application-level SQL-to-object mapping:

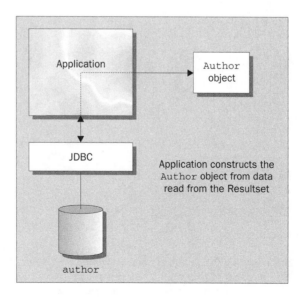

Try It Out—A Simple Mapping from SQL Rows to Java Objects

1 The **authors** table in the sample database is a good example of a simple mapping. To recap, this table has the following definition:

Column	Datatype	Description
authid	int	Unique identifier for each author
lastname	char(25)	Last name of author
firstname	char(15)	First name of author
address1	char(25)	First line of address
address2	char(25)	Second line of address
city	char(25)	City
state_prov	char(25)	State or province
postcode	char(10)	Postal code
country	char(15)	Country
phone	char(20)	Daytime phone number
fax	char(20)	Fax number
email	char(25)	Email address

2 Let's define a Java class for the authors. Take a look back at the table which shows you how to map SQL to Java data types. Based on those mappings, we can define the member variables for an **Author** class, and add a constructor, member access methods and a **toString()** method.

```
public class Author
{
  int authid;
  String lastname;
  String firstname;
  String address[];
  String city;
  String state;
  String postcode;
  String country;
  String phone;
  String fax;
  String email;

  public Author() {}

  public Author(int authid, String lastname, String firstname,
          String address[], String city, String state,
          String postcode, String country,
          String phone, String fax, String email)
```

```
{
  this.authid = authid;
  this.lastname = lastname;
  this.firstname = firstname;
  this.address = address;
  this.city = city;
  this.state = state;
  this.postcode = postcode;
  this.country = country;
  this.phone = phone;
  this.fax = fax;
  this.email = email;
}

public int getId()
{
    return authid;
}

public String getLastName()
{
    return lastname;
}

public String getFirstName()
{
    return firstname;
}

public String[] getAddress()
{
    return address;
}

public String getAddressText()
{
    String addr = new String("");

    int n;
    for (n = 0; n < this.address.length; n++)
        addr.concat(this.address[n]);

    return addr;
}

public String getCity()
{
  return city;
}

public String getState()
{
```

```
      return state;
   }

   public String getCountry()
   {
      return country;
   }

   public String getPostCode()
   {
      return postcode;
   }

   public String getPhone()
   {
      return phone;
   }

   public String getFax()
   {
      return fax;
   }

   public String getEmail()
   {
      return email;
   }

   public String toString()
   {
      return new String
            ("auth       : " + Integer.toString(authid) +
             "\nname      : " + lastname + "," + firstname +
             "\naddress   : " + address[0] +
             "\n          : " + address[1] +
             "\n          : " + city + " " + state +
             "\n          : " + postcode + " " + country +
             "\nphone     : " + phone +
             "\nfax       : " + fax +
             "\nemail     : " + email);
   }
}
```

3 Next, we need to get the data from the database into the **Author** object. Our first strategy for doing this is pretty basic—the application class will create the **Connection**, **Statement** and **ResultSet**, and read the data from the database. The **Author** class constructor will be called using each row of data read. For this example, I'll use a SQL statement that is a literal string in the code, rather than creating a **PreparedStatement**.

```
import java.sql.*;

public class TrySimpleMapping
{
  Connection databaseConnection;
  String driverName;
  String sourceURL;

  public static void main (String[] args)
  {
    TrySimpleMapping SQLtoJavaExample;
    try
    {
      SQLtoJavaExample = new TrySimpleMapping();
      SQLtoJavaExample.listAuthors();
    }
    catch(SQLException sqle)
    {
      System.out.println("SQL Exception: " + sqle.toString());
    }
    catch(ClassNotFoundException cnfe)
    {
      System.out.println(cnfe.toString());
    }
  }

  public TrySimpleMapping() throws SQLException, ClassNotFoundException
  {
    driverName = "sun.jdbc.odbc.JdbcOdbcDriver";
    sourceURL = "jdbc:odbc:technical_library";

    Class.forName (driverName);
    databaseConnection = DriverManager.getConnection(sourceURL);
  }

  public void listAuthors() throws SQLException
  {
    Statement getAuthors;
    ResultSet theAuthors;
    Author anAuthor;

    int id;
    String lastname;
    String firstname;
    String address1;
    String address2;
    String city;
    String state;
    String postcode;
    String country;
    String phone;
```

```
    String fax;
    String email;

    String query = "select authid, lastname, firstname, address1,
                ↳ address2, city, state_prov, postcode, country,
                ↳ phone, fax, email from authors";

    getAuthors = databaseConnection.createStatement();
    theAuthors = getAuthors.executeQuery(query);

    while(theAuthors.next())
    {
      id  = theAuthors.getInt(1);
      lastname  = theAuthors.getString(2);
      firstname  = theAuthors.getString(3);
      address1  = theAuthors.getString(4);
      address2  = theAuthors.getString(5);
      city  = theAuthors.getString(6);
      state  = theAuthors.getString(7);
      postcode  = theAuthors.getString(8);
      country  = theAuthors.getString(9);
      phone  = theAuthors.getString(10);
      fax  = theAuthors.getString(11);
      email  = theAuthors.getString(12);
      String addr[] = new String[2];
      addr[0] = address1;
      addr[1] = address2;

      anAuthor = new Author(id, lastname, firstname,
                            addr, city, state, postcode,
                            country, phone, fax, email);

      System.out.println("\n" + anAuthor.toString());
    }
    getAuthors.close();
    databaseConnection.close();
  }
}
```

You should get the following results:

```
auth     : 1
name     : Gross                      ,Christian
address  : 1234 Corporate Drive
         : Suite 374
         : Anytown AnyProvince
         : VVV 888 Canada
phone    : null
fax      : null
email    : cgross@anynet.net

...
```

How It Works

Everything in this example should look pretty familiar, but there are just a couple of new things we need to cover.

Note first that there's an extra step after the data is read, which creates the **Author** object by calling its constructor with that data. Also in the code that follows, as each row is read from the **ResultSet**, the application uses the appropriate **getXXX()** method of the **ResultSet** object to perform the mapping from SQL to Java data types. In order to print out each product, we simply call **System.out.println()** and pass it the string returned by the **Author**'s **toString()** method. Notice that in the output, the literal **null** appears where there are null values in the database.

This example uses the JDBC-ODBC bridge driver with a datasource that does not require a user name or password. If you need a user name and password to access that data source, simply modify the code in the **TrySimpleMapping** constructor to use the appropriate driver, URL and **getConnection()** method of the **DriverManager**.

At the time of writing, the **getXXX(columnname)** (for example, **getString("lastname")**) methods of the **ResultSet** as implemented by the mSQL JDBC driver do not work properly. The corresponding functions using column numbers, however, do work correctly. In order to ensure code compatibility with mSQL, I've used the **getXXX(columnnumber)** form of these methods throughout this chapter.

A Better Mapping Strategy

As you saw, the simple strategy described above does in fact get the data between the relational database and the Java objects (and can be used in reverse to get data back to the database, as we'll see shortly). It does, however, leave a little to be desired. The moving of data between the database and the Java object is left completely to the application class.

A better, more object-oriented strategy, is to let the **Author** class handle its own data extraction from the **ResultSet** object. We'll add a static factory method (a method that manufactures **Author** objects) to the **Author** class. The code calling the factory method must do the work of creating the **Connection**, the **Statement** and executing the **Statement**, and ensuring that the **ResultSet** contains the columns required for populating the **Author** object.

The following figure shows this encapsulated SQL-to-object mapping.

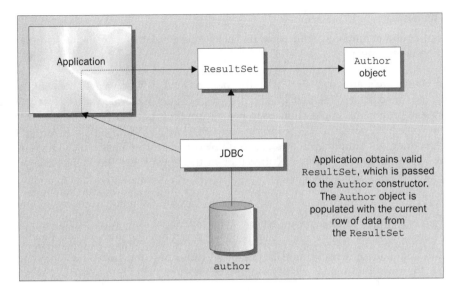

We need to establish an implied 'contract' between this factory method and any code that calls it:

▶ The current row of the **ResultSet** object passed to the factory method is positioned at a valid row

▶ The factory method retrieves data from the **ResultSet** by column position, so the **ResultSet** must contain the following columns:

Column position	Column data	Data type
1	Product id	**int**
2	Last name	**String**
3	First name	**String**
4	Address1	**String**
5	Address2	**String**
6	City	**String**
7	State	**String**
8	Postcode	**String**
9	Country	**String**
10	Phone	**String**
11	Fax	**String**
12	Email	**String**

Let's extend the **Author** class with a subclass, and rewrite the previous example to use this strategy.

Try It Out—Encapsulated Mapping of SQL Rows to Java Objects

1 Create the application class. This class is nearly identical to `TrySimpleMapping`, except that there's less code in the `listAuthors()` method.

```java
import java.sql.*;

public class TryEncapsulatedMapping
{
  Connection databaseConnection;
  String driverName;
  String sourceURL;

  public static void main (String[] args)
  {
    TryEncapsulatedMapping SQLtoJavaExample;
    try
    {
      SQLtoJavaExample = new TryEncapsulatedMapping();
      SQLtoJavaExample.listAuthors();
    }
    catch(SQLException sqle)
    {
      System.out.println("SQL Exception: " + sqle);
    }
    catch(ClassNotFoundException cnfe)
    {
      System.out.println(cnfe);
    }
  }

  public TryEncapsulatedMapping() throws SQLException,
                                         ClassNotFoundException
  {
    driverName = "sun.jdbc.odbc.JdbcOdbcDriver";
    sourceURL = "jdbc:odbc:technical_library";
    Class.forName (driverName);
    databaseConnection = DriverManager.getConnection(sourceURL);
  }
```

2 Instead of reading from the `ResultSet` and instantiating a new `Author` for each row, we'll just call the static `fromResults()` method of the `SelfExtractingAuthor` class, which will create a new `SelfExtractingAuthor` object from the `ResultSet` data.

```java
  public void listAuthors() throws SQLException
  {
    Statement getAuthors;
    ResultSet theAuthors;

    SelfExtractingAuthor anAuthor;
```

```
        String query = "select authid, lastname, firstname, address1,
                    ⇘ address2, city, state_prov, postcode, country,
                    ⇘ phone, fax, email from authors";

        getAuthors = databaseConnection.createStatement();
        theAuthors = getAuthors.executeQuery(query);

        while(theAuthors.next())
        {
          anAuthor = SelfExtractingAuthor.fromResults(theAuthors);
          System.out.println("\n" + anAuthor.toString());
        }

        getAuthors.close();
        databaseConnection.close();
    }
}
```

3 Create a new source file and build a subclass of **Author** called
SelfExtractingAuthor. This class will have two methods: a constructor and the
static fromResults() method. Notice that the code in the **fromResults()** method
is nearly identical to the **listAuthors()** code in the **TrySimpleMapping** class.

```
import java.sql.*;

public class SelfExtractingAuthor extends Author
{
  public static SelfExtractingAuthor fromResults(ResultSet theAuthors)
                                                throws SQLException
  {
    int id;
    String lastname;
    String firstname;
    String address1;
    String address2;
    String city;
    String state;
    String postcode;
    String country;
    String phone;
    String fax;
    String email;

    id  = theAuthors.getInt(1);
    lastname  = theAuthors.getString(2);
    firstname  = theAuthors.getString(3);
    address1  = theAuthors.getString(4);
    address2  = theAuthors.getString(5);
    city  = theAuthors.getString(6);
    state  = theAuthors.getString(7);
```

```
          postcode  = theAuthors.getString(8);
          country   = theAuthors.getString(9);
          phone  = theAuthors.getString(10);
          fax  = theAuthors.getString(11);
          email  = theAuthors.getString(12);
          String addr[] = new String[2];
          addr[0] = address1;
          addr[1] = address2;

          return new SelfExtractingAuthor(id, lastname, firstname,
                                          addr, city, state, postcode,
                                          country, phone, fax, email);
      }

      public SelfExtractingAuthor(int id, String lastname, String firstname,
                                  String address[], String city, String state,
                                  String postcode, String country,
                                  String phone, String fax, String email)
      {
        super(id, lastname, firstname, address, city, state,
              postcode, country, phone, fax, email);
      }
  }
```

When you run the example, you should get results exactly like those of the previous example.

How It Works

All we've really done in this example is pushed the work of extracting Java types from the **ResultSet** to the class that is using the data. In order to do that, the new **SelfExtractingProduct** class has to import the **java.sql** package because it's now using that package. It then implements the code that was previously in the **TrySimpleMapping** application, as a static factory method.

> *As we saw in Chapter 5, a static method is used so that the method call can reference the class instead of an object of that class—otherwise you'd have a "chicken and egg" problem!*

Why It's Better

This method is better because the class itself is responsible for ensuring that the correct mapping is performed between the database and the Java object. That way, applications don't have to duplicate that logic, and can't mess up by implementing bad mappings (such as casting a **REAL** to an **int**). Encapsulation also lends itself well to classes that can be reused within and between applications, so, although it's a little more work than the simple mapping method, it's worth it.

The Statement and PreparedStatement Interfaces

In this section we're going to look in some detail at the `Statement` and `PreparedStatement` interfaces.

We start with the `Statement` interface, where we learn about the methods that allow you to constrain the query, and how to handle data definition and data manipulation. Next, we'll look at the `PreparedStatement`, discuss the differences between static and dynamic statements, and working with the `PreparedStatement` interface

The Statement Interface

You were introduced to the `Statement` in the last chapter. Now it's time to look at how you can better tune and use this interface.

The `Statement` interface defines a set of methods implemented by an object that is returned to your program by the `Connection` object. The `Statement` is always obtained by calling the `createStatement()` method of the `Connection` with no parameters:

```
try
{
  Statement queryStatement = databaseConnection.createStatement();
  // ...
}
catch(SQLException sqle)
{
  System.out.println(sqle);
}
```

Like pretty much every other method defined by JDBC, this code must be within a `try` clause, and include a `catch` statement for `SQLException`.

Defining and Executing a Query

Once the `Statement` has been created, defining the query is as simple as building a `String` containing a valid SQL statement and passing that statement as a parameter to the `executeQuery()` method of the `Statement`. The SQL query can be a literal value, or it can be a `String` value built at runtime, as is the case in the InteractiveSQL application where the application obtains the SQL string from the text field just before the statement is executed.

So, the following `Statement` objects will produce identical results:

```
String sqlString = "select lastname from authors where authid = ";
int authid = 27;

ResultsFromLiteralSQL = stmtLiteral.executeQuery(
            "select lastname from authors where authid = 27");
```

```
ResultsFromBuiltString = stmtBuilt.executeQuery(
                    sqlString + Integer.toString(authid));
```

A static SQL query is executed by passing the SQL string to the **executeQuery()** method of the **Statement**. This method returns an object that implements the **ResultSet** interface, as you saw in the examples in the last chapter.

Query Constraints

The **Statement** interface allows you to determine and change constraints on a query. These constraints include:

- Maximum number of rows
- Maximum field size
- Query timeout

Maximum Number of Rows

The JDBC driver may impose limitation on how many rows may be returned by a query, or you may wish to impose a limit on how many rows to return. The **Statement** methods **getMaxRows()** and **setMaxRows()** allow you to query and set the maximum rows returned, respectively. The value 0 is defined as no limit.

A particular JDBC driver may default to practical row limits, or may have implementation restrictions that limit the returned rows. To determine the row limit, simply call the **getMaxRows()** method of the **Statement**:

```
Statement SQLStatement = libraryConnection.createStatement();

int maxRows = SQLStatement.getMaxRows();
```

You may wish to limit the number of returned rows for a query in an application. For example, you may want to limit the number of rows returned to prevent an extremely lengthy query process. You can call **setMaxRows()** to limit the number of returned rows:

```
SQLStatement.setMaxRows(30);
```

> *It's important to note that, when the maximum row count is set to a non-zero value, you will not get an indication when data are truncated. If the number of rows hits the maximum value, any remaining rows that meet the query criteria will be silently left behind.*

Maximum Field Size

The **Statement** interface also enables you to query and set the maximum field size for all column values returned in a **ResultSet**. Querying this value will tell you if the JDBC driver imposes a practical or physical limit on the size of returned column. The value 0 is defined as no limit.

At the time of this writing, this feature does not work correctly with the Access ODBC driver.

To determine the maximum field size for statement results, simply call the `getMaxFieldSize()` method of the `Statement`:

```
Statement SQLStatement = libraryConnection.createStatement();

int maxFieldSize = SQLStatement.getMaxFieldSize();
```

Like the maximum row method pair, there is a corresponding `setMaxFieldSize()` method to set the maximum field size:

```
SQLStatement.setMaxFieldSize(4096);
```

Note that the `setMaxFieldSize()` only applies to columns with the following SQL data types:

BINARY	VARBINARY	LONGVARBINARY
CHAR	VARCHAR	LONGVARCHAR.

Query Time-out

Depending on your JDBC driver and the database to which it is attached, there may be an execution time-out period after which a `Statement` will fail and raise an exception. You can test the time-out period with the `getQueryTimeout()` method, or set the time-out period (for instance, if you want a query to fail after a fixed time period) using the `setQueryTimeout()` method. The time-out period is defined in seconds. A time-out value of 0 indicates that there is no time-out.

Here's a quick program that will test the default query constraints for your JDBC driver. As always, substitute an appropriate URL and driver name if yours differs.

*Note that if you're using the JDBC-ODBC bridge, you may get a **SQLException** reporting **"Driver not capable"** when executing **getQueryTimeout()** or **setQueryTimeout()**. This is most likely due to the fact that the underlying ODBC driver doesn't support time-out—for example, if you are using a driver for a local database such as Access. Drivers that access remote database servers over a network should support these methods.*

Try It Out—Query Constraints

1 Since this program is tiny, we'll incorporate everything into the `main()` method:

```
import java.sql.*;

public class TestQueryTimeOut
{
```

```
   public static void main(String[] args)
   {
     try
     {
       String url =
            "jdbc:msql://zorak.happykitty.com:4333/technical_library";
       String driver = "imaginary.sql.iMsqlDriver";
       String username = "guest";
       String password = "guest";

       Class.forName(driver);
       Connection libraryConnection =
               DriverManager.getConnection(url, username, password);
```

2 Create the statement, query and display the values for maximum rows, maximum field
size and time-out.

```
       Statement SQLStatement = libraryConnection.createStatement();

       int maxRows = SQLStatement.getMaxRows();
       int maxFieldSize = SQLStatement.getMaxFieldSize();
       int queryTimeout = SQLStatement.getQueryTimeout();

       System.out.println("Driver  :   " + driver);
       System.out.println("Maximum rows    :   " +
               (maxRows == 0?"None":Integer.toString(maxRows)));
       System.out.println("Max field size  :   " +
           (maxFieldSize == 0?"None":Integer.toString(maxFieldSize)));
       System.out.println("Timeout         :   " +
           (queryTimeout == 0?"None":Integer.toString(queryTimeout)));
     }
     catch (ClassNotFoundException cnfe)
     {
       System.out.println(cnfe);
     }
     catch (SQLException sqle)
     {
       System.out.println(sqle);
     }
   }
}
```

Running this should result in the following output:

```
Driver  :    imaginary.sql.iMsqlDriver
Maximum rows    :    4096
Max field size  :    None
Timeout         :    None
```

How It Works

This code is pretty simple. It creates a **Connection** using an URL defining an mSQL database called **technical_library** on the host **zorak.happykitty.com**. Once the connection is established, a **Statement** is created, and from there the values for the query timeout period, as well as the maximum column size and maximum number of rows can be queried.

Executing DDL and DML

The **executeQuery()** method is used to execute a SQL statement that is a query—that is, the **Statement** is expected to return some results. There are other types of SQL statements, however, that do not return results. These statements fall into two primary categories: data definition language (DDL) and data manipulation language (DML). As you might guess from the name, DDL statements are those that affect the structure of a database, such as **CREATE TABLE**, and **DROP TABLE**. DML statements are those that affect the contents of the database, such as **INSERT**, **UPDATE** and **DELETE** statements.

So far, all of the example code including the InteractiveSQL application has used the **executeQuery()** method. If, in the last chapter, you tried to execute a SQL statement that didn't produce a result set, such as any DDL or DML, you will have seen an exception reported on the status line:

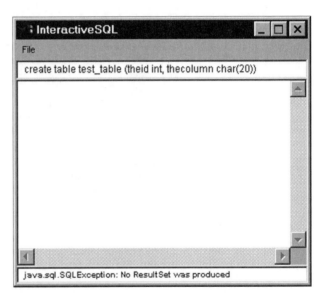

The exception **"No ResultSet was produced"** is raised because the **executeQuery()** method expects a SQL statement that generates results (note that, even though an exception is raised, the SQL statement is still executed).

To execute statements that do not return results, the **Statement** interface provides the **executeUpdate()** method. Like **executeQuery()**, the **executeUpdate()** method accepts a single **String** as a parameter. The method returns an integer value indicating the number of rows affected by the operation in the case of DML, or 0 if the statement returned nothing. The code fragment below illustrates use of the **executeUpdate()** method to add a row to the **products** table.

```
int rowsAdded;

Statement SQLStatement = libraryConnection.createStatement();
rowsAdded = SQLStatement.executeUpdate(
            "insert into authors (authid, lastname, firstname) values
         ↳ (65,'Poe','Edgar'");
```

Using the **executeUpdate()** method, it's pretty easy to write a utility to create and populate a table. This example does exactly that. In fact, this example is similar in principle the **build_tables** utility included with the book's source code. Rather than reading SQL statements from a file, however, this example keeps them as string literals in the code.

Try It Out—Executing DDL and DML

1 Again, this is a small example, so the code will all be contained in the **main()** method. The URL and the driver are identified by the **url** and **driver** strings.

```
import java.sql.*;

public class BuildTables2
{
  public static void main(String[] args)
  {
    try
    {
      String url = "jdbc:odbc:technical_library";
      String driver = "sun.jdbc.odbc.JdbcOdbcDriver";
```

2 The **SQLStatements String** array contains the DDL and DML that will be executed by this program.

```
String SQLStatements[] = {
        "create table online_resources
     ↳ (pub_id int, name char(48), url char(80))",
        "insert into online_resources values
     ↳ (1, 'Wrox Home Page', 'http://www.wrox.com')",
        "insert into online_resources values
     ↳ (2, 'JavaSoft Home Page', 'http://www.javasoft.com')",
        "insert into online_resources values
     ↳ (3, 'Imaginary Home Page',
        'http://www.imaginary.com')"};

    int statementIndex;
    String username = "guest";
    String password = "guest";
    Class.forName(driver);
```

```
        Connection bugTrackerConnection = DriverManager.getConnection
                                        (url, username, password);
        Statement SQLStatement = bugTrackerConnection.createStatement();
```

3 Here's where the work is done. This **for** loop simply iterates through each statement in the array, and executes it using the **executeUpdate()** method of the **Statement**.

```
        for (statementIndex = 0; statementIndex < SQLStatements.length;
            statementIndex++)
        {
          SQLStatement.executeUpdate(SQLStatements[statementIndex]);
          System.out.println(SQLStatements[statementIndex]);
        }
      }
      catch (ClassNotFoundException cnfe)
      {
        System.out.println(cnfe);
      }
      catch (SQLException sqle)
      {
        System.out.println(sqle);
      }
    }
  }
```

You can check the results by running the **InteractiveSQL** application on the table you created and the rows were inserted. To do this, start that application and execute the SQL statement:

```
select * from online_resources
```

After you're satisfied with your results, feel free to delete the table. Using a new instance of the **InteractiveSQL** application, execute the statement:

```
drop table online_resources
```

InteractiveSQL will complain that no **ResultSet** is produced, but will dispose of the table nevertheless.

How It Works

BuildTables2 is pretty simple. The **String** array **SQLStatements** contains all of the SQL statements that we want to execute with **executeUpdate()**. The **for** loop simply iterates through that array, and executes and prints each statement in turn. As usual, the code lives inside a **try** clause to trap any **SQLExceptions**.

The only substantial difference between this example and the other examples you've seen is that the SQL statements are executed with the **executeUpdate()** method instead of the **executeQuery()** method of the **Statement**, and instead of a **ResultSet** being returned, the method returns the number of rows affected by the operation.

The PreparedStatement Interface

Earlier in this chapter, you saw that you can build SQL strings on the fly and execute them with the **executeQuery()** method of a **Statement**. That is one way to introduce parameters into a SQL statement, but not the only way, nor the most convenient.

The **PreparedStatement** interface enables you to define an SQL statement with **placeholders** for arguments. Placeholders are tokens that appear in the SQL statement, and are replaced with actual values before the SQL statement is executed. This is often much easier than building an SQL statement with specific values by concatenating strings.

A **PreparedStatement** object, like a **Statement** object, is created by a **Connection** object. Instead of calling the **createStatement()** method of the **Connection** object however, the **PreparedStatement**object is created by calling the **prepareStatement()** method. Unlike the **Statement** object, the SQL statement must be defined, with the placeholders for the values, at the time that **prepareStatement()** is called:

```
PreparedStatement SQLStatement;
String changeLastName =
            "update authors set lastname = ? where authid = ?";

SQLStatement = libraryConnection.prepareStatement(changeLastName);
```

Setting Query Parameters

The question marks that appear in the **changeLastName** variable in the code fragment above are the placeholders in the statement. After the statement has been created, and before the statement is executed, the placeholders are filled by calling one or more of the **setXXX()** methods of the **PreparedStatement** interface:

setAsciiStream()	setBigDecimal()	setBinaryStream()
setBoolean()	setByte()	setBytes()
setDate()	setDouble()	setFloat()
setInt()	setLong()	setNull()
setObject()	setShort()	setString()
setTime()	setTimestamp()	setUnicodeStream()

These methods accept, minimally, a position argument and a value argument. The **setXXX()** method replaces the placeholder in the **PreparedStatement** object before it is executed. The following figure shows the **PreparedStatement** placeholder value replacement in action:

statement executed	SQL statement executed as

SQLStatement =
    libraryConnection.prepareStatement(
    "update authors set lastname = ? where authid = ?")
	update authors set lastname = ? authid = ?

SQLStatement.setString(1, "Burk");	update authors set lastname = 'Burk' where authid = ?
SQLStatement.setInt(2, 27);	update authors set lastname = 'Burk' where authid = 27

Note that placeholders for string arguments are not quoted—the **PreparedStatement** automatically takes care of that. Also, it's perfectly OK to set parameters in whatever order you choose—you don't have to set the first placeholder first, the second one next and so forth.

The following example demonstrates using a **PreparedStatement** object to plug in placeholder values. The code in this example will change the last name of the author whose authid is 27.

Try It Out—Using a *PreparedStatement Object*

Try out the following code:

```java
import java.sql.*;

public class TryPlaceHolders
{
  public static void main(String[] args)
  {
    try
    {
      int rowsUpdated;
      String url = "jdbc:odbc:technical_library";
      String driver = "sun.jdbc.odbc.JdbcOdbcDriver";

      Class.forName(driver);
      Connection libraryConnection = DriverManager.getConnection(url);

      PreparedStatement SQLStatement;
      String changeLastName =
              "update authors set lastname = ?  where authid = ?";

      SQLStatement =
              libraryConnection.prepareStatement(changeLastName);

      SQLStatement.setString(1, "Burk");
      SQLStatement.setInt(2, 27);

      rowsUpdated = SQLStatement.executeUpdate();
      System.out.println("rows affected: " + rowsUpdated);
    }
    catch (ClassNotFoundException cnfe)
    {
      System.out.println(cnfe);
    }
    catch (SQLException sqle)
    {
      System.out.println(sqle);
    }
  }
}
```

How It Works

The **PreparedStatement** object is created from the **Connection** object by calling the **prepareStatement()** method. The statement is also defined with the placeholders marked as question marks. Those placeholders, for the last name and author ID columns respectively, are then filled with values at runtime by the **setString()** and **setInt()** methods of the **PreparedStatement**.

The statement is executed by calling the **executeUpdate()** method which returns the number of rows affected by the update operation. Notice that no parameters are passed to the method.

Statement versus PreparedStatement

There will be times where the choice between using a **Statement** object or a **PreparedStatement** object may not be entirely clear. **PreparedStatement** objects are great when:

▶ You need to execute the same statement several times, and only need to change specific values

▶ You are working with large chunks of data that make concatenation unwieldy

▶ You are working with a large number of parameters that make concatenation unwieldy

Conversely, **Statement** objects work well when you have simple statements, and they are essential if your JDBC driver doesn't support the **PreparedStatement** interface. The mSQL driver, for example, does not support **PreparedStatement**s at the time of writing. Applications that will rely on mSQL have no choice but to use **Statement** objects and **String** concatenation if they need to build SQL statements at runtime.

Working with Input Streams

One of the most intriguing features of the **PreparedStatement** interface is the ability to use streams as input. It's very often more convenient to deal with streams when you're working with data types like **LONGVARCHAR** and **LONGVARBINARY**. For example, an application storing binary images can very efficiently populate a **LONGVARBINARY** column by creating a **FileInputStream** from a source file.

The **PreparedStatement** interface provides three methods for extracting data from input streams:

Method	Description
setAsciiStream()	Use for **LONGVARCHAR** columns
setBinaryStream()	Use for **LONGVARBINARY** columns
setUnicodeStream()	Use for **LONGVARCHAR** columns

All of these methods take a parameter to indicate the placeholder position, an **InputStream** object, and the number of bytes to read from the stream. If an end-of-file is encountered before the designated number of bytes are read, the methods throws a **SQLException**.

The next example shows a simple example of using the **setAsciiStream()** method of the **PreparedStatement** to store Java source code in a database. It opens a Java source code file to an **InputStream** object, and uses that **InputStream** to populate a column in the database.

Try It Out—*PreparedStatement and Input Streams*

1 The program starts out with the usual code. Then a **FileInputStream** object is created from the source code file for this program. The number of bytes contained by the file is obtained by calling the **available()** method:

```java
import java.sql.*;
import java.io.*;

public class TryInputStream
{
  public static void main(String[] args)
  {
    try
    {
      int rowsUpdated;
      String url = "jdbc:odbc:technical_library";
      String driver = "sun.jdbc.odbc.JdbcOdbcDriver";

      FileInputStream fis = new FileInputStream("TryInputStream.java");
      int length = fis.available();

      Class.forName(driver);
      Connection libraryConnection =
                      DriverManager.getConnection(url);
```

2 This table hasn't been created yet, so we'll take care of that here. The table simply consists of an identifier column and the source code contained in the file

```java
      Statement createTable = libraryConnection.createStatement();
      createTable.executeUpdate("create table source_code
                      (name char(20), source longtext)");
```

3 A **PreparedStatement** is instantiated by the **Connection**, and the first placeholder value is set with **setString()**. The second placeholder value, which will contain the source code read from the file, is set by calling **setAsciiStream()**. The **PreparedStatement** will read the entire file from the stream for the source column value.

```
        PreparedStatement SQLStatement;
        String ins = "insert into source_code values (?,?)";
        SQLStatement = libraryConnection.prepareStatement(ins);

        SQLStatement.setString(1, "TryInputStream");
        SQLStatement.setAsciiStream(2, fis, length);

        rowsUpdated = SQLStatement.executeUpdate();
        System.out.println("rows affected: " + rowsUpdated);
       libraryConnection.close();
    }
    catch (ClassNotFoundException cnfe)
    {
      System.out.println(cnfe);
    }
    catch (SQLException sqle)
    {
      System.out.println(sqle);
    }
```

4 **IOException**s need to be caught both for the **FileInputStream** constructor and the
setAsciiStream() method of the **PreparedStatement** interface. We'll catch them
both here.

```
    catch (IOException ioe)
    {
      System.out.println(ioe);
    }
  }
}
```

You might want to check your results, by running the InteractiveSQL application, to verify
that the table was created and the rows were inserted. Start that application and execute the
SQL statement

```
select * from source_code
```

After you're satisfied with your results, feel free to delete the table. Having restarted the
InteractiveSQL application, execute the statement:

```
drop table source_code
```

How It Works

This program is very similar to the previous example. A **FileInputStream**, which is a type
of **InputStream**, is created from the file **TryInputStream.java**. Since the **set*XXX*Stream()**
methods need to know how many bytes to read from the stream, we have to get the file
size of the **TryInputStream.java** file by calling the **available()** method of the
FileInputStream.

I've elected to create the table within the example code. Then the **PreparedStatement** object is created by the **Connection**, and the placeholder value for the first column is set by calling the **setString()** method of the **PreparedStatement**. The real magic happens in the **setAsciiStream()** method—all you have to do is supply the method with the placeholder position, the **InputStream**, and the number of bytes to read. When the statement is executed, the bytes are read from the stream and saved to the database.

If your JDBC applications will be dealing with large chunks of data, the **Stream** methods of the **PreparedStatement** interface are a real help.

The ResultSet

In the last section, we took another look at the **Statement** and **PreparedStatement** interfaces. By now, you should have a pretty good understanding of how to create a query and, now that you do, it's time to dig into the details of getting the data back from the query. In this section, we'll extend what you learnt about the **ResultSet** object in the last chapter.

Retrieving Column Data for Specified Data Types

So far we've retrieved mostly **String** data types. Like the **Statement** and **PreparedStatement**, though, the **ResultSet** provides methods for working with several data types.

Most of these methods work alike, and follow the form:

```
XXXvalue ResultSet.getXXX(String columnName)
```

and

```
XXXvalue ResultSet.getXXX(int columnPosition)
```

The mechanics of calling these methods is pretty straightforward. But to use these methods effectively, you need to understand what Java data types can be mapped from SQL data types, and vice versa.

The following table illustrates the mappings between SQL data types and the appropriate **ResultSet getXXX()** methods. When you're deciding what **getXXX()** method to use, use the table to map the column data type to the appropriate method. The 'preferred' method for a type is indicated with the ✓ symbol. That means that it is the closest mapping to the SQL type. Other methods may also work, however. Those methods are indicated in by the ± symbol.

ResultSet method to SQL Data Type Mapping	TINYINT	SMALLINT	INTEGER	BIGINT	REAL	FLOAT	DOUBLE	DECIMAL	NUMERIC	BIT	CHAR	VARCHAR	LONGVARCHAR	BINARY	VARBINARY	LONGVARBINARY	DATE	TIME	TIMESTAMP
getByte()	✓	+	+	+	+	+	+	+	+	+	+	+							
getShort()	+	✓	+	+	+	+	+	+	+	+	+	+							
getInt()	+	+	✓	+	+	+	+	+	+	+	+	+							
getLong()	+	+	+	✓	+	+	+	+	+	+	+	+							
getFloat()	+	+	+	+	✓	+	+	+	+	+	+	+							
getDouble()	+	+	+	+	+	✓	✓	+	+	+	+	+							
getBigDecimal()	+	+	+	+	+	+	+	✓	✓	+	+	+							
getBoolean()	+	+	+	+	+	+	+	+	+	✓	+	+							
getString()	+	+	+	+	+	+	+	+	+	+	✓	✓	+	+	+	+	+	+	+
getBytes()														✓	✓	+			
getDate()											+	+	+				✓		
getTime()											+	+	+					✓	+
getTimeStamp()											+	+	+				+		✓
getAsciiStream()											+	+	✓	+	+	+			
getUnicodeStream()											+	+	✓	+	+	+			
getBinaryStream()														+	✓	✓			
getObject()	+	+	+	+	+	+	+	+	+	+	+	+	+	+	+	+	+	+	+

Working with Null Values

Null is a special value in the world of SQL. Null is not the same thing as an empty string, for text columns, nor is it the same thing as zero. Null means that no data is defined for a column value within a relation. For example, recall the **authors** table, which has several values that may or may not have values assigned, including the **email** column. In order to determine which authors do not have an email address recorded, you could use the query:

```
select authid from authors where email = null
```

This query will return the ID for each author without an email address.

The **ResultSet** interface provides a method for testing a column value within a result set to determine if it is null. The **wasNull()** method returns a **boolean** value indicating if the last column read was a null or some other value.

The ability to detect a null value in your code is pretty important unless you created your tables with each column defined as **NOT NULL**, which would tell the database to never allow a null value in those columns. That's not always a practical or desirable way to design tables.

893

Consider the following example, which selects and prints the author id, last name, first name, phone number and email address for each row in the **authors** table. If any of these values are not assigned a value, the code will throw a **NullPointerException** when the program attempts to print out the value. In order to avoid that sort of bad program behavior, this class uses the **wasNull()** method of the **ResultSet**. Notice that the **wasNull()** method is called after the value is retrieved from the **ResultSet**:

Try It Out—Testing for Null Values in the *ResultSet*

Try entering the following code:

```
import java.sql.*;

public class TestNullValues
{
  public static void main(String[] args)
  {
    String url = "jdbc:odbc:technical_library";
    String driver = "sun.jdbc.odbc.JdbcOdbcDriver";

    String theStatement =
            "select authid, lastname, firstname, email from authors";

    try
    {
      Class.forName(driver);
      Connection libraryConnection =
                DriverManager.getConnection(url, "guest", "guest");
      Statement queryAuthors = libraryConnection.createStatement();
      ResultSet theResults = queryAuthors.executeQuery(theStatement);

      while(theResults.next())
      {
        String lastname, firstname, email;
        int id;

        id = theResults.getInt(1);
        lastname = theResults.getString(2);
        firstname = theResults.getString(3);
        email = theResults.getString(4);

        if (theResults.wasNull())
          email = "no email";

        System.out.println(Integer.toString(id) + ", " +
                          lastname.trim() + ", " +
                          firstname.trim() +", " +
                          email.trim());
      }
      queryAuthors.close();
```

```
        }
        catch (ClassNotFoundException cnfe)
        {
          System.out.println(cnfe);
        }
        catch (SQLException sqle)
        {
          System.out.println(sqle);
        }
    }
  }
```

Running this code produces the following results:

```
1, Gross, Christian, no email
2, Roche, Kevin, no email
3, Tracy, Michael, no email
4, Horton, Ivor, no email
. . .
```

How It Works

In **TestNullValues**, the SQL statement is executed, and the values for the author id, last name, first name and email address are extracted into local variables. Notice that after reading the value for **email**, we've called the **wasNull()** method to test if the last value read was a null value. If so, we'll replace a literal string so the report will work. Since the **authid**, **lastname** and **firstname** columns are required, I didn't have to test those column values for null values.

Working with Special Data Types

In addition to providing access methods for standard Java data types, the JDBC **java.sql** package also defines objects for some handy data types.

Date

The **java.sql.Date** class defines the object that is returned by the **ResultSet.getDate()** method. This class subclasses the **Date** class defined in the **java.util** package, so all of the methods for that class can be applied against this class. The **java.sql.Date** class overrides many of these methods, and provides a static **valueOf()** method that converts a string representation (*yyyy-mm-dd* form) of a date into a **Date** object.

Time

Like **java.sql.Date**, the **java.sql.Time** class wraps the **java.util.Date** class as a subclass, and provides a static **valueOf()** method that returns a **Time** object from a string representation (*hh:mm:ss* form) of time into a **Time** object.

Timestamp

The **java.sql.Timestamp** class also subclasses **java.util.Date**, but provides additional support for SQL timestamps with support for nanoseconds (**java.util.Date** only supports time to the seconds). The static **valueOf()** method creates a **Timestamp** object from a string representation (*yyyy-mm-dd hh:mm:ss.fffffffff* form). It also overloads accessor methods and comparison methods (before, after) to support nanoseconds.

Big Numbers

The designers of the first version of JDBC needed a means of working with the SQL **NUMERIC** and **DECIMAL** types, and created the **java.sql.Numeric** class (subsequently the **java.lang.BigNum** class) which provides very high precision for fixed point or numeric values. This has since been split into two and these moved to their own package, **java.math**. They are the **BigInteger** and **BigDecimal** classes.

These classes are worth taking the time to look into. You may never need this degree of precision, but it's nice to know it's there when you do. The **math** classes are very useful for applications that require a high degree of numeric precision, such as security keys, very large monetary values, and so forth.

BigInteger and **BigDecimal** objects are characterized by:

Precision	The total number of digits that make up the number (both to the left and to the right of the decimal place).
Scale	The total number of digits to the right of the decimal place.
Sign	Can be positive or negative.
Value	The sequence of digits that comprise the number.

The **BigInteger** and **BigDecimal** classes provides mathematical methods for addition, subtraction, multiplication and division, as well as comparison methods, methods for obtaining their value as standard Java types, and methods for tailoring the rounding behavior.

Like Java **String** objects, the value of a **BigInteger** or **BigDecimal** object is immutable. That is, once it's been created, you can't change the value. You can create new **BigInteger** and **BigDecimal** objects using their methods, such as **multiply()** and **divide()**, much as you'd create a new string using the **concat()** or **substring()** methods of **String**.

Consider the difficulties you might have if you had to compute very large sums and needed a great deal of accuracy. Suppose you had to accurately calculate the product of the following two floating point numbers:

```
98765423462576235623562346234623462.35632456234567890
```

and

```
98982345232356246643764376346474373436547.34586558
```

You might be tempted to write the following code:

```
class BigMultiplication
{
  public static void main(String[] args)
```

```
  {
    Double d1, d2;
    double d3;

    d1 = Double.valueOf(
        "9876542346257623562356234623462.35632456234567890");
    d2 = Double.valueOf(
        "98982345232356246643764376346747373436547.34586558");

    d3 = d1.doubleValue() * d2.doubleValue();
    System.out.println(Double.toString(d3));
  }
}
```

And then be very disappointed when your code produced the result:

```
9.776033242192577E74
```

Considering the number of digits of precision you entered for the factors you would probably find this unacceptable. Enter the **BigInteger** and **BigDecimal** classes. Try the following code:

Try It Out—The *BigDecimal* Class

1 Declare three **BigDecimal** objects.

```
import java.math.*;

public class TestBigDecimal
{
  public static void main(String[] args)
  {
    BigDecimal bn1, bn2, bn3;
```

2 Create the new **BigDecimal** objects using the string literal of the numbers:

```
    bn1 = new
    BigDecimal("9876542346257623562356234623462.35632456234567890");
    bn2 = new
    BigDecimal("98982345232356246643764376346747373436547.34586558");
```

3 Create the third **BigDecimal** by multiplying the first by the second. Then print out the results using the **BigDecimal** method.

```
    bn3 = bn1.multiply(bn2);
    System.out.println(bn3);
  }
}
```

When you run the code the program prints the results:

```
97760332421925786372389351223148078503101925277904720859519667576821933944
8.77331351021069269324226208
```

How It Works

The **BigDecimal** class is pretty remarkable. It can support numbers of virtually limitless precision (the precision and scale are both 32-bit signed integer values, so can be as large as 2,147,483,647—and that's a huge number of digits!).

The **BigInteger** class is just as impressive—it provides the same arbitrary precision characteristics for integer values. The **BigInteger** has the following constructors:

Constructors	Description
BigInteger(byte[] val)	Create an integer from two's complement (signed) array of bytes. Assumes that the most significant bytes are at the beginning of the array (**big endian order**).
BigInteger(int signum, byte[] magnitude)	Creates an integer from an array of bytes in big endian order. The sign integer indicate that the number is positive, zero or negative when its values are 1, 0 or -1, respectively.
BigInteger(String val, int radix)	Creates an integer from a string representation using the base indicated by the radix value.
BigInteger(int numBits, Random rndSrc)	Creates a non-negative random integer

A useful factory method is also provided to create a **BigInteger** from a **long** value:

public static BigInteger valueOf(long val)   Create a **BigInteger** object from a **long** value.

Like the **BigDecimal** class, the **BigInteger** class provides operator methods for multiplication, division, subtraction and addition, as well as other methods for calculating modulus, greatest common denominator, exponents and bitwise operations.

Try out the following code:

Try It Out—The *BigInteger Class*

1 First, we declare three **BigInteger** objects.

```
import java.math.*;

public class TestBigInteger
{
```

```
  public static void main(String[] args)
  {
    BigInteger bi1, bi2, bi3;
```

2 Create the first **BigInteger** object using the string literal of hexadecimal (base 16) numbers:

```
    bi1 = new
    BigInteger("cafebabecabbeefdeaffeeddead", 16);
```

3 Create another **BigInteger** object using the **valueOf()** factory method to create a **BigInteger** from a **long** literal

```
    bi2 = BigInteger.valueOf(35);
```

4 Calculate the greatest common denominator of the two numbers and display the resulting **BigInteger**

```
    bi3 = bi1.gcd(bi2);
    System.out.println(bi3);
  }
}
```

Running this code produces the resulting greatest common denominator, 7.

How It Works

The **BigInteger** constructors enable creation of **BigInteger** objects from big endian byte arrays, and as this example shows, from literal string values. Like the **BigDecimal** class, this class provides arbitrarily large precision integers, and some very powerful methods for manipulating those values. This example uses the built-in **gcd()** method to calculate the greatest common denominator without much code at all.

Of course, there is a price to pay for that precision. Computations using the **BigInteger** and **BigDecimal** classes are notably slower than their counterparts using native Java types. The **BigInteger** and **BigDecimal** classes manages digits as objects in a vector, so size and computing time are the tradeoff. Nonetheless, this class is invaluable for many applications.

Working with Streams

Earlier, we looked at using streams to populate **LONGVARCHAR** and **LONGVARBINARY** columns, because it's frequently much easier to deal with streams when you're working with large objects.

The **ResultSet** provides methods for retrieving data from a database as streams, much like the **PreparedStatement** provides methods for populating a database from streams. The methods are the direct correlates:

Method	Description
setAsciiStream()	Use for **LONGVARCHAR** columns
setBinaryStream()	Use for **LONGVARBINARY** columns
setUnicodeStream()	Use for **LONGVARCHAR** columns

All of these methods take a parameter to indicate the column name or column position, and return an **InputStream** object.

The next example shows a simple example of using the **getAsciiStream()** method of the **ResultSet**. This code extends **TryInputStream.java** in the previous chapter, so please refer back to that section if you need some clarification on anything in this code prior to the comments below.

Try It Out—ResultSet Columns as Streams

1 If we open **TryInputStream.java** and make the following changes:

```java
import java.sql.*;
import java.io.*;

public class TryInputStream2
{
  public static void main(String[] args)
  {
    try
    {
      int rowsUpdated;
      String url = "jdbc:odbc:technical_library";
      String driver = "sun.jdbc.odbc.JdbcOdbcDriver";

      FileInputStream fis = new FileInputStream("TryInputStream2.java");
      int length = fis.available();

      Class.forName(driver);

      Connection libraryConnection = DriverManager.getConnection(url);
      Statement createTable = libraryConnection.createStatement();
      createTable.executeUpdate("create table source_code
                        ↳ (name char(20), source longtext)");

      PreparedStatement SQLStatement;
      String ins = "insert into source_code values (?,?)";
      SQLStatement = libraryConnection.prepareStatement(ins);

      SQLStatement.setString(1, "TryInputStream2");
      SQLStatement.setAsciiStream(2, fis, length);
```

```
rowsUpdated = SQLStatement.executeUpdate();
System.out.println("rows affected: " + rowsUpdated);
```

2 Create a new **Statement** for selecting the name and source from the **source_code** table. Execute the query and save the resulting **ResultSet** in the local variable **theCode**

```
Statement getCode = libraryConnection.createStatement();
ResultSet theCode = getCode.executeQuery("select name,
                              ⤷ source from source_code");
```

3 Loop through each row in the **ResultSet**. Since we've just added a single row, this should only have one row returned.

```
while(theCode.next())
{
  boolean done = false;
```

4 Create a **BufferedReader** object using the **InputStream** object returned from the **getAsciiStream()** method of the **ResultSet** in the constructor argument. The **BufferedReader** class will make it easier to extract the source code data a line at a time.

```
BufferedReader br = new BufferedReader(
                    new InputStreamReader(
                    theCode.getAsciiStream(2)));
```

5 Loop through the data behind the **BufferedReader**, and extract and print each line in turn.

```
while(!done)
{
  String theLine = br.readLine();
  if (theLine == null)
    done = true;
  else
    System.out.println(theLine);
}
}
```

6 Close the connection:

```
libraryConnection.close();
}
catch (ClassNotFoundException cnfe)
{
  System.out.println(cnfe);
}
```

```
      catch (SQLException sqle)
      {
        System.out.println(sqle);
      }
      catch (IOException ioe)
      {
        System.out.println(ioe);
      }
    }
  }
```

You should see the text of the source code printed out.

After you're satisfied with your results, feel free to delete the table. Using the InteractiveSQL application, execute the statement:

```
drop table source_code
```

How It Works

Most of this code sets up and populates the **source_code** table. Once the **ResultSet** is returned from **executeQuery()**, we can get an **InputStream** from the **ResultSet**. This code is going to loop through each row of data returned, and create a new **InputStream** object for the data in the **source** column of the **source_code** table. We use the **InputStream** object to create a new **BufferedReader** object. The **BufferedReader** class provides methods that will scan the input and return data a line at a time, which is exactly what we want. While there is still data to read, the program reads and prints each line of the source code. When it is done, the **next()** method of the **ResultSet** gets executed again, and the process repeats until there are no more rows.

Exceptions

So far, in all of the examples that we've used, we've glossed over the issue of errors, warnings and exceptions. The examples up until this point have all been predicated on the hope that everything will work OK.

Unfortunately, life is a bit less predictable than that, and you need to take some extra steps in your JDBC applications to handle conditions that generate warnings or errors. In this section, you'll see how to build mechanisms to trap errors, how to use the facilities built into JDBC to get detailed warning and error information from the data source, and how to gracefully recover from JDBC exceptions.

SQLException

Every example that you've seen so far has had the basic format

```
try
{
   //do JDBC stuff
}
catch(SQLException sqle)
{
   // print out the error
}
```

Every method of every JDBC class and interface can throw a **SQLException**. The **SQLException** exception is a pretty broad-brush way of handling exceptions in JDBC, and in all of our previous examples, we've not done a great deal with these exceptions.

In order to do useful things with the **SQLException**, you need to know that there are three important pieces of information available from the thrown exception. How you use these pieces of information pretty much depends on your application.

Exception Message

First, a string that describes the exception is available through the **getMessage()** method. For the examples that we've presented so far, this is the most useful piece of information. This string, however, varies, depending on the JDBC driver that you're using, so while this information is useful for humans, it's difficult for programs to make decisions based on this information.

SQL State

There is another piece of information—the SQL state—that can be used by a program. The SQL state is a string that contains a state as defined by the X/Open SQL standard. The SQL state value can be obtained from the **SQLException** by calling the **getSQLState()** method.

The X/Open standard defines the SQL state as a five character string. The first two characters of the string define the class of the state—for example, the characters **01** represent the SQL state **"success with warning"**.

The next three characters define the subclass of the state. The X/Open standard defines specific subclasses, and also provides the value **000** as a general subclass. Specific implementations may define state subclasses using the values **900** through **ZZZ** where the standard does not provide a specific subclass.

The following table shows the SQL state strings defined in the X/Open standard. These state codes may not be directly attributable to your JDBC code, but may reflect an error occurring in the underlying driver. For example, if you are using the ODBC bridge, a SQL state can reflect an error occurring at the ODBC driver level.

Class	Subclass	Description
01		Success with warning
	002	Disconnect error
	004	String data, right truncation
	006	Privilege not revoked
02	000	No data
07		Dynamic SQL error
	001	Using-clause does not match dynamic parameters
	006	Restricted data type attribute violation
	008	Invalid descriptor count
08		Connection exception
	001	Server rejected the connection
	002	Connection name in use
	003	Connection does not exist
	004	Client unable to establish connection
	007	Transaction state unknown
	S01	Communication failure
21		Cardinality violation
	S01	Insert value list does not match column list
	S02	Degree of derived table does not match column list
22		Data exception
	001	String data, right truncation
	003	Numeric value out of range
	005	Error in assignment
	012	Divide by zero
23	000	Integrity constraint violation
24	000	Invalid cursor state
25	000	Invalid transaction state
	S02	Transaction still active
	S03	Transaction is rolled back
2D	000	Invalid transaction termination
34	000	Invalid cursor name

Class	Subclass	Description
37	000	Syntax error or access violation
40	000	Transaction rollback
	001	Statement completion unknown
42	000	Syntax error or access violation
HZ	000-ZZZ	RDA errors
S0		Invalid name
	001	Base table or view already exists
	002	Base table not found
	011	Index already exists
	012	Index not found
	021	Column already exists
S1		Call Level Interface specific
	001	Memory allocation error
	002	Invalid column number
	003	Program type out of range
	004	SQL data type out of range
	008	Operation canceled
	009	Invalid argument value
	010	Function sequence error
	012	Invalid transaction operation code
	013	Memory management error
	015	No cursor name available
	900-ZZZ	Implementation defined

The SQL state string is a very useful piece of information if you want to programmatically handle exceptions. Using the SQL state value, you can make decisions in your program to help recover from exceptions. For example, if your application creates tables, an exception indicating SQL state S0001 means that the table already exists. Depending on your application, this may not represent a fatal error, and your program can continue.

Vendor Error Code

Another bit of information that you can get from the **SQLException** is a vendor-specific code. This value is returned as an integer, and its meaning is completely defined by the driver vendor. This value can be obtained by calling the **getErrorCode()** method of the **SQLException**.

Try It Out—Extracting information from *SQLException*

In this short example, we will intentionally create errors in the executed SQL statements to generate exceptions, and then extract the message, vendor code and SQL state from the exception. In order to generate the exception, I've misspelled the name of the table in the variable **theStatement**.

```java
import java.sql.*;

public class ExtractSQLExceptionInfo
{
  public static void main(String[] args)
  {
    String url = "jdbc:odbc:technical_library";
    String driver = "sun.jdbc.odbc.JdbcOdbcDriver";

    String theStatement = "select lastname, firstname from autors";

    try
    {
      Class.forName(driver);
      Connection libraryConnection = DriverManager.getConnection(url);
      Statement queryAuthors = libraryConnection.createStatement();
      ResultSet theResults =  queryAuthors.executeQuery(theStatement);

      queryAuthors.close();
    }
    catch (ClassNotFoundException cnfe)
    {
      System.out.println(cnfe);
    }
    catch (SQLException sqle)
    {
      String sqlMessage = sqle.getMessage();
      String sqlState  = sqle.getSQLState();
      int vendorCode = sqle.getErrorCode();
      System.out.println("Exception occurred:");
      System.out.println("Message: " + sqlMessage);
      System.out.println("SQL state: " + sqlState);
      System.out.println("Vendor code: " + vendorCode);
    }
  }
}
```

When I ran this example, it produced the following:

```
Exception occurred:
Message: [Microsoft][ODBC Microsoft Access 97 Driver] The Microsoft Jet
database engine cannot find the input table or query 'autors'.  Make sure
it exists and that its name is spelled correctly.
SQL state: S0002
Vendor code: -1305
```

How It Works

In the **SQLException** exception handler, instead of simply printing out the text of the exception, we extract the message, the SQL state, and the vendor-specific error code. In this simple example, this information is formatted and printed to the console. In a more sophisticated application, you might want to log this information to a file to help you troubleshoot your application.

The message returned is pretty self-explanatory. The format of the text will vary, of course, from driver to driver. Hence the importance of the SQL state value. If you look back to the previous table, you will see that the SQL state reported in this exception corresponds to the SQL state "Base table not found" which correctly identifies the problem. Finally, the vendor code returned indicates the driver vendor's numeric code for the exception.

Chaining SQLExceptions

When SQL exceptions occur, there may be more than one exception associated with the occurrence. In order to handle this situation, the **SQLException** may be linked to another in a chain of exceptions.

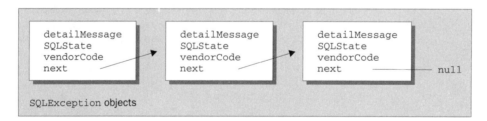

The **SQLException** class is essentially a linked list, and provides the **setNextException()** method for JDBC drivers and applications to link one exception to the next.

The **SQLException getNextException()** method is used to return the next exception in the chain if one exists. This method returns a **SQLException** object, or **null** if there are no more exceptions in the chain.

When your program traps a **SQLException**, you should call the **getNextException()** method to get each exception until the **getNextException()** method returns **null**, indicating that there are no more exceptions in the chain. The code fragment below illustrates a simple technique for looping.

```
try
{
  // call a method that can throw SQLException
  theProgram.doSQLQuery();
}
catch(SQLException sqle)
{
  SQLException thisException;

  thisException = sqle;
  // loop through each exception
  while(thisException != null)
  {
    // do something with each exception
    doSomething(thisException);
    thisException = thisException.getNextException();
  }
}
```

This example shows how an application can create a chain of **SQLException** objects in its exception handling. This technique is handy if you are writing a reusable class library that wraps JDBC, and want to provide additional information when an exception is thrown.

Try It Out—Chaining *SQLExceptions*

1 Having created a **ChainSQLExceptions** object in **main()**, we then call the object's **doQuery()** method. Since this can throw a **SQLException**, we must catch this exception:

```
import java.sql.*;

public class ChainSQLExceptions
{
  public static void main(String[] args)
  {
    ChainSQLExceptions theProgram = new ChainSQLExceptions();
    try
    {
      theProgram.doQuery();
    }
    catch(SQLException sqle)
    {
      SQLException thisException;
      thisException = sqle;
```

2 Within the **catch** clause, we loop through each exception in the chain. For each exception, get the description, **SQLState** and vendor code, and print it out. When the last **SQLException** is reached, **thisException** will be **null**, and the program will terminate.

```
      while(thisException != null)
      {
        String sqlMessage = thisException.getMessage();
        String sqlState = thisException.getSQLState();
        int vendorCode = thisException.getErrorCode();
        System.out.println("Exception occurred:");
        System.out.println("Message: " + sqlMessage);
        System.out.println("SQL state: " + sqlState);
        System.out.println("Vendor code: " + vendorCode +
                        ⮑ "\n----------------");

        thisException = thisException.getNextException();
      }
    }
  }
```

3   Now for that `SQLException` throwing `doQuery()` method.

```
public void doQuery() throws SQLException
{
  String url = "jdbc:odbc:technical_library";
  String driver = "sun.jdbc.odbc.JdbcOdbcDriver";
  String theStatement = "select lastname, firstname from autors";

  try
  {
    Class.forName(driver);
    Connection libraryConnection =
    DriverManager.getConnection(url);
    Statement queryAuthors = libraryConnection.createStatement();
    ResultSet theResults = queryAuthors.executeQuery(theStatement);

    queryAuthors.close();
  }
  catch (ClassNotFoundException cnfe)
  {
    System.out.println(cnfe);
  }
```

4   In the exception handling routine, we'll add a new exception to the end of the chain, indicating that the operation was canceled. Create a new instance of the `SQLException`.

```
  catch (SQLException sqle)
  {
    SQLException generatedException =
              new SQLException("SQL operation canceled","S1008", 0);
```

5 To make sure that we're adding the exception to the end of the list, run through the exception chain until we find the end. The last exception in the chain will return a **null** when its **getNextException()** method is called.

```
    SQLException lastException = sqle;
    while(lastException.getNextException() != null)
      lastException = lastException.getNextException();
    lastException.setNextException(generatedException);
    throw sqle;
  }
 }
}
```

When I ran the program with the JDBC_ODBC driver I got:

```
Exception occurred:
Message: [Microsoft][ODBC Microsoft Access 97 Driver] The Microsoft Jet
database engine cannot find the input table or query 'autors'.  Make sure
it exists and that its name is spelled correctly.
SQL state: S0002
Vendor code: -1305
----------------
Exception occurred:
Message: SQL operation canceled
SQL state: S1008
Vendor code: 0
----------------
```

How It Works

This example demonstrates how your application can not only handle chains of **SQLException** objects, but also how it can add exceptions to the chain.

The **main()** method calls the **doQuery()** method, which throws a **SQLException**. The exception handler in **main()** starts with the exception passed to the exception handler, and follows the chain of exceptions. For each exception, the message, **SQLState** and vendor code are displayed.

The **doQuery()** method contains an exception handler that appends a new **SQLException** to the chain. Notice that the exception handler doesn't just assume that the exception is the last one in the chain, and call **setNextException()** to add another exception to the one caught. Instead, the code ensures that the new exception is correctly appended to the end of the chain by following the chain until the last exception is found.

SQLWarning

JDBC provides another means of obtaining warning information from JDBC objects. Sometimes conditions may arise that may not be serious enough to throw an exception, but merits the program being able to determine that all is not completely well.

The **SQLWarning** class is derived from **SQLException**. Like the **SQLException**, it defines a message, a **SQLState** code, and a vendor code. It can also be chained to one or more other **SQLWarning** objects. The techniques described in the previous section for traversing **SQLException**s apply to **SQLWarning**s as well. In most respects, the **SQLWarning** looks a lot like **SQLException**, except for one very important distinction: you have to ask for a **SQLWarning** explicitly. They do not occur as exceptions.

The **ResultSet**, **Connection** and **Statement** interfaces all provide the **getWarnings()** method, which returns a **SQLWarning** object if warnings are present, and **null** otherwise.

To better understand how **SQLWarning**s come into play, consider one special class of warnings—data truncation. For example, there is nothing preventing an application from retrieving data from a floating point column as an integer. In order to notify the application that potential data loss or any other warning condition has occurred, the application can call the **getWarnings()** method of the result set.

Since data truncation is a common type of warning, JDBC provides a **DataTruncation** class that is itself derived from **SQLWarning**.

Try It Out—Using *SQLWarning*

This example intentionally retrieves floating point values from the **PRODUCTS** table as an integer in order to force a warning. In order to simplify this example, the **SQLWarning** chain is not traversed—we'll simply print the text of the **SQLWarning** message.

```java
import java.sql.*;

public class TestSQLWarning
{
  public static void main(String[] args)
  {
    TestSQLWarning theProgram = new TestSQLWarning();
    try
    {
      theProgram.doQuery();
    }
    catch(SQLException sqle)
    {
      SQLException thisException;
      thisException = sqle;
      while(thisException != null)
      {
        String sqlMessage = thisException.getMessage();
        String sqlState = thisException.getSQLState();
        int vendorCode = thisException.getErrorCode();
        System.out.println("Exception occurred:");
        System.out.println("Message: " + sqlMessage);
        System.out.println("SQL state: " + sqlState);
```

```
          System.out.println("Vendor code: " + vendorCode +
                                "\n----------------");

        thisException = thisException.getNextException();
      }
    }
  }

  public void doQuery() throws SQLException
  {
    String url = "jdbc:odbc:technical_library";
    String driver = "sun.jdbc.odbc.JdbcOdbcDriver";
    String theStatement =
            "select title, price from books where price <> null";
    try
    {
      Class.forName(driver);
      Connection libraryConnection = DriverManager.getConnection(url);
      Statement queryBooks = libraryConnection.createStatement();
      ResultSet theResults = queryBooks.executeQuery(theStatement);
      while(theResults.next())
      {
        int price;
        String title;

        title = theResults.getString("title");
        SQLWarning sqlw = theResults.getWarnings();
        if (sqlw != null)
          System.out.println(sqlw.getMessage());

        price = theResults.getInt("price");

        sqlw = theResults.getWarnings();
        if (sqlw != null)
          System.out.println(sqlw.getMessage());

        System.out.println(title + " " + Integer.toString(price));
      }
      queryBooks.close();
    }
    catch (ClassNotFoundException cnfe)
    {
      System.out.println(cnfe);
    }
    catch (SQLException sqle)
    {
      SQLException generatedException =
              new SQLException("SQL operation canceled","S1008", 0);
      SQLException lastException = sqle;
      while(lastException.getNextException() != null)
        lastException = lastException.getNextException();
      lastException.setNextException(generatedException);
```

911

```
        throw sqle;
      }
    }
  }
```

When you run the program you should see:

```
Professional Java Fundamentals
 35
Data truncation
Design Patterns
 45
```

How It Works

Since **SQLWarning** objects are not thrown, the code needs to check the **ResultSet** after extracting values to find out if any warnings were produced. The **ResultSet.getWarnings()** method returns a **SQLWarning** object if any warnings were generated, and **null** otherwise. If a non-null **SQLWarning** is returned, the code prints out the text of the warning immediately before printing out the title and the price of the book.

The results displayed by running the program reflect the fact that the book "Professional Java Fundamentals" has a price of $35.00. Retrieving the price as an integer doesn't result in any data truncation. "Design Patterns", however, has a price of $45.25, and the **SQLWarning** is generated.

Summary

In this chapter, you've used and extended the basic JDBC skills and topics we learned in the previous chapter. Specifically, we've:

- ▶ Looked at a couple of strategies for creating Java objects from JDBC data sources
- ▶ Created, updated and deleted database objects
- ▶ Looked at different techniques for defining and executing SQL statements, and explored when to use which flavor
- ▶ Presented a table to allow accurate mappings between SQL and Java
- ▶ Used the **java.math** classes for applications that need numeric precision beyond the capabilities of the base numeric types
- ▶ Integrated rational handling of errors and warnings into our JDBC applications

Exercises

With some additional features, you will find the InteractiveSQL utility very useful. Add the following features to InteractiveSQL:

1 Keep the last ten queries that were executed, and allow the user to select from that list of previously run queries

2 Provide a menu option that lets the user close the current **Connection** and open a new one. Prompt the user for the URL, driver name, user name and password.

3 Trap **SQLException**s and provide full, detailed information about the exception. You may want to use a separate window that provides more space and keeps a running list of exceptions until these are cleared by the user.

Introducing Remote Method Invocation

In today's world of technology, Distributed Object Computing (DOC) is quickly proving itself as a viable technique for designing and building network-centric applications. It replaces the tiered architecture found in traditional client-server systems by allowing objects to communicate with each other over the network. Distributed computing techniques allow you to develop objects across the network, and invoke each other's methods through a pre-defined interface.

Java's Remote Method Invocation (RMI) package is a set of classes and interfaces that enables one Java object to call the public methods of another Java object running on a different virtual machine. In keeping with the spirit of distributed computing, the RMI allows objects to communicate through a pre-defined interface that allows them to function as if the objects are local to them so they can invoke their methods directly.

As you begin to develop distributed applications written entirely in Java, it is important to consider the RMI as your primary design alternative. It offers several advantages over other solutions, and also retains the ability to take complete advantage of Java's ubiquity. (We will briefly review other design alternatives later on in this chapter, such as Sockets, CGI and IDL, and see how the RMI compares to them).

Within the following pages, we will explore the RMI more fully in order to understand what situations it is useful in, how to develop distributed objects with the RMI, and special considerations you need to make when you design RMI applications.

In this chapter you will learn:

- What the RMI is
- The components of the RMI architecture
- How to build a distributed application using the RMI
- How to manage multiple clients
- How the RMI deals with garbage collection
- How the RMI compares to other distributed computing techniques

What is Remote Method Invocation?

Remote Method Invocation is an object-based distributed computing architecture written completely in Java. Before we analyze the RMI, let's review the topology of a distributed object environment:

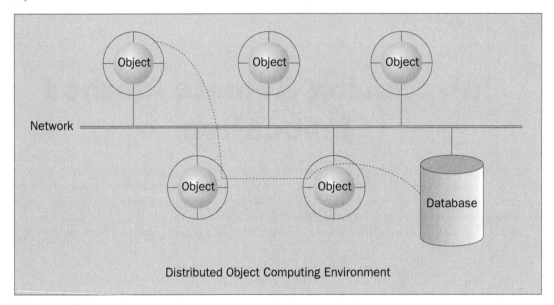

In distributed object computing, an object calls procedures contained within another object. The second object, in turn, may call yet another object's procedures. These objects may or may not reside on the same physical machine. If not, then the access is made through the network. The diagram displays several objects communicating with each other over the network. The third object is the only one that interacts with the database. Through a distributed object architecture that is capable of querying databases, we can reduce data access methods to a single object. The main advantage to such a design is the ability to build reusable objects across the network.

In distributed object environments, we loosely refer to various objects as clients and servers. Any object that calls another object is named the **client**. The second object, in turn, is referred to as the **server**. If it again calls procedures contained within yet another object, it becomes the client for that call, and the receiving object becomes the server. (Because there are multiple clients and servers associated within distributed object environments, they are often referred to as **n-tier** architectures.)

RMI is Java's way of delivering distributed object computing to Java objects. Through the RMI, a Java object (client) can call a public method contained within another Java object (server). In fact, 'RMI' was named specifically as a result of the client's ability to **invoke** a **remote** object's **methods**.

Suppose, for example, you wish to create a Java applet that connects to a relational database and performs some queries and updates. One option is to make the applet a self-contained application and program the database access directly within it using the JDBC (Java Database Connectivity) API. This design is typical of client-server applications:

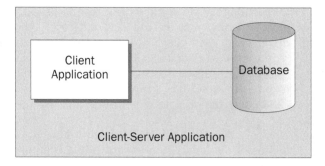

Client-Server Application

Traditional client-server computing originally addressed the need to distribute work across the network and provide centralized utilities where it made most sense (such as database storage). The typical problem with this approach, however, is that every machine that runs the client application also needs to have the native database drivers installed, since the client itself manages the database access directly. Additionally, since it is the application's responsibility to process the information, the network can be burdened with additional traffic as the client repeatedly communicates with the database. Finally, if the database engine is ever changed, the application and associated database drivers need to be modified and redistributed to every client.

An alternative approach in designing this application is to use RMI. Through RMI, a Java client can access another Java object running on a separate virtual machine (the "remote object"), where the database access is performed:

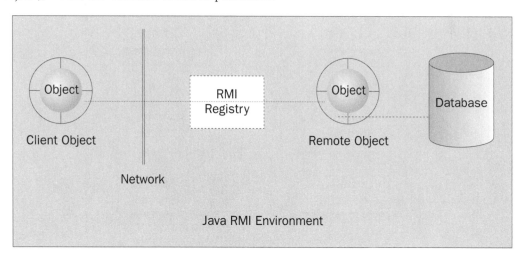

Comparing the RMI view to the traditional client-server approach, the Java applet (client object) invokes methods contained within the remote object, which in turn issue the database call and return the results back to the client. The applet still behaves as if it were a self-contained applet. It 'thinks' these methods are local to itself, passing values and receiving results with the remote object. It does this through the use of a **registry**, which we will learn more about later.

By partitioning the work across the network in this way, the client can function independently from the back-end database. There is no need to install native database drivers with each client. The remote object can manage the database accesses centrally, thus reducing network traffic. Changes can be made to the database by modifying the remote object, which means that no changes to the client are required. Lastly, other applications that require the same data access logic as this one can use the same remote object, thus eliminating the need to rebuild this code within another program.

Not only does RMI allow you to distribute the work more effectively across the network, it reinforces the Java vision—to provide a computing platform that can perform without regard to the specific hardware on which it runs, using the virtual machine.

It's time now to explore the underlying architecture of the RMI to see how all this happens.

The RMI Architecture

As stated above, the RMI environment consists of a client process and a remote object running on separate virtual machines. The two are logically linked to each other through a registry. Consider the following illustration:

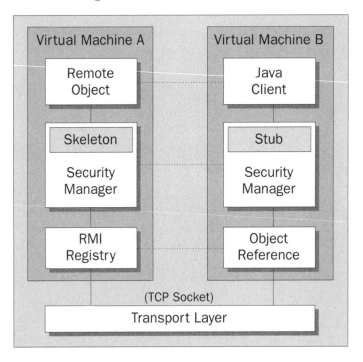

At the start of the process, a Java application executes as a server process on Virtual Machine A. This application, which is referred to as the **remote object**, identifies itself with the **RMI registry**, on that same virtual machine. The registry is another Java application whose role is to maintain active references to remote objects. These references are stored within an internal table contained within the registry program. Through the registry, the remote object is able to offer its services to RMI clients.

Next, a Java client running on Virtual Machine B wishes to invoke a method contained within the remote object. Before it can attempt this, however, it needs to request the service from the registry. It does this by accessing the RMI registry on the host where the remote object resides (Virtual Machine A) through a TCP socket connection. Once the registry accepts the client's request, it delivers a reference to the remote object in the form of a **stub** back to the client.

The client now invokes a method contained within the remote object's stub. This invocation may also involve the exchange of additional objects as parameters, and the receipt of return values from the method call. These communications occur through the network streams made available by the TCP socket, using **object serialization**.

Parameters are forwarded to the remote object through a **skeleton** object. The skeleton then dispatches them to the remote object and invokes the object's method. (A security manager governs the access as the stub and skeleton objects communicate with each other.) When the remote object's method completes, the return value is sent back through the skeleton and stub objects and finally received by the client. (More detail will be provided on stubs and skeletons shortly.)

The transport layer performs the underlying session and network management, using TCP sockets. It listens for incoming calls from the client and passes requests to the server.

The RMI Security Manager

As with all well-designed distributed applications, security measures must be implemented to make sure that the application is well behaved and doesn't violate the client's interests. In Java, security is controlled through the class loader that is associated with each object. We are already aware of two class loaders and their security measures:

▶ The default class loader. By default, Java applications will load class files through the virtual machine's **CLASSPATH** environment. This class loader is non-restrictive, allowing the application to load classes anywhere on the network

▶ The **AppletClassLoader**. This class loader is implemented within the browser that is used when you run your applets. It uses the **AppletSecurity** class as its security manager to control the applet's ability to load other classes. Typical features of this security manager include:

> Restricting access only to classes that are stored on the same host where the applet was loaded (i.e. its **codebase**).
> Preventing the applet from accessing sensitive functions, such as reading and writing files stored on the client's hard disk.

In addition to these, the RMI uses another class loader, called **RMIClassLoader**, to load stubs, skeletons, and other classes contained within the RMI that are necessary to manage the RMI session. Under normal conditions, the class loader is called internally by the RMI runtime system, so you needn't concern yourself about it other than to know that it exists. You do need to know, however, about the security restrictions contained within the RMI class loader.

In keeping with the security policy defined by the original Java specification, the RMI requires that a security manager be active before any class can be loaded through it. This requirement ensures that RMI objects interact only with other trusted objects. In the case where your RMI client is an applet, the applet's own security manager is sufficient. If your client is an application, however, you need to install the security manager that will be used by the RMI.

The `java.rmi` package contains a class, `RMISecurityManager`, which can be used for this purpose. Similar to the `AppletSecurity` class, it restricts access to trusted objects, such as those stored on the same host where the application was loaded. If you need special access privileges that are not available through `RMISecurityManager`, you are free to write and implement your own custom security manager. (We will not get into the specifics of building your own security manager here, since it is beyond the scope of this chapter.)

Regardless of the specific security manager you choose; its primary goal is to define the policies that govern the object while it runs on the client. It is for this reason alone that the security manager must be in place before any attempt is made to access a remote object. If no security manager is installed, the object will revert to the virtual machine's own `CLASSPATH` to load objects locally.

Except for applets (since they have their own security manager by default), we typically install the security manager through a **bootstrap process** created specifically for the RMI object. This bootstrap process, which we will learn more about later in this chapter, usually loads the RMI security manager as its first step in order to guarantee that it is active before any RMI call is made. (In the case of remote objects, the bootstrap also offers the object up to the RMI server and binds it to the registry. More on this later on.)

Parameterization with Object Serialization

Generally speaking, with calls made to methods contained within local objects, arguments may be passed, and a result may be returned. For example, consider the following method:

```
public Employee getRecord (String lastName) {
  Employee employee;
  ...
  ...
  ...
  return employee;
}
```

An application may invoke this method as follows:

```
Employee e = getRecord("Smith");
```

This example shows a last name of **"Smith"** being sent as an argument to the `getRecord()` method. In return, an object of type **Employee** is sent back to the application.

With calls to local methods, the transfer of these objects is performed 'by reference'. In other words, the receiving method doesn't receive the actual object, or even a copy of it. Instead, it receives a reference point to that object, representing its physical location in the Java virtual machine.

With calls to remote methods, however, the client and server objects operate under different virtual machines, and are unable to pass objects by their physical reference. Instead, copies of these objects are passed between the client and server processes through object serialization. When objects are sent, or **serialized**, between the client and server, only the non-static, non-transient fields are copied. If the serialized object is yet another remote object, it is copied by reference to that object's stub, which represents the public interface used to define it.

The RMI system automatically manages the exchange ('marshalling' and 'unmarshalling') of objects for you, so you are not required to build this logic explicitly into your program. You must make sure, however, that all parameters and return objects are serializable, otherwise your code will throw a **NotSerializableException** exception when an attempt is made to serialize the object.

Most of the classes contained within the **java.lang** and **java.util** packages have already been defined as serializable. If you use or extend any of these classes to create your own object, your class will implicitly be serializable as well. For objects that you create yourself, you can make them serializable simply by implementing the **Serializable** interface contained within the **java.io** package as we saw in Chapter 8.

Stubs and Skeletons

To understand stubs and skeletons, let's step through the RMI process, which we've just outlined. A **stub** is a proxy for the remote object, implementing its public interface. When a client object references a remote object, it does so by referencing its stub. The stub's purpose is to manage the communication with the remote object, and dispatch requests initiated by the client object.

The client and remote objects use the RMI registry to locate each other. When the client first issues a call to the remote object, it must perform a lookup in the remote registry. The registry sends it back the stub, which the client will use from this point onward.

A **skeleton** is the stub's counterpart running on the remote server. Similar to the stub, it provides the mechanism for accepting client requests, forwarding them to the actual remote object, and sending results back to the client. Stubs and skeletons are loaded dynamically at run time.

Generally speaking, stubs and skeletons serve as the vehicle for dispatching requests between the client and remote objects. They contain a 'blueprint' of the remote object's public methods (its public interface), and not the actual values or logic contained within the object. They communicate with each other through the transport layer of the RMI system by marshalling and unmarshalling parameters between the client and the remote objects using object serialization.

Let's look at a brief example. Suppose we create a remote object called **QuoteOfTheDay**. The purpose of this object is to deliver a quote of the day, or a message the varies on a daily basis, to a client object. Suppose further that the remote object contains a method, called **getMessage()**, that returns the quote as a string value. Let's step through the process that is used through the RMI to perform this task.

▶ The **QuoteOfTheDay** object registers itself, through a bootstrap routine that we will see more of later in this chapter, to the RMI registry. A reference to this object's skeleton is stored in the registry table. Once the registration occurs, the remote object is available for use over the network

▶ A Java applet wishes to access the **QuoteOfTheDay** object to obtain the current day's message. First, through the transport layer, it opens up a connection with the RMI registry on the host where **QuoteOfTheDay** is located, and searches for its entry within the registry. Next, the registry finds a match for this object and sends (marshals) the **QuoteOfTheDay**'s stub back through the transport layer. Finally, the applet receives (unmarshals) the stub and stores a reference to it

▶ The applet calls the stub's **getMessage()** method. If there were any parameters, they would be serialized by the stub and sent to the remote object's skeleton through the transport layer. Along with the parameters, the stub sends an internal indicator to the skeleton identifying the method that it wishes to invoke. In our example, **getMessage()** contains no parameters, so the stub only sends the internal indicator

▶ The skeleton receives the incoming objects through the transport layer. In our case, it is the internal indicator telling it which method to invoke within the remote object. If there were parameters sent to it as well, it would also pass them along to the actual remote object and invoke the specified method

▶ Once the remote object's method completes, its return value is serialized and sent back through the skeleton, transport layer and stub and, in turn, processed by the applet

As you can see, stubs and skeletons serve a critical function—the exchange of information between the client and remote objects.

Let's Build an Application

Now that we have explained the RMI architecture, let's start building our own distributed RMI application. We'll create an on-line employee directory for a company. The flow of this system will look as follows:

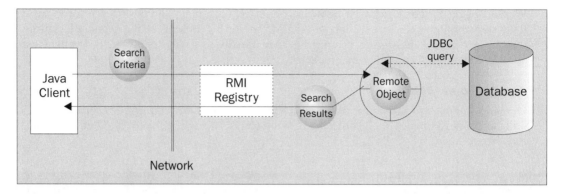

The Java client wishes to perform a database lookup against the corporate database. We will use the RMI to perform this task. First, we establish the RMI connection between the client and remote objects. Next, the client sends some search criteria to the remote object. Finally, the remote object issues the database call using the JDBC, and returns the results to the client.

The RMI design is being used for the following reasons:

▶ We wish to keep the client object independent from any database-specific activity. This eliminates the need to install database drivers on every client machine

▶ If we decide to change database engines in the future, we can do so by modifying the remote object. Because the client has no direct connection to the database, it is unaware of the change and can continue to operate without any further modification

▶ Unlike some stateless alternatives (such as CGI), the RMI offers the ability to maintain a persistent connection between the client and remote objects. As a result, we eliminate the extra overhead that would otherwise be required to manage the stateless sessions. (We'll explain this in more detail as we compare the RMI to other alternatives.)

In our Java client, the following search options will be allowed:

▶ Search by last name
▶ Search by title
▶ Search by department

Once the search is performed, we will display the resulting employee names, titles, departments and telephone numbers based on the match.

We will first illustrate the RMI-based system using a Java application as the client to explain the concepts. The application will make a simple connection to retrieve all employees contained within the directory. Once this is done, we will illustrate the same process using an applet that contains the search options listed above.

We will begin by constructing a database object representing the employee record. We will then step through the construction of an RMI server by looking at the registry, creating the remote object, and registering it with the RMI. Finally, we will create the RMI client using an application and an applet to invoke the remote object.

The Employee Object

Our application will make use of an object that represents an employee record. This object will be passed between the client and server objects and will contain the data retrieved from a database lookup.

Try It Out—Constructing the Employee Object

1   First, let's look at the database definition of our employee table:

Column Name	Description	Data Type	Length
LAST	Last name	**VARCHAR**	30
FIRST	First name	**VARCHAR**	30
TITLE	Job title	**VARCHAR**	30
DEPARTMENT	Employee's department	**VARCHAR**	30
TELEPHONE	Telephone number	**VARCHAR**	16

2   Using this table definition, we can define our **Employee** object as follows:

```
/* Employee
 * This class defines the attributes and access methods for
 * creating an Employee object.
 */

import java.sql.*;
import java.io.*;

public class Employee implements Serializable
{
  // Employee attributes
  private String lastName;
  private String firstName;
  private String title;
  private String department;
  private String telephone;

  // Constructor to load Employee data from a previously executed
  // database query
```

```
    public Employee(ResultSet rs)
    {
      try
      {
        setLastName(rs.getString(1));
        setFirstName(rs.getString(2));
        setTitle(rs.getString(3));
        setDepartment(rs.getString(4));
        setTelephone(rs.getString(5));
      }
      catch (SQLException sqle)
      {
        sqle.printStackTrace();
      }
    }

    public String getLastName()    { return lastName; }
    public String getFirstName()   { return firstName; }
    public String getTitle()       { return title; }
    public String getDepartment()  { return department; }
    public String getTelephone()   { return telephone; }

    public void setLastName(String s)    { lastName = s; }
    public void setFirstName(String s)   { firstName = s; }
    public void setTitle(String s)       { title = s; }
    public void setDepartment(String s)  { department = s; }
    public void setTelephone(String s)   { telephone = s; }
  }
```

How It Works

Let's briefly explore a few important features of the **Employee** object. Since we will be using the JDBC to access our database, we must first import the **java.sql** package.

Next, we need to make the object serializable in order to exchange it between the RMI client and server objects. To do so, we import the **java.io** package and implement the **Serializable** interface.

Prior to instantiating an **Employee** object, our remote object will execute a JDBC call that queries the database and generates a **ResultSet** object. The **Employee** object's constructor receives this **ResultSet** object and populates its own instance variables with the current row in the result set. The **getString()** method contained within the **ResultSet** is used to extract the necessary column values.

Finally, the **getXXXX()** and **setXXXX()** access methods are used to retrieve and set the values of the **Employee**'s private instance variables respectively.

> *A sample Microsoft Access database,* Employee.mdb, *is provided with the source code. The examples that follow make use of this database through the JDBC-ODBC bridge, which is included with the Java Developer's Kit. To set up your system to use this database, you must create an ODBC data source name,* **empldir,** *to reference it. (Under Windows 95, you may do so using the 32-bit ODBC utility found within the Control Panel. If this utility is missing, you must install it from your Microsoft Access installation disk or CD.)*
> *If you wish to use the sample* Employee *database with another database system, a SQL script, called* empldir.sql, *has been provided with the source code. You may use this script to build and populate the database tables. Be sure to modify the JDBC portion of the remote object as necessary to reflect your particular database as we proceed.*

The RMI Server

The RMI Server consists of a registry table and a set of objects. The registry contains an index of all the objects on this host that have offered themselves to the RMI. Each of these objects is a server-side Java application running on the same host. These objects become the remote objects that will be accessed later on by RMI clients.

We'll explore the registry in more detail now, and then continue with the creation of the remote object.

The RMI Registry

The RMI Registry is actually a Java application running on the server. Its basic role is to act as a control point for communications that occur between the client and the server. Consequently, it performs the following functions:

> Registers the remote objects that may be accessed over the network. Through the registry, the remote object becomes available to the network

> Dispatches the remote object's stub and skeleton objects when requests are made from the client to the server

You must start the registry as a background process on your server. It uses a TCP socket as the transport mechanism between the client and the remote object. By default, the registry uses port 1099, but you may override this if you choose. The command for starting the registry is as follows:

```
rmiregistry [port]
```

If you are running Windows 95 or NT, you can start this as a background process as follows:

```
start /min rmiregistry
```

If you are running Solaris, you can start it similarly as follows:

```
rmiregistry &
```

FYI

Each of the commands listed above starts the registry on the default port. If you wish to run the registry on another port, you can do so by specifying it as the optional parameter on the command line. For example, to start the registry on port 8099, you would do the following: `rmiregistry 8099`. This command does not display any message on execution indicating that the registry has been started.

In order for the RMI registry and objects to perform, an active TCP/IP network connection must be available.

Creating a Remote Interface

The remote interface is an abstract object that defines the public methods that will be accessed through the RMI. Like all other interfaces, it does not contain any actual program logic, but only serves as the template for objects that implement it.

The remote interface will be used for two purposes in the RMI model:

▶ To define the public methods contained within the remote object

▶ To define the structure of the remote object once accessed by the RMI client

Let's create a remote interface for our employee directory application.

Try It Out—The Remote Interface

Type in the following code:

```
/* EmplDir
 * This is a remote interface to be used with the RMI application
 * for retrieval of employee information to be displayed as part
 * of a directory listing.
 */

import java.rmi.*;

public interface EmplDir extends Remote
{
  // Open employee directory
  public void openDirectory() throws RemoteException;

  // Close employee directory
  public void closeDirectory() throws RemoteException;
```

```
    // Search employee directory using criteria specified
    public void searchDirectory(String criteria) throws RemoteException;

    // Retrieve next employee's record found in the search
    public Employee getNextEmployee() throws RemoteException;
}
```

How It Works

First, we must tell our interface that it will use the **java.rmi** package. This is done because our **EmplDir** class is inherited from the **Remote** object contained within that package.

The interface contains four **public** methods:

Method	Description
openDirectory()	Establishes a JDBC connection through the remote object to the database containing our employee directory.
closeDirectory()	Closes the JDBC connection that was previously opened within the remote object.
searchDirectory()	Accepts a search string from the client and executes a query on the database.
getNextEmployee()	Retrieves the next employee record obtained from the most recent database search. An **Employee** object is returned if a record is available, or a **null** value if no more records are found.

Each of these methods must be declared to throw **RemoteException**, in case an error occurs within the RMI process.

Remote Exceptions

Remote exceptions are ones that are generated by the RMI system, as opposed to exceptions that are generated locally. They are usually generated because of an I/O error that occurs with a distributed object.

The **RemoteException** class is the superclass of all other exceptions that may be thrown by the RMI. Because of this hierarchy, the generic **RemoteException** class can be handled in the same way the **Exception** class is used for local exceptions. If you wish to handle specific remote exceptions, however, the following is a list of some of the more common ones you may encounter:

Exception	Description
AlreadyBoundException	The attempt to bind a remote object to the RMI cannot be made because another object was previously registered with the same name.
ConnectException	The RMI registry is not available on the specified host or port.

Exception	Description
`MalformedURLException`	The syntax used to reference the remote object's registry name (i.e. URL) is invalid.
`NotBoundException`	There is no entry for this remote object in the RMI registry on the specified host.
`RMISecurityException`	There is no active security manager in place for the RMI.
`SkeletonNotFoundException`	The remote object's skeleton object cannot be located within the server's **CLASSPATH**.
`StubNotFoundException`	The remote object's stub object cannot be located within the client's **CLASSPATH** or **CODEBASE**.
`UnknownHostException`	The host name specified for the RMI connection is invalid.

As we proceed further in our explanation of the RMI, we will see some of the conditions under which these exceptions may be thrown.

Creating a Remote Object

As stated earlier, the remote object is actually a server-side Java application that runs on the RMI host alongside the registry. It makes itself known to the RMI by registering, or binding, itself to the registry. This object is responsible for executing the actual logic that will be invoked by the RMI client through the stub and skeleton.

The remote object is created by implementing the remote interface, inserting program code and variables for the object. It is then registered with the RMI, and exceptions that arise are handled. Let's explore each of these steps separately.

Try It Out—Creating the Remote Object

1 Start by importing the **java.rmi** and **java.sql** packages in their entirety, along with the **java.rmi.server.UnicastRemoteObject** class. **UnicastRemoteObject** is the class that allows the remote object to function as a server on the RMI host (more of this anon).

Next we declare the class, implementing the remote interface **EmplDir**, and define three private variables that will be used for the database work in our remote object. Finally, we define the object's constructor, **EmplDirImpl()**, which throws **RemoteException**. It is a requirement of the RMI that the remote object's default constructor be defined, throwing this exception. (You may also add other constructors with different parameters, again throwing **RemoteException**. If you do so, you still need to define the default constructor for this object.)

```
/* EmplDirImpl
 * This class implements the remote interface, EmplDir, for use
 * as a remote object through the RMI. It executes on the RMI
 * server and performs database calls to access employee
 * information for display within directory listing.
 */

import java.rmi.*;
import java.rmi.server.UnicastRemoteObject;
import java.sql.*;

public class EmplDirImpl extends UnicastRemoteObject implements EmplDir
{
  private Connection con = null;
  private Statement stmt = null;
  private ResultSet rs = null;

  public EmplDirImpl() throws RemoteException { }
```

2 Earlier, we created the remote interface which declares the public methods contained within `EmplDirImpl`. To create the remote object, we now need to implement the methods of this interface. We'll start with the `openDirectory()` method:

```
public void openDirectory() throws RemoteException
{
  try
  {
    // Load the JDBC-ODBC bridge driver
    Class.forName ("sun.jdbc.odbc.JdbcOdbcDriver");

    // Connect to the database
    con = DriverManager.getConnection("jdbc:odbc:empldir", "", "");
  }
  catch (Exception ex)
  {
    ex.printStackTrace();
  }
}
```

3 Next we implement the `closeDirectory()` method.

```
public void closeDirectory() throws RemoteException
{
  // close all open database objects
  try
  {
    if (rs != null)
    {
      rs.close();
      rs = null;
```

```
      }
      if (stmt != null)
      {
        stmt.close();
        stmt = null;
      }
      if (con != null)
      {
        con.close();
        con = null;
      }
    }
    catch (SQLException sqle)
    {
      sqle.printStackTrace();
    }
  }
```

4 We can search through the employee directory using the specified criteria.

```
  public void searchDirectory(String criteria) throws RemoteException
  {
    String query;

    try
    {
      // Create the query statement
      query = "SELECT Last, First, Title, Department, Telephone
              ↳ FROM EMPLDIR WHERE " + criteria;

      // Open the query and execute it
      stmt = con.createStatement();
      rs = stmt.executeQuery(query);
    }
    catch (SQLException sqle)
    {
      sqle.printStackTrace();
    }
  }
```

5 We need a method to retrieve the next employee's record.

```
  public Employee getNextEmployee() throws RemoteException
  {
    try
    {
      // Get the next row in the result set and return it as an employee
object
      if (rs.next())
        return new Employee(rs);
```

```
      }
      catch (SQLException sqle)
      {
        sqle.printStackTrace();
      }

      // null means no more employee records
      return null;
    }
```

6 Finally, we have a **main()** method to start the object as a background process and bind it to the RMI registry. This is the 'bootstrap' that we alluded to earlier.

The bootstrap's purpose is to install the object's security manager and register the object with the RMI. We'll explain this in more detail under *Registering a Remote Object*.

```
public static void main(String[] args)
{
  System.out.println("Starting Employee Directory...");

  // Install the security manager
  System.setSecurityManager(new RMISecurityManager());

  try
  {
    // Instantiate the remote object and register it
    EmplDirImpl empldir = new EmplDirImpl ();
    Naming.rebind("empldir", empldir);
    System.out.println("Employee Directory is running.");
  }
  catch (Exception e)
  {
    System.out.println("EmplDirImpl.main: an exception occurred: "
                       + e.getMessage());
    e.printStackTrace();
  }
}
```

How It Works

Our remote object, **EmplDirImpl**, implements the remote interface, **EmplDir**, which we created earlier. Additionally, it extends the **UnicastRemoteObject** class contained within the **java.rmi.server** package. The **UnicastRemoteObject** class declares the object as a remote object and allows it to perform as an RMI server. Let's see how it accomplishes this.

The **java.rmi** and **java.rmi.server** packages contain the RMI classes that are used by our remote object. Within **java.rmi.server** are three classes that make up the remote object. Their class hierarchy is as follows:

```
java.lang.RemoteObject
        │
        └──── java.rmi.server.RemoteServer
                        │
                        └──── java.rmi.server.UnicastRemoteObject
```

RemoteObject is the parent class of all remote objects. Its purpose is to define the high-level behaviors for all remote objects.

RemoteServer contains the common methods required by all remote objects in order to be implemented as servers. One such method is **getClientHost()**, used to determine the hostname of the client that is accessing it.

UnicastRemoteObject implements the support necessary to marshal remote objects and method invocations through the transport layer.

After we define the object's constructor and **public** methods, we create the bootstrap process. In order for a remote object to be recognized through the RMI, it must bind itself with the registry on that host. The **main()** routine is defined for this purpose. The next section explains the bootstrap in more detail.

FYI The remote object can also define other methods that are not included in its interface. These methods remain local to the virtual machine on which the remote object executes and are not accessible to RMI clients.

Registering a Remote Object

Now that we have defined the remote object behavior through its methods and variables, we need to register it as a server process. This is done through a bootstrap routine, which is simply a procedure that executes the remote object as a server. In our example, we accomplish this through the **main()** method. Within **main()**, we perform a number of tasks:

▶ We load the **RMISecurityManager** class as our object's security manager. The RMI security manager prevents this object from accessing 'untrusted' remote objects, such as those loaded from another host. It also allows the object to interact with the RMI, such as binding itself to the registry. As stated earlier, the security manager must be installed before any RMI activity can occur. It is easiest to accomplish this by making it the first action in our **main()** method

▶ We instantiate the remote object, **EmplDirImpl**. This instance of the remote object serves as its reference within the RMI registry

▶ Finally, we register, or bind, the remote object to the RMI registry, using the **rebind()** method contained within the **Naming** class. This method accepts two parameters: the name to be associated with the remote object and the instance of the remote object

Exception Handling

During the registration process, it is possible for an exception to be thrown. Two of the more common ones that can occur at this point are:

Exception	Description
`MalformedURLException`	The name used to register the remote object is not a valid URL. Refer to the later section, *The RMI Naming Protocol*, for more details on the proper syntax for the RMI protocol.
`UnknownHostException`	The host on which the bind attempt is made cannot be resolved. To correct this error, insert the server's hostname into the system host table or make sure it is available through the Domain Name Server (DNS).

We should try to trap all exceptions within the remote object's **main()** method. We do so and display the error on the system console if one is caught.

Compiling a Remote Object

This completes the creation of our remote object. We can now compile it:

```
javac EmplDirImpl.java
```

There is a last step, however, in constructing a remote object; this to create its stub and skeleton classes. As stated earlier, the stub and skeleton allow the exchange of information between the client and server objects through object serialization. These classes are created using the **rmic** tool. We will invoke this command as follows:

```
rmic EmplDirImpl
```

When this command completes, you will see two new class files stored with the remote object: **EmplDirImpl_Stub.class** (the stub class) and **EmplDirImpl_Skel.class** (the skeleton class).

Prior to executing this command, our system's CLASSPATH environment must point to the `classes.zip` file and to the path where our remote object is stored. If you wish to override the default CLASSPATH, you may do so by specifying an alternative classpath on the `rmic` command line as follows:

```
rmic -classpath path objectname
```

Furthermore, if your object is defined as part of another package, then you must also specify the name of the package as part of the object name:

```
rmic -classpath path package.objectname
```

Suppose, for example, the JDK is stored in C:\JDK1.1.1 and your remote object is stored in C:\OBJS (assuming a Windows workstation). Suppose also your remote object is contained with a package called apps. The proper syntax for rmic is:

```
rmic -classpath C:\JDK1.1.1\lib\classes.zip;C:\OBJS apps.EmplDirImpl
```

Under Solaris, the command would look something like the following, depending on the actual location of your JDK and remote objects:

```
rmic -classpath /jdk1.1.1/lib/classes.zip:/objs apps.EmplDirImpl
```

Running the RMI Server

It's time to execute the remote object and start it as a server application. We do so by running it as a background process. (If you haven't already done so, you need to start the RMI registry before you proceed.)

Windows 95/NT   `start /min java EmplDirImpl`

Solaris   `java EmplDirImpl &`

When the application starts, it displays its progress through the **System.out.println()** calls contained within it:

```
Starting Employee Directory...
Employee Directory is running.
```

The remote object is now registered with the RMI and ready to accept calls from a client.

Again, make sure your remote object, as well as its stub and skeleton, can be located within the system's CLASSPATH environment. If necessary, you may override the default CLASSPATH through the -classpath switch of the java command. Additionally, if the remote object is defined as part of a package, its package name must be specified as well.

Viewing the Registry

Now that the remote object has successfully bound itself to the registry, you can create and execute the following program to view its entry on the registry. This program makes use of the **Registry** and **LocateRegistry** classes of the **java.rmi.registry** package to access the registry's table.

Try the following code:

```
import java.rmi.registry.*;

public class RMIList
{
  public static void main(String[] args) throws Exception
  {
    // access the registry for our current machine
    Registry reg = LocateRegistry.getRegistry();

    // retrieve all name entries for this registry
    String [] entries = reg.list();

    // display the list of name entries on the console
    for (int i = 0; i < entries.length; i++)
    {
      System.out.println(entries[i]);
    }
  }
}
```

How It Works

The **LocateRegistry** class, contained within the **java.rmi.registry** package, allows you to access the RMI registry on a given host. The **getRegistry()** method, when invoked, returns a **Registry** object for that particular host.

The generic syntax of **getRegistry()** is as follows:

```
getRegistry(String host, int port)
```

Either or both of the parameters are optional and, when omitted, will retrieve the registry for the current host on the default port. If you specify the host and/or port, you are able to locate registries running on other servers.

The **Registry** interface, also found within the **java.rmi.registry** package, contains several methods, such as **bind()** and **unbind()**, that allow you to store and remove remote objects within it. In our example above, we invoke the registry's **list()** method to obtain a listing of all objects that previously registered themselves with the registry on our current host.

The RMI Client

We have successfully installed an RMI server by creating and registering a remote object. We will now create a client that will issue calls to the remote object's methods and interact with it. Our first attempt at creating such a client will be in the form of a Java application. Let's begin creating it now. (The listing below contains the complete client application. We will explore the different aspects of it separately as we proceed.)

Try It Out—The RMI Client Application

We import the necessary RMI packages, **java.rmi** and **java.rmi.registry**.

```
/* Directory
 * This Java application acts as an RMI client, accessing a remote
 * object that retrieves employee information from a database. It
 * sends a search command to the remote object, calls its remote
 * methods to access the database, and displays the results on the
 * screen. This client illustrates a distributed application
 * using the RMI.
 */

import java.rmi.*;
import java.rmi.registry.*;

public class Directory
{
  public static void main(String[] args) throws RemoteException
  {
    Employee empl;
    EmplDir dir;
    String registryName;

    // Set the registry name for the remote object
    registryName = "empldir";

    try
    {
      // Install the RMI security manager
      System.setSecurityManager(new RMISecurityManager());

      // Obtain a reference to the remote object
      dir = (EmplDir)Naming.lookup(registryName);
    }
    catch (Exception e)
    {
      System.err.println("Cannot connect to RMI registry for "
                        + registryName);
      return;
    }

    dir.openDirectory();
    dir.searchDirectory("LAST LIKE 'G%'");
    while ((empl = dir.getNextEmployee()) != null)
    {
      System.out.println("Employee Name: " +
          empl.getFirstName() + " " + empl.getLastName());
      System.out.println("Title: " + empl.getTitle());
      System.out.println("Department: " + empl.getDepartment());
```

```
            System.out.println("Telephone: " + empl.getTelephone());
            System.out.println("====================");
        }
        dir.closeDirectory();
    }
}
```

Let's compile the client and run it. The output of the client is a listing of all employees whose last name begins with the letter G:

```
Employee Name:  Hyacinthe Greene
Title: Technician
Department: Operations
Telephone: (513) 555-6123
====================
Employee Name: Cathleen Georgeson
Title: Sales Manager
Department: Sales
Telephone: (513) 555-9015
====================
```

 The remote object's stub object must be available in the client's CLASSPATH.

How It Works

The **Directory** class is small enough for everything to be handled by the **main()** method, which we again declare as throwing **RemoteException**. Then we load the RMI security manager that governs the client application's ability to access the remote object.

Reading the RMI Registry

In order for the client to access the remote object, we need to obtain a reference to it through the registry. You may recall that the remote object bound itself to the RMI registry through the **rebind()** method of the **Naming** class. This time, we will call the **Naming** class' **lookup()** method to access the remote object from the client.

First, we specify the name that was used by the remote object when it registered itself, **empldir**. This name is then passed to the **lookup()** method to determine whether there is an entry of that name in the registry table on the current host. If there is a match, the **lookup()** method returns a reference to the remote object.

The RMI Naming Protocol

The complete registry name takes the form of a URL string as follows:

```
rmi://hostname:port/name
```

where:

`rmi`	The name of the protocol
`hostname`	The name of the RMI host
`port`	The port number of the RMI registry
`name`	The name of the object's registry entry

Using the full URL notation, our remote object's registry name is (assuming `rmihostname` is the name of the RMI host):

```
rmi://rmihostname:1099/empldir
```

Accessing a Remote Object

The `Naming.lookup()` call that we saw above returns a reference to the remote object's stub in the form of a `Remote` interface. You may recall that our own remote interface was also defined as an extension of `Remote`. To access the object's stub, we do so by retrieving the return value of `Naming.lookup()` and casting it to the name of our remote interface:

```
// Obtain a reference to the remote object
EmplDir dir = (EmplDir)Naming.lookup(registryName);
```

Invoking a Remote Method

At this point we hold a reference to the remote object through its stub. We can now call any of the remote object's methods, as if the object were local to the client.

In the sample code listed above, we use the `dir` object that was returned from our earlier registry lookup. Using this object, we invoke its `openDirectory()`, `searchDirectory()`, `getNextEmployee()` and `closeDirectory()` methods. Our example uses a search parameter, `"LAST LIKE 'G%'"`, to refine the search by retrieving only employees whose last name begins with the letter G. The results of the search are displayed on the system console within the `while` loop.

Exception Handling

Any of several exceptions may occur as the client attempts to access the remote object. A few of the more common ones are explained below:

Exception	Reason
`NotBoundException`	The name used within the registry lookup is not available on the RMI server. Make sure you are using the correct spelling and that the remote object has bound itself successfully with the RMI registry.
`MalformedURLException`	As we saw earlier, the URL used within the registry lookup is not valid.
`UnknownHostException`	As we saw earlier, the hostname specified in the RMI URL cannot be resolved.
`ConnectException`	The client cannot connect to the RMI registry. Make sure the registry is actively running on the RMI host and that the hostname in the registry lookup is spelled properly.

We can trap any or all of these exceptions using a standard **try-catch** block.

Using Remote Objects with Applet Clients

Apart from the obvious, applet clients differ from applications in two regards:

▶ When we created our application, we specified that the **RMISecurityManager** would be used to control the RMI security. With applets, its default security manager is sufficient for controlling the RMI security. Therefore, there is no need to explicitly load any other security manager

▶ When we perform a lookup on the RMI registry, we must specify the hostname of the RMI server through the naming protocol. Since the applet's security restricts access only to objects on the same host from which it was loaded, we will access the remote object by its name on the current host (as specified by its codebase):

```
String registryName = "rmi: //" + getCodeBase().getHost() + "/empldir";
```

Let's create our applet client. In our original specification, we had stated that we were going to allow three search options in our RMI system:

▶ Search by last name

▶ Search by title

▶ Search by department

Our applet will have an option that allows the user to select any of these search criteria and display the results within it. The following figure shows the applet's screen display:

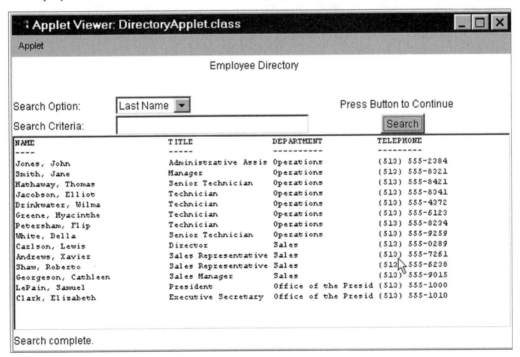

The Search Option listbox allows the choice of Last Name, Title or Department. The Search Criteria textbox is a free-form field to allow entry of the search text. Once the user selects a search option, enters the search criteria, and presses the Search button, the applet will call the remote object to perform the database search and display the results.

We won't explain the line-by-line details of how the applet screen is formatted, as this should all familiar to you from Chapter 11, but we give the full source code below:

Try It Out—The RMI Client Applet

1 We first declare the AWT objects and some useful constants:

```
/* DirectoryApplet
 * This Java applet acts as an RMI client, accessing a remote
 * object that retrieves employee information from a database.
 * It sends a search command to the remote object, calls its
 * remote methods to access the database, and displays the
 * results on the screen. This client illustrates a distributed
 * application using the RMI.
 */

import java.awt.*;
import java.awt.event.*;
import java.applet.Applet;
import java.rmi.*;
import java.rmi.registry.*;

public class DirectoryApplet extends Applet
implements ActionListener
{
  // Remote object name and directory objects
  String registryName;
  EmplDir dir;

  // Applet panels and layouts
  Panel north, center, south;
  GridBagLayout gbl;
  GridBagConstraints gbs;

  // Applet panel components
  Choice searchOption;
  TextField searchCriteria;
  Button searchButton;
  List searchResults;
  // GridBag constants
  private int WEST = GridBagConstraints.WEST;
  private int CENTER = GridBagConstraints.CENTER;
  private int RELATIVE = GridBagConstraints.RELATIVE;
  private int REMAINDER = GridBagConstraints.REMAINDER;
```

2 Now we initialize the applet:

```java
public void init()
{
  // Build the applet's panels
  buildPanels();
}
```

3 Next we need the code for when the applet starts.

```java
public void start()
{
  // Open the RMI connection
  try
  {
    // Build the URL for the remote object
    registryName = "rmi://" + getCodeBase().getHost() + "/empldir";
    showStatus("Opening connection: " + registryName);

    // Obtain a reference to the remote object
    dir = (EmplDir)Naming.lookup(registryName);
    showStatus("Remote connection ready.");
  }
  catch (Exception ex)
  {
    showStatus("Cannot connect to remote object: " + ex);
    return;
  }
}
```

4 Now we deal with the button press event:

```java
/* handle applet's action events */
public void actionPerformed(ActionEvent e)
{
  if (e.getActionCommand().equals("Search"))
  {
    try
    {
      performLookup();
    }
    catch (Exception ex)
    {
      showStatus("Error: " + ex);
    }
  }
}
```

5 The next method performs database lookup and processes search results:

```
private void performLookup() throws Exception
{
  String searchBy = "";          // Search option
  String query = "";             // SQL query string
  Employee empl;                 // Employee object

  // Clear the search result listbox
  searchResults.setVisible(false);
  clearSearchList();

  // Get search option
  switch (searchOption.getSelectedIndex())
  {
    case 0: searchBy = "LAST"; break;
    case 1: searchBy = "TITLE"; break;
    case 2: searchBy = "DEPARTMENT"; break;
  }

  // Build the complete query string
  query = searchBy + " LIKE '" + searchCriteria.getText() + "%'";
  showStatus("Executing search...");

  // Call the remote object's methods
  dir.openDirectory();
  dir.searchDirectory(query);
  while ((empl = dir.getNextEmployee()) != null)
  {
    addListItem(empl.getLastName() + ", " + empl.getFirstName(),
                empl.getTitle(), empl.getDepartment(),
                empl.getTelephone());
  }
  dir.closeDirectory();
  searchResults.setVisible(true);
  showStatus("Search complete.");
}
```

6 Following on from our `init()` method, we build and display the applet's panels in `buildPanels()`:

```
private void buildPanels()
{
  // Set the applet's layout
  setLayout(new BorderLayout());

  // Create GridBag layout and constraints
  gbl = new GridBagLayout();
  gbs = new GridBagConstraints();
```

```
      // Create the applet's panels
      north = new Panel();
      north.setLayout(gbl);
      add("North", north);

      center = new Panel();
      center.setLayout(new GridLayout());
      add("Center", center);

      // create applet's components
      searchOption = new Choice();
      searchOption.addItem("Last Name");
      searchOption.addItem("Title");
      searchOption.addItem("Department");
      searchOption.select(0);
      searchCriteria = new TextField(30);
      searchButton = new Button("Search");
      searchButton.addActionListener(this);
      searchResults = new List();
      clearSearchList();

      // Set the listbox to a fixed font
      searchResults.setFont(new Font("Courier", Font.PLAIN, 10));

      // Add components to the north panel
      addComponent(new Label("Employee Directory"), CENTER, REMAINDER);
      addComponent(new Label(), CENTER, REMAINDER);
      addComponent(new Label("Search Option:"), WEST, 1);
      addComponent(searchOption, WEST, 1);
      addComponent(new Label("Press Button to Continue"), CENTER, RELATIVE);
      addComponent(new Label(), CENTER, REMAINDER);
      addComponent(new Label("Search Criteria:"), WEST, 1);
      addComponent(searchCriteria, WEST, 1);
      addComponent(searchButton, CENTER, RELATIVE);
      addComponent(new Label(), CENTER, REMAINDER);

      // Add components to the center panel
      center.add(searchResults);

      // Validate and display the panels
      validate();
      setVisible(true);
   }
```

7 To add a `GridBagLayout` component to the north panel we use `addComponent()`:

```
private void addComponent(Component c, int anchor, int width)
{
   // Set GridBag constraint values
   gbs.fill = GridBagConstraints.NONE;
   gbs.weightx = 1.0;
   gbs.anchor = anchor;
```

```
        gbs.gridwidth = width;

        // Set component's constraints
        gbl.setConstraints (c, gbs);

        // Add component to the north panel
        north.add(c);
    }
```

8 The last three methods clear out the search result listbox, add a row to that listbox and pad a string with spaces to the specified length:

```
    private void clearSearchList()
    {
      searchResults.removeAll();
      addListItem("NAME", "TITLE", "DEPARTMENT", "TELEPHONE");
      addListItem("----", "-----", "----------", "---------");
    }

    private void addListItem(String col1, String col2,
                             String col3, String col4)
    {
      String listItem = padString(col1, 30) + " " +
                        padString(col2, 20) + " " +
                        padString(col3, 20) + " " +
                        padString(col4, 14);
      searchResults.add(listItem);
    }

    private String padString(String s, int size)
    {
      String fs = s;
      while (fs.length() < size)
        fs += " ";
      return fs.substring(0, size);
    }
  }
```

How It Works

Our applet, **DirectoryApplet**, uses its **init()** method to build the GUI panels. The connection to our remote object is made within the applet's **start()** method. Notice that the logic used to access the remote object from an applet is identical to that used within our application, except for the object's registry name and the use of the applet security manager:

We use the applet's **actionPerformed()** method to trap the Search button. When we press the Search button, we call **performLookup()**, which will perform the database lookup using RMI. If an exception occurs during the remote process, the **action()** method will trap it and display a message on the applet's status line. Our **performLookup()** method will accept the search parameters specified by the user on the applet's input screen, create a search condition (that is, query) using the SQL **LIKE** statement, and pass it to the remote object for execution.

As you can see, the calls to the remote object within the applet are very similar to those made by our client application earlier in this chapter. The only difference lies in the formatting of the information for display within the applet.

You can run this applet with the following HTML document to load it:

```
<HTML>
<HEAD>
<TITLE>Directory Applet</TITLE>
</HEAD>
<BODY>
<H1>Directory Applet</H1>
<APPLET CODE="DirectoryApplet.class" HEIGHT=400 WIDTH=600>
</APPLET>
</BODY>
</HTML>
```

If the name of our HTML document is **directory.html**, then we can use the **appletviewer** tool to execute it as follows:

```
appletviewer directory.html
```

The remote object's stub object must be available in the applet's CODEBASE. If you are loading the applet from a Web server, then you must store a copy of the remote object's stub file in the same location as the applet on the server.

This applet uses features contained within JDK 1.1 and requires a browser that supports this version of the JDK. The applet will not function properly with browsers that implement earlier releases of the JDK.

Distributed Computing using RMI

The sample application and applet in this chapter has so far illustrated the distributed computing architecture when using the RMI with two objects:

- RMI Client (application or applet)
- RMI Server (remote object)

As it is currently designed, however, the remote object can only support a single user on the network. To understand why, let's take another look at this diagram:

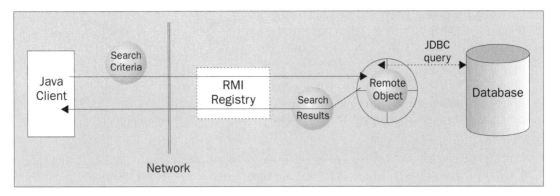

Remember that the remote object binds itself to the RMI registry. As it does so, it stores a single reference to itself within the registry table. Since there is only one reference to this remote object, all clients share this same reference and, as a result, the same internal variables.

Internally, the RMI contains built-in threaded support for client calls. Different virtual machines may implement threading differently, however. For example, calls to the remote object from the same client virtual machine may operate on a single thread or on separate threads, depending on the remote machine's implementation of threads. Calls from different client virtual machines, however, always operate on separate threads.

In order to create robust applications with the RMI for multiple users, we cannot rely upon its own built-in mechanisms. Instead, we must develop multi-user access within the application ourselves. We will do so through multithreading and database session management. The following section will step through this process.

Multithreading

One way we can manage multiple client calls to our remote object is by binding the object to the registry several times, each time with a different registry name. Using our **EmplDirImpl** object, we could accomplish this through some changes to the **main()** method as follows:

```
/* Main routine to start the object as a background process
 * and bind itself to the RMI registry
 */
public static void main(String[] args)
{
  System.out.println("Starting Employee Directory...");

  // Install the security manager
  System.setSecurityManager(new RMISecurityManager());
```

```
    for (int i = 0; i < 10; i++)
    {
      try
      {
        // Instantiate and register the remote object
        EmplDirImpl empldir = new EmplDirImpl ();
        Naming.rebind("empldir" + i, empldir);
        System.out.println("empldir" + i + " is running.");
      }
      catch (Exception e)
      {
        System.out.println("EmplDirImpl.main: " + e.getMessage());
        e.printStackTrace();
      }
    }
  }
```

This example shows how the **EmplDirImpl** object is instantiated ten times from within a loop. Each instance is bound sequentially to the registry using a unique name (**empldir1**, **empldir2**, **empldir3**, etc.). Up to ten clients can access these separate objects by connecting themselves to a different registry name. Of course, all this assumes that there is a predetermined one-to-one relationship between the client and server objects. In practice, however, this is not a good design and should never be considered.

A more flexible and generic approach is to activate threads within the remote object. Consider, for example, the technique shown in the following diagram:

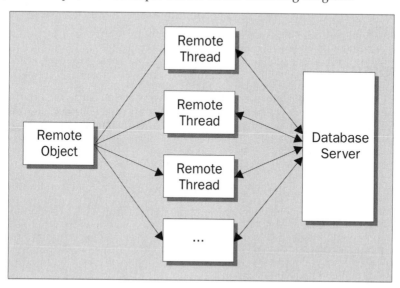

Every time a client attaches itself to the remote object, we generate a unique thread that is assigned to this client. With this approach, the thread contains the actual program logic that was formerly contained within the remote object, for example, connecting to a database. The remote object is simply responsible for managing the remote threads.

Going back to our Employee Directory application, the **EmplDir** interface object can be modified to support multiple threads as follows. Let's call our new interface **EmplDirMulti**:

Try It Out—A Multi-user Remote Interface

Make the following highlighted changes to the **EmplDir** interface:

```
/* EmplDirMulti
 * This interface is a remote interface to be used with the RMI
 * for retrieval of employee information to be displayed as part
 * of a directory listing.
 * This interface enables support of multiple users through
 * threads.
 */

import java.rmi.*;

public interface EmplDirMulti extends Remote
{
    // Open employee directory
    public int openDirectory() throws RemoteException;

    // Close employee directory
    public void closeDirectory(int id) throws RemoteException;

    // Search employee directory using criteria specified
    public void searchDirectory(int id, String criteria) throws
        RemoteException;

    // Retrieve next employee's record found in the search
    public Employee getNextEmployee(int id) throws RemoteException;
}
```

How It Works

When the RMI client calls **openDirectory()**, it will receive an integer value representing the session ID for the thread that will be used to identify it within the remote object. This ID is passed to all the other methods as an additional parameter.

Next, let's modify our remote object, **EmplDirImpl**, to manage the multiple threads. We'll call our new object **EmplDirThreadManager**:

Try It Out—A Multithreaded Remote Object

The following code implements the **EmplDirMulti** interface. It makes calls to **EmplDirThread** (the code which we'll see in a moment) to make the database connection we used earlier, so it can't be compiled until after **EmplDirThread** has been compiled.

949

```
/* EmplDirThreadManager
 * This class implements the remote interface, EmplDir, for use as
 * a remote object through the RMI. It executes on the RMI server
 * and performs database calls to access employee information for
 * display within directory listing.
 * This class enables support of multiple users.
 */

import java.rmi.*;
import java.rmi.server.UnicastRemoteObject;

public class EmplDirThreadManager extends UnicastRemoteObject implements
                                                            EmplDirMulti
{
  private final int MAXTHREADS = 10;
  private EmplDirThread threads[] = new EmplDirThread [MAXTHREADS];

  public EmplDirThreadManager() throws RemoteException
  {
  }

  // Open a directory on a new thread
  public int openDirectory() throws RemoteException
  {
    int id;

    // Synchronize this logic to prevent collisions
    synchronized (threads)
    {
      // loop through the thread table until an empty slot is found
      for (id = 0; id < MAXTHREADS; id++)
      {
        if (threads[id] == null)
          break;
      }

      // If no empty slots found, generate an error
      if (id >= MAXTHREADS)
      {
        return -1;
      }

      // Create a new thread and store it
      threads[id] = new EmplDirThread();
    }

    // Start the new thread
    threads[id].start();
```

```
    // Call the thread's openDirectory() method
    threads[id].openDirectory();

    // Return the thread identifier
    return id;
  }

  // Close employee directory
  public void closeDirectory(int id) throws RemoteException
  {
    // Call the thread's closeDirectory() method
    threads[id].closeDirectory();

    // Shut down the thread
    threads[id].stop();
    threads[id] = null;
  }

  // Search employee directory using criteria specified
  public void searchDirectory(int id, String criteria) throws
RemoteException
  {
    // Call the thread's searchDirectory() method
    threads[id].searchDirectory(criteria);
  }

  // Retrieve next employee's record found in the search
  public Employee getNextEmployee(int id) throws RemoteException
  {
    // Call the thread's getNextEmployee() method
    return threads[id].getNextEmployee();
  }

  // Main routine to start the object as a background process and
  // bind itself to the RMI registry
  public static void main(String[] args)
  {
    System.out.println("Starting Employee Directory...");

    // Install the security manager
    System.setSecurityManager(new RMISecurityManager());

    try
    {
      // Instantiate and register the remote object
      EmplDirThreadManager emplmdir = new EmplDirThreadManager ();
      Naming.rebind("emplmdir", emplmdir);
      System.out.println("Employee Directory (threaded) is running.");
    }
```

```
      catch (Exception e)
      {
        System.out.println("EmplDirThreadManager.main: an exception
                occurred: " + e.getMessage());
        e.printStackTrace();
      }
    }
  }
```

How It Works

In this modified remote object, we have removed all the code that uses the JDBC. The object's role now is strictly to manage the multiple users that may connect to it. Let's explore a few highlights of this object's code.

Firstly, note that we can keep track of up to ten threaded sessions, using an array. The object's **openDirectory()** method initiates a new thread using the **EmplDirThread** class (which we will look at next). This is done by looping through our **threads** array until a **null** slot is found. This array must be **synchronized** in order to prevent multiple people from looping through at the same time. When a new thread is created, it is stored in the **threads** array, and we call its **start()** and **openDirectory()** methods. Finally, we return the array index for this thread, representing the session ID for the client to access it in the future.

Each remaining method simply invokes the respective method contained within the remote thread, based on the session ID passed to it. The **closeDirectory()** method also stops the thread and removes it from the **threads** array.

Finally, the **main()** method bootstraps and binds our new thread manager object to the RMI registry, using the name **emplmdir** to distinguish it as a multi-user object, separate from the its single-user predecessor **empldir**.

The last step in creating a multithreaded remote object is to create the remote thread. This thread is a normal object that contains what remains of the original object. We'll call our remote thread **EmplDirThread**:

Try It Out—The Remote Thread

Now we recreate the database session code within a thread object:

```
/* EmplDirThread
 * This class is a threaded object that performs the database
 * calls to access employee information for display within a
 * directory listing.
 */

import java.sql.*;

public class EmplDirThread extends Thread
```

```
{
  private Connection con=null;
  private Statement  stmt=null;
  private ResultSet  rs=null;

  public void run()
  {
    try
    {
      while (true)
      {
        sleep(Long.MAX_VALUE);
      }
    }
    catch (InterruptedException ie) { }
  }

  // Open employee directory
  public void openDirectory()
  {
    try
    {
      // Load the JDBC-ODBC bridge driver
      Class.forName ("sun.jdbc.odbc.JdbcOdbcDriver");

      // Connect to the database
      con = DriverManager.getConnection("jdbc:odbc:empldir", "", "");
    }
    catch (Exception ex)
    {
      ex.printStackTrace();
    }
  }

  // Close employee directory
  public void closeDirectory()
  {
    // Close all open database objects
    try
    {
      if (rs != null)
      {
        rs.close();
        rs = null;
      }
      if (stmt != null)
      {
        stmt.close();
        stmt = null;
      }
      if (con != null)
```

```java
      {
        con.close();
        con = null;
      }
    }
    catch (SQLException sqle)
    {
      sqle.printStackTrace();
    }
  }

  // Search employee directory using criteria specified
  public void searchDirectory(String criteria)
  {
    String query;

    try
    {
      // Create a query statement
      query = "SELECT Last, First, Title, Department, Telephone
              ↳ FROM EMPLDIR WHERE " + criteria;

      // Open the query and execute it
      stmt = con.createStatement();
      rs = stmt.executeQuery(query);
    }
    catch (SQLException sqle)
    {
      sqle.printStackTrace();
    }
  }

  // Retrieve next employee's record found in the search
  public Employee getNextEmployee()
  {
    try
    {
      // Get the next row in the result set
      // and return it as an employee object
      if (rs.next())
        return new Employee(rs);
    }
    catch (SQLException sqle)
    {
      sqle.printStackTrace();
    }

    // Null means no more employee records
    return null;
  }
}
```

How It Works

The thread is identical to our original remote object, except there is no need to throw **RemoteException**. Since it is called from within the remote object, it neither instantiates itself nor registers itself with the RMI.

EmplDirThread is declared as a subclass of **Thread** and requires a **run()** method to provide any startup instructions. You will note that this method contains an infinite **while** loop that simply calls the thread's **sleep()** method. The purpose of this is to keep the thread actively running on the server in order for the remote object to call its methods. (Once the **run()** method completes, the thread terminates execution.) In larger-scale multithreaded applications, any special processing required by the thread can be inserted at this point as well.

Finally, to use our new remote object, we need to modify the RMI client. The new application, which we will call **DirectoryMulti**, will make use of the modified interface and methods:

Try It Out—The Modified Client Application

The necessary changes to the **Directory** class are shown highlighted:

```
/* DirectoryMulti (multi-user)
 * This Java application acts as an RMI client, accessing a remote
 * object that retrieves employee information from a database.
 * It sends a search command to the remote object, calls its
 * remote methods to access the database, and displays the results
 * on the screen. This client illustrates a distributed
 * application using the RMI.
 */

import java.rmi.*;
import java.rmi.registry.*;

public class DirectoryMulti
{
  public static void main(String[] args) throws RemoteException
  {
    Employee empl;
    EmplDirMulti dir;
    String registryName;
    int sessionId;

    // Set the registry name string for the remote object
    registryName = "emplmdir";

    try
    {
      // Install the RMI security manager
      System.setSecurityManager(new RMISecurityManager());
```

```
                    // Obtain a reference to the remote object
                 dir = (EmplDirMulti)Naming.lookup(registryName);
         }
         catch (Exception e)
         {
           System.err.println("Cannot connect to RMI registry for "
                               + registryName);
           System.out.println(e.toString());
           return;
         }

           sessionId = dir.openDirectory();
           dir.searchDirectory(sessionId, "LAST LIKE 'G%'");
           while ((empl = dir.getNextEmployee(sessionId)) != null)
           {
             System.out.println("Employee Name: " +
               empl.getFirstName() + " " + empl.getLastName());
             System.out.println("Title: " + empl.getTitle());
             System.out.println("Department: " + empl.getDepartment());
             System.out.println("Telephone: " + empl.getTelephone());
             System.out.println("====================");
       }
           dir.closeDirectory(sessionId);
       }
     }
```

Note that the **dir** object obtains a reference to the newly defined **EmplDirMulti** interface. The integer ID returned from the **openDirectory()** method is used as a session ID for subsequent calls to the remote object.

The changes to the applet are similar to those listed above for the application, so we will not illustrate them here.

Run it!

Now that all the elements have been created (or suitably altered), let's compile our multithreaded objects and generate the remote object stub and skeleton:

```
javac EmplDirThreadManager.java
rmic EmplDirThreadManager
javac DirectoryMulti.java
```

If the registry is not still running from our earlier exercise, then you need to start it now:

Windows 95	**start /min rmiregistry**
Solaris	**rmiregistry &**

Now start the remote object:

Windows 95	**start /min java EmplDirThreadManager**
Solaris	**java EmplDirThreadManager &**

If you are still running the single-user EmplDirImpl **object from earlier in the chapter, you may run the** RMIList **program again to see both remote objects running on the server.**

Finally, run the client application:

```
java DirectoryMulti
```

The output of this command is the same as that which we saw with the single-user **Directory** class, a listing of all employees whose last name begins with the letter G:

```
Employee Name:  Hyacinthe Greene
Title: Technician
Department: Operations
Telephone: (513) 555-6123
====================
Employee Name: Cathleen Georgeson
Title: Sales Manager
Department: Sales
Telephone: (513) 555-9015
====================
```

Our multi-threaded remote object allows you to manage up to ten concurrent client sessions. You can make this even more flexible by increasing the size of the array to a larger number, or by using **Vector** or **Hashtable** objects to manage a dynamic number of threads.

This application is too small for us to truly experience the merits of multi-user access. The rewards are great, however, once you begin building more advanced objects requiring continuous database access and/or complex processing.

Database Connectivity

The RMI architecture is a persistent one, meaning the network session between the client and remote objects remains open as long as both continue to be active. This is different from some other Internet-based protocols, such as HTTP and CGI, which are stateless. When database connections are managed in a persistent environment like the RMI, there are certain considerations you need to make when designing your applications.

First of all, it is preferable to perform the database calls within the server process. This allows the creation of a 'thin' client, where database drivers only need to be installed on the server and not on each client. Our examples so far in this chapter have illustrated this technique by encapsulating the JDBC calls within the remote object.

Next, in managing a multi-user environment, you need to decide how best to manage the database sessions. Ask yourself the following questions:

▶ Do you want everyone to use a different user ID and password, or to share a common one?

> If you wish to assign a unique ID and password to your users, then you need to build a logon screen requesting this information from the user through the client object. The ID and password are then passed along to the remote object for signing on to the database.
>
> If you use a common ID that will be shared by all users, you can then program the ID and password directly in the remote object and avoid the need for a logon screen.

▶ Do you wish to open the database once at the start of the client process and close it at the end? Or, would you rather open and close the database only when you need to access it?

> If you open the database at the start and close it at the end of the process, then your RMI application will preserve the connection and reduce the amount of time it takes to make subsequent database calls. Be aware, however, that this means extra overhead in your database server and can cause it to experience performance problems with large numbers of concurrent connections.
>
> If, on the other hand, you open and close the database only when you need to access it, you minimize the overhead required by your database server, thus reducing the load on it. The tradeoff, however, is a slight degradation of performance with every access because of the extra steps involved.

▶ Do you want to control the number of open sessions made to your remote object? This may be important if you have to limit the number of open database connections you may have at any one time.

> You can limit the number of open sessions as we did in our multithreaded object through an array of a fixed size (refer to the **threads** array in our **EmplDirThreadManager** object). Because we limited the number of threads in the remote object, we implicitly limited the number of concurrent connections we could make to the database.
>
> Another approach is to open a fixed number of database sessions and store the JDBC **Connection** objects in an array. This technique, often referred to as a *session pool*, allows you to share a limited number of database connections across a large number of clients. By managing the session pool, you can add logic into your program to 'poll' the pool until a session opens up and assign it to the client for the duration of a single query or transaction.
>
> If you don't wish to limit the number of client connections within your remote object, you can store the threads within a **Vector** or **Hashtable** object, dynamically adding and removing them as clients open and close the database.

How do you want to handle database errors?

> Our examples so far have ignored the **SQLException** errors that can possibly be thrown by the JDBC calls. In practice, you should decide how to handle these exceptions and include the necessary error handling logic in your object.

These are just a few issues to get you thinking about how to architect your distributed application. Although they are not necessarily unique to the RMI, it is important to consider them when you're building your own RMI-based application.

Distributed Garbage Collection

There is one final package that we have not yet explored: **java.rmi.dgc**. This package defines the interfaces and classes that are used to manage garbage collection for the RMI. We will briefly cover some of the highlights of this package.

When a client first issues a call to a remote object, it receives a reference to its interface through the registry. During this process, the RMI environment keeps a record of all clients that have active references to the objects. It does this through the client's unique Virtual Machine Identifier (VMID). The **VMID** class is used to store the client's particular ID.

Next, as the RMI server dispatches the remote object's stub to the client, it issues a 'lease' to the remote object. In other words, the client is granted access to the object for a period of time that is determined by the server. The **Lease** class represents this lease and contains the client's VMID and lease duration.

The **DGC** interface is an abstraction that defines the methods that will be used by the server to manage the garbage collection tasks of the RMI. When it is implemented, it keeps track of all active leases to remote objects through its internal algorithms. The **DGC** interface contains two methods: **dirty()** and **clean()**. A 'dirty' call is made when the client first unmarshals the remote stub through the registry. A 'clean' call is made when the client no longer has an active lease on the remote object.

When no more clients have an active reference to the remote object, the RMI refers to the object using a 'weak' reference. This allows the Java virtual machine to process it through its local garbage collector provided there are no more local references to the object.

There is no need to concern yourself with the garbage collection of remote objects. There is no special coding required in your client and remote objects to manage these activities. The RMI runtime automatically does this for you, so you simply need to be aware that it exists.

RMI vs. Other Distributed Computing Techniques

We've just shown how RMI can be used to build a distributed computing environment, written purely in Java. There are several other distributed computing environments available as well. In this section we will explore a few of them, comparing and contrasting them to the RMI.

CGI

The Common Gateway Interface (CGI) is a standard interface that allows Web developers to execute programs on an HTTP server. It is a crude form of client-server computing whereby an HTTP client invokes a program running on the server (often passing it some data), and the program sends some results back to the client for display on a browser.

Java applications can be written to act as CGI programs running on the server. CGI programs operate in a stateless mode—that is, no persistent connection is maintained between the client and server program. Every time the CGI program is invoked, its runtime environment (memory, system variables, input/output streams etc.) is re-established, the program executes and sends information back to the client, and the process shuts down. The recurring startup and shutdown activities generate extra overhead in the server's load and cause some delay in performance.

The CGI is effective in scenarios where the client doesn't have the Java Virtual Machine available to it. By running the Java applications on the server, the client can communicate with it through most Web browsers using HTML.

In contrast to CGI, however, RMI operates in a persistent mode. In other words the network session between the client and remote objects remains active until the connection is closed by the client or by the server. With RMI, the TCP stream is automatically closed by the garbage collection process when the remote object is no longer referenced by the client.

Because of its persistence, RMI is more effective than CGI in cases where the client is running within the Java virtual machine. The extra overhead associated with CGI is eliminated, and performance is improved.

JDBC

Earlier in the chapter, we looked a scenario where JDBC calls were managed directly by the Java client. We saw that this requires that the JDBC drivers be accessible to the client.

Some JDBC drivers require direct interaction with native database drivers, such as Microsoft's ODBC or Oracle's SQL*Net. The security contained within most commercial browsers prohibit the execution of native code by Java applets. In this case, a security violation will be thrown when the attempt is made to connect to the database.

Other JDBC drivers remove the native calls from the client by introducing an application server. The application server operates as a form of middleware, performing all the database interaction and session management on the server. The Java client has no direct contact with the database or its drivers as a result. This middleware is usually proprietary in nature.

Incorporating JDBC calls directly within the Java client may be useful in small-scale applications that are not widely distributed. With large-scale applications, it would be extremely difficult to maintain the up-to-date database drivers on every client. Additionally, if either the database engine or middleware (if used) were replaced by another product, every client application that accessed it would require modification.

Finally, the JDBC client is responsible for managing the database session and processing the information. In some cases, the network may be burdened with additional traffic as the client repeatedly communicates with the database.

RMI allows you to partition the data access and workload apart from the client by encapsulating the JDBC code within a remote object. (This was the technique we used in our earlier examples.) By following this approach, you eliminate the added maintenance of client-side drivers. You are also able to reduce network utilization by placing the RMI server physically closer to the database server on the network.

Sockets

When we explored the RMI architecture, we learned that the exchange of information between the client and server is performed through TCP sockets. That begs the question: why don't we just implement Java networking using the `Socket` class?

Architecturally, the RMI process operates in the same way as one written with `Socket` objects. The client and server objects communicate with each other through a TCP stream. Both environments support persistent network connections between the client and server.

The exchange of information between the client and server objects is performed through object serialization. When you use sockets, you must create the program logic to marshal and unmarshal the objects that are serialized. With the RMI, this activity is managed automatically through the remote object's stub and skeleton.

Generally speaking, objects that make direct use of sockets will perform faster than those that use the RMI API. They do not require interaction with the registry, security manager and transport mechanism.

The RMI is a higher-level architecture than sockets. Although the two perform similar functions, the RMI allows you to concentrate on value-added program logic and not have to deal with network or object transports. The tradeoff is with the added processing required by the RMI to manage these things for you. As machines continue to get faster, however, this becomes less of an issue.

IDL

Recall from our earlier discussion that the first step in building a remote object is to create its remote interface. The interface defines the public methods contained within the remote object so that it may be referenced by the client.

The IDL, or Interface Definition Language, is a standard defined by the Object Management Group for defining object interfaces. Included within the Common Object Request Broker Architecture (CORBA), it is intended to establish the object's interface definition regardless of the programming language and environment within which it is implemented. For example, a C++ object can interact with a Java object using the IDL.

The IDL operates in a model that is similar to the RMI. It makes use of stubs and skeletons to marshal parameters between objects. Unlike the RMI, it is able to operate within a heterogeneous environment whereby not all objects are written or implemented in the same language or operating environment.

The RMI is useful in brokering object requests when the objects are written purely in Java. The IDL is advantageous when you need to interact with objects written in other languages. (At the time of writing, development of the Java IDL package by Sun Microsystems has not been completed. Once it is finalized, it will be included within Java's core API.)

Conclusion

Although there are many alternatives for building distributed applications, the RMI shows its strengths in several areas. It is easy to use and, because it is written in Java, is completely portable. It facilitates application partitioning by allowing you to communicate across virtual machines. Longer term, you can reduce your application development cycle by building objects that are reusable and accessible by many clients.

Summary

In this chapter you have learned what Remote Method Invocation is and how you can use it to create distributed applications written completely in Java. Hopefully, this will have convinced you to seriously consider RMI as a practical approach to Java development and distributed object computing.

The important concepts we explored in this chapter are:

> ▶ The RMI architecture allows an applet or application to call methods contained within an object running on a remote host

> ▶ The RMI registry is an application that works as the 'gateway' between the remote object and the RMI client

> ▶ A security manager must be present within the architecture to govern the access attempts made by the client to the remote object. RMI applications use the **RMISecurityManager** class as their security manager, and applets use their own built-in security manager

▶ Stub and skeleton objects perform the exchange of information between the client and remote objects using TCP sockets and object serialization

▶ Objects which are passed between the client and remote objects must implement the **Serializable** interface

▶ The **Remote** interface is used to define the structure of the remote object

▶ The **UnicastRemoteObject** class is used to create the remote object as an RMI server process. This remote object *binds* itself to the RMI registry through the **Naming** class in order to be seen and accessed by RMI clients

▶ Several **Exception** classes may be thrown by the RMI process. These exceptions should be caught by the client and remote objects in order to control the activity of your program if an error is generated

▶ RMI clients access the remote object by obtaining a reference to it through the RMI registry using the **Naming** class. This reference is performed through the remote object's stub

▶ Multi-user support can be enabled through the use of threads. Since threads are not serializable, they must be implemented and managed within the remote object and not the RMI client

▶ Session management is effective in controlling database connectivity for multi-user support. We saw several ways in which database sessions can be managed and the pros and cons of each

▶ We looked quickly at the RMI's distributed garbage collection package and learned about the **DGC** interface and the **VMID** and **Lease** classes. Garbage collection is managed automatically by the RMI runtime environment

▶ We saw how RMI applications compare to other distributed environments, such as CGI, Sockets and IDL. It has many advantages over the other options and offers many benefits

Exercises

1 Write a client program as an application that will accept a string, send it to a remote object, and return it in reverse order. Use the RMI to build this.

2 Modify this client program to work as an applet.

3 Modify the **EmplDirThreadManager** object to store the threads in a **Hashtable** instead of an array. Modify the **DirectoryMulti** class to utilize this change. (Hint: use the **Thread.toString()** method as the unique key for the thread.)

4 Modify the **DirectoryApplet** object to work with the new **EmplDirThreadManager** class that you created in Exercise 3.

Setting Up

In this appendix we'll briefly summarize the use of the main JDK 1.1 tools you'll need in this book, and give you some tips for setting up the source code that accompanies it.

The JDK

The book is based on Javasoft's Java Development Kit version 1.1 (and subsequent releases). At the time of writing, the JDK 1.1.1 is available from **http://java.sun.com** for the following platforms:

- Windows 95 and NT
- Solaris 2.4, 2.5 for SPARC
- Solaris 2.5 for x86

with a MacOS port pending. Ports exist for a large number of other platforms. They are encouraged, but not officially supported, by JavaSoft. For more information take a look at the following URLs:

- **http://www.javasoft.com/products/jdk/jdk-ports.html**—JavaSoft links to porting projects
- **http://www.ibm.com/Java/**—IBM's contribution
- **http://www.blackdown.org/java-linux.html**—Linux Port

All these development kits will vary subtly, but should be easy to install. There are two key things to remember:

- The JDK tools (in the **bin** directory) should be available to the command line, using a **PATH** variable in your environment
- The JDK tools reference the Java class library when they're in use, using the **CLASSPATH** environment variable to reference the **lib/classes.zip** file and any other classes you're using

It's also customary to include the current directory `'.'` in your **CLASSPATH** so that you can compile and run code from within the directory.

When you're using packages you need only reference the top-level directory, whose subdirectories correspond to the package name. For example, with the package **wrox.Sketcher**, we could create a **classes** directory underneath the Java folder, reference the **classes** directory in the **CLASSPATH**, and then put the Sketcher files in the folder **/classes/wrox/Sketcher**.

Once the JDK is set up, you can use any of its tools. We will look at the use of some more tools in Appendix B, but for now, the three crucial ones you need to know are:

▶ **javac**—Compiles Java source code, generating a **class** file of Java bytecodes ready for the Java virtual machine to run.

▶ **java**—Runs Java applications in the platform's implementation of the Java virtual machine.

▶ **appletviewer**—Reads HTML files and executes the applet classes embedded within them. This is currently pretty much the only way to run JDK 1.1 compiled applets (apart from the HotJava browser).

The syntax for compiling Java classes is:

```
javac ClassName.java
javac Class1.java Class2.java
javac *.java
```

Note that the **.java** extension must be included, and **ClassName** must match the name of the public class defined within the source code. Other non-public classes can be defined within the same source code file, so long as they aren't referenced from other source files, but each public file must be stored in a separate source file.

The Java compiler will attempt to resolve all the links (to other classes) referenced in your code (hence the need for a **CLASSPATH** variable). If it can't find the **.class** files, but finds the correct **.java** files it will compile those instead. And if the source file is newer than the class file, it will recompile the source code.

java creates an instance of the Java Virtual Machine and runs the specified class file within it. It has the syntax:

```
java ClassName
```

You shouldn't type any file extension here, just the class name.

The **java** command complains if the class file doesn't contain a **public static void main()** method at which it can start execution, and from which it can instantiate objects of the classes referenced in the code.

appletviewer has the syntax:

```
appletviewer ClassName.html
```

where the **.html** file contains an applet tag that calls the class file. The **APPLET** tag has the following form:

```
<APPLET CODE="ClassName.class" WIDTH=300 HEIGHT=300> </APPLET>
```

The applet, a stripped down web-based Java program, derived from the **Applet** class, starts execution with an **init()** method. Its bytecodes can be downloaded from the web server and executed locally in a virtual machine within a browser. The applet's interaction with the system is severely constrained to provide security for the environment in which it is executing—it cannot access system properties or the local hard drive on the client machine, and cannot maintain a network connection with anything apart from its host server machine. The introduction of trusted applets in JDK 1.1 is discussed in Appendix B.

The Book Source Code

The book's source code is available from:

```
http://www.wrox.com
http://www.wrox.co.uk
```

as a JAR file (standing for Java ARchive). To extract the contents of the file:

```
jar xvf BegJava.jar
```

To use the **jar** tool more fully, take a look at Appendix B.

The code is divided into chapters and sub-divided into further directories that reflect the progression in program development within the chapter. Only the Java source files with any necessary supporting files (for example, html documents and sample databases) are included.

The networking chapter assumes that your computer has TCP/IP enabled and an active connection to the Internet, or at least to a LAN Ethernet. We thought this a fair assumption as Java is a web-based language and environment. Of course you can use Java to develop full-featured local applications, but the main reason for using Java, the reason that brushes the issue of execution speed aside, is that Java allows diverse computers to communicate very easily. In that vein, some of the sample code requires a running web server to test applets out. I used the JavaSoft web server, but any web server will do just fine.

Setting up the Sample Databases

In Chapters 17, 18 and 19, we use sample databases to illustrate the JDBC and RMI packages. The examples are, for the most part, shown using Access databases connected to the Java code with the JDBC-ODBC bridge which comes as part of the JDK.

Where some of the JDBC functionality is not available in Access, we've looked to mSQL, a widespread database for Unix platforms. You can get mSQL, subject to a license agreement from **http://hughes.com.au** and the JDBC driver from **http://www.imaginary.com/Java/**

JDBC is intended to facilitate the connection of Java programs to many different kinds of databases, provided there is a suitable driver implementation available. You can find out whether such a driver exists by looking at **http://splash.javasoft.com/jdbc/jdbc.drivers.html**

Because of the variety of possible connections, the whole issue of covering database access becomes a little fraught. The source code of the book provides a Java tool to construct the sample tables for the database. Called **build_tables**, it uses a text file of SQL commands to communicate with the database in question (via the JDBC driver) to create the database. Versions of the text file used as input to **build_tables** are provided for Access and mSQL, and these should be easily configurable to suit other databases.

Distributing Java Classes

Once upon a time, distributing a completed program was as easy as slapping a label on a floppy disk and mailing it off. It was too good to last. The Internet has thrust today's developers into a worldwide market, should they desire it. They need to anticipate, so far as is possible, the environments in which their products will be asked to run, and then provide for their users' needs. Thankfully, help is at hand!

The Java Development Kit comes with a number of tools to make distributing your classes easier:

> **jar**—Creating, accessing and distributing Java Archives (JAR files)

> **javakey**—Dealing with issues of security and authentication

> **Locale** and **ResourceBundle** classes—Help with internationalization

> **javadoc**—Documenting your code

Using Java and these tools, you can address these considerations, conform to accepted standards, be sympathetic to users and produce polished applications. Applications that ignore such questions also ignore a significant chunk of their target audience and condemn themselves to perceptions of mediocrity.

JAR Files

Platform-dependent executables are often distributed using one of a variety of commercial compression algorithms such as ZIP, LHA or ARJ. Not only do they make more efficient use of space, but they also combine multiple files into an archive. This is more convenient, both for the developer and for the end-user, than keeping track of many image, sound and data files and runnable programs.

With the introduction of the Java Archive, or JAR, specification, a platform independent archive format has been created for Java programs. JAR files have all the features of the previously mentioned formats, such as recursing subdirectories and sender authentication, but they are intended for deploying Java code.

Compressing Java classes and their support files (sounds and images) keeps the download time down. You also need only one network connection to download the JAR file containing *n* files. This is especially useful as operating systems have limits on the number of simultaneous network connections, and downloading an applet with lots of images can take some time. It also reduces the network bandwidth necessary for Java web pages and the load on the HTTP server.

The JAR File Format

The JAR specification is based heavily on the well-known ZIP format, making only minor modifications to its parent algorithm. In fact, WinZip 6.3 can read the contents of a JAR, even reporting relative paths and file sizes; the only thing it can't do is extract them!

Until someone develops a graphical JAR utility, programmers can rely on the command-line tool provided with each release of JDK 1.1, named, appropriately enough, **jar**. Not to worry, though—a few commands are enough to take care of everyday tasks like adding to and extracting from archives.

> *Interestingly enough, the DOS version of PKZIP 2.04g handles JARs perfectly, except for the matter of long file names. Because of this, it isn't a viable utility for Java development—but it does reassure programmers that the JAR specification doesn't depart radically from the tried-and-true ZIP standard.*

Using the jar Utility

The basic syntax for using the **jar** utility is:

```
jar <option string> [output JAR] [manifest file] [input files]
```

The option string is used to specify the action performed by **jar**—the same utility handles creating archives and extracting files. Of these options, one of **c**, **t** or **x** is required at all times, which is why the option string is shown enclosed in sharp brackets. Various combinations of other options then affect what those three do. The table below summarizes the basic commands recognized by **jar**:

Option	Description
c	Creates a new JAR file.
f	Indicates that the file to be processed comes from the command line.
m	Indicates that the user will supply a manifest file for the JAR.
M	Tells **jar** not to generate a manifest file for the archive.
t	Lists the table of contents of the specified JAR.
v	Selects verbose output.
x	Extracts files from an existing JAR.
0 (zero)	Stores, but doesn't compress, files.

For example, the following command lists all of the files contained in `fakejar.jar`:

```
jar tf fakejar.jar
```

Some of these options are a little non-intuitive in their application, and they deserve further explanation.

Creating a JAR, c

Creating a JAR is as easy as specifying the `jar` utility's `c` flag. If no other options or files are specified, `jar` will create an empty archive and output it to the standard output (usually the screen). If you want to do anything else with it, you had better investigate the other options.

> *Recursing subdirectories is easy with `jar`; if you pass it the name of a directory, all its contents and its subdirectories are automatically included in the archive.*

Specifying Files, f

For some reason, you have to tell `jar` that you're sending it files, or it will neither create nor extract archives correctly. The `f` option indicates that all parameters beyond the option string are filenames. When making a new archive, `jar` will look for the output file as well as the input files on the command line if you invoke this option. When extracting or viewing existing JARs, it will likewise get the filename from the parameter list.

You will normally always want to use this option.

Selecting a Manifest File, m

Manifest files describe the contents of a JAR, as well as its authentication information. They will be discussed in more detail a little later on, but for now all you need to know is that `jar` produces a default manifest if you don't send it one yourself. Should you wish to override this behavior, the **m** option tells it to look for a manifest as the next parameter after the jar file.

Preventing Generation of a Manifest, M

This option prevents `jar` from generating a manifest file. However, it's always best to include a manifest with any JAR you distribute.

Displaying the Contents, t

If you want to see what's in a JAR without extracting it, use the **t** option. This lists the JAR file's table of contents to the screen.

Selecting Verbose Output, v

Normally, `jar`'s output is limited to filenames only. This option tells it to include a little more, such as file sizes and timestamps.

Extracting files, x

Extraction can behave in two ways. The **x** option alone will cause all files to be extracted. If you name a group of files along with it, only they will be produced (assuming they are contained within the archive, of course). The directory structure of the archive is automatically preserved. In fact, there's no way to get just a file without its full path.

As with creation, **jar** assumes its default input to be the standard input; to make it look at the command line, combine this with the **f** option.

Bypassing ZIP Compression, 0

If you want to use a JAR file in your **CLASSPATH**, you should use this option, which concatenates several files into one, but doesn't apply ZIP compression.

Manifest Files Revisited

As mentioned before, manifest files help **jar** track the contents of an archive. They also contain information about who signed a security-sensitive archive and are instrumental in detecting tampering in such cases.

The JAR specification says that manifests should always be named **MANIFEST.MF**, and should reside in a subdirectory of the archive's root directory named **META-INF**. However, **jar** takes care of these technical details for you. Should you wish to create your own manifest for some reason, it handles the renaming and places it in the correct location. You only have to worry that your manifest follows the right format.

An average manifest consists of three items, in text format. The first line gives the manifest file format version. At this time, there's only one possible value for this, because there have been no modifications to the manifest specification. Therefore, the first line of a manifest should always be:

```
Manifest-Version: 1.0
```

The second line is optional; it allows you to specify the manifest format version required (and therefore, the version of jar that should be used). It reads:

```
Required-Version: 1.0
```

This allows for backward compatibility, or lack thereof. At present the default manifests generated by **jar** don't contain this line, since there's no backward compatibility in a first version.

The final item gives information about each file contained in the archive. Most of this is incomprehensible to the casual reader; it relates to compression and authentication, and it is dealt with entirely behind the scenes. A typical file description looks like this:

```
Name: relative_path/filename
Digest-Algorithms: MD5 SHA
```

```
MD5-Digest: <24 characters>
SHA-Digest: <28 characters>
```

The **Name** field is obvious; it specifies the location of each file relative to the root of the archive. The other fields are best left alone; their inner workings serve no purpose here. **Digest-Algorithms** remains the same for all **jar**-generated manifests, and the final two lines contain gibberish incomprehensible to humans.

In most cases, you will simply let **jar** generate manifests for you. However, knowing how to read manifests can give you information about an archive. There's much more to the manifest format than there's room to describe here; the most important extensions have to do with the security options, which will be described in the next section.

Try It Out—Putting jar to Use

1 Now that we understand the theory behind **jar**, we'll give it a try in real life. To do this, let's produce a few simple files. The first simply prints a line of text on the screen. Here's its listing:

```
public class Jardemo
{
  public static void main(String[] args)
  {
    System.out.println("I'm ready to be zipped up!");
  }
}
```

Compile this code and put both **Jardemo** files in a directory of their own.

2 Now let's just create a simple archive called **jardemo.jar**. We can do this with the following line. The resulting output is quite descriptive.

```
jar cvf jardemo.jar *
adding: Jardemo.class (in=480) (out=333) (deflated 30%)
adding: Jardemo.java (in=135) (out=118) (deflated 12%)
```

*Alternatively we could list the individual files, but using wildcards is more efficient. As a rule of thumb, any use of wildcards that works with directory listings will also work with **jar**. Notice too that verbose output gives you all sorts of information about the compression ratio and file sizes. With these you can verify that every file you wanted in the archive did end up there.*

3 To view the contents of the archive you just created, use the following command, which provides basic information on each of the files contained within the archive:

```
jar tf jardemo.jar
META-INF/MANIFEST.MF
Jardemo.class
Jardemo.java
```

975

4 If you want to know a little more about them, use the verbose option.

```
jar tvf jardemo.jar
   288 Tue Apr 15 16:28:04 GMT+01:00 1997 META-INF/MANIFEST.MF
   480 Tue Apr 15 16:25:02 GMT+01:00 1997 Jardemo.class
   135 Tue Apr 15 16:24:36 GMT+01:00 1997 Jardemo.java
```

5 Now, let's extract all of the files from the archive, to verify that they come out the same way they went in.

```
jar xvf jardemo.jar
 extracted: META-INF\MANIFEST.MF
 extracted: Jardemo.class
 extracted: Jardemo.java
```

6 `jar` automatically created a subdirectory called **META-INF** to preserve the file structure of the archive. If you change to this directory, you can view the manifest file that it generated for your classes. It will be something like:

```
Manifest-Version: 1.0

Name: Jardemo.class
Digest-Algorithms: SHA MD5
SHA-Digest: ftpSeUfwKPv9Y5gDkSbNfICHZ/o=
MD5-Digest: MUmja2m6W3tj5u0+ahEmaw==

Name: Jardemo.java
Digest-Algorithms: SHA MD5
SHA-Digest: TB0T1oqgpaervWBoWsS2GG61xLI=
MD5-Digest: IvBfDl3Bq/HqN8WtXt7xUA==
```

JARs and Applets

JARs come in handy, not only for physical-medium distribution, but also for Internet delivery. For this reason, in the JDK 1.1 there's an extra parameter in the **APPLET** HTML tag.

To refresh your memory, the traditional **APPLET** tag contained four parameters:

```
<APPLET CODE=AnyClass.class CODEBASE=MyPrograms/ WIDTH=100 HEIGHT=100>
```

All but **CODEBASE** were mandatory, and remain so. In addition, if the class specified in the code parameter, or any resource accessed by it, resides in a JAR, you should use the **ARCHIVE** parameter to indicate this. For example:

```
<APPLET CODE=AnyClass.class ARCHIVE="class1.jar, extras/class2.jar"
WIDTH=100 HEIGHT=100>
```

As you can see, archive names are enclosed in quotes and specified by their paths relative to the **CODEBASE**. If you need to access more than one JAR, you should separate each archive name with a comma.

That wraps up our discussion of JARs. By using this simple utility, you save on the headache of managing huge collections of files, as well as conserving drive space and oftentimes Internet bandwidth.

Security Issues

Security is another concern that has special ramifications for Java code. Most customers scrupulously protect their systems from the myriad threats that haunt computer programs. This is especially true when working in a distributed environment. In JDK 1.1, therefore, the Java security system has been refined and expanded.

Let's first expand our previous discussion of the JAR specification to touch on some of its newly implemented security features

Signed JARs

More and more, the Internet is becoming a significant distribution medium, and as it does so, questions of its security take on ever greater importance. How do your customers verify that their new program actually originated from you, not from some malicious third party? Since you aren't there to physically deliver your products, the next best thing you can do is attach a **signature** that is uniquely yours, thereby authenticating it.

Although the security model in JDK 1.1 is quite extensive, we're only going to touch on its most common application, signing JAR files. This is a simple way of letting everyone who views your archives know who you are. You generate a signature file, using the `javakey` utility, and include it in the archive just as you would any other file.

Java's signature model is based upon the popular public key/private key combination. If you've used PGP, or seen others publish their public keys over the Internet, then you're familiar with the process. Your public key is meant to be seen by others; your private key should never be shared with anyone else. The two are like pieces of a puzzle—you 'sign' documents with your private key, and your public key fits with it better than any forgery could. The algorithms that generate your keys were designed by mathematical wizards to ensure that neither key can be 'guessed' from the other one.

Therefore, in managing your security, you have two tasks. You must store your own keys, and you must maintain a database of others' keys as well. The `javakey` utility takes care of both of these jobs.

First, we need to look at some terminology. To sign a JAR, you need to be a **signer**, that is, you need to have generated your public and private key combination. From that you, or some other trusted body, create a **certificate**. A certificate is a digital assurance that your public key has a particular value. With your certificate, someone can receive signed documents from you, and verify that the private key in the document is compatible with the public key from the certificate. Surprisingly, you can also sign code.

977

Whenever someone trusts you sufficiently to want to use your signed code, they need to set you up on their system as an **identity**. That involves importing your certificate. Then whenever signed code from you is downloaded, the signature within the code is checked against your certificate, and the code is run—hopefully!

The fact that `javakey` takes care of both jobs, maintaining a persistent database of both signers and identities, can be a little confusing!

The table below summarizes the main options you'll need when using `javakey`. You'll only need to use most of the commands once, to create the keys. Then signing is easy…

Option	Description
-c	Creates a new identity.
-cs	Creates a new signer.
-ld	Lists information about registered identities and signers.
-gc	Generates a certificate.
-gk	Generates public and private keys.
-gs	Signs a JAR file.
-ld	Takes a look at the database contents.
-ic	Import a certificate for an identity.
-r	Removes the specified username from the database.

These commands are enough for us to sign the `jar` we created in the last section. But first we must become a signatory, and have the necessary keys and certificate.

Try It Out—Becoming a Signatory

1 First, let's register a signer named Jack in the `javakey` database:

```
javakey -cs Jack true
Created identity [Signer]Jack[identitydb.obj][trusted]
```

As mentioned before, the **-cs** option creates a signer, which means that `javakey` will expect to create a private key for Jack sooner or later. If we had used the **-c** option, `javakey` would have created an identity named Jack and would then only expect a public key. The next parameter is the name by which that signer will be known in your database. The final argument specifies trust level, and it can be either **true** or **false**. In this case, you obviously trust yourself, so you should select **true**.

2 Next, let's create some keys for Jack:

```
javakey -gk Jack DSA 512 pubkey.txt privkey.txt
Generated DSA keys for Jack (strength: 512).
```

```
Saved public key to pubkey.txt.
Saved private key to privkey.txt.
```

Note that you can only create keys for signers. Identities are people who distribute signed JARs to you, so they are supposed to give you their public key, too.

3 The third step in this process involves generating a certificate file. This includes information such as the signer's real name, and the dates for which his or her public key is valid. A directive file assists **javakey** in obtaining this information:

```
#Listing of JackDirective.txt
#Directive file for Certificate Generation

#Comments are indicated by the '#' character

#name of person issuing the certificate, must be a registered signer
issuer.name=Jack

#Certificate number to be used in signing (1 because this is the first
#generated certificate for this username)
issuer.cert = 1

#Information about the subject
subject.name=Jack
subject.real.name=Jack Jackson
subject.org.unit=Sales Department
subject.org=Beanstalks International
subject.country=Fantasyland

#Dates for which the certificate is valid. serial.number is for internal
#identification only
start.date=1 Jan 1997
end.date=1 Jan 1999
serial.number=1234

#Filename to which the certificate should be written
out.file=Jack.cer
```

4 Make sure this file is saved as **JackDirective.txt**, then type in the following command:

```
javakey -gc JackDirective.txt
Generated certificate from directive file JackDirective.txt.
```

It dutifully outputs a file named **Jack.cer**. Like the key files, this means nothing to the human eye, but you can view the contents with the command **javakey -dc Jack.cer**.

How It Works

DSA stands for Digital Signature Algorithm, whose inner workings are beyond our concern right now. The next number is the length of the keys in bits: this must range from 512 to 1024. The more bits in a key, the harder it is to crack! Lastly, the last two parameters represent filenames in which the public and private keys will be stored respectively.

> *Under normal operation, you should never save your private key to a file because if anyone else gets hold of it, your security is instantly compromised! To do this, simply omit the* `privkey.txt` *file from the command line.*

Don't be alarmed if the process of generating signatures takes quite a long time—your computer is doing some heavy-duty math behind the scenes. Eventually, it will report back, and you can view the contents of Jack's keys in **pubkey.txt** and **privkey.txt**, although they only contain a combined 1024 bytes of gibberish.

Take heart, though, as once the certificate file has been generated, Jack is finally qualified to sign JARs, and he will not need to go through process again! Once a key pair and a certificate is generated for any person, they can sign any number of JARs until the certificate expires.

Now, let's have Jack sign **jardemo.jar**.

Try It Out—Signing a JAR File

1 The bad news is that we need another directive file for this. The good news is, it contains only four lines (excluding comments).

```
#JackSign.txt
#Directive file for signing a JAR

#signer designates a database userID for the archive's signer
signer=Jack

#The certificate number to use, if more than one certificate exists for
#the same person.  1 represents the first certificate.
cert=1

#This parameter has not been implemented yet, and should always be left
#like this.
chain=0

#Two files will be generated by javakey, one with extension DSA, the
#other with extension SF. Both will begin with this name, which must be
#8 characters or less.
signature.file=VERIFY
```

2 Now, back to our original business of signing the archive.

```
javakey -gs JackSign.txt jardemo.jar
Adding entry: META-INF/MANIFEST.MF
Creating entry: META-INF\VERIFY.SF
Creating entry: META-INF\VERIFY.DSA
Adding entry: Jardemo.class
Adding entry: Jardemo.java
Signed JAR file jardemo.jar using directive file JackSign.txt.
```

How It Works

In the end, signing a JAR is as easy as that—first, you specify the directive file, then the archive to be signed. This outputs a new JAR named **jardemo.jar.sig**, indicating that it is signed. Its contents are identical to its parent JAR, except that two files have been added to the **META-INF** directory: **VERIFY.DSA** and **VERIFY.SF** (as noted in the previous listing).

Verifying JAR files

Let's assume now that your friend Jack has an applet on his web page that reads your user name from the system. While this action is legal in an application, it causes a **SecurityException** to be thrown when it's attempted in an applet. You really want to run his Java program, but you have no way to tell the Java security manager that you trust Jack! How can you convince it to let you run his applet?

If Jack has had the forethought to sign the archive containing the offending applet, all you need is his public key (as part of a certificate) to put your worries to rest.

Try It Out—Creating an Identity

1 First, you need to create an identity for Jack in your **javakey** database. Recall that identities are personas from the external world and they only have a public key associated with them. This identity is easily created with the following command:

```
javakey -c Jack1 true
```

2 Next, we give **javakey** Jack's signing certificate.

```
javakey -ic Jack1 Jack.cer
```

How It Works

The **-c** option creates Jack's identity; we use **Jack1** as his username because we already have a signer named Jack. Usernames may not be duplicated, even if one refers to a signer and the other to an identity. Lastly, we tell **javakey** that we trust Jack by specifying **true** as the final parameter. Only trusted identities may subvert the Java security manager.

The **-ic** option stands for 'import certificate'. **Javakey** then needs to know who the certificate belongs to, and which file contains it. It's as simple as that.

Now, any time you execute an applet contained in an archive signed by Jack, the security manager authenticates his signature in the background, and it allows the applet the same freedom afforded to applications. You don't have to intervene at all.

Likewise, you can publish applets of your own over the Internet, and if you sign all of your archives, people who trust you will be able to run them even if you try to do something unconventional like writing a file to their hard drive.

Since your **javakey** database knows that you trust Jack, let's try out applet verification. This example requires you to have access to a web server because only applets downloaded off the Internet have security restrictions placed on them. That web server can quite happily be on your local machine.

First, let's write an applet that performs a restricted action, like reading your username. This is stored as a property along with your current OS and some other relevant information. However, in the interest of privacy, not every applet you view has the privilege of finding out who you are. This is a good example of a Java security restriction—applets stored on your hard drive are permitted to read your name while applets viewed over the Internet aren't.

Try It Out—A Sneaking, Peeking Applet

1 The code looks like this:

```java
import java.awt.*;
import java.applet.*;

public class ReadName extends Applet
{
  // This applet attempts to learn your username.  If successful, it
  // prints it onscreen.  If not, it indicates that it has caught a
  // SecurityException.
  public void paint (Graphics g)
  {
    try
    {
     g.drawString ("username: " + System.getProperty("user.name"),50,30);
    }
    catch (SecurityException e)
    {
     g.drawString ("Security Exception: can't display username!",50, 30);
    }
  }

  public void repaint ()
  {
    paint (getGraphics ());
  }
}
```

2 Having compiled `ReadName.java` we need an HTML file named `ReadName.html` so that you can access your applet from a web browser.

```
<HTML>
<HEAD>
<TITLE>ReadName</TITLE>
</HEAD>
<BODY>

<APPLET CODE="ReadName.class" WIDTH=300 HEIGHT=100>
</APPLET>

</BODY>
</HTML>
```

How It Works

This code is exceedingly basic—reading the username is as simple as making a single call to `System.getProperty`, with the `String "user.name"` as the single parameter. Any other system-dependent environment variable can be read in a similar manner, providing you know its name.

Verify that our program works by invoking it with the `appletviewer`. Recall that because we're running it from a local hard drive, we're exempt from security restrictions. Sure enough, `ReadName` successfully printed my username; your program will naturally display your own name.

Now upload `ReadName.class` and `ReadName.html` to a web server and view the file again. Although you're running the same applet, you get a completely different result!

We've proven that the Java security manager does its job correctly; now let's see how we can negotiate with it to make `ReadName` run from a web server just as it does from a local drive.

Try It Out—Granting Access to System Properties

1 The first step is to store `ReadName.class` in a JAR file, just as we learned in the last section.

```
jar -cf ReadName.jar ReadName.class
```

2 Next, we need to sign this `jar` using Jack's identity—remember, when we retrieve it, the signature on the archive must match one of the identities we've entered into the database.

```
javakey -gs JackSign.txt ReadName.jar
```

> *Signing our second archive is far easier than signing the first one was. We've already generated Jack's certificate and signing directive, and they can be used over again until the certificate expires.*

983

3 Next, we need to rename the signed archive to `ReadName.jar`. `javakey` automatically names it `ReadName.jar.sig`—but for compatibility purposes, JARs should always end with the `.jar` extension, whether or not they are signed. Don't worry about overwriting the original archive, we won't need it again.

4 Lastly, we have to modify `readname.html` slightly, to take into account the fact that `ReadName.class` resides in a JAR. We'll also change the file to `SignedRead.html`, to preserve the original HTML document.

```
<HTML>
<HEAD>
<TITLE>Signed ReadName</TITLE>
</HEAD>
<BODY>

<APPLET CODE="ReadName.class" ARCHIVE="ReadName.jar" WIDTH=300 HEIGHT=100>
</APPLET>

</BODY>
</HTML>
```

The one change we have made is to add the **ARCHIVE** parameter to the **APPLET** tag. This tells the Java runtime to look in `ReadName.jar` for any resources (like `ReadName.class`) that it needs.

Upload these files to your web server and view `SignedRead.html`. Magically, the online applet now possesses the same capabilities as its offline counterpart!

This is only the tip of the iceberg of `javakey`'s capabilities. And the Java Security API is going to be added to considerably in the near future to allow finer-grained and configurable control over access.

Internationalization

Of ever-growing importance in the software industry is the need for software to run in countries other than those in which it was designed. Five years ago, the solution to this dilemma was to compile separate versions of programs for each target country, and so one routinely received distributions with a significant amount of extraneous language support. This isn't only inefficient, it also defeats the purpose of a 'write once, run anywhere' language. Therefore, internationalization has been incorporated at the heart of JDK 1.1.

Under the Java Internationalization specification, you include multiple versions of text strings, images, or sounds in languages of your choosing and the object your user actually sees is determined dynamically, that is, at runtime. The JDK itself also provides a number of utilities, such as the **NumberFormat** class, which will localize monetary displays, and the

Date class, which prints dates according to the local convention (as we saw in Chapter 9). However, here we're going to focus on the most common application of internationalization—printing text in multiple languages.

Locales

Your first question is probably—how can a program know where it is being run? In Java, it's simple: geographically sensitive operations access a **Locale** object, which contains a location field and a language field. The operation then formats its output appropriately. We saw quite a bit of the **Locale** class back in Chapter 9 but let's review it briefly.

An object of the **Locale** class, which is defined in the **java.util** package, does no language conversion work, it just identifies a country and a language. The **Locale** class has the simple constructor:

```
public Locale(String language, String country);
```

Both parameters are two-letter codes, some of which are summarized in the table below.

The following is a partial listing of country and language codes. There are many, many more, and if the region you're looking for isn't here, you can certainly find it on the Internet. The document is ISO-3166, and one site that currently has it is:

http://www.chemie.fu-berlin.de/diverse/doc/ISO_3166.html

You can also find a list of language codes (ISO-639) at:

http://www.ics.uci.edu/pub/ietf/http/related/iso639.txt

Java supports a subset of these codes. However, the full meaning of 'supported' hasn't been defined yet, so you're on your own until the standards settle down into their final form.

Country	Country Code	Language	LanguageCode
Canada	CA	English	en
China	CN	Chinese (Simplified)	zh
France	FR	French	fr
French-speaking Canada	CA	French	fr
Germany	GE	German	de
Japan	JP	Japanese	ja
Korea	KR	Korean	ko
Taiwan	TW	Chinese (Traditional)	zh
United Kingdom	GB	English	en
United States	US	English	en

In addition, the `Locale` class provides constants—`Locale` objects representing some of the more commonly used countries and languages. You have the option of using these instead of creating your own `Locale` objects.

For example, to create a `Locale` for Germany, you could write:

```
Locale here = new Locale("de", "GE");
```

> *Notice that language codes are always lower case, and the country codes are upper case.*

Alternatively, the `Locale` class defines a constant for Germany so instead of creating the object yourself, you can just use the object `Locale.GERMANY`.

The following `Locale` objects representing languages are defined in the `Locale` class:

ENGLISH	**FRENCH**	**GERMAN**
ITALIAN	**JAPANESE**	**KOREAN**
CHINESE	**SIMPLIFIED_CHINESE**	**TRADITIONAL_CHINESE**

and the following objects representing countries are defined in the class:

FRANCE	**GERMANY**	**ITALY**
JAPAN	**KOREA**	**CHINA**
PRC	**TAIWAN**	**UK**
US	**CANADA**	**CANADA_FRENCH**

Resource Bundles

Here comes the other half of the background we need before we can actually demonstrate internationalization. Under JDK 1.1, your localized resources, be they text, images or sounds, aren't stored within your program itself. Instead, they reside in a separate class that encapsulates what is called a **resource bundle**.

Actually, `ResourceBundle` is a class defined in the **java.util** package. It contains handy static methods such as `getString()`, which will retrieve localized strings from a given `ResourceBundle`. Since it's **abstract**, you must subclass it in order to use it in your applications. You're only required to implement two methods when you do this.

```
public Object handleGetObject(String key)
public Enumeration getKeys()
```

The first matches a key to a localized text string. The second returns an **Enumeration** object letting your application know which keys it can look for when using **handleGetObject**.

If you are going to the trouble of creating your own resource bundles, you are obviously going to be in the business of supporting two or more languages. To do this, you need to create a default resource bundle class, as well as other language specific resource bundle classes. Let's create a default resource bundle first.

Try It Out—Subclassing ResourceBundle

Here's a simple subclass of **ResourceBundle**.

```
// Default class for HelloResources
import java.util.*;

public class HelloResources extends ResourceBundle
{
  Hashtable resources;                        // Stores keys and resources

  // Constructor
  public HelloResources()
  {
    resources = new Hashtable();              // Create the hash table

    // Insert keys and resources into the hash table
    resources.put("helloKey", "Hello World!");
    resources.put("goodbyeKey", "Goodbye!");
  }

  public Object handleGetObject(String key)
  {
    return resources.get(key);       // Return the object for the key
  }

  public Enumeration getKeys()
  {
    return resources.keys();         // Return an enumeration of the keys
  }
}
```

How It Works

As you can see, we store the resources in a hash table. This has the merit that we store the keys along with the resources, and we can use the **Hashtable** class methods to help implement the methods we need. The **handleGetObject()** is really quite trivial. It just calls the **get()** method for the **Hashtable** object, **resources**. If the key is not found, the **get()** method returns **null**.

The implementation of **getKeys()** is also trivial. We just call the **keys()** method for the resources object to get an **Enumeration** for the keys.

987

For every **Locale** object you wish to support, you must define another version of **HelloResources**. You distinguish them from one another by appending the language and/or country codes to the classname. For instance, the French version of **HelloResources** should be named **HelloResources_FR**. Should you need to specify both a language and a country (as in the case of French Canada), put the language first, and capitalize both symbols—**HelloResources_FR_CA**. If you don't conform to this pattern, your application won't be able to find your resources!

With all this in mind, here's the listing for **HelloResources_FR.java**.

Try It Out—A Resource Class for the French

Notice that the exact same keys, **"helloKey"** and **"goodbyeKey"** are defined. Normally, you'll use your default **ResourceBundle** as a template for all your other resource classes. Only the resource strings stored in the **Hashtable** object, **resources**, in the class constructor will change.

```java
// Resources for French
import java.util.*;

public class HelloResources_FR extends ResourceBundle
{
  Hashtable resources;                        // Stores keys and resources

  // Constructor
  public HelloResources_FR()
  {
    resources = new Hashtable();              // Create the hash table

    // Insert keys and resources into the hash table
    resources.put("helloKey", "Bonjour tout le monde!");
    resources.put("goodbyeKey", "Au revoir!");
  }

  public Object handleGetObject(String key)
  {
    return resources.get(key);                // Return the object for the key
  }

  public Enumeration getKeys()
  {
    return resources.keys();                  // Return an enumeration of the keys
  }
}
```

Apart from the class name, the only changes are the resources corresponding to the keys are in French. You would do exactly the same for each language you want to support.

In providing resources, you are by no means limited to just `Strings`**. Images and sounds can also be referenced by keys. Plus you can store any object in a** `Hashtable`**.**

Of course, if we now want to support Frecnch Canada, the resources required are the same, so all we need to do is to derive the class:

```
// Resources for French Canada
public class HelloResources_FR_CA extends HelloResources_FR
{}
```

All that is required is inherited from the base class.

You need to compile all your resource class explicitly. Your program that uses resources will not refer to these classes directly, even though it uses them, so they will not be compiled along with your program code.

That's all there is to building resource bundles. It doesn't get much more complicated than **HelloResources**, only longer, as you define more resources.

Putting Internationalization to Work

Now that you have resources and know how to make **Locale** objects, it's time to put the two together. Obtaining resources is as easy as passing a **Locale** object to the static method **Resource.getResourceBundle()**. It tries to find resources for that **Locale** and returns them to you.

So how do you go about internationalizing your programs? First, you must gather up everything that needs to be represented differently in different locales—menus, messages, button labels or whatever. You then need to define a resource bundle class for each of the languages that you intend to support, which contains a key/resource pair for every resource that your program uses. Your program should then follow a general algorithm during initialization to set up the program for the environment in which it is running:

▶ Obtain the **Locale** object for the current environment by calling the static method **getDefault()** in the **Locale** class

▶ Obtain a **ResourceBundle** object corresponding to this locale from which it can obtain the resources in the local language, and arrange to make this available to all the classes in the program that need access to it

▶ You then need to make sure that all methods that create and use menus, messages, button labels etc., retrieve the appropriate resource from the resource bundle to use for the item

You can use **static** methods from the **ResourceBundle** class to extract the resource for any key. There are a variety of such methods, each tailored to work with a different kind of resource.

Method	Function
getMenu()	Retrieves a **Menu** object.
getMenuBar()	Retrieves a **MenuBar** object.
getObject()	Retrieves any **Object**—**Button** objects, pictures, sound etc.
getString()	Retrieves a **String**.
getStringArray()	Retrieves an array of **String**s.

For example, given that you have retrieved a **Locale** object for the current locale, and used that to obtain the corresponding **ResourceBundle** object and stored it in a variable, **resources**, you can then create a menu by using a statement such as:

```
Menu fileMenu = resources.getMenu("Edit");
```

where **"Edit"** is the key to the resource that you want here. You do the same sort of thing for everything in your program that needs internationalizing. Of course, if you design your program to be international from the outset, the whole process will be very easy.

Try It Out—Hello and Goodbye

Here's a program that retrieves and displays the resources in the resource bundle classes that we defined earlier:

```
// Try out some resource bundles
import java.util.*;

public class IntlDemo
{
  public static void main(String[] args)
  {
    try
    {
      // Retrieve resource bundles for three Locales.
      ResourceBundle englishText = ResourceBundle.getBundle(
                            "HelloResources", Locale.ENGLISH);
      ResourceBundle frenchText = ResourceBundle.getBundle(
                            "HelloResources", Locale.FRENCH);
      ResourceBundle frcaText = ResourceBundle.getBundle(
                            "HelloResources", Locale.CANADA_FRENCH);

      // Output the keys and resources for English
      String key;
      System.out.println("-----------------English-----------------");
      for(Enumeration e = englishText.getKeys(); e.hasMoreElements(); )
      {
        key=(String)e.nextElement();
        System.out.println(key + ": " + englishText.getString(key));
      }
```

```
        // Output the keys and resources for French
        System.out.println("\n----------------French----------------");
        for(Enumeration e = frenchText.getKeys(); e.hasMoreElements(); )
        {
          key=(String)e.nextElement();
          System.out.println(key + ": " + frenchText.getString(key));
        }

        // Output the keys and resources for French Canada
        System.out.println("\n----------------French Canada-----------");
        for(Enumeration e = frcaText.getKeys(); e.hasMoreElements(); )
        {
          key=(String)e.nextElement();
          System.out.println(key + ": " + frcaText.getString(key));
        }
      }
    catch(MissingResourceException e)
    {
      System.out.println(e);          // Resource bundle class missing
    }
  }
}
```

Running the application, you should see:

```
----------------English----------------
goodbyeKey: Goodbye!
helloKey: Hello World!

----------------French----------------
goodbyeKey: Au revoir!
helloKey: Bonjour tout le monde!

----------------French Canada-----------
goodbyeKey: Au revoir!
helloKey: Bonjour tout le monde!
```

How It Works

The code is in a **try** block because the **getBundle()** method can throw a
MissingResourceException—usually because you forgot to compile the class defining the
resources. You've already seen most of the code in the **try** block in one form or another.
The **ResourceBundle** objects are retrieved using constants from the **Locale** class. Retrieving
the key names from the resource bundle should also be familiar. You've used this same
method before, to obtain an **Enumeration** object in a **for** loop, with its
hasMoreElements() method controlling when the **for** loop ends. Within the loop we
retrieve each resource key in turn, and output the key along with the resource, which we
obtain by using the **getString()** method inherited from the **ResourceBundle** class.

Note that we did not define a **HelloResources** class for English. The default class,
HelloResources, was selected automatically and this happens to have English resources. Of

991

course, if you had defined a **HelloResources_EN** class, that would have been selected instead. You could try this by adding such a class, and defining resources that are different from the default class. Don't forget to compile your resources class explicitly. Since it is not used directly, it will not be compiled as part of the **IntlDemo** program.

There you have it—internationalization in a nutshell. This covers the bulk of Java's localization capabilities. You don't have to worry about formatting dates, times and numbers correctly, as it's already been handled for a variety of **Locale** classes.

Documentation

At this point, you've made your killer application as slick as it will ever be... almost. The one task that remains is to explain to your customers exactly how to use it!

Luckily, the JDK comes with a tool named **javadoc** that allows you to concentrate your efforts into documenting the code accurately, leaving the presentation of the text to the tool. If you've ever glanced at the API documentation, available at **http://www.javasoft.com**, then you're familiar with **javadoc**'s output.

javadoc parses your source files, looking for class signatures, method signatures, field names and special comments and tags that you've embedded yourself. It produces descriptions of each package, class and method in HTML format. These are linked in a hierarchical structure and designed to be easily readable, so you don't even need to edit them before you send them off to your users.

You can run **javadoc** on all of the source code you've seen, and it will pick out the names of everything it's concerned with. By default, this includes every public and protected class, method and variable (referred to as fields by **javadoc**). However, these don't mean much without some human elaboration describing what each one actually does, which is why you should always add **javadoc** comments to your Java code.

Each description must be embedded in special comment tags.

```
/**
I'm a javadoc comment!
*/
```

As you can see, they resemble one of the two regular comment tags, except that the opening tag contains two stars instead of one.

These comments can appear before a class, method or field declaration. Although the Java compiler won't complain if you insert them elsewhere, **javadoc** won't catch your descriptions if you do. Furthermore, it will always associate comments with the declarations that immediately follow them. Keep in mind that if you don't place them correctly, they either won't show up, or they will appear next to the wrong element!

Because **javadoc** comments are viewed in a web browser, you can use any standard HTML tag, other than **<H1>** and **<H2>**, in your comments. Why the exceptions? Well, **javadoc** itself inserts these tags into the output file. If your tags happen to conflict with tags already there, your browser will get confused and render your page incorrectly.

This is a legal **javadoc** comment, somewhat more pleasing to the eye than our first version.

```
/**
 * <H3>
 * I'm a <CODE>javadoc</CODE> comment!
 * </H3>
 */
```

Don't worry if you don't know HTML. It helps, but it isn't necessary to produce meaningful explanations of your software.

There are a few special fields we can insert into our comments, to tell **javadoc** who wrote the classes, how old they are and so on. We saw these tags quickly in Chapter 2. When your documentation pages are displayed, these fields will be emphasized. They are summarized in the table below.

Tag name	Legal usage	Function
@author	Class declaration	Describes the authors of a class.
@exception	Method declaration	Lists exceptions thrown by method (fully qualified names). A description of the exception is also required.
@param	Method declaration	Lists parameters taken by method.
@return	Method declaration	Describes value returned by method.
@since	Class declaration	Describes age of class (in terms of version numbers).
@see	Class, method, field declaration	References another **javadoc**-generated item.
@version	Class declaration	Lists version of class.

Except for the **@param** tag, descriptions should take up no more than a line, and each item should have its own tag. For example, a method which throws two exceptions needs two **@exception** tags, grouped together, before it. Be sure only to include your own descriptions first in each comment block—tagged fields should be the last thing to appear before the closing comment symbol. Again, this is because **javadoc** won't format your text correctly unless you follow a set pattern.

The **@see** tag deserves some special attention. Any text that appears after it is interpreted as a hyperlink to another relevant page. You use this to reference another package, class or method—any other code that might help the user understand the current topic.

To reference a **javadoc**-generated class, you simply type its name. If the class is in another package, you should include its package name as well. For example:

```
/**
 * @see java.util.ResourceBundle
 */
```

What about methods and fields? You can link to them, too, by inserting the name of the class in which they reside, followed by a **#**, and the name of the desired method or field:

```
/**
 * @see java.lang.Integer#parseInt
 */
```

Lastly, you can insert a conventional hyperlink to any document using the standard HTML format.

```
/**
 * @see <a href = http://www.javasoft.com>Java API Docs</a>
 */
```

By default, **@author** and **@version** don't appear onscreen, although we'll see later how you can enable them.

Try It Out—Commenting Source Code

Now let's add comments to **IntlDemo** to demonstrate how all of this works.

```
// Try out some resource bundles
import java.util.*;

/**
 * IntlDemo.java demonstrates the internationalization capabilities of
 * JDK 1.1 by accessing resource bundles for three different locales.
 *
 * @author Ivor Horton
 * @version 1.0
 */
public class IntlDemo
{
  /**
   * The method main() loads resources
   * for English, French, and French Canada.
   *
   * @exception java.util.MissingResourceException
   *               Signals a missing resource
   * @see java.util.ResourceBundle
   */
```

```java
public static void main(String[] args)
{
  try
  {
    // Retrieve resource bundles for three Locales.
    ResourceBundle englishText = ResourceBundle.getBundle(
                              "HelloResources", Locale.ENGLISH);
    ResourceBundle frenchText = ResourceBundle.getBundle(
                              "HelloResources", Locale.FRENCH);
    ResourceBundle frcaText = ResourceBundle.getBundle(
                              "HelloResources", Locale.CANADA_FRENCH);

    /**
     * useless javadoc comment won't be picked up!
     */
    // Output the keys and resources for English
    String key;
    System.out.println("----------------English----------------");
    for(Enumeration e = englishText.getKeys(); e.hasMoreElements(); )
    {
      key=(String)e.nextElement();
      System.out.println(key + ": " + englishText.getString(key));
    }

    // Output the keys and resources for French
    System.out.println("\n----------------French----------------");
    for(Enumeration e = frenchText.getKeys(); e.hasMoreElements(); )
    {
      key=(String)e.nextElement();
      System.out.println(key + ": " + frenchText.getString(key));
    }

    // Output the keys and resources for French Canada
    System.out.println("\n----------------French Canada----------");
    for(Enumeration e = frcaText.getKeys(); e.hasMoreElements(); )
    {
      key=(String)e.nextElement();
      System.out.println(key + ": " + frcaText.getString(key));
    }
  }
  catch(MissingResourceException e)
  {
    System.out.println(e);              // Resource bundle class missing
  }
}
}
```

How It Works

Keep the comments neat—someday, when you're writing version 2 of your masterpiece, you will appreciate them! Believe it or not, code that once made perfect sense mutates into gibberish after six months of neglect.

All of the **javadoc** comments are straightforward enough; the only thing you must remember is that your general comments should precede the special, tagged comments.

To generate the actual HTML files containing your explanations, you need to invoke **javadoc**.

```
javadoc [option string] <source file names>
```

You can document single **.java** files by passing their names to **javadoc** one at a time (with the **.java** extension), separating them with spaces. To speed things up, you can also process package names, and every file in the package will be processed.

We won't worry about options until later, because we just want to see **javadoc**'s default output. Therefore, we execute the following command from the same directory as **IntlDemo.java**:

```
javadoc IntlDemo.java
```

It thinks for a little while, and produces some output.

```
Generating package.html
Generating documentation for class IntlDemo
Generating index
Sorting 2 items...done
Generating tree
```

You should also find four new files in your work directory: **packages.html**, **AllNames.html**, **IntlDemo.html** and **tree.html**. This is quite a bit more than we bargained for, but it comes in handy when you want to organize a large program's classes and methods. Covering the output files one by one:

▶ **packages.html** lists the packages we parsed. Since **IntlDemo** just belongs to the default package, you won't find anything listed in this file, although it still contains a pretty heading

▶ **AllNames.html** shows you every method name and field name, arranged in alphabetical order

▶ **IntlDemo.html** contains our comments, and it's the one you're probably most interested in

▶ Lastly, **tree.html** shows you a visual class hierarchy—not very informative since we just have one class and **Object**

Take a look at **IntlDemo.html** in your favorite web browser. Don't be alarmed at all the images it can't find—these are bullets and other eye candy. You can copy the **\doc\api\images** directory across to your folder to make them visible. Notice that the useless **javadoc** comment we inserted in the middle of **IntlDemo.java** doesn't appear anywhere. It was ignored! However, all of the descriptions were taken straight from our legal comments.

This process is easily extrapolated to larger projects—the only differences are that you have to write more comments and **javadoc** produces more output—one HTML file for each source file you give it.

Now is a good time to turn to some of **javadoc's** fine-tuning options. By default, it only produces output for public and protected methods, assuming your customer's don't need to know about the innards of your application. What if you want to produce documentation for yourself, detailing every member method? The command-line switches handle several special cases like these.

Command Line Switches	Description
-author	Displays author tags (not shown by default).
-d	Specifies destination directory for HTML files.
-nodeprecated	Doesn't show documentation with the **deprecated** tag (obsolete methods).
-noindex	Doesn't generate **AllNames.html**.
-notree	Doesn't generate **tree.html**.
-package	Documents all classes and methods with package, public or protected scope.
-private	Documents all classes, methods and fields.
-protected	Documents public and protected classes, methods and fields.
-public	Documents only public classes, methods and fields.
-verbose	Generates verbose output.
-version	Displays version tags (not shown by default).

Let's put some of these to work!

```
javadoc -author -noindex -notree -verbose -version IntlDemo.java
```

The output is more detailed, though how useful the new information is, you will have to judge.

```
[parsed IntlDemo.java in 770 ms]
Generating package.html
Generating documentation for class IntlDemo
[loaded C:\JDK1.1.1\LIB\CLASSES.ZIP(java/lang/Object.class) in 50 ms]
[loaded C:\JDK1.1.1\LIB\CLASSES.ZIP(java/util/
                              MissingResourceException.class)in 0 ms]
[loaded C:\JDK1.1.1\LIB\CLASSES.ZIP(java/lang/RuntimeException.class)
                                                            in 0 ms]
[loaded C:\JDK1.1.1\LIB\CLASSES.ZIP(java/lang/Exception.class) in 60 ms]
[loaded C:\JDK1.1.1\LIB\CLASSES.ZIP(java/lang/Throwable.class) in 50 ms]
[done in 3570 ms]
```

997

This time, if you examine `IntlDemo.java`, you'll see that the author and version which you specified are visible, and if you check the timestamps on `AllNames.html` and `tree.html`, you can confirm that `javadoc` did not produce new versions of them.

I leave it to you as an exercise to document the other classes that `IntlDemo` depends on: `HelloResources HelloResources_FR`, and `HelloResources_FR_CA`. You should be able to describe them, insert references to each other, and just about anything else that strikes your fancy.

Documenting your applications isn't hard, but it is a step you shouldn't ignore, either. If you give it the time and effort it deserves, you'll be rewarded with satisfied customers and time off from technical support.

Summary

In this appendix, you have learned how to radically expand the target audience of your Java programs.

▶ By distributing applications and their associated images, sounds and resources in JAR files, you appeal to customers using the Internet

▶ You can also cater for the security requirements necessitated by the Internet itself, by signing and authenticating your JAR files

▶ You can attract customers not only in your own country, but worldwide, by drawing on Java's internationalization capabilities

▶ Lastly, you can quickly generate clear and concise documentation in HTML format for distribution with your application or inclusion on your web site

Utilizing each of these features makes your application more useful to your customers. Slick distribution is as important as intelligent design in the world of commercial software—no matter how cool your programming, potential buyers will only look twice if their first impression is favorable.

Keywords

The following keywords are reserved in Java, so you must not use them as names in your programs:

abstract	int
boolean	interface
break	long
byte	native
case	new
catch	package
char	private
class	protected
const	public
continue	return
default	short
do	static
double	super
else	switch
extends	synchronized
final	this
finally	throw
float	throws
for	transient
goto	try
if	void
implements	volatile
import	while
instanceof	

You should also not attempt to use the boolean values **true** and **false**, or **null** as names in your programs.

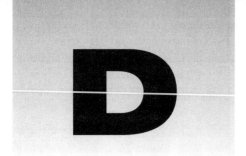

The ASCII Table

The American Standard Code for Information Interchange or ASCII assigns values between 0 and 255 for upper and lower case letters, numeric digits, punctuation marks and other symbols. ASCII characters can be split into the following sections:

0 – 31   Control functions.

32 – 127   Standard, implementation-independent characters.

128 – 255   Special symbols, international character sets—generally, non-standard characters.

Since the latter 128 characters are implementation-dependent and have no fixed entry in the ASCII table, we shall only cover the first two groups in the following table:

ASCII Characters 0 - 31

Decimal	Hexadecimal	Character	Control
000	00	null	NUL
001	01	☺	SOH
002	02	•	STX
003	03	♥	ETX
004	04	♦	EOT
005	05	♣	ENQ
006	06	♠	ACK
007	07	•	BEL (Audible bell)
008	08		Backspace
009	09		HT
010	0A		LF (Line feed)
011	0B		VT (Vertical feed)
012	0C		FF (Form feed)
013	0D		CR (Carriage return)
014	0E		SO
015	0F	¤	SI
016	10		DLE
017	11		DC1

Decimal	Hexadecimal	Character Control	
018	12		DC2
019	13		DC3
020	14		DC4
021	15		NAK
022	16		SYN
023	17		ETB
024	18		CAN
025	19		EM
026	1A	→	SUB
027	1B	←	ESC (Escape)
028	1C	L	FS
029	1D		GS
030	1E		RS
031	1F		US

ASCII Characters 32 - 127

Decimal	Hexadecimal	Character	Decimal	Hexadecimal	Character
032	20	space	060	3C	<
033	21	!	061	3D	=
034	22	"	062	3E	>
035	23	#	063	3F	?
036	24	$	064	40	@
037	25	%	065	41	A
038	26	&	066	42	B
039	27	'	067	43	C
040	28	(	068	44	D
041	29	)	069	45	E
042	2A	*	070	46	F
043	2B	+	071	47	G
044	2C	,	072	48	H
045	2D	-	073	49	I
046	2E	.	074	4A	J
047	2F	/	075	4B	K
048	30	0	076	4C	L
049	31	1	077	4D	M
050	32	2	078	4E	N
051	33	3	079	4F	O
052	34	4	080	50	P
053	35	5	081	51	Q
054	36	6	082	52	R
055	37	7	083	53	S
056	38	8	084	54	T
057	39	9	085	55	U
058	3A	:	086	56	V
059	3B	;	087	57	W

Decimal	Hexadecimal	Character	Decimal	Hexadecimal	Character
088	58	X	108	6C	l
089	59	Y	109	6D	m
090	5A	Z	110	6E	n
091	5B	[	111	6F	o
092	5C	\	112	70	p
093	5D	]	113	71	q
094	5E	^	114	72	r
095	5F	_	115	73	s
096	60	´	116	74	t
097	61	a	117	75	u
098	62	b	118	76	v
099	63	c	119	77	w
100	64	d	120	78	x
101	65	e	121	79	y
102	66	f	122	7A	z
103	67	g	123	7B	{
104	68	h	124	7C	ç
105	69	i	125	7D	}
106	6A	j	126	7E	~
107	6B	k	127	7F	delete

Beginning
Java

Symbols

Instant HTML Programmers Reference

Author: Steve Wright
ISBN: 1861000766
Price: $15.00 C$21.00 £13.99

This book is a fast paced guide to the latest version of the HTML language, including the extensions to the standards added by Netscape and Microsoft. Aimed at programmers, it assumes a basic knowledge of the Internet. It starts by looking at the basics of HTML including document structure, formatting tags, inserting hyperlinks and images and image mapping, and then moves on to cover more advanced issues such as tables, frames, creating forms to interact with users, animation, incorporating scripts (such as JavaScript) into HTML documents, and style sheets.

The book includes a full list of all the HTML tags, organised by category for easy reference.

Instant VBScript

Authors: Alex Homer, Darren Gill
ISBN: 1861000448
Price: $25.00 C$35.00 £22.99

This is the guide for programmers who already know HTML and another programming language and want to waste no time getting up to speed. This book takes developers right into the code, straight from the beginning of Chapter 1. The first object is to get the programmer to create their own 'reactive' web pages as quickly as possible while introducing the most important HTML and ActiveX controls. This new knowledge is quickly incorporated into more complex examples with a complete sample site built early in the book.

As Internet Explorer is the browser that introduced VBScript, we also take a detailed look at how to use VBScript to access different objects within the browser. We create our own tools to help us with the development of applications, in particular a debugging tool to aid error-trapping. Information is provided on how to build your own controls and sign them to secure Internet download. Finally we take a look at server side scripting and how with VBScript you can get the clients and server communicating freely. The book is supported by our web site which contains all of the examples in the book in an easily executable form.

Wrox Press
http://www.wrox.com/

Professional Web Site Optimization

Authors: Ware, Barker, Slothouber
and Gross
ISBN: 186100074x
Price: $40.00 C$56.00 £36.99

OK, you've installed your web server, and it's working fine and you've even got people interested in visiting your site - too many people, in fact. The real challenge is just starting you need to make it run faster, better and more flexibly.

This is the book for every webmaster who needs to improve site performance. You could just buy that new T-1 you've had your eye on, but what if the problem is really in your disk controller? Or maybe it's the way you've designed your pages or the ISP you're using.

The book covers web server optimization for all major platforms and includes coverage of LAN performance, ISP performance, basic limits imposed by the nature of HTTP, IP and TCP. We also cover field-proven methods to improve static & dynamic page content from database access and the mysteries of graphic file manipulation and tuning.

If you've got the choice between spending fifteen thousand on a new line, or two hundred dollars in new hardware plus the cost of this book, which decision would your boss prefer?

Professional Visual C++ ISAPI Programming

Author: Michael Tracy
ISBN: 1861000664
Price: $40.00 C$56.00 £36.99

This is a working developer's guide to customizing Microsoft's Internet Information Server, which is now an integrated and free addition to the NT4.0 platform. This is essential reading for real-world web site development and expects readers to already be competent C++ and C programmers. Although all techniques in the book are workable under various C++ compilers, users of Visual C++ 4.1 will benefit from the ISAPI extensions supplied in its AppWizard.

This book covers extension and filter programming in depth. There is a walk through the API structure but not a reference to endless calls. Instead, we illustrate the key specifications with example programs.

HTTP and HTML instructions are issued as an appendix. We introduce extensions by mimicking popular CGI scripts and there's a specific chapter on controlling cookies. With filters we are not just re-running generic web code - these are leading-edge filter methods specifically designed for the IIS API.

Beginning Visual Basic 5

Author: Peter Wright
ISBN: 1861000081
Price: $29.95 C$41.95 £27.49

The third edition of the best selling Beginner's Guide to Visual Basic is the most comprehensive guide for the complete beginner to Visual Basic 5. Peter Wright's unique style and humour have long been a favourite with beginners and, because the book has just the one author, you can be sure that the text has a consistent voice and flow.

As with all Wrox Beginning guides, every topic is illustrated with a Try It Out, where each new concept is accompanied by a focused example and explanatory text. This way, you get to create an example program that demonstrates some theory, and then you get to examine the code behind it in detail.

Peter starts with a lightning tour of the Visual Basic 5 environment, before moving on to the creation of a Visual Basic 5 program. Critical concepts such as events, properties and methods are given the attention they deserve. You'll find yourself starting with basics, such as "What is a control and how does VB5 use them?", but you'll quickly be able to move on to more complex topics such as graphics, object-oriented programming, control creation and creating databases. By the end of the book, you'll be able to build your own application from scratch, with very impressive results.

Instant VB5 ActiveX Control Creation

Authors: Alex Homer, Stephen Jakab and Darren Gill
ISBN: 1861000235
Price: $29.95 C$41.95 £27.99

Aimed at experienced Visual Basic programmers who want to be able to create their own controls using the freely downloadable Visual Basic 5 CCE, this book takes you from an overview of VB5 CCE, right up to how to create your own, highly customized controls. It explains in detail how to create different types of control, including sub-classed, aggregate and owner-draw controls, and also includes coverage of the issues you need to be aware of when distributing your controls.

Wrox Press
http://www.wrox.com/

Professional Java Fundamentals

Authors: Cohen, Mitchell, Gonzalez,
Rodrigues and Hammil
ISBN: 1861000383
Price: $35.00 C$49.00 £32.49

Professional Java Fundamentals is a high-level, developer's book that gives you the detailed information and extended coverage you need to program Java for real, making the most of Java's potential.

It starts by thoroughly recapping the basics of Java, providing a language reference, looking at object-oriented programming issues and then at Java's fundamental classes. The book then details advanced language features, such as multithreading, networking, file I/O and native methods. There are five Abstract Windowing Toolkit chapters which provide in-depth coverage of event handling, graphics and animation, GUI building blocks and layout managers. Lastly, the book shows you how to design and implement class libraries in Java.

The book is supported by the Wrox web site, from which the complete source code is available.

Beginning Access 95 VBA Programming

Authors: Robert Smith, David Sussman
ISBN: 1874416508
Price: $29.95 C$41.95 £27.99

This book is for the Access user who has a knowledge of databases and the basic objects of an Access database such as tables, queries, forms and reports, but wants to learn how to program. You will need no prior programming experience, in any language.
This book looks in depth at the language that acts as the cornerstone of Microsoft Office 95. Focusing on the sample application provided, it explains the concepts and techniques you need to get to grips with VBA.

The book starts by explaining why you actually need to learn VBA to harness the full power of Access and why macros just aren't enough for some tasks. It then introduces you to the Visual Basic programming environment in Access and explains the common programming techniques and terminology, such as loops, conditions and arrays. Each feature of the language is fully illustrated with practical examples.

The later chapters concentrate on several diverse topics, such as debugging and error handling, multi-user situations, libraries, add-ons and optimization issues. At the end of the book you will have a solid grounding in all the important aspects of VBA. The disk contains the sample application used in the book, plus all the sample VBA code used.

Beginning Linux Programming

Authors: Neil Matthew, Richard Stones
ISBN: 187441680
Price: $36.95 C$51.95 £33.99

The book is unique in that it teaches UNIX programming in a simple and structured way, using Linux and its associated and freely available development tools as the main platform. Assuming familiarity with the UNIX environment and a basic knowledge of C, the book teaches you how to put together UNIX applications that make the most of your time, your OS and your machine's capabilities.

Having introduced the programming environment and basic tools, the authors turn their attention initially on shell programming. The chapters then concentrate on programming UNIX with C, showing you how to work with files, access the UNIX environment, input and output data using terminals and curses, and manage data. After another round with development and debugging tools, the book discusses processes and signals, pipes and other IPC mechanisms, culminating with a chapter on sockets. Programming the X-Window system is introduced with Tcl/Tk and Java. Finally, the book covers programming for the Internet using HTML and CGI.

The book aims to discuss UNIX programming as described in the relevant POSIX and X/Open specifications, so the code is tested with that in mind. All the source code from the book is available under the terms of the Gnu Public License from the Wrox web site.

Professional SQL Server 6.5 Admin

Authors: Various   ISBN: 1874416494
Price: $44.95 C$62.95 £41.49

This book is not a tutorial in the complete product, but is for those who need to become either professionally competent in preparation for Microsoft exams or those DBAs needing real-world advice to do their job better. It assumes knowledge of databases and wastes no time on getting novices up to speed on the basics of data structure and using a database server in a Client-Server arena.

The book covers everything from installation and configuration right through to the actual managing of the server. There are whole chapters devoted to essential administrative issues such as transaction management and locking, replication, security, monitoring of the system and database backup and recovery. We've used proven techniques to bring robust code and script that will increase your ability to troubleshoot your database structure and improve its performance. Finally, we have looked very carefully at the new features in 6.5, such as the Web Assistant and Distributed Transaction Controller (DTC) and provided you with key practical examples. Where possible, throughout the book we have described a DBA solution in Transact SQL, Visual Basic and the Enterprise Manager.

Instant SQL Programming

Author: Joe Celko   ISBN: 1874416508
Price: $29.95 C$41.95 £27.99

This is the fastest guide for developers to the most common database management language. If you want to get the most out of your database design, you will need to master Structured Query Language. SQL is the standard database language supported by almost every database management system on the market. This book takes you into the concepts and implementation of this key language quickly and painlessly, covering the complete ANSI standard SQL '92 from basic database design through to some of the more complex topics such as NULLS and 3-valued logic. We take you through the theory step-by-step, as you put into practice what you learn at each stage, gradually building up an example database while mastering essential techniques.

Beginning Visual C++ 5

Author: Ivor Horton   ISBN: 1861000081
Price: $39.95 C$55.95 £36.99

Visual Basic is a great tool for generating applications quickly and easily, but if you really want to create fast, tight programs using the latest technologies, Visual C++ is the only way to go.

Ivor Horton's Beginning Visual C++ 5 is for anyone who wants to learn C++ and Windows programming with Visual C++ 5 and MFC, and the combination of the programming discipline you've learned from this book and Ivor's relaxed and informal teaching style will make it even easier for you to succeed in taming structured programming and writing real Windows applications.

The book begins with a fast-paced but comprehensive tutorial to the C++ language. You'll then go on to learn about object orientation with C++ and how this relates to Windows programming, culminating with the design and implementation of a sizable class-based C++ application. The next part of the book walks you through creating Windows applications using MFC, including sections on output to the screen and printer, how to program menus, toolbars and dialogs, and how to respond to a user's actions. The final few chapters comprise an introduction COM and examples of how to create ActiveX controls using both MFC and the Active Template Library (ATL).

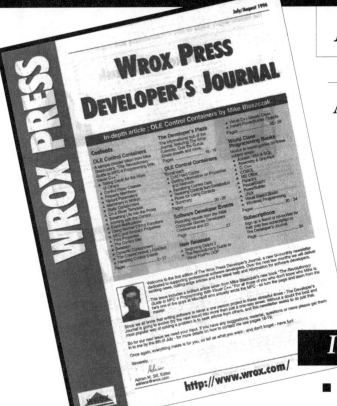

Learn online at ZDNet University –
the best value in continuing education

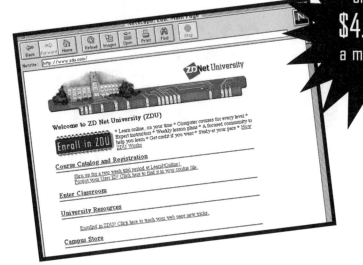